PRODUCT MANAGEMENT

THE IRWIN SERIES IN MARKETING

Alreck & Settle
The Survey Research Handbook
Second Edition

Arens
Contemporary Advertising
Sixth Edition

Bearden, Ingram & LaForge
Marketing: Principles & Perspectives
First Edition

Belch & Belch
Introduction to Advertising and Promotion: An Integrated Marketing Communications Approach
Third Edition

Bernhardt & Kinnear
Cases in Marketing Management
Seventh Edition

Berkowitz, Kerin, Hartley & Rudelius
Marketing
Fifth Edition

Boyd, Walker & Larréché
Marketing Management: A Strategic Approach with a Global Orientation
Second Edition

Cateora
International Marketing
Ninth Edition

Churchill, Ford & Walker
Sales Force Management
Fifth Edition

Cole & Mishler
Consumer and Business Credit Management
Tenth Edition

Cravens
Strategic Marketing
Fifth Edition

Cravens
Strategic Marketing Management Cases
Fifth Edition

Crawford
New Products Management
Fifth Edition

Dillon, Madden & Firtle
Essentials of Marketing Research
Second Edition

Dillon, Madden & Firtle
Marketing Research in a Marketing Environment
Third Edition

Faria, Nulsen & Roussos
Compete
Fourth Edition

Futrell
ABC's of Relationship Selling
Fifth Edition

Futrell
Fundamentals of Selling
Fifth Edition

Gretz, Drozdeck & Weisenhutter
Professional Selling: A Consultative Approach
First Edition

Hawkins, Best & Coney
Consumer Behavior
Sixth Edition

Hayes, Jenster & Aaby
Business to Business Marketing
First Edition

Johansson
Global Marketing
First Edition

Lambert & Stock
Strategic Logistics Management
Third Edition

Lehmann & Winer
Analysis for Marketing Planning
Fourth Edition

Lehmann & Winer
Product Management
Second Edition

Levy & Weitz
Retailing Management
Second Edition

Levy & Weitz
Essentials of Retailing
First Edition

Mason, Mayer & Ezell
Retailing
Fifth Edition

Mason & Pereault
The Marketing Game!
Second Edition

Meloan & Graham
International and Global Marketing Concepts and Cases
First Edition

Patton
Sales Force: A Sales Management Simulation Game
First Edition

Pelton, Strutton & Lumpkin
Marketing Channels: A Relationship Management Approach
First Edition

Perreault & McCarthy
Basic Marketing: A Global Managerial Approach
Twelfth Edition

Perreault & McCarthy
Essentials of Marketing: A Global Managerial Approach
Seventh Edition

Peter & Donnelly
A Preface to Marketing Management
Seventh Edition

Peter & Donnelly
Marketing Management: Knowledge and Skills
Fourth Edition

Peter & Olson
Consumer Behavior and Marketing Strategy
Fourth Edition

Peter & Olson
Understanding Consumer Behavior
First Edition

Quelch
Cases in Product Management
First Edition

Quelch, Dolan & Kosnik
Marketing Management: Text & Cases
First Edition

Quelch & Farris
Cases in Advertising and Promotion Management
Fourth Edition

Quelch, Kashani & Vandermerwe
European Cases in Marketing Management
First Edition

Rangan
Business Marketing Strategy: Cases, Concepts & Applications
First Edition

Rangan, Shapiro & Moriarty
Business Marketing Strategy: Concepts & Applications
First Edition

Smith & Quelch
Ethics in Marketing
First Edition

Stanton, Buskirk & Spiro
Management of a Sales Force
Ninth Edition

Thompson & Stappenbeck
The Marketing Strategy Game
First Edition

Walker, Boyd & Larréché
Marketing Strategy: Planning and Implementation
Second Edition

Weitz, Castleberry & Tanner
Selling: Building Partnerships
Second Edition

SECOND EDITION

PRODUCT MANAGEMENT

Donald R. Lehmann
Graduate School of Business
Columbia University

Russell S. Winer
Haas School of Business
University of California, Berkeley

Boston, Massachusetts Burr Ridge, Illinois Dubuque, Iowa
Madison, Wisconsin New York, New York San Francisco, California St. Louis, Missouri

To those who helped shape our thinking and especially those like Kris who helped on the book.

Irwin/McGraw-Hill

A Division of The ***McGraw-Hill*** *Companies*

Irwin Book Team

Publisher: *Rob Zwettler*
Senior sponsoring editor: *Stephen M. Patterson*
Editorial assistant: *Andrea Hlavacek*
Marketing manager: *Colleen Suljic*
Senior project supervisor: *Mary Conzachi*
Senior production supervisor: *Laurie Sander*
Designer: *Matthew Baldwin*
Assistant manager, desktop services: *Jon Christopher*
Compositor: *Carlisle Communications, Ltd.*
Typeface: *10/12 Times Roman*
Printer: *R. R. Donnelley & Sons Company*

Library of Congress Cataloging-in-Publication Data

Lehmann, Donald R.
Product management / Donald R. Lehmann, Russell S. Winer.
p. cm.—(The Irwin series in marketing)
Includes indexes.
ISBN 0-256-21439-5
1. Product management. I. Winer, Russell S. II. Title.
III. Series.
HF5415. 15.L44 1997
658.5'6—dc20 96-28869

Printed in the United States of America
3 4 5 6 7 8 9 0 DO 3 2 1 0 9 8

PREFACE

The focus of this book is on those individuals who have the primary responsibility for the market success of the company's products and services. In many companies, particularly packaged goods companies, this person has the title *product manager.* Although, as we note in Chapter 1, the title is not always the same, there are always individuals in the company who must be the "expert" for the product, someone to whom senior managers can assign responsibility for the execution of marketing plans and someone who advances or fails as a result of the product's performance.

The product manager's job is becoming increasingly complex. Due to, among other things, changes in information technology, increasing global competition, changing customer needs and wants, the job of the product manager involves continually collecting and synthesizing information, forecasting changes in competition and market conditions, revising market strategies, and adapting decisions such as price and communications to rapidly changing market conditions. This is true even for so-called mature product categories.

In the second edition of *Product Management,* we have attempted to cover the three major tasks facing product managers:

1. Analyzing the market.
2. Developing objectives and strategies for the product or service in question.
3. Making decisions about price, advertising, promotion, channels of distribution, and service.

We use as a unifying framework the development of the marketing plan, a process that integrates the three tasks and provides a written record of the brand's history, prospects, and hopes.

Why We Wrote the Book

Many fine textbooks deal with marketing management and strategy issues. These books either are general introductions to marketing management or focus more exclusively on strategic issues. One way to look at the existing set of textbooks is to relate them to job responsibilities. The general marketing management texts are excellent devices for introducing marketing concepts to all employees in an organization. The strategy books are more advanced and fit well with the jobs of senior marketing managers such as group product managers, VPs of marketing, and the like. These people usually manage "portfolios" of products and, sometimes, many product managers.

We have found that most existing textbooks do not really cover the middle ground. This middle ground consists of marketing managers who have day-to-day responsibilities for managing either a single product or service or a closely related product line. These managers know what the marketing concept is and understand the general pros and cons of basic strategy decisions (e.g., which segment should I pursue?). What they need to know is how to write product marketing plans, how to select specific marketing strategies, and how to implement those strategies by making decisions regarding so-called marketing mix instruments. That is the focus of this book.

A second reason for writing this book is our belief that much of the research marketing academics have produced has great relevance for practicing managers but is generally inaccessible to them. In this book, we attempt to bridge this gap. Particularly in the chapters on marketing decision making, we have attempted to integrate findings from academic research in the marketing management, consumer behavior, and marketing science literature.

The differences, then, between *Product Management* and other marketing textbooks are (1) its hands-on approach, (2) the focus on decision making, and (3) the attempt to simulate what the product manager's job is actually like.

As a result, we do not aim to be comprehensive, but rather focus on the key tasks facing product managers. For example, there is no chapter on sales force management because typically the product manager has little influence on sales force size, compensation, territory design, reward systems, and so on. We also omit a very important part of any managerial position: interpersonal skills. Clearly, a large part of a product manager's success is usually related to an overall ability to get things done in a complex and often political organizational setting. We leave discussions of these issues to the appropriate experts.

What Is New in the Second Edition

While we are gratified with the reception given the first edition, we also received many suggestions from colleagues and reviewers about things to change. The most important changes are as follows:

- We have included a chapter on the role of product management in new-product development (Chapter 9).

- We have reorganized the book somewhat. The material from old Chapter 12, "Brand Value Maintenance and Product Modification," has been included either in the new Chapter 9 or in Chapter 8, "Developing Product Strategy."
- One of the features readers liked best about the first edition, the running examples (formerly bottled water and computer workstations), have been updated. The two new examples are ready-to-drink fruit drinks (e.g., Snapple) and personal digital assistants (PDAs).
- Many references are made to Internet-based marketing and marketing on the World Wide Web.

The basic outline of the book is the same, so past users and readers will be comfortable with the new edition.

The Structure of the Book

As noted previously, the book covers three major areas of product manager responsibilities. The structure of the book uses the operating product marketing plan as a unifying theme. The marketing plan guide, given in the appendix to Chapter 2, is also an outline for the book:

- Part 1 (Chapters 2 through 7) describes the marketing planning process and the background analyses necessary for constructing a successful marketing plan. Rather than taking a checklist or fill-in-the-blank approach as do many books on marketing planning, we attempt to keep the process as simple as possible while giving a sound rationale for answering the necessary major questions.
- Part 2 (Chapters 8 and 9) describes how to set sound product objectives and develop a product strategy as a result of the market analysis conducted in Part 1. Chapter 9 presents this material in the context of new products.
- Part 3 (Chapters 10 through 14) covers the marketing mix with an emphasis on decisions. While Managing Service Quality (Chapter 14) is not a classic marketing mix topic, it has become critical for product managers in the 1990s.
- Part 4 (Chapters 15 and 16) covers important ancillary topics, such as financial analysis, and expected future trends in product management, including the strategic use of information technology and advertising and channels issues in the context of the Internet.

Intended Audience for this Book

This book can be used at both the undergraduate and graduate levels. At the undergraduate level, the book can be used in a capstone course for seniors who have had several other marketing courses. At the MBA level, the book works best in a course positioned between the core marketing course and an advanced marketing strategy course. Those three courses make a very nice three-course sequence for marketing majors or those with a serious interest in marketing and exist (not surprisingly) at both Berkeley and Columbia.

We also planned for the book to have a practitioner audience. As we have noted, *Product Management* is meant to be a practical, "hands-on" book based on actual product manager experiences across a wide variety of product categories. As a result, the book is not purely academic but attempts to integrate practical results from academic research that are not otherwise easily available to practicing managers. A product manager could read this book and immediately apply the concepts to his or her situation. Positive feedback from participants in executive education courses and other practicing managers support this contention.

In some ways, *Brand Management* would be a clearer title for the book. However, we chose to title the book *Product Management* to connote the applicability of the concepts to high-tech, low-tech, and no-tech manufacturing, and service situations. Our examples are purposefully diverse and, we hope, make the book equally useful to a toothpaste brand manager, a computer software product manager, and a product manager in the financial services sector.

We always appreciate feedback. In this electronic age, maintaining communications with customers is easier than ever. We invite you to send us e-mail with comments, suggestions, and questions.

Donald R. Lehmann
dlehmann@research.gsb.columbia.edu
Russell S. Winer
winer@haas.berkeley.edu
http://www.haas.berkeley.edu/~market/

CONTENTS IN BRIEF

C O N T E N T S

10 Pricing Decisions 276

11 Advertising Decisions 309

C H A P T E R

1 Introduction to Product Management

Overview

This book focuses on the job of the product manager. Not every marketing organization has a person with that exact title; while many such jobs exist, the people who fill them could be called "brand managers," "marketing managers," or the like. We intend the generic title *product manager* to apply to different kinds of organizational structures and different kinds of companies, whether they provide consumer goods, industrial products, or services.

What makes this book different from the large number of books on "marketing management" or "marketing strategy"? We take the perspective of a manager whose primary responsibility is a product or a closely related product line. Broadly speaking, the product manager has two responsibilities. First, the product manager is responsible for the planning activities related to the product or product line.[1] Thus, the product manager's job involves analyzing the market, including customers, competitors, and the external environment, and turning this information into marketing objectives and strategies for the product. Second, the product manager must get the organization to support the marketing programs recommended in the plan. This may involve coordinating with other areas of the firm, such as research and development for product-line extensions, manufacturing, marketing research, and finance. It also involves internal marketing of the product to obtain the assistance and support of more senior managers in the firm. Figure 1–1 gives a perspective on a product manager's interactions within and outside the firm.

What, then, are the differences between a focus on the product manager and a more general marketing management perspective? Figure 1–2 indicates what separates the two. One key difference is that marketing managers in charge of a division or

[1] When we use the term *product* throughout the book, we are referring to all kinds of products, including services. *Product* is simpler to use than *product/service.* While there are well-documented differences between marketing manufactured goods and services, the structure we present in this book is meant to be a template that can be used for all products.

FIGURE 1–1 A Product Manager's Potential Interactions

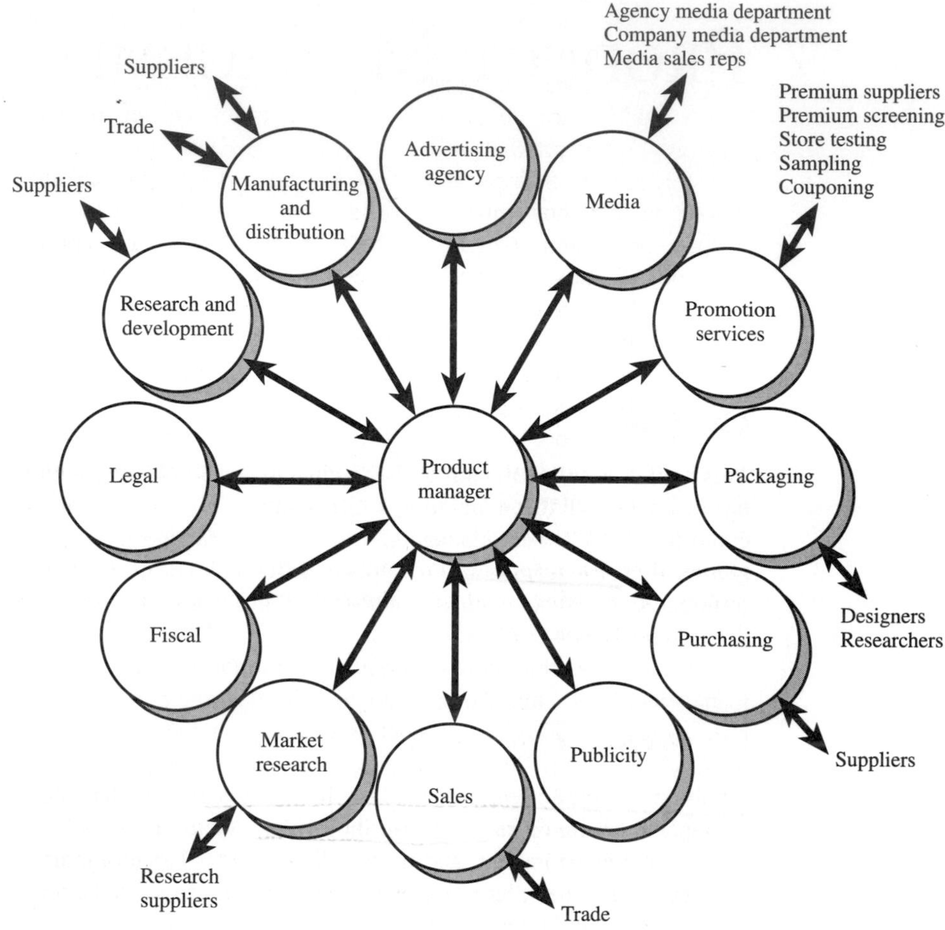

Source: Philip Kotler, *Marketing Management: Analysis, Planning, Implementation, & Control.* 8th ed. ©1994, p. 724. Reprinted with permission of Prentice Hall, Englewood Cliffs, New Jersey.

FIGURE 1–2 Product versus General Marketing Management

	Product Management	*General Marketing Management*
Scope of responsibility	Narrow: Single product or product line	Broad: Portfolio of products
Nature of decision making	Mainly tactical	Mainly strategic
Time horizon	Short-run (often annual or shorter)	Long-run

strategic business unit have more concerns about managing "portfolios" of products and about the long-term strategic direction of their business groups. Because product managers in our sense are in charge of a single product or a closely related product line, they are not concerned on a day-to-day basis about the health of the general business area in which they operate.[2] A second key contrast is in the nature of decision making. Divisional marketing managers typically make strategic decisions about which products to add or drop and manage to meet an overall divisional financial objective. While product managers are involved with developing marketing objectives and strategies for their products, their key decisions are tactical and revolve around the marketing mix: how much to spend on advertising, how to react to a competitor's coupon promotion, which channels of distribution are appropriate, and similar questions. Finally, product managers and marketing managers face different time horizons. Product managers face substantial pressure to attain and hence focus on short-run market share, volume, or profit targets. Marketing managers are also concerned with short-run targets, but they more often take a longer-term perspective of where the business is going.

Thus, this book focuses on the product manager's tasks of marketing planning, developing product strategy, and implementing that strategy through various marketing tools. The intended audience includes those who manage individual products and services or want to know how this is done. This book is not intended for senior managers whose responsibilities include managing groups of products.[3] It also focuses largely on existing products, although we devote a chapter, Chapter 9, to the management of new products.

Marketing Organization

Although we briefly described the tasks of the "typical" product manager, they vary quite widely from organization to organization. The kinds of tasks product managers perform are highly related to how marketing is organized.[4] Three organizational structures for marketing have been identified: organizing by product, by market, and by function.[5]

---

[2] This problem with the traditional product management structure is discussed later in this chapter. The narrow product or brand focus at the expense of the product category as a whole has given rise to a new position at many packaged goods companies: the category manager.

[3] Excellent books for higher-level marketing managers include David A. Aaker, *Strategic Market Management,* 4th ed. (New York: John Wiley & Sons, 1995); David W. Cravens, *Strategic Marketing,* 3rd ed. (Homewood, Ill.: Richard D. Irwin, 1991); and Glen L. Urban and Steven H. Star, *Advanced Marketing Strategy* (Englewood Cliffs, N.J.: Prentice-Hall, 1991).

[4] Note that we resist referring to the marketing "function" within an organization. Referring to marketing as a functional area of the firm implies that only people in the marketing function perform marketing tasks. Nothing could be further from the truth; as service and other businesses are discovering, in today's business environment, with its growing emphasis on customer service, marketing is often looked at as everyone's job. More will be said about this in Chapter 14.

[5] This section draws on Frank V. Cespedes, "Aspects of Marketing Organization: An Introduction," Harvard Business School case study 9–589–062, 1988.

FIGURE 1–3 Product-Focused Structure

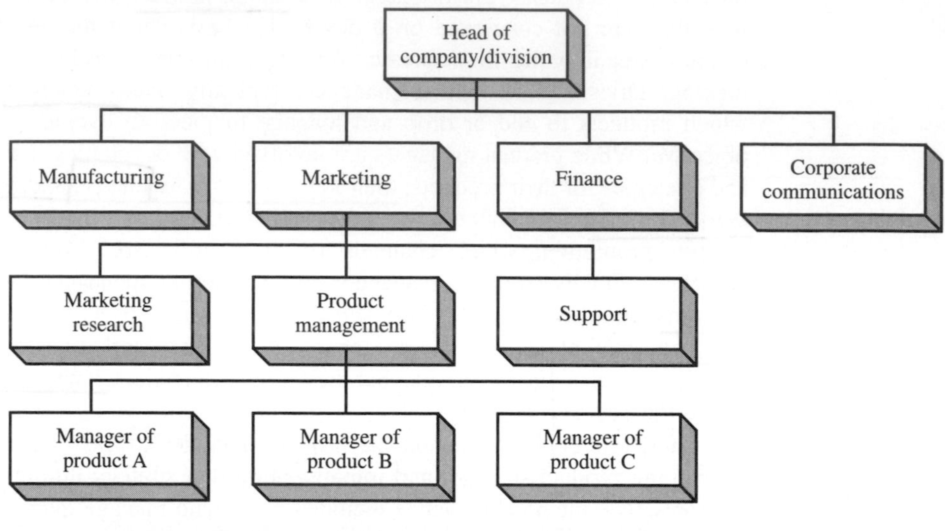

Product-Focused Organizations

Figure 1–3 provides a general view of this form of marketing organization. This is the classic "brand" management structure that Procter & Gamble developed in the 1930s. It is most often found in packaged goods industries, but it also exists in other industries. It is commonly used where different products use the same channels of distribution.

In this structure, the product manager acts as a "mini-CEO," taking responsibility for the overall health of the brand. Over time, a well-defined hierarchy within the product management system has developed, with key roles assigned to assistant and associate product managers. Often these jobs are entry-level positions for individuals who want careers in product management.

The tasks of these elements of the hierarchy are typically the following. The assistant product manager's job includes market and share forecasting, budgeting, coordinating with production, executing promotions, and packaging. In general, the brand assistant's tasks involve becoming more familiar with the category within which the brand competes. Associate product managers have more freedom to develop brand extensions, and sometimes even manage a small brand. The product manager, of course, has the ultimate responsibility for the brand. Figure 1–4 shows an illustration from General Foods Corporation's Desserts Division (from around 1984).[6]

As previously noted, this structure is not limited to packaged goods companies. Figure 1–5 illustrates the organizational structure of Adobe Systems Inc., a computer

[6] Since then, of course, General Foods has merged with Kraft and become part of Philip Morris, Inc.

Figure 1–4 General Foods Corporation (ca. 1984): Desserts Division Organizational Chart

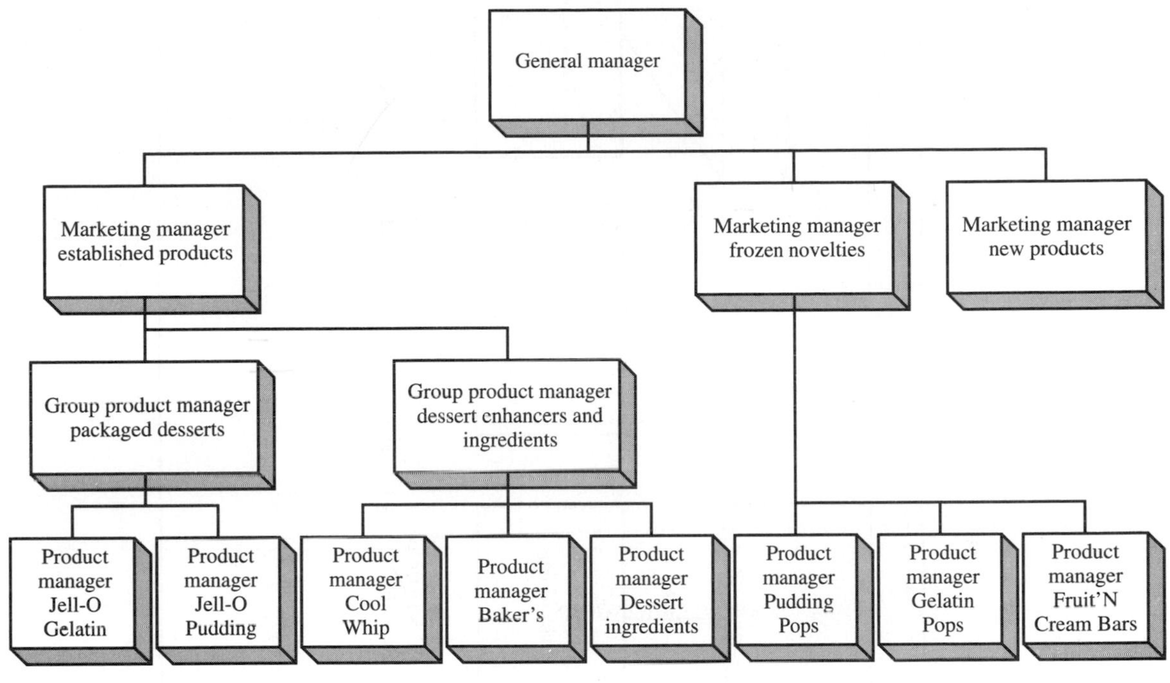

software company. The product marketing group has product managers whose responsibility is to put together marketing strategies and programs for their products such as Acrobat, Photoshop, Persuasion, and Pagemaker. In this organization, product marketing differs from "marketing" in that the latter is more tactical in nature; that is, marketing offers support to product managers in the form of designing promotional events, trade show displays, and so forth. Also, note that the sales organization is responsible for all promotional programs oriented toward the channels.

The product management system has several advantages. The locus of responsibility is clear because the person responsible for the success of the product is the product manager and no one else. Because of this, it is also clear to whom the organization can turn for information about the product. Product managers' training and experience are invaluable; they develop the ability to work with other areas of the organization and the persuasion and communication skills necessary to be an advocate for the product. In fact, companies with product-focused marketing organizations are often breeding grounds for senior executives of other companies that highly value the training received.

The product management system also has its weaknesses. The narrow focus on one product can lead to an inability to step back and ask more fundamental questions about customer needs. It can also be a very centralized structure in which the product manager is somewhat removed from "where the action is" in the field. One of the

FIGURE 1–5 Adobe Systems Marketing Organization

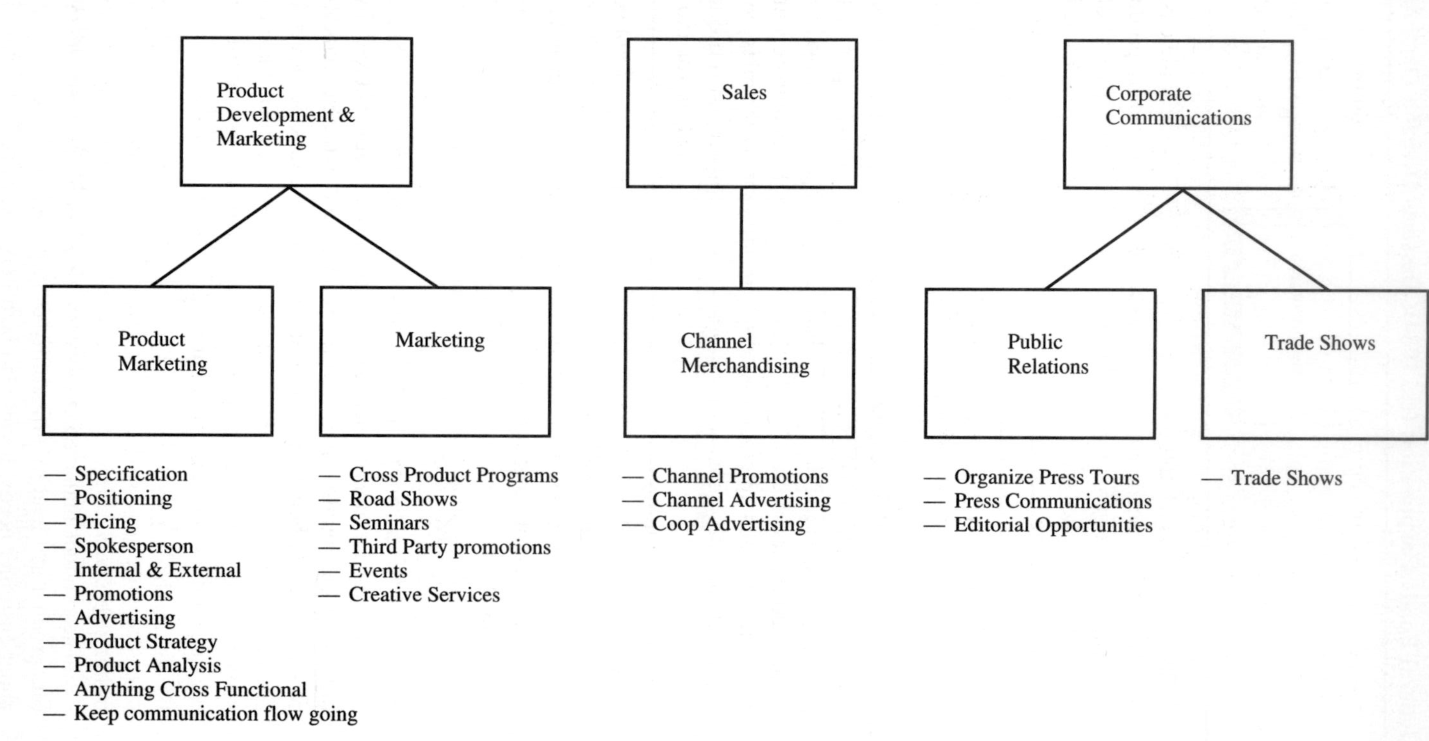

changes in marketing organizations we will discuss later is an attempt to flatten the organization and decentralize product management, particularly when significant differences exist in regional tastes for a product. In addition, some people complain that product managers are too myopic in their quest for quarterly or even shorter-term sales and market share goals. One result of this perspective has been the dramatic increase in the use of short-term marketing tools, such as sales promotions, for consumer packaged goods. A final risk in a product-focused organization, particularly for industrial products, is that it could result in several salespeople representing different products from the same company calling on the same customer. This problem is most likely to occur when the sales force is organized by product specialties and is not necessarily a general characteristic of product management organizations.

These and other problems faced by product managers have led some to predict the "death" of the product management system and widespread "burnout" among product managers.[7] Some of the factors leading to burnout are senior managers who have a short-term focus that stifles innovation, an explosion of marketing data leading to information overload, corporate downsizing, and more responsibility and pressure with less autonomy.

At the same time, the product management system continues to flourish in many consumer and industrial product companies. One study reported that hospitals with a product management organization outperformed those without it on nearly all performance indicators, including occupancy rate, gross patient-revenue per bed, average profit margin, and return on assets.[8] In addition, companies continue to adopt the organizational structure. Two notable recent examples are Ford and General Motors. Ford has adopted a structure that has a brand manager for closely related product "families": "Youthful vehicles" (e.g., Aspire), "Family vehicles" (e.g., Taurus), "Sporting cars" (e.g., Mustang), "Expressive cars" (e.g., Explorer), and "Tough vehicles" (e.g., F-Series pickups).[9] In addition, packaged goods managers with brand management experience have been hired by computer software companies such as Intuit, SoftKey, and Micrografx.[10]

Market-Focused Organizations

Figure 1–6 describes the market-focused organization. This structure defines marketing authority by market segment. Segments can be defined by industry, channel, regions of the country or the world, or customer size. The market-focused structure is clearly useful when there are significant differences in buyer behavior among the market segments that lead to differences in the marketing strategies and tactics used to appeal to them. For example, banks often define their activities in terms of corporate

---

[7] See George S. Low and Ronald Fullerton, "Brands, Brand Management, and the Brand Manager System: A Critical-Historical Evaluation," *Journal of Marketing Research,* May 1994, pp. 173–190; Tracy Carlson, "Brand Burnout," *Brandweek,* January 17, 1994, p. 23.

[8] Linda M. Gorchels, "Traditional Product Management Evolves," *Marketing News,* January 30, 1995, p. 4.

[9] Raymond Serafin, "Ford Taps Insiders as Brand Managers," *Advertising Age,* January 1, 1996, p. 3.

[10] Tim Clark, "Package-Goods Execs Flood into Software," *Advertising Age,* May 16, 1994, p. S–4.

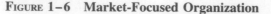

FIGURE 1–6 Market-Focused Organization

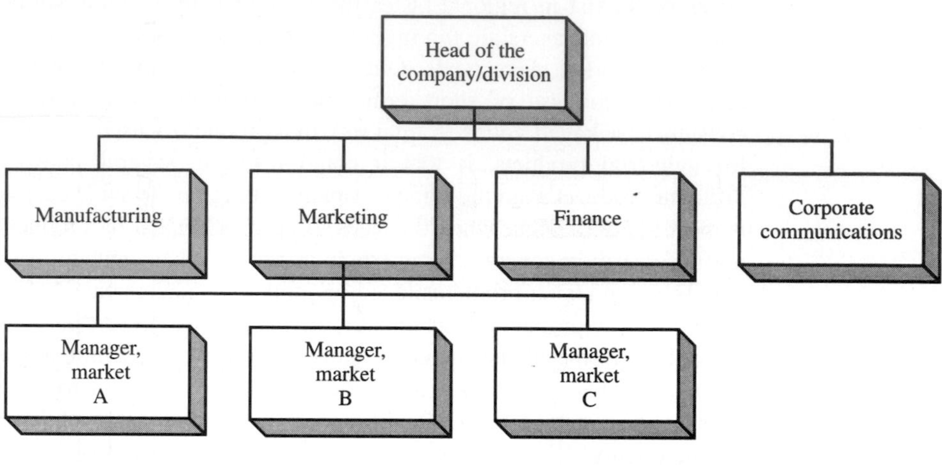

versus consumer business, and within the corporate business they often define market segments in terms of customer size.

Figure 1–7 shows the marketing organization of one of the regional Bell Telephone operating companies (often referred to as RBOCs). This organizational chart divides marketing into three large groups: consumer, business, and interindustry (business with other carriers, such as US Sprint). Within each business market are different operational functions and product management. For example, within the consumer sector are product managers for custom-calling features such as call waiting and special phone directory listings. Within the business sector are product managers for pay telephones, central office phone services, local area network planning services, and many other services. This type of organization, however, does not give managers full responsibility for their services and products. Product managers are instead more like coordinators who implement marketing programs developed by the staffs of the three business managers.

Clearly the big advantage of this market-based structure is its focus on the customer. This focus on customers as assets makes it easier to consider changes in customer tastes and when necessary modify or eliminate some of the products currently being marketed. It is particularly useful when the product being marketed is a system that bundles a number of products made by the company or when the customer purchases many different products from the company. A product management structure offers insufficient motivation to spend time on a system sale, which may involve little revenue for a particular product. The market-based structure makes it easier to get the product managers to pull together. These managers often have better knowledge about the company's lines of products than do the product managers in a product-focused company.

A drawback of this structure is the potential conflict with the product management structure that may lie beneath it. In addition, some of the mini-CEO training and experience of traditional product managers is lost. Importantly, however, most of the

Figure 1–7 Marketing Organization: Regional Bell Operating Company

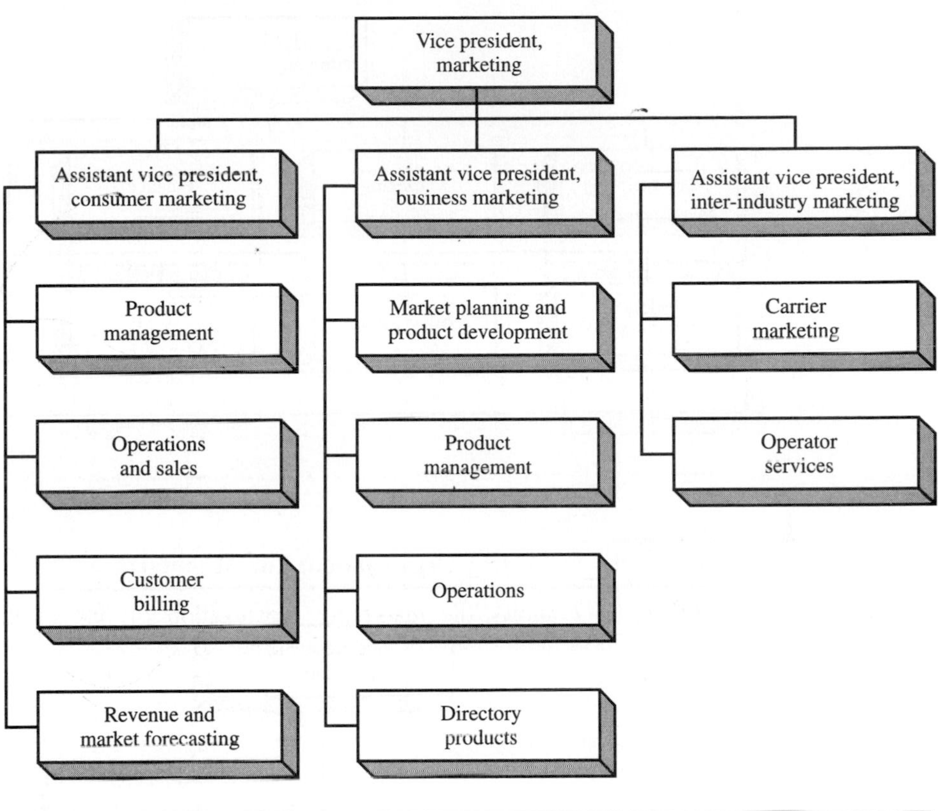

skills, procedures, and activities required to be a good product manager are critical for market focused management as well.

Functionally Focused Organizations

As opposed to the product-focused and market-focused organizations previously described, functionally focused organizations align themselves by marketing functions such as advertising and sales promotion. A general illustration of this type of structure appears in Figure 1–8. Most marketing organizations have some aspect of this structure; it is common, for example, for sales and marketing research to be separate functions. However, in functionally focused structures, no single person is responsible for the day-to-day health of a product. Marketing strategies are designed and implemented through the coordinated activities.

Figure 1–9 represents the organizational structure of a well-known toy manufacturer that markets three different products. Reporting to the vice president–marketing are marketing support, advertising and public relations, publications (a magazine targeted toward product users), and merchandising, which deals with retailers and

FIGURE 1–8 Functionally Focused Organization

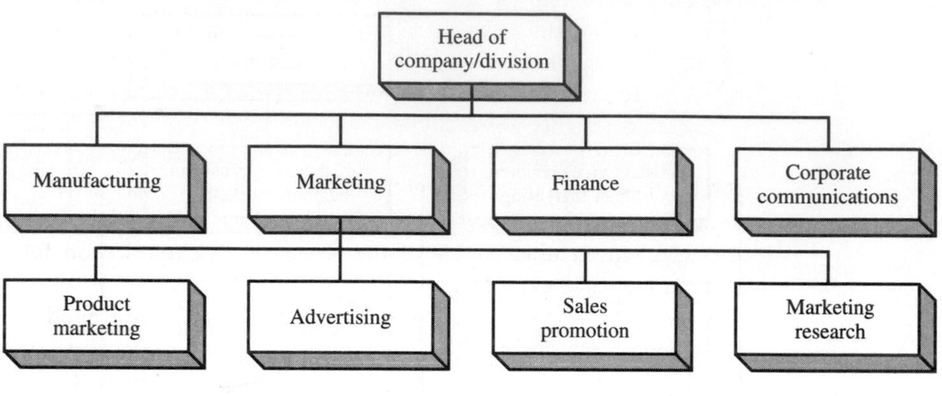

FIGURE 1–9 Marketing Organization: Toy Manufacturer

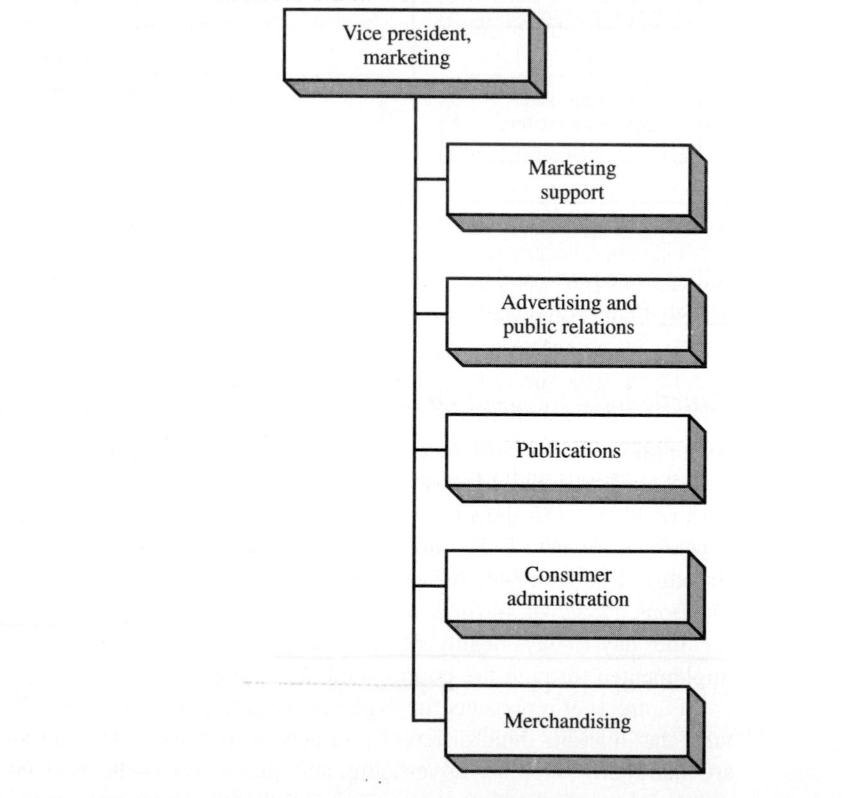

point-of-purchase displays. In this company, the CEO and the vice presidents make marketing strategy decisions. Strategies are implemented through discussion and coordination among the functional areas. This structure serves the company well when it is producing only two products. As the company adds products, however, the increased coordination needed raises the potential for confusion and makes it questionable whether the company can continue to sustain its success.

This highlights one of the drawbacks of the functionally oriented structure: Who is responsible for the product? Someone must take day-to-day responsibility for each product or service marketed by the organization. Conflicts between product marketing strategies can be resolved only by spending substantial time in meetings. The management training aspect of the structure also focuses on functional rather than general management education.

However, this kind of structure has some advantages. It is administratively simple: The groups are designed to be parallel to normal marketing activities. Functional training is better; for example, a person whose sole responsibility is to develop sales promotions will bring better skills to that area. Also, it may be desirable that the marketing vice president does much of the planning because of that person's broader business perspective.

The Role of the Sales Force

The previous discussion focused on the organizational structure of marketing management within companies. Although sales is an element of the marketing mix, most companies have separate sales organizations with their own structures and coordinating relationship with marketing organizations (see, for example, the Adobe marketing organization chart in Figure 1–5).

Briefly, there are three kinds of sales organizational structures. One structure is organized around product lines. This product/product structure sells a product or product line to all markets and often coexists with a product-focused organization. The second structure, product/market, has a product-oriented marketing structure, but each salesperson sells all products marketed by a division to a single market. Finally, the market/market structure has a market-based marketing organization and a sales force that sells a complete product line to a single market.

These structures have different advantages and disadvantages, with the product/product and the market/market structures exhibiting the most extreme characteristics. Advantages often cited for the product/product structure are easy administration, clear communications with manufacturing and operations, and effective cost control of product expenses. As in the product management system, a disadvantage is lack of concern with and communication about customer needs as well as duplication of effort. In the market/market structure, customer needs may be better served by both existing and new products. However, lines of responsibility for individual products are blurry.

Marketing Organization Implications of Global Marketing

Global marketing is the attempt to market a product or service using a common strategy around the world with only minor tactical changes in packaging, advertisement, language, and the like. Some companies, most often producers of consumer products, have been successful global marketers. These include Coca-Cola, McDonald's, British Airways, Nike, Unilever, Procter & Gamble, and Tambrands.

Unfortunately, global marketing often conflicts with companies' organizational structures. Most companies do not become global companies overnight. Usually they begin by exporting their products to some countries outside the domestic market, often using local agents for distribution. These evolve into rather strong local organizations that can have substantial power in making decisions involving pricing, packaging, and even brand names. Thus, this typical international marketing structure limits the ability to market globally or even market a product using a similar strategy in a specific region of the world. Strong, centralized product management systems that can globally market a product are rare.

An example of this problem was the situation facing Henkel Corporation, the large German manufacturer of household products, adhesives, chemicals, and cosmetics, in the mid-1980s. Henkel is headquartered in Dusseldorf and has subsidiaries throughout Europe. Traditionally, the subsidiaries operated as regional profit centers and had a substantial amount of local autonomy; they even had different brand names in different countries. Marketing managers in the company began to advocate the notion of global marketing. However, the country managers opposed the global marketing concept because they believed the standardized marketing strategy developed in Dusseldorf would be inappropriate for their countries. This highlights the difficulty of mixing a centralized product management structure, strong country managers, and a standardized marketing strategy in a region of the world.

Clearly the traditional role of the country manager is changing due to global competition, global customers, global integration, regional trading blocs, and strategic alliances. The role of the country manager as "king" or "queen" in his or her region is shifting to multinational companies using sales managers who report to either regional managers or centralized product managers. However, some kind of local management will always be necessary to allow a company to stay close to local customers and government authorities.[11]

Product Management: Fact versus Fiction

Much of the preceding description of the product manager's job and the types of organizational structures that affect the role of product managers was general. As is always the case, there are exceptions to the rules. Even within a specific organization type, the product manager's job varies among industries and among products.

A survey of 25 product managers at a wide variety of firms sheds some light on the product manager's job.[12] Figure 1–10 shows the variety of product management

[11] For more on this topic, see John A. Quelch, "The New Country Managers," *The McKinsey Quarterly,* no. 4 (1992), pp. 155–165, and Erich A. Joachimsthaler, "A Note on the Organizational Implications of Globalization," IESE case number 594–042–6, University of Navarra, Barcelona-Madrid.

[12] This section is based on Trevor Traina, "A Comparison of Product Marketing Management Across Industries," master's thesis, Haas School of Business, University of California at Berkeley, 1996.

FIGURE 1–10 Sample Composition of Product Manager Survey

	"Small" (<$500M)	*"Large" (>$500M)*
Consumer products		
Packaged goods	3	5
Clothing/retail	1	1
Financial services	0	2
Industrial products		
Computer hardware	0	2
Computer software	2	2
Industrial	1	1
Services	0	1
Consulting	1	1

jobs represented in the sample. To get a flavor for the responses to the survey, summaries from four of the interviews are provided in the appendix to this chapter. Although the sample is not large or randomly selected, we can draw some general implications.

Qualifications. The respondents reported a large number of different routes to the product manager job. Some of the firms preferred people with MBA degrees, some were indifferent, and, interestingly, one firm preferred that applicants *not* have an MBA, as the firm has its own internal training program complete with classes taught by professors using the case method. About half of the product managers did have an MBA, without any particular pattern across industries. Industry and/or general business experience was widely believed to be more important than the degree. In the large consumer products companies, half of the product managers had experience at those companies and worked their way up, while the other half had some experience at other large consumer products companies. Not surprisingly, at the smaller firms, most had worked at a large firm before joining the smaller company. In the industrial product sector, the product managers interviewed tended to have backgrounds in an appropriate technical area or degrees in a relevant area of science (e.g., the product manager at a chemical company had an undergraduate degree in chemical engineering). The computer companies in the sample tended to hire product managers with more technical skills as well as some with more unusual or creative backgrounds, such as musicians and architects.

Responsibilities. Most of the product managers have general manager-type duties to oversee the day-to-day operations of their products. They generally, but not always, have profit-and-loss responsibility and profit targets they have to meet or exceed. This is most typical of the larger consumer product companies; these managers are also charged with building and maintaining brand images (also referred to as brand "equity," as we discuss shortly) over a long period of time. Consumer product brand managers emphasize data analysis more than their industrial product counterparts do and are thus more analytical in nature. These managers also devote more time to volume targets, whereas non–consumer product managers focus more on profit or other objectives. Along with meeting their objectives, high-technology marketers spend a large amount of time tracking their competitors. Several of these companies are organized like the regional Bell operating company shown in Figure 1–7, with both product managers who focus on the day-to-day operations of the brand and market managers who worry more about the different market segments and how to satisfy their needs.

The Marketing Plan. There was almost universal agreement among the respondents that the marketing plan is an essential component of the marketing function. While the specific parameters of the plan vary by company, all the product managers devote considerable time to its development. Large consumer product companies have mastered the formal marketing planning process. Small consumer product companies have more loosely formed plans that are prone to shift quickly in response to changing market conditions (this is, of course, one of the strategic advantages of a small firm against larger competitors). Industrial product companies tend to have very detailed plans, particularly the technology-based firms. One of the industrial companies in the sample is adopting a "rolling" marketing plan that is continuously updated rather than reworked every year in the traditional fashion, which it hopes will lead to greater focus and the kind of quick market response that characterizes smaller firms.

Critical Skills Needed. A common question the authors often get is: What kind of people are successful product managers? This question was put to the sample of product managers. Successful product managers appear to have the following qualities:

1. They are organized. Product managers are expected to be the "hub of the wheel," with broad knowledge of other business functions. Thus, they spend a large amount of time in meetings coordinating with production, finance, sales, human resources, and other functions. People who are not able to handle the large amount of interaction will not be successful product managers.
2. They are efficient. A "typical" day (although respondents unanimously said there is no such thing) has mornings spent responding to electronic mail, afternoons spent in meetings, and constant "fires" to be extinguished. Somehow, in between all of these activities, the work—planning and executing the marketing of the product—has to get done.
3. They have excellent interpersonal skills. Once again, as the "hub," the manager spends his or her day in constant contact with other people. Successful product managers are team players and able to work well in cross-functional teams.
4. They are persuasive. Often product managers compete against other divisions and brands for resources and attention. They cannot do their jobs without winning support from those around them.
5. They are aware of the business environment. Good product managers have the ability to spot trends and gather relevant data, which they then translate into appropriate action in the marketplace.

Trends in Product Management. The product managers surveyed were asked to comment on what they saw as some key trends in product management, in particular, how their jobs were changing. The most frequently mentioned trends were as follows:

- Corporations starting to emphasize profit over volume or market share targets.
- Targeted promotions and one-to-one marketing.
- The routine use of electronic mail (e-mail) for communicating within the firm.
- The use of the Internet for a variety of activities, including market research, competitor analysis, communications, data transfer, and even finding employees.
- More data.
- More emphasis on the end user by industrial product companies.
- Firms starting to think more in global terms.
- Marketing growing in importance.

We will expand on some of these trends in the next section.

Changes Affecting Product Management

It is often said that the only constant is change. Product managers such as those in the study we reported on in the previous section face many challenges in adapting to the changes in the marketing environment. Some of the key changes are as follows:

1. *New ways of reaching customers.* In the mid-1990s, the World Wide Web on the Internet is replacing interactive television as the "hot" medium of the decade. Any company not having a web site in 1996 is considered to be hopelessly out of date.[13] The hard part is not creating the site. Many large and small firms exist to do that. The big issue is whether or not the web will actually be useful for marketers. The current major application of web sites is information dissemination and product positioning; little is actually being sold over the web. The main advantage of the web for product managers is the ability to customize messages, services, and products to the individuals accessing the web site (this concept of micromarketing is discussed further in Chapter 6). In addition to the Internet, increases in the use of direct marketing, telemarketing, and cable/satellite TV will make the product manager's job of selecting alternative modes of communication more complex.

2. *The data explosion.* As the product managers interviewed for this book noted, effective marketing today requires sophisticated information management. For consumer packaged goods companies, this means better and more timely information on market shares, sales, and distribution due to the proliferation of scanners in supermarkets. Almost all products sold through the retail system are more effectively tracked by both the retailer and the manufacturer due to increased use of information technology. The use of laptop computers and fax machines means quicker transmission of competitor information and sales call reports from the field. Database marketing—launching marketing programs from computerized customer lists—is becoming a key approach for obtaining and keeping customers.

3. *The increased value of brands.* The 1980s was clearly the era of sales promotion and price discounts. These activities may increase short-term volume, but

[13] The same could be said for marketing departments in business schools.

they have negative long-term effects on how consumers see the brand. A brand once associated with quality becomes associated with low price and discounting. A major trend in the mid-1990s is the realization that one of the greatest assets a company has is its set of brands and the image and confidence customers have in them. For example, Ohgo, the chairman and CEO of Sony, suggested the new president's job had one key priority:

> 'Our biggest asset is four letters: Sony. It's not so much our buildings or our engineers or our factories, but our name. Idei-san will have to do things his own way, of course, but a new president must above all else preserve and build our reputation, because that determines the value of the company in the 21st century.' He pauses, then adds with a chuckle, 'If Idei-san can't do that, I'll just have to fire him.'[14]

As a result, a key term used by product managers is brand "equity," the value of the brand name. Brand names such as Coke, IBM, Compaq, and Federal Express are not just descriptive labels but are product attributes that require consistent investment for maintenance and enhancement. We expand on this issue in Chapter 8.

4. *Product life cycles are shortening.* A key phenomenon in technology-based industries and many others is the shortening of product life cycles.[15] The time it takes for most product categories to reach maturity has been reduced by increased rates of innovation among increased numbers of competitors. This puts pressure on product managers to constantly seek ways to extend their brands' life cycles by repositioning, changing features, looking for new uses, or developing other ways to extend the period in which profits can be generated. Because shortening product life cycles implies that profit life cycles are also becoming shorter, it is more important than ever to be right when the product is first brought to market. This increases the importance of market research and the interaction of new-product development teams and marketing.

5. *Increased power of sellers.* Prior to the mid-1980s, manufacturers held the upper hand in dealing with retailers due to asymmetry in information: Manufacturers had a better idea of what was selling than retailers because of better data collection methods. Today improvements in information technology and partnerships between manufacturers and sellers in developing measurement systems have given both parties equal access to sales and market share data. As a result, the balance of power in distribution channels has shifted from the manufacturer to the retailer. This has created more manufacturer awareness, even among manufacturers with powerful brand names, that retailers must be treated as key customers and that it is as important to be close to them as it is to the end customer.

6. *Significant spending on sales promotion versus advertising.* This trend is mainly characteristic of consumer products. The high rates of spending on sales promotion, particularly on trade promotion, coupled with downward pressure on prices (due in large part to successful private label products), have lowered profit margins dramatically. Investments in brand equity and concomitant calls by some managers to reduce spending on trade promotions have attempted to reverse this process, but have not been universally accepted. This has had the unfortunate effect of making product

---

[14] *Fortune,* June 12, 1995.

[15] William Qualls, Richard Olshavsky, and Ronald Michaels, "Shortening of the PLC—An Empirical Test," *Journal of Marketing,* (Fall 1981), pp. 76–80.

management even more short-term oriented as the battle for market share has intensified.

7. *Pricing and value.* These two terms are often confused. Companies are more interested in pricing their products at a level commensurate with customer value, that is, the economic value customers place on the products. However, during the recessionary period of the early 1990s, value pricing came to mean offering greater value to the customer than is justified by the price. Product managers therefore seek ways to offer increased value in products while reducing prices, producing "bargains."

8. *Increased importance of customer retention programs.* Companies are becoming very attuned to the lifetime value of a customer concept, whereby one measures the value of a customer by the discounted stream of income from future purchases. By focusing more on keeping customers than on attracting brand switchers, who have a greater overall propensity to switch to someone else eventually, product managers are paying more attention to customer service and satisfaction programs, database marketing, and advertising and promotion programs aimed at satisfying current customers and/or getting them to buy more of the product.

9. *Increased global competition.* Unquestionably, product managers have to be equipped to deal with worldwide competition—not only by having appropriate organizational structures, as discussed earlier in this chapter, but also by obtaining experience and knowledge about how a variety of cultures conduct business.

Impact of Change on Organizational Structure: Category Management

As noted previously, companies have used a variety of organizational forms for their marketing function. Most of the changes in the environment noted earlier have led to important shifts in resource allocation within the firm rather than to massive shifts in the organizational structure. These include investments in the new interactive methods for reaching customers, data processing capabilities, and so on.

One change mentioned earlier that has had a strong impact on marketing organizations is the increased power of the retailer in the channel of distribution system, particularly for consumer products. The perspectives of manufacturers and retailers are quite different. Retailers' scarce resource is their selling space, and they care less about how a particular brand is selling than what is happening to the sales of a product category, department, or store as a whole. In other words, retailers are more interested in a category perspective than a brand perspective. Of course, the reverse is true for manufacturers.

This category perspective can be coupled with the data explosion that has given retailers, manufacturers, and data suppliers a microscope under which to analyze the performance of different product categories in different parts of the country, different parts of a state, and different areas within a city. To optimize their product mix, retailers not only want to offer the appropriate brands in a category; they want the mix of brands and product varieties to be appropriate for the ethnic and socioeconomic composition of the shopping areas in which particular stores are located.

Thus, the early 1990s introduced a concept called *category management* into the product manager's lexicon. Category management has been defined as a process that considers product categories to be business units that should be customized on a store-by-store basis in a way that satisfies customer needs.[16] Retailers have category managers who, like product managers and their brands, are empowered to operate their categories as separate businesses.

The category management phenomenon has had an important impact on product management organizations from the perspective of the responsibilities of product managers and the sales force. This is highlighted in Figure 1–11. Under the traditional approach (that is, when manufacturers had information about which products were selling and which were not), the sales force focused on gaining distribution, getting retailers to promote their brands, and pushing the product managers for trade-oriented promotions to increase short-run volume. As noted earlier in this chapter, the product manager's job has traditionally been to develop the marketing strategies and programs for his or her product.

More recently, however, marketing organizations have begun to view the retailer as a partner whereby the objective is to provide a mix of products that best satisfy customer needs. Under a category management system, manufacturers have to be concerned about meeting not only their objectives but also the retailer's. This has meant that within the manufacturer, the product management, sales, and marketing research organizations also have to work together as a team, since typically a salesperson sells a large number of a company's products managed by an equivalently large number of product managers. Salespeople are working closely with product managers, and marketing research/MIS people are providing information to both product managers and salespeople, the former interested in customer behavior toward brands and the latter concerned with customer behavior toward the whole product category. Interestingly, in this era of category management, the salesperson is really the key person since she or he is the link between product managers interested primarily in their brands and retailers interested mainly in their categories. The job of the salesperson is to become intimately familiar with the needs of both the retailer and the customer so that he or she can configure the company's offerings appropriately to a particular store.

---

[16] A good source on category management is a publication by A. C. Nielsen, *Category Management: Positioning Your Organization to Win,* (Chicago: NTC Business Books, 1992), see also Laurie Petersen, "Brand Managing's New Accent," *Marketing Week,* April 15, 1991, pp. 17–22.

FIGURE 1–11 Changing Organization Structures

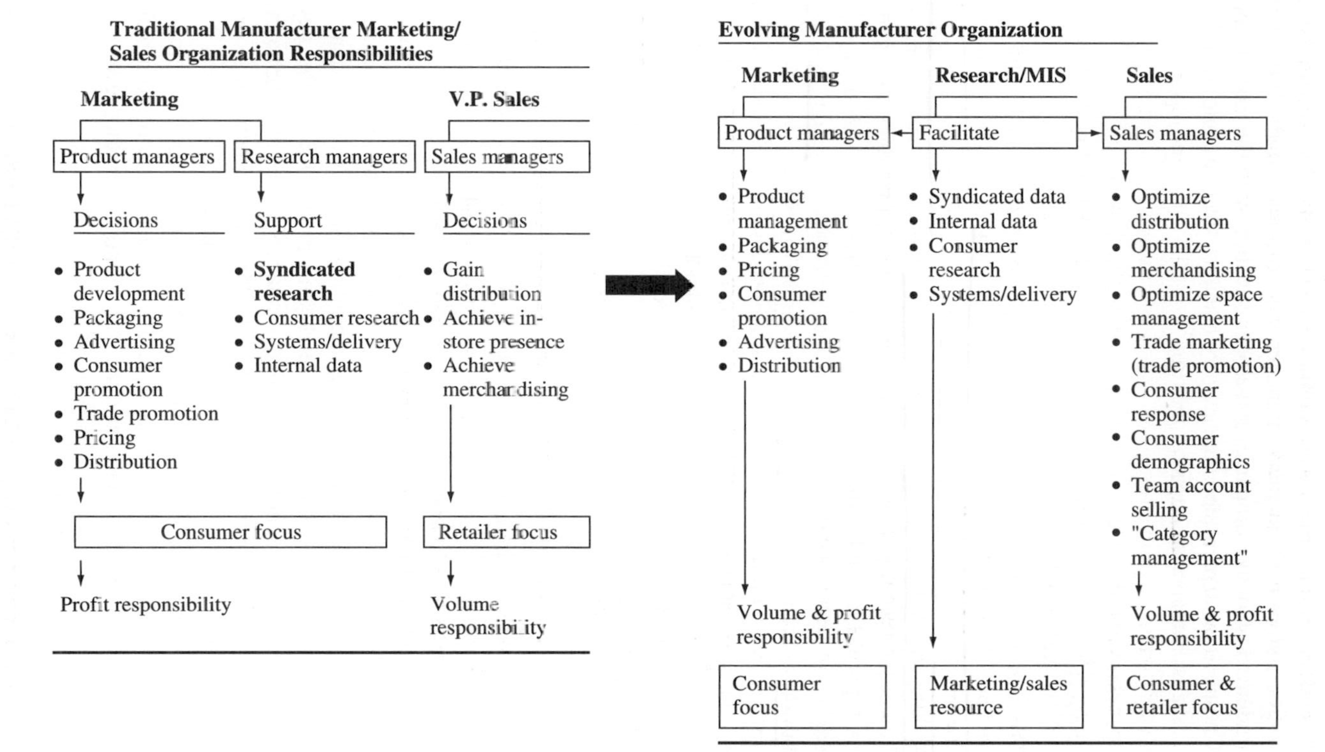

Source: A. C. Nielsen, *Category Management: Positioning Your Organization to Win* (Chicago: NTC Business Books, 1992), pp. 106–7.

In some cases, companies such as Procter & Gamble and Clorox have adopted category managers to whom product managers report that are parallel to the retailer's categories. Coca-Cola Foods defines its categories by trademarks, such as Minute Maid, and has a trademark manager who oversees marketing all brands with that trademark. Not all companies have been satisfied with the extra layer of management; Campbell Soup instituted the category manager structure and then dropped it to reduce costs and streamline decision making.[17]

Summary

We characterize the product manager's job by three distinct activities: (1) collecting and analyzing background product category data, (2) utilizing the background analysis for marketing strategy development, and (3) implementing the marketing strategy through marketing mix and related decisions. Doing an excellent job at these activities, however, does not guarantee a successful career in product management. As indicated in Figure 1–1 and supported by the interviews with product managers described earlier in the chapter, the interpersonal activities of leadership, coordination, team building, and communications are becoming increasingly critical aspects of the job and often determine a person's rate of advancement in the company. In this book, we do not attempt to prescribe how an existing or aspiring product manager can become successful at those activities; we leave that to other books and courses. Rather we concentrate on monitoring the marketing environment and the planning, strategy, and decision-making aspects of the job.

Marketing Planning

The first seven chapters of the book cover the background analysis for developing marketing plans.[18] A distinctive feature of the marketing planning chapters is the use of two running illustrations of the material presented, Ready-to-Drink (RTD) fruit drinks (e.g., Snapple) and personal digital assistants (PDAs). These illustrations are introduced in Chapter 2. Chapter 2 also presents an overview of marketing planning, including a rationale for developing marketing plans. An important part of this chapter is a comprehensive outline of a marketing plan. One of the key changes in the marketing environment facing product managers is the shifting nature of competition. Chapter 3 discusses the importance of looking at competition from a broad perspective, one beyond the narrowly defined product category. Chapters 4, 5, and 6 describe the core background analyses for marketing plans: category, competitor, and customer analysis. Chapter 7 discusses how to develop estimates of both market potential and future sales or market share, at either the brand or product level.

---

[17] Judann Dagnoli, "Campbell Cuts Category Slot," *Advertising Age,* May 17, 1990, p. 4.

[18] See also Donald R. Lehmann and Russell S. Winer, *Analysis for Marketing Planning,* 4th ed. (Burr Ridge, Ill.: Richard D. Irwin, 1997).

Marketing Strategy

Chapter 8 discusses how objectives and a complete marketing strategy are developed based on the background analyses from Chapters 4 through 7. While the book is intended to be a template for all kinds of products and services, there are some aspects of being a product manager on a new product that are different and need additional discussion. Chapter 9 covers the marketing planning and strategy process from the perspective of new products.

Marketing Program Decisions

The rest of the book focuses on decisions product managers typically have to make as part of their jobs. Our approach to this section is unusual in two ways. First, we do not attempt to cover all aspects of an area. As a result, for example, we do not cover the creative aspects of advertising in depth. Instead, we discuss the issues we believe are most critical to product managers, such as setting budgets and evaluating advertising effectiveness. Second, where appropriate, we discuss recent results from the academic marketing research literature and make them accessible to practicing product managers.

We cover key marketing mix variables, including pricing (Chapter 10), advertising (Chapter 11), and sales promotion (Chapter 12). We do not cover sales management in this book. While the sales force is a key resource and, as the discussion about category management illustrated, is increasingly becoming a partner with product management in working with retail and end customers, the survey discussed earlier indicated that most product managers do not have authority over decisions about its size, allocation of resources, and other functions. In fact, as we noted in this chapter, sales and marketing are usually separate organizations.

The last four decision-oriented chapters of the book cover some topics not usually discussed in other marketing management texts that are extremely important for product management in the 1990s. In Chapter 13, we discuss how decisions about channels of distribution and the general problem of reaching customers have become more complex. For example, substantially increased spending on direct marketing is one new way companies are reaching customers. In Chapter 14 we focus on managing customer service, which, as noted earlier, is critical to a successful customer retention program. In Chapter 15, we discuss financial analysis and profit planning. Many marketing students underestimate the importance of a solid background in financial analysis and cost accounting in a product management career. We pay particular attention to alternative definitions of profit.

In sum, this book is intended to give the reader background and knowledge essential to being a successful product manager. At the same time, we try to communicate the excitement of being involved with the day-to-day decisions that determine the success of products, brands, and services.

Appendix 1.1
Sample Responses from Product Managers

1. *Company:* Large computer software company
   Title: Product manager
   Background: After an architecture undergraduate degree, worked in various marketing positions in architecture firms up to the level of director of marketing. After an MBA program, worked as an international marketing manager for a sporting goods company. Subsequently founded a toy company.

   Typical day: Meetings related to product development, launching a new product line, the marketing mix, marketing staff, and with other product managers for integration/compatibility issues. E-mail and telephone to third-party developers, check up on sales force and product support. Work on marketing plan.

   Marketing planning activities: The marketing plan is the most critical thing for which the product manager holds full responsibility. In this company, the product manager is responsible for both strategy and tactics.

   Marketing mix: The product manager is ultimately responsible for the marketing mix, except for price and sales. With respect to pricing, the product manager makes recommendations to a Corporate Pricing Committee that recommends to Executive Staff for final decision. Advertising is under the manager's responsibility; focus groups for positioning, other qualitative research, and cost-benefit analyses are done. Manager also makes channel decisions concerning which to use and the budget.

   How the job is changing: Technology has had a huge impact particularly on distribution, as the company is now distributing the product electronically. Technology also is being used for communications with customers and other strategic partners.

2. *Company:* Large financial services company
   Title: Product manager, customer development and retention
   Background: Undergraduate major in art history. Worked for a small financial services firm for five years in marketing (mutual funds), then a large commercial bank for three years in mutual funds, then to current company.

   Typical day: A very meeting-intensive environment. Often four to five meetings per day, which occupies half of the day. Meetings involve whoever is affected by direct mail in the company. Spends a great deal of time on e-mail communications for the product's marketing programs.

   Marketing planning activities: Annual marketing plan submitted to director who is ultimately responsible for the plan. Heavy direct-mail orientation. Responsible for a "strategic document" for each mailing done during the year, including budget, creative plan, etc., which are submitted and approved by director. The overall marketing plan is reviewed quarterly.

   Marketing mix: Responsibilities include direct mail (60 percent of the job), communicating industry/pricing changes to customers, quarterly statements to customers, field training (working with the four call centers to prepare them for direct-mail responses), coordinating with advertising agency.

   How the job is changing: With the introduction of electronic financial services and the ability of customers to work with their brokers in more ways, such as through home computers, the World Wide Web, etc., the product manager's job has changed how they work with their customers. Information systems are much more sophisticated, and therefore promotions can be much targeted.

3. *Company:* Large commodity-based consumer packaged goods company

   Title: Senior product manager

   Background: Sold high-end medical equipment after undergraduate degree. Received an MBA. Worked as an assistant brand manager at a large consumer products company, then changed firms and received successive promotions to associate and then product manager. Went to current firm as a senior product manager.

   Typical day: Seventy-five percent of the day goes to issues that come up and require immediate attention, only 25 percent to planning, strategy, and other management decisions. Organization is very lean, and so involvement in even small decisions is important and exposure to "fires" is high.

   Marketing planning activities: Fiscal year runs July 1–June 30, annual planning process starts in November/December. The key to planning is volume forecasting since unsold inventory is perishable. Budget and profit goals never change once they are negotiated.

   Marketing mix: Approximately one-third of time spent on pricing issues, both list and trade prices, 20 percent on consumer-oriented promotions, very little on advertising (the president personally handles most advertising), about 15 percent of time on distribution issues, very little on sales force and customer service.

   How the job is changing: The biggest change has been the amount of trade (channel) spending and the time spent on channel issues. These issues get as much weight as consumer issues. In this kind of business, product managers must work with all customers and understand their individual needs.

4. *Company:* Small company manufacturing packaging materials

   Title: Sales and marketing manager

   Background: Went to company straight from undergraduate school. Built the current marketing position and reports directly to the president of the holding company owning his employer.

   Typical day: This includes capacity planning, a critical task since the company cannot meet current demand. Other responsibilities include making sales calls, developing marketing materials, attending trade shows, and working on customer service issues.

   Marketing planning activities: This is a critical document for the company. They have chosen 100 companies to target and have focused very specifically on them, directing their spending to get the maximum benefit. The plan is instrumental in shaping this process and as a check throughout the year to measure effectiveness. Building the plan was initially very time consuming but has become quicker and easier in recent years.

   Marketing mix: Price: has some leeway but within guidelines. Promotion: in charge of these, which are limited to generating new business. Sales force: this person is the sales force. Advertising/distribution: not responsible. Customer service: major part of the job and is responsible for this activity. Fifty percent of time is spent on programs oriented toward new business.

   How the job is changing: Communications technology has had the most impact in the last few years. Uses e-mail to target communications to key customers. Internally, it makes accomplishing tasks much easier. Extensive use of teleconferencing with two other managers in different parts of the country creating a virtual office. More emphasis on international business.

C H A P T E R

2 Marketing Planning

Overview

Definition and Objectives of Plans

The discussion in Chapter 1 about the product manager's job noted that developing a marketing plan is a key responsibility. In fact, some people believe the development of the annual marketing plan is the single most important activity of the product manager.[1]

Marketing planning has become a major activity in most firms. One survey found that over 90 percent of marketing executives engaged in formal planning.[2] These executives spent, on average, 45 days each year on planning, relying most heavily on information from the sales force, management information systems, and internal marketing research. The development of marketing plans, which are generally annual and focus on a product or one or more product lines, is thus an important function for marketers, one that is believed to improve both coordination and performance.

The marketing plan can be divided into two general parts: the situation analysis, which analyzes the background of the market for the product, and the objectives, strategy, and programs based on the background analysis that direct the product manager's actions. While most books and the popular press concentrate on the latter, incorrect or inadequate analysis often leads to poor decisions about pricing, advertising, and the like. The next few chapters of this book are devoted to the critical task of providing the analysis on which to base an action plan—in short, the marketing homework.

---

[1]See, for example, Stanley Stasch and Patricia Lanktree, "Can Your Marketing Planning Procedures Be Improved?" *Journal of Marketing*, Summer 1980, pp. 79–90.

[2]James Hulbert, Donald Lehmann, and Scott Hoenig, "Practices and Impacts of Marketing Planning," working paper, Columbia University, 1987. A comment made by a reviewer, with which we agree, is that the firms with product managers who do not develop marketing plans are usually small manufacturers of industrial products.

What is a marketing plan? A working definition is:

> A **marketing plan** is a *written* document containing the guidelines for the *business center's* marketing programs and allocations over the *planning period.*

Several parts of this definition have been emphasized and merit further explanation.

First, note that the plan is a *written* document, not something stored in a product manager's head. This characteristic of marketing plans produces multiple benefits. Requiring that the plan be written calls for disciplined thinking. It also ensures that prior strategies that succeeded or failed are not forgotten. In addition, a written plan provides a vehicle for communications between functional areas of the firm, such as manufacturing, finance, and sales, which is vital to the successful implementation of the plan. Also, a written marketing plan pinpoints responsibility for achieving results by a specified date. Finally, a written plan provides continuity when management turnover occurs (a significant issue for the product manager position) and quickly introduces new employees to the situation facing the business.

A second aspect of the marketing plan definition to note is that it is usually written at the *business center* level. This is purposely vague because the precise level at which plans are written varies from organization to organization. For example, in a company using a brand management organizational structure, a marketing plan is written for each brand which is (at least nominally) a profit center. Alternatively, some companies write plans for groups of brands or products, particularly when fixed costs are difficult to allocate by individual product. Thus, while marketing planning is common, it occurs at different organizational levels. In this book, we focus on specific products or closely related product lines.

For example, Kraft develops a separate marketing plan for each brand of cereal marketed by the Post Division, such as Raisin Bran. Alternatively, the medical equipment company referred to in Chapter 1 develops an overall marketing plan for reagents, the chemicals added to blood before it is analyzed, despite the fact that many different reagents exist. The reagents are grouped by application type, and parts of the overall reagent marketing plan are devoted to each group.

A final item to note from the definition of a marketing plan is that the *planning period* or horizon varies from product to product. Retailing, for example, traditionally has short planning cycles to match the seasonality and vagaries of fashion trends. Industrial firms and firms manufacturing consumer durables tend more than frequently purchased consumer product or service firms to have longer than annual marketing plans. Automobiles, for example, have longer planning cycles because lead times for product development or modifications are longer. With such long lead times, the plan would cover several years with annual updates and would focus on tactical issues such as promotion.[3] Other factors contributing to variation in the length of planning horizons are rates of technological change, intensity of competition, and frequency of shifts in the tastes of relevant groups of customers. The typical horizon, however, is annual, as the data in Figure 2–1 indicate.

---

[3]This may change with the recent trend in automobile companies to move to brand management systems.

FIGURE 2–1 Time Horizons for Marketing Plans

Time Period	*Consumer Products*	*Industrial Products*	*Services*
1 year	62%	45%	65%
3 years	5	5	8
5 years	15	17	3
Long term	4	3	6
Indefinite	0	2	2
Other	14	28	16

Source: Howard Sutton, *The Marketing Plan in the 1990s* (New York: The Conference Board, 1990), p. 25.

FIGURE 2–2 Hierarchy of Planning

Often there is confusion between *strategic* planning and *marketing* planning, which are distinct in two ways. First, strategic planning usually takes place at a higher level in the organization than marketing planning. As Figure 2–2 shows, strategic planning takes place at the corporate, group, or strategic business unit levels. At these levels, objectives are broad (e.g., return on investment or assets) and strategies are general (e.g., divesting of manufacturing nuclear power generating plants and investing in entertainment, such as Westinghouse did with its purchase of CBS). Marketing planning takes place at the business center level and has specific objectives (e.g., market share) and strategies (e.g., pursuing the small-business segment). A second difference is that due to the long-term nature of strategic plans, they usually have a longer time horizon than marketing plans; three to five years or more with annual updates is not uncommon.

In summary, the marketing plan is an operational document. It contains strategies for a product, but it focuses on a shorter time span than the strategic plan. Marketing plans are specific statements of how to achieve short-term, usually annual, results.

The objectives of a marketing plan can be stated concisely as follows:

1. To define the current situation facing the product (and how we got there).
2. To define problems and opportunities facing the business.
3. To establish objectives.
4. To define the strategies and programs necessary to achieve the objectives.
5. To pinpoint responsibility for achieving product objectives.
6. To encourage careful and disciplined thinking.
7. To establish a customer-competitor orientation.

The last objective is particularly important. Today most product managers are aware of the *marketing concept,* popularized in the 1960s, dictating that marketers must develop strategies that maintain a customer orientation. This customer orientation was reinforced in the 1980s by Peters and Waterman's book *In Search of Excellence* and the total quality management (TQM) movement. Today the marketing concept has been translated into a strong focus on customer retention and service (an issue we explore in Chapter 15). Less commonly acknowledged is the fact that a *competitor* orientation, especially in today's business environment of more competitors and shorter life cycles, is equally important. In recent years, a few books with the word *warfare* in their titles have focused on the competitive nature of marketing.[4] The vast majority of products and services are not monopolies; competitors often determine a brand's profits as much as any action taken by the product manager does. By emphasizing the importance of having both a customer orientation and a competitor orientation, the marketing plan focuses on the two most important components of the strategy development process. This is consistent with recent research at the firm level showing that a significant and positive relationship exists between a firm's degree of market orientation (as measured by customer, competitor, and interfunctional coordination) and performance.[5]

Frequent Mistakes in the Planning Process

Unfortunately, not all organizations attempting to develop marketing plans have been pleased with the process. The Strategic Planning Institute and the authors have

[4]For example, Al Ries and Jack Trout, *Marketing Warfare* (New York: McGraw-Hill, 1986).

[5]For example, Stanley F. Slater and John C. Narver, "Does Competitive Environment Moderate the Market Orientation-Performance Relationship?" *Journal of Marketing*, January 1994, pp. 46–55.

identified the most common mistakes in planning (generally defined) that are relevant to marketing planning as well.[6]

The Speed of the Process. The planning process can either be so slow that it seems to go on forever or so fast that managers rush out a plan in a burst of activity. In the former case, managers required to constantly complete forms that distract them from operational tasks burn out. In the latter case, a hastily developed plan can easily lead to critical oversights that impede the strategies developed.

The Amount of Data Collected. It is important to collect sufficient data to properly estimate customer needs and competitive trends. However, as in many other situations, the economic law of diminishing marginal returns quickly sets in on data collection. Usually a small percentage of all the data available produces a large percentage of the insights obtainable. What is the "right" amount of information? Although we could say that product managers ought to collect about 10 pounds of magazine articles, no prescription for data collection effort would be sensible. One of the purposes of this book is to point product managers toward the most important areas for data collection to avoid both under- and overcollecting information.

Who Does the Planning? In the late 1960s, strategic planning models developed by the Boston Consulting Group, McKinsey & Company, General Electric, Shell Petroleum, and others led to the formation of formal strategic planning groups in many major corporations. Essentially the planning process was delegated to professional planners, while implementation of the plans was left to line managers. Naturally, line managers resented the process. They thought the planners had no "feel" for the markets for which they were planning, and were managing by the numbers rather than considering market intuition gleaned from experience. As a result, hostility between the staff planners and line managers led to strategies that were either poorly implemented or ignored. Presently, poor results from staff-directed planning and recent economic recessions have led to cuts in non-revenue-producing jobs, making line managers get more involved with planning, both strategic and marketing. At many successful companies, such as Emerson Electric, "the people who plan are the people who execute."[7] Besides leaving planning to those who will implement the plans, it is important to involve managers from other functions in the firm. This helps to ensure buy-in from all relevant parties.

The Structure. Any formal planning effort involves some structure. The advantage of structure is that it forces discipline on the planners; that is, certain data must be collected and analyzed. Interestingly, many firms believe the most important result of planning is not the plan itself but the necessity of structuring thought about the strategic issues facing the business. However, an apparent danger is that the structure can take precedence over the content so that planning becomes mere form filling or number crunching with little thought for its purposes. Thus, although there must be

---

[6]See also Zuhair M. Suidan, "Ten Commandments for Marketing Planning," *Marketing News*, September 26, 1994, pp. 4–5.

[7]Charles Knight, "Emerson Electric: Consistent Profits, Consistently," *Harvard Business Review*, January–February 1992, pp. 57–70.

FIGURE 2–3 Lengths of Marketing Plans

Length	*Consumer Products*	*Industrial Products*	*Services*
10 pages or fewer	28%	23%	26%
11–20	17	22	22
21–30	18	11	15
31–50	21	17	12
51 or more	16	27	24

Source: Howard Sutton, *The Marketing Plan in the 1990s* (New York: The Conference Board, 1990), p. 25.

enough structure, the process should not be too bureaucratic. A good solution to this dilemma is to use the plan format shown in the appendix to this chapter as a guide but to set a rigid timetable. A flexible format helps to prevent the plan from deteriorating into mindless paper shuffling.[8]

Length of the Plan. The length of a marketing plan must be balanced, neither so long that both line and senior managers ignore it nor so brief that it omits key details. Many organizations have formal guidelines for the optimal length of plans (similar to Procter & Gamble's dreaded one-page limit on memos), so what is long for one firm is optimal for another.

Figure 2–3 provides some data on lengths of plans. The data show an interesting U-shaped pattern: Many plans are 20 pages or fewer, and many are 51 pages or more. However, the median lengths are 30 pages for industrial products, 25 for consumer products, and 21 for service businesses. Thus, typical marketing plans are between 20 and 30 pages in length.

Frequency of Planning. A potential problem occurs if the product manager plans either more or less frequently than necessary. Frequent reevaluation of strategies can lead to erratic firm behavior and make the planning process more burdensome. However, if plans are not revised as needed, the product's marketing strategies may not adapt quickly enough to changes in the environment, and its competitive position may deteriorate. Often a company adopts its fiscal year as its planning cycle. Sometimes it is difficult to determine the appropriate planning interval with precision. However, after several planning cycles and some experimentation, the appropriate amount of time becomes apparent.

Number of Courses of Action Considered. Too few alternatives may be discussed, thus raising the likelihood of failure, or too many, which increases the time and cost of the planning effort. It is important to have diverse strategic options (e.g., both growth and hold strategies) because discarded strategies often prove useful as contingency plans. In fact, one job of the product manager is to prioritize possible marketing

[8]For an example of a marketing planning approach based on completing forms, see Malcolm McDonald, *Marketing Plans: How to Prepare Them, How to Use Them*, 3rd ed. (Oxford, U.K.: Butterworth-Heinemann Ltd., 1995).

strategies at a given point in time. The most appropriate strategy clearly should be implemented first, and the others should become contingency plans.

Who Sees the Plan. The successful implementation of a marketing plan requires a broad consensus from as many corporate departments as possible. Increasing the "buy-in" to the marketing plan increases its likelihood of success. For example, a strategy emphasizing high quality is difficult to implement if manufacturing does not simultaneously emphasize quality control. Growth objectives may be achievable only by relaxing credit policies. A common mistake is to view the plan as the proprietary possession of the marketing department.

Not Using the Plan as a Sales Document. A major but often overlooked purpose of a plan is to generate funds from either internal sources (e.g., to gain budget approval) or external sources (e.g., to gain a partner for a joint venture). The plan and its proponents compete with other plans and their proponents for scarce resources. Therefore, the more appealing the plan and the better the product managers' track records, the better the chance of budget approval.

Insufficient Senior Management Leadership. As with many intrafirm programs, commitment from senior management is essential to the success of a marketing planning effort. Mere training is insufficient. One organization with which we are familiar did and said all the right things about implementing a marketing planning process, but frequent turnover of marketing vice presidents with different backgrounds, values, and attitudes toward the development of marketing plans prevented a successful planning effort.

Not Tying Compensation to Successful Planning Efforts. Managers are usually driven by their compensation plans. Product managers' compensation should be oriented toward the achievements of the objectives stated in the plan. If the organization rewards profit margins and the negotiated objective of the plan is market share, a fundamental conflict will arise that will lead to a concentration on margins rather than on what is best for the product at that time.

HR issue

What Makes a Good Planning System: Some Empirical Results

Although few systematic studies of marketing planning systems have been published, some useful guidelines for improving planning have appeared in the marketing literature. A major component of a "good" marketing planning system is its thoroughness. A marketing planning process is considered to be thorough if it does the following:

1. Utilizes experience from several managerial levels rather than just from product managers. Particularly in organizations in which senior marketing managers have risen through the ranks, considerable knowledge exists of past successful and unsuccessful product marketing strategies.
2. Employs a variety of both internal and external sources of information rather than just internal information. For example, the advertising agency working on the product account often can be a valuable source of information.

3. Extends over a period of time sufficient to collect and analyze the data necessary for developing the marketing strategies.

4. Employs a number of incentives for the product managers in addition to employment security or advancement.[9]

Is Planning Worthwhile?

Again, few studies empirically link the quality of planning systems to performance as measured in terms of higher profitability or increased market share. One study found that strategic planning in general is not positively related to levels of performance, but firms with formal planning systems have less variation in profitability than those without them.[10] Using a sample of six firms, another study found a generally positive relationship between the thoroughness of the marketing planning effort and various performance measures.[11] Although it is difficult to directly relate marketing planning to improved market performance, most managers believe planning provides intangible benefits such as a disciplined approach to strategy development and the assurance that the external environment is considered at all times.

The Planning Process

Approaches to Planning

In general, the planning process works as shown in Figure 2–4. Whereas the collection and analysis of data and the development of product strategies take place over a limited time frame, there is no beginning or ending to the planning process as a whole. The formal part of the process is followed by implementation, during which programs such as distribution, promotion, advertising, and the like are executed. Monitoring and evaluating both the performance of the plan and changes in competition or customers in the external environment are also continuous tasks. This information feeds back into the formal planning part of the process. This circular aspect of marketing planning ensures that the plan is not "cast in stone" and can be revised as necessary. It also guarantees that information obtained from the market concerning the performance of the plan is integrated into next year's plan.

Two general approaches to planning have been developed. In *top-down* planning, the marketing plans are formulated by either senior or middle management with the aid of staff and product management and then implemented by the latter. In *bottom-up* planning, the lower ranks down to field salespeople are actively involved in the planning process through collecting competitor and customer information and making forecasts. The information is subject to higher-level review, but lower management personnel play key roles in the process.

---

[9]See Stasch and Lanktree, "Can Your Marketing Planning Procedures Be Improved?", pp. 79–90.

[10]Hulbert, Lehmann, and Hoenig, "Practices and Impacts of Marketing Planning."

[11]Stasch and Lanktree, "Can Your Marketing Planning Procedures Be Improved?", pp. 79–90.

FIGURE 2–4 **The Planning Process**

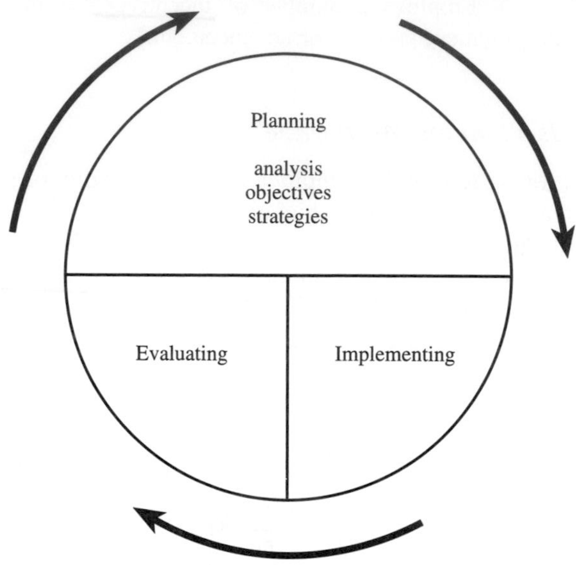

Source: Mary Ann Pezzullo, *Marketing for Bankers* (American Bankers Association, 1982), Washington, D.C. p. 32.

Both systems have some commendable characteristics. The rationale often used for top-down planning is that the higher the level the person occupies in the organization, the better the perspective on the problems facing the business. Field salespeople, for example, tend to consider the competitive battleground as their sales territories and not necessarily the national or even international market. Bottom-up planning systems are often characterized by better implementation than top-down approaches, since the people primarily charged with executing the plan are involved in its development.

Steps in the Planning Process

In most organizations, collecting information and structuring the marketing plan require a sequential planning process. This process generally includes eight steps, as shown in Figure 2–5.

Step 1: Update the facts about the past. Data collected for marketing planning purposes are often provisional or estimated. For example, planning for 1997 takes place in 1996. At that time, annual data on market sales or share would be available only for 1995 at best and often only for 1994 due to delays in the data collection process. As a result, planners often use forecasts or extrapolations of partial results. However, when new data become available, they should replace figures that were estimated or forecasted.

FIGURE 2–5 Marketing Planning Sequence

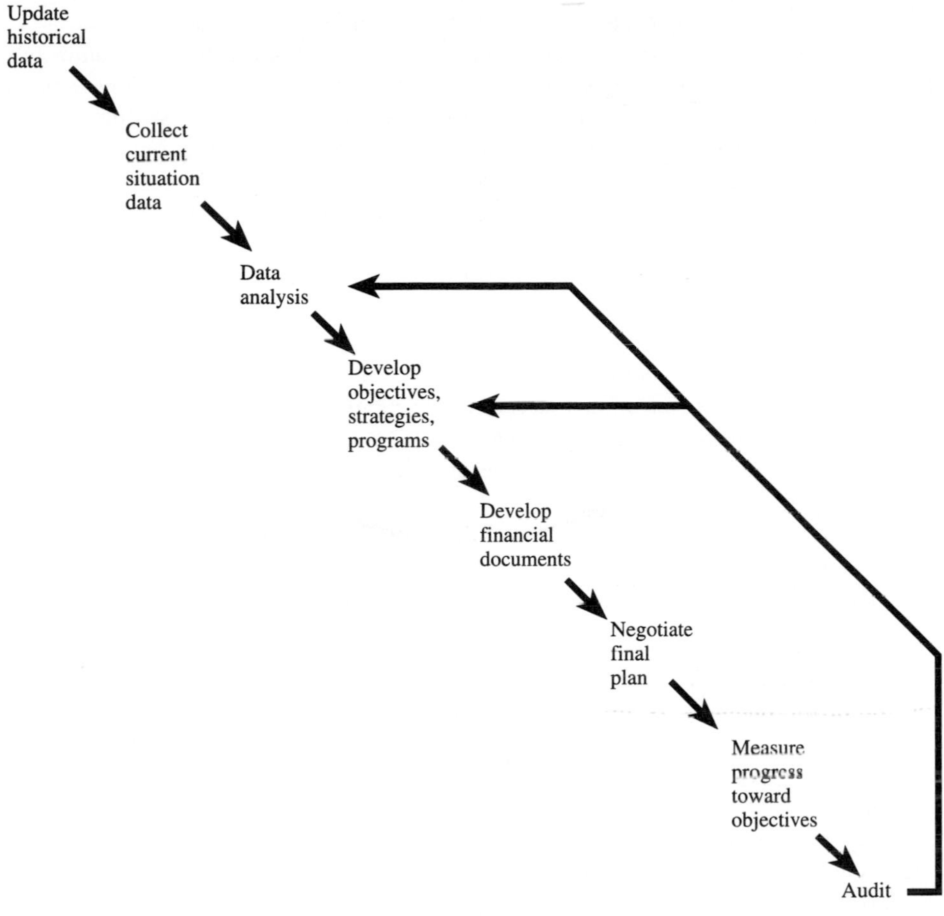

Step 2: Collect background data. Data collection focuses on information available about the current situation, which forms the situation analysis part of the plan. Again, lags in collecting data about an industry or product category mean that the time period of the data often does not match the period of analysis.

Step 3: Analyze historical and background data. Analyze the existing data to forecast competitors' actions, the behavior of customers, economic conditions, and so forth. Such an analysis need not be quantitative; in fact, as later chapters show, much of the analysis is qualitative and draws implications from nonnumerical data. This analysis leads to delineating key opportunities and threats to the business.

Step 4: Develop objectives, strategies, and action programs. Use the implications drawn from the background data (see step 3) to formulate brand objectives, strategies, and marketing mix decisions. This is, in fact, the critical activity of the planning process because it outlines in detail what will be done with the brand during the year (or the appropriate planning period). However, the order of the steps indicates that logical strategic thinking cannot be done without considering the facts at hand.

Objectives, strategies, and mix decisions are constrained by the company's mission, objectives and strategy, policies, resources, and legal considerations, among other factors. Thus, this part of the process generally involves (1) setting product objectives, (2) developing strategies and programs to achieve the objectives, (3) comparing programs in terms of their abilities to achieve objectives (e.g., market share) within the terms of company policies and legal constraints, and (4) selecting a basic objective, strategy, and program combination.

Step 5: Develop pro forma financial statements. Such statements typically include budgets and profit-and-loss figures.

Step 6: Negotiate. Rarely, if ever, is the marketing plan generated from steps 1 to 5 implemented without several rounds of negotiations with senior management. In a brand management organizational structure, the plans themselves must be marketed both inside and outside marketing as managers compete for their desired portions of corporate or divisional resources. In large organizations, this negotiation process can last as long as all the prior steps.

Step 7: Measure progress. To correct the plan if the environment changes within the planning period, progress toward stated objectives must be monitored. This implies that marketing research and other information relevant to measuring the quantities stated as objectives (e.g., market share or sales) must continue to be collected.

Step 8: Audit. After a planning period, it is customary to determine variances of planned versus actual results and sources of the variances. This audit provides important diagnostic information for both current and future planning efforts and thus acts as a source of feedback on the planning effort.

The planning sequence is therefore a logical flow of events leading from data collection and analysis to strategy formulation to auditing the performance of the plan. It implies that sound strategic thinking cannot occur until the product manager has used all available information to draw implications about future market conditions.

Components of the Marketing Plan

Although nearly every firm has its own format,[12] most marketing plans do have a common set of elements. The appendix to this chapter provides a sample marketing plan outline, which is summarized in Figure 2–6. This outline describes the major areas of analysis and data collection required for a "typical" marketing plan. The

[12]For some further examples, see David Hopkins, *The Marketing Plan* (New York: The Conference Board, 1981), and Howard Sutton, *The Marketing Plan in the 1990s* (New York: The Conference Board, 1990).

FIGURE 2–6 Marketing Plan Summary

I. Executive summary
II. Background assessment:
  A. Historical appraisal
  B. Situation analysis
  C. Planning assumptions
III. Marketing objectives
IV. Marketing strategy
V. Marketing programs
VI. Financial documents
VII. Monitors and controls
VIII. Contingency plans

rationale and a brief description of each major component of the plan follow, giving an overview of the plan and a context for the planning chapters of the book.

The Executive Summary

A senior manager often must review many marketing plans, so a brief summary of the marketing plan focusing on the objectives, strategies, and expected financial performance is necessary. This brief overview is useful for quickly reviewing the major elements of the plan and easily comparing product plans.

Background Assessment

The data and concomitant analysis so vital to developing sound marketing strategies contain three parts. First, the historical appraisal seeks to identify long-term trends and short-term changes in the market. This section applies to past data; that is, if we are planning for 1997 in 1996, historical data will include information from 1995 and before. The major areas of interest in this part include general market data, such as sales and market shares; market activity information, such as advertising and pricing histories; historical cost and profit data; and facts related to changes in technology, regulations, or other general environmental conditions. Since the amount of data is usually considerable, data are often stored in a separate document called a product fact book.

The situation analysis, the second major component of the background analysis, is a detailed study of current events composed of several parts.

The *sales analysis* is an intensive study of a brand's sales records intended to uncover problems hidden by aggregate numbers. For example, an overall sales increase for a line of shoes may hide the fact that sales of a particular size or color are dropping.

The *category attractiveness analysis* identifies factors that can be used to assess the attractiveness of a product category (or industry if more appropriate) in which the product competes at a given point in time. Since all markets are dynamic in that competitors, customers, technology, and sales growth rates change, the underlying attractiveness of a product category as a target for investment can also change.

The *competitor analysis* asks who the key competitors are in the market and what their likely future strategies are. Competitor analysis is becoming an increasingly important activity. A critical section of the competitor analysis component is what is often termed a *resource analysis* or self-assessment. By comparing the product to its key competitors the strengths and weaknesses become clear.

The aim of the *customer analysis* is to guarantee that the product manager retains a customer focus at all times. This customer focus is critical to success in today's competitive marketplace. It is vital to understand not only who the customers are but also how and why they behave the way they do.

The third part of the background assessment deals with a wide variety of *planning assumptions*. First, the product's market potential is a key number in making decisions about expected future category growth, resource allocation, and many other areas. Market and brand forecasts and assumptions about uncontrollable factors, such as raw materials or labor supply, are also relevant.

The background assessment is the "homework" to be done before formulating marketing objectives and strategies. It may be more enjoyable to develop the marketing strategy for a product during the next planning horizon, but the preliminary data collection and analysis are more vital because drawing implications from the background data often makes the optimal strategies apparent.

The Marketing Strategy

It is logical to follow the background assessment by the strategy portion of the plan, which includes three sections: a statement of marketing objectives (where do we want to go?), the marketing strategy itself (how are we going to get there?), and the marketing mix elements (exactly what do we do and in what order?).

The Rest of the Plan

The final three parts of the marketing plan do not form a cohesive unit, but they are nevertheless important components. The financial documents report the budgets and pro forma profit-and-loss (P&L) or income statements. Senior managers, naturally, inspect the expected financial outcome carefully. In fact, the P&L statements are often the key element in securing approval for the plan. The monitors and controls section specifies the type of marketing research and other information necessary to measure progress toward achieving the stated objectives. The kind of information collected depends on the objectives; for example, if a market share increase is the objective, information must be collected in time to check for possible shortfalls. Finally, contingency plans are helpful, particularly in dynamic markets where either new products or new competitors create the need for changes in strategy before the end of the plan's horizon. These contingencies are often previously considered strategies that were discarded.

Example

Figure 2–7 shows one company's planning form.[13] As can be seen, this company limits the plan to 20 pages, excluding exhibits. Sections IV, V, and VI cover the situation analysis. The rest of the plan describes the marketing objectives, strategies, and action programs. Note the separate objective, strategy, and program sections for different market segments (group and transient customers) and products (food and beverage). Clearly, advertising and public relations are viewed as very important to the hotel industry because they merit distinct sections of the plan. In general, the two major parts of the plan—the situation analysis and the objectives, strategies, and programs—are covered well by this structure. This company's plan differs from the general format previously described in several ways. For example, the company prefers an initial description of its differential advantage over competitors (Section II), as opposed to discussing this as part of the product positioning.

Two Case Studies

In Chapters 3 through 7, we illustrate the concepts presented with two running examples. In these examples, objectives and strategies will be developed from the background analyses. Because most product strategies, particularly those in high-technology industries, are subject to considerable change, the two examples are meant to illustrate the use of background analyses for developing the marketing plan; they do not necessarily provide current data about the products and brands involved.

Ready-to-Drink Fruit Drinks (ca. 1995)[14]

Fruit beverages account for 12.3 percent of total beverage consumption. A total of 3.3 billion gallons of juice were consumed in 1994, averaging 12.7 gallons per capita, good for third place in the beverage wars behind soft drinks and beer (see Figure 2–8 for U.S. fruit beverage sales since 1970). For the last 10 years, the category has been growing at a compound annual growth rate of 3 percent, with a growth rate of 3.8 percent from 1993 to 1994. The 3.3 billion gallons in 1994 were worth $9.6 billion at the wholesale level and $12.2 billion at retail.

The fruit beverage market is divided into two product segments: 100 percent fruit juices and fruit drinks that contain less than 100 percent fruit juice. For the last 10 years, fruit drinks have been gaining share from fruit juices due to innovations in marketing and from the partial insulation fruit drinks have from price swings caused by variations in the world's fruit crops. In 1994, fruit drinks were 39 percent of the market, up from 32 percent 10 years ago.

---

[13]Other examples of marketing plans appear in William A. Cohen, *The Marketing Plan* (New York: John Wiley & Sons, 1995).

[14]This illustration is based on Fabio Bellotti, Olivier Girard, and Omar Tellez, "Snapple 1996 Marketing Plan," master's thesis, Haas School of Business, University of California at Berkeley, 1995.

FIGURE 2–7 Sonesta Hotels Marketing Plan Outline

***Note: Please keep the plan concise—Maximum of 20 pages plus summary pages. Include title page and table of contents. Number all pages.

I. *Introduction.* Set the stage for the plan. Specifically identify marketing objectives such as "increase average rate," "more group business," "greater occupancy," or "penetrate new markets." Identify particular problems.

II. *Marketing Position.* Begin with a single statement that presents a consumer benefit in a way that distinguishes us from the competition.

III. *The Product.* Identify all facility and service changes that occurred last year and are planned for next year.

IV. *Marketplace Overview.* Briefly describe what is occurring in your marketplace that might impact on your business or marketing strategy, such as the economy, the competitive situation, etc.

V. *The Competition.* Briefly identify your primary competition (3 or fewer) specifying number of rooms, what is new in their facilities, and marketing and pricing strategy.

VI. *Marketing Data*
   - A. Identify top 5 geographic areas for transient business, with percentages of total room nights compared to the previous year.
   - B. Briefly describe the guests at your hotel, considering age, sex, occupation, what they want, why they come, etc.
   - C. Identify market segments with percentage of business achieved in each segment in current years (actual and projected) and project for next year.

VII. *Strategy by Market Segment*
   - A. Group
     1. *Objectives:* Identify what you specifically wish to achieve in this segment. (For example, more high-rated businesses, more weekend business, larger groups).
     2. *Strategy:* Identify how sales, advertising and public relations will work together to reach the objectives.
     3. *Sales Activities:* Divide by specific market segments.
        - a. Corporate
        - b. Association
        - c. Incentives
        - d. Travel agent
        - e. Tours
        - f. Other

        Under each category include a narrative description of specific sales activities geared toward each market segment, including geographically targeted areas, travel plans, group site inspections, correspondence, telephone solicitation and trade shows. Be specific on action plans, and designate responsibility and target months.
     4. *Sales Materials:* Identify all items, so they will be budgeted.
     5. *Direct Mail:* Briefly describe the direct mail program planned, including objectives, message, and content. Identify whether we will use existing material or create a new piece.
     6. *Research:* Indicate any research projects you plan to conduct next year, identifying what you wish to learn.

B. Transient (The format here should be the same as group throughout)
   1. *Objective*
   2. *Strategy*
   3. *Sales Activities:* Divide by specific segments.
      a. Consumer (rack rate)
      b. Corporate (prime and other)
      c. Travel Agent: business, leisure, consortia
      d. Wholesale/Airline/Tour (foreign & domestic)
      e. Packages (specify names of packages)
      f. Government/Military/Education
      g. Special Interest/Other
   4. *Sales Materials*
   5. *Direct Mail*
   6. *Research*

C. Other Sonesta Hotels

D. Local/Food & Beverage
   1. *Objectives*
   2. *Strategy*
   3. *Sales Activities:* Divide by specific market segments.
      a. Restaurant and Lounge, external promotion
      b. Restaurant and Lounge, internal promotion
      c. Catering
      d. Community Relation/Other
   4. *Sales Materials* (e.g., banquet menus, signage, etc.)
   5. *Direct Mail*
   6. *Research*

VIII. *Advertising*

A. Subdivide advertising by market segment and campaign, paralleling the sales activities (group, transient, F&B).

B. Describe objectives of each advertising campaign, identifying whether it should be promotional (immediate bookings) or image (long-term awareness).

C. Briefly describe contents of advertising, identifying key benefit to promote.

D. Identify target media by location and type (e.g., newspaper, magazine, radio, etc.).

E. Indicate percent of the advertising budget to be allocated to each market segment.

IX. *Public Relations*

A. Describe objectives of public relations as it supports the sales and marketing priorities.

B. Write a brief statement on overall goals by market segment paralleling the sales activities. Identify what proportion of your effort will be spent on each segment.

X. *Summary:* Close the plan with general statement concerning the major challenges you will face in upcoming year and how you will overcome these challenges.

Source: Howard Sutton, *The Marketing Plan in the 1990s,* (New York: The Conference Board, 1990), pp. 34–35.

FIGURE 2–8 US Fruit Beverage Market

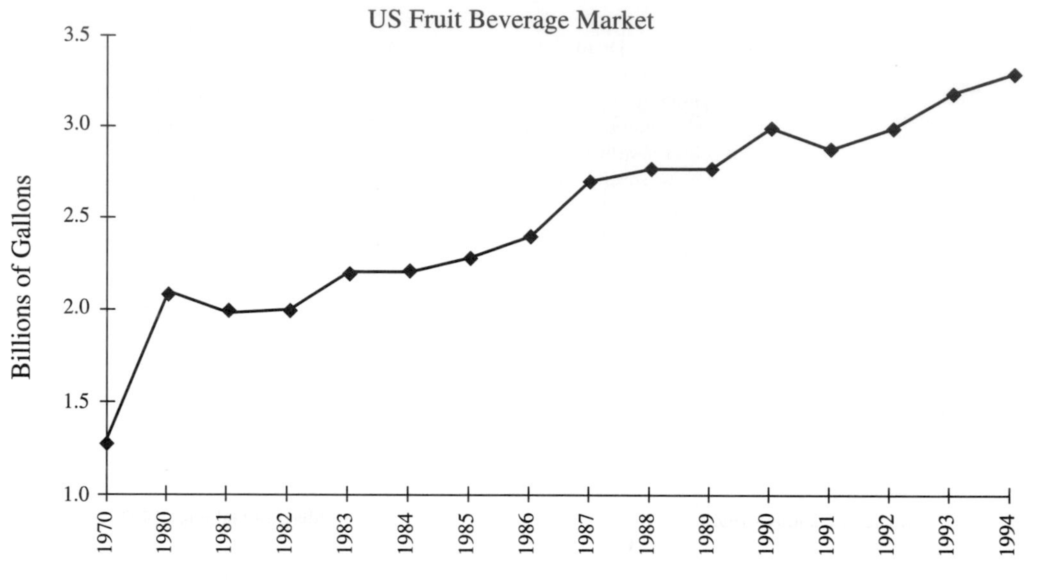

Source: Beverage Marketing Corporation.

The market for fruit drinks can be further divided into three subsegments: shelf-stable ready-to-drink products, chilled ready-to-drink products, and frozen concentrate products. The first two subsegments dominate the market with about 85 percent of sales, and over 75 percent of these sales occur at retail (supermarkets, convenience stores, etc.).

Ready-to-drink (RTD) fruit drinks, both shelf-stable and chilled, are commonly included in a larger segment called the New Age beverage segment. This category includes a large variety of beverages as diverse as sports drinks (e.g., Gatorade), flavored waters (e.g., Clearly Canadian), sparkling juices (e.g., Orangina), RTD teas (e.g., Snapple), and RTD coffees. The dollar sales and volume of this market have been steadily increasing during the 1990s (see Figure 2–9). Within the New Age category, RTD fruit drinks have been increasing their share of gallons, as Figure 2–10 shows.

Our analyses will be conducted from the perspective of the Snapple brand. Snapple was founded in 1972 when three friends became associated with a California juice manufacturer to distribute 100 percent natural fruit juices in New York City via health food distributors. In 1978, the company adopted the Snapple name and began to produce a line of pure, natural fruit juices at an upstate New York production plant. Over the next several years, Snapple introduced natural sodas, seltzers, fruit drinks, and iced teas. In 1995, Snapple had 20 plants in the United States and distributed its products in 17 countries in North America, Europe, Asia, and the Far East. The company offers 15 flavors of RTD fruit drinks. References used for this category are shown in Figure 2–11.

FIGURE 2–9 New Age Beverage Market, 1990–93

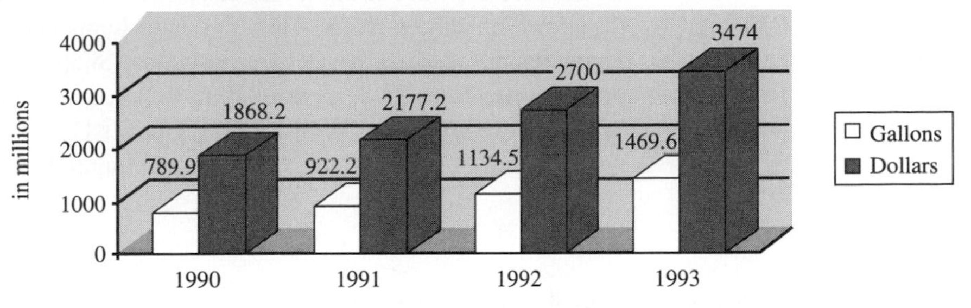

Source: *Beverage World* 1994–95 database/Beverage Marketing Corporation.

FIGURE 2–10 New Age Beverage Market, Share of Gallons, 1992–93

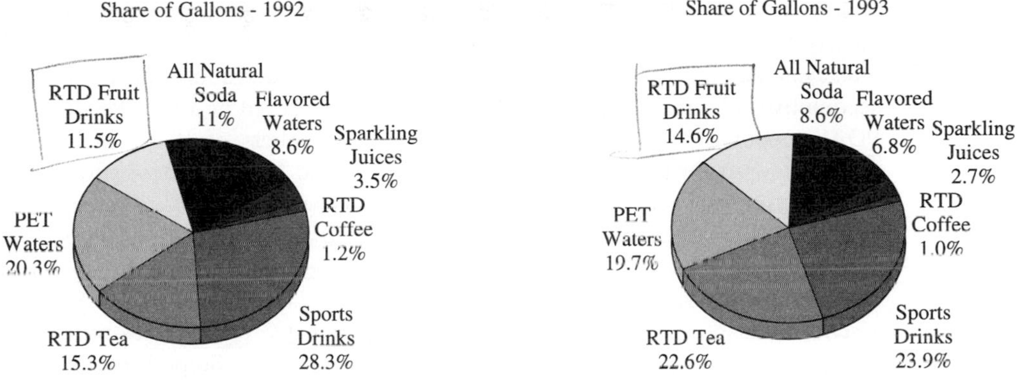

Source: *Beverage World* 1994–95 database/Beverage Marketing Corporation.

FIGURE 2–11 Reference Sources for RTD Fruit Drink Category

Advertising Age
Beverage Industry
Beverage World
Brandweek
Business Week
Direct Marketing
Market Share Reporter
Brand Ad Index
Various annual reports

In November 1994, Snapple was acquired by Quaker Oats, Inc., for $1.7 billion; Quaker also markets the Gatorade brand. Quaker Oats successfully expanded the Gatorade brand franchise after acquiring it and obviously felt it could do the same with Snapple. At the time of this writing, this has not happened; due to increased competition, management turnover, and other problems, Snapple's share of the RTD fruit drink market dropped from 34 percent in 1993 to 26 percent in 1994. Turning the brand around is one of the highest priorities facing Quaker Oats management. In fact, Quaker CEO William Smithburg personally assumed command of the business in late 1995.[15]

Personal Digital Assistants (ca. 1995)[16]

A growing need for smaller and lighter mobile computing devices to organize, store personal data, and communicate while on the road has created an emerging market for a class of electronic devices known as personal digital assistants (PDAs). Often called by other names such as high-end electronic organizers, palmtop computers, and personal communicators, PDAs are handheld computers that combine communications, personal organization, and word processing capabilities.

PDAs generally weigh less than one pound, measure less than 4″ × 7″ × 1″, and display less than one-fourth the number of pixels of a subnotebook PC (they have much smaller screens and less brightness). Device navigation and data entry are accomplished by using either a built-in miniature keyboard or a penlike stylus. Some PDAs support both methods of input. Leading suppliers of PDAs include Sharp, Apple, Hewlett-Packard (HP), Psion, Casio, Sony, and Motorola. Most PDAs are sold to mobile professionals, white-collar workers who spend more than 20 percent of their time away from their desks. The remainder are sold to technology gadget enthusiasts, early adopters who seek out the latest in consumer electronics.

The well-publicized introduction in 1993 of the Apple Newton MessagePad essentially marked the beginning of the PDA product category (electronic personal organizers existed prior to 1993). Since then Sharp, Casio, Sony, Motorola, and HP have introduced devices ranging in price from $350 to $1,150. There has already been an exit from the category: EO, a well-funded subsidiary of AT&T, which attempted to develop a tablet-form personal communicator priced at $2,000.

The PDA market can be divided into three subclasses based on feature set emphasis: general purpose, communicator, and personal information management (PIM). General-purpose PDAs are full-featured computing devices that offer a rich set of third-party (software vendor) applications usually based on an open (nonproprietary) operating system. The HP200LX, Apple Newton, and Sharp Zaurus are examples of this subclass. The communicator subclass emphasizes built-in communi-

---

[15]Judith Crown, "Snapple Is Now Up to Smithburg," *Advertising Age*, October 30, 1995, p. 8.

[16]This illustration is based on Doug Etzel, Paul Musembwa, Henri Uehara, and Kenichiro Yamada, "US Marketing Plan for the Sharp 'Wiz' Personal Digital Assistant," master's thesis, Haas School of Business, University of California at Berkeley, 1995.

FIGURE 2–12 U.S. Personal Digital Assistant Category, 1992–96

Standard Handhelds	*1992*	*1993*	*1994*	*1995*	*1996*
Hewlett-Packard	1	1	1	1	1
Psion	1	1	1	1	1
Apple	0	1	1	1	1
Sharp	0	1	0	1	1
Tandy/Casio	0	1	1	1	1
AST	0	0	1	0	0
EO/GO	0	1	0	0	0
Motorola	0	0	1	1	1
Sony	0	0	1	1	1
Bell South	0	0	1	1	1
Samsung	0	0	0	0	1
IBM	0	0	0	0	1
Compaq	0	0	0	0	1
Panasonic	0	0	0	0	1
Total	2	6	8	8	12

Note: 0 = no product on the market; 1 = at least one product on the market.

FIGURE 2–13 PDA Sales, 1992–95

Year	*Sales (thousands of units)*
1992	63
1993	130
1994	200
1995	285

cations capabilities such as wireless messaging. Sony's Magiclink and Motorola's Marc and Envoy are examples. The PIM subclass focuses mainly on providing personal information management functionality such as note taking, address/phone lists, datebooks, and so on. These devices are typically limited in features and are used primarily to carry around personal information. The HP OmniGo, Psion 3a, and Sharp Wiz fall into this subclass. Figure 2–12 shows the different entrants in the category since 1992, and Figure 2–13 shows PDA sales.

We will take the perspective of Sharp in performing the marketing plan background analyses. Sharp, a Japanese company with 1994 sales of over $15 billion, is best known for being the world's largest supplier of LCD flat panels used in laptop/notebook computers. It is the leading supplier of electronic organizers and PDAs worldwide with its own brands, Wiz and Zaurus; it also manufactures for other companies.

Although it has been sold in Japan since 1994, the Zaurus was introduced in the United States in 1995. The U.S. Zaurus features a built-in miniature keyboard (the

FIGURE 2–14 **Reference Sources for the PDS Category**

Mobile Office
Dataquest, Inc.
Frost & Sullivan
BIS *Strategic Decisions*
The Red Herring
Computer Letter
Mobile Letter
Microprocessor Report
Businessweek
Computerworld
MacWEEK
PCWeek
Computer Reseller News
InfoWorld
New York Times
San Francisco Chronicle

Japanese model uses a pen-based system like the Apple Newton). Sales in 1995 were disappointing; under 100,000 units were sold.

The Wiz was also sold in Japan first. It is a lower-end model with less functionality than the Zaurus and a commensurately lower price. The Wiz is scheduled to be launched in the United States in 1996. Sources used in this illustration are shown in Figure 2–14.

Summary

The marketing plan provides a unifying theme for the job of the product manager. While product managers have responsibility for many tasks, such as arranging trade shows, checking print advertising copy, and managing distribution channel members, day-to-day tasks should have the marketing strategy as a guiding theme. This theme emanates from a careful analysis of the market, giving the product manager ideas on how to differentiate his or her product from the others from which customers can choose. The tasks (marketing tactics), guiding theme (marketing strategy), and analysis (situation or background analysis) are what marketing plans and planning are about.

APPENDIX
MARKETING PLAN OUTLINE

I. *Executive Summary.* A one- to three-page synopsis of the plan providing highlights of the current situation, objectives, strategies, principal action programs, and financial expectations.
II. *Situation Analysis.*
  A. Category analysis.
    1. Market.
      a. Size, scope, and share of the category sales history of all competitors and their market shares.
      b. Market potential and major trends in supply and demand of this and related products.
    2. Category activity.
      a. Pricing history through all levels of distribution and reasons for principal fluctuations.
      b. The distribution channels.
      c. Selling policies and practices.
      d. Advertising and promotion.
    3. Sales, costs, and gross profits on our product.
      a. Sales history by grades, varieties; by sales district; by end use; by industry.
      b. Cost history.
      c. Profit history.
      d. Changes in volume and profit rankings of product lines and items in a product line.
    4. Technology—product and process improvements.
      a. Rate (life cycle).
      b. Lead time required for design and development of a new product.
      c. Market impact (primary versus selective demand).
      d. Relation of product and process?
    5. Category characteristics:
      a. Industry use patterns.
      b. End-use patterns.
      c. Frequency, quantity, and timing of purchase.
      d. Buying procedures and practices.
      e. Service.
    6. Government and social.
      a. Regulatory climate.
      b. Fiscal and monetary policy.
      c. Consumerism.
      d. Environmental impact.
    7. Category attractiveness analysis:
      a. Aggregate market factors:
        1) Size.
        2) Growth.
        3) Cyclicity.
        4) Seasonality.

- b. Category factors:
  - 1) Capacity.
  - 2) New-product entry prospects.
  - 3) Rivalry.
  - 4) Power of suppliers.
  - 5) Power of buyers.
  - 6) Threat of substitutes.
- c. Environmental factors:
  - 1) Social.
  - 2) Political.
  - 3) Demographic.
  - 4) Technological.
  - 5) Regulatory.

B. Sales analysis: Evaluate performance.
1. Market area performance versus company average.
2. Trends of sales, costs, and profits by products.
3. Performance of distributors, end-users, key customers.
4. Past versus current results by area, product, channel, and so on.

C. Competitor analysis.
1. For each major competitor and your own company, ask:
   - a. How are results measured and evaluated?
   - b. How were the results achieved and what factors helped or hurt along the way?
   - c. What are the important strengths and liabilities and how are these likely to change?
   - d. What is the future strategy likely to be?
2. Thorough analysis requires:
   - a. Exploration of past results.
   - b. Reconstruction of past strategy.
   - c. Evaluation of resources.
     - 1) Ability to conceive and design new products.
     - 2) Ability to produce or manufacture.
     - 3) Ability to market.
     - 4) Ability to finance.
     - 5) Ability to manage.
     - 6) Will to succeed in this category.
   - d. Comparative analysis of existing and anticipated future products.
   - e. Prediction of future marketing strategies.

D. Customer analysis.
1. Who are your customers?
2. What do they buy?
3. How do they choose?
4. Why do they select a particular product?
5. Where do they buy it?
6. When do they buy it?
7. So what?
   - a. What are the implications of changes in your customers' behavior?
   - b. What is the expected impact on you and your competitors?

E. Planning assumptions.
1. Explicit statement of assumptions about the future.
2. Market potential estimates.
3. Category and product sales forecasts.
4. Implications for marketing strategy.

III. *Objectives*
   A. Corporate objectives (if appropriate).
   B. Divisional objectives (if appropriate).
   C. Marketing objectives.
      1. Quantity (sales, share, profits, etc.).
      2. Direction.
      3. Number.
      4. Time frame.
      5. Rationale.
   D. Program objectives.
      1. Pricing.
      2. Advertising/promotion.
      3. Sales/distribution.
      4. Product.
      5. Service.
IV. *Marketing Strategy.* How the objectives will be achieved.
   A. Strategic alternative(s).
   B. Customer targets.
   C. Competitor targets.
   D. Core strategy.
V. *Marketing Programs.*
   A. Pricing.
   B. Advertising/promotion.
      1. Copy.
      2. Media.
      3. Trade versus consumer promotion.
   C. Sales/distribution.
   D. Product development.
   E. Service.
   F. Market research.
VI. *Financial Documents.*
   A. Budgets.
      1. Advertising/promotion.
      2. Sales.
      3. Research.
      4. Product development.
   B. Pro forma statements.
      1. Costs.
         a. Dollar, unit.
         b. Variable, fixed.
      2. Revenues (forecasted).
      3. Profits.
         a. Dollars, dollars per unit.
         b. ROI.
         c. Versus company average.
VII. *Monitors and Controls.* Specific research information to be used:
   A. Secondary data.
      1. Sales reports.
      2. Orders.
      3. Informal sources.

B. Primary data.
   1. Sales records (Nielsen, IRI).
   2. Specialized consulting firms.
   3. Consumer panel.

VIII. *Contingency Plans and Other Miscellaneous Documents.*
   A. Contingency plans.
   B. Alternative strategies considered.
   C. Miscellaneous.

C H A P T E R

3 Defining the Competitive Set

Overview

In Chapter 2, we presented an overview of marketing planning and an outline of a marketing plan that can be used to develop a similar document in virtually any product management situation. Of particular importance to the marketing plan is the background analysis of "homework," which focuses on the existing category and the competitive and customer situations. However, before beginning the analysis, the product manager must have a good conceptual definition of the product category to serve as the focus for data collection and analysis. This chapter provides tools to develop that category definition. In particular, we point out several possible ways to define the competition for a product or product line.

In our view, product managers tend to view competition too narrowly. For example, a product manager for a line of notebook computers would likely view other notebook computers as the major competitors. This is a natural outgrowth of the short-term orientation discussed earlier that pervades product management; competitor products or services that are most similar receive the most attention. However, as we argue in more detail later in this chapter, a myopic view of competition can be dangerous.

In some sense, everything competes with everything else. Since this concept of competition is not useful to the product manager, the key question in defining competition is not whether two products compete but the extent to which they compete. The degree of competition is a continuum, not a discrete *yes* or *no*. Defining competition therefore requires a balance between identifying too many competitors (and therefore complicating instead of simplifying decision making) and identifying too few (and thus overlooking a key competitor).

This chapter focuses on customer-based competition; in other words, a competitor is defined as one competing for the same customers. Competitors tangle on other bases as well. For example, IBM and Emerson Electric, although noncompetitors in terms of customers, compete for electrical engineers—the same labor supply. Kodak and

FIGURE 3–1 Bases of Competition

1. Customer oriented
   Who they are: competition for the same budget
   When they use it
   Why they use it: benefits sought
2. Marketing oriented: advertising and promotion
   Theme/copy strategy
   Media
   Distribution
   Price
3. Resource-oriented
   Raw materials
   Employees
   Financial resources
4. Geographic

jewelers compete for silver—raw materials. Suppliers are also a basis for competition; in 1990, hard disk drive manufacturer Conner Peripherals sued rival Seagate Technology on the grounds that Seagate blocked Conner's supplies of a critical component. Avon and Tupperware compete for home demonstration sales—the same channel of distribution. Similarly, frozen food manufacturers that use the freezer cabinets in supermarkets compete for shelf space. Geographically based competition is important for local retailers—for example, hardware stores—and multinational firms in the market for telecommunications equipment such as Ericsson (Sweden), NEC (Japan), and Northern Telecom (Canada). In other words, competition exists across many dimensions. Figure 3–1 summarizes these different bases of competition.

As Figure 3–1 suggests, competitors can be defined using several criteria. Competition can exist for customers in terms of their budgets (disposable income: vacations versus financial products), when they use a product (evenings: a basketball game versus a movie), and benefits sought (cancer treatments: bioengineered drugs versus chemotherapy). Competition is also related to marketing activities such as advertising (time on network television programs) and distribution (shelf space). The battle for shelf facings in supermarkets has led to a variety of manufacturer concessions to retailers to obtain desirable shelf positions, and the struggle for shelf space occurs across as well as within traditional product category boundaries. Examples of resource-based and geographic-based competition have already been mentioned.

Perhaps the most crucial competition occurs *within* a company, when different units in an organization request funds for their marketing plans. In this form of competition, the plan serves mainly as a sales document, and its financial projections often become the key to the "sale." This competition is often intentional; it puts pressure on product managers to develop sound marketing plans.

Misidentification of the competitive set can have a serious impact on the success of a marketing plan, especially in the long run. Overlooking an important competitive threat can be disastrous. For example, for many years the Swiss controlled the market for premium watches and Timex dominated the market for inexpensive watches. When

Japanese firms such as Casio developed electronic watches in the 1970s, they were not viewed as a threat or serious competition in either business. Today both Timex and Swiss firms offer electronic models, and only the strong success of the Swatch brand of inexpensive fashion watches has saved the Swiss watch industry.

A second illustration comes from the U.S. coffee industry. Coffee manufacturers traditionally felt free to pass along increased costs to consumers when a freeze in Colombia or another coffee-producing country restricted the supply of coffee beans. However, during 1977 and 1978, retail coffee sales dropped nearly 20 percent due to price increases. Much of this decrease can be accounted for by the concurrent rapid increase in demand for soft drinks and juices.[1] Witness also the recent attempt by Pepsi to compete with coffee manufacturers by introducing a morning cola, Pepsi A.M. (which, unfortunately, failed). In fact, share of occasion and so-called share of stomach competition is a major consideration of food and drink producers.

Pity the owner of a small "mom and pop" video store in 1996. Strong competitors such as Blockbuster exist with greater selection and considerably more marketing muscle due to national advertising and direct-mail campaigns. Moreover, the video store owner now also competes against another giant, Sony, which sells the small satellite dishes that, when combined with a home entertainment service, can deliver video on demand. In addition, every regional Bell operating company, such as US West, wants to get into the video-on-demand business shipping video images over telephone lines. And why not add your local electric utility, which also has a "pipeline" into your home?

Ambiguous definition of the competition creates uncertainty in market definition and therefore ambiguity in market-related statistics such as market share. This leaves open the possible manipulation of market boundaries, particularly when compensation or allocation decisions are at stake. For example, assume an objective for a subnotebook computer (weighing four pounds with a hard disk drive but no floppy disk drive) is to gain 10 percent market share. The ability to achieve this objective depends on whether the "market" is defined as all subnotebook products, all portable computers (subnotebooks plus notebook/laptops with floppy drives), all portable Windows-based computers, all desktop computers plus portables, and so on. A chocolate-covered granola bar could have a large share if measured in the snack bar category or a very small share if considered in the snack food category.

The data in Figure 3–2[2] provide a further example. As can be seen, Ore-Ida is the largest brand of frozen potatoes, with 55.3 percent of the market in 1994. The brand thus has a very large share of its "market" if the product manager views the market as limited to frozen potatoes. However, if one considers that frozen potatoes are only one possible alternative starch to have with a meal (among stuffing, rice, etc.), Ore-Ida's market share of the "starch accompaniments" category is much smaller and more realistically represents the competition.

In this chapter, therefore, we take the view that the definition of the competitive set ultimately affects what strategy is pursued, and the definition can be too narrow or

---

[1] See George Yip and Jeffrey Williams, "U.S. Retail Coffee Market (A)," Harvard Business School case no. 9-586-134, 1986.

[2] These data are from *Advertising Age*, January 30, 1995, p. 20.

Figure 3–2 Frozen Potato Market Shares

Rank			Dollar Sales to Date		Market Share	
1994	*1993*	*Brand*	*1994*	*% Change*	*1994*	*1993*
1	1	Ore-Ida	$470.6	2.1	55.3	56.5
2	2	Private labels	170.7	7.3	20.1	19.5
3	5	McCain	24.9	34.7	2.9	2.3
4	4	J.R. Simplot	23.7	5.4	2.8	2.8
5	3	Inland Valley	22.5	−9.7	2.6	3.1
6	9	Simply Fresh Potatoes	14.5	22.3	1.7	1.5
7	6	Weight Watchers	14.4	−13.7	1.7	2.1
8	7	Lean Cuisine	14.4	12.4	1.7	1.6
9	8	Lynden Farms	11.6	−5.9	1.4	1.5
10	10	Larrys	10.5	1.6	1.2	1.3
Total frozen potatoes			851.5	4.5	100.0	100.0

Dollars in millions for 52 weeks ending November 12, 1994. Source: Reprinted with permission from *Advertising Age*, January 30, 1995.

too broad for the market conditions at the time. Not all authors subscribe to this approach;[3] some believe the corporate mission or business definition selected affects the set of competitors for a firm. In other words, the definition of competition is a decision made by the product manager. Unfortunately, competitors usually do not care how a company chooses to define itself or how a product manager defines competition, and they are thus free to compete against a firm's products even if that firm does not define itself to include them as competitors.

In this chapter, we describe several levels of competition that can be useful for conceptualizing the competitive set. In addition, we discuss methods that can help determine the competition at the various levels. Finally, we describe the notion of enterprise competition.

Levels of Market Competition

Definitions

One way to delineate the set of competitors facing a brand is to consider the proximity of other products to the physical attributes of the product in question.[4] As Figure 3–3 shows, the problem of defining competition can be viewed as defining a set of concentric circles with the product or brand in question at the center.

Before discussing the definitions of competition, let us define the term *product feature*. A product's features are defined as the presence (or absence) of a characteristic or attribute (e.g., calories, weight). The *value* of a feature is the level of the

[3]See Derek Abell, *Defining the Business* (Englewood Cliffs, N.J.: Prentice Hall, 1980).

[4]Again, the use of the term *physical* does not preclude services from utilizing the proposed method for identifying competitors. Services can also be described in terms of their actual characteristics, for example, interest rate for a mortgage.

FIGURE 3–3 Example of Levels of Competition

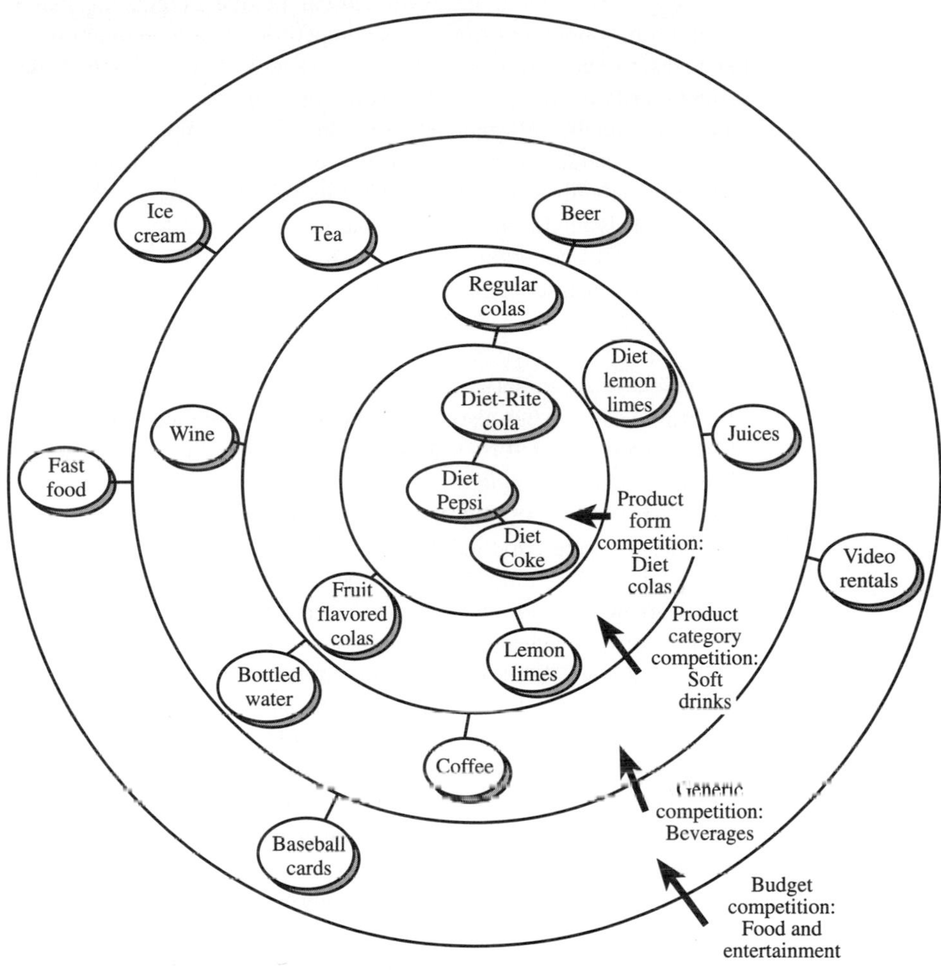

characteristic (e.g., 0 calories, 5 pounds). Thus, Coke and Diet Coke share the same features—carbonation, cola taste, sweetness, and the like—but have different values of some of the features since Diet Coke has fewer calories and is artificially sweetened.

The narrowest perspective one can take of competition is called *product form*. These products typically pursue the same market segment, and their features therefore have similar values. As Figure 3–3 shows, from Diet Coke's perspective, a narrow view of competition would include only diet colas, such as Diet-Rite and Diet Pepsi. These brands appeal to similar consumers: those seeking a cola taste with low calories. Similarly, Compaq, Gateway 2000, Dell, IBM, Toshiba, and others compete in the Windows-based notebook/laptop computer category. Again, although the brands differ slightly on some characteristics, they use the same operating system and are fairly similar in weight. Apple's Powerbook might not be included in this product form competition, since it has a different operating system. Interestingly, competition in the notebook market could be asymmetrical in that companies that produce Windows machines may not view Apple as a competitor, but Apple might be interested in selling machines to customers who currently have Windows-based desktop computers. To further clarify the definition of product form competition, subnotebook products would comprise a totally different set of product form competitors.

Thus, product form competition is a narrow view of competition because it considers only those products that "look" the same as the product or service in question. This might be an acceptable perspective in the short run, as these would be the most serious competitors on a day-to-day basis. It is also a convenient definition of competition because it mimics the way commercial data services often measure market shares. For example, A. C. Nielsen, a major provider of market share information to consumer packaged goods companies (along with its main competitor, Information Resources, Inc., or IRI), provides market share information not only on the entire soft-drink category but also on the diet product segment alone. This narrow definition of the market supplied by a data collection service can have the unfortunate effect of setting an industry standard for looking at competition and market shares in a way that does not represent the true underlying competitive dynamics in the industry (the data in Figure 3–2 are supplied by Nielsen, for example). Thus, the product form view, while perhaps providing the set of the closest competitors in a product feature sense, is too narrow for a longer-run view of competition.

The second level of competition is based on those products or services with similar features. This type of competition, called *product category*, is what product managers naturally think of as the industry. For example, personal computers, fast food, televisions, and the like describe sets of competitors that are aggregates, or composites, of narrower product forms. All soft drinks (Figure 3–3) form a market as well. This is, in fact, the traditional way to determine the composition of a competitive set. While somewhat broader than product form competition, this product category definition of competition still takes a short-run view of market definition. To recall an earlier example, the video store "industry" faces critical competition from the telecommunications "industry."

The third level of competition is longer term and focuses on substitutable product categories. Termed *form competition* by Kotler,[5] it defines the competition, and therefore the market, as consisting of those products and services fulfilling the same customer need. Thus, soft drinks compete with orange juice in the "thirst-quenching" market, fast-food outlets compete against frozen entries in the "convenience" eating market, and so on. PepsiCo introduced a new brand, Pepsi XL, in 1995 to compete against the RTD fruit drink category.

This need-based perspective is essential if a manager wishes to avoid both overlooking threats and ignoring opportunities. This perspective is well described in Levitt's classic article that admonishes several industries for defining their businesses

[5]Philip Kotler, *Marketing Management*, 8th ed. (Englewood Cliffs, N.J.: Prentice Hall, 1994).

FIGURE 3–4 InterNex Ad

Top 10 Reasons Your Business Needs Frame Relay Internet Access from Internex

10. 75% of all new Internet sites are business systems going on line. These days, if your business isn't on the Net, you're not in business.
9. Your FedEx bill averages about $10,000/mo.
8. The World Wide Web has been referred to as "a global Yellow Pages for the 21st century". Do you want your business to be unlisted?
7. Have you tried downloading 10 megabytes of product, pricing and competitive data from the Net, using only an analog modem?
6. InterNex understands your mission-critical business applications. We provision Internet feeds for some of America's largest companies.
5. You have to get meeting minutes to five hundred different people within, oh, about two minutes.
4. InterNex provides you with turn-key solutions: preconfigured hardware, on-site installations, training, and support 24 hours/day, 7 days/week.
3. We provide an untroubled night's sleep.
2. InterNex Frame Relay service is available in speeds from 28 Kbps to 1.544 Mbps. InterNex's dedicated lines, SMDS and ATM have even more growth built in: all the way to 45 Mbps and higher.
1. Your competition may already have it.

Source: *The Wall Street Journal,* November 20, 1995. Reprinted by permission of InterNex.

too narrowly.[6] Railroads viewed themselves as providing rail-based rather than general transportation services and lost much of their business to trucks and airlines. Steel companies thought they were providing steel rather than general structural material. Some firms, on the other hand, do take a generic perspective in defining themselves and their competitors. FedEx, for example, sees its competitors as not only DHL, UPS, Emery, and the U.S. Postal Service but also other companies providing quick transmission of information. As a result, it tried to develop a facsimile business as an alternative to overnight package and small-letter delivery. Interestingly, the reverse is now happening to FedEx. As Figure 3–4 shows, new Internet-based services view themselves as substituting for FedEx.

A critical difference between generically defined competitors and either product form or product category competition is that the former is *outward* oriented while the latter two are *inward.* Product form and product category competitors are defined by products that look like those we are producing. Generic competitors are defined by looking outside the firm to the customers. After all, who really defines competition, the firm or the customer? It is the customer who determines what alternative products and services solve the problem at hand. Although in some cases there may be a limited number of ways to solve the same problem or provide the same benefit, in most instances focusing on the physical product alone ignores viable competitors.

An even more general level of competition is *budget* competition. This is the broadest view of competition: It considers all products and services competing for the same customer dollar as forming a market. For example, a consumer who has $500 in

[6]Theodore Levitt, "Marketing Myopia," *Harvard Business Review*, July–August 1960, pp. 45–56.

FIGURE 3–5 **Levels of Competition: Implications for Product Strategy**

Competitive Level	*Product Management Task*
Product form	Convince customers that the brand is better than others in the product form
Product category	Convince customers that the product form is the best in the category
Generic	Convince customers that the product category is the best way to satisfy needs
Budget	Convince customers that the generic benefits are the most appropriate way to spend the discretionary budget

discretionary disposable income could spend it on a vacation, a ring, a money market instrument, or a variety of other things. A purchasing manager may have a fixed budget for office equipment that includes copy machines, word processing software upgrades, or a new water cooler service. For example, a senior manager at Union Pacific Corporation decided to hold the line on personal computer purchases so that the railroad could purchase more equipment it really needed, such as a new diesel engine.[7] While this view of competition is conceptually useful, it is very difficult to implement strategically since it implies an enormous number of competitors.

Product Strategy Implications

The four-level model of competition just described has significant implications for developing product strategy and for a product manager's marketing problems. A different set of tasks must be accomplished at each level of competition for a product to be successful in the market. Figure 3–5 shows these tasks in conjunction with the appropriate level of competition.

At each level of competition, part of the job of the product manager is fairly clear, and marketing managers are trained to handle it: Convince the customer that your company's version of the product, your brand, is better than others available. In other words, your most direct competitors are other brands of like product form. What differs at each level is how much additional marketing has to be done beyond touting your own brand's advantages. At the product form level, none is required: clearly, when the competition is viewed as consisting only of other products with similar levels of features, marketing activities directly aimed at the similar competitors are all that is required (e.g., Toshiba is a better laptop computer than IBM). However, the problem becomes more complex as the competitor set widens. At the product category level, the product manager must also convince customers that the product form is best in the product category (e.g., subnotebooks are better than notebook/laptop computers). At the generic competition level, the product manager must also convince customers that the product category solution to the customer's problem (the benefit derived from the product category) is superior to the solution provided by other product categories (e.g.,

[7]Bart Ziegler and Thomas E. Weber, "PC Sales Growth Slows as Corporate Ardor for New Models Cools," *The Wall Street Journal*, March 25, 1996, p. A-1.

taking an airplane is superior to taking a train). This is most likely to occur when a totally new product category is introduced. For example, when Procter and Gamble introduced disposable diapers in the 1970s, the main marketing job was to convince mothers to switch from the generic competitors, cloth diapers and diaper services. Finally, it might also be necessary to convince customers that the generic benefit of the product is better than other ways to spend discretionary money (e.g., taking a cruise versus putting a down payment on a new car).

To illustrate the product strategy implications of competition, consider the problem facing the marketing manager for a line of low-priced stereo components such as Pioneer. What competition does this product manager face? First, competitors are fighting for the same segment of the stereo market (product form competitors), so the manager must show that Pioneer is superior to others competing in the low-priced segment. Second, there are other, higher-priced component manufacturers (product category competitors), and the Pioneer manager must communicate to customers the advantages of low-priced components over more expensive alternatives (e.g., Bang and Olufsen). Third, the manager must consider generic competitors. These could include all-in-one systems ("boom boxes") or lower-priced rack stereo systems as well as the manufacturers of other entertainment consumer durables such as TVs, video game systems, and videocassette recorders (Sony, Nintendo, Panasonic, Sanyo). Customers must be convinced to buy stereos rather than these other products. Finally, alternative ways to spend the money could be relevant (budget competition). As a result, customers might have to be informed about the benefits of buying stereos instead of taking a vacation or buying stocks. While this latter problem may seem a little farfetched, it is undoubtedly true that stockbrokers, retail jewelers, travel agents, and many other businesspeople worry about customer alternatives for spending a certain amount of money.

It is also important to note that as one moves from product form toward budget competition, customer targets also begin to change. Product form competition suggests battling for exactly the same customers in terms of who they are and why they buy (although not necessarily where or when they buy: one soft-drink manufacturer [Coca-Cola] may concentrate on fountain sales and another [Pepsi] on grocery store sales). As the company moves toward budget competition, both who its customers are and why they buy begin to differ as the need to be satisfied becomes more general. Because the key to success in business is obtaining and keeping customers, the most crucial form of competition will *generally* be product form, in which competition occurs for the same customers. On the other hand, generic competition can destroy entire product categories when a major innovation occurs, and thus it too requires attention, especially for long-run planning.

Note that products thought of as substitutes, and therefore generic or budget competitors, may also be viewed as complements. For example, a customer might be trying to decide between purchasing word processing or spreadsheet software (budget competition). These potential competitors could be turned into allies through joint ventures or cobranding (e.g., Dreyer's Ice Cream and M&Ms) or bundling (Microsoft's Office suite of applications). Thus, this delineation of competitive levels defines *potential* competitors and not necessarily mortal foes.

Figure 3–6 RTD Fruit Drinks Competitors

Level of Competition	*Definition*	*Competitors*	*Need Satisfied*
Product form	New Age chilled ready-to-drink fruit drinks	Snapple Fruitopia Ocean Spray Arizona Private labels	Healthy Convenience Single-serve Thirst quenching
Product category	Fruit beverage	Minute Maid Tropicana Sunny Delight Hi-C	Healthy Thirst quenching
Generic	Beverages	Powdered drinks Frozen concentrates Ready-to-drink teas Bottled water Soft drinks Sports drinks Flavored waters Others	Thirst quenching
Budget	Other supermarket, convenience store, vending machine products	Many: Candy Pretzels	Used at home Thirst-quenching Energy filling treat

Illustrations

The two illustrations introduced in Chapter 2 were RTD fruit drinks and personal digital assistants (PDAs). Let's look at competitor definitions in light of the information provided in that chapter and some use of "managerial judgment."

RTD Fruit Drinks. Figure 3–6 shows the competitive structure of the RTD fruit drink product category. The narrowest form of competition for Snapple would be with other RTD drinks such as Fruitopia, Arizona, Ocean Spray, and private label entrants. All these brands are advertised as being healthy, easy to serve and drink, and thirst quenching. The New Age category is somewhat trendy, reflecting the younger demographics of the target audience. The product category would be expanded to include other fruit drinks such as orange juice (Minute Maid, Tropicana) and other fruit drinks and "punches." These brands are usually not single-serving, can be sold in frozen concentrate form, and are targeted for other use occasions. The generic category, of course, is very broad and includes a large number of beverages such as soft drinks, sports drinks, bottled waters, and so on, as well as to some extent snack foods. The key point here is that for a consumer, many substitutes for RTD fruit drinks are available. Budget competition here would mainly be other grocery products purchased in the supermarket.[8]

[8]This assumes the product is purchased for consumption at home. If the consumption situation is in an out-of-home location, the most general competitive set would be the generic set because in that situation, the consumer would be looking for a beverage of some kind.

FIGURE 3–7 PDA Competition

Level of Competition	*Definition*	*Competitors*	*Need Satisfied*
Product form	PIMs	HP OmniGo Psion 3a Sharp Wiz	Personal information management
Product category	Full-featured PDAs	Apple Newton HP 200LX Motorola Envoy/Marco Sony Magic Link Sharp Zaurus	PIM plus integrated communications
Generic	Notebook/subnotebook computers	IBM Toshiba Many others	Other solutions to the above
	Paper-based solutions	Rolodex Day Timer	
Budget	Business items costing $100–$1,000	Fax machines Personal copiers Cellular phones Furniture (e.g. Steelcase)	

If we take the perspective of the Snapple product manager, the key short-run competitors therefore are Fruitopia, Ocean Spray, and Arizona. The manager must convince consumers that Snapple is the best alternative and delivers product benefits better than those brands. However, the product manager must also convince consumers of the advantages of the RTD fruit drinks over the other fruit beverages, most notably convenience, image, and healthiness. The main advantage of the RTD fruit drinks over the generic competitors is the healthiness (fruit) aspect, since some of them are convenient (e.g., bottled waters) and have a strong, upscale image (e.g., Perrier).

Personal Digital Assistants. Figure 3–7 indicates the different levels of competition for the PDA category. The closest competitors are those PDAs that are essentially high-end personal information managers (PIMs) and offer address/telephone/fax recordkeeping, calculators, financial calculations, and optional links to personal computers and modems. The major competitors to Sharp's Wiz are the HP OmniGo and the Psion 3a. These products are marketed as offering many of the functions needed by businesspeople away from the office at a moderate price. The product category would consist of the full-featured PDAs, which include integrated communications capabilities, larger screens, more software, and a higher price. These products are a "bridge" between the lower-end PDAs such as the Sharp Wiz and notebook computers and offer more functionality than the Wiz-type products. The job of the Wiz product manager, then, is to differentiate it from these higher-end models, primarily on the basis of price but perhaps also by indicating that a simpler product may be all that is needed, particularly if the user also has a notebook computer. The generic competition consists of two quite different kinds of products. First, notebook

FIGURE 3–8 Defining Competition Using Customer Segments

	Market Segments		
Generic Competitors	*Business Travelers*	*Tourists*	*Students*
Airline	X	X	
Bus		X	X
Train		X	X
Automobile (own)		X	
Automobile (rent)		X	

and subnotebook computers can provide all the benefits of PDAs at a larger size, a higher price, and slower access to the information. However, manual, paper-based solutions still exist. One can still use a Rolodex, a Day Timer, or just paper files to obtain many of the benefits of the PDAs. Add a cellular phone and this combination matches the full-featured PDAs as well. There are many serious budget competitors. If we consider other business-related personal productivity items, portable printers, home fax machines, and similar items compete with PDAs. Of course, other durable goods may also compete for the same dollar if the purchase is not just for business purposes.

Overlapping Market Segments

An additional and valuable way to conceptualize the definition of competitors is based on market segments. Consider the market for travel services shown in Figure 3–8. The modes of travel listed on the left are generic competitors in that they satisfy the benefits of providing transportation. The market segments across the top could be defined in many ways, depending on the benefit being analyzed.

The generic competitors in the first column indicate how a customer would look at the travel problem. Consider the route between San Francisco and Los Angeles (a nine-hour drive or one-hour flight). For the business traveler, the major competitors would be airlines, primarily Southwest and United. For tourists, airlines, trains, car rental agencies, or their own cars would be substitutes if time is not critical.[9] Students on a budget might consider buses and trains as competitors.

Methods for Determining Competitors

The easiest way to define competition is to let someone else do it for you. For example, you can use the predefined categories provided by a commercial data service as the definition of the competitive set (as we showed earlier in this chapter using

[9]It is interesting to note that a small airline in the southeast United States, ValuJet, has been successful in attracting new leisure flyers who would otherwise be driving due to its low prices (see *Fortune*, November 27, 1995, p. 111). In addition, the new Eurotunnel connecting England and France has taken business away from airlines (*WorldBusiness*, January–February 1996, p. 13).

FIGURE 3–9 Managerial Judgment of Competition

	Product/Services	
Markets	*Same*	*Different*
Same	A	B
Different	C	D

Figure 3–2). A second example of an external definition of markets is the Standard Industrial Classification (SIC) code used by the U.S. government. This system assigns products to two-digit major groups (e.g., 34, Fabricated Metal), three-digit groups (e.g., 342, Cutlery and Hand Tools), four-digit industries (e.g., 3423, Hand and Edge Tools), and five- or more digit representations of products (e.g., 34231,11 Pliers). Clearly, both of these external sources of information define competition based on physical product similarities (product form or category definitions). As a result, relying exclusively on these categorizations will overlook both generic and budget competitors.

Two alternative approaches to assessing the set of competitors facing a brand permit a broader definition advocated in this chapter: managerial judgment and customer-based evaluation.

Managerial Judgment

Through experience, salesperson call reports, distributors, or other company sources, product managers can often develop judgments about the sources of present and future competition.

One way to structure the thought process is to use a tabular structure such as that shown in Figure 3–9 (a variant of Ansoff's well-known growth matrix[10]). Box A represents product form competiton, that is, those products or services that are basically the same and are pursuing the same customers. Box C represents product form competitors that target other customers.

The most interesting cell of Figure 3–9 is B. This cell represents potential future competitors that already have a franchise with our customers but do not offer the same product or service. In this case, the product manager might try to forecast which firms falling into B are likely to become more direct competitors. Examples of companies capitalizing on prior customer familiarity are numerous. In telecommunications, IBM had a considerable franchise with large business customers through its mainframe computer business. IBM easily moved to cell A through its investments in MCI and Rolm. In the orange juice category, Procter & Gamble had perhaps the best franchise of any consumer product manufacturer with both supermarkets and consumers, which it used to develop the Citrus Hill brand. Disney's recent purchase of Capital Cities/ABC is consistent with its entertainment franchise. In financial services, AT&T's surprise introduction of a credit card, which put it into direct competition with

[10]H. Igor Ansoff, *Corporate Strategy* (New York: McGraw-Hill, 1965).

VISA, American Express, and others, was based on its wide franchise with consumers. This type of movement into new product areas is common in consumer businesses; companies often try to leverage their brand equity in one category to grab sales in others that serve the same customers. Managers should assess the likelihood of such horizontal movements as well as their chances of success, although some moves, such as AT&T's, will always be difficult to predict.

Cell D competitors are the most difficult to predict, as they currently sell different products to different customers. One example of the impact of such a competitor in consumer durables was Litton Industries' commercialization of microwave technology, which created a new competitor for General Electric in the kitchen appliance market.

Perhaps the least scientific but most useful way to see what a product or service might compete with is to imagine the item as a "prop" for a stand-up comedian. The comedian, unencumbered by convention (and sometimes good taste), can create many uses for a product, therefore suggesting different competitive products.

Technology substitution is particularly relevant for technological products. Judgments by engineers, marketing managers, and other experts may suggest other products or technologies that substitute for current ones. For example, in many telecommunications and computer networking applications, infrared or wireless communications are substituting for optical fiber, which in turn substituted for wire or "twisted pair," thus producing successive technological generations of competitors.

Customer-Based Measures

Two types of customer data are commonly used to assess market structures: actual purchase or usage data and judgments.[11] The former are particularly useful for understanding product form and category competition; because it is difficult to understand what alternatives were considered when purchases were actually made, the usual assumption is that purchases are made within a narrow definition of competition. However, what customers have actually done does not necessarily indicate what they would have preferred to do in the past or are likely to do in the future. Judgmental data are needed to understand broader definitions of competition as well as to estimate how a new product affects the structure of competition.

Using Purchase Data. A key source of purchase data used in consumer packaged goods applications is data collected from electronic scanners. Households enroll with a commercial firm, either A. C. Nielsen or Information Resources, Inc. (IRI). Before scanning in their purchases at the cash register, the cashier scans an identification code indicating that the purchases to follow are for a particular household. The brands and package sizes are coded by Universal Product Code (UPC or bar codes). Alternatively, since many products have substantial purchase volume outside supermarkets (e.g., convenience stores, vending machines), A. C. Nielsen has developed an in-home scanning system in which the panel member scans the UPC codes at home with an

[11]George S. Day, Allan D. Shocker, and Rajendra V. Srivastava, "Customer-Oriented Approaches to Identifying Product Markets," *Journal of Marketing,* Fall 1979, pp. 8–19.

FIGURE 3–10 Brand-Switching Matrix

		Time t + 1				
		A	B	C	D	E
Time t	A	.6	.2	.2	0	0
	B	.2	.3	.4	.1	0
	C	.2	.3	.5	0	0
	D	0	.1	.1	.5	.3
	E	.1	0	0	.4	.5

infrared "wand" and the data are dumped into a computer and downloaded via modem. While most of the data collected from consumers using these technologies are aggregated to estimate sales and market shares for brands, the household-level data are very useful for noting patterns of repeat purchasing of brands and brand switching.[12]

Figure 3–10 shows a common way to organize the data from scanners. The figure is a brand-switching matrix for a specific product category. Because most of these analyses concern predetermined product categories, patterns of competition within categories or subcategories (product form) but not cross-category (generic) can be determined. This approach is usually best applied to determine segment competitors for frequently purchased goods or services. The numbers in the table represent purchase probabilities calculated across panel households from one purchase occasion (time *t*) to the next (time *t+1*) for a set of brands, A through E. Probabilities of brand switching have been proposed as measures of customers' perceived similarities, and therefore substitutability, among brands.[13] High brand-switching probabilities suggest a high degree of competition.

The diagonal elements represent the degree of brand loyalty; for example, 60 percent of the households buying brand A on one occasion repurchased it on the next purchase occasion. The off-diagonal elements represent brand-switching behavior; for example, 20 percent of the time purchases of brand A were followed by a purchase of B. The row numbers must sum to 1, as a household must buy one of the five brands.

While sophisticated methods of analysis are needed for large brand-switching matrixes, Figure 3–10 was constructed for easy eyeballing. From observing the

---

[12]Interestingly, the different companies sometimes produce different market share estimates. Both PepsiCo and Coca-Cola recently claimed to have increased share more than the other in 1995; PepsiCo uses IRI and Coca-Cola uses Nielsen. See Robert Frank, "Conflicting Market Data on Coca-Cola and PepsiCo Roil Beverage Industry," *The Wall Street Journal*, January 4, 1996, p. B5.

[13]See Manohar Kalwani and Donald Morrison, "A Parsimonious Description of the Hendry System," *Management Science*, January 1977, pp. 467–77; Donald Lehmann, "Judged Similarity and Brand-Switching Data as Similarity Measures," *Journal of Marketing Research*, August 1972, pp. 331–34; Frank M. Bass, Moshe Givon, Manohar U. Kalwani, David Reibstein, and Gordon P. Wright, "An Investigation into the Order of the Brand Choice Process," *Marketing Science,* Fall 1984, pp. 267–87.

FIGURE 3–11 Defining Competition with Brand Choice Data

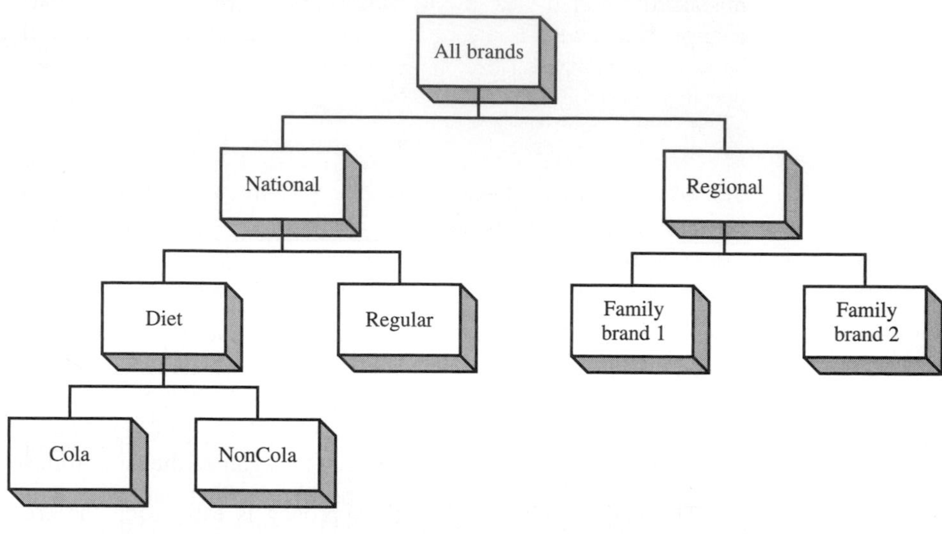

Source: Reprinted by permission from Vithela Rao and Darins Sabavala, "Inference of Hierarchical Choice Processes from Panel Data," in JOURNAL OF CONSUMER RESEARCH, June 1981, published by the University of Chicago Press. © 1981 by the University of Chicago.

patterns of brand switching, there are clearly two main groups of brands, A-B-C and D-E. In addition, within the A-B-C cluster, B and C seem to form another group. We could conclude that within the market for this product, there are two sets of product form and an even narrower set of two within one of the clusters.

An example of this kind of analysis on real consumer purchasing data for soft drinks appears in Figure 3–11.[14] These analyses typically create a treelike diagram with the branch structure indicating the competition implied by consumer purchasing patterns. As the figure indicates, the competition for a national brand is other national brands, while the major competition for a regional brand is the other regional or family brand. Within the national brand competition, the regular brands compete against one another, as do the diet brands. Finally, there is an extremely narrow range of competition within national diet colas and national diet noncolas.

A problem with using purchase data to understand product form and category competition is that brand switches occur across complements as well as substitutes. Consumers might purchase complements when they want variety.[15] For example, consider a consumer who views Coke and Pepsi as direct substitutes but sometimes likes a lemon-lime drink such as 7UP as a break from Coke/Pepsi. Now suppose a

[14]This illustration is taken from Vithala Rao and Darius Sabavala, "Inference of Hierarchical Choice Processes from Panel Data," *Journal of Consumer Research*, June 1981, pp. 85–96.

[15]See Leigh McAlister and James Lattin, "Using a Variety-Seeking Model to Identify Substitute and Complementary Relationships among Competing Products," *Journal of Marketing Research*, August 1985, pp. 330–39.

recording of purchases shows a purchase sequence of Coke–Coke–7UP–Coke. A researcher might analyze the brand switch from Coke to 7UP for that consumer and mistakenly infer it was due to substitutability reasons rather than to the desire for a change. If this were true for a large number of consumers, the product manager would believe that Coke and 7UP were competitors and might design his or her strategy with that in mind when the truth is that 7UP is not really a competitive threat in the usual sense.

Another problem with using purchase data is one of its strengths: The data are at the household level. Observed switching between two brands could be due to different household members' preferences rather than to any substitutability reasons. For example, purchases of Coke and Pepsi could be for two different people or a true switch of brands by one individual. The difference is crucial.

Panel or sales data can be used to calculate cross-elasticities of demand, another basis for estimating patterns of competition. A cross-elasticity is the percentage change in one brand's sales compared to a percentage change in a marketing variable for another brand, such as price. If a cross-elasticity with respect to price is positive (a brand's sales decline when another brand's price drops), the two brands or products in question are considered to be competitive.[16]

The major problem with this approach is estimating the cross-elasticities: It is assumed there is no competitive reaction to the price cut and the market is static with respect to new entrants, product design, and so forth. In addition, a positive cross-elasticity does not imply cause and effect, that is, that the price decline (increase) of the brand in question actually caused the other brand's sales to decline (increase). As with measuring brand switching, the set of brands or products usually must be defined a priori.

In summary, the estimates of competition using purchasing behavior are useful because they represent what consumers *actually* do, not what they *might* do, which surveys indicate. For the most part, however, without specially designed and expensive data collection, these estimates apply primarily to frequently purchased, nondurable goods. In addition, they tend to be most appropriate when a product class is defined a priori and when a set of market definitions based on product form or category is sought.

Using Customer Judgments. Several methods have been proposed for estimating competition from customer judgments. All are essentially paper-and-pencil exercises in which customers are surveyed in focus groups, shopping mall intercepts, or other environments. Although not based on actual customer behavior, they have the advantages of providing insight into potential future market structures, producing broader definitions of current structures, and being applicable to all types of products and services, including industrial products and consumer durables.

Judged overall similarity measures between pairs of products or brands can be used to create geometric representations in multidimensional spaces called *perceptual maps*. The brands or products are represented by points in the space, while the

[16]See, for example, Lee Cooper, "Competitive Maps: The Structure Underlying Asymmetric Cross-elasticities," *Management Science*, June 1988, pp. 707–23.

FIGURE 3–12 Defining Competition with Perceptual Mapping

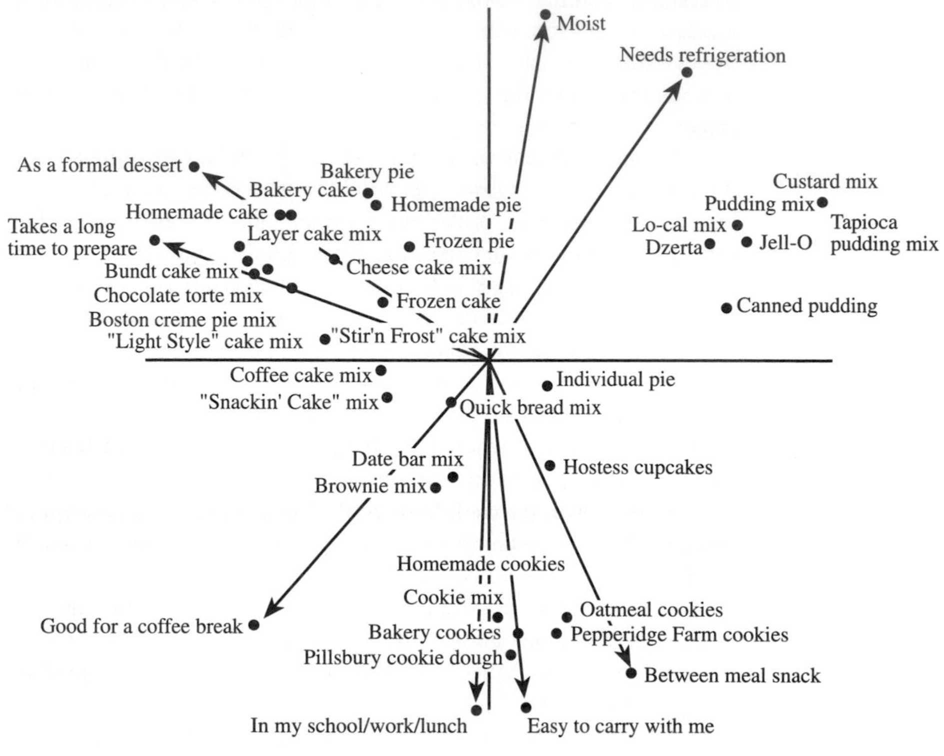

Source: *Marketing News,* May 14, 1982, p. 3.

dimensions represent the attributes customers use to make the similarity judgments. Brands located close to one another are judged to be similar and thus form a defined market.[17] If brands are the objects of the mapping exercise, only product category or product form competition can be assessed. However, if a larger set of products is used, more interesting generic competition can be identified.

As an example, Figure 3–12 presents a perceptual map from the generic category of desserts. The analysis must begin with a prespecified set of the relevant of alternatives, which can be developed through focus group research that identifies products satisfying a given need. The points not attached to the vectors represent the various products the focus group identified as filling the need for dessert. The vectors help determine attributes for defining the space, but are not relevant to the market competition issue. Information about the competitive sets is obtained by examining

[17]There are other methods for constructing perceptual maps besides similarity ratings, for example, factor and discriminant analysis of attribute ratings.

clusters of points. The upper-right quadrant would be very useful to, say, the brand manager for Jell-O. From the map, it is clear that Jell-O is perceived to be quite similar to custard, pudding, tapioca, lo-Cal mix, and Dzerta, a mixture of gelatin and other products.

Similarity of consideration sets is an approach developed by Bourgeois, Haines, and Sommers that asks customers to take a large set of products and divide them into groups of items that can be substituted for one another, that is, items that would be considered together on a purchase occasion.[18] The customers are then asked to judge the similarity of the products within each group. By accumulating similarity judgments across the customers, a perceptual map can be developed. Thus, this approach is somewhat similar to the preceding one, but it collects the similarity judgments after consideration sets have been formed. Other variants of this approach use verbal protocol data gathered as customers think aloud while considering a purchase decision.

The consideration set concept itself has been extensively explored.[19] A customer faces a choice simplification problem when making a purchase decision. It is hypothesized that customers simplify the process by reducing the number of available products and brands that can satisfy a need to a smaller set from which they make the ultimate decision. Clearly, the options in this smaller set closely compete against one another. However, the usefulness of the consideration set concept is limited by the sets' variability across customers and across distribution channels and by the fact that they are dynamic: Consideration sets change from one purchase occasion to another.

Product deletion is an interesting approach to defining competition based on customer reaction to product unavailability.[20] Products or brands in a set are presumed to be substitutes and consequently form a market if, when one of them is deleted from the choice set, customers are more likely to buy from the remaining products than from products outside the original set. For example, suppose a choice set of stereos consists of Pioneer, Sansui, Technics, and others. If, when Pioneer is eliminated from the set, customers are more likely to choose Sansui or Technics than any other brand, the three brands are presumed to form a market.

Although its authors describe product deletion as useful primarily to partition product form markets into submarkets, there is no reason the approach could not be used in a more general setting. For example, if milk is unavailable and orange juice and soft drinks are subsequently chosen more often than tea or coffee, then milk, juice, and soft drinks apparently compete at the generic level.

---

[18] Jacques Bourgeois, George Haines, and Montrose Sommers, "Defining an Industry," paper presented at the ORSA/TIMS Market Measurement Conference, Stanford, 1979.

[19] See John R. Hauser and Birger Wernerfelt, "An Evaluation Cost Model of Consideration Sets," *Journal of Consumer Research*, March 1990, pp. 391–405; John H. Roberts and James M. Lattin, "Development and Testing of a Model of Consideration Set Composition," *Journal of Marketing Research*, November 1991, pp. 429–40; Rick L. Andrews and T.C. Srinivasan, "Studying Consideration Effects in Empirical Choice Models Using Scanner Panel Data," *Journal of Marketing Research*, February 1995, pp. 30–41.

[20] Glen Urban, Philip Johnson, and John Hauser, "Testing Competitive Market Structures," *Marketing Science*, Spring 1984, pp. 83–112.

Substitution in use estimates degree of competitiveness through judged similarities of products in usage contexts.[21] First, customers list all possible uses and contexts (e.g., a party or one's own use) for a target product or brand. Next, either the original sample or a fresh sample of respondents list other products or brands that provide the same benefits or uses and rate their appropriateness for the different contexts or use occasions. This method clearly has the potential to produce a large number of generic competitors or even budget competitors.

As an illustration, suppose the target product of interest is a baseball game. A brief sketch of the analysis is as follows:

Target:	Baseball game	
Uses:	Sports event	Entertainment
Substitutes:	Horse racing	Movies
		Dinner at a restaurant
		Visiting a sports bar

Thus, substitution in use can produce a fairly diverse set of competitors.

Summary

Figure 3–13 summarizes the methods for determining competition along two dimensions: (1) the usefulness of each method for determining competition at a certain level and (2) the kind of research data typically used to implement the method. With respect to the latter, information is divided into primary sources (data collected specifically to determine competitors) and secondary sources (data collected for some general purpose other than to determine the structure of the market).

As Figure 3–13 indicates, all the methods are useful for determining product form competition. Managerial judgment and behavior-based customer data are useful mainly for developing product form and product category markets. Customer information that is judgment based, however, can also be used to assess generic competition. Since cross-elasticities, judged similarity, technology substitution, product deletion, and substitution in use either start with an a priori market definition (which could be very broad) or are usage based, they cannot really be used to define budget competition, that is, those products fighting for the same customer dollar. Since the consideration set approach has no such restrictions, it can be used to assess budget competition.

With respect to data requirements, the judgment-based customer evaluations require primary data while behavior-based methods can use secondary data. When

[21]See Volney Stefflre, "Some Applications of Multidimensional Scaling to Social Science Problems," in *Multidimensional Scaling: Theory and Applications in the Behavioral Sciences*, Vol. III, ed. A. K. Romney, R. N. Shepard, and S. B. Nerlove (New York: Seminar Press, 1972); S. Ratneshwar and Allan Shocker, "Substitution in Use and the Role of Usage Context in Product Category Structures," *Journal of Marketing Research*, August 1991, pp. 281–95.

FIGURE 3–13 Methods versus Competition Levels and Information Required

	Level of Competition				Typical Data Sources	
Approach	*Product Form*	*Product Category*	*Generic*	*Budget*	*Primary*	*Secondary*
Existing definitions	X	X				X
Technology substitution	X	X	X		X	
Managerial judgment	X	X			X	X
Customer behavior based:						
Brand switching	X	X				X
Interpurchase times	X	X				X
Cross-elasticities	X	X	X			X
Customer evaluation based:						
Overall similarity	X	X	X		X	
Similarity of consideration sets	X	X	X	X	X	
Product deletion	X	X	X		X	
Substitution in use	X	X	X		X	

Note: An X indicates that either the method is useful for determining competition at that level or it employs data of a certain type.

applied to consumer packaged goods, the behavior-based methods utilize commercially available scanner panel data. Consumer judgments might supplement purchase data with primary data, for example, from interviews focusing on motivations for brand switching. Managerial judgment can (and at least implicitly does) utilize both primary data (e.g., discussions with distributors) and secondary data (e.g., salesperson call reports).

Competitor Selection

Examining competition at four levels makes intuitive sense, and the practical implications for a product manager are substantial. One implication already mentioned is that marketing strategy must be developed with an eye toward four different problems: (1) convincing customers in your market segment that your brand is best (product form competition); (2) convincing buyers that your product form is best (product category competition); (3) convincing buyers that your product category is best (generic competition); and, occasionally, (4) convincing buyers that the basic need your product fulfills is an important one. A product manager must decide what percentage of his or her budget to spend on each problem.

A second implication of the four levels of competition is that product managers must choose a selective competitor focus. A product manager cannot focus either analysis or strategy on every product in the market perceived to be a competitor due to limited available resources. Choosing who to compete against has major implications for both performance standards (e.g., determing share of what) and strategy (e.g., competitive advertising). For example, the Pioneer marketing manager described earlier must select which other low-priced stereos, other stereos, or other entertainment forms (and therefore which manufacturers or service suppliers) to compete against.

The product manager can decide which competitors to focus on by examining three factors: (1) the time horizon of the marketing plan being developed, (2) the stage of the product life cycle relevant for the product, and (3) the rate of change in the technological base of the product.

In the one-year operating marketing plan most common for product managers, competition *must* be defined primarily on a product form basis and secondarily using any other appropriate bases. Clearly, the brands that compete with the one in question on a day-to-day basis are in the product form or a subcategory. For these brands, the product manager must have intimate knowledge of the customers, the competitors, and the effects of environmental changes such as demographics. For example, in an annual planning cycle, Sanka's major competitors are primarily other decaffeinated instant coffees. What about other decaffeinated or regular coffees? The selection of other competitors in the product category (coffee) or generic group is a judgment call based on where the product manager sees potential growth opportunities or whether a category or a generic competitor is attacking the product form. In this example, Sanka also competes more against other decaffeinated coffee brands than regular brands. As we mentioned earlier, competition such as soft drinks and juices is a serious issue for the category, and efforts to compete are funded by the coffee trade association. For longer-term plans, all four levels of competition are relevant, with special emphasis placed on the generic level to identify important competitive threats.

The stage of the product life cycle may be relevant to defining competition because the breadth of view of the industry varies over time. In the early growth stages of a product, particularly a new technology, competition must be broadly defined (generic competition) since a large part of the marketing task is to convince customers to substitute a new product for an existing one that was previously satisfying their needs. On the other hand, in mature markets, the focus should generally be on product form and category competitors to best assess whether or not to stay in a market.

Finally, where the rate of technological change is rapid, competition should be conceived as broadly as possible. This is characteristic of the communications field, in which such diverse products as word processors, fax machines, the Internet, home computers, cable TV, and satellites compete for certain services. Alternatively, narrow definitions are sufficient for fields in which new technical advances occur less frequently, as is the case with food products.

Given that the appropriate levels of competition have been selected, that is, that the "market" has been defined by the product manager, attention shifts to choosing relevant competitors. This assessment may require preparing a preliminary competitor analysis or at least updating the previous plan's competitor analysis. The factors determining which competitors are relevant relate to forecasts of competitors' likely strategies, which the competitor analysis should provide. However, the resources the competitors can bring to bear in the market are also critical. This focus on resources highlights a final perspective on competition called *enterprise competition.*

Enterprise Competition

Ultimately products and services do not compete against one another; companies do. The resources a company has to support the product are a key determinant of its ability to successfully implement a marketing strategy. Thus, while we have examined competition in this chapter from the perspective of a brand or product, it is important to note that firm versus firm or enterprise competition involves a higher-level perspective in developing strategies.

For example, in the computer workstation market, the Hewlett-Packard product line competes against Sun, IBM, Silicon Graphics, and DEC, among others. However, not all competitors are created equal. When HP develops a marketing strategy against IBM, it competes not only in terms of product features and benefits communicated but also against IBM's resources: its financial support, sales force, and image. HP must develop different strategies to compete against IBM than those it uses to compete against Sun, which is many times smaller than IBM.

Figure 3–14 shows the diverse set of companies competing in the financial services industry.[22] This could easily be expanded to include companies such as Fidelity, Vanguard, Citibank, etc., and products such as IRAs and annuities. As a traditional financial services company, American Express is used to competing against Merrill Lynch and Prudential in insurance, commercial lending, and securities. However, General Motors, General Electric, and Ford, typically thought of as industrial powers, also compete with American Express for consumer loans, credit/debit cards, commercial lending, and insurance. Thus, the American Express green card product manager competes against products with a very diverse set of corporate parents with among the deepest pockets in the world.

It is often difficult to understand brand-level competition without understanding the broader context in which it occurs. For example, the Bic versus Cricket cigarette lighter battle may make little sense without recognizing the general competition

FIGURE 3–14 Enterprise Competition in Financial Services

	FDIC-insured depository	*Consumer loans*	*Credit/debit cards*	*Mortgage banking*	*Commercial lending*	*Mutual funds*	*Securities*	*Insurance*
American Express	X	X	X			X	X	X
Ford		X	X	X	X			X
General Electric	X	X	X	X	X	X		X
General Motors		X	X	X	X			X
Merrill Lynch	X		X	X	X	X	X	X
Prudential	X	X	X	X	X	X	X	X

Source: *Fortune,* May 15, 1995, p. 178.

[22]*Fortune*, May 15, 1995, p. 178.

between Bic and Gillette, which includes razors and pens as well as lighters. In addition, Kimberly Clark, a fierce competitor with Procter & Gamble (P&G) in the disposable diaper market, acquired Scott Paper with the intention of using the Scott brands (e.g., toilet tissue) to compete against P&G (Charmin) and therefore help dilute P&G's resources to compete in the more lucrative diaper category.

Enterprise competition is often characterized by asymmetries in competitive perspectives. For example, Microsoft probably views Lotus's (now IBM's) 1-2-3 as its most serious spreadsheet software competitor to Excel and ignores others. However, Corel's Quattro Pro has to view Microsoft as a key competitor, since it dominates the market. In other words, Excel competes against Quattro Pro from Corel's perspective, but Quattro Pro does not compete against Excel from Microsoft's perspective.

Summary

In this chapter, we argued that the set of competitors that pose a threat to a product can be highly varied and can come from a variety of what have traditionally been referred to as industries. Therefore, a "market" or an "industry" is often dynamic and difficult to define; often the labels are used more for convenience than to accurately describe the underlying patterns of competition. We presented a framework to conceptualize competition and methods to help form ideas about the competitive set. Finally, we discussed approaches to selecting competitors by choosing the relevant levels and specific brands.

Essentially, we suggest that competitors are those companies whose products or services compete for the same customers either directly through offering similar products or services (product form or category competition), indirectly through satisfying similar basic needs (generic competition), or in terms of budget. The product manager in charge of an existing product in an established category would generally be most interested in product form or category competition, since those are the products that immediately threaten his or her "livelihood." However, for new-product plans, a generic perspective is very important since the new product is substituting for another category satisfying similar customer needs.

C H A P T E R

4 Category Attractiveness Analysis

Overview

For either new or existing products, product managers must ask whether the category of interest is sufficiently attractive to warrant new or continued investment—by their company, current competitors, or potential new entrants—before the planning process begins. For example, the product portfolio approach popularized by the Boston Consulting Group uses the market growth rate to indicate attractiveness. Other models utilize a two-dimensional strategic grid consisting of market attractiveness and business position.[1]

The kind of analysis described in this chapter is often characterized as "industry" or "market" analysis. Because the focus of this book is on the individual product management level, we focus on the product category, which defines the set of competitors against which one most often competes on a daily basis. While this may seem to be a narrow definition, particularly after the discussion in the preceding chapter, in many cases it is no easier to define an industry than a product category. In general, a product manager can adapt the analysis presented in this chapter to the definition of product category or industry most appropriate for the circumstances.

An essential component of the marketing planning process is an analysis of a product's potential to achieve a desired level of return on the company's investment. An analysis of this type not only assesses financial opportunities but also provides ideas about how to compete better given structural characteristics of the category.

The characteristics of a product category rarely point in the same direction. As a result, categories that some firms find attractive will be of little interest to others. For example, most food categories are characterized by low but steady sales volume growth. Thus, a growth rate of 4.5 percent in the frozen potato category (see Figure 3–2 on page 52) would probably seem high to the Ore-Ida product manager but quite low to a Microsoft marketer. In the automobile market, most observers consider the luxury car segment (over $30,000) overpopulated with models from every major car

[1]See, for example, David W. Cravens *Strategic Marketing*, 4th ed. (Burr Ridge, IL: Richard D. Irwin, 1994), ch. 2.

FIGURE 4–1 Category Attractiveness Summary

Aggregate category factors:
- Category size
- Category growth
- Stage in product life cycle
- Sales cyclicity
- Seasonality
- Profits

Category factors:
- Threat of new entrants
- Bargaining power of buyers
- Bargaining power of suppliers
- Current category rivalry
- Pressure from substitutes
- Category capacity

Environmental factors:
- Technological
- Political
- Economic
- Regulatory
- Social

manufacturer in the world. However, Ford chose to purchase Jaguar because of the considerable brand equity in the name and because Ford management believed the brand gave the company an instant entry into the luxury car field.

Besides the product manager for the manufacturer or service provider, another interested party to this analysis is the distribution channel. As we noted in Chapter 1, more channel members, particularly retailers, are interested in category management, the profitable management of entire product categories. Clearly, retailers will give more space and/or selling time to those categories that are "attractive," as this implies faster inventory turnover and greater total profits and less space for categories that are "unattractive." Thus the product manager must realize that the kind of analysis described in this chapter is also relevant to (and probably is also being performed by) the channel members in the distribution system.

In this chapter, we examine the factors (summarized in Figure 4–1) considered important in assessing the underlying attractiveness of a product category. The three main areas of inquiry include basic aggregate factors, category factors related to the major participants, and environmental factors. We also discuss sources of information for the attractiveness analysis components and apply the concepts to the RTD fruit drink and PDA categories.

Aggregate Market Factors

Category Size

Category size (measured in both units and dollars) is an important piece of data about any market. It is clearly an important determinant of the likelihood that a product will generate revenues to support a given investment. In general, larger markets are better than smaller ones. Besides having more market potential, large categories usually offer more opportunities for segmentation than small ones (see Chapter 6). Therefore, both large firms and entrepreneurial organizations might find large markets attractive. Large markets, however, tend to draw competitors with considerable resources, thus making them unattractive for small firms. Witness the soft-drink category. Coca-Cola and PepsiCo spent over $248 million in 1995 on advertising alone supporting Coke, Diet Coke, Pepsi, and Diet Pepsi, and this did not include money spent on promotion.[2] Thus, absolute size by itself is not sufficient to warrant new or continuing investment.

Market Growth

As mentioned previously, market growth is a key market factor advocated by various planning models. Not only is current growth important, but growth projections over the horizon of the plan are also critical. Fast-growing categories are almost universally desired due to their abilities to support high margins and sustain profits in future years. However, like large categories, fast-growing ones also attract competitors. For example, while Procter & Gamble developed the U.S. market for disposable diapers, the projected high market growth rate supported the entry of other firms such as Johnson & Johnson and Kimberly Clark. In technology-based markets, fast growth often means dramatic shifts in market shares and the virtual disappearance of rival products. In the Internet browser market, a market growing at a rate in the triple digits, Netscape had 13 percent of the market and Mosaic had 60 percent in 1994. However, in 1995, Netscape had 79 percent while Mosaic was down to 3 percent.[3] In 1996, the shares are changing dramatically again as Microsoft begins actively marketing its own browser.

Product Life Cycle

Category size and category growth are often portrayed simultaneously in the form of the product life cycle (see Figure 4–2). Usually presumed to be S shaped, this curve breaks down product sales into four segments: introduction, growth, maturity, and decline. The introduction and growth phases are the early phases of the life cycle when sales are growing rapidly, maturity represents a leveling off in sales, and the decline phase represents the end of the life cycle.

Figure 4–2 also presents a general assessment of the attractiveness of a category at each stage of the life cycle. In the introductory phase, both the growth rate and the size of the market are low, thus making it unattractive for most prospective participants, who would rather wait on the sidelines for a period of time. When market growth and sales start to take off, the market becomes more attractive. In the maturity phase, the assessment is unclear; while the growth rate is low, the market size could be at its peak. This is the classic pattern for soft drinks, fast food, and many other

---

[2] *Advertising Age*, May 6, 1996, p. 36.

[3] David Kirkpatrick, "As the Big Guys Awake, Can Netscape Prevail?" *Fortune*, January 15, 1996, p. 16.

FIGURE 4–2 Category Attractiveness over the Product Life Cycle

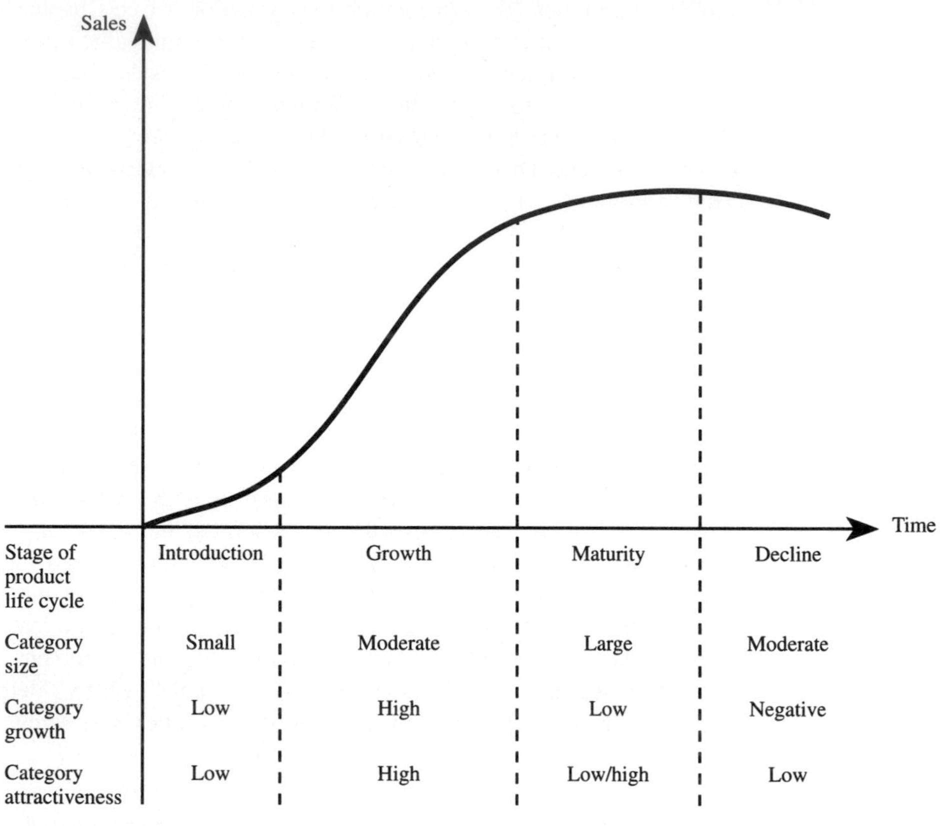

consumer packaged goods: large dollar volume with slow growth. Finally, the decline phase usually is so unattractive that most competitors flee the category.

However, the attractiveness of products in different phases of the life cycle is not always clear. While the introductory phase has low growth and sales volume, it can be attractive to be the pioneer from a long-run market share perspective.[4] Products in the growth phase are not ensured success; witness the failures of Osborne and Commodore in the early days of personal computers, and even "big name" companies such as AT&T and Hewlett-Packard have had difficulties in the home segment of the personal computer market. Even products in the decline phase, the "last ice man," can be very profitable. Lansdale Semiconductor and Rochester Electronics are the last companies

---

[4]See, for example, Glen L. Urban, Theresa Carter, Steven Gaskin, and Zofia Mucha, "Market Share Rewards to Pioneering Brands: An Empirical Analysis and Strategic Implications," *Management Science*, June 1986, pp. 645–59, and Gurumurthy Kalynanaram, William T. Robinson, and Glen L. Urban, "Order of Market Entry: Established Empirical Generalizations, Emerging Empirical Generalizations, and Future Research," *Marketing Science*, Part 2 of 2 (1995), pp. G212–G221.

to manufacture the 8080 microprocessor introduced by Intel in 1974. Some companies in the toy, defense, and telecommunications industries make products or need spare parts that use these old chips.

Sales Cyclicality

Many categories experience substantial interyear variation in demand. Highly capital-intensive businesses such as automobiles, steel, and machine tools, are often tied to general business conditions and therefore suffer through peaks and valleys of sales as gross domestic product (GDP) varies. Similarly, businesses tied to interest rates, such as real estate and other financial services, are susceptible to cycles. Products based on agricultural commodities are affected by yearly climactic conditions. This is clearly not an attractive characteristic of a category, as these sales swings affect profits, employment levels, and cash available for new-product development. Many firms attempt to develop products and acquire other businesses to eliminate interyear sales cyclicity.

Seasonality

Seasonality—intrayear cycles in sales—is generally not viewed positively. For example, in the last few years, the toy industry has reduced its reliance on the Christmas period to generate most of its sales. Such seasonal business tends to generate price wars because there may be few other opportunities to make substantial sales. However, most products are seasonal to some extent. Some, such as cold remedies, lawn mowers, fuel oil, and ice cream, are very seasonal.

Profits

While profits vary across products or brands in a category, large interindustry differences also exist. For example, the average profit margins for grocery stores, machine tools, automobiles, and computer software were 5.23 percent, 9.22 percent, 17.54 percent, and 26.82 percent, respectively, in 1994.[5]

These differences in profitability across industries are actually based on a variety of underlying factors. Differences can be due to factors of production (e.g., labor versus capital intensity, raw materials), manufacturing technology, and competitive rivalry, to name a few. Suffice it to say that product categories that are chronically low in profitability are less attractive than those that offer higher returns.

A second aspect of profitability is that it varies over time. Variance in profitability is often used as a measure of industry risk. Semiconductors offer abnormally high returns when demand is good but concomitant poor returns when demand slumps. Food-related businesses, on the other hand, produce steady, if unspectacular, profits. As is usually the case, product managers must make a risk-return trade-off, evaluating the expected returns against the variability in those returns. Figure 4–3 summarizes these variables.

---

[5]*S&P Analysts' Handbook, 1995 Annual Edition.*

Figure 4–3 Attractiveness of Market Variables

	Attractiveness	
	High	*Low*
Market size	+	–
Market growth	+	–
Sales cyclicity	–	+
Sales seasonality	–	+
Profit level	+	–
Profit variability	–	+

Category Factors

Although the aggregate factors just described are important indicators of the attractiveness of a product category, they do not provide information about underlying structural factors affecting the category. A classic model developed by Porter[6] considers five factors in assessing the structure of industries:

- The threat of new entrants.
- The bargaining power of buyers.
- The bargaining power of suppliers.
- The amount of intracategory rivalry.
- The threat of substitute products or services.

We adapt these factors to the category analysis and add a sixth factor, production or service capacity.

Threat of New Entrants

If the threat of new entrants into the product category is high, the attractiveness of the category is diminished. Except for the early stages of market development, when new entrants can help a market to expand, new entrants bring additional capacity and resources that usually heighten the competitiveness of the market and diminish profit margins. Even at early stages of market growth, the enthusiasm with which new entrants are greeted is tempered by who the competitor is. For example, while Apple publicly welcomed IBM's entry into the personal computer market, it is unlikely that there was considerable private elation in Cupertino, California.

The barriers to entry erected by the existing competition are key to the likelihood that new competitors will enter the market. This sounds anticompetitive and illegal, but it is only definitely anticompetitive; making it difficult for new competitors through legal means is a common strategic weapon of product managers. Some of the potential barriers to entry follow.

[6]Michael E. Porter, *Competitive Strategy* (New York: The Free Press, 1980).

Economies of Scale. An important barrier to entry in the automobile industry is the large plant size needed to operate efficiently, obtain quantity discounts on raw materials, and so on. Small manufacturers (e.g., Rolls-Royce, Aston Martin) must be content with serving the high-priced market segment. Economies of scale are obtainable in areas other than manufacturing. For example, in the hospital supply business, profit margins are better on larger orders because the costs of taking and fulfilling an order are largely fixed. Service costs are also subject to economies of scale because it costs about the same to set up a service center to service many customers or retailers as it does to service a few. Large advertisers usually get quantity discounts when buying blocks of media time on TV, radio, and other media.

Product Differentiation. Well-established brand names or company reputations can make it difficult for new competitors to enter. In the ready-to-eat breakfast cereal industry, the big four—Kellogg, Kraft/General Foods, General Mills, and Quaker Oats—have such long-established reputations that a new branded competitor would find it difficult to establish a brand franchise. The high barriers in the cereal industry were the subject of a lawsuit (ultimately unsuccessful) by the U.S. government.

Capital Requirements. Large amounts of capital may be necessary to establish manufacturing facilities, chain store locations, or marketing programs. It is easy to think of very capital-intensive industries, such as chemicals and aircraft, that require enormous amounts of money to set up plants. However, many categories are much more marketing intensive, through either advertising or distribution. For example, some mail-order computer companies buy their machines from other companies and spend most of their money on advertising, distribution, and service. Thus, capital barriers are clearly not confined to plant and equipment. The fast-food category has enormous fixed costs for marketing (advertising and promotion) and distribution.

Switching Costs. These are the costs of switching from one supplier to another. *Supplier* can be interpreted in a business-to-business sense or in an end-customer context. If switching costs are high, as they are in the mainframe computer and computer software businesses, it is difficult to convert a competitor's existing customers. Federal Express has given its business customers software that enables them to monitor the status of their own packages in the FedEx system. This creates a barrier to potential new entrants as well as making it difficult for competitors to get FedEx customers to switch package delivery firms. It is more difficult to build in switching costs into consumer products, particularly supermarket items, as consumers can simply change brands the next time they shop. However, a notable exception is Gillette, which tries to sell the notion of a shaving "system" and thus promote the use of its blades with its razors. Another example is home video game manufacturers such as Nintendo and Sega, which have security devices in their game cartridges and proprietary hardware that allow only games made by each company or their licensees to be used with the system.

Distribution. New products can find it difficult to obtain shelf space. Coca-Cola and PepsiCo have created so many varieties of their basic colas that branded rivals such as 7Up have found it more difficult to gain shelf space, particularly since private labels have made significant inroads into the soft-drink category. Supermarkets, drugstores, and other chain retailers often charge "slotting allowances," payments from manufacturers for placing their goods on shelves. This practice obviously creates a barrier to entry, particularly for smaller firms that find it difficult to pay the fees. Similarly, some analysts have argued that United's and American's airline reservation systems provide an unfair advantage to those companies.

The willingness of the competitors in the category to vigorously retaliate against newcomers can also act as a barrier. When small Minnetonka, Inc., innovated with a pump for hand soap, both Colgate-Palmolive and Procter & Gamble immediately copied the package and outspent Minnetonka in promotion. That story has been repeated in the toothpaste category.

Barriers change over time. When Xerox's patent on its basic copying process expired, the number of competitors in the copier market expanded dramatically. Likewise, when a prescription drug's patent protection ends, a generic with a much lower price is invariably introduced.

It is important not only that product managers note the likelihood of a new entrant based on the above factors, but that they also assess the ability of a product to heighten entry barriers. Again, although raising barriers to entry has a negative connotation, particularly to a company's lawyers, there are legal means of inhibiting competition in a product category. Thus, a product manager could ask: Is there anything I can do to make it more difficult for a new entrant or even a current competitor to compete against me? The answers are related to the factors noted above. For example, if threat of entry is easy (a negative for the category), then (1) differentiate more, (2) raise the stakes (capital) required to compete effectively, (3) build in switching costs, thus making it harder for customers to switch brands, (4) lock up distribution and/or supply to the extent it is legal, or (5) if appropriate, signal your intention to strongly retaliate. Product managers commonly attempt most of these tactics. Note that brand extensions occupy shelf space, and consumer product companies are spending more money trying to limit brand switching through database marketing and loyalty programs, that is, tracking individual customer buying habits and offering promotions via direct mail or telemarketing.

Bargaining Power of Buyers

The following diagram is useful for discussing the power of both buyers and suppliers:

Suppliers → Category of Concern → Buyers

Buyers are any people or institutions that receive finished goods or services from the organizations in the category being analyzed. Buyers can be distributors, original equipment manufacturers (OEMs), or end customers. Suppliers are any institutions that supply the category of concern with factors of production such as labor, capital, raw materials, and machinery.

High buyer bargaining power is negatively related to industry attractiveness. In such circumstances, buyers can force down prices and play competitors off against one another for benefits such as service. Some conditions that occur when buyer bargaining power is high include the following:

1. *When the product bought is a large percentage of the buyer's costs.* Historically, the automobile industry (the buyer) had little buying power over the steel industry (the industry of concern) because steel has been so important to car manufacturing. This power, however, is increasing as car manufacturers replace steel with plastics and reduce the number of suppliers they use to gain price concessions and productivity improvements.

2. *When the product bought is undifferentiated.* If product managers in the category of concern view what they sell as a commodity, buyers will have a great deal of power. Good examples of this include the leverage held by customers of commodity chemicals or bulk semiconductors. In such situations, buyers view the offerings as indistinguishable and bear down on price.

3. *When the buyers earn low profits.* Ailing industries such as farm equipment can generally extract better terms from supplier industries than can healthy industries.

4. *When the buyer threatens to backward integrate.* Among other pressures felt by semiconductor manufacturers is the constant threat by computer companies to make their own chips. IBM's purchase of part of Intel is such an example. Consumers also backward integrate, as the growth of do-it-yourself hardware and furniture stores indicates.

5. *When the buyer has full information.* Consumers can exert more power in retail stores if they are fully aware of competitive offerings. For example, car dealers are more willing to negotiate on price when a buyer demonstrates he or she has collected dealer cost information from a source such as *Consumer Reports*.

6. *When substitutes exist for the seller's product or service.* Although this is a separate category factor, described below, it also clearly affects buyer power.

In general, consumers wield their buyer power only on an individual and generally limited basis. This is not true in industrial businesses in which customers such as the U.S. government can wield large amounts of power. However, if consumers can be motivated as a group, they become a more important customer and thus exert more power than would otherwise be the case. For example, the large population of retired consumers are powerfully linked through the American Association of Retired Persons (AARP). Similarly, buying cooperatives have increased power.

Again, the product manager's concern is to decrease buyer power. This is accomplished, for example, by increasing product differentiation (e.g., making your product an essential component), helping customers become more profitable through services such as technical assistance or manufacturing-related consulting, and building in switching costs. Thus, the implications of this analysis of buyer power are as critical as is the overall concept of buyer power.

Bargaining Power of Suppliers

This assessment is really the mirror image of the buyer power analysis. High supplier power is clearly not an attractive situation because it allows suppliers to dictate price and other terms, such as delivery dates, to the buying category. Some conditions that prevail when supplier bargaining power is high are:

1. *When suppliers are highly concentrated, that is, dominated by a few firms.* Organizations in need of supercomputers face strong suppliers because very few exist worldwide.

2. *When there is no substitute for the product supplied.* The supercomputer falls in this category, although this power is diminishing with the increased computing speed offered by workstations. In contrast, the power of OPEC has diminished since the 1970s as many industries have converted plants to use oil and coal.

3. *When the supplier has differentiated its product or built in switching costs.* Armco Inc., a steelmaker, increased its power with the automobile industry by offering General Motors a delayed payment plan, a guarantee of no work stoppages, a demonstration of how cheaper steel could be substituted in certain areas, and extra service such as supplying steel already prepared with adhesives for some applications.

4. *When supply is limited.* Clearly when capacity and output are limited buyers have little opportunity to extract special terms.

Product managers should be concerned with reducing supplier power by looking for new sources of supply, substitute materials, and other strategies.

Current Category Rivalry

Product categories characterized by intense competition among the major participants are not as attractive as those in which the rivalry is more sedate. A high degree of rivalry can result in escalated marketing expenditures, price wars, employee raids, and related activities. Such actions can exceed what is considered "normal" market competition and can result in decreased welfare for both consumers and competitors.

Several examples highlight the negative aspects of rivalry. In the soft-drink category, PepsiCo and Coca-Cola are continually at each other's throats, increasing advertising, cutting prices, and running coupon and other sales promotions. Although advertising wearout is rapid in this category and the advertising does buy "share of mind," usually the big effect is on profits—and this effect is negative. Even the famous Ray Charles "uh huh" Diet Pepsi advertising campaign, into which PepsiCo poured a lot of money, had little impact on the brand's market position versus Diet Coke.[7] In the airline industry, American was the first with its frequent-flier program, but it was quickly copied by others, leaving no one with a marketing advantage and everyone with increased costs.[8] Compaq and Dell are well known to be bitter rivals in the personal computer industry; situated 200 miles apart in Texas, they steal each other's employees, trade vicious attacks in the press, and hire focus groups to find holes in the rival's strategies.[9] Other well-known intense rivalries are AT&T, MCI, and Sprint in the long-distance telephone market, chipmakers Intel and Cyrix, amusement park operators Six Flags and Disney, and giant Japanese trading companies Matsushita and Sony in consumer electronics.[10]

Some of the major characteristics of categories exhibiting intensive rivalries are:

1. *Many or balanced competitors.* The fast-food, automobile, and personal computer industries each have several large, well-endowed competitors. Alternatively,

---

[7]Laurie Petersen, "Pepsi Buys the Month of April, But Will It Sell?" *Marketing Week*, February 24, 1992, p. 9.

[8]Frequent-flier programs do increase switching costs and thus decrease buyer power.

[9]Kyle Pope, "For Compaq and Dell, Accent Is on Personal in the Computer Wars," *The Wall Street Journal*, July 2, 1993, p. A1.

[10]Jaclyn Fierman, "When Genteel Rivals Become Mortal Enemies," *Fortune*, May 15, 1995, p. 90.

the commercial aircraft manufacturing industry has one strong entrant, Boeing, and two weaker companies, McDonnell Douglas and Airbus.

2. *Slow growth.* The relevant issue here, of course, is that in mature markets, growth can come only from a competitor.

3. *High fixed costs.* In such categories, there is intense pressure to keep operations running at full capacity to lower average unit costs. For this reason, capital-intensive industries such as paper and chemicals are highly competitive.

4. *Lack of product differentiation.* When little differentiation exists, products and services look like commodities to customers and price warfare is rampant.

5. *Personal rivalries.* In some industries, personal rivalries develop around strong personalities who exhibit strong competitive instincts. High-technology industries such as computer software and telecommunications are examples, with company leaders such as Ray Smith (Bell Atlantic), Larry Ellison (Oracle), and Bill Gates (Microsoft) shaping their companies' intensely competitive behavior.

Except for product differentiation, it is more difficult for the product manager to have an impact on category rivalry than on the other categories of factors.

Pressure from Substitutes

Categories making products or delivering services for which there are a large number of substitutes are less attractive than those that deliver a relatively proprietary product, one that uniquely fills a customer need or solves a problem. Since almost all categories suffer from the availability of substitutes (recall the discussion from Chapter 3), this may not be a determinant of an unattractive product category. However, some of the highest rates of return are earned in categories in which the range of substitutes is small. For example, the broadcast media industry, which had few substitutes (although that is changing rapidly), earned much higher margins (nearly 30 percent) than coal (under 10 percent), which definitely has available alternatives.

Determining the degree to which substitutes exist relates to the definition of the category. However, as noted in Chapter 2, some products, such as soft drinks, clearly have more generic competitors, whereas others, such as farm tractors, find their main competition within the category.

Category Capacity

Chronic overcapacity is not a positive sign for long-term profitability. When a category is operating at capacity, its costs stay low and its bargaining power with buyers is normally high. Thus, a key indicator of the health of a category is whether there is a consistent tendency toward operating at or under capacity. For example, during recessions, consumer spending on travel services is low, resulting in overcapacity at many worldwide resorts. This leads to low bargaining power with buyers, who can bargain down rates on cruises and other vacations.

Figure 4–4 summarizes the category analysis. For an actual marketing plan, each of the major categories in the figure should be expanded to include the factors discussed in this chapter. In addition, the implications of the analysis should be stated, not just whether or not the category is attractive. Since, as a product manager, you are in the

FIGURE 4–4 Attractiveness of Category Factors

	High Attractiveness	*Low Attractiveness*
Threat of new entrants	–	+
Power of buyers	–	+
Power of suppliers	–	+
Rivalry	–	+
Pressure from substitutes	–	+
Unused capacity situations	–	+

category whether you like it or not, the important output of the category analysis is what the product manager learns about how to better compete in the product category.

Environmental Analysis

Consider the following diagram of the relationship of a firm to its environment. A definition of *environment* might include those factors outside the control of both the firm and its industry, or, stated another way, the external factors unrelated to the product's customers and competitors that affect marketing strategies. The vulnerability of a product category to changes in the environment is an unattractive characteristic, but virtually all product managers must deal with it. As mentioned earlier in the chapter, if a category's sales are tied to the domestic economic situation, cyclicity can result. Alternatively, categories that are well positioned to take advantage of environmental changes may prosper, as will product managers who view these changes as opportunities to gain competitive advantage.

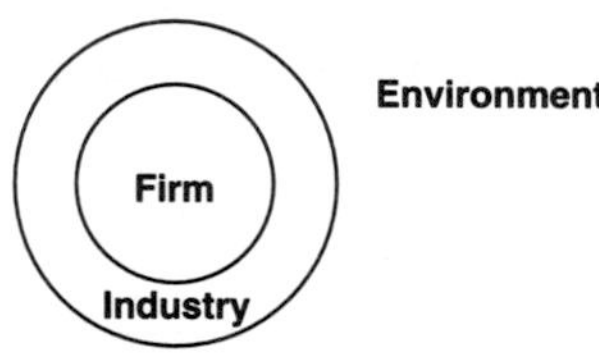

Environmental factors fall into five groups: technological, political, economic, regulatory, and social. These factors should be examined to assess category attractiveness and to determine if any forecasted changes dictate changes in strategy.

Technological Factors

Figure 4–5 displays a model of the technological environment that is useful for conceptualizing sources of technological change in an industry[11] (adapted here for a

[11]Adapted from Philip S. Thomas, "Environmental Analysis for Corporate Planning," *Business Horizons* 17 (October 1974), p. 27.

FIGURE 4–5 Typology of Technical Developments

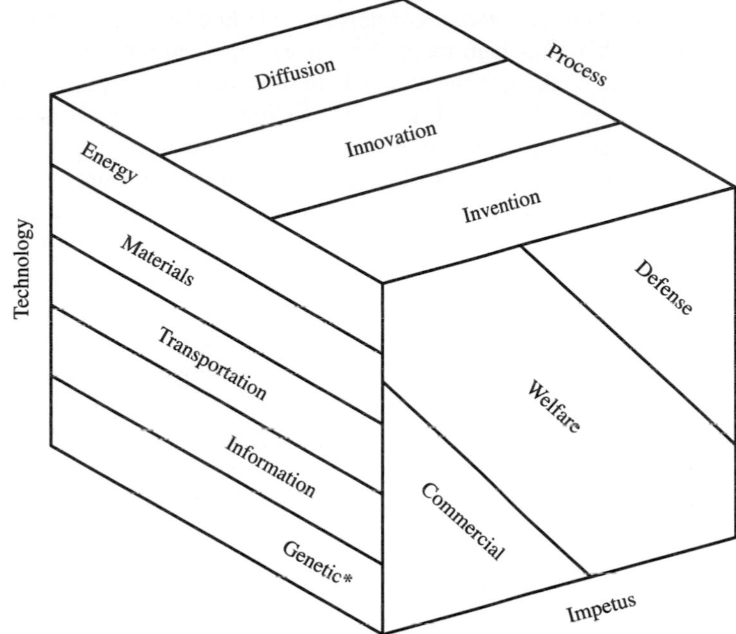

*Includes agronomic and biomedical developments.

Source: Philip S. Thomas, "Environmental Analysis for Corporate Planning," *Business Horizons* 17 (October 1974), p. 27.

product category). The "technology" and "impetus" dimensions are self-explanatory. The "process" dimension draws a distinction among the development of a new product (invention), the introduction of the product (innovation), and the spread of the product through the population (diffusion).

The two key dimensions used to assess a category's attractiveness are technology and process. Major changes are occurring in the energy, materials, transportation, information, and genetic (bioengineering) areas. With respect to information, for example, electronic scanning systems installed at supermarket cash registers enable retailers to closely monitor sales of different items for both inventory and shelf space allocation decisions. Bioengineering research is being used to both improve crop yields and find cures for various diseases such as cancer.

Product categories that are weaker on the technology dimension are particularly vulnerable to competition both from new products and from foreign competitors that have made the necessary investment. For example, in the 1980s most major U.S. steel firms used blast furnace technology developed in the 1800s. Foreign steel firms and domestic companies that invested in modern manufacturing technology have been highly successful in the past decade. On the positive side, U.S. strength has been computer software. Thus, an attractive product category is one that is well positioned to take advantage of technological changes that may be necessary to remain competitive against new, substitute technologies.

There is, however, a point beyond which technology can create a backlash, particularly among consumers. This has been referred to by John Naisbitt as "high tech versus high touch."[12] For example, automatic teller machines have depersonalized banking to the point where some consumers yearn for the human contact afforded by tellers. Several years ago, Citibank in New York proposed to allow only its wealthiest customers to make transactions through personal contact; other customers would have been forced to use machines. Consumers protested so vehemently that Citibank scrapped the idea. Although frequently touted as a wave of the future, home banking through personal computers has never really caught on with consumers. Similarly, home shopping through the computer-based services still accounts for a minuscule fraction of retail sales.

Attractive product categories are strong in invention, innovation, or diffusion of new products or services. Most technologically based companies must continually innovate because the life cycles for those products are extremely short. In contrast, success in frequently purchased packaged goods, while continuously being upgraded in various ways (e.g., packaging, flavor), is determined more by the quality of the marketing programs such as promotion, advertising, and the like.

Political Factors

A second environmental factor relates to the category's sensitivity to political factors. These are particularly relevant for products with substantial foreign markets. Figure 4–6 conceptualizes the sources of political risk, the groups that generate political risk, and political problems in operating the business.

For example, many multinational companies are either actively marketing or considering marketing products in China and other countries experiencing economic reform, such as Vietnam and Cambodia. Following Figure 4–6, the sources of political risk are competing political philosophies (the risk that communism or some form of autocracy hostile to market reforms could return) and possible social unrest and disorder. The results of these risks could be a halt to conducting business, damage to property, and personal risk to employees.

Such an analysis would not imply that an entire product line would be assessed as unattractive; it aids in evaluating geographically defined market segments for the line. If a sufficient percentage of a product's sales came from risky foreign markets, however, such a product could in fact look unattractive relative to others.

Domestic U.S. political risk is generally not as great, but it is still important. Domestic risk is usually related to which political party is in power. Republicans tend to favor free market economies. Therefore, products hard hit by foreign competition (e.g., shoes, commodity semiconductors, automobiles) would probably receive no relief through quotas or increased tariffs. With Democrats, defense spending has

---

[12]John Naisbitt, *Megatrends: Ten New Directions for Tranforming Our Lives* (New York: Warner Books, 1984).

FIGURE 4–6 Conceptualizing Political Risks

Sources of Political Risk	*Groups through Which Political Risk Can Be Generated*	*Effects on International Business Operations*
Competing political philosophies (nationalism, socialism, communism) Social unrest and disorder Vested interests of local business groups Recent and impending political independence Armed conflicts and internal rebellions for political power New international alliances	Government in power and its operating agencies Parliamentary opposition groups Nonparliamentary opposition groups (Algerian "FLN," guerrilla movements working within or outside country) Nonorganized common interest groups: students, workers, peasants, minorities, and so on Foreign governments or intergovernmental agencies such as the EEC Foreign governments willing to enter into armed conflict or to support internal rebellion	Confiscation: loss of assets without compensation Expropriation with compensation: loss of freedom to operate Operational restrictions: market shares, product characteristics, employment policies, locally shared ownership, and so on Loss of transfer freedom: financial (dividends, interest payments, goods, personnel, or ownership rights, for example) Breaches or unilateral revisions in contracts and agreements Discrimination such as taxes or compulsory subcontractings Damage to property or personnel from riots, insurrections, revolutions, and wars

Source: Stefan H. Robock, "Political Risk: Identification and Assessment," *Columbia Journal of World Business,* July–August 1971, p. 7.

historically been a target, and hence the fortunes of defense-related products are at risk. However, these political risks are dynamic. With the lowering of world tensions following the demise of the Soviet Union and the Eastern European communist bloc, even Republican presidents would have a hard time sustaining large defense spending. In addition, Democrats are becoming increasingly conservative on economic issues due to the mood of the country favoring balanced budgets.

Economic Factors

A wide variety of economic factors exist, and the product manager must consider how sensitive the product in question is to these factors.

Almost all capital goods industries (machine tools, farm equipment, mainframe computers) are sensitive to *interest rate fluctuations*, since their high costs to buyers are often financed at short-term interest rates. Consumer durables such as homes, cars, and stereos are also sensitive to interest rates, although consumer credit card rates do not react as much to changes in the prime lending rate as do commercial rates. Inflation rates, of course, are tied to interest rate fluctuations.

The financial impact of having foreign markets or producing in other countries can vary widely over time depending on *currency exchange rates*.

Since service businesses often hire relatively unskilled labor at low wage rates, they are highly dependent on *employment conditions*. When employment rates are high, for example, fast-food employees are hard to find or it is necessary to pay them more because higher-paying jobs are available. Demand and supply of labor for each industry must be considered as well. The supply of engineers is cyclical. When supply is down, many firms in technically related businesses suffer from a shortage of skilled labor.

Products such as automobiles and other consumer durables that have broad customer bases are often sensitive to *fluctuations in GDP growth*. When the country is in a recession, the sales of these products decline.

Regulatory Factors

Government and other agencies have an impact on category attractiveness through regulations. Some product categories have become less attractive over time because of laws that restrict product managers' abilities to market or that raise the overall cost of doing business. Government regulations, for example, restrict the media the tobacco industry can use for advertising. Pharmaceutical companies and many companies that make medical products are subject to stringent testing requirements that can change over time. Alternatively, government intervention can help some product categories. The U.S. government's restrictions on Japanese auto exports is an example, as is the subsidy given to certain agricultural commodities.

A good example of the impact of regulation on a pharmaceutical product is Genentech's tPA, an anticlotting drug. The company was so confident that the drug would succeed that it invested a considerable amount of money in manufacturing equipment, employees, premarketing, and product inventory. However, the Food and Drug Administration rejected the drug in May 1987, and within a week Genentech's market value dropped by nearly $1 billion.

It is not possible to generalize about the sources of regulatory impact because each product category is affected by different regulatory bodies. As a result, this part of the analysis must be highly category specific.

Social Factors

Trends in demographics, lifestyles, attitudes, and personal values among the general population are of particular concern for consumer product manufacturers and services. First, new products have been developed to fit into today's lifestyles. Frozen entrées, for example, were developed to suit dual-career households with a need for convenience and easy preparation. Second, new features have been added to existing products. Upper-income consumers can have ice water dispensers in refrigerators, fancy stereos with CD players in cars, and telephones with built-in calculators. Finally, promotion has changed. The aging "baby boomer" (look-alikes for the authors) is commonplace today in television ads, as is the mysterious "Generation X" (young adults) consumer.

What is not generally recognized is the importance of understanding trends in lifestyles and demographics for business-to-business products. Because the demand for such products is often derived demand, that is, ultimately generated by consumers, changes in the source of that demand can clearly affect demand for an industrial product. For example, the chemical manufacturer making polymers used in paints is affected by the amount of money consumers spend in fixing up houses and in new construction. For companies that provide business-to-business products, the key question to ask in assessing attractiveness is whether the *customers* of the product being considered are in the "right" industries. Clearly, firms supplying the "hot" categories will do well, and those that are heavily tied to declining consumer products will not.

For consumer products, the key question to ask is whether the product category under consideration is well positioned to take advantage of current trends. Some products are "hot" because they appeal to the large and increasingly affluent baby boomer group; these include furniture and electronic appliances, upscale fast-food chains, clothing, and financial and travel services. Other products have been developed for consumers at the older end of the baby boom generation (those now reaching 50). For example, a large part of the market for the Mazda Miata and other recently introduced sports cars by BMW and Porsche are people over 40 who wish to reduce their psychological age. Products having trouble, on the other hand, include coffee, cigarettes, and brown alcohol, which are being buffeted by demographic and taste trends.

Because of the importance of these lifestyle and demographic changes, we will examine further some of those occurring in the United States.

1. *The widening gap in incomes.* Over the past 15 years, the gap between the rich and the poor has increased. As Figure 4–7 shows, from 1977 to 1992, the 60 percent of families with the lowest income levels all experienced a decline in real income growth, while those in the top 20 percent saw their incomes increase by nearly 30 percent.[13] This phenomenon is supported by Figure 4–8, which shows the shares of national income accounted for by the quartiles of income levels as well as the associated average family incomes.[14] This so-called demise of the middle class is partly attributed to the decline of unions and their well-paying, secure jobs and may affect educational levels as well due to the decreased ability of some families to afford college tuition.

This bifurcation of income has significant implications for product management. It signifies growth in two broad segments: buyers of expensive goods and buyers of low-priced goods. Products or companies positioned in the middle, including some retailers, face the evaporation of their markets. Many retailers positioned at the middle class such as Emporium and J. C. Penney, are either going out of business or suffering financial difficulties. Those positioned at the lower price range, such as Wal-Mart, are doing very well, as are the category "killers" that feature low prices, such as Home Depot. Upscale retailers, such as Nordstrom and Neiman Marcus, are doing well, as are direct-mail retailers, such as Lands' End and L. L. Bean.

---

[13]Karen Pennar, "The Rich Are Richer—and America May Be the Poorer," *Business Week*, November 18, 1991, p. 85.

[14]Aaron Bernstein, "Inequality—How the Gap Between Rich and Poor Hurts the Economy," *Business Week*, August 15, 1994, p. 78.

FIGURE 4–7 Changes in Income Distribution in the United States

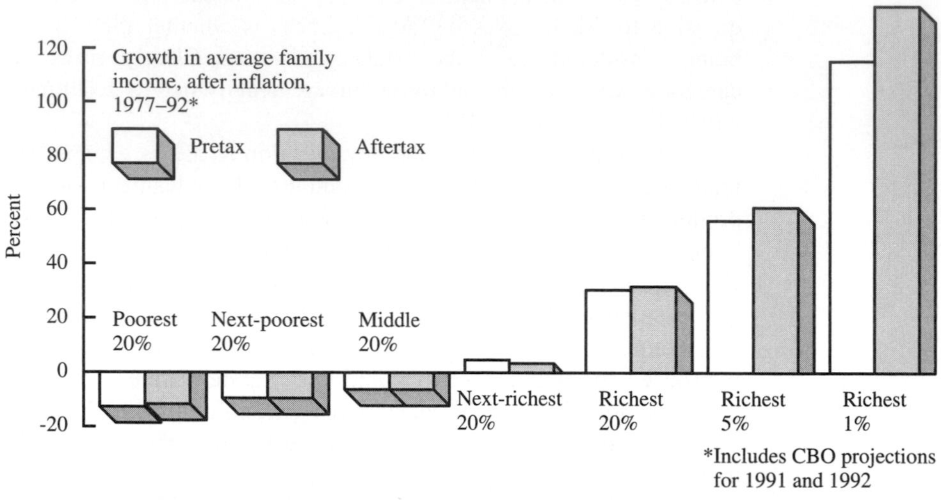

Source: Reprinted from November 18, 1991, issue of *Business Week,* by special permission, copyright © 1991 by McGraw-Hill, Inc.

2. *The increasing birth rate*. A recent trend is that younger women seem more interested in starting families earlier than their older sisters did.[15] In 1989, the Census Bureau predicted 3.7 million births in 1990. The actual number was 4.2 million (see Figure 4–9). This is the highest birth rate since near the end of the baby boom period, 1961, when there were 4.3 million births. Compare these figures to the birth rate in the 1980s, which averaged 1.8 million births per year. Larger families are also expected, if survey results are correct.

Again, product managers should take heed. The market for products related to baby needs will be important, but day care could be negatively affected if more mothers, the traditional caregivers, choose not to work. Fast-food outlets and other eating establishments could also suffer, since eating out decreases after a baby's arrival. However, spending on at-home entertainment products (e.g., stereo equipment) and services (video-on-demand) could increase.

3. *The changing ethnic and geographic mix of the population*. Projections based on 1990 U.S. census data through 1999 show dramatic shifts in the ethnic and geographic composition of the country. The Asian population is projected to grow 22.5 percent and Hispanics 16.6 percent. In terms of geographic patterns, the western states are expected to grow 8.5 percent and the South 6.2 percent.[16]

[15]Joshua Mendes, "The Baby Boomlet Is for Real," *Business Week*, February 10, 1992, p. 101.
[16]*Advertising Age*, September 19, 1994, p. 3

FIGURE 4–8 A Growing Gap between Rich and Poor Families

	Average Family Income as Share of National Income		Average Family Income in Thousands of 1992 Dollars		
Income Level	*1980*	*1992*	*1980*	*1992*	*Percent Change*
Top 25%	48.2%	51.3%	$78,844	$91,368	Up 15.9%
Second 25%	26.9	26.3	44,041	46,471	Up 5.5%
Third 25%	17.3	16.0	28,249	28,434	Up 0.7%
Bottom 25%	7.6	6.5	12,359	11,530	Down 6.8%

Source: Reprinted from August 15, 1994, issue of *Business Week* by special permission, Copyright 1994 by The McGraw-Hill Companies, Inc.

FIGURE 4–9 Births in the United States: 1960–2000

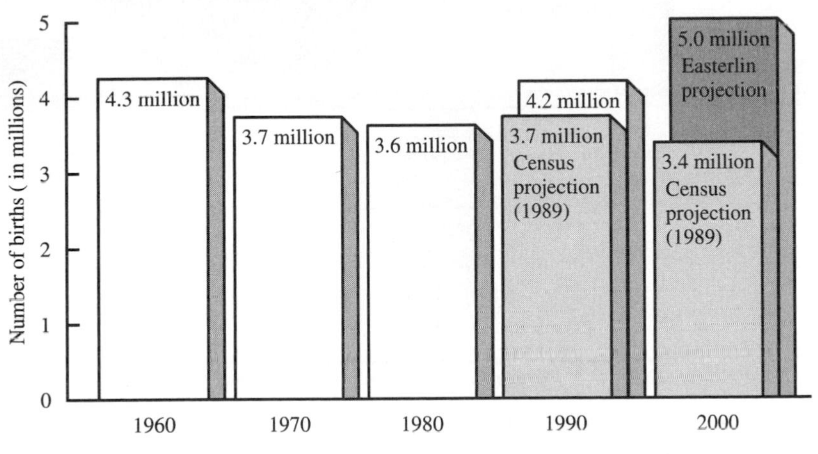

These shifts have already affected product management. As noted in Chapter 1, many consumer products companies are flattening their organizations to respond to product needs in different parts of the country and for different ethnic groups. New media choices, such as cable TV channels focused on Asian Americans and African Americans, have increased. Some supermarkets target particular ethnic audiences.

4. *The changing age mix of the U.S. population.* Figure 4–10 highlights the projected change in the age of the U.S. population in the year 2005.[17] As a result of the birth rates shown in Figure 4–9, there will be a big bulge in the age 40–59 group and in the 10–19 group (referred to as "echo boomers," since they are children of the baby boomers) but a decline in the 30–39 group. There will also be a dramatic increase in the number of people over 80.

[17]Erick Schonfeld, "Betting on the Boomers," *Fortune*, December 25, 1995, p. 80.

Figure 4–10 Projected Change in U.S. Population 1995–2005

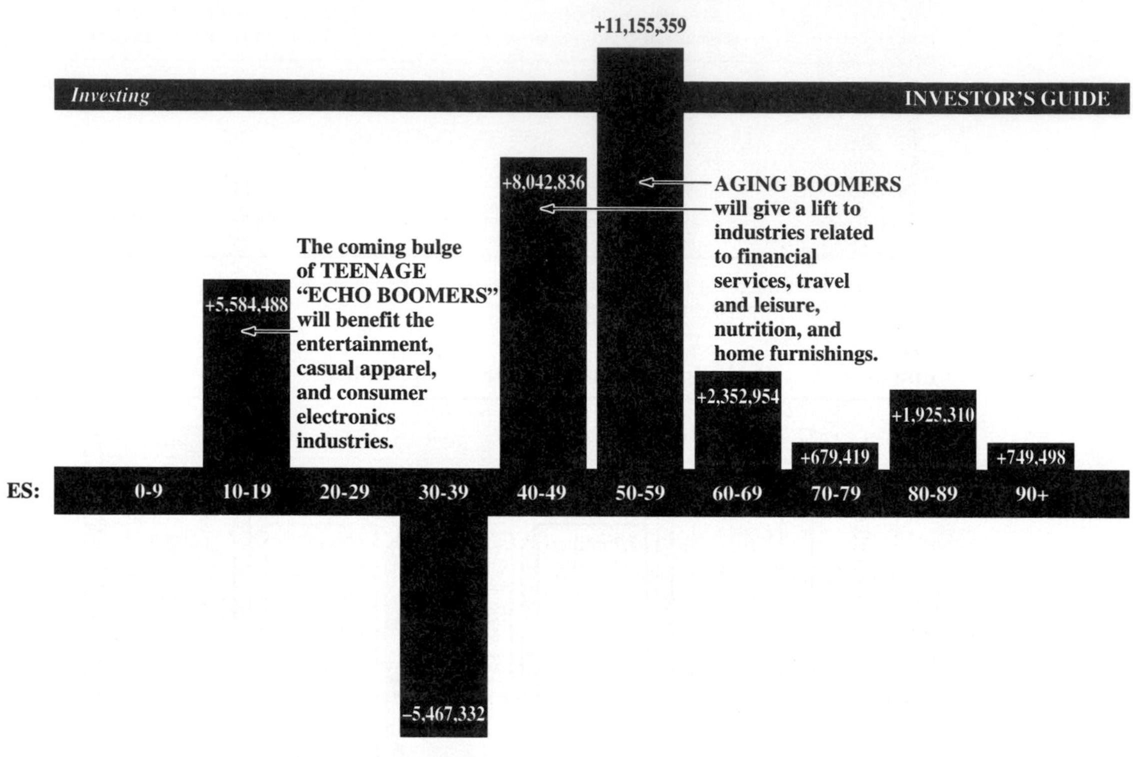

Source: Reprinted with permission from "Betting on the Boomers," by Erick Schonfeld, *Fortune*, December 2, 1995.

Again, a variety of product categories and brands may benefit from the age distribution. In the teen group, services such as MTV may gain audience. Nostalgic brands such as Harley-Davidson may be (and are) popular (the median age of a Harley owner today is 42, whereas 10 years ago it was 34). Healthcare-related services and products and retirement real estate developments are on tap for the retired group. In fact, the general aging of the population is having a substantial impact on product design. For example, telephones are being made with larger buttons and cars with controls that are easier to reach. RJR Nabisco introduced miniature Oreos in 1991 to give baby boomers a taste from childhood without increasing their waistlines. Lee's Jeans introduced an advertising campaign targeting jeans wearers who think young but have expanding rear ends (clothing manufacturers refer to this euphemistically as "relaxed" fit). Procter & Gamble replaced the cardboard tab on its giant-size Tide box with a reclosable snap top that carries a seal of approval from the National Arthritis Foundation.[18]

[18]Jamie Beckett, "U.S. Adjusts to Older Population," San Francisco *Chronicle*, October 7, 1991.

FIGURE 4–11 A Sample of Firms Specializing in Trendspotting

Firm	*Location*
SRI International	Menlo Park, CA
Yankelovich, Clancy, Shulman	Westport, CT
BrainReserve	New York
Institute for the Future	Menlo Park, CA
Inferential Focus	New York
Langer Associates	New York
Trend Union	Paris, New York
Weiner Edrich Brown	New York
The Naisbitt Group	Washington, DC

5. *The increased spread of home technology*. As noted in Chapter 1, one of the main shifts in the product manager's job is due to the increased levels of technology available to consumers. This environmental change is not simply technological; it affects where we shop, what kinds of communications we are exposed to, and, more generally, how we live and work. Nearly 40 percent of all U.S. homes have personal computers, and it is predicted that by 1999 almost 60 percent of these will have modems.[19] Projections from a 1995 study using a random sample of over 50,000 households found that 37 million persons age 16 and above in the United States and Canada have access to the Internet.[20] While the current demographics of this usage are heavily tilted toward more highly educated/higher-income households, the reduction in prices of personal computers, product innovation such as the targeted $500 Internet-only computer being championed by Oracle, and increased access to high speed home connections through cable modems and better telephone (Integrated Services Digital Network, or ISDN) lines will broaden the base of usage. Product managers will have to adapt to this technologically based world.

Because of these and other changes in the U.S. population, a significant industry in trendspotting has emerged. Typically, trendspotting organizations use extensive focus groups, magazines and newspapers, and some guesswork to try to forecast future trends. Figure 4–11 lists some consulting firms that specialize in lifestyle trendspotting, and Figure 4–12 gives some sample forecasts from some of the experts.[21] Interested readers should track the forecasts to see how good these people really are!

An alternative to hiring a consultant is to design an environmental scanning function within the company. A committee of managers representing different functional areas of the firm can be established. The committee would essentially replicate the activities of the consulting firms by scanning the environment. Popular scanning resources are national and regional newspapers, journals reporting new

[19]Todd Harris, "On-Line and Upward," *FORECAST*, September–October 1995.
[20]CommerceNet, *The CommerceNet/Nielsen Internet Demographics Survey,* 1995.
[21]"Packaging in the '90s," San Francisco *Chronicle*, October 3, 1991.

Figure 4–12 A Sampling of Trend Forecasts

Tom Mandel *Director, Leading Edge, a division of SRI International. Menlo Park.*

Work: Look for a growing global business class. Your new boss will be Japanese, German, French. Boundaries that define the workplace will get fuzzier. You'll work on the road, at home, in hotel rooms, wherever you happen to be at the moment.

Family: Your kids will be part of a new global youth culture emerging through music, fashion, TV. They will be more tuned into the world than you are. White kids will find themselves the new minority.

Health: We will see some sort of national health insurance in place by the year 2000. Lots of self-help, active attention to health. The trend against smoking and excessive drinking will continue.

Leisure Time: Increasing quest for new personal challenges—rock climbing for paraplegics (though maybe not Half Dome). The home will become an important place for play as well, as technology advances—you can play chess by computer with someone in Europe.

Sex: If cure for AIDS is found, more sexual freedom. If the epidemic worsens, more controls on sexual activity, probably some sort of voluntary national register to keep track of your past and present sexual contacts.

Prediction: So many pseudoevents celebrating the millennium, starting around 1996, that Americans will be sick of the entire concept by the year 2000.

Ian Morrison *President, Institute for the Future. Menlo Park.*

Work: The new "just in time" professional will emerge—people who opt out, move to less expensive cities to become independent consultants.

Family: Education will finally be a priority, as the boom-boom generation invades the school system.

Health: Will boomers want to preserve their youth forever or just say to hell with it and buy bigger clothes? Remains to be seen.

Leisure Time: A new leisure underclass will surface. The underemployed or unemployed who have time, but little money to spend. They will be angry and resentful.

Sex: Three words—no time for.

Prediction: The millennium—the mother of all New Year's Eve parties is coming. It's going to be a major focus starting in two years.

Watts Wacker *Executive vice president, Yankelovich, Clancy, Shulman, which conducts annual nationwide surveys on values, lifestyle, and attitudes. Westport, Conn.*

Work: There will not be a mass migration from office to home. People will stay in the office because it will become a critical place for social connection.

Family: Kids will be savvier and more independent because their parents are leaving them alone more. The legal driver's license age will drop to 14 by the year 2000.

Health: Attitudes will shift from "Life is too short" to "Life is too long." At 70, people will start eating rich foods and smoking again.

Leisure Time: We'll use leisure time to be productive, but we're still me-oriented—we'll build a playground for our kids to use rather than collect food for those 100 miles away.

Sex: Men are perilously close to becoming pets. Women are starting to see that their lives can go on quite famously without them. Men are no longer the only breadwinners in society.

Prediction: The car will give way to the home entertainment system as the ultimate status symbol. The coolest thing to carry will be a remote control that fits on your key chain and takes care of everything.

Faith Popcorn *CEO, BrainReserve, author of "The Popcorn Report," New York.*
Work: Home-based businesses; flex-time and job-sharing; employee empowerment.
Family: Mom-and-pop businesses; unintended family (kids moving back home; grandparents living with parents).
Health: Life extension. Self-health care. "Foodaceuticals": food with nutritional qualities; blending of drug therapy and nutrition (cancer-preventing vegetables).
Leisure Time: Ecotourism—whole family volunteering to clean up national parks as part of vacation. Learning vacations. Safe, fantasy adventures: Tank diving (individual tanks as replicas of exotic bodies of water).
Sex: Sex as theater (porno movies, sex-chat lines); sexy lingerie; men's lingerie and makeup. Monogamy.
Prediction: A leader will emerge in the '90s similar to Will Rogers—someone who will come up through a grass-roots movement, not the political system.

Peter Schwartz *President, Global Business Network, author of "The Art of the Long View." Emeryville.*
Work: Jobs will no longer be stable and forever. Secondly, office life will profoundly change around the new technology.
Family: The family dinner hour will return. We are going to spend more time with our kids. The social problems of society will be best dealt with in the family.
Health: A resurgence of individual responsibility paired with a move toward easily accessible self-diagnosis technology—sophisticated testers for blood cholesterol, diabetes, etc.
Leisure Time: Increasing urban gridlock will make it harder to get anywhere. People will be staying home more on a day-to-day basis, but going farther away to exotic locales on vacation.
Sex: We may go back to a more open sexual behavior once they find a cure for AIDS. That pent-up energy will have to go somewhere.
Prediction: Taking responsibility for things; companies, families, political leaders will have to answer to social responsibilities.

Source: Reprinted from "Packaging the 90's," by Sylvia Rubin, October 3, 1991. © 1991 San Francisco Chronicle. Reprinted by permission.

scientific developments (*Psychology Today*, *Scientific American*), "fringe" literature (*Mother Earth News*, *Heavy Metal*), trend-tracking publications (*The Futurist*, *World Future Society Bulletin*), and Internet-based resources on the World Wide Web, bulletin boards, and so on. Some publications are useful for monitoring particular areas of interest. For example, *Wired* has become a magazine of choice for those interested in the impact of technology on society. This committee would be charged with clipping and abstracting relevant items, summarizing the data into a small number of key issues, and, finally, recommending strategies to deal with the issues.

Illustrations

RTD Fruit Drinks

Figure 4–13 summarizes a category attractiveness analysis for the RTD fruit drink category. Sources of information for this and the PDA illustration are listed in Chapter 2 in Figures 2–11 and 2–14.

Favorable aggregate market factors are the size of the market (in both dollar sales and volume) and the growth rate (1994 data) and profit margins. Profits are high due to the relatively low costs of ingredients (water and some fruit concentrate). Although the market growth rate seems low at 3 percent, for a food category this is quite good. A key point is that the growth rate is slowing, moving the category from the growth era to an early maturity era. This may imply more intense competition, as sales growth is more likely to come from rival brands than from growth in aggregate sales. The Snapple brand manager therefore has to monitor marketing tactics by other brands targeted at Snapple. In addition, in a mature category, brand identification becomes critical for survival. Thus, the Snapple brand manager should emphasize brand-building activities in the marketing program area. A problem for the category is its seasonality, an issue for any beverage of its kind. Clearly, one of the tasks of the Snapple brand manager is to reduce the category's dependence on the hotter summer months, perhaps by timing promotions during the off season.

The category factors lean toward the negative side of the ledger. The threat of new entrants is relatively low given the high expenses for advertising and distribution. However, since product can be manufactured under license, a new entrant does not have to establish its own bottling capabilities. Even distribution can be obtained through a joint agreement. The bargaining power of suppliers is low, since the ingredients are readily available. Bargaining power of buyers, both consumers and retailers, is high given the available substitutes and limited shelf space. The product manager's job, then, is to develop excellent relations with the large retailers that sell the category and determine what their needs are. The number of beverage substitutes also makes this a difficult marketing category, as some of the marketing effort must be targeted at the generic competitors.

The environmental factors are generally either not applicable or positive. The biggest benefit is the social dimension, as the product category fits right into modern lifestyles (and, in fact, was developed expressly for that purpose).

Personal Digital Assistants

Figure 4–14 shows the category attractiveness analysis for PDAs. The aggregate market factors show a market that is in the growth stage of the product life cycle. Sales levels are still relatively low as producers gear up their marketing efforts and attempt to find a product configuration that satisfies customer needs. The failure of the Newton is still on everyone's mind here. However, the market is beginning to grow more rapidly, as product improvements tailor models to fit different segment needs. While margins are still low, as volume increases they should improve. The Sharp product manager (and others in the category) needs to focus on building primary demand for the PDAs, that is, use advertising to communicate the benefits of a high degree of portability and quick

Figure 4–13 Category Attractiveness Analysis: RTD Fruit Juices

		Attractiveness
Aggregate market factors:		
Market size	Retail 1994: $12.2 billion, 3.3 billion gallons	+
Market growth	3% in volume	+
Product life cycle	Late growth maturity	−
Profits	High	+
Sales cyclicity	Slight	0
Seasonality	Strong	−
Category factors:		
Threat of new entrants	Low; barriers are economies of scale, well-established brands, huge advertising budgets, distribution	+
Bargaining power of buyers	High; large selection of substitutes, limited retailer shelf space	−
Bargaining power of suppliers	Low; big players like Coca-Cola, PepsiCo, Quaker Oats; percentage of fruit juice is usually less than 15%	+
Category rivalry	High: big players, slow growth	−
Pressure from substitutes	High: many beverage substitutes	−
Category capacity	Medium	0
Environmental factors:		
Technological	Not applicable	+
Political	Not applicable	+
Economic	Low to moderate	0
Social	High; New age; healthier habits	+
Regulatory	Moderate: labeling must describe all ingredients very clearly	−/+

access to information relative to notebook computers, as well as the price advantage. This need to build generic demand is in sharp contrast to the RTD fruit drink situation.

Several category factors are also relatively positive. Although almost any maker of consumer electronics could enter this market, there is a need to expend research and development dollars on the product category. Distribution in crowded consumer electronics chains such as Circuit City and The Good Guys is essential. Once a purchase is made, switching costs and the high price compared to grocery products inhibit changing to another brand. Thus, the bargaining power of buyers is low. The components are standard but are also in demand by PC manufacturers, thus increasing the need to lock in supply. The main negative factor is the availability of numerous substitutes, including the no-purchase option. Keeping an electronic calendar is not a necessity of life as quenching a thirst is. Thus, part of the product manager's job is to convince customers that they need a product like this.

FIGURE 4–14 **Category Attractiveness Analysis: Personal Digital Assistants**

		Attractiveness
Aggregate market factors:		
Market size	$500 million	0
Market growth	20–30%	+
Product life cycle	Growth	+
Profits	Low but growing	0
Sales cyclicity	None	+
Sales seasonality	Some	0
Category factors:		
Threat of new entrants	Moderate; R&D required, distribution	0
Bargaining power of buyers	Low; high switching costs	+
Bargaining power of suppliers	Moderate; PCs use similar components	0
Category rivalry	Moderate	0
Pressure from substitutes	High	–
Category capacity	Not a problem for now	+
Environmental factors:		
Technological	Ahead of curve	+
Political/regulatory	Telecommunications deregulation	+
Economic	Some income effects	0
Social	More work done on the road	+

The environmental factors are positive. PDAs are on the leading edge of technology. Further deregulation of the telecommunications industry will help the high-end PDAs due to their extensive communications capabilities. The main plus for the product category from this set of factors is that it is right in line with the way work is changing: more work out of the office and on the road increases the need for quick convenient ways to take notes and keep records of phone numbers and appointments.

Summary

As we went through the three major groups of factors for assessing category attractiveness, we stressed the importance of qualitative assessment: indicating whether the factor had a positive or negative (or possibly neutral) impact on product management in that category of analysis. Clearly, certain factors have the potential to affect some products in a category more than others. For example, a product with a strong brand name is better able than one without strong brand identification to create a barrier to entry as a potential limit to brand switching. Thus, the purpose of this analysis is to develop a general perspective of the effects of the major factors on product managers in the category.

C H A P T E R

5 Competitor Analysis

Overview

Consider the following story reported in *Fortune* in 1988.[1] In the summer of 1986, six employees of Marriott Corporation checked into a hotel near the Atlanta airport. Once in their $30 rooms, the team went into their standard routine. One employee called the front desk for a new shoelace; another noted the brands of soap, shampoo, and towels; and the third began making noises to test for the soundproofing of the room. The team collected data for six months on the competitors in the economy hotel business, a segment in which Marriott had strong interest. With the detailed data collected in this manner, Marriott knew the strengths and weaknesses of the competitors and believed its new chain, Fairfield Inn, could easily improve on the existing hotels in that segment. Launched in the fall of 1986, by 1988 the hotel chain had an occupancy rate 10 percent higher than the rest of the category.

The collection of competitor intelligence is of course not limited to domestic companies or ethical behavior. Consider this quote from a 50-year veteran of Japan's corporate industrial "spy wars" on how he obtains information from corporate employees:

> We follow our targets to their favorite bars, make friends with them and find out what their weak spots are. If they don't have any, we make them.[2]

Here we emphasize that useful competitor analysis does not require illegal or unethical activities.

For most of the reasons mentioned in Chapter 1 concerning the difficulties of the product manager's job, competitor analysis has received more attention in recent years. In slow-growth markets, sales growth must come from the competitors. With

[1]Brian Dumaine, "Corporate Spies Snoop to Conquer," *Fortune*, November 2, 1988, pp. 68–76.

[2]Benjamin Fulford, "Spy Biz Thrives on Sex, Lies, Audiotapes," *The Nikkei Weekly*, December 23, 1995, p.1.

shorter product life cycles, product managers must recoup investments in a shorter period of time, which makes errors of judgment about competition difficult to overcome. Technology available to managers makes collecting and disseminating information within the organization easier as well as quicker. Finally, given the generally high level of turbulence product managers face from increased foreign competition, dramatically changing technology and rates of innovation, large shifts in interest rates (both up and down), and changing customer tastes, it is becoming more important than ever to keep abreast of changes in all factors exogenous to the firm, including competition.

In fact, given the number of marketing books with the term *warfare* in the title,[3] the 1980s and the 1990s have been as oriented toward competitors as the 1960s were toward the customer. The traditional view of the marketing concept is a focus on the needs and wants of the customer. Since the 1980s, however, it has become increasingly clear that meeting customer needs is not enough for success. What is critical to a product's success is meeting customer needs *better* than a competitor can, often at a lower cost. This implies an equally strong focus on understanding competitors' marketing strategies and capabilities.

Many companies have, of course, discovered the importance of competitor analysis. Here are some examples:[4]

- *Corning*: Employees from the janitor to the CEO send information collected about competitors to a central database that analyzes the data and feeds them to employees worldwide. Divisions hire intelligence consultants to profile competitors.
- *Nutrasweet*: The "strategic and business information" group creates personality profiles of key decision makers at the company's competitors to help anticipate and explain their strategies. It also monitors competitors' junior executives who rise through the ranks.
- *Prime Computer*: A manager of competitor intelligence and sales analysis for the Computervision division collects sales and product development data on U.S. and foreign competitors. The unit also publishes an electronic tip sheet of unfavorable information about competitors for use by its salespeople.
- *Helene Curtis*: A new "strategy and productivity development" department, run by a group that includes a former army intelligence officer, tries to obtain information that will help cut costs and improve product quality.
- *FCB/Leber Katz Partners*: This advertising agency has a dedicated group of strategists called the "Chess Team" whose job is to act as the competitor and "live" two to three moves out into the future.

It would be a mistake to assume that competitor intelligence gathering is only for large companies. An example illustrates that small companies can profit from such

---

[3]For example, Al Ries and Jack Trout, *Marketing Warfare* (New York: McGraw-Hill, 1985).

[4]Michele Galen, "These Guys Aren't Spooks. They're 'Competitive Analysts,' " *Business Week*, October 14, 1991, p. 97; Joe Mandese, "Critical Intelligence Hitting Every Desktop," *Advertising Age*, July 24, 1995, p. S-1.

activity as well.[5] The CEO of a small company turned a discussion with a customer into a problem for a competitor. The company, an importer of lamps and office furniture, had recently faced increased competition. The CEO learned from a retailer that one of the company's competitors had just raised the prices of some expensive lamps. The executive quickly relayed the information to the firm's salespeople, who used the information to win new business.

It is a fact that competitors, both large and small, constantly provide information to the marketplace, what economists refer to as *signals*.[6] Signals can be of two varieties. *Costly* signals are actual actions taken by a competitor such as the construction of a new plant, the introduction of a new product, a change in price, and so forth. The other variety are communications through the media, with customers, and with other marketplace actors. These have been referred to as *cheap talk* signals as they are costless,[7] nonbinding, nonverifiable communications. An example of this kind of signal is the marketing manager who announces in an interview that she intends to match a competitor's price if it is lowered. The job of the product manager is to collect both kinds of information and be wary about cheap talk signals that may be less than truthful.

Why don't all firms have a formal reporting system designed to collect and analyze information about competitors? After all, in some companies (e.g., Japanese firms), managers are trained to make competitive intelligence gathering everyone's business. Yet the Conference Board estimates that fewer than 5 percent of U.S. companies have sophisticated intelligence systems.

Overconfidence about a product's continued success can reduce willingness to collect competitor information. An impressive list of such companies (General Motors, Coca-Cola, McDonald's) that were somewhat overconfident at one time can be produced, along with a list of competitors that were ignored until they made significant inroads into the markets (Toyota, Pepsi, Burger King). A second reason for insensitivity to competition is uncertainty about where to collect the necessary information and how to analyze it. This excuse grows weaker all the time as consultants specializing in competitive intelligence gathering, articles and books containing tips on where to collect information,[8] and computerized databases containing articles about companies proliferate. A final reason for not collecting competitive intelligence is an ethical consideration: the fear that either illegal methods or otherwise "dirty tricks" have to be used to obtain such information. Many examples of such approaches to collecting information exist, and some of these are mentioned later in the chapter. However, information can almost always be obtained ethically.

At the very minimum, firms should view methods for collecting information about competitors from a defensive perspective, that is, how they can prevent information

[5]" 'Competitor Intelligence': A New Grapevine," *The Wall Street Journal*, April 12, 1989, p. B-2.

[6]For those readers with an interest in this economics approach, see Thomas C. Schelling, *The Strategy of Conflict* (Cambridge, Mass.: Harvard University Press, 1960).

[7]Actually they are not entirely costless. Some companies, such as Apple, have been sued by stockholders for not delivering on new products that the company announced.

[8]See, for example, Leonard M. Fuld, *Competitor Intelligence: How to Get It; How to Use It* (New York: John Wiley & Sons, 1985).

about themselves from landing in the laps of important competitors. John Sculley, the former CEO of Apple, became so alarmed at the number of leaks of important secrets that he had a six-minute video made for new employees warning them about the implications of "loose lips."[9] This is becoming increasingly problematic for companies as improved technology for "eavesdropping" and decreased employee loyalty from corporate downsizings increase competitors' ability to obtain corporate secrets. A 1995 survey of Fortune 1000 companies showed that about 75 percent believe theft or attempted theft by computer of customer information, trade secrets, and new-product plans increased over the previous five years.[10]

To analyze competitors, a commitment to developing a competitive strategy that includes a willingness to expend resources on collecting data is necessary. However, the data themselves are usually not the major problem product managers face. There are many sources of competitive intelligence. What is often lacking is a structure to guide the collection and analysis of the data, that is, a clear idea of what questions the data should address.

Figure 5–1 shows the competitor analysis model used in this chapter. At the top of the figure, the key inputs to the model are, of course, data. The first part of this chapter describes the data sources available for competitor analysis. It may seem to make more sense to first identify the questions to be answered, but the data collection process for understanding competitor behavior is somewhat unstructured, and information is continually being received and processed. It is thus useful to first understand the major sources of information and then apply them to the important questions that must be addressed. The two kinds of data described are *secondary* data, or data that have already been collected by someone else for some other purpose (i.e., "library" data), and *primary* data, or information derived from studies specially designed to answer a particular set of questions.

The data analysis portion of the process is the second major area of this chapter and is represented by the three questions in Figure 5–1. These cover three major areas of interest:

- Who are the major competitors?
- What are the objectives of the major competitor products?
- What is the current strategy being employed to achieve the objectives?

We addressed the first question in Chapter 3. The next two parts of the analysis assess the current objectives and strategy of the competing products. Differential competitor advantage analysis assesses the strengths and weaknesses of competing products based on information about the competitors' capabilities along a set of dimensions. The final element of the competitor analysis could be called the "bottom line." The purpose of examining the competitors is to be able to forecast what they are likely to do over the

---

[9]G. Pascal Zachary, "At Apple Computer Proper Office Attire Includes a Muzzle," *The Wall Street Journal*, October 6, 1989, p. A-1.

[10]Milo Geyelin, "Why Many Businesses Can't Keep Their Secrets," *The Wall Street Journal*, November 20, 1995, p. B-1.

FIGURE 5–1 Competitor Analysis System

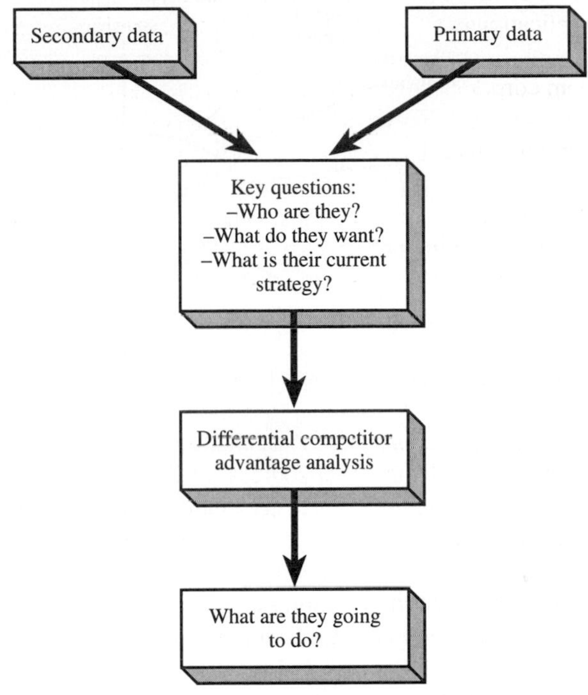

next planning cycle so we can then incorporate that forecast into our own strategies. Taken together, the issues shown in Figure 5–1 comprise a fairly complete picture of the activities of competing products.

A caveat to this chapter is that an intensive analysis of competition cannot substitute for a customer focus. In the end, it is better for a product manager to satisfy customer needs and ignore competition than do the reverse. Placing too much importance on keeping up with competitors can result in inadequately monitoring shifts in customer tastes. One benefit of the systematic approach to marketing planning advocated in this book is that it does not favor or ignore either customers or competitors.

Sources of Information

Secondary Sources of Information

As with marketing research in general, product managers should always begin a competitor analysis with a search of secondary sources of information. Secondary sources are generally less expensive and easier to obtain than primary data and often

Figure 5–2 Secondary Sources of Competitor Information

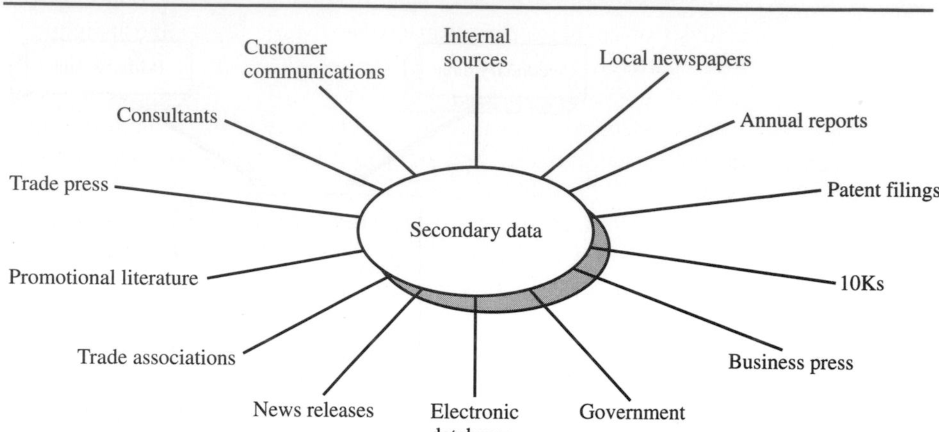

cover most of the important questions we need to ask about competitors. Figure 5–2 identifies popular secondary sources used by companies. An exhaustive listing of all secondary sources of information is beyond the scope of this book; however, many good listings of these sources exist.[11] Many of these sources are also useful for tracking foreign companies doing business in the United States or other markets.[12]

Internal Sources. Good information about competing products probably already exists within the company or division. Data can be found in past marketing plans, special studies commissioned by strategic planning groups, or simply in someone's office. As noted at the beginning of the chapter, some companies establish competitor hot lines or databases that can be accessed easily.

Local Newspapers. An excellent inexpensive source of information about competitors is local newspapers. For example, if a key competitor's product is manufactured in a small town, subscribing to the local newspaper is an excellent way to keep tabs on hirings and other changes. A U.S. medical supply manufacturer was shocked when a Japanese competitor significantly increased output at a new plant in Kentucky. The U.S. company had to reduce prices to maintain market share. What is interesting is that many details about the new plant—cost, number of employees, the products to be produced—were reported in the Lexington *Herald-Leader* in 1987, three years before the plant opened.[13]

---

[11]See, for example, Gordon L. Patzer, *Using Secondary Data in Marketing Research: United States and Worldwide* (Westport, Conn.: Quorum Books, 1995).

[12]For additional information on tracking foreign companies, see Leonard M. Fuld, "How to Gather Foreign Intelligence without Leaving Home," *Marketing News*, January 4, 1988, p. 24.

[13]Richard S. Teitelbaum, "The New Race for Intelligence," *Fortune*, November 2, 1992, pp. 104–7.

Annual Reports. Much of the information in an annual report is for public relations value, and the discussion is on the corporate, not the product, level. However, careful analysis of annual reports can produce some interesting insights even at the product level, particularly by examining the product areas the report does *not* mention. Often one can get useful information about areas of corporate emphasis from the message from the chairman or the text. Annual reports sometimes mention locations of manufacturing facilities and the names of key corporate decision makers. Although the financial information is aggregate, some data on cost of goods sold can be useful. These reports are, of course, available only for publicly held companies. For private companies, Dun & Bradstreet publishes its famous D&B reports, which estimate the financial performance of those firms.

10K Statements. Another reporting requirement for publicly held corporations is the 10K statement. Often this is more useful than the annual report because it is broken down by line of business and does not have the "gloss" of the annual report.

One clear implication of these two sources of information is that a cheap way to keep up with the corporate parent of a competitor is to become a shareholder (preferably a small one!). Shareholders receive the annual reports and 10Ks as well as admission to the annual shareholder meetings, which can be another useful resource.

Financial documents, including annual reports and 10Ks, are also available at most business libraries and stockbrokerage offices, where other useful financial documents such as new business prospectuses can be found.

Patent/Trademark Filings. Within the last decade, commercially available data networks such as CompuServe have made patent filings available. Obviously, patents give some notion of the manufacturing process and technology underlying the product. However, companies have been known to apply for patents on mistakes or on products that they have no intention to market. A company called MicroPatent recently introduced a new six-CD-ROM set called MarkSearch, which contains the text and images from the more than 1.5 million trademarks registered in the United States since 1884.

General Business Publications. Excellent sources of information about products and companies are general business publications such as *Business Week*, *Fortune*, *Forbes*, and *The Wall Street Journal*. One might wonder why companies are often so willing to disclose what should be proprietary information concerning, for example, future marketing strategies. Some potential audiences are investors, employees, and perhaps even competitors who might be the target for strategic warnings. To get information from these publications, product managers can subscribe to clipping services and electronic databases or clip appropriate articles themselves. For example, *Fortune* started a service in 1992 that charged $29.95 for a 15-page report on over 8,000 public companies. The reports can be ordered simply by calling an 800 telephone number.

News Releases. Companies usually retain public relations firms to release information to the press concerning new products, senior management appointments, and the like. These releases often show up in newspapers and trade publications, but it is possible to get on a direct distribution list.

Promotional Literature. Sales brochures (often referred to as *collateral material*) or other promotional literature focusing on a competing product or product line are extraordinarily valuable. Sales literature is a rich source of information concerning the product's strategy, since it usually has details about how the product is being positioned and differentiated versus those of competitors (including your product), product attribute and performance data, key phone numbers, and even personnel to contact.

Trade Press. These periodicals narrowly focus around a particular industry or product category. Representing this class of literature is *Women's Wear Daily* for the retail clothing trade, *Billboard* for the record and video industry, *Rubber Age* and *Chemical Week* for their respective industries, and *Test and Measurement World* for semiconductor testing equipment. This class of publications is obviously a rich source of information concerning new-product announcements, personnel shifts, advertisements for products, and industry or category data on sales and market shares. Virtually every product category has its own set of publications.

Consultants. Competitor analysis is a fertile area for consulting services. Many of these firms sell industry reports to different companies. They usually develop these reports from secondary sources and thus sell a service that substitutes for the firm's own efforts. One type of company services all industries. For example, New York–based FIND/SVP distributes a bimonthly catalog of available reports. The November–December 1995 issue offered a 150-page report on the "Fiery Foods Market" covering chili peppers, sauces, spices, condiments, and prepared food at a price of $2,150. There are also individual company reports such as the one on Rohm & Haas, a chemical company, which has 88 pages, costs $750, and covers the firm's product lines, financial performance, expected future strategies, and other topics. MarkIntel, a subsidiary of Thomson Financial Services in Boston, acts as a clearinghouse for reports of other companies. For example, one can purchase Datamonitor's 1995 report on the Belgian canned food market from them. Disclosure, Inc., focuses on the collection and analysis of financial reports such as prospectuses and annual reports.

Employee Communications. Companies often publish internal newsletters targeted toward employees. These newsletters may report on new vendors, new employees, and so forth.

Trade Associations. Most companies are members of trade associations (a listing of such associations is available in business libraries). These associations are usually formed for public relations or lobbying purposes, but they also often perform market research for the member firms. While usually focused on customers, this research may also provide some information about market shares, price levels, and so on.

Government Sources. The U.S. government collects a considerable amount of information about industries. However, as noted in Chapter 3, the data are usually at the SIC level and therefore are not very useful for understanding specific product competitors. More useful information is collected by agencies such as the Federal Communications Commission, the Food and Drug Administration, and state agencies. For example, if Pacific Bell submits a request for a rate increase, competitors such as Sprint and MCI can obtain cost information from the filing since the request is public information.

Electronic Data Services. Much of the information just described can be found on electronic databases or networks accessible via personal computer and modem or compact disks. Most good business libraries provide access to the latter, and most companies subscribe to the computer-based services.

An example of such a database is DIALOG Information Services. DIALOG offers access to such databases as the following:

- PIERS (Port Import Export Reporting Service).
- *Financial Times*.
- Moody's.
- Standard & Poor's.
- Dun & Bradstreet.
- Press releases issued by more than 10,000 U.S. corporations.
- The full text of more than 30 major newspapers.
- Regional business journals.

For European companies, DATA-STAR gives trade statistics, databases on U.K. and French importers and exporters, and the texts of many European newspapers.

Today, much information is also available through the World Wide Web. A convenient way to search through the web is with a search "engine" or "spider," a web site that allows the user to search for information by key words. One very popular spider is Yahoo; the Business and Economy page is shown in Figure 5-3. The user can type a company name (the search entry location is not shown), such as "Sony," and (eventually) reach Sony's home page and other pages linked to Sony. At Hewlett-Packard's page (www.hp.com), a browser can find product information and news about HP. HP's chemistry and bioscience site even lets users study supercritical fluid extractors before picking out a high-end scanner. Most national and international newspapers and magazines now have pages displaying up-to-the-minute business news.

Primary Sources of Information

Figure 5–4 lists the most important primary sources of information about competitors. Many of these are also sources of secondary information, depending on when the information was originally collected.

Sales Force/Customers. One of the most underutilized sources of information in companies is the sales force. Salespeople are trained to sell, but how many are trained to be part of a competitor intelligence force? Since they interact with customers on a regular basis, salespeople are in an excellent position to find out about recent competitor sales pitches, pricing, and many other dimensions. Depending on the

FIGURE 5–3

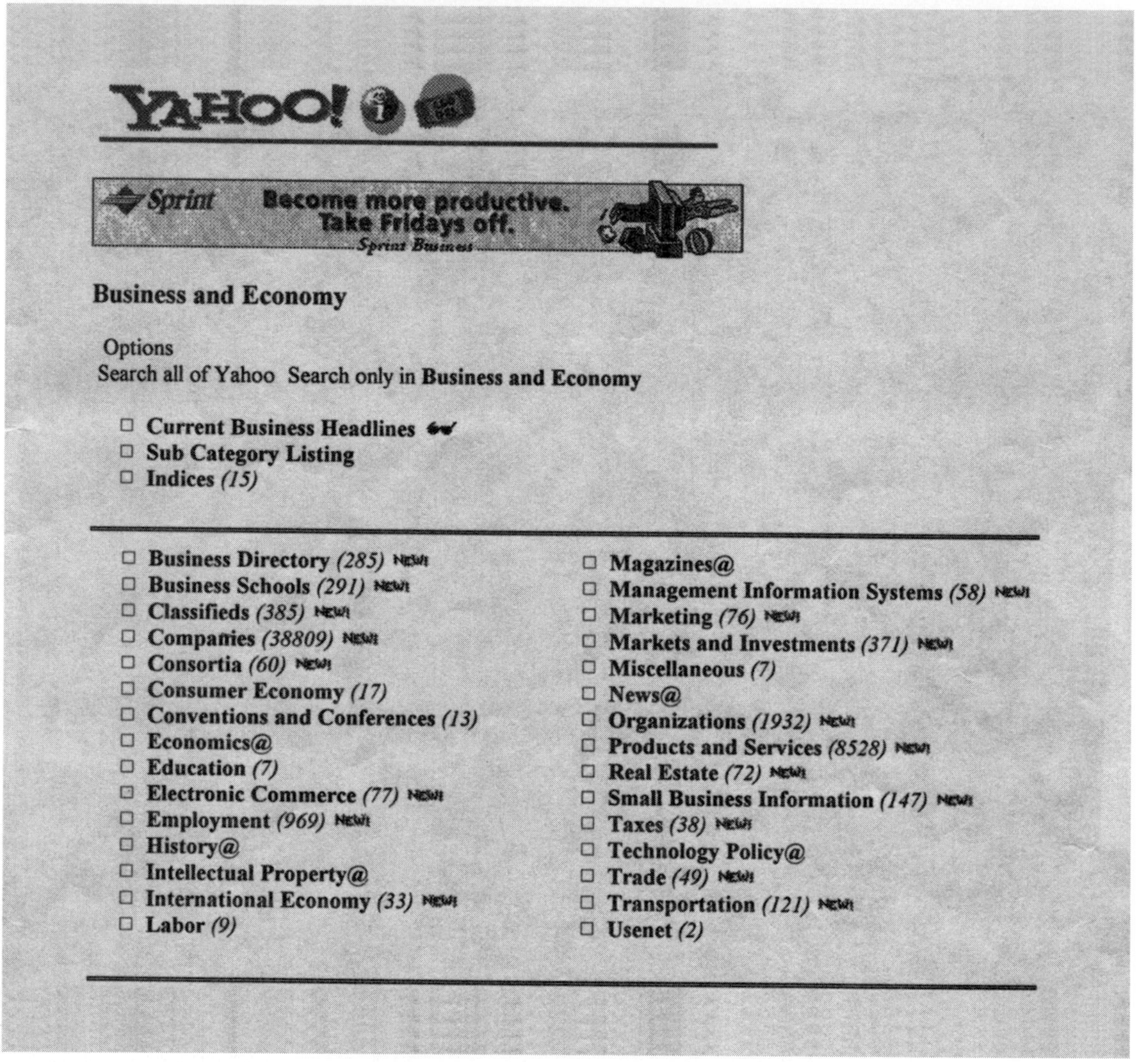

YAHOO!

Sprint Become more productive. Take Fridays off. Sprint Business

Business and Economy

Options
Search all of Yahoo Search only in **Business and Economy**

- **Current Business Headlines**
- **Sub Category Listing**
- **Indices** *(15)*

- **Business Directory** *(285)* NEW!
- **Business Schools** *(291)* NEW!
- **Classifieds** *(385)* NEW!
- **Companies** *(38809)* NEW!
- **Consortia** *(60)* NEW!
- **Consumer Economy** *(17)*
- **Conventions and Conferences** *(13)*
- **Economics@**
- **Education** *(7)*
- **Electronic Commerce** *(77)* NEW!
- **Employment** *(969)* NEW!
- **History@**
- **Intellectual Property@**
- **International Economy** *(33)* NEW!
- **Labor** *(9)*
- **Magazines@**
- **Management Information Systems** *(58)* NEW!
- **Marketing** *(76)* NEW!
- **Markets and Investments** *(371)* NEW!
- **Miscellaneous** *(7)*
- **News@**
- **Organizations** *(1932)* NEW!
- **Products and Services** *(8528)* NEW!
- **Real Estate** *(72)* NEW!
- **Small Business Information** *(147)* NEW!
- **Taxes** *(38)* NEW!
- **Technology Policy@**
- **Trade** *(49)* NEW!
- **Transportation** *(121)* NEW!
- **Usenet** *(2)*

Source: Reprinted from Yahoo! January 25, 1996. Copyright 1996 Ziff-Davis Publishing Company.

product, salespeople are often in a position to collect information merely by being trained observers. Xerox salespeople, for example, are trained to note competitor copiers. Forward-looking companies use information from salespeople for quick updates on competition. With notebook computers, salespeople can make their calls, fill out call reports electronically, and send the information back to the local office or headquarters via modem. For competitor tracking, the call report should have a section related to noting anything new or different picked up during the call.

FIGURE 5–4 Primary Sources of Competitor Information

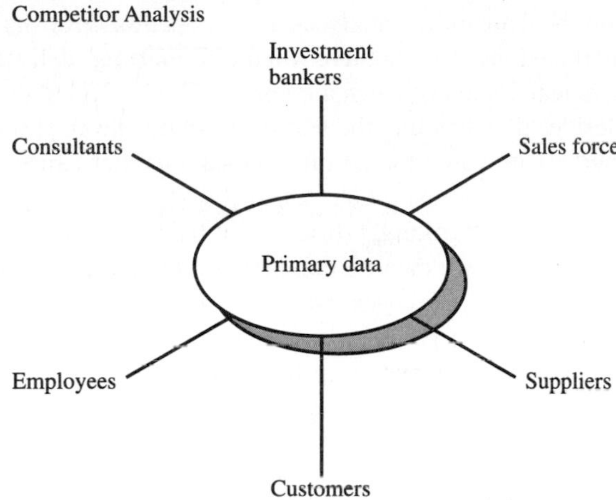

Of course, the salespeople must get the information from customers. Every attempt by suppliers and vendors to cultivate a potential customer involves the transmission of information. Unfortunately, customers may be reluctant to give away such information, believing it means playing "dirty tricks" on the competition. To aid in overcoming this reluctance, the data collection can be positioned as giving the vendor an opportunity to provide better service or products to the customer, that is, clearly show that the customer will benefit by passing along the information. Usually the data can be obtained from public sources anyway; it is just quicker for the vendor to obtain it from the customer.[14]

Employees. Generalizing from the use of salespeople to collect competitor intelligence, much can be learned about competition from observation in the marketplace by any company employee. If the product category in question is sold in the supermarket, the employee can easily observe changes in price, packaging, and shelf display. Competitors' TV ads also give important information about their marketing strategies.

Suppliers. Often competitors' suppliers are willing to give information about shipments to impress potential buyers. Imprints on packaging cartons can provide useful information because they often disclose the name and address of the carton's maker. Following up with the carton manufacturer may lead to estimates of sales volume.

Consultants. Consultants can often be used to develop special-purpose reports, as opposed to the off-the-shelf variety referred to under secondary sources. For example,

[14]B. G. Yovovich, "Customers Can Offer Competitive Insights," *Business Marketing*, March 1995, p. 13.

Adscope, Inc., tracks advertising spending, campaigns, and media placement for the high-tech industry. One of the largest consulting/accounting firms in the country, Deloitte & Touche, markets a service called Peer*Scape* that conducts detailed financial and benchmarking analyses of competitors for its clients. An innovative service marketed by Competitive Media Reporting delivers a warning signal through a personal computer when a competitor ran a TV ad during the previous 36 to 48 hours. Besides downloading the text of the copy, the customer receives information about the markets in which the ad ran, the stations that carried it, and the times it ran.

Investment Bankers. Investment bank reports are excellent sources of both secondary and primary data on competitors, particularly if a bank wishes to gain the firm as a new client. Analysts employed by the investment banks develop very detailed analyses of the prospects of different firms and products in an industry. While their perspective is financial performance, much of the information is useful to product managers.

Other Sources

Help-Wanted Advertisements. Often help-wanted ads contain valuable information, such as job requirements and salary levels. Other information is available as well; sometimes the purpose of the ad is to fill positions opened by an expansion of business or a new plant opening. Although many ads disclose only a box number for a reply, many provide information about the organization paying for the ad.

Trade Shows. Company representatives often attempt to obtain information at the booths of competitors. This is becoming more difficult, however, as companies increasingly try to screen the people to whom they provide information to keep it away from competitors. In addition, spying is now so common at trade shows that hot new products are usually displayed only in hotel suites open to major customers, joint venture partners, and industry reporters who agree not to disclose information until product release dates. This is particularly true at large trade shows such as Comdex, the computer industry trade show, where industry players like Michael Dell, founder of Dell Computer Corporation, roam through the aisles trying to pick up information quickly before they are recognized.[15] Even if some information is gained, however, about as much is lost from your own company, so usually the net gain is small.

Plant Tours. This is a rapidly disappearing phenomenon, largely because companies are becoming skittish about giving away valuable information. The most popular tourist destination in Battle Creek, Michigan, was Kellogg's cereal plant until the company stopped giving tours several years ago, citing competitor information gathering as the reason. Gerber stopped its Fremont, Michigan, plant tours in 1990 after spotting sales representatives from competitor firms taking the tour. Although

[15] " 'Go to IBM's Booth. Avoid Recognition. Skulk.' " *The Wall Street Journal*, November 17, 1994, p. B-1.

there are some exceptions,[16] most tours today are like the amusement park–like tour at Hershey Foods' facility in Hershey, Pennsylvania, which offer little to be learned about how the products are really made.

Reverse Engineering. A common way to analyze a competitor's product is to purchase it and take it apart. This is referred to as *reverse engineering* in high-technology industries and sometimes as *benchmarking* in service markets.[17] In general, it is wise to become a customer of a competitor by, for example, purchasing a computer or software, opening a small bank account, and so forth. One important reason to do so is to estimate the competitor's costs of manufacturing or assembly. Another objective is to assess the product's strengths and weaknesses. Companies such as Emerson Electric, General Motors, and Xerox perform this kind of analysis routinely. For example, in the late 1970s, Xerox benchmarked Canon's copiers and tried to beat each component of the latter's machines on cost and quality. In designing the Lexus, Toyota bought competitors' cars, including four Mercedes, a Jaguar XJ6, and two BMWs, put them through performance tests, and then took them apart.[18]

Analyzing Test Markets. Some companies test market products in limited areas of the country or the world to better understand decisions about pricing, advertising, and distribution. While this is often useful, test markets can be fertile grounds for competitors to get an early view of the product and how it will eventually be marketed after rollout to the larger market.

Hiring Key Employees. This practice obviously provides a considerable amount of information. However, new employees may not legally transmit what are considered to be trade secrets to new employers. Trade secrets can have a narrow interpretation, however, that does not cover marketing strategies or complete plans. Some companies attempt to hinder employees, particularly senior managers, from jumping to a competitor by including a special clause in the employment contract. At Hewlett-Packard, new employees are asked to sign nondisclosure agreements and attend a training program, complete with video, that defines how HP interprets "trade secrets."[19]

Some Sources with Ethical Considerations

Our purpose in describing some of the unethical approaches to collecting competitor information is not to encourage readers to use them but to point out that such activities do occur. As mentioned earlier in the chapter, a key reason to learn about the various

[16]Robert L. Rose, "Vacation Paradise on a Factory Floor," *The Wall Street Journal*, July 7, 1995, p. B-1.

[17]The term *benchmarking* is also used more generally to refer to the tracking and analysis of any process, such as manufacturing, billing, and so on, in competing and noncompeting organizations.

[18]Jeremy Main, "How to Steal the Best Ideas Around," *Fortune*, October 19, 1992, pp. 102–6.

[19]Julian Guthrie, "Brain Drain," San Francisco *Focus*, October 1993, p. 24.

approaches to collecting information about competitors is to become more defensive minded. Of course, it is virtually impossible to completely defend against lying and cheating. However, on a hopeful note, these approaches rarely uncover something an ethical approach cannot; there are usually several ways to collect a key piece of information.

Aerial Reconnaissance. It is illegal in the United States for a company to hire an airplane or a helicopter to take aerial photographs of a competitor's facilities as they are being constructed, because this action is interpreted as trespassing. Procter & Gamble won a lawsuit against Keebler for spying on a new soft-cookie-making facility being constructed in Tennessee in 1984. Companies can, apparently legally, purchase photographs taken from satellites: Sweden and France are partners in a satellite joint venture that sets aside a limited percentage of the transponder time for commercial purposes (usually mapmaking and municipal planning). In 1994, Lockheed Missiles & Space Company, a subsidiary of Lockheed Corporation, received the first license from the U.S. government to sell spy-quality satellite pictures for commercial use. Lockheed has the technology to photograph a car from 400 miles in space.

Buying/Stealing Trash. It is not illegal to take a company's trash after it leaves the firm's facility. However, companies have been known to either bribe employees or otherwise obtain access to discarded documents. Recently Avon admitted it had hired private detectives to run through rival Mary Kay's trash to attempt to defend against a takeover attempt by the latter. The maneuver was not illegal because Mary Kay's dumpster was in a public parking lot.[20] People are always looking through the trash of high-profile companies such as Apple Computer. Simple defensive mechanisms include shredders and incinerators. Unfortunately, in today's online world, "trash" also means electronic mail that had been thought to be discarded but was not.

Bribing Printers. Some companies attempt to obtain predistribution copies of catalogs and other collateral.

Running Phony Want Ads. Not all help-wanted ads are for actual positions. Some companies run ads in an attempt to get disgruntled employees from competitors to apply. These applicants then can be probed for information.

The ethics of various data collection methods is a continuum from methods that are clearly illegal (stealing a competitor's marketing plans) to obviously legal (reading an article in a trade magazine). Today there is more pressure than ever to uncover information about competitors. The Society of Competitive Intelligence Professionals, now numbering nearly 3,000 members, has established an ethical code that requires members to comply with the law, identify themselves when seeking information about competitors, and respect requests for confidentiality. However, those bent on violating legal and ethical standards do not tend to join such societies. It is therefore incumbent

---

[20]Wendy Zellner and Bruce Hager, "Dumpster Raids? That's Not Very Ladylike, Avon," *Business Week*, April 1, 1991, p. 32.

on companies to develop policy statements that clearly define the standards expected from employees in this area of competitor intelligence gathering and strongly enforce them.[21]

Assessing Competitors' Current Objectives

The first step in a competitor analysis is to assess what the current objectives are for the major competitor products. An assessment of current objectives provides valuable information concerning the intended aggressiveness of the competitors in the market in the future. It also provides a context for assessing the capabilities of competitors; that is, does the firm marketing brand A have the resources to successfully pursue such an objective?

When discussing objectives, it is important to define the term precisely, for many different types of objectives exist. In the context of marketing planning, three basic product objectives can be identified. A *growth* objective usually implies increasing the brand's units or market share, with profit conditions being secondary. The *hold* objective could also be termed a *consolidation* objective. A hold scenario might be logical for a brand that is losing market share in that a reasonable first step in reversing its fortunes is to stop the slide. Finally, a *harvest* objective, also referred to as *milking*, describes a situation in which profit is paramount relative to market share.

In other words, at the product level, objectives are typically stated in terms of either market share or profits. At the corporate level, return on investment or other, more aggregate statistics becomes more relevant.

Determination of Competitor Objectives

While a brand's objective determines, to a great extent, what strategies will be pursued and hence what actions will be taken in the marketplace, usually it does not take a substantial amount of research to uncover it. What is required is sensitivity to competitors' actions through observation, salesperson call reports, and many other resources mentioned in the previous section of this chapter.

Let us consider the two major options outlined above: the growth versus harvest choice. If a competitor's brand is being pushed to improve its market position at the expense of short-term profits, some of the following are likely to occur: a cut in price, increased advertising expenditures, increased promotional activity to both consumers and distributors, or increased distribution expenses.

In other words, a product manager who is trying to expand a brand's market share will spend money on market-related activities and/or reducing price. Such actions can be easily monitored by brand managers, advertising account representatives, and other parties with access to information about the rival brand's actions.

[21]For further reading on the ethical aspects of competitor analysis, see U. Srinivasa Rangan and Michael E. Porter, "Ethical Dimensions of Competitive Analysis," Harvard Business School case study 9-792-088, 1992.

Brands being harvested would be marketed in the opposite way. An increase in a competitor's price, decreases in marketing budgets, and so on can be interpreted as a retreat (perhaps only temporary) from active and aggressive competition in the market. While the product manager cannot exactly estimate the size of the share loss expected, it is not difficult to establish the direction of the objective, which is the most important competitor information.

Two other factors are relevant to the assessment of competitors' objectives. First, the product objectives of a firm with a foreign-based parent are often affected by the country of origin. In many cases, such firms have financial backing from a government or major banks and are not as concerned with short-term losses as they are with establishing a viable market position or obtaining foreign currency. Although at one time Japanese firms were the ones usually referred to in this context, other countries, such as Korea and Singapore, are also homes to firms that are strongly interested in building market share in the United States. Thus, depending on the competitor, cues concerning the competitor brand's objectives can be obtained from the geographical home of the parent firm.

A second relevant factor is whether the ownership of the competitor firm is private, public, or government. Since private firms do not have to account to stock analysts, long-term profits may be more important than showing consistent positive quarterly returns. On the other hand, if a family depends on the firm for current income, profits may be more important than market share. Finally, government controlled firms may have objectives such as maintaining employment, providing service, or currency exchange.

An interesting variant of the impact of private ownership on objectives occurs if the privatization resulted from a leveraged buyout (LBO). In these cases, even though the company is private, it is often more interested in profits and cash flow to pay down debt than it is in plowing money into market share gains. An excellent example is the well-publicized LBO by Kohlberg Kravis Roberts & Company (KKR) of RJR Nabisco in 1988. Because of the large load of debt the firm took on, many of RJR's brands became vulnerable to competitors that took advantage of the opportunity to go for market share gains. These included Philip Morris in tobacco products because RJR was reluctant to enter the low-price cigarette category, and competitors in snack foods, which took advantage of large cuts in advertising and promotion expenditures for Ritz crackers and Planters products. As of 1995, RJR was free of KKR, and began to attempt to regain the market share lost to Philip Morris, particularly for its flagship Winston brand.[22]

A less apparent level of objectives can be deduced from a firm's operating philosophy and procedures. For example, a firm that seeks to minimize capital investment will be slow to respond to a competitor that makes a heavy capital outlay. (For example, Emery Air Freight when Federal Express bought its own airplanes in the mid-1970s). Similarly, firms that compensate sales staffs with commissions based on a percentage of sales indicate that volume rather than profitability is a key objective. In

---

[22]Ira Teinowitz, "Marketing, Ad Woes Choking RJR Brands," *Advertising Age*, June 26, 1995, p. 3.

fact, the key performance measure by which employees are judged often has a distinct influence on a firm's performance.

Sometimes the objectives being pursued by a competing product or company are made public by the management. For example, the chairman of Cabot Corporation, a manufacturer of carbon black (an oil-derived substance used in tires, inks, and many other products), which is heavily dependent on high levels of utilized manufacturing capacity for profitability, put it this way: "They'll carry me out of here on a stretcher before I lose market share."[23] Matsushita announced it would begin to emphasize profits over market share, a switch from its previous product objectives.[24]

Estimates of the objectives pursued by competitors provide important information for the development of strategy. Certainly a brand that is aggressive in its pursuit of market share must be viewed as a different type of competitor than one that is attempting primarily to maximize profits. The latter would clearly be more vulnerable to an attack on its customers, whereas a confrontation with the former brand might be avoided. In other words, a study of the brands' objectives provides a first-level analysis of the competitor brand's likely strategy.

This type of analysis has been profitably applied. During the late 1970s, Coca-Cola was concerned primarily with holding market share and improving profits. PepsiCo, on the other hand, viewed its rival's drowsiness as an opportunity and became more aggressive, gaining share points and improving its position versus Coca-Cola in store sales. Miller Brewing's successful attack on Budweiser during the 1970s was prompted by a similar observation.

Assessing Competitors' Current Strategies

The second stage in competitor analysis is to determine how competitors are attempting to achieve their objectives. This question is addressed by examining their past and current marketing strategies.

Marketing Strategy

Many authors have attempted to define the concept of strategy. At the product level, a marketing strategy can be thought of in terms of three major components: target market selection, core strategy (i.e., positioning and differential advantage), and implementation (i.e., supporting marketing mix). These components are described in more detail in Chapter 8; we will briefly discuss them here in the context of understanding a competitor's product strategy rather than developing one for your company.

The first major component is the description of the market segment(s) to which competing brands are being marketed. Market segments can be described in various

[23]Keith Hammonds, "Can Cabot Go Home Again?" *Business Week*, December 10, 1990, p. 52.

[24]Yumiko Ono and Michael Williams, "Matsushita's Overhaul Effort Puts Emphasis on Profits," *The Wall Street Journal*, October 7, 1992, p. B-3.

ways, as shown in Chapter 6 (Figures 6–2 and 6–5). Since few brands are truly mass marketed, that is, marketed equally to all potential customers, the key is to determine which group(s) each competitor has targeted. This is important to avoid segments in which there may be intense competition and to determine under- or nontargeted segments that may represent opportunities.

The second strategy component is what is called the *core strategy*.[25] This is the basis on which the rival is competing, that is, its key claimed differential advantage(s). Differential advantage is a critical component of strategy because it usually forms the basic selling proposition around which the brand's communications are formed. It is also called the brand's *positioning*.

Product managers essentially have a choice between two types of differential advantage: price/cost based and product feature based. In other words, products are usually positioned on price or quality dimensions, although some marketers choose a "value" positioning with mid-range price and quality. Concentration on price often follows the classic approach developed by the Boston Consulting Group,[26] which advocates taking advantage of the experience curve that assumes costs are driven down with increases in cumulative production volume and thus allows the product manager to cut prices and maintain margins over time. The quality differential advantage is superiority on some other product dimension (real or psychological) such as service, packaging, or delivery terms. Necessary conditions for such a core strategy to be successful are that customers value the characteristics claimed as advantages and that the differential can be maintained for a significant period of time without being copied.

An important characteristic of quality differential advantages is that they can be perceived rather than actual differences. For example, IBM's core strategy since its inception has been service based. This is an actual differential advantage because it can be supported by hard data (e.g., number of field service representatives, mean response time, and so on). On the other hand, Reebok's claimed differential advantage during its "U B U" campaign was related to individuality. Such positioning is clearly outside the domain of physical product differences, but can still be effective in differentiating Reebok from Nike. Physical product differences are often stressed in industrial, durable, or new frequently purchased product strategies. Companies producing mature frequently purchased products that are physically similar or "commodities" often emphasize perceptual differences.

The final strategy component of competitors that must be assessed is the supporting marketing mix. The mix provides insight into the basic strategy of the competitor and specific tactical decisions. These decisions are what customers actually see in the marketplace; they neither are exposed to nor do they particularly care about a product's marketing strategy. However, customers are exposed to price, advertising, and other marketing mix elements. The areas to consider and some questions to address follow.

---

[25]This concept first appeared in David J. Luck and Arthur E. Prell, *Market Strategy* (New York: Appleton-Century-Crofts, 1968).

[26]Bruce D. Henderson, "The Experience Curve Revisited," *Perspectives* 220 (Boston: Boston Consulting Group, 1980).

Pricing. Pricing is a highly visible element of a competitor's marketing mix; therefore, it raises several questions. For example, if a brand's differential advantage is price based, is the list price uniform in all markets? If the strategy is quality based, what is the price differential claimed? Are discounts being offered? What is the pattern of price changes over time? In general, any price-related information pertaining to the implementation of strategy is relevant.

Promotion. With respect to sales management, what kinds of selling approaches are being employed? Are the salespeople aggressive in obtaining new accounts? What are their commission rates? In terms of advertising, what media are being used? What creative activities? Are competitors referred to either directly or indirectly? Sales promotion activities—for example, which types and how often—are also important.

Distribution. Have the channels of distribution shifted? Is the brand being emphasized in certain channels? Is the manufacturer of the competing product changing the entire system, for example, by opening its own retail outlets or putting more emphasis on direct marketing?

Product/Service Capabilities. A major determinant of a company's capabilities, at least in the short run, is the physical makeup of its product or service, which in general is less easily changed than, say, price or advertising. A product filled with expensive parts is unlikely to be positioned as a low-end product. Similarly, physical properties (e.g., stability under high temperatures) go a long way toward dictating target market uses and hence strategy. Many engineering plastics categories are segmented on the basis of physical properties, for example, DuPont's Delrin versus Celanese's Celcon. Different applications can be dominated by a different company's offerings. Therefore, a comparison of the competitive product offerings, the physical product or service, and how it is presented and sold should be performed.

How to Assess Competitors' Strategies

Detailed information about competitors is not yet necessary for the analyses discussed so far. Up to this stage in the competitor analysis process, only qualitative assessments of objectives and strategies are required.

Recall that the two key elements of a strategy are the segments it appeals to and the core strategy. For industrial products, both can be easily determined by examining three sources of information: product sales literature, the company's own sales force, and trade advertising. The former provides information about the core strategy because brochures usually detail the points of difference the competitor wants to emphasize. Even if the sales literature does not present a specific table comparing the product in question to competitors' products in different areas, the sales literature should indicate the brand's major strengths. A firm's own sales force can provide some data concerning targeted companies or industries, much of it resulting from informal contacts, trade show discussions, and the like. Finally, trade advertising is useful because it reveals the segments being targeted and the differential advantage being touted. One can determine the differential advantage directly from the ad copy and the target segments at least partially by the publication in which the ad appears.

For consumer goods or other products targeted toward a large audience, simply tracking competitors' ads, either yourself or by using one of the services such as those mentioned earlier this chapter, provides most of the necessary information. Television ads can be examined for their messages (differential advantage) and for the programs in which they appear (target segment[s]). TV advertising is quite useful for determining the core strategy because the nature of the medium prohibits communicating all but the most important messages. Similarly, print advertising can provide equivalent information, but with greater elaboration of the core strategy.

For example, consider the copy for a print ad in *PC Magazine* for Sun's Ultra 1 workstation, shown in Figure 5–5. At least part of Sun's marketing strategy for the product can be determined by the fact that the ad appeared in that particular magazine and from the copy itself. From data obtained from Mediamark Research's *Magazine Total Audiences Report, Spring 1994*, we know that the median age of the *PC Magazine* readers is 37.2 years, the median income is $51,000, and 47.1 percent graduated from college (among many other variables measured by Mediamark Research). One could obtain information from the publication itself about the proportion of readers who are decision makers in their organizations versus users. Looking at the copy itself, this ad attempts to describe some of the product features and indicate that the Ultra 1 is the most powerful workstation on the market at the time the ad ran (January 1996). Thus, the product is being positioned as a technological leader in the product category. Note that the ad does not mention Sun's major competitors, HP, IBM, and Silicon Graphics. The differentiation therefore is not explicit with side-by-side comparisons but implies that Sun is the undisputed leader and is not really concerned about the competition. This ad reveals only part of the strategy for the product, because other ads could be oriented toward different segments and indicate a different positioning. The product manager might also be interested in the price of the ad; these data are obtainable from publications such as *Marketer's Guide to Media*.

Information about implementing current strategies is also easily found. Pricing information can be obtained from basic market observation: Distributors, salespeople, customers, advertising agencies, or even a firm's own employees acting as customers on their own behalf can be the sources of pricing data. Promotion, distribution, and product information can be obtained from similar sources. In other words, as in determining competitors' objectives, it takes market sensitivity rather than sophisticated management information systems to assess much of the competitive activity.

One apparent but often overlooked source of information mentioned earlier in this chapter is being a customer or stockholder of competitors. Both customers and stockholders get special mailings and information that makes strategy assessment easier. Furthermore, personal use of competitors' products often gives one a feeling for them that does not come through even the best-prepared research. Thus, policies that forbid or discourage the use of competitive products are usually foolish.

FIGURE 5–5 Sun Advertisement

Introducing Sun Ultra 1. A box so revolutionary, it allows you to think outside of it.
Forget incremental advancements. Forget compromises. In short, forget everyone else. UltraComputing™ is here, and the only way you can get it is the Sun™ Ultra™ 1. The new workstation that converges all the best computing technology. A powerful 64-bit processor, real-time video and audio, imaging, 2D and 3D graphics, and the ability to run over 10,000 existing applications. It even offers networking that's 10 times faster than today's standards. And with supercomputing power on your desktop, you can collaborate in ways once thought impossible. Sun Ultra 1. You'll never look at computing the same way again. To learn more, call 1-800-786-0785, Ext. 360. Or see us at http://www.sun.com
Sun
THE NETWORK IS THE COMPUTER™

Technology Strategy

An important task is to assess the technological strategies of the major competitors. This can be done using the following framework of six criteria:[27]

1. Technology selection or specialization.
2. Level of competence.
3. Sources of capability: internal versus external.
4. R&D investment level.
5. Competitive timing: initiate versus respond.
6. R&D organization and policies.

These decisions generally lead to four basic strategies, each of which has different requirements for success, listed in Figure 5–6.

As an illustration of Figure 5–6 for assessing competition, consider the blank audiocassette market in the early 1970s. This was the early stage of the product life cycle, with no major competitors. Gillette's Safety Razor Division was considering entering this market, as was Memorex, a manufacturer of computer tape and related products. Gillette had competitive advantages over Memorex in marketing and finance, but it was decidedly at a disadvantage in terms of R&D, manufacturing, and the apparent match of its skills and image to the cassette category in the minds of customers. The end result was a success for Memorex and a failure for Gillette in test marketing.[28]

At this point in the analysis, it is often useful to summarize the products of the major competitors. Figure 5–7 provides a general format that is useful for both summarizing the results and for communicating them.

Differential Advantage Analysis

Several frameworks have been proposed to indicate what information to collect about competitors.[29] A useful way to examine competitors' capabilities is to divide the necessary information into five categories that include the competitors' abilities to conceive and design, to produce, to market, to finance, and to manage. You might need information from both the corporate and product levels. For example, the financial capabilities of a corporate parent are important in determining the amount of money that could support a specific product.

[27]Modesto A. Maidique and Peter Patch, "Corporate Strategy and Technological Policy," unpublished working paper, Harvard Business School, 1978.

[28]See "Gillette Safety Razor Division: The Blank Cassette Project," Harvard Business School case study 9-574-058, 1974.

[29]These include H. Igor Ansoff, *Corporate Strategy* (Hammondsworth, U.K.: Penguin Books, 1979); D.E. Hussey, *Introducing Corporate Planning* (Oxford, U.K.: Pergamon Press, 1971); and William E. Rothschild, *Putting It All Together* (New York: AMACOM, 1979).

Figure 5–6 Typical Functional Requirements of Alternative Technological Strategies

	R&D	*Manufacturing*	*Marketing*	*Finance*	*Organization*	*Timing*
First to market	State-of-the-art R&D	Pilot and medium scale manufacturing	Stimulating primary demand	Access to risk capital	Flexibility over efficiency; encourage risk taking	Early-entry inaugurates the product life cycle
Second to market	Flexible, responsive, and advanced R&D capability	Agility in setting up manufacturing medium scale	Differentiating the product; stimulating secondary demand	Rapid commitment of medium to large quantities of capital	Flexibility and efficiency	Entry early in growth stage
Late to market or cost minimization	Skill in process development and cost-effective production	Efficiency and automation for large-scale production	Minimizing selling and distribution costs	Access to capital in large amounts	Efficiency and hierarchical control; procedures rigidly enforced	Entry during late growth or early maturity
Market segmentation	Ability in applications, custom engineering, and advanced product design	Flexibility on short to medium runs	Identifying and reaching favorable segments	Access to capital in medium or large amounts	Flexibility and control required in serving different customers' requirements	Entry during growth stage

FIGURE 5–7 Format for Competitive Product Analysis

	Competitor A Brand $1 \ldots K_A$	Competitor B Brand $1 \ldots K_B$
Product:		
Quality		
Features		
Benefits		
Target segment:		
Who		
Where		
When		
Why		
Place:		
Distribution method		
Distribution coverage		
Promotion:		
Total effort ($)		
Methods		
Advertising:		
Strategy/copy		
Media		
Timing		
Total effort ($)		
Price:		
Retail		
To trade		
Technological strategy		

Ability to Conceive and Design. This category measures the quality of competitors' new-product development efforts. Clearly, a firm with a high ability to develop new products is a serious long-term threat in a product category. The use of such procedures as total quality management generally improves product design capabilities.

Ability to Produce. This category concerns the production capabilities of the firm. For a service, it might be termed the ability to deliver the service. A firm operating at capacity to produce a product is not as much of a threat to increase sales or share in the short run as is a firm that has slack capacity, assuming a substantial period of time is required to bring new capacity online. Product quality issues would also be important here.

Ability to Market. How aggressive, inventive, and so on are the firms in marketing their products? Do they have access to distribution channels? A competitor could have strong product development capabilities and slack capacity but be ineffective at marketing.

Ability to Finance. Limited financial resources hamper effective competition. Companies with highly publicized financial problems such as the now defunct airlines

Eastern, Pan Am, and Braniff, firms going through LBOs, and companies or divisions for sale (which have limited marketing expenditures) become vulnerable to competitors in their product lines. While financial ratios are key pieces of information, how the competitor allocates its resources among products is also critical.

Ability to Manage. In the mid-1980s, Procter & Gamble replaced the manager of its U.S. coffee business with the coffee general manager from the United Kingdom. This new manager had a reputation for developing new products; in a 15-month period, for example, he oversaw the launch of four new brands, which was above average for the company. The message to competitors such as General Foods was clear: New products were likely to be a focus of the Folgers division. A stronger emphasis on marketing at RJR Nabisco's tobacco division emerged in 1989 when a former senior manager who had a reputation for building brands was named CEO. He was in charge when the controversial but successful "Joe Camel" advertising campaign was developed.

Figure 5–8 gives examples of specific information to collect about competitors. While the list is not exhaustive, it highlights major areas that should be researched.

What to Do with the Information

This is the stage at which many competitor analysis efforts fall flat. What do we do with all the information we collected? We need a useful format for synthesizing this information.

A first step toward making sense out of the data is to construct a table patterned after Figure 5–9. This forces the product manager to boil down the information to its essential parts and provides a quick summary of a large amount of data.

A critical part of the analysis is including the product for which the plan is written. This would be done in the column of Figure 5–9 labeled "Our Product." Detecting the strengths and weaknesses of the company's product is sometimes referred to as an *internal* or *resource* analysis. However, in our context, this comparison forms the basis of the differential competitor advantage analysis shown in Figure 5–1.

One outcome of this analysis could be a structured comparison of the competing firms and products on a small set (5 to 10) of factors that are critical to success in the relevant product category. Such a comparison could be structured along the lines of Figure 5–10. In this figure, the entries in the cells of the tables can be rated from, say, 1 to 10 to evaluate each firm or product on the critical success factor. This by itself forces the product manager of "our" product to evaluate (as honestly as possible) his or her product's capabilities versus those of competitors on a factor-by-factor basis. In addition, an overall rating gives the product manager a more global feel for the toughest competitors in the market, which may not necessarily be reflected in market shares or profits.

Assessing a Competitor's Will

Even the strongest competitor can be overcome if it is not committed to the market. Similarly, a weak competitor can cause massive damage if it is fanatically committed.

At some point, it is crucial to assess competitors' strength of will or commitment. This requires going beyond objectives (what do they want?) to assess the intensity

Figure 5–8 Examples of Competitor Information to Collect

A. Ability to conceive and design
   1. Technical resources:
      a. Concepts
      b. Patents and copyrights
      c. Technological sophistication
      d. Technical integration
   2. Human resources:
      a. Key people and skills
      b. Use of external technical groups
   3. R&D funding:
      a. Total
      b. Percentage of sales
      c. Consistency over time
      d. Internally generated
      e. Government supplied
   4. Technological strategy:
      a. Specialization
      b. Competence
      c. Source of capability
      d. Timing: initiate versus imitate
   5. Management processes:
      a. TQM
      b. House of Quality

B. Ability to produce:
   1. Physical resources:
      a. Capacity
      b. Plant
         (1) Size
         (2) Location
         (3) Age
      c. Equipment
         (1) Automation
         (2) Maintenance
         (3) Flexibility
      d. Processes
         (1) Uniqueness
         (2) Flexibility
      e. Degree of integration
   2. Human resources:
      a. Key people and skills
      b. Work force
         (1) Skills mix
         (2) Union
   3. Suppliers
      a. Capacity
      b. Quality
      c. Commitment

C. Ability to market:
   1. Sales force:
      a. Skills
      b. Size
      c. Type
      d. Location
   2. Distribution network:
      a. Skills
      b. Type
   3. Service and sales policies
   4. Advertising:
      a. Skills
      b. Type
   5. Human resources:
      a. Key people and skills
      b. Turnover
   6. Funding:
      a. Total
      b. Consistency over time
      c. Percentage of sales
      d. Reward system

D. Ability to finance:
   1. Long term:
      a. Debt/equity ratio
      b. Cost of debt
   2. Short term:
      a. Cash or equivalent
      b. Line of credit
      c. Type of debt
      d. Cost of debt
   3. Liquidity
   4. Cash flow:
      a. Days of receivables
      b. Inventory turnover
      c. Accounting practices
   5. Human resources:
      a. Key people and skills
      b. Turnover
   6. System:
      a. Budgeting
      b. Forecasting
      c. Controlling

E. Ability to manage:
   1. Key people:
      a. Objectives and priorities
      b. Values
      c. Reward systems
   2. Decision making:
      a. Location
      b. Type
      c. Speed
   3. Planning:
      a. Type
      b. Emphasis
      c. Time span
   4. Staffing:
      a. Longevity and turnover
      b. Experience
      c. Replacement policies
   5. Organization:
      a. Centralization
      b. Functions
      c. Use of staff

with which they approach the task (how badly do they want it?). Most competitions involve several key times when each competitor has the choice of backing down or continuing the fight. In assessing the likelihood that a competitor will continue the fight (an act that sometimes is not rational in a profit sense), one should assess the following factors.

1. How crucial is this product to the firm? The more crucial the product is in terms of sales and profits, number of employees, or strategic thrust, the more committed most companies will be to it. This helps explain why efforts to unseat a market leader by attacking the heart of the market provoke violent reactions, whereas a strategy that nibbles away at secondary markets is more likely to go unmatched. For example, Clorox's key product is bleach. Attempts by Procter & Gamble to develop rival products are met by strong responses in terms of promotions, line extensions, and other moves.

2. How visible is the commitment to the market? It may be difficult for companies to admit they are wrong once they are publicly committed. A good example of this is Exxon's Office Systems Division, which was clearly in trouble for a long time before it was sold in 1985. Also, Coca-Cola has held on to New Coke and repositioned it several times even though it has not sold well since its introduction.

3. How aggressive are the managers? Personality differences exist, and some individuals are more combative than others. This aspect of management may not be detected in the management analysis in Figure 5–9.

Only by knowing how badly a competitor "wants it" can one successfully approach the next task: predicting future competitor strategies.

Predicting Future Strategies

We now have three sets of information about the competitors in the product category. First, we have assessed what their likely objectives are, that is, for what reward they are currently playing the game. Second, we have made a judgment about their current product marketing strategy. Finally, we have some idea about their resources and how they compare to ours. The final step is to put it all together and answer the question: What are they likely to do in the future? In particular, we are interested in their likely strategies over the subsequent planning horizon, usually a year.

Sometimes competitors will actually signal their likely future strategies through sources previously discussed. For example, in an article in a major newspaper, MCI gave six-months' notice to the regional Bell operating companies (RBOCs) by stating the 10 U.S. cities where it was going to begin offering local phone service to businesses. While a major target of the article was the investment analyst community, we are sure the RBOCs were also quite interested in the announcement.[30] Of course,

[30]"MCI Details Assault on the Baby Bells," San Francisco *Chronicle*, March 7, 1995, p. D-2.

FIGURE 5–9 Competitor Capabilities Matrix

	Firm/Product				
	A	*B*	*C*	*D*	*Our Product*
Conceive and design:					
• Technical resources					
• Human resources					
• Funding					
•					
•					
•					
•					
Produce:					
• Physical resources					
• Human resources					
•					
•					
•					
•					
•					
Market:					
• Sales force					
• Distribution					
• Service and sales policies					
• Advertising					
• Human resources					
• Funding					
•					
Finance:					
• Debt					
• Liquidity					
• Cash flow					
• Budget system					
•					
•					
•					
Manage:					
• Key people					
• Decision process					
• Planning					
• Staffing					
• Organization structure					
•					
•					

FIGURE 5–10 Differential Competitor Advantage Analysis

Critical Success Factors	Firm/Product					
	A	*B*	*C*	*D*	*E*	*Our Product*
1						
2						
3						
4						
5						
Overall Rating						

the product manager must be aware that such signals could be of the "cheap talk" variety mentioned at the beginning of the chapter.

Often, however, the competition does not come right out and indicate what strategies they will pursue. In that case, subjective estimates can be based on the information previously collected and analyzed. One way to approach the problem is to emulate what forecasters do with historical data. With historical observations on both a dependent variable (in our context, a competitor's strategy) and independent variables useful to predict the dependent variable (in our context, the resource variables), the forecaster might do one of two things. First, the forecaster might assume the trend will continue, that is, suppose that the only relevant information is the historical pattern of past strategies. For example, if the brand has a track record of positioning with a high-quality, high-price program, one could extrapolate into the future and assume the trend will continue. Similarly, if a brand has been appealing to increasingly mature consumers, a manager might assume it will continue to do so. An alternative way for the forecaster to proceed is to try to establish a cause-and-effect relationship between the resource variables and the strategy, in other words, to link changes in resources or abilities to the strategies to be pursued.

Some examples will help clarify this approach. Several years ago, Merrill Lynch spent heavily to bring in managers with packaged goods experience to develop the markets for its financial services. Competitors (Dean Witter, E. F. Hutton) could forecast that this would result in an emphasis on market segmentation (pursuing high-potential customers) and increased spending on marketing-related activities such as advertising. Similarly, Bethlehem Steel invested billions of dollars to upgrade its flat-rolled steel facilities. Competitors could forecast that this investment in highly efficient capacity would improve Bethlehem's ability to simultaneously cut price and protect margins.

A third approach to strategy forecasting does not explicitly employ historical data but rather makes use of data in a different way. Corning Glass's highly profitable Corning Ware line was coming off patent. At the same time, it was well known that several companies (Libby-Owens-Ford, Anchor Hocking) were looking at that business. Corning was interested in finding out how a competitor would enter to preempt the entry strategy. To forecast the probable entry strategy, it asked senior managers to role-play (i.e., simulate) a competitor and determine how, if they were managing the entry, they would attack Corning Ware. This exercise provided useful defensive information for Corning.

Thus, a third approach to forecasting competitors' possible actions is to simulate them. One can take the existing data already collected, have different managers play the roles of the product managers for the competitors, and develop competitor action scenarios. SmithKline Beecham, the pharmaceutical company, did exactly that when Tagamet (an antiulcer drug), then the largest-selling prescription drug in the world, was coming off patent. In this case, it knew who the competitor was going to be: Glaxo Holdings. SmithKline prepared its salespeople for Glaxo's anticipated promotion of its drug, Zantac, in terms of differential advantage (fewer doses needed per day) and for counteracting arguments against Tagamet. Although Zantac has since replaced Tagamet as the category leader, SmithKline believed the simulation helped dampen the impact of Zantac. Another company using the simulation approach is Intel, which has a full-time group within the company that develops strategies that competitors may follow.

In general, there has been little systematic study of how to predict competitor moves.[31] Using the airline industry as a case history, some recent research has studied how competitors react to a competitive move as defined by the following characteristics of the action: the competitive impact (pervasiveness of the impact across competition), the intensity of the attack (degree to which the action affects a given competitor's key markets), implementation requirement (how much effort it takes to execute the action), and the type of action (strategic versus tactical).[32] The main empirical findings were:

- The greater the competitive impact, the greater the number of responses made.
- The greater the intensity of the move, the greater the number of counteractions.
- The greater the implementation requirement, the smaller the number of responses.
- The more tactical the move, the greater the competitive response.

While limited to a single industry, these results provide some insight about how competitors might respond to a product manager's move or how to respond to a competitor's move.

---

[31]An approach similar to simulation is to use economic game theory. While game theory is theoretically elegant, it is limited in its ability to model real-world situations involving large numbers of competitors and many possible moves. For a brief description of game theory, see F. William Barnett, "Making Game Theory Work in Practice," *The Wall Street Journal*, February 13, 1995, p. A-14.

[32]Ming-Jer Chen, Ken G. Smith, and Curtis M. Grimm, "Action Characteristics as Predictors of Competitive Responses," *Management Science*, March 1992, pp. 439–55.

Illustrations

RTD Fruit Drinks (ca. 1995)

To conserve space, we concentrate on three major brands in the product category: Snapple, Ocean Spray, and Fruitopia. There are many entrants in this category that are more regional in nature (e.g., Arizona, Koala) and private labels. In a real situation, the product manager would choose the set of brands based on his or her judgment concerning the most vital and direct set of competitors and possibly include an "other" category to account for smaller brands. In addition, since we have been performing the analyses from the perspective of the Snapple brand manager, most of the discussion will focus on Ocean Spray and Fruitopia. Figure 5–11 shows market shares of the major brands.

Brand Objectives. *Ocean Spray:* As Figure 5–11 indicates, this brand has been very successful in increasing market share. As the solid number two brand in the category, the product manager sees that Snapple is vulnerable and therefore looks to increase sales volume and market share, that is, grow.

Fruitopia: This is a new brand in the segment, launched at the beginning of 1994 by Coca-Cola. It gained 1.2 percent of the market in its first year of existence. Clearly, this brand will also have a volume/share growth objective to increase its position in the market and stave off competition from regional and private label brands.

Brand Strategies. *Ocean Spray:* This brand has succeeded by investing heavily in advertising and forming a joint venture with PepsiCo using its national distribution network. Ocean Spray tries to target consumers from 15 to 35 years old, sponsoring sport competitions and active sports in general through its campaign "Juice Jam '95: Crave the Wave." Ocean Spray is also strong on promotions, for example, sponsoring National Football League tie-ins. Finally, the brand is also being offered at a reduced price in some markets.

FIGURE 5–11 RTD Fruit Drink Market Share, 1992–94

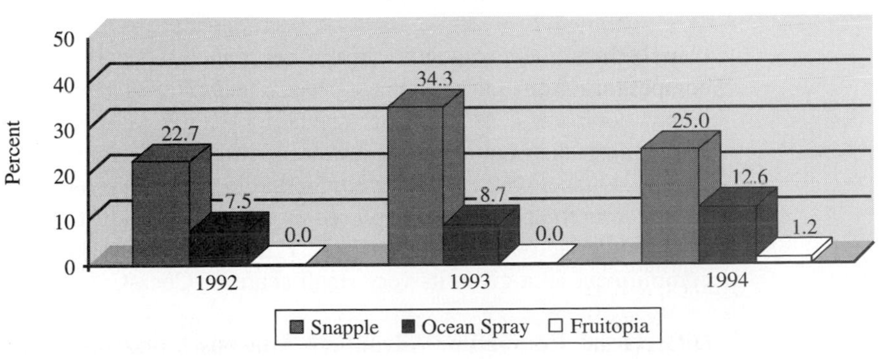

FIGURE 5–12 Competitor Capabilities Matrix for RTD Fruit Drinks

	Quaker Oats	*Ocean Spray/Pepsi*	*Coca-Cola*
Major brands	Snapple	Ocean Spray	Fruitopia
Corporate share as 1994 estimates	25.0%	12.6%	1.2%
Pricing	Moderate price	Moderate price	Moderate price
Sales estimates as of 1994	US $470 million	US $240 million	US $20.4 million
Commitment to RTD fruit drink segment	Deeply commited; represents 7.6% of Quaker world sales	Ocean Spray: entirely committed Pepsi: low commitment; represents 0.8% of PepsiCo world sales	Low commitment; represents 0.1% of Coca-Cola world sales
Ability to develop new products	Excellent	Excellent	Excellent
Ability to market:	Invest heavily	Invest heavily	Invest heavily
Advertising:			
1992	US $27.7 million	US $32.0 million	US $30.0 million
1993	US $18.2 million	US $18.9 million	—
1994	US $3.1 million	US $22.9 million	—
Advertising mix as of 1994	Outdoor, Network, spot and cable TV, Spot radio	Newspaper, Syndicated spot and cable TV, Network radio	Not available
Distribution network	National, but stronger on the West Coast and in the Northeast	National (uses Pepsi distribution network)	Gradually getting national (new product)
Relations with retailers	Medium: facing problems	Very good	Very good
Ability to finance	Strong financial parent company	Strong financial parent company	Strong financial parent company
Ability to produce	Strong	Strong	Strong

Fruitopia: The managers of this brand invested heavily in marketing expenses, spending $30 million in 1994. Fruitopia is targeting the Woodstock generation, an older crowd than Ocean Spray's. Its appeal is heavy on 1960s nostalgia, featuring peace-and-love themes and psychedelic labels. Fruitopia uses the Coca-Cola distribution system.

Capabilities. A competitor capabilities matrix appears in Figure 5–12. All three competitors seem fairly well matched in capabilities, and all are financed by large parent companies. All three are spending heavily to support their brands and have outstanding distribution networks. One difference might be level of commitment. Clearly, Quaker Oats is heavily committed to Snapple given the discussion in Chapter 2 indicating the priority being placed on recovering its lost share. RTD fruit drinks are also a major activity for Ocean Spray. Fruitopia is somewhat more questionable in the commitment area given its very small share of Coca-Cola business.

Differential Competitor Advantage Analysis. *Snapple:* This brand's major competitive advantages are an established customer base, high awareness (theme: "Made from the best stuff on earth"), and brand equity. Disadvantages are some management problems stemming from the Quaker takeover that have resulted in distribution difficulties and lack of strategic direction.

Fruitopia: Strengths are financial support and the distribution system of Coca-Cola. Disadvantages are the fact that it is a very small brand in the Coke empire and question marks about the 1960s positioning.

Ocean Spray: Strengths are the distribution alliance with Pepsi and the brand equity in the Ocean Spray name and logo. A disadvantage is the lack of flavor variety and the perhaps overly close perceptual relationship with cranberries, which have a taste that is not to everyone's liking.

Expected Future Strategies. *Fruitopia:* Coca-Cola has aggressive expansion plans for Fruitopia and is expected to continue investing heavily in advertising and promotion. It will try to establish the brand equity that Snapple enjoys. If the strategy does not appear to be working, Coca-Cola will likely lower price to gain supermarket volume to get a bigger share of the market.

Ocean Spray: Indications suggest that Pepsi is not completely satisfied with its partnership with Ocean Spray and is thinking about launching its own fruit drink products. This would completely change the scenario for Ocean Spray (and for the other market players), which would be deprived of an efficient national distribution network. Until then, the joint venture will continue to invest in advertising and promotion.

Personal Digital Assistants

In the PDA analysis, the perspective is that of the Sharp Wiz, and the competitors are the Apple Newton MessagePad 120, the HP200LX and OmniGo, the Motorola Envoy and Marco, and the Sony Magic Link.

Brand Objectives. Since the PDA is in the early stages of the life cycle, all of the products are trying to gain volume to bring down costs. This has resulted in a recent price drop of the major entrants following the usual early skimming approach to grab those who need to be the first with the latest technology (at the highest price).

Brand Strategies. Figure 5–13 gives a technical comparison of the major products.

Apple MessagePad 120: Apple has corrected many of the well-publicized technical problems of the Newton with the release of version 2.0 of the Newton operating system (OS). Handwriting recognition has been improved, sluggish search speeds increased, and communications capabilities greatly improved. Apple is targeting industry-specific applications (called *vertical markets*) such as insurance and health care. Advertising expenditures and price have dropped significantly. Figure 5–14 shows an Apple ad from *The Wall Street Journal.* The ad clearly shows what Apple product managers view as the product's differential advantages: it is an organizer with handwriting recognition capabilities, it is a communicator with wireless technology, and it can connect to both Macintosh and Windows-based computers; in other words, it is flexible.

Figure 5–13 Competitive Product Analysis: PDA Category

	Apple Newton MessagePad 120	*HP200LX*	*HP OmniGo*	*Sharp Zaurus K-PDA*	*Sony Magic Link*	*Motorola Marco*	*Motorola Envoy*	*High-End Organizer*
Features:								
Unit size	1.25″x4″x8″	1″x3.4″x6.3″	1″x3.7″x6″	1″x3.9″x6.7″	1″x5.2″x7.5″	1.4″x5.8″x7.5″	1.2″x5.7″x7.5″	0.7″x3.5″x6.3″
Weight	19.6 oz.	11 oz.	11.6 oz.	13.6 oz.	1.2 lbs.	1.8 lbs.	1.7 lbs.	9.3 oz.
Screen size	3″x6″	?		4″x2.6″	4.5″x3″	3″x6″	4.5″x3″	N/A
Screen resolution	320x240	?	240x240	320x240	480x320	320x240	480x320	N/A
Input	Pen	Keyboard	Keyboard + pen	Keyboard + pen	Pen	Pen	Pen	Keyboard
OS	Newton OS 2.0	DOS	GEOS	Proprietary	Magic Cap	Newton OS	Magic Cap	Proprietary
RAM/ROM	1MB/4MB	1MB/3MB	1MB/3MB	1MB/4MB	1MB/4MB	1MB/5MB	1MB/4MB	256K–4MB/ 1MB
PCMCIA slots	1	1	1	1	1	1	2	Proprietary
Built-In								
Address book	Yes	Yes	Yes	Yes	Yes	Yes	Yes	Yes
Appointment book	Yes	Yes	Yes	Yes	Yes	Yes	Yes	Yes
Alarm clock	Yes	Yes	Yes	Yes	Yes	Yes	Yes	Yes
Scratchpad/ notepad	Yes	Yes	Yes	Yes	Yes	Yes	Yes	Yes (Psion), no (Sharp, Casio)
To-do list	Yes	Yes	Yes	Yes	Yes	Yes	Yes	Yes
Calculator	Basic	Advanced	Advanced	Basic	Basic	Basic	Basic	Yes
Spreadsheet	Third-party option	Lotus 123	Yes	No	Yes	Third-party option	Option	Yes (Psion), no (Sharp, Casio)
Database	List manager	No	No	Yes	No	No	No	Yes
Word processor	No	Memo editor	Jotter	Yes	Option	No	Option	No
Dictionary	13,000 words	?	?	No	Yes	10,000 words	Option	Yes
Finance	No	Quicken	No	No	Quicken	No	No	Yes
Spellchecker	No	?	?	No	Yes	No	Option	No
E-mail	Yes	Yes	Yes	Terminal emulator, CompuServe	ATT, AOL, CompuServe	CompuServe (optional), Newtonmail	AOL, CompuServe, ATT (optional)	Yes
Standard communications	None	None	None	None	Modem	Radio modem	Modem, radio modem	None
Optional communications	Modem, radio modem, pager	Modem, radio modem, cellular modem	Modem, two-way pager, radio modem	Modem, cellular modem	Two-way pager	Pager	Pager	Optional extended modem (some models) Radio modem

Market Positions:								
Strengths	S/W availability, improved writing recognition	Built-in applications, DOS compatible	Keyboard or pen input, standard PDA OS	Keyboard or pen input, tightly integrated built-in applications	Communications, industrial design, ease of use	Wireless communications	Wireless communications	Built-in, well-integrated applications, low entry price
Weaknesses	Built-in applications, size	No pen	?	Proprietary OS	Size	High price	High price	Proprietary OS
Target segment	Professionals	Professionals, corporations	Professionals	Professionals	Professionals	Professionals, corporations	Professionals, corporations	Professionals
Distribution:								
Channels	Computer, electronics, office supply, retailers, mail order	Computer, electronics, office supply, retailers, mail order	Computer, electronics, office supply, retailers, mail order	Computer, electronics, office supply, retailers, mail order	Computer, electronics, retailers, mail order	Electronic retailers with expertise	Electronic retailers with expertise	Computer, electronics, office supply, retailers, mail order
Coverage	Nationwide	Nationwide	Nationwide	Nationwide	Nationwide	Limited	Limited	Nationwide
Promotion:								
Effort	N/A	N/A	N/A	N/A	N/A	N/A	N/A	N/A
Method	N/A	N/A	N/A	N/A	N/A	N/A	N/A	N/A
Advertising:								
Strategy/copy	Personal organizer	S/W availability	"The Power of Organization"	Portability, communications	"Intelligent Communicator"	Built-in wireless	Built-in wireless	PIM (Sharp, Casio) PC compatibility and memory capacity (Psion)
Media	Print	Print	Print	TV, print	Print	Print	Print	Print
Effort	High	Medium	n/a	High	Medium	Low	Low	Medium
Pricing (MRP)	$699	$549	$349	$749 $499 (street)	$699 $399 (street)	$900–1,400	$1,000–1,500	$150–$300 (Casio) $399–$599 (Psion)
Key highlights	First to market with pen product	First to market with DOS product	Second to market with pen+keyboard product, improved w/ std OS	First to market with pen+keyboard product	Targeting heavy online users, easy to use, elegant design	First to market with built-in wireless	First to market with built-in wireless	Cost, size, ease of use and integration objectives achieved via proprietary hardware and software strategy

FIGURE 5–14 1995 Apple Message Pad Ad

The New, Enhanced Apple MessagePad 120.

The new Apple® MessagePad® 120 is powered by the just-released Newton® 2.0 operating system, recent winner of "Best of COMDEX" in its category at COMDEX '95.

You're organized while you're mobilized.

Weighing only 1 lb., the MessagePad 120 has the functions of an electronic organizer, and more. It stores hundreds of names, phone and fax numbers, street and e-mail addresses. It keeps track of your schedule. You can write to-do lists, notes, memos, or even make sketches. Its handwriting recognition has been greatly improved.

BEST OF BYTE COMDEX/Fall '95

Info to go.

It not only organizes, it communicates.

The MessagePad 120 works with the way you communicate today. It can send and receive faxes. It also allows you to receive wireless paging messages and news bulletins. You can exchange e-mail via the Internet. It even has an optional keyboard so you don't have to carry a laptop.

An easy connection to your PC.

The new MessagePad 120 connects to both Windows and Mac™ OS-based computers. So you'll be able to create backup files, take your PC files with you, or access your PC from the road. That's because, with new connection software, you can easily download and upload data from your personal computer to your MessagePad 120.

To see the MessagePad in action, call for your free video. You'll soon discover how the new Apple MessagePad 120 can make you more efficient and productive when you're on the go.

To see how people on the go use the MessagePad 120, call for a free video:
1 800 423-3300
or, for more information, surf over to
http://www.info.apple.com/newton

The New Apple MessagePad 120

HP200LX and OmniGo: The HP200LX is priced somewhat higher than the OmniGo, giving HP a two-tiered approach to the market. The former is targeted to corporate users and the latter to individuals. HP is using an aggressive pricing strategy combined with a full set of features to position the product as the optimal combination of both. It hopes to create significant generic demand for PDAs with this strategy.

Motorola Envoy and Marco: These products are targeted at mobile professionals who need wireless access anytime and anywhere. The sales brochures mention as possible users salespeople who need to enter order information from a customer's location and service technicians who want to access product warranty and repair information. These two products are the only PDAs available with built-in two-way wireless communications, but they are expensive. They are also using a more limited distribution strategy, choosing to sell the products only through those resellers, distributors, system integrators, and specialty retailers who can offer customers strong technical support.

Sony Magic Link: Sony refers to this product as a PIC (personal intelligent communicator) rather than as a PDA. It is targeting users with heavy communication needs; the Magic Link comes with a built-in data/fax modem and, with the optional headset, can be used as a telephone while viewing, inputting, and processing data. The product is also expensive.

Capabilities. Figure 5–15 shows a competitive capabilities matrix. Sharp seems to be well positioned to succeed in this market, its only notable competitive weakness being marketing expertise compared to Apple and HP (not a minor weakness, of course). Apple has major long-term problems with its management in turmoil and its future somewhat in doubt. Therefore, the future of the Newton, hardly one of Apple's success stories, is somewhat uncertain. HP is a very strong entrant and a likely market leader. Sony is also a very strong competitor, with significant expertise and experience in marketing electronic devices. Motorola's differential advantage in this market is questionable. While it has outstanding technical capabilities in communications (e.g., cellular phones), it is unproven as a marketer for these kinds of products. In addition, Motorola has been siphoning off R&D money from developing future PDAs to give to current marketing efforts.

Expected Future Strategies. *Apple Newton:* As noted earlier, the future of this product is uncertain. Apple has been talking to Oracle about a joint venture in PDAs. This may permit Apple to concentrate more on its Macintosh computer line and allow it to leverage Oracle's expertise in networking.

HP200LX and OmniGo: HP is likely to continue aggressively marketing these products to try to dominate the category. It is also likely to drop price below $300 sometime in 1996. It is not likely to try to integrate telephone, pager, or radio WAN (wide area network) technology directly into its PDA hardware as it tries to keep the price down.

Motorola Envoy and Marco: In 1995, Motorola announced that it is shrinking its wireless data group staff by about 20 percent due to poor demand for these products. As noted earlier, Motorola is also shifting R&D funds to marketing. Given the poor sales results from marketing the products to individuals, it seems likely that Motorola

FIGURE 5–15 Competitive Capabilities Matrix: PDA Category

	Apple Newton Message Pad	*HP200LX and OmniGo*	*Sharp Zaurus K-PDA*	*Sony Magic Link*	*Motorola Marco and Envoy*	*High-End Organizers*	*Sharp Wiz*
Conceive and design:							
Technical resources	Good; in-depth knowledge of computer market, strength in both hardware and software	Excellent; expertise in computers and miniature devices (calculators)	Excellent; expertise in LCDs, ICs, consumer electronics, and miniaturization	Excellent; expertise in consumer electronics, batteries, ICs, and miniaturization	Excellent; expertise in wireless, ICs, and miniaturization	Casio: Good; expertise in consumer electronics Psion: Fair; experience in PDAs but not components	Excellent; expertise in LCDs, ICs, consumer electronics, and miniaturization
Human resources	Good; still able to attract innovative engineers	Excellent; one of the most popular firms among engineers in U.S.	Good; able to attract high-quality engineers in Japan	Excellent; one of the most popular firms among engineers in Japan	Fair; recent cut of 20% of PDA group may hurt morale	Good	Good; able to attract high-quality engineers in Japan
R&D funding	Poor, looking to refocus R&D on computers	Good; HP calculator and palmtop computer groups doing well	Good; success of Japan Zaurus and Wiz line should provide funding	Good; willing to make long-term investments in emerging technology	Poor; transferring R&D funds to market current products	Casio: Fair; not keeping up with Sharp Psion: Fair; small firm, earns most revenue from PDAs	Good; success of other lines should provide funding
Technology strategy	Will continue focusing on pen-based PDA using Newton OS	Will offer "product line," not tied to one OS; likely to rely on third parties for communications	Likely to stick with proprietary OS and keyboard+pen devices in U.S.	Likely to stay with Magic Cap–based communicator in short term.	Leverage expertise in wireless; use "standard" operating systems	Casio: Leverage expertise in low-cost manufacturing Psion: Exploit superior ease of use/integration of proprietary system	Leverage expertise in components and miniaturization; employs standard OS and works with application developers to ensure software availability
Produce:							
Physical resources	Fair, relies on contract manufacturers for production	Excellent; owns plant in Singapore	Excellent; already mass produces Zaurus and Wizards	Excellent	Good	Casio: Excellent Psion: Fair; produces model 3a in high volume	Excellent
Human resources	Fair	Excellent	Excellent	Excellent	Good	Casio: Good Psion: Fair	Excellent
Market	Excellent	Excellent	Good	Excellent	Good	Good	Good
Finance	Fair to poor	Good	Good	Fair	Good	Good	Good
Manage	Fair; turmoil in executive ranks	Good	Good	Good	Fair; recent downsizing	Casio: Fair Psion: Good	Good

will target more vertical applications for its PDA products and focus on business customers more generally.

Sony Magic Link: Sony will continue to make product improvements and decrease prices. It will not expand the product line and focus marketing on the Magic Link, but in the longer term it may use its expertise in consumer electronics to offer lower-priced, mass-marketed PDA models.

Summary

Competitive analysis is an important component of strategy development. Many approaches have been followed and this chapter provides a framework that integrates several of these. Like most other analyses, however, the key ingredient is not clever devices, unethical behavior, or elegant presentation. Rather the quality of competitor analysis depends heavily on the effort devoted to it.

C H A P T E R

6 Customer Analysis

Overview

Without customers, a business cannot survive. Although this may seem obvious, many product managers have regretted not obtaining sufficient information about their customers to develop products or strategies that meet customer needs. This can occur despite the widespread adoption of the "marketing concept," which stresses keeping close to customers. Despite spending millions of dollars on marketing research, automobile manufacturers missed the female market segment for years because they failed to adapt products and the sales environment to the fact that women were both influencing and making more automobile purchases.

This chapter describes some ways to structure a customer analysis. First, note that in this chapter the term *customer* refers not only to current customers of a given product but also to both customers of competitors and current noncustomers of the product category. For useful marketing planning to occur, it is important to consider the potential market for the product and not just its current market and customers.[1]

Each customer is unique to some degree. Since it is time consuming and not very profitable to develop a strategy for each customer, some grouping of customers into segments is required.[2] This segmentation is a compromise between treating each customer as unique and assuming all customers are equal. The latter approach, often

[1]Customers can, of course, include channel members. In this chapter, however, we consider only end customers for the product or service, although most of the analyses discussed apply equally to channel members.

[2]Some categories have so few customers that each can be treated as a separate segment and analyzed separately. Examples are passenger aircraft, military products (e.g., battle tanks), and nuclear generators. In addition, there is a trend in marketing today called *mass customization,* developing ways to market products and services to individuals rather than to segments. Examples are Levis custom-tailored jeans for women and Internet-based information services that the user can customize. For further reading on this concept, see B. Joseph Pine II, Bart Victor, and Andrew C. Boynton, "Making Mass Customization Work," *Harvard Business Review,* September–October 1993, pp. 108–19.

FIGURE 6–1 What We Need to Know about Current and Potential Customers

1. Who are they?
2. What do they buy?
3. How do they choose?
4. Why do they select a product? (customer value)
5. Where do they buy it?
6. When do they buy it?

termed *mass marketing,* is rarely used today. Segmentation programs, in contrast, both provide insights about different kinds of customer behavior and make marketing programs more efficient.

In this chapter, we suggest an approach to systematically analyze a product's customers. Figure 6–1 shows the main parts of this analysis. Product managers need to answer a set of six questions. First, who are the customers for this product or service? Second, what are customers buying? (Note that customers buy benefits rather than simply product features or characteristics.) Third, how do customers make purchase decisions? Fourth, why do customers choose a particular product? In other words, how do they value one option over another? Fifth, where do customers buy products? Finally, when are purchase decisions made? The purchase timing issue affects communications, production, logistical, and other tactical decisions.

Who Buys the Product?

Product Definition

In Chapter 3, we suggested there are various ways to define a product and its competition. Clearly, the product manager must begin to answer the question "Who buys the product?" with a definition of the product category. If the product category is defined generically, a large number of potential kinds of customers might exist. For example, if the bottled water category is defined to include soft drinks, coffee, and other beverages, customers would include people who buy these other products as well as bottled water. The marketing manager for a mutual fund would analyze not only customers who purchase mutual funds but also people who invest in individual stocks, real estate, certificates of deposit, and so on.

Buyers versus Users

When a product manager analyzes the customers in the product category, the first question is "Who are the customers?" For most industrial goods and many consumer products, the *who* must be broken into several different buyers within the organization or household, including the following:

1. Initiator (who identifies the need for product).
2. Influencer (who has informational or preference input to the decision).

FIGURE 6–2 Buying Roles and Needs/Benefits Sought

	Needs/Benefits			
Buying Roles	*A*	*B*	*C*	*D*
1. Initiator(s)				
2. Influencer(s)				
3. Decider(s)				
4. Purchaser(s)				
5. User(s)				

3. Decider (who makes the final decision through budget authorization).
4. Purchaser (who makes the actual purchase).
5. User.

The identities of the above customers can differ widely, particularly the user and the buyer. For example, in an industrial market, the end user may be an engineer who is concerned mainly with technical features, whereas the purchasing agent emphasizes cost and reliability of delivery. One reason for the success of Federal Express was its ability to take the decision on how to send overnight packages away from the shipping clerk by making the user the purchaser. Similarly, adults often purchase cereal, toys, or fast-food meals even though the user of the product is a child. McDonald's ads clearly recognize this and attempt to target both teenagers (who have money of their own) and the family meal segment, in which the child is likely to influence where the family goes to eat. Products targeted toward gift givers, such as Corning Ware, also recognize the difference between the buyer and the user.

This distinction among buyer, user, and other purchase influencers is particularly important for industrial products. In fact, the mark of a top salesperson is the ability to identify the different people involved in making a decision, understand the relative power over the purchase each person holds, and learn what they value. For example, in selling word processing software to a law firm, the needs of the secretaries (ease of use, mouse support, readable screen) differ from those of the office manager (high productivity, no bugs in the software, good service) and from the person approving the purchase (low cost, reliable delivery). Product managers in industrial goods businesses or consumer product categories that generate substantial discussion within the household (e.g., durable goods purchases such as automobiles or houses, in addition to fast food, toys, and other categories already mentioned) will find Figure 6–2 useful as a template for this kind of analysis.

Descriptor Variables

Assume for simplicity that customers, potential customers, and the different buying roles can all be considered under the umbrella term *customer.* Obviously we need some set of variables to use to identify customers.

Consumer Products. The most obvious and popular basis for describing consumers is their general characteristics. Figure 6–3 lists many of the variables used to describe consumers for segmentation purposes. The general categories are as follows:

1. *Demographic.* The most commonly used demographics are age, sex, geographic location, and stage in the family life cycle. These characteristics have the advantage of being relatively easy to ascertain. Unfortunately, in many cases, segments based on demographics are not clearly differentiated in their behavior toward the product.

2. *Socioeconomic.* Socioeconomic variables include income and such related variables as education, occupation, and social class, with income and education generally being more useful. As in the case of demographics, the relationship between these variables and purchase behavior can be weak.

3. *Personality.* Given the relatively limited predictive power of demographic and socioeconomic variables, the fact that many marketing people are trained in psychology and the natural desire to find a general basis for dividing up consumers that will be useful across many situations, it is not surprising that marketers have attempted to use personality traits as a basis for segmentation. Unfortunately, personality variables have proven even less useful than demographic or socioeconomic variables in predicting purchasing behavior.

4. *Psychographics and values.* Psychographics basically represent an evolution from general personality variables to attitudes and behaviors more closely related to consumption of goods and services. Like personality variables, psychographics describe differences among people that demographic and socioeconomic variables cannot capture. Also known as lifestyle variables, psychographics generally fall into three categories: activities (cooking, sports, traveling, etc.), interests (e.g., art, music), and opinions. They are thus, not surprisingly, often referred to as AIO variables. These have been widely used as bases for segmentation by many companies and for the creation of advertising themes by ad agencies. Many researchers have used the VALS (Values and Lifestyles) typology (see Figure 6–4) and its updated version, VALS2, developed by SRI International as a basis for defining segments.[3] Figure 6–4 also shows the lifestyle typology, GLOBALSCAN, which was developed by the advertising agency Backer Spielvogel Bates Worldwide. GLOBALSCAN was based on a survey of 15,000 adults in 14 countries.

Another typology, the List of Values (LOV) Scale,[4] delineates nine basic values:

1. Self-respect.
2. Security.
3. Warm relationship with others.
4. Sense of accomplishment.
5. Self-fulfillment.
6. Sense of belonging.
7. Respect from others.
8. Fun and enjoyment.
9. Excitement.

---

[3]Readers interested in categorizing themselves on the VALS2 scale can do this through the World Wide Web site http://future.sri.com/vals/survey.html.

[4]Lynn P. Kahle, Sharon E. Beatty, and Pamela Homer, "Alternative Measurement Approaches to Customer Values: The List of Values (LOV) and Values and Life Styles (VALS)," *Journal of Consumer Research,* December 1986, pp. 405–9.

FIGURE 6–3 Major Segmentation Variables for Consumer Markets

Variable	*Typical Breakdown*
Geographic	
Region	Pacific, Mountain, West North Central, West South Central, East North Central, East South Central, South Atlantic, Middle Atlantic, New England
City or metro size	Under 5,000; 5,000–20,000; 20,000–50,000; 50,000–100,000; 100,000–250,000; 250,000–500,000; 500,000–1,000,000; 1,000,000–4,000,000; 4,000,000 or over
Density	Urban, suburban, rural
Climate	Northern, southern
Demographic	
Age	Under 6, 6–11, 12–19, 20–34, 35–49, 50–64, 65+
Gender	Male, female
Family size	1–2, 3–4, 5+
Family life cycle	Young, single; young, married, no children; young, married, youngest child under 6; young, married, youngest child 6 or over; older, married, with children; older, married, no children under 18; older, single; other
Income	Under $10,000; $10,000–$15,000; $15,000–$20,000; $20,000–$30,000; $30,000–$50,000; $50,000–$100,000; $100,000 and over
Occupation	Professional and technical; managers, officials, and proprietors; clerical, sales; craftspeople, foremen; operatives; farmers; retired; students; homemakers; unemployed
Education	Grade school or less; some high school; high school graduate; some college; college graduate
Religion	Catholic, Protestant, Jewish, Muslim, Hindu, other
Race	White, black, Asian
Nationality	American, British, French, German, Italian, Japanese
Psychograhic	
Social class	Lower lowers, upper lowers, working class, middle class, upper middles, lower uppers, upper uppers
Lifestyle	Straights, swingers, longhairs
Personality	Compulsive, gregarious, authoritarian, ambitious
Behavioral	
Occasions	Regular occasion, special occasion
Benefits	Quality, service, economy, speed
User status	Nonuser, ex-user, potential user, first-time user, regular user
Usage rate	Light user, medium user, heavy user
Loyalty status	None, medium, strong, absolute
Readiness stage	Unaware, aware, informed, interested, desirous, intending to buy
Attitude toward product	Enthusiastic, positive, indifferent, negative, hostile

Source: Philip Kotler, *Marketing Management,* 8th ed. (Upper Saddle River, N.J.: Prentice Hall, 1994), p. 271. Adapted with permission.

FIGURE 6–4 Lifestyle Typologies

VALS	*VALS2*	*GLOBALSCAN*
Inner-directed consumers	Principle-oriented consumers	Strivers
Societally conscious	Fulfilleds	Achievers
Experientials	Believers	
I-am-me consumers		
Outer-directed consumers	Status-oriented consumers	Pressured
Achievers	Achievers	
Emulators	Strivers	Adapters
Belongers		
Need-driven consumers	Action-oriented consumers	Traditionals
Sustainers	Experiencers	
Survivors	Makers	
	Strugglers	

These typologies help managers understand different purchasing patterns and afford the product manager the opportunity to match potential buyers with appropriate media to communicate with them.[5]

5. *Behavioral variables.* Other segmentation variables describe consumers' behavior toward products. Included in this set are quantity purchased (e.g., heavy versus light), degree of brand loyalty, benefits sought, and other variables.

Industrial Products. Many of the variables used to describe consumers can also be used to describe organizations (see Figure 6–5 for a list of some of the most popular variables used). For industrial product customers, the traditional focus has been on firm characteristics such as size of the company, industry, and location, that is, the demographic variables appropriate for describing companies. However, a variety of other kinds of variables can be used, such as operating variables (e.g., customer technology), purchasing approaches (e.g., centralized versus decentralized purchasing operations), situational factors (e.g., size of the order), and "personal" characteristics (e.g., attitude toward risk).

It is interesting that concepts of personality and psychographics, the last category of variables mentioned earlier, can be applied in the context of organizations. Although it may be unusual to think of a firm as having a personality, one important segmentation variable in technologically oriented industries is innovativeness. The

[5]See, for example, Kim P. Corfman, Donald R. Lehmann, and Sundar Narayanan, "The Role of Consumer Values in the Utility and Ownership of Durables," *Journal of Retailing,* Summer 1991, pp. 184–204.

Figure 6–5 Major Segmentation Variables for Business Markets

Demographic
- *Industry:* Which industries should we focus on?
- *Company size:* What size companies should we focus on?
- *Location:* What geographical areas should we focus on?

Operating Variables
- *Technology:* What customer technologies should we focus on?
- *User/nonuser status:* Should we focus on heavy, medium, light users, or nonusers?
- *Customer capabilities:* Should we focus on customers needing many or few services?

Purchasing Approaches
- *Purchasing-function organization:* Should we focus on companies with highly centralized or decentralized purchasing organizations?
- *Power structure:* Should we focus on companies that are engineering dominated, financially dominated, etc.?
- *Nature of existing relationships:* Should we focus on companies with which we have strong relationships or simply go after the most desirable companies?
- *General purchase policies:* Should we focus on companies that prefer leasing? Service contracts? Systems purchases? Sealed bidding?
- *Purchasing criteria:* Should we focus on companies that are seeking quality? Service? Price?

Situational Factors
- *Urgency:* Should we focus on companies that need quick and sudden delivery or service?
- *Specific application:* Should we focus on certain applications of our product rather than all applications?
- *Size of order:* Should we focus on large or small orders?

Personal Characteristics
- *Buyer-seller similarity:* Should we focus on companies whose people and values are similar to ours?
- *Attitudes toward risk:* Should we focus on risk-taking or risk-avoiding customers?
- *Loyalty:* Should we focus on companies that show high loyalty to their suppliers?

Source: Philip Kotler, *Marketing Management,* 8th ed. (Upper Saddle River, N.J.: Prentice Hall, 1994), p. 278. Adapted with permission.

innovators, organizations that adopt new technologies earlier than others in their industry, are often referred to as "lead users." Lead users have two characteristics: (1) They face general needs but face them months or years before the bulk of the industry does, and (2) they can benefit significantly by obtaining an early solution to those needs.[6] These are obviously valuable customers, as they not only provide early sales and spread (hopefully favorable) word of mouth information but also help the company make necessary product modifications and improvements.

Industrial customers can also be segmented on the basis of reactions to marketing mix variables.[7] For example, a large industrial product company segmented its

[6]Glen L. Urban and Eric von Hippel, "Lead User Analyses for the Development of New Industrial Products," *Management Science,* May 1988, pp. 569–82.

[7]V. Kasturi Rangan, Rowland R. Moriarty, and Gordon S. Swartz, "Segmenting Customers in Mature Industrial Markets," *Journal of Marketing,* October 1992, pp. 72–82.

national accounts based on the trade-offs made between price and service to form four segments:

- Programmed buyers: small customers that do not consider the product important and make routine purchases.
- Relationship buyers: small buyers, loyal to the supplier, that pay low prices and obtain high service levels.
- Transaction buyers: large buyers for which the product is important and that obtain price discounts, expect high service levels, and switch suppliers.
- Bargain hunters: large buyers that get the lowest prices and the highest service.

Foreign Markets. Many of the same variables used to segment markets for consumer and industrial goods are used to segment markets internationally. Figure 6–6 lists key segmentation variables used in direct marketing campaigns in Europe.

Segmenting Databases. As we mentioned in Chapter 1, one key trend in product management is the increased use of customer databases for target marketing and customer retention programs. Database marketers often use three criteria for segmenting customers in their databases:

1. Recency: How recently has the customer bought from you?
2. Frequency: How many different products does the customer buy, and what are the time intervals?
3. Monetary value: What is the value of the customer's purchases in terms of profits?

This RFM approach is used to rate each customer in the database on a scale, perhaps by multiplying the three criteria and then rank ordering customers in terms of attractiveness. For prospecting for new customers, top-ranked customers can be profiled using the descriptors noted above, and then potential customers can be matched against these descriptors.

Analysis for Market Segmentation

Developing methods for market segmentation has been one of the most popular areas for marketing researchers. Many of the methods developed, particularly by marketing academics, are highly technical and are not in widespread use among product managers. In this section, we focus on three methods that are simple to apply and for which there is easy-to-use computer software: (1) cluster analysis, (2) cross-tabular analysis, and (3) regression analysis.[8] We assume the product manager has customer data from surveys or other sources measuring both descriptive information and information about behavior toward the product in question. Again, we interpret the

[8]Our intention in this section is not to completely describe the methods but to give the reader an idea of how they can be applied to develop a customer analysis. The interested reader is referred to a marketing research textbook such as Donald R. Lehmann, *Marketing Research and Analysis,* 3rd ed. (Burr Ridge, Ill.: Richard D. Irwin, 1989).

FIGURE 6–6 Key Segmentation Variables Used in Direct Marketing Campaigns in Europe

	Belgium	*Denmark*	*France*	*Germany*	*Greece*	*Ireland*	*Italy*	*Netherlands*	*Portugal*	*Spain*	*UK*
Most commonly used consumer segmentation criteria	Social class Nielsen zones Geographic Database	Demographic from census Database	Sociodemographic Database	Age Profession Income Family status Lifestyle	Urban/rural Profession Database	Age Income Profession Family status Database	Age Sex Profession Housing types	Age Sex Geographic Lifestyle Database	Income Urban/rural Education Political bias Database	Age Sex Education Urban/rural Geographic proximity Database	Age Sex Profession Lifestyle Database
Most commonly used business segmentation criteria	SIC* Size VAT	SIC Size Turnover Decision	SIC Size Turnover	SIC Turnover Size	Size Turnover SIC	Size Turnover Location Liquidity	SIC Size Turnover Number of telephone lines	Size/SIC Turnover Branches Credit rating Decision makers	Size SIC	Size Turnover	SIC Sizee

Source: *Marketing Director International,* 1991.
*SIC: Standard Industrial Classification.

FIGURE 6–7 **Cluster Analysis Illustration**

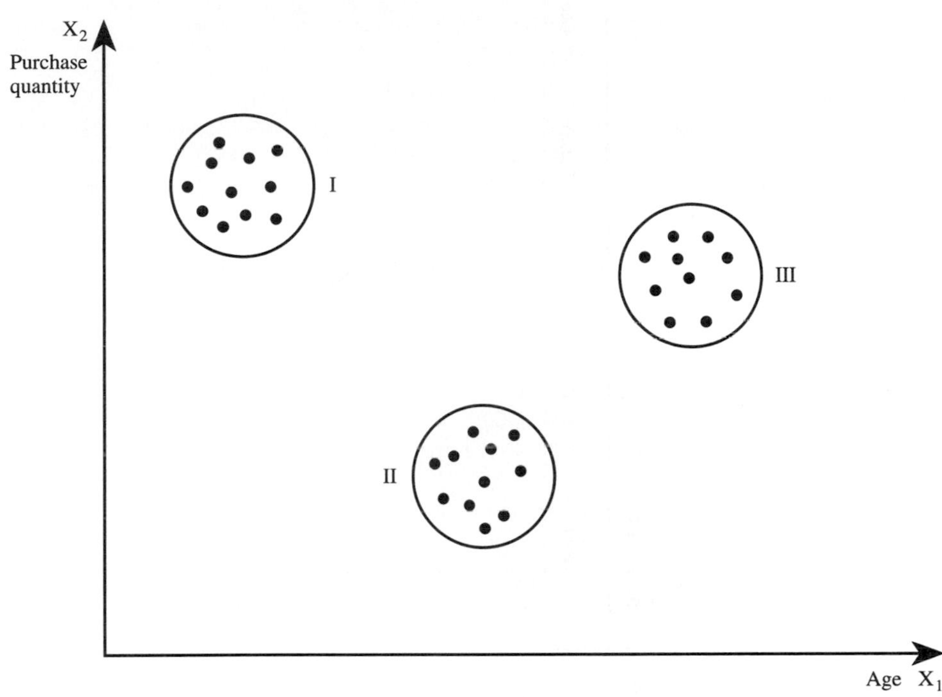

term *customer* broadly to imply that data should be collected from former and potential as well as current customers.

The basic underlying notion of segmentation analyses is to relate information about the two kinds of segmentation variables: descriptors and behavioral variables. Neither type by itself is useful for segmentation. Suppose we know that 50 percent of the population consists of men and 50 percent of women (only guessing). This information is not helpful to the product manager because it does not indicate whether men or women have a greater propensity to buy our product. Alternatively, suppose we know that 20 percent of the population consists of heavy buyers, 40 percent of medium buyers, and 40 percent of light buyers. Again, this information is not very useful because we do not know who these buyers are (in terms of income, geography, and so forth); that is, we have no way to reach any of the groups. As a result, the methods on which we focus relate descriptor and behavioral data about customers in different ways to form useful market segments.

Cluster Analysis. One way to generate segments is to collect data about the descriptor and behavioral variables from a sample of customers and then form groups by means of cluster analysis. Cluster analysis examines the values of the variables for each respondent (from the sample of customers) and then groups respondents with similar values. Consider Figure 6–7. Each dot represents a combination of factors, say,

FIGURE 6–8 Cluster Analysis: Phone Company Market Segmentation Scheme

	Fledglings	*Thrifties*	*Contenteds*	*Climbers*	*Techies*	*Executives*
Mean age	37	51	44	43	38	40
Mean income	\$26k	\$27k	\$37k	\$31k	\$40k	\$48k
Occupation	Blue collar	Retired/blue collar	Administrative/ professionals	Administrative/ sales	White collar	White collar
Education	14	12	14	16	18	18
Married	60%	72%	76%	65%	33%	72%
Children	44%	38%	51%	54%	75%	33%
Mobility	High	Low	Medium	Medium	High	Low
Home value	\$70–85k	\$60–80k	\$70–85k	\$60–80k	\$80k+	\$90k+
Dual income	Low	Medium	Medium	High	Highest	Medium
Number of phones	Low	Low	Medium	Medium	High	High
Type of phones	Basic/standard	Basic/standard	Medium mix	Medium mix	All types	All types
Monthly bill	Low	Low	Medium	Very high	Very high	Very high
Technology adoption	Late adopters	Laggards	Late adopter	Early adopter	Innovator	Early adopter
Purchase criteria	Value/money	Security	Convenience	Status	Environmental control	Quality
Application	Social interaction	Safety and protection	Social interaction	Social interaction	Personalized systems	Time saving

age (X_1) and purchase quantity (X_2). In this case, three obvious clusters emerge. These clusters are appealing in that the members of each cluster are similar to one another and different from members of other clusters in terms of age and purchase quantity. The product manager would conclude from this analysis that the youngest customers purchase the most and the oldest customers the second most and that the product does not appeal to middle-aged people. Cluster analysis programs are widely available on commercial computer software packages for personal computers such as SAS, SPSS, and Statgraphics. (Unfortunately, such clear clusters rarely emerge.)

A standard application of this approach was made by a regional phone company that was attempting to understand its residential customers. The company collected information on descriptors, attitudes, and behavior (usage was measured in dollars) and formed six segments based on clustering those households that "looked the same" based on the variables:

1. Low income/blue collar: "Fledglings."
2. Frugal/retired: "Thrifties."
3. Contented middle class: "Contenteds."
4. Aspiring middle-class status seekers: "Climbers."
5. Technology-driven strivers: "Techies."
6. Contented upper middle class: "Executives."

A more detailed profile of the segments is shown in Figure 6–8.

Mobil Corporation also applied cluster analysis to gasoline buyers to tailor different stations to neighborhoods with different profiles and needs.[9] The company identified five segments of gasoline buyers:

1. Road warriors: higher-income, middle-aged men who drive 25,000 to 50,000 miles per year, buy premium gas with a credit card, and buy sandwiches and drinks from the convenience store (16% of buyers).
2. True blues: men and women with moderate to high incomes who are loyal to a brand and sometimes to a particular station (16%).
3. Generation F3 (fuel, food, and fast): upwardly mobile men and women, half under 25 years old, who are constantly on the go; drive and snack a lot (27%).
4. Homebodies: usually homemakers who shuttle their kids around during the day and buy gas from whatever station is along the way (21%).
5. Price shoppers: not loyal to a brand or station, rarely buy premium (20%).

Most gas companies have targeted the last group. However, Mobil has emphasized better service and amenities to customers in the first two segments and has been able to charge 2 cents more per gallon than competitors in some markets.

A third example highlights the use of a geodemographic system called PRIZM (Potential Rating Index by Zip Market), which is marketed by Claritas Corporation. PRIZM's basic analysis is performed on U.S. ZIP codes. Based on the 1990 census, the PRIZM system examines the means of a set of demographic variables for all of the nearly 40,000 U.S. ZIP codes. Based on the demographic variables, the ZIP codes are then clustered into 62 different groups. These 62 groups are given catchy names based on the mean levels of the variables, such as "Norma Rae–ville," "Cashmere & Country Clubs," and "American Dreams." The final crucial step, of course, is to relate membership in the geodemographic clusters to purchasing of various products and services (the behavior variable).

Figure 6–9 shows an application of PRIZM to the beer market.[10] The graphs clearly indicate the different amounts of market potential for various kinds of beer in the various PRIZM segments. Families in the "Blue Blood Estates" and "Urban Gold Coast" clusters are particularly good targets for imported beer (they are about seven times more likely to drink imported beer than malt liquor), whereas "Southside City" families show the reverse behavior.[11]

Figure 6–10 provides another example from Strategic Mapping, Inc.'s Cluster-PLUS 2000 for the disposable diaper market. This analysis develops 60 segments using similar data to PRIZM. Figure 6–10 provides the number of households in each

---

[9]Allanna Sullivan, "Mobil Bets Drivers Pick Cappuccino over Low Prices," *The Wall Street Journal,* January 30, 1995, p. B-1.

[10]Justin Martin, "Make Them Drink Beer," *FORECAST,* July–August 1994, pp. 34–40.

[11]This kind of analysis must be treated with caution, as there is a "chicken and egg" problem; Do "Southside City" families have a naturally high propensity to drink malt liquor, or is it high due to intensive marketing efforts? Products that are developed for particular segments and are heavily marketed to them will naturally have higher purchase incidence rates unless there is a total market/product mismatch. The reader should also note the ethical implications of target marketing by demographic/ethnicity variables for certain kinds of products, such as malt liquor.

FIGURE 6–9 Prizm Geodemographic Segmentation

Why Geodemographic Marketing Works

Beer companies can market their brews by neighborhood, thanks to geodemographic systems. Research shows that residents in different neighborhoods drink different amounts and types of beer. By using geodemographic systems, which categorize neighborhoods by their life-style characteristics, including household purchasing patterns, age and income, beer marketers can concentrate their marketing and distribution dollars on the areas where they'll be most effective. Here are a sampling of different types of neighborhoods and their beer consumption indexes (100=national average), as recorded by Claritas Inc.'s Prizm geodemographic system. A beer consumption index of 300, for instance, indicates that the neighborhood drinks three times as much beer as the national average.

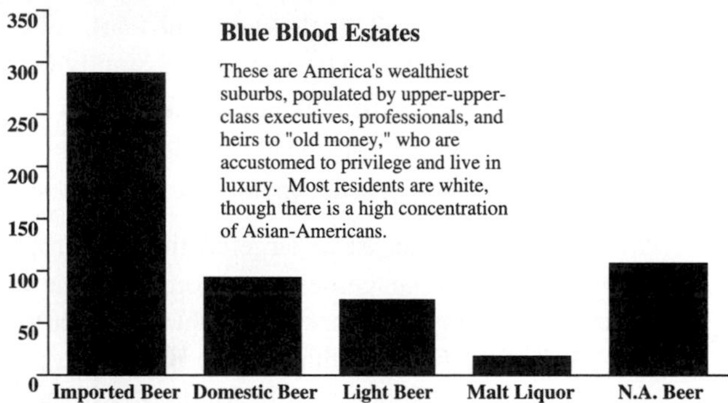

350
300
250
200
150
100
50
0
Blue Blood Estates
These are America's wealthiest suburbs, populated by upper-upper-class executives, professionals, and heirs to "old money," who are accustomed to privilege and live in luxury. Most residents are white, though there is a high concentration of Asian-Americans.
Imported Beer
Domestic Beer
Light Beer
Malt Liquor
N.A. Beer

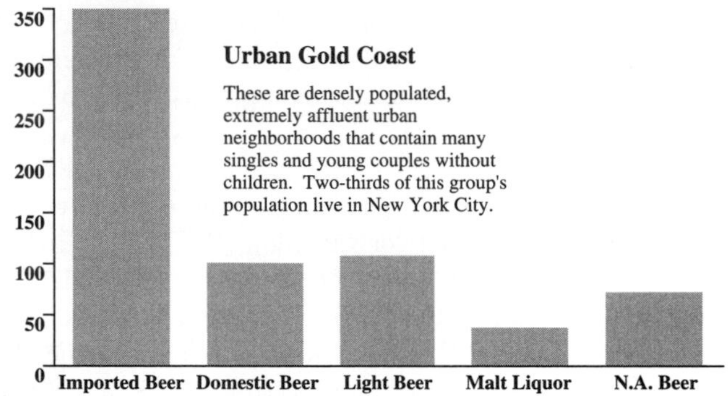

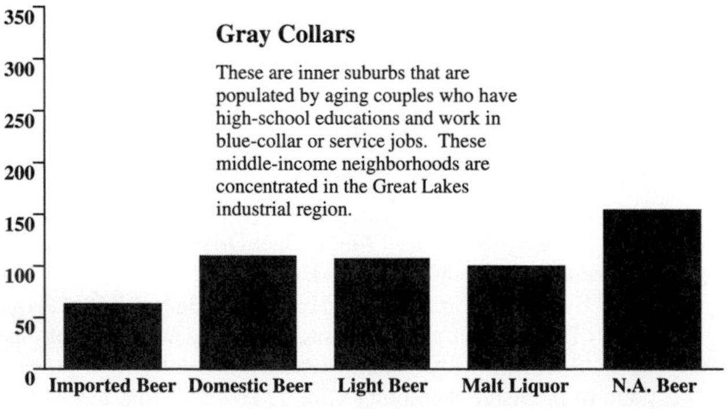

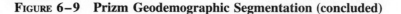

Figure 6–9 Prizm Geodemographic Segmentation (concluded)

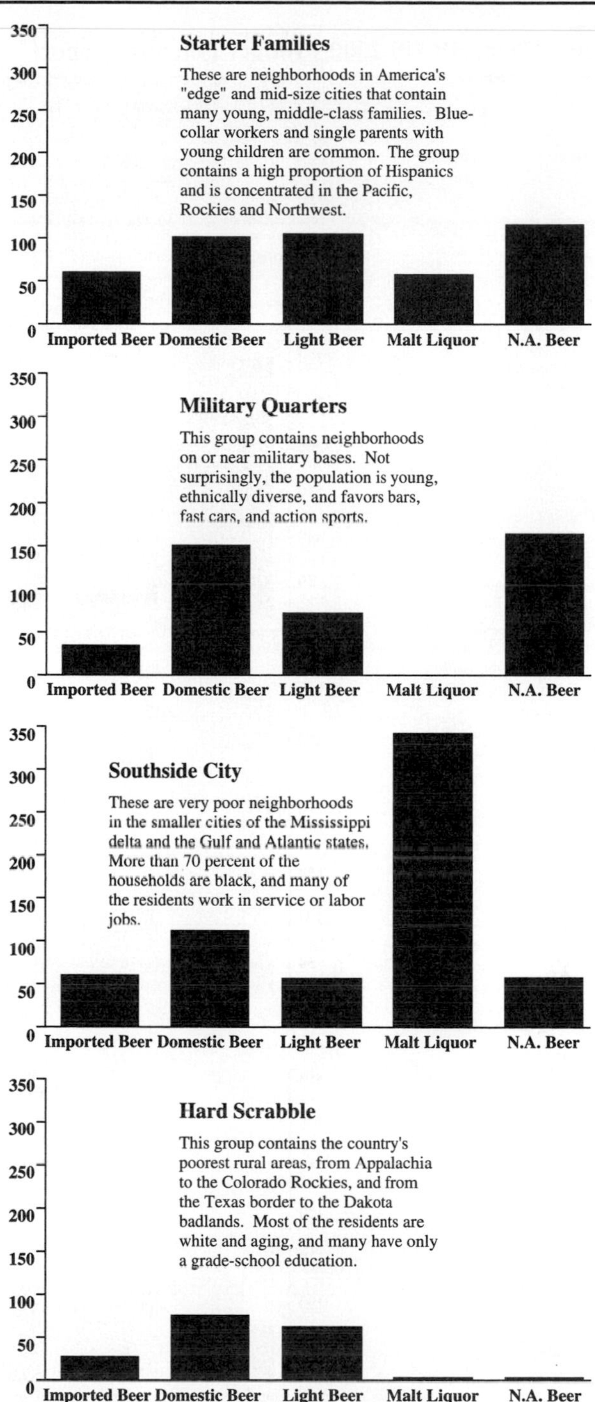

Starter Families
These are neighborhoods in America's "edge" and mid-size cities that contain many young, middle-class families. Blue-collar workers and single parents with young children are common. The group contains a high proportion of Hispanics and is concentrated in the Pacific, Rockies and Northwest.
0
50
100
150
200
250
300
350
Imported Beer
Domestic Beer
Light Beer
Malt Liquor
N.A. Beer
Military Quarters
This group contains neighborhoods on or near military bases. Not surprisingly, the population is young, ethnically diverse, and favors bars, fast cars, and action sports.
Southside City
These are very poor neighborhoods in the smaller cities of the Mississippi delta and the Gulf and Atlantic states. More than 70 percent of the households are black, and many of the residents work in service or labor jobs.
Hard Scrabble
This group contains the country's poorest rural areas, from Appalachia to the Colorado Rockies, and from the Texas border to the Dakota badlands. Most of the residents are white and aging, and many have only a grade-school education.

Source: Justin Martin, "Make Them Drink Beer," *Forecast,* July–August 1994, pp. 38–39.

FIGURE 6–10 ClusterPLUS 2000 Product Potential Report

Item: SI150: NUMBER OF DISPOSABLE DIAPERS USED IN HH ON AVG DAY
Market: U.S.
Demographic Base: Households
Group Set: Clusters

Description	*Base Count*	*% Base*	*Usage*	*% Usage*	*Avg Use*	*Index*
Totals: U.S.	96,976,894	100.00	44,435,425	100.00	0.46	100
C54:Young Blacks with Kids	796,378	0.82	656,588	1.48	0.82	180
S45:Low Income Younger Blacks	794,712	0.82	623,785	1.40	0.78	171
C40:Younger Mobile Singles	1,551,509	1.60	1,072,648	2.41	0.69	151
U10:New Families, New Homes	1,794,370	1.85	1,208,366	2.72	0.67	147
S22:Young Families Dual Income	2,545,890	2.63	1,696,654	3.82	0.67	145
S07:High Inc, Young Families	1,582,765	1.63	1,026,304	2.31	0.65	142
T53:Low Income Ethnic Mix	2,408,568	2.48	1,532,643	3.45	0.64	139
U44:Young Black Families	1,097,859	1.13	694,500	1.56	0.63	138
U48:VYng BCollar Hispanic Fams	887,710	0.92	544,265	1.22	0.61	134
C57:Black Lowest Inc Fem Hd HH	1,102,997	1.14	670,655	1.51	0.61	133
S35:Avg Age/Inc, Blue Collars	3,111,554	3.21	1,831,753	4.12	0.59	128
C27:Yng Avg Inc Hispanics Apts	1,606,595	1.66	922,631	2.08	0.57	125
R26:Yngr Settld BCollar Fams	2,202,399	2.27	1,224,826	2.76	0.56	121
U30:Yngr Homeowners, LVal Home	1,777,653	1.83	946,531	2.13	0.53	116
R47:Below Avg Inc Work Couples	3,295,708	3.40	1,732,530	3.90	0.53	115
U18:Yngr Hisp/Asian Homeowners	1,336,855	1.38	696,558	1.57	0.52	114
U23:Yngr Families Lo Val Homes	2,342,629	2.42	1,195,549	2.69	0.51	111
C52:Mid-Age Old Apts	1,111,753	1.15	562,416	1.27	0.51	110
T37:Below Avg Inc Blue Collar	2,726,056	2.81	1,343,793	3.02	0.49	108
R28:Settld Couples Lo Val Homes	5,259,551	5.42	2,547,153	5.73	0.48	106
U46:Above Avg Age Low Inc/Rent	1,281,639	1.32	597,541	1.34	0.47	102
C55:Low Inc Mobile Hispanics	1,725,271	1.78	800,347	1.80	0.46	101
R43:Below Avg Inc Blue Collars	3,991,458	4.12	1,802,116	4.06	0.45	99
S03:Well Educated Professional	1,972,176	2.03	877,473	1.97	0.44	97
S50:Very Young Hispanics	560,158	0.58	243,992	0.55	0.44	95
S12:High Inc Settled Families	2,208,503	2.28	960,122	2.16	0.43	95
U08:Hi Inc Urban Professionals	1,390,450	1.43	593,088	1.33	0.43	93
U04:Upscale Urban Couples	1,635,493	1.69	671,429	1.51	0.41	90
C29:Avg Age & Inc Few Kids	1,731,043	1.79	700,570	1.58	0.40	88
C25:Young WCollar Singles Apts	2,472,066	2.55	954,393	2.15	0.39	84
U31:Very Young Apt Dwellers	3,196,517	3.30	1,202,506	2.71	0.38	82
S05:Younger Affluent w/Kids	1,812,746	1.87	676,769	1.52	0.37	81
T19:Above Avg Age White Collar	2,141,629	2.21	793,668	1.79	0.37	81
U24:Avg Inc Apts Fewer Kids	1,728,593	1.78	611,974	1.38	0.35	77
U36:Avg Income Hispanics	1,098,132	1.13	380,782	0.86	0.35	76
U14:High Inc WCollar Apt/Condo	2,741,736	2.83	945,426	2.13	0.34	75
C34:Younger, Hispanics/Asians	2,031,995	2.10	699,422	1.57	0.34	75
S13:WCollar High Value Homes	1,539,106	1.59	519,431	1.17	0.34	74
S21:Suburban Married Couples	1,989,228	2.05	619,096	1.39	0.31	68
S38:Retired Homeowners	1,187,663	1.22	368,475	0.83	0.31	68
R06:Rural Affluents, New Homes	919,158	0.95	281,294	0.63	0.31	67
C15:Single Prof High Rent Apts	2,159,119	2.23	634,909	1.43	0.29	64
S09:Mature Couples Profs	1,139,545	1.18	321,101	0.72	0.28	61
R16:Younger Couples with Kids	2,509,079	2.59	681,097	1.53	0.27	59
S02:Mid-Age Affluent w/Kids	718,314	0.74	194,525	0.44	0.27	59
S01:Established Wealthy	543,731	0.56	135,722	0.31	0.25	54
C17:Prof & Retirees Apt/Condo	1,266,237	1.31	274,325	0.62	0.22	47
C11:Ctr City Affluent Few Kids	968,301	1.00	185,212	0.42	0.19	42
*G59:GQtrs: Military	45,649	0.05	29,083	0.07	0.64	139

*Results should be viewed with caution—insufficient sample size.
Note: Calculations are based on Source Market Usage.

Source: Simmons Market Research Bureau.

segment, the percentage of U.S. households in the segment (%Base), the estimated number of disposable diapers used in one day in the segment (Usage), the percentage of U.S. daily disposable diaper use (% Usage), the average number of diapers used per household in that segment (Avg. Use), and an index that is the ratio of %Usage/%Base and gives some idea about the usage rate of that segment relative to the size of the segment. The indexes are rank ordered for easy analysis by the product manager. While this index obviously is not the only criterion for choosing to target a segment (e.g., no data by brand are shown), the information is a useful part of an overall picture of consumer behavior in the disposable diaper category.

Using electronic scanner data combined with ZIP code information and other data sources, product managers now can segment not only by ZIP code but also by store. For example, Kraft can alter the mix of flavors of cream cheeses sold by supermarkets across different neighborhoods. This micromarketing permits the manager to define even narrower segments. Retailers also can use this analysis. Dayton-Hudson Corporation's Target store on Phoenix's eastern edge sells prayer candles (the area is heavily populated by Catholic Hispanics) but no child-toting bicycle trailers. The Target 15 minutes away in affluent Scottsdale sells the trailers but no portable heaters. Heaters can be found 20 minutes south in Mesa, which has a cooler climate.[12]

Cross-Tabular Analysis.[13] This analysis uses categorical variables constructed from customer membership in a category. For example, surveys usually ask respondents to identify the range in which their incomes fall, such as "$20,000–$29,999," "$30,000–$39,999," and so on, or what their favorite brand is. Sometimes surveys ask questions that are continuously "scaled," for example, "How many times did you go to the movies last month?" The answers can then either be analyzed as given or be placed in categories (e.g., 0–2 times, 3–5 times, 6 or more).

As an illustration, consider the data in Figure 6–11. These data were taken from a survey of 1,004 users of cranberry sauce.[14] The descriptor variables, located in the leftmost column, are based on some prior analyses of data concerning attitudes toward cooking. These four categories are "convenience oriented," "enthusiastic cook," "disinterested," and "decorator." The descriptor variable is referred to as the *independent* variable. The behavioral categories, located across the top, are divided into three groups based on self-reported usage: heavy, medium, and light. This variable is referred to as the *dependent* variable. Entries in the table or cells indicate the number of consumers who simultaneously satisfy both a descriptor group and a behavioral group. In other words, 81 people were both heavy users of cranberry sauce and convenience oriented. The row sums and the column sums are called *marginals.*

The basic issue facing the product manager, assuming she or he is interested in understanding how to segment the market based on the behavioral variable of usage quantity, is whether attitude toward cooking is a useful variable. Product managers

[12]Gregory A. Patterson, "Target 'Micromarkets' Its Way to Success: No 2 Stores Are Alike," *The Wall Street Journal,* May 31, 1995, p. A-1.

[13]The reader uninterested in somewhat more technical material can skip the remainder of this section.

[14]See F. Steward De Bruicker, "Ocean Spray Cranberries (A)" and "Ocean Spray Cranberries (B)," Harvard Business School case studies 9–575–039 and 9–575–040, 1974.

FIGURE 6–11 Raw Data: Cranberry Sauce Usage

Cooking Attitude	*Heavy Users*	*Medium Users*	*Light Users*	*Total (row marginal)*
Convenience oriented	81	144	74	299
Enthusiastic cook	97	115	45	257
Disinterested	35	108	127	270
Decorator	45	96	37	178
Column total (marginal)	258	463	283	1004

have many descriptor variables to choose from, not to mention several behavioral variables. An important task is to sift through the candidate descriptors to find some that are useful to describe the heavy, medium, and light buyers.

Before analyzing the results in great detail, it is useful to first determine if there is a *significant* relationship between the independent variable, cooking attitude, and the dependent variable, usage quantity. The most common and simplest approach to this task is a *chi-square* test. In this statistical test, each cell based on the survey results (e.g., Figure 6–11) is compared to an *expected* cell size or the number of people that would be expected in that cell if attitude toward cooking were independent of usage quantity. The expected cell size can be calculated by multiplying the marginal for the row in which the cell is located by the marginal for the column in which the cell is located and dividing by the total sample size. For example, the expected cell size for the convenience-oriented–heavy usage cell is $(299 \times 258)/1{,}004 = 77$. Then the chi-square value is determined by taking the sum over all cells of the $(\text{observed} - \text{expected})^2/\text{expected}$. For Figure 6–11, the chi-square value of 86, together with the number of degrees of freedom of the table (the number of rows minus 1 times the number of columns minus 1) and the significance level of the test, is compared to a table of chi-square values found in any statistics book. In this example, the chi-square value of 86 with 6 degrees of freedom exceeds the table value of 12.6 at the 95 percent confidence level; hence the relationship is significant. Thus, we can conclude that there is a significant relationship between consumers' attitudes toward cooking and their reported cranberry sauce usage levels.[15]

A second step in the analysis is to better understand the nature of the relationship between the two variables[16] by calculating percentages. The two most common ways

[15]Using a computer program, the chi-square tests from many descriptor variables could be compared to see which of the sets the product manager should consider further in the segmentation analysis. This is actually more complicated than it sounds, as the chi-square values of tables with different numbers of rows and/or columns (degrees of freedom) cannot be directly compared. One alternative is to standardize all the tables to the same size. A second alternative is to use a computer program such as SAS that prints out the exact level of significance of each chi-square result and rank orders the descriptors by this number.

[16]Cross-tabular analysis can easily be extended to tables with more than one independent variable. The same logic for the chi-square test holds.

FIGURE 6–12 Cranberry Sauce Usage Percentages

Cooking Attitude	*Heavy Users*	*Medium Users*	*Light Users*
Convenience oriented			
Row %	27%	48%	25%
Column %	31	31	26
Enthusiastic cook			
Row %	38	45	18
Column %	38	25	16
Disinterested			
Row %	13	40	47
Column %	14	23	45
Decorater			
Row %	25	54	21
Column %	17	21	13

to calculate percentages are to divide each cell by its row marginal to obtain row percentages or divide each cell by its column marginal to obtain column percentages. Figure 6–12 shows the row and column percentages for the cranberry sauce data.

The row percentage indicates what percentage of the row category customers are in the column group. In the example, 27 percent of convenience-oriented consumers are heavy users. The column percentage indicates what percentage of the column category is in the row group. In the example, 31 percent of heavy users are convenience oriented. Of course the product manager must interpret these two types of percentages differently.[17]

To use cross tabular analysis, the product manager needs to first establish which behavioral category is of interest. In the cranberry sauce example, assume the manager is interested in medium users because heavy users are saturated and light users probably cannot be convinced to consume more cranberry sauce. Which customers should the product manager pursue? One obvious group is the convenience-oriented cooks, as this group has the largest number of medium buyers (31 percent) and is the second most "concentrated" (48 percent); that is, 52 percent of them are not medium buyers, so advertising to them would waste 52 percent of the dollars. Perhaps enthusiastic cooks should also be targeted, as they are the largest group of heavy users (38 percent). In sum, the discussion of which group(s) to target should focus on the percentages.

Note that the cranberry sauce example illustrates the use of psychographics as potential segmenting variables. However, since media typically are not measured by psychographics (which magazines know their readers' attitudes toward cooking?), an additional cross-tabular analysis matching demographic or socioeconomic variables

[17]To see this more clearly, consider the descriptor "men" and the behavioral variable "reads *Playboy* magazine." In this case, a large percentage of *Playboy* readers are men, but a small percentage of men are *Playboy* readers.

with the lifestyle variable may be necessary for lifestyle segmentation. In other words, if the product manager wishes to target convenience-oriented customers, it is useful to know income, geographic, and other information about them to implement the segmentation strategy.

Regression Analysis. Like cross-tabular analysis, regression analysis is used when the product manager can specify an explicit relationship between a dependent (behavioral) variable and one or more descriptor (independent) variables.[18] However, unlike cross-tabular analysis, regression assumes a continuously measured dependent variable. Using the cranberry sauce illustration, if the dependent variable is reported usage in number of cans rather than categories of consumption, then regression will be more appropriate.

Suppose we believe that income and family size are key segmentation variables in addition to the categories of cooking attitudes. Assume three categories of income (low, medium, and high) are reported on the survey as well as the actual number of people in the family. We can then specify a *model* of the following form:

$$Usage = f(\text{CO, EC, DI, DE, LOWY, MEDY, HIGHY, FAMSIZE}),$$

where the dependent variable is the reported usage rate of cranberry sauce and the independent variables are the descriptors: convenience oriented, enthusiastic cooks, disinterested, decorator, low income, medium income, high income, and family size, respectively.

Generally, one person can be in only one category of cooking attitude and one category of income. In addition, assume these two variables cannot be represented by continuously measured numbers such as reported usage (number of cans) and family size (number of people). To understand the segmentation implications of this model, we need to create *dummy variables* to represent the cooking attitude and income variables. These variables are simply 0 or 1, indicating membership in one of the categories.

Figure 6–13 provides a hypothetical representation of the survey responses of five individuals. The first column contains values of the dependent variable, usage of cranberry sauce in number of cans. The next four columns represent cooking attitude. However, each respondent can have 1 in only one of the columns and must have a 1 in one of them because the categories are mutually exclusive and collectively exhaustive. The next three columns represent the income variable, which has the same characteristics as the cooking attitude variable. Finally, family size is reported as the actual number.

Due to statistical (and logical) restrictions, if a dummy variable has n categories, only n–1 are needed in the regression. Therefore, rewriting the regression model in equation form, we obtain

$$Usage = a + b\text{CO} + c\text{EC} + d\text{DI} + e\text{LOWY} + f\text{MEDY} + g\text{FAMSIZE},$$

where a to f are regression coefficients estimated using the data in Figure 6–13 and some computer software (e.g., Excel).

[18]We assume in this section that the reader has some working knowledge of regression analysis.

FIGURE 6–13 Dummy Variable Illustration: Data Matrix

		Cooking Attitudes				Income			
Person	*Cranberry Sauce Usage (Number of cans)*	*CO*	*EC*	*DIS*	*DEC*	*LO*	*MED*	*HI*	*Family Size*
1	5	0	1	0	0	0	1	0	4
2	2	1	0	0	0	0	0	1	3
3	0	0	0	1	0	1	0	0	5
4	6	0	0	0	1	0	1	0	4
5	3	1	0	0	0	1	0	0	3

The interpretation of the coefficients differs between the continuously measured variable, FAMSIZE, and the dummy variables. The coefficient g is interpreted in the usual way: For a one-person change in family size, usage changes by g units. For example, if g is positive, a one-person increase (decrease) in family size is predicted to increase (decrease) usage by g units. The coefficients b, c, d, e, and f, however, are interpreted differently. Recall that these variables are measured either as 0 or 1 depending on membership in that category. For each set of dummies, a coefficient is interpreted as the *contrast* from the omitted category. For example, b, the coefficient of the dummy variable "convenience oriented," is interpreted as the estimated difference in cranberry sauce usage between a person who is convenience oriented versus one who is a decorator (the omitted category). Likewise, f, the coefficient on "medium income," is the estimated difference in usage between a person who reports having medium income versus one who has high income. It is irrelevant which category is dropped, as the estimated differences would be the same even though the coefficients themselves would change.

Suppose we estimated the regression equation using a computer program and obtained the following results:[19]

$$\begin{aligned} Usage = {} & 10.3 + 2.1 \times \text{CO} - 1.9 \times \text{EC} - 3.5 \times \text{DI} - 2.5 \times \text{LOWY} - 1.1 \times \text{MEDY} \\ & + 0.9 \times \text{FAMSIZE}. \end{aligned}$$

What would be the market segmentation implications? In this case, convenience-oriented cooks have the highest usage rate: 2.1 units more, on average, than the omitted category, decorators. Both of the other categories of cooking attitude use less than decorators, as the negative signs on their coefficients indicate. In terms of income, high-income consumers are estimated to have the highest usage rate (both signs on the other income variables are negative). Finally, for every one-person increase in family size, reported usage increases an estimated .9 units (i.e, cans). Thus, the profile of the largest cranberry sauce users is (hypothetically) high-income, convenience-oriented cooks with large families.

[19]For those readers knowledgeable about regression, we assume all the coefficients are statistically significant and have sufficiently large t-statistics.

An important statistic produced with regression equations is R^2, which measures the degree to which the equation "fits" the data on a 0 to 1 scale, with 1 being a perfect fit. Unfortunately, for frequently purchased products, these kinds of equations tend to have low R^2 values. However, despite the poor fits, these regressions often point to useful bases for segmentation. Figure 6–14 shows that significant differences in product consumption can be determined from the variables represented by the regression coefficients on the dummy variables even when the R^2 values are low.

Summary. These kinds of analyses can be applied to any product, consumer or industrial, low-tech or high-tech. What is needed are survey or other primary data in which customers report information about themselves or their organizations and their buying behavior.

Many other methods have been used for segmentation. Two methods discussed later in this chapter, conjoint analysis and multidimensional scaling, are good examples. In addition, other multivariate techniques (analysis of variance, logit/probit, Automatic Interaction Detector, to name just a few) can be applied to obtain information about existing market segments.

Analyses of the types described here can help winnow down the possible segments to a manageable number. Additional criteria for selecting market segments, some of which are accounted for in the analyses described here, include the following:

1. The segments must be large enough to be profitable.
2. The segments must be identifiable. This issue is addressed by the analyses utilizing demographic and socioeconomic data.
3. The segments must be reachable by media.
4. The segments should respond differently to the marketing mix. If all segments can be reached with the same marketing programs, there is no need to separate them.
5. The segments should be stable in terms of size.
6. The segments should be reasonably coherent; that is, the members should behave as similarly as possible.

Other useful criteria can be identified:

7. The segments should be growing.
8. The segments should not be so heavily dominated by competitors that our product cannot be successful

Finally, with existing products and services, the product manager rarely has to start from "ground zero" in understanding the various segments for the product. Presumably there is an existing marketing strategy based on some understanding of the various potential target markets. In addition, there are often industry or category customs for defining segments. For example, banks typically define their merchant (business) customers in terms of the size of their revenues. Many consumer product companies segment their markets based on the variables that MRI (Mediamark Research Inc.) and a competitor, Simmons Market Research Bureau, Inc. (SMRB), use

FIGURE 6–14 **Light and Heavy Buyers by Mean Purchase Rates for Different Socioeconomic Cells**

		Description		Mean Consumption Rate Ranges		
R^2	*Product*	*Light Buyers*	*Heavy Buyers*	*Light Buyers*	*Heavy Buyers*	*Ratio of Highest to Lowest Rate*
.08	Catsup	Unmarried or married over age 50 without children	Under 50, three or more children	.74–1.82	2.73-5.79	7.8
.07	Frozen orange juice	Under 35 or over 65, income less than $10,000, not college grads, two or less children	College grads, income over $10,000, between 35 and 65	1.12–2.24	3.53–9.00	8.0
.04	Pancake mix	Some college, two or less children	Three or more children, high school or less education	.48–.52	1.10–1.51	3.3
.08	Candy bars	Under 35, no children	35 or over, three or more children	1.01–4.31	6.65–22.29	21.9
.08	Cake mix	Not married or under 35, no children, income under $10,000, TV less than 3½ hours	35 or over, three or more children, income over $10,000	.55–1.10	2.22–3.80	6.9
.09	Beer	Under 25 or over 50, college education, nonprofessional, TV less than 2 hours	Between 25 and 50, not college graduate, TV more than 3½ hours	0–12.33	17.26–40.30	—
.02	Cream shampoo	Income less than $8,000, at least some college, less than five children	Income $10,000 or over with high school or less education	.16–.35	.44–.87	5.5
.06	Hair spray	Over 65, under $8,000 income	Under 65, over $10,000 income, not college graduate	0–.41	.52–1.68	—
.09	Toothpaste	Over 50, less than three children, income less than $8,000	Under 50, three or more children, over $10,000 income	1.41–2.01	2.22–4.39	3.1
.03	Mouthwash	Under 35 or over 65, less than $8,000 income, some college	Between 35 and 65, income over $8,000, high school or less education	.46–.85	.98–1.17	2.5

Source: Frank Bass, Douglas Tigert, and Ronald Lonsdale, "Market Segmentation—Group versus Individual Behavior," Reprinted from *Journal of Marketing Research,* published by the American Marketing Association 5 (August 1968), p. 267.

to define customer purchasing and media use habits. These include gender, education, age, employment status, income, geography, marital status, household size and composition, and race.

What Do Customers Buy?

Benefits

Though many product managers do not realize it, customers do not purchase products and services for the features of the product; rather, customers purchase the *benefits* the product provides. Another way to look at this issue is that the firm produces features but customers purchase benefits. Recognizing this distinction is a particular problem in technology-driven companies that tend to focus on the development of new technologies and fancy products without concern about whether the benefits the technology provides solve the customers' problems better than the old products do.

As noted in Chapter 3, focusing on benefits is also important in understanding the competitive set. The old story about the drill manufacturer that recognized it was selling holes, not drills, not only indicates that benefits are more important than the physical product but also helps to define the competition based on the benefit (we referred to this idea in Chapter 3 as *generic competition*).

Thus, a key problem facing the product manager with respect to customer analysis is to understand through marketing research what benefits different customer groups or market segments are seeking. As Figure 6–2 shows, the needs or benefits sought can vary with the buying role in the decision-making unit. In addition, the product manager must uncover how benefits and needs vary by segments.

For example, consider the selling of a Cadillac Seville. The following distinction can be drawn between features and benefits:

Feature	*Benefit*
300 horsepower engine	The ability to pull away quickly from potentially dangerous situations. With the increased city traffic, you'll feel much safer in this car.
Northstar engine	This engine will not need a tuneup for the first 100,000 miles. You'll enjoy a smooth-running engine with fewer trips to the dealer for service.
Adjustable seats	These controls allow you to make easy adjustments to your seating position so you'll stay fit, alert, and comfortable throughout your trip.
ABS brakes	Even if you step hard on these brakes, your wheels won't lock up and skid. This means you'll have an extra margin of safety.

As you can see, this kind of description, which can be used in a print ad or as part of a sales pitch, appeals both to the features-hungry customer and to the customer who needs the features translated into terms he or she can understand.

Typically, product managers can ascertain *what* benefits are sought through focus group research or judgment. The advantage of using focus groups in this context is that through an informal group discussion led by a professional moderator, customers get a better chance to thoroughly explain their problems and how they can be solved than they usually can through structured interviews.

Product Assortment

A second useful piece of information related to the "what" question involves the number of different brands purchased by customers in the segments. For many frequently purchased consumer goods, panel or similar data are available that provide purchase histories for individual consumers (e.g., brands purchased were A, A, A, B, A, A, C, A, A, A). Such data can be analyzed by a variety of means to measure competitive patterns, as Figure 3–10 in Chapter 3 shows. For industrial products, it is useful to understand how many different vendors a customer employs and the assortment of models, quality levels, and the like from which the customer chooses.

Product Uses

A classic illustration of a company making significant profit from studying how the product is used is Arm & Hammer. The company relies on customers mailing in suggestions about new ways to apply its popular baking soda. From customers, Arm & Hammer found out about putting a box in the refrigerator, using baking soda to deodorize drains, and many other applications. Often customers find many uses for a product that the company never dreamed of. Interestingly, the way a product is used may or may not be related to why customers originally bought it.

In addition, defining the exact situation in which the product or service is used is crucial to understanding customers. This includes both where they use it (e.g., at home or in the office) and on what occasions (e.g., for entertaining or everyday use).

How Do Customers Choose?

The Multiattribute Model

The problem of understanding the process of customer behavior has been extensively studied by marketing academics. Excellent textbooks exist that thoroughly describe the elements of customer choice behavior.[20] In addition, comprehensive conceptual models have been developed that focus on consumer decision processes,[21] information processing,[22] and organizational buying behavior.[23] It is thus impossible to provide a comprehensive discussion here of how customers make choices.

[20]See, for example, William L. Wilkie, *Consumer Behavior,* 2d ed. (New York: John Wiley & Sons, 1990).

[21]For example, John A. Howard, *Consumer Behavior in Marketing Strategy* (Englewood Cliffs, N.J.: Prentice Hall, 1989).

[22]James R. Bettman, *An Information Processing Theory of Consumer Choice* (Reading, Mass.: Addison-Wesley, 1979).

[23]Wesley J. Johnston and Jeffrey E. Lewin, "Organizational Buying Behavior: Toward an Integrative Framework," *Journal of Business Research* 35 (1996), pp. 1–15.

However, a concise and practical conceptualization of customer decision making that is useful in both consumer and industrial product contexts is the multiattribute model. The multiattribute model of decision making is composed of several parts. First, the products or alternatives in a product category are assumed to be collections of attributes. Attributes can be defined in terms of physical characteristics or, as described earlier, as benefits sought. In addition, each customer is assumed to have a perception about how much of each attribute the alternatives in a product category contain. Third, each customer is assumed to place an importance value or weight on obtaining each attribute when making a choice in the category. Finally, customers are assumed to combine the attribute and importance weight information using some process, or *rule,* to develop their most preferred option in the product category.

The model raises four key questions:

1. Which attributes do customers use to define a product?
2. How do customers determine how much of each attribute a brand possesses?
3. How are the importance weights determined?
4. What decision rule is used to combine the information?

Determining the Attributes. To apply the multiattribute model, one must define the set of relevant attributes. This is not as easy as it sounds; using managerial judgment alone can seriously underestimate the number and types of attributes used in making decisions. The set of attributes is useful information for the product manager, particularly for communications purposes.

One way to collect such information is through focus group research. The participants in the focus group are first selected from the actual or possible target segment(s). The moderator of the focus group elicits from the set of respondents what characteristics or benefits the customers want to see in a product.

A second approach is through survey-based methods. Determining the set of attributes would be accomplished through open-ended rather than fixed-alternative questions. For example, to determine the set of attributes for a notebook computer, the product manager would not predefine the set and ask the respondent to mark those used in making a decision; instead she or he would use a survey instrument that first asks the respondent to write down the 5 or 10 key attributes used in making a purchase decision.

Determining Perceptions. Once the set of attributes has been estimated, the next step is to determine customers' perceptions of the amount of each attribute possessed by each brand or product option in the category. This is often done by direct questioning through primary data collection methods. Suppose it was determined that weight is a key attribute of a notebook computer. Then the following question could be asked: "On a 1 to 7 scale where 1 is the lightest and 7 is the heaviest, how heavy is the —— brand of laptop computer?" This question would be asked for all the brands or models of interest to the product manager, and similar questions would be used for the other attributes. There are variations in the way the question could be asked as well as in the number of scale points used, but this is a typical format.

FIGURE 6–15 Bank Perceptual Map

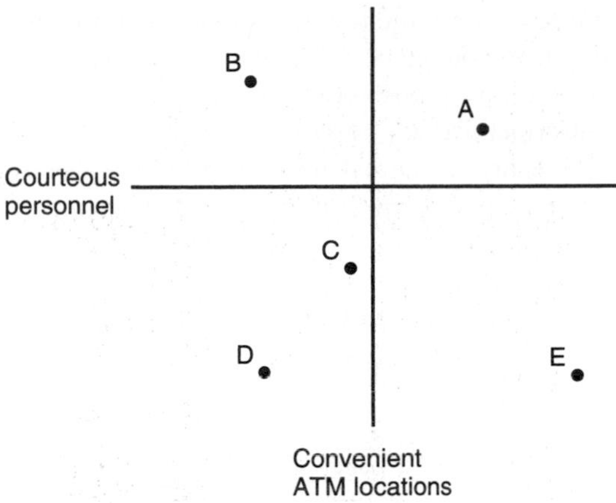

An indirect approach to determining perceptions uses a marketing research methodology called *multidimensional scaling* (also referred to as *perceptual mapping*). This method provides a spatial representation of the brands in a product category based on customers' perceptions of similarity (or dissimilarity, depending on the exact method used). The characteristics used to differentiate customers' perceptions of the brands are inferred from their relative locations in the product space. The perceptions of the characteristics are inferred from their positions along the axes in the space (see Figure 3–11 for an example of multidimensional scaling).

As an example, suppose a bank manager is interested in better understanding customers' perceptions of the five retail (consumer) banks in a city. The manager would first enlist a sample of respondents, perhaps 100. The task could take several forms. One approach is to take all the possible pairs of the five banks (10) and ask each respondent to rate on some scale—say, 1 to 7, with 7 being the most similar—how similar each pair is. A computer program[24] would then be used to locate the banks in a multidimensional space such that the number of dimensions was as small as possible but that also replicated the implied perceptual distances between the banks. Figure 6–15 shows a representative output of such a program.

Each bank is represented by a point in the two-dimensional space. The distances between the points closely replicate the information given by the respondents. For example, banks B and E are the farthest apart in the space. This means that across all the respondents, those two banks were perceived to be the most dissimilar. The labels on the two axes (the attributes) could be determined by two methods: judgmentally based on the manager's knowledge of the market, or estimated based on other

[24]Several widely available computer programs for multidimensional scaling exist, such as SAS's ALSCAL.

information collected from the respondents. The map leads to two major implications. First, the two key characteristics used by bank customers in this city are the courtesy of the personnel and the convenience of the locations of the automated teller machines (ATMs). Second, the perceived performance of the banks on those attributes differs. Bank E is perceived to have the surliest personnel, and bank D has the most convenient ATM locations.

Thus, perceptual mapping can give useful information about both the characteristics being used in assessing perceived similarities and dissimilarities among products and perceptions of the products on those characteristics. It is not generally thought of as a substitute for direct questioning, but it can provide useful supplemental information. Although perceptual mapping can be done for each respondent individually, it is more useful to perform the analysis segment by segment.

Importance Weights. Like the product attribute ratings, attribute importance weights can be assessed through direct questioning. Returning to the notebook computer example, a sample question could be the following: "On a 1 to 7 scale with 7 being very important, how important is weight in your purchase decision?" The same question would then be asked on the other attributes, such as speed of the microprocessor, screen viewing characteristics, and so on. The respondent could also be asked to rank order the attributes in terms of importance.

An alternative approach is to use a popular marketing research technique called *conjoint analysis.* This method permits the product manager to infer the importance of different product attributes from customer rank orderings of alternative product bundles of attributes.

As an example, assume there are three important attributes in a notebook/subnotebook computer purchase decision: weight, battery life, and brand name.[25] The product manager would like to determine the relative importance of the three attributes for product development and communications decisions. Assume also that each characteristic can have two different levels or values, as shown in Figure 6–16. The respondent's task is to rank order the eight combinations from the most preferred to the least preferred.

In Figure 6–16, a hypothetical response to the rank ordering task gives a 1 to the most preferred combination and an 8 to the least preferred. One combination (3 pounds, 4 hours, and a Compaq) clearly dominates, and another (5 pounds, 2 hours, and a Gateway) is clearly the least preferred. However, trade-offs must be made for the combinations of attributes between those two options. In this case, the average rank for the 3-pound options is 2.5 ([1 + 2 + 3 + 4]/4); for the 5-pound options, 6.5; for the 4-hour options, 4.0; for the 2-hour option, 5.0; for the Compaq, 3.5; and for Gateway, 5.5. Looking at the differences in the average ranks, the most important characteristic to this respondent is weight (difference = 4.0), followed by the the brand name (2.0) and finally battery life (1.0). While the actual analysis and design of studies are obviously

[25]For a more complete illustration of conjoint analysis, see Paul E. Green and Yoram Wind, "New Way to Measure Consumers' Judgments," *Harvard Business Review,* July–August 1975, pp. 107–17.

FIGURE 6–16 Conjoint Analysis: Notebook Computers

Assume 3 attributes of laptop computer choice:
Weight (3 pounds or 5 pounds)
Battery life (2 hours or 4 hours)
Brand Name (Gateway, Compaq)
Task: Rank order the following combinations of these characteristics from 1 = Most preferred to 8 = Least preferred

Combination	*Rank*
3 pounds, 2 hours, Gateway	4
5 pounds, 4 hours, Compaq	5
5 pounds, 2 hours, Gateway	8
3 pounds, 4 hours, Gateway	3
3 pounds, 2 hours, Compaq	2
5 pounds, 4 hours, Gateway	7
5 pounds, 2 hours, Compaq	6
3 pounds, 4 hours, Compaq	1

more complicated than this one, the basic ideas are the same. This analysis can be done at the individual level, but generally it is more useful when conducted at the segment level.[26]

An example of how importance weights can vary by market segment is shown in Figure 6–17 for the personal computer market. As can be seen, there is a dramatic difference in the rankings of the attributes when comparing the attributes/benefits among home users, information systems (IS) professionals, and managers. Note also how price, commonly thought to always be the most important attribute, is way down the list for IS professionals and not even on the lists for the home and manager users.

Rules for Combining the Information. The most common way to combine attribute information is to use a *compensatory* rule, which simply multiplies each attribute importance weight by the attribute value and sums all the attributes for each person and product. Figure 6–18 demonstrates this process for one product at the market segment level. It assumes each market segment has an average perceived value for each product attribute and importance weight. The product of importance weight times rating is simply summed down each column of the table to get a score for each segment. A separate table should be constructed for each competing brand.

However, it is possible that the compensatory rule is incorrect. Although it is difficult to determine the correct combination rule, if the implied ranking of the brands from the algebraic combination of importance weights and attribute perceptions does not generally match the rank order of market shares, other rules may be in effect.[27] For

[26]Clearly, conjoint analysis has uses other than estimating relative importances of the characteristics. Some of them are new-product design and estimating price sensitivity, among many others.

[27]Of course, there are other explanations, such as a dominated brand being a more effective marketer in terms of distribution. Many of the brands rated highly by *Consumer Reports* do not have the highest market shares in their categories.

FIGURE 6–17 Importance Weight Variation by Segment

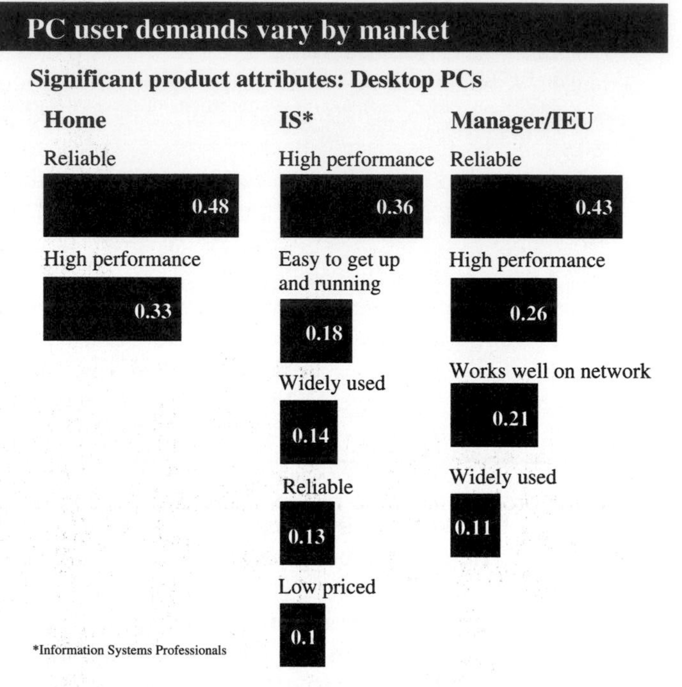

Source: *Brandweek,* December 5, 1994, p. 21. © 1994 ASM Communications, Inc. Used with permission.

FIGURE 6–18 Multiattribute Decision Making: Compensatory Rule

	Segment 1	*Segment 2*	*Segment 3*
Attribute A	Weight × Rating = Score_{1a}		
Attribute B	Score_{1b}		
Attribute C	Score_{1c}		
Attribute D	Score_{1d}		
Attribute E	Score_{1e}		
Segment Score	$\text{Score}_{1a} + \ldots + \text{Score}_{1e}$		

example, a *lexicographic* rule compares all products on the most important characteristic alone. A *conjunctive* rule assumes the customer sets minimum cutoffs on each dimension and rejects a product if it has any characteristic below the cutoff.

From the product manager's perspective, it is important to understand how the information is being combined. A compensatory rule implies that all attributes are being considered and that weakness in one can be compensated for (hence the name of the rule) by strength in another. However, the conjunctive rule is not compensatory at all, so weakness on one dimension may rule out purchasing by many customers.

Customers as Problem Solvers

Customers can be described in terms of the difficulty of the problem they are attempting to solve.[28] In extensive problem-solving (EPS) situations, customers are concerned mainly with understanding how the product works, what it competes with, and how they would use it. EPS is generally found among first-time purchasers and with products that are technologically new. Limited problem solving (LPS) occurs when the customer understands the basic functioning of the product and what it competes with, and is concerned with evaluating the brand on a small number of attributes, typically in comparison to alternatives. This is generally the approach to most large-ticket purchases when the customer has made purchases in the category before (e.g., consumer durables). The third basic type of purchase is routinized (RRB). In this stage, customers essentially follow a predetermined rule for making decisions. Most routine order purchases fall into this category, but so do many big-ticket items (e.g., some people always buy a Volvo). Since customers who follow this approach can be expected to ignore most information because they have already reached a decision, the implications for marketing strategy are dramatic. Product managers with a winning product that is bought routinely should make it easy for the customer to keep buying. If the product has little market share and the objective is to increase it, the product manager must "shock" the customer into considering the product to break him or her of the routine. Promotions, significant price breaks, and free samples are useful shock devices.

Why They Prefer a Product: Customer Value

The fourth component of the customer analysis examines why customers make purchase decisions. Central to this question is the concept of *customer value:* what the product is worth to the customer. Customer value thus depends on the benefits offered (from the customer's perspective) and the costs involved (price, maintenance, etc.). The concept of value is very different from cost: An item costing only pennies to produce may be worth thousands of dollars if it solves an important problem in a timely and efficient manner, and a product that is expensive to produce may have little value. Knowing the value customers place on a product makes it much easier to make various key decisions such as setting price (see Chapter 13).

The customer value of a brand is composed of three basic elements:

1. Importance of the usage situation.
2. Effectiveness of the product category in the situation.
3. Relative effectiveness of the brand in the situation.

Thus, customer value involves two basic notions of value: *absolute* value, which essentially assumes no competing brand exists (points 1 and 2 above) and *relative*

[28]See Howard, *Consumer Behavior in Marketing Strategy.*

value, which involves comparison of the brand with other brands. Because new markets eventually attract competitors, it is the relative effectiveness of a brand that determines its eventual share and profitability. Put differently, customer value encompasses both product form and product category competitors. It is therefore important to determine not only the usage situations for which the product category has value but also how various competitive products compare (e.g., most chemical product categories in which brand formulations vary eventually are chosen based on physical properties such as rigidity and stability under different temperatures).

Sources of Customer Value

Functional Characteristics. Knowing the total value of a brand is useful for both entry/exit and pricing decisions, but understanding the components of the product that produce its value is also important. Functional value is defined by considering those aspects of a product that provide functional or utilitarian benefits to customers. In other words, value is provided by the performance features of a product (e.g., luggage capacity, fuel economy) and not by any psychological or benefit-based characteristics.

Service. Much criticism has been leveled at the quality of some products made in the United States. This criticism encompasses two main thrusts: The functional attributes are at low levels and unreliable, and the other aspects of the product, specifically service, have been neglected. Customers derive value from three kinds of service. Before-sales service involves providing information. Time-of-sales service facilitates purchase, such as reliable and fast delivery, installation and startup, and convenient financial terms. After-sales service involves providing both routine and emergency maintenance. Nothing is more likely to cement a long-term customer relationship than speedy and effective reaction to a problem or more apt to destroy one than a slow and bureaucratic response. Monitoring service quality has (appropriately) become a much more important activity. More will be said about customer service in Chapter 15.

Image. A third source of value is the image of the product. This includes how the product "feels" (e.g., sporty, luxurious, high-tech) and whether that feeling matches the image the customer wants to project. Price is clearly part of product image; some customers may prefer a high price (either because they view price as a signal of quality or to engage in conspicuous consumption), whereas others prefer a low price. The importance of image (as opposed to functional attributes) was highlighted by adverse reaction to Coke's formula change (even though it was preferred in blind taste tests) and the strong positive reaction to the reintroduction of Classic Coca-Cola.

Brand Equity. Recently, partly inspired by a wave of corporate takeovers, the value of the brand name per se has received much attention.[29] Brand equity is the value of a product to a customer *beyond* that explainable by functional, service, and image

[29]See David A. Aaker, *Managing Brand Equity* (New York: The Free Press, 1991), and David A. Aaker, *Building Strong Brands* (New York: The Free Press, 1996).

attributes. It can be represented by the premium a customer would pay for one product over another when those three sets of attributes are identical.

Manifestations of Customer Value

While all products presumably have some value, a variety of signs of the value of a product are evident even without special efforts to measure them:

- *Price.* Price is the company's assessment of the product's value.
- *Price sensitivity.* A product with constant sales when prices increase generally is of greater value than one for which demand slumps.
- *Satisfaction.* Survey-based satisfaction measures are standard practice in my businesses (e.g., course evaluations).
- *Complaints and compliments.* The number of complaints or compliments the company receives indicates the product's value.
- *Word of mouth.* Although difficult to measure, spoken comments provide a useful subjective assessment of a product's value.
- *Margin/profit contribution.* Generally, higher margins indicate partially monopolistic positions due to greater communicated value.
- *Dollar sales.* Total dollar sales provide an aggregate measure of the value of a product as assessed by the market.
- *Competitive activity.* Competitive activity such as new-product introductions indicates that the total gap between customer value and company costs is sufficiently large to allow for profits even when more companies divide the market.
- *Repeat purchase rate.* High loyalty indicates high brand value.

Assessing the Value of the Product Category

Many ways can be devised to estimate the value of a product category. One particularly useful method focuses on the value of different uses or applications of a product.

1. Determine the uses of the product. Like the value-in-use approach discussed in Chapter 3 on generating generic competitors, a first step is to determine the present and potential uses to which a particular product category can be put.
2. Estimate the importance of the uses. This estimate could focus on individual customers or market segments and may simply be projected sales to the segment.
3. List the competing products for the uses.
4. Determine the relative effectiveness of the product category in each usage situation.

The value of the product category (VPC) is then indicated by the sum over all uses of the importance of the use times the relative effectiveness of the product category:

$$VPC = \Sigma\,(Importance) \times (Relative\ effectiveness).$$

FIGURE 6–19 Microcomputer Product Category Value Estimation

Use	*(IMP) Importance*	*Competitive Products*	*(REL) Relative Effectiveness*	*Category Value (IMP) × (REL)*
Video games	Some 20	TV attachments, board games	Very good	High
Bookkeeping	None 1	Accountant, service bureau, "books"	Marginal	Low
Learning skills	Very low 4	Books, school	Inferior	Low
Data analysis	Large 65	Large-scale computer, time sharing, consultant, calculator	Good	High
Report preparation	A little 10 (total 100)	Typewriter, word processor, secretarial service	OK	Fairly low

More important than the total VPC, however, is the relative effectiveness of the product category for each usage situation, since this generally defines separate markets.

A hypothetical example of this approach, based on the microcomputer industry, appears in Figure 6–19. Rather than using numbers, this scale uses adjectives. A numerical system is better, but only after the analysis has been performed on enough product categories to know which numbers are good and which are not. It should be noted that although it is fairly easy to structure the table in Figure 6–19, some of the entries will be hard to quantify. However, it is obvious that the value of the exercise is to generate broad indicators toward which particular uses of the microcomputer should be targeted.

Where Customers Buy

An analysis of where customers make purchase decisions is a critical input into decisions about the channels of distribution (see Chapter 13). Many product managers think of channels as being fixed and traditional; this is a big mistake, because customers migrate to other channels as their information needs and other market conditions change.

Take, for example, the home stereo market. During the 1960s, consumers started replacing consoles (the turntable, tuner, and amplifier housed in what looks like a piece of furniture) with stereo components. The locus of purchase was mainly small stereo stores and some mail-order firms. Today most of these purchases occur in electronics superstores such as Circuit City.

Why did this happen? Several important changes occurred. First, consumers' need for information has diminished over time. The component system is no longer a novelty; most people today are not buying their first system but upgrading an old one. Media such as *Consumer Reports* provide excellent information on features and quality. Thus, whereas customers relied on salespeople for technical information and product comparisons in the 1960s, the Circuit City salesperson merely indicates what is on sale and whether it is in stock. In addition, more products are available, which has brought down margins. Only large-volume retailers can prosper in such a pricing environment.

A similar picture is emerging in personal computers. The small computer retailers have given way to large hardware and software superstores such as CompUSA, specialized software discounters such as Egghead, and huge mail-order firms such as Dell and Gateway 2000.

Therefore, tracking trends in where customers are making purchases is very important. Part of the phenomenon of moving from specialty retailer to discounter is due to the traditional migration of channels and may be predictable. However, the timing of that migration is uncertain. In addition, new technologies for shopping emerge. Witness the growth in shopping via cable TV on home-shopping channels and the potential growth on the Internet.

When Customers Buy

The final dimension to understanding customers is the timing issue. When they buy encompasses time of year, time of month, and even, potentially, time of day. Fast-food operators, for example, are known to segment by "daypart," that is, breakfast, lunch, dinner, and even snacking times. *When* can also include when customers buy in terms of sales or price breaks and rebates, on the assumption that those who buy because of a special deal may be different than those who pay full price, as well as seasonal sales patterns.

Some sales variation is predictable due to the nature of the product. Snowblower sales to end users are most likely to be highest during winter or in late fall; sales to channels will occur earlier. Capital equipment sales are often made near the end of a fiscal year to spend money that may not be there next year. However, as noted in Chapter 4, highly seasonal categories are unattractive due to the pressures placed on manufacturing, personnel, and cash flow. Thus, competitors in such categories look for ways to even out demand as much as possible. For example, cold remedies are marketed well before the major cold seasons to get households to stock up and lock out competing brands. Such timing trends must be watched closely.

Illustrations

RTD Fruit Drinks

Who Are the Customers? Descriptive data on the RTD customers were obtained from Mediamark Research, Inc.'s spring 1994 report. Demographics by usage volume are shown in Figure 6–20, and a comparison of Ocean Spray and Snapple's segments appears in Figure 6–21.

Figure 6–20 RTD Fruit Drinks

		GLASSES/AVERAGE DAY														
		ALL				HEAVY MORE THAN 3				MEDIUM 2–3				LIGHT LESS THAN 2		
	TOTAL U.S.	A	B %	C %	D	A	B %	C %	D	A	B %	C %	D	A	B %	C %	D
BASE: FEMALE HOMEMAKERS	'000	'000	DOWN	ACROSS	INDEX	'000	DOWN	ACROSS	INDEX	'000	DOWN	ACROSS	INDEX	'000	DOWN	ACROSS	INDEX
All Female Homemakers	86474	**45066**	100.0	52.1	100	**11974**	100.0	13.8	100	**12362**	100.0	14.3	**100**	20729	100.0	24.0	100
Women	86474	**45066**	100.0	52.1	100	**11974**	100.0	13.8	100	**12362**	100.0	14.3	**100**	20729	100.0	24.0	100
Household Heads	35551	**16974**	37.7	47.7	92	**3976**	33.2	11.2	81	**4829**	39.1	13.6	**95**	8169	39.4	23.0	96
Homemakers	86474	**45066**	100.0	52.1	100	**11974**	100.0	13.8	100	**12362**	100.0	14.3	**100**	20729	100.0	24.0	100
Graduated College	15478	**8326**	18.5	53.8	103	**2015**	16.8	13.0	94	**2364**	19.1	15.3	**107**	3947	19.0	25.5	106
Attended College	20440	**11508**	25.5	56.3	108	**2874**	24.0	14.1	102	**3225**	26.1	15.8	**110**	5409	26.1	26.5	110
Graduated High School	32802	**17302**	38.4	52.7	101	**4771**	39.8	14.5	105	**4630**	37.5	14.1	**99**	7902	38.1	24.1	100
Did not Graduate High School	17755	**7928**	17.6	44.7	86	**2314**	19.3	13.0	94	**2143**	17.3	12.1	**84**	3471	16.7	19.5	82
18–24	7578	**3910**	8.7	51.6	99	**1057**	8.8	13.9	101	**1021**	8.3	13.5	**94**	1832	8.8	24.2	101
25–34	19632	**11407**	25.3	58.1	111	**3801**	31.7	19.4	140	**3228**	26.1	16.4	**115**	4379	21.1	22.3	93
35–44	18954	**10779**	23.9	56.9	109	**3475**	29.0	18.3	132	**2917**	23.6	15.4	**108**	4387	21.2	23.1	97
45–54	13220	**7264**	16.1	54.9	105	**1717**	14.3	13.0	94	**1959**	15.8	14.8	**104**	3588	17.3	27.1	113
55–64	10669	**4789**	10.6	44.9	86	**1094**	9.1	10.3	74	**1084**	8.8	10.2	**71**	2611	12.6	24.5	102
65 or over	16421	**6915**	15.3	42.1	81	**830**	6.9	5.1	37	**2153**	17.4	13.1	**92**	3932	19.0	23.9	100
18–34	27211	**15318**	34.0	56.3	108	**4858**	40.6	17.9	129	**4248**	34.4	15.6	**109**	6211	30.0	22.8	95
18–49	53395	**30336**	67.3	56.8	109	**9235**	77.1	17.3	125	**8330**	67.4	15.6	**109**	12772	61.6	23.9	100
25–54	51806	**29451**	65.4	56.8	109	**8993**	75.1	17.4	125	**8104**	65.6	15.6	**109**	12354	59.6	23.8	99
Employed Full Time	37988	**20093**	44.6	52.9	101	**4873**	40.7	12.8	93	**5695**	46.1	15.0	**105**	9526	46.0	25.1	105
Part-time	9424	**5358**	11.9	56.9	109	**1733**	14.5	18.4	133	**1566**	12.7	16.6	**116**	2058	9.9	21.8	91
Sole Wage Earner	12125	**5805**	12.9	47.9	92	**1483**	12.4	12.2	88	**1489**	12.0	12.3	**86**	2833	13.7	23.4	97
Not Employed	39062	**19615**	43.5	50.2	96	**5368**	44.8	13.7	99	**5101**	41.3	13.1	**91**	9146	44.1	23.4	98
Professional	8012	**4441**	9.9	55.4	106	**1208**	10.1	15.1	109	**1371**	11.1	17.1	**120**	1862	9.0	23.2	97
Executive/Admin./Managerial	6082	**3380**	7.5	55.6	107	**869**	7.3	14.3	103	**767**	6.2	12.6	**88**	1744	8.4	28.7	120
Clerical/Sales/Technical	20370	**10974**	24.4	53.9	103	**2649**	22.1	13.0	94	**3152**	25.5	15.5	**108**	5173	25.0	25.4	106
Precision/Crafts/Repair	1059	**512**	1.1	48.3	93	***130**	1.1	12.3	89	***195**	1.6	18.4	**129**	*187	.9	17.7	74
Other Employed	11890	**6144**	13.6	51.7	99	**1750**	14.6	14.7	106	**1776**	14.4	14.9	**104**	2618	12.6	22.0	92
H/D Income $75,000 or More	10095	**5319**	11.8	52.7	101	**1200**	10.0	11.9	86	**1446**	11.7	14.3	**100**	2673	12.9	26.5	110
$60,000–74,999	6870	**4068**	9.0	59.2	114	**1199**	10.0	17.5	126	**1134**	9.2	16.5	**115**	1735	8.4	25.3	105
$50,000–59,999	7349	**3864**	8.6	52.6	101	**921**	7.7	12.5	91	**1154**	9.3	15.7	**110**	1788	8.6	24.3	101
$40,000–49,999	9587	**5633**	12.5	58.8	113	**1354**	11.3	14.1	102	**1743**	14.1	18.2	**127**	2536	12.2	26.5	110
$30,000–39,999	11920	**6741**	15.0	56.6	109	**2100**	17.5	17.6	127	**1708**	13.8	14.3	**100**	2934	14.2	24.6	103
$20,000–29,999	14082	**7264**	16.1	51.6	99	**1790**	14.9	12.7	92	**1755**	14.2	12.5	**87**	3719	17.9	26.4	110
$10,000–19,999	14661	**6690**	14.8	45.6	88	**1627**	13.6	11.1	80	**2050**	16.6	14.0	**98**	3013	14.5	20.6	86
Less than $10,000	11910	**5487**	12.2	46.1	88	**1784**	14.9	15.0	108	**1373**	11.1	11.5	**81**	2330	11.2	19.6	82
Census Region: North East	18002	**10168**	22.6	56.5	108	**3080**	25.7	17.1	124	**2680**	21.7	14.9	**104**	4408	21.3	24.5	102
North Central	20735	**11616**	25.8	56.0	107	**3100**	25.9	15.0	108	**3041**	24.6	14.7	**103**	5476	26.4	26.4	110
South	30561	**13729**	30.5	44.9	86	**3551**	29.7	11.6	84	**4142**	33.5	13.6	**95**	6036	29.1	19.8	82
West	17176	**9553**	21.2	55.6	107	**2243**	18.7	13.1	94	**2499**	20.2	14.5	**102**	4810	23.2	28.0	117
Marketing Reg.: New England	4677	**2858**	6.3	61.1	117	**1018**	8.5	21.8	157	**739**	6.0	15.8	**111**	1100	5.3	23.5	98
Middle Atlantic	15145	**8216**	18.2	54.2	104	**2389**	20.0	15.8	114	**2217**	17.9	14.6	**102**	3610	17.4	23.8	99
East Central	11962	**6760**	15.0	56.5	108	**1855**	15.5	15.5	112	**1851**	15.0	15.5	**108**	3053	14.7	25.5	106
West Central	13278	**7379**	16.4	55.6	107	**1825**	15.2	13.7	99	**1968**	15.9	14.8	**104**	3585	17.3	27.0	113
South East	16710	**7105**	15.8	42.5	82	**1835**	15.3	11.0	79	**1926**	15.6	11.5	**81**	3344	16.1	20.0	83

South West	9667	**4426**	9.8	45.8	88	**1112**	9.2	11.4	82	**1400**	11.3	14.5	**101**	1924	9.3	19.9	83
Pacific	15035	**8322**	18.5	55.4	106	**1949**	16.3	13.0	94	**2260**	18.3	15.0	**105**	4113	19.8	27.4	114
County Size A	34913	**18913**	42.0	54.2	104	**5089**	42.1	14.4	104	**5116**	41.4	14.7	**103**	8759	42.3	25.1	105
County Size B	25829	**13843**	30.7	53.6	103	**3773**	31.5	14.6	105	**4012**	32.5	15.5	**109**	6058	29.2	23.5	98
County Size C	12476	**5957**	13.2	47.7	92	**1656**	13.9	13.4	96	**1506**	12.2	12.1	**84**	2785	13.4	22.3	93
County Size D	13256	**6352**	14.1	47.9	92	**1447**	12.5	11.3	82	**1727**	14.0	13.0	**91**	3128	15.1	23.6	98
MSA Central City	30912	**15610**	34.6	50.5	97	**3975**	33.2	12.9	93	**4392**	35.5	14.2	**99**	7243	34.9	23.4	98
MSA Suburban	36298	**20346**	45.1	56.1	108	**5731**	47.6	15.7	113	**5601**	45.3	15.4	**108**	9044	43.6	24.9	104
Non-MSA	19264	**9110**	20.2	47.3	91	**2238**	19.2	11.9	86	**2369**	19.2	12.3	**86**	4442	21.4	23.1	96
Single	12608	**6400**	14.2	50.8	97	**1716**	14.3	13.6	98	**1710**	13.8	13.6	**95**	2975	14.4	23.6	98
Married	51692	**28484**	63.2	55.1	106	**8138**	68.5	15.9	115	**7587**	61.4	14.7	**103**	12698	61.3	24.6	102
Other	22175	**10182**	22.6	45.9	88	**2061**	17.2	9.3	67	**3065**	24.8	13.8	**97**	5056	24.4	22.8	95
Parents	34159	**20767**	46.1	60.8	117	**7831**	65.1	22.8	165	**5690**	46.0	16.7	**117**	7276	35.1	21.3	89
Working Parents	21523	**12928**	28.7	60.1	115	**4546**	38.0	21.1	153	**3761**	30.4	17.5	**122**	4620	22.3	21.5	90
Household Size: 1 Person	14545	**6116**	13.6	42.0	81	**753**	6.3	5.2	37	**1633**	13.2	11.2	**79**	3730	18.0	25.6	107
2 Persons	26910	**12621**	28.0	46.9	90	**2028**	16.9	7.5	54	**3563**	28.8	13.2	**93**	7029	33.9	26.1	109
3 or More	45020	**26329**	58.4	58.5	112	**9133**	76.8	20.4	147	**7166**	58.0	15.9	**111**	9970	48.1	22.1	92
Any Child in Household	37210	**22234**	49.3	59.8	115	**8432**	70.2	22.6	163	**6111**	49.4	16.4	**115**	7721	37.2	20.7	87
Under 2 Years	7801	**4849**	10.8	62.2	119	**1830**	15.0	23.1	167	**1288**	10.4	16.5	**115**	1762	8.5	22.6	94
2–5 Years	15245	**9451**	21.0	62.0	119	**4232**	35.8	28.2	203	**2330**	18.8	15.3	**107**	2829	13.6	18.6	77
6–11 Years	17131	**10177**	22.6	59.4	114	**4138**	34.3	24.0	173	**2657**	21.5	15.5	**108**	3412	16.5	19.9	83
12–17 Years	15418	**9007**	20.0	58.4	112	**3235**	26.8	20.8	150	**2591**	21.0	16.8	**118**	3211	15.5	20.8	87
White	74214	**38961**	86.5	52.5	101	**9731**	81.3	13.1	95	**10622**	85.9	14.3	**100**	18606	89.8	25.1	105
Black	9630	**4770**	10.6	49.5	95	**1872**	15.6	19.4	140	**1326**	10.7	13.8	**96**	1573	7.6	16.3	68
Spanish Speaking	5328	**2496**	5.5	46.8	90	**756**	6.4	14.4	104	**583**	4.7	10.9	**77**	1147	5.5	21.5	90
Home Owned	57985	**30774**	68.3	53.1	102	**7847**	65.5	13.5	98	**8674**	70.2	15.0	**105**	14252	68.8	24.6	103
Daily Newspapers: Read Any	48473	**25311**	56.2	52.2	100	**6513**	54.4	13.4	97	**7091**	57.4	14.6	**102**	11707	56.5	24.2	101
Read One Daily	40398	**21166**	47.0	52.4	101	**5348**	45.0	13.3	96	**5918**	47.9	14.6	**102**	9860	47.6	24.4	102
Read Two or More Dailies	8075	**4146**	9.2	51.3	99	**1125**	9.4	13.9	101	**1174**	9.5	14.5	**102**	1847	8.9	22.9	95
Sunday Newspapers: Read Any	58565	**31528**	70.0	53.8	103	**8346**	69.4	14.2	102	**8988**	72.7	15.3	**107**	14234	68.7	24.3	101
Read One Sunday	52047	**27891**	61.9	53.6	103	**7312**	61.3	14.1	102	**7948**	64.3	15.3	**107**	12601	60.8	24.2	101
Read Two or More Sundays	6518	**3637**	8.1	55.8	107	**954**	8.1	14.8	107	**1040**	8.4	16.0	**112**	1633	7.9	25.1	105
Quintile I - Outdoor	16907	**9003**	20.0	53.3	102	**2471**	20.6	14.6	106	**2340**	18.9	13.8	**97**	4193	20.2	24.8	103
Quintile II	17393	**9399**	20.9	54.0	104	**2325**	19.4	13.4	97	**2755**	22.3	15.8	**111**	4319	20.8	24.8	104
Quintile III	17429	**9303**	20.6	53.4	102	**2325**	19.4	13.3	96	**2816**	22.8	16.2	**113**	4162	20.1	23.9	100
Quintile IV	17410	**8720**	19.3	50.1	96	**2571**	21.5	14.8	107	**2333**	18.9	13.4	**94**	3815	18.4	21.9	91
Quintile V	17335	**8640**	19.2	49.8	96	**2213**	19.1	13.2	95	**2118**	17.1	12.2	**85**	4240	20.5	24.5	102
Quintile I - Magazines	16484	**8945**	19.8	54.3	104	**2939**	24.5	17.8	129	**2483**	20.1	15.1	**105**	3523	17.0	21.4	89
Quintile II	17363	**9411**	20.9	54.2	104	**2471**	20.6	14.2	103	**2465**	19.9	14.2	**99**	4474	21.6	25.8	107
Quintile III	17533	**9053**	20.1	51.6	99	**2470**	20.6	14.1	102	**2573**	20.8	14.7	**103**	4010	19.3	22.9	95
Quintile IV	17505	**8900**	19.7	50.8	98	**2015**	17.4	11.9	86	**2473**	20.0	14.1	**99**	4342	20.9	24.8	103
Quintile V	17590	**8756**	19.4	49.8	96	**2049**	15.8	11.4	82	**2367**	19.1	13.5	**94**	4380	21.1	24.9	104
Quintile I - Newspapers	17144	**8989**	19.9	52.4	101	**2447**	20.1	14.0	101	**2522**	20.4	14.7	**103**	4059	19.6	23.7	99
Quintile II	17420	**8947**	19.9	51.4	99	**2041**	17.5	12.0	87	**2533**	20.5	14.5	**102**	4323	20.9	24.8	104
Quintile III	17221	**9216**	20.5	53.5	103	**2673**	22.3	15.5	112	**2399**	19.4	13.9	**97**	4143	20.0	24.1	100
Quintile IV	17454	**9326**	20.7	53.4	103	**2426**	20.3	13.9	100	**2916**	23.6	16.7	**117**	3984	19.2	22.8	95
Quintile V	17236	**8588**	19.1	49.8	96	**2377**	19.9	13.8	100	**1991**	16.1	11.6	**81**	4220	20.4	24.5	102
Quintile I - Radio	16686	**9010**	20.0	54.0	104	**2669**	22.3	16.0	116	**2465**	19.9	14.8	**103**	3875	18.7	23.2	97
Quintile II	17211	**9198**	20.4	53.4	103	**2570**	21.5	14.9	108	**2497**	20.2	14.5	**101**	4131	19.9	24.0	100
Quintile III	17235	**8990**	19.9	52.2	100	**2254**	18.8	13.1	94	**2505**	20.3	14.5	**102**	4231	20.4	24.5	102
Quintile IV	17724	**9423**	20.9	53.2	102	**2645**	22.1	14.9	108	**2548**	20.6	14.4	**101**	4231	20.4	23.9	100
Quintile V	17618	**8445**	18.7	47.9	92	**1836**	15.3	10.4	75	**2346**	19.0	13.3	**93**	4262	20.6	24.2	101

Source: *Mediamark Research Beverages Report,* Spring 1994, p. 254.

FIGURE 6–21 RTD Fruit Drinks: by Brand

	TOTAL U.S.	SNAPPLE A	B	C	D	OCEAN SPRAY A	B	C	D
BASE: FEMALE HOMEMAKERS	'000	'000	% DOWN	% ACROSS	INDEX	'000	% DOWN	% ACROSS	INDEX
All Female Homemakers	86474	3310	100.0	3.8	100	12340	100.0	14.3	100
Women	86474	3310	100.0	3.8	100	12340	100.0	14.3	100
Household Heads	35551	1272	38.4	3.6	93	5163	41.8	14.5	102
Homemakers	86474	3310	100.0	3.8	100	12340	100.0	14.3	100
Graduated College	15478	789	23.8	5.1	133	2568	20.8	16.6	116
Attended College	20440	962	29.1	4.7	123	3296	26.7	16.1	113
Graduated High School	32802	1120	33.8	3.4	89	4943	40.1	15.1	106
Did not Graduate High School	17755	*438	13.2	2.5	64	1533	12.4	8.6	61
18–24	7578	*426	12.9	5.6	147	772	6.3	10.2	71
25–34	19632	960	29.0	4.9	128	2334	18.9	11.9	83
35–44	18954	842	25.4	4.4	116	2512	20.4	13.3	93
45–54	13220	695	21.0	5.3	137	2451	19.9	18.5	130
55–64	10669	*221	6.7	2.1	54	1669	13.5	15.6	110
65 or over	16421	*166	5.0	1.0	26	2602	21.1	15.8	111
18–34	27211	1385	41.8	5.1	133	3106	25.2	11.4	80
18–49	53395	2650	80.1	5.0	130	7089	57.4	13.3	93
25–54	51806	2497	75.4	4.8	126	7297	59.1	14.1	99
Employed Full Time	37988	1773	53.6	4.7	122	5925	48.0	15.6	109
Part-time	9424	449	13.6	4.8	124	1374	11.1	14.6	102
Sole Wage Earner	12125	595	18.0	4.9	128	1589	12.9	13.1	92
Not Employed	39062	1087	32.8	2.8	73	5041	40.9	12.9	90
Professional	8012	424	12.8	5.3	138	1286	10.4	16.1	112
Executive/Admin./Managerial	6082	*433	13.1	7.1	186	983	8.0	16.2	113
Clerical/Sales/Technical	20370	824	24.9	4.0	106	3120	25.3	15.3	107
Precision/Crafts/Repair	1059	*22	.7	2.1	54	*153	1.2	14.4	101
Other Employed	11890	519	15.7	4.4	114	1757	14.2	14.8	104
H/D Income $75,000 or More	10095	589	17.8	5.8	152	1861	15.1	18.4	129
$60,000–74,999	6870	*383	11.6	5.6	146	1209	9.8	17.6	123
$50,000–59,999	7349	*322	9.7	4.4	114	1223	9.9	16.6	117
$40,000–49,999	9587	375	11.3	3.9	102	1416	11.5	14.8	104
$30,000–39,999	11920	481	14.5	4.0	105	1887	15.3	15.8	111
$20,000–29,999	14082	580	17.5	4.1	108	1853	15.0	13.2	92
$10,000–19,999	14661	*343	10.4	2.3	61	1610	13.0	11.0	77
Less than $10,000	11910	*236	7.1	2.0	52	1281	10.4	10.8	75
Census Region: North East	18002	1043	31.5	5.8	151	3056	24.8	17.0	119
North Central	20735	645	19.5	3.1	81	3143	25.5	15.2	106
South	30561	720	21.8	2.4	62	2945	23.9	9.6	68
West	17176	901	27.2	5.2	137	3196	25.9	18.6	130
Marketing Reg.: New England	4677	*120	3.6	2.6	67	1017	8.2	21.7	152
Middle Atlantic	15145	1002	30.3	6.6	173	2369	19.2	15.6	110
East Central	11962	*394	11.9	3.3	86	1715	13.9	14.3	100
West Central	13278	*348	10.5	2.6	68	2220	18.0	16.7	117
South East	16710	*308	9.3	1.8	48	1413	11.5	8.5	59
South West	9667	*284	8.6	2.9	77	988	8.0	10.2	72
Pacific	15035	853	25.8	5.7	148	2619	21.2	17.4	122
County Size A	34913	1953	59.0	5.6	146	5659	45.9	16.2	114
County Size B	25829	744	22.5	2.9	75	3546	28.7	13.7	96
County Size C	12476	*422	12.7	3.4	88	1709	13.8	13.7	96
County Size D	13256	*190	5.7	1.4	37	1426	11.6	10.8	75
MSA Central City	30912	1410	42.6	4.6	119	4399	35.6	14.2	100
MSA Suburban	36298	1488	45.0	4.1	107	5746	46.6	15.8	111
Non-MSA	19264	*412	12.4	2.1	56	2196	17.8	11.4	80
Single	12608	826	25.0	6.6	171	1697	13.8	13.5	94
Married	51692	1872	56.6	3.6	95	7580	61.4	14.7	103
Other	22175	612	18.5	2.8	72	3063	24.8	13.8	97
Parents	34159	1519	45.9	4.4	116	3871	31.4	11.3	79
Working Parents	21523	1057	31.9	4.9	128	2776	22.5	12.9	90
Household Size: 1 Person	14545	367	11.1	2.5	66	2016	16.3	13.9	97
2 Persons	26910	814	24.6	3.0	79	4316	35.0	16.0	112
3 or More	45020	2128	64.3	4.7	123	6008	48.7	13.3	94
Any Child in Household	37210	1628	49.2	4.4	114	4333	35.1	11.6	82
Under 2 Years	7801	*319	9.6	4.1	107	768	6.2	9.8	69
2–5 Years	15245	525	15.9	3.4	90	1553	12.6	10.2	71
6–11 Years	17131	636	19.2	3.7	97	1748	14.2	10.2	72
12–17 Years	15418	798	24.1	5.2	135	1993	16.2	12.9	91
White	74214	2817	85.1	3.8	99	11033	89.4	14.9	104
Black	9630	*370	11.2	3.8	100	1042	8.4	10.8	76
Spanish Speaking	5328	*248	7.5	4.7	122	629	5.1	11.8	83
Home Owned	57985	2032	61.4	3.5	92	8901	72.1	15.4	108

Source: *Mediamark Research Beverages Report,* Spring 1994, pp. 266–267.

A quick examination of the figures can be done by using the "Index" column, which, following a discussion earlier in this chapter, shows whether a particular row group is behaving greater than (index > 100) or less than (index < 100) the proportion of that group in the population. A heavy user profile is as follows: 25 to 44 years old, the female homemaker is employed part time, moderate family income, New England residents, young children, and black. The Ocean Spray consumer (Figure 6–21) is educated, 45 to 54 years old, professional, upper income, New England/Pacific resident, and a member of a two-person household. The female Snapple consumer is educated, age 18 to 54, is an employed homemaker, an executive/professional, with high income, a Middle Atlantic/Pacific urban resident, and single. An analysis of Simmons Market Research Bureau data (not shown) describes the Fruitopia consumer as 35 to 54 years old, educated, professional, medium-high income, a Midwest/Pacific resident, married with children in larger households, and black. Thus, quite distinct differences exist in the markets for the three brands.

What Are They Buying? Customers usually buy juices because they are thirsty. They drink fruit beverages because of health concerns and they appreciate their natural characteristics compared to soft drinks. They also buy RTD fruit drinks for their convenience. Another point of preference is the fact that RTD drinks usually have wide distribution, which facilitates the purchase. Thus, the main benefits are

- Refreshment.
- Healthiness.
- Natural.
- Convenient to drink.
- Convenient to purchase.

How Do They Buy? Advertising and image are important factors in the purchase decision, along with availability from the strong distribution networks. Supermarket purchases are influenced by price and other in-store promotions. Special displays and contests/sweepstakes are commonly used.

Where Do They Buy? Vending machines close to or in offices and schools are extensively used for RTD fruit drink purchases. Cafés, delicatessens, and small restaurants (e.g., pizza parlors) are also popular. Of course, the most common channels are supermarkets, convenience stores, and warehouse clubs.

When Do They Buy? Since the main purpose of fruit beverages is refreshment, periods of warmer weather exhibit greater sales. Customers usually buy RTD drinks from vending machines during the day while on a break from their work. RTD drinks are also heavily purchased on normal shopping trips.

Personal Digital Assistants

Who Are the Customers? The customers for PDAs are primarily mobile professionals. The current general profile of users is predominantly male, analytical and quantitative in nature, well educated, and over 21 years of age.

Figure 6–22 PDA Market Segments

Segment	Size	Characteristics	Distinctive Attribute
Wide area travelers:			
Globetrotters	10%	Age 45–54; mostly male Employed in senior positions	Innovators, have modems installed in their portable PCs
Road Warriors	20%	Mostly in corporate management and sales, property management and real estate	High cellular phone usage Overall computer usage lower than for other mobile pros
Corporate Wanderers	12%	Travel less than Globetrotters or Road Warriors; spend most time visiting employees within their own companies	Employ portable PCs least Heaviest fax users (on PCs) High e-mail users Longest owners of cellular phones
Local area travelers:			
Collaborators	8%	Age 25–44 Well-educated young professionals, tend to hold advanced degrees Team leaders, project managers	Innovators High use of pagers (20% of segment) Not very mobile but need mobile products
Corridor Cruisers	15%	Similar profile to Collaborators	Not as likely to adopt new products as collaborators
Hermits	8%	Least mobile Youngest segment (many under 35) Seldom work with others Mostly finance and telemarketing	Heavy e-mail users Virtually all are PC users but not portable users
Solo Practitioners	16%	Like Hermits but older Diverse collection of technical professionals in small to medium-size companies	Typically connect to corporate network when traveling Highest connect times of any group
Small-Site Bosses	11%	Run small businesses	Highest portable PC purchase intention in next 12 months; shifting to portable PC as primary computer

Mobile professionals, the key target market, can be segmented using the scheme shown in Figure 6–22. In addition, the buyers in the market for these devices in 1996 would be classified as "early adopters" of new technology. These labels do not help the product manager locate these people, of course. However, early adopters of PDAs probably have a high incidence of purchasing other high-tech consumer products such as personal and laptop computers, home fax machines, cellular phones, and so forth.

What Do They Buy? Buyers and potential buyers of PDAs seek the following features in decreasing order of importance:

- Small size/light weight.
- PC connectivity.
- E-mail communications capability.

- Phone/address book.
- Appointment book/calendar/alarm.
- One-way paging.

Despite the above list, PDAs are valued primarily as organizers and less as communications devices by current users. This implies that two benefit segments are emerging: (1) those who value PDAs solely for their organizer features and (2) a smaller but growing group who value them for communications. As communications capabilities improve, this latter group is likely to grow.

How Do They Buy? Advertising and marketing have not been key influencers in PDA purchase decisions to this point. Current users sought out the devices themselves. Again, this is not unusual for a product at the early stage of the product life cycle. Later users, however, will rely more on information-based advertising and recommendations from colleagues and friends.

Where Do They Buy? Customers buy lower-priced, low-feature devices from consumer electronics stores and office supply superstores (e.g., Office Max, Office Depot). Higher-end PDAs are purchased from computer stores or through mail order.

Summary

Customers are the essential component of a business and analyzing customers is the fundamental task for developing marketing strategy. Customer analysis should be both qualitative and quantitative. As in the case of competitor analysis, however, the value of the analysis depends on the effort put into the analysis, including being systematic, and the insights gleaned from the analysis.

C H A P T E R

7 Market Potential and Forecasting

Overview

A critical part of the background assessment is the specification of key planning assumptions. Often product managers must make assumptions about factors beyond their control. Most of these are environmentally related factors, such as those covered in Chapter 4. For example, the product manager for Lean Cuisine must make assumptions about the likelihood of continuing interest in low-calorie entrées. The product manager for Fuji film must make assumptions about the worldwide supply of silver. Marketing personnel in the home construction business make assumptions about future home mortgage interest rates. Hence many plans list a series of assumptions as a way of summarizing earlier analyses and establishing the basis for potential estimates and forecasts.

In this chapter, we describe methods for thinking about the future results of the marketing plan, namely sales or market share. Two key constructs relevant to results-based marketing planning are *potential* and *forecast*.

Definitions

The terms *potential* and *forecast* are used in many contexts, and they are frequently confused. We use the following definitions:

> *Potential*: The maximum sales reasonably attainable under a given set of conditions within a specified period of time.
>
> *Forecast*: The amount of sales expected to be achieved under a set of conditions within a specified period of time.

Another related term is *quota*. Quotas are set by senior managers and are what an individual in the company, for example a salesperson, is expected to achieve.

Figure 7–1 shows the distinction between potential and forecast in a sales context. The key difference between the concepts is that *potential* represents what *could*

FIGURE 7–1 Forecasts versus Potential

	Expectations	*Possibilities*
Firm/brand	Sales forecast	Sales potential
Category	Market forecast	Market potential

happen in a category if all the competitors (market potential) or the product in question (sales potential) had full distribution, heavy advertising and promotion, and appeal to all the customers who could possibly purchase the product. Alternatively, *forecasts* represent expectations, which could (and usually do) fall far below the potential in a market.

In this chapter, we consider market potential and sales forecasting in a product category context. These concepts can have different meanings depending on how the product manager views the structure of the market. If the product manager believes the market should be defined broadly, this perspective should be incorporated into the analyses.

Market Potential

Overview

Although market potential estimates are often an input to forecasts, they are important in their own right. However, market potential is one of the most difficult concepts in the planning process to grasp. Not only is it difficult to develop a concrete number; it is also hard to conceive of the upper limit or maximum of sales. In addition, based on our earlier definition, although most managers may perceive potential as a fixed number, it is in fact a dynamic concept and can change dramatically over time. The key to understanding this point is the clause "under a given set of conditions within a specified period of time." In other words, market or sales potential can change depending on market factors such as average category price or general economic conditions.

For example, when Texas Instruments introduced its first hand-held calculator, the SR10, which made slide rules largely obsolete, it had four functions (add, subtract, multiply, divide), had no memory, and it cost over $100. Compare that to the calculators of the 1990s; today calculators far better than the SR10 are given away for free as promotions. The market potential of the original calculator was limited to those individuals, usually scientists or college students, who needed to make many math calculations and could afford the price. When the number of functions offered dramatically increased and the price rapidly fell, more people could both use and afford one. Not only did sales increase but so did market potential.

Estimates of potential have several uses. First, estimates can help allocate resources over a product line. A manager may allocate resources to products based on their total market potential, not just according to current sales levels.

Second, estimates can help determine the stage of the product life cycle. Often the product life cycle is used as a tool to help determine different kinds of objectives and strategies. However, the product life cycle measures actual sales of a category over time, not potential sales. This is a critical difference and can lead to myopic decisions, particularly in assessing a mature or saturated market (defined as a market in which sales equal potential). An interesting illustration of the differences between conventional product life cycle thinking and market potential thinking can be found in the running shoe category. In the 1960s, a buyer could get sneakers cut either high or low and in either black or white. The major brands were Keds and Converse. The product life cycle indicated maturity. In the 1970s, the market shot up with the introduction of performance shoes such as Nike, Adidas, and Puma. It became commonplace to wear running shoes to work and then change into work shoes. However, the market again became mature. What happened in the 1980s? Brands such as Reebok and L.A. Gear appealed to segments (e.g., aerobics) and fashion, and again the market jumped. The important point is that maturity is in the eye of the beholder; that is, one product manager's mature market is another's growth market in which growth (actually, potential growth) is defined as the gap between actual sales and market potential. Thus, as many writers have warned,[1] the product life cycle concept must be used carefully.

Third, estimates can help set product objectives. A product's sales gains are limited by the difference between current and potential sales, as well as by market potential.

Fourth, estimates can help sales managers. Market potential (or, more accurately, geographic area potential) can help sales managers in two ways. First, sales territories are often designed to have equal market potential so that different salespersons can be better judged on the basis of actual sales. Second, sales quotas are sometimes set based on the potential sales in a territory.

Fifth, estimates can help develop marketing strategies. As we will discuss later in this chapter, perhaps the most important use of market potential is for the product manager to compare actual to potential sales and ask, "Why is there such a difference?" Often this leads to new uses, new market segments, or other changes in marketing strategy.

Sixth, estimates can help make location decisions. Manufacturing plants, distribution facilities, and retail stores tend to be located based on potential estimates.

Finally, estimates can be an input to forecasts. To construct the market potential figure, product managers must understand various underlying factors in a category, such as who the customers are. These factors can also be used in developing a forecasting model.

Estimating Market and Sales Potential: Basics

Market potential may be estimated in a variety of ways. Clearly, the details involved depend heavily on the particular industry and the product under consideration. This section suggests some general approaches to assessing potential.

---

[1]See, for example, Nariman K. Dhalla and Sonia Yuspeh, "Forget the Product Life Cycle Concept!" *Harvard Business Review,* January–February 1976, pp. 102–12.

FIGURE 7–2 Deriving Potential Estimates

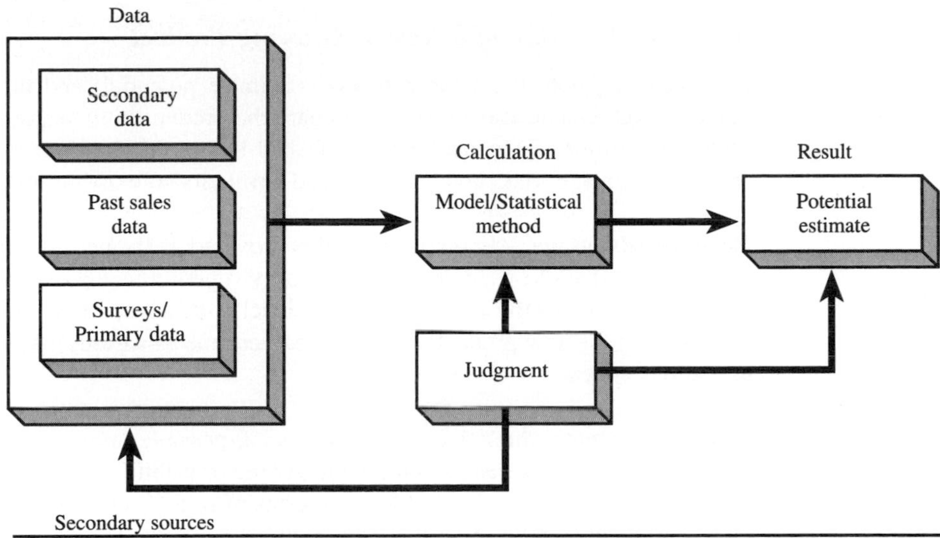

Past sales data are useful, and for a stable market they provide the necessary information for both a potential estimate and a sales forecast. In new markets, however, such data may be unavailable, inaccurate, or unduly influenced by isolated events. Even when such data are available, other data should *not* be ignored.

Figure 7–2 summarizes a general process for deriving potential estimates (which is also useful for forecast development). The exact data collected and calculations used depend on the situation. Some of the sources useful for potential estimates are already familiar to readers.

Government Sources. Market size estimates are available for many industries from sources such as the U.S. Department of Commerce and the Bureau of the Census (e.g., *Survey of Current Business*, *Current Industrial Reports*). Even when specific forecasts for an industry or a product are not available, government data may be useful as inputs to the potential estimate. Examples include breakdowns of industry by location, size, and SIC code and forecasts of general economic conditions.

Trade Associations. These groups are a good source of information for particular industries or product categories, although they may be a bit optimistic.

Private Companies. A number of private companies track and forecast sales for various industries (e.g., FIND/SVP, mentioned in Chapter 5). Some also survey capital spending plans (e.g., McGraw-Hill), consumer sentiment, and durable purchasing plans (e.g., the Survey Research Center at the University of Michigan).

Financial Analysts. Industry specialists often provide forecasts or potential estimates for various industries (e.g., Gartner Group and Dataquest for computers).

Assessing the Value of a New or Growing Product

In considering both the saturation level (ultimate potential) and the time pattern of market development, it is useful to compare the product to its major (and presumably older) competitors. This can be accomplished by considering four major dimensions: relative advantage, risk, compatibility, and similarity to existing products.

Relative Advantage. In terms of benefits provided, is the new product superior in all respects and, if so, to what degree? Noticeably superior benefits will increase both the saturation level and the rate at which the level is achieved. Also, in general, relative advantage of the new product will increase over time as various modifications and line extensions appear.

Risk. The greater the risk involved (financial, possible impact on product quality if a new component fails, and so on), the lower the probability that someone will buy the new product. Typically, risk—at least in terms of price—tends to drop over time, thus increasing the potential.

Compatibility. The fewer and less important the changes required to adopt a new product, the faster it will be adopted. Compatibility issues relate not only to customers but also to intermediaries, the company itself (e.g., sales staff), and, if customers use a certain product as a component in another product, their customers as well. Therefore, if a chemical company is planning to manufacture a new product, issues of manufacturing compatibility and sales staff effort arise within the company along with potential problems regarding the behavior of wholesalers (assuming the product is sold through that channel), customer problems (is retooling required?), and eventual customer acceptance. As in the case of risk, incompatibility tends to decrease over time. Finally, incompatibility may be primarily psychological (i.e., "We just don't do things that way here"), and failure to consider the psychological barriers to adoption is often disastrous, at least in assessing short-term potential.

Role of Analogous Products. Examining the pattern of use and adoption of analogous products or services is often quite useful, especially for growing or new products. For either, the previous adoption patterns of similar products provide a clue to the likely pattern and rate of adoption and the eventual saturation level. As will be seen later in this chapter, analogies are also useful for sales forecasting.

The problem with using analogies is that two products are rarely perfectly comparable. To be reasonably comparable, both the newer product and its older analogue should be targeted to a similar market; be similar in perceived value, both in toto and in terms of the major benefits provided; and be similar in price. Under these criteria, a microwave oven could be compared to a dishwasher in that both are targeted at households, stress convenience and time savings, and cost about the same. In contrast, a mainframe computer from 1960 and a microcomputer from 1984 are not analogous, even though one is a direct descendant of the other, because the target market (a company versus individuals), perceived value (number crunching and billing versus convenience and word processing), and price (a million dollars versus a few hundred) all differ dramatically.

Mature Product Potentials

For many products, the more mature they are, the more sales will come from reorders from past customers. Reorders in a mature market are of two types. For a consumable product, ordering will be in proportion to the market need (if an industrial product) or usage rate (if a consumer product). For a durable product, ordering will occur to replace a worn-out product, to upgrade to get new features, or to add an additional model (e.g., a second TV).

Methods of Estimating Market and Sales Potential

The role of managerial judgment in deriving potential is crucial and ubiquitous. It influences the type of data examined, the model used to derive the estimate, and often the estimate itself. Although statistical knowledge is useful, logic or common sense is much more important. Therefore, after calculating market potential, the product manager should always step back and ask, "Does this estimate make sense?"

Analysis-Based Estimates

A formula-based method can be developed based largely on the potential users or buyers of the product in question. This is a three-step process.

1. *Determine the potential buyers or users of the product.* The buyers should be interpreted very broadly as the customers who have the need, the resources necessary to use the product, and the ability to pay. This often results in the product manager assessing that almost all customers are in the potential market (and maybe they are). An alternative approach is to work backward: Who *cannot* qualify as a potential customer? This might include apartment dwellers for lawn mowers, diabetics for regular ice cream, and so on. The product manager can determine potential customers judgmentally. In addition, other data sources that could be useful are surveys, commercial sources such as data from Simmons Market Research Bureau, and government documents.

As an example, consider the problem of estimating the market potential for laptop computers. One judgmental approach to determining the number of potential users is to divide the market into five categories: (1) "fleet workers" who are not in an office but need portable computing capabilities in a warehouse or manufacturing line, (2) "road warriors" who are on the road full time and need a virtual office, (3) "office functionalists" who work mainly out of the office but sometimes from home, (4) "corridor cruisers" who need their office computers when they go to business meetings, and (5) "road runners" who need a second office but less intensively than "road warriors" do.[2]

2. *Determine how many are in the potential group of buyers defined by step 1.* Often steps 1 and 2 are done simultaneously. If defined in terms of a particular demographic group, for example, people above age 60, sources such as the *Statistical Abstract of the United States* can help determine how many people are in the group. For the previous example of laptop computers, the estimated group sizes were 15 million "fleet workers," 10 million "road warriors," 8 million "office functionalists," 6 million "corridor cruisers," and 5 million "road runners."

3. *Estimate the potential purchasing or usage rate.* This can be done by taking either the average purchasing rate determined by surveys or other research or by assuming the potential usage rate is characterized by the heaviest buyers. The latter notion would be based on the assumption that all buyers could be convinced to purchase at that heavy rate. Market potential is then calculated by simply multiplying the number obtained from step 2 by the number from step 3, that is, the number of potential customers times their potential usage rate. For example, if we assume one laptop computer per potential user, the market potential is simply 44 million units. The market potential estimate derived in this manner usually results in a large number when compared to current industry sales. However, the number itself is not nearly as important as the process of trying to get the number. Estimating market potential using this kind of analysis forces the product manager to think about who the potential customers for the product are. As noted earlier, this can often result in new thinking about untapped segments. A second impact of the market potential estimate is that it usually reveals a significant amount of untapped purchasing power in the market that is waiting for a new strategy, a new product formulation, or perhaps a new competitor.

Two examples will help illustrate this method. The first illustration is from the infant/toddler disposable diaper category. The potential users are rather obvious in this case. As noted in Figure 4–9 (page 84), there were 4.2 million births in 1990. The average child goes through 7,800 diapers in the first 130 weeks of life until toilet training.[3] To compute the potential sales, this 7,800 figure can be used to represent a mix of children at different ages. Thus, the market potential for disposable diapers in 1990[4] was 32,760,000 diapers. This figure is somewhat exaggerated because it does not exclude babies who are allergic to the diapers, but it does include all those households using cloth diapers or diaper services. This is important: Those households using cloth diapers are still potential customers, but the competitors (Procter & Gamble, Kimberly-Clark, and private labels) have not figured out how to convert them to disposables. They certainly are trying, though, with different colors for boys and girls and myriad other tactics.

---

[2]Jenny E. Beeh, "PCs Are Taking to the Streets," *Advertising Age,* October 31, 1994, p. 28.

[3]Kathleen Deveny, "States Mull Rash of Diaper Regulations," *The Wall Street Journal,* June 15, 1990, p. B-1.

[4]This is a key point; as we noted earlier in the chapter, market potential is defined at a point in time by the relevant market conditions. If the birth rate increased in a given year, then, assuming usage rate remains stable, market potential would be higher.

FIGURE 7–3 Market Potential: Electric Coil

SIC	*Industry*	*Purchases of Product*	*Number of Workers*	*Average Purchase/ Worker*	*National Number of Workers*	*Estimated Potential*
3611	Electrical measuring	$160	3,200	$.05	34,913	$1,746
3612	Power transformers	5,015	4,616	1.09	42,587	46,249
3621	Motors and generators	2,840	10,896	.26	119,330	31,145
3622	Electrical industry controls	4,010	4,678	.86	46,805	40,112
		$12,025				$119,252

A second application is shown in Figure 7–3 and is typical of estimates of market potential for industrial products.[5] In this case, the potential customers are identified by SIC code. How much they can buy is extrapolated from an activity measure, in this case dollars of purchases per employee. A defect of this approach, however, is that current nonbuying SIC codes that are potential buyers are not be included in the analysis.

Continuing our analysis of the ready-to-drink fruit juice market, we assume that for the majority of the United States there is no income constraint since the drinks are very low priced. Juices are also assumed to be healthy, since they provide several vitamins and other nutrients and therefore no particular group of people is restricted from drinking them. The potential buyers would then be the total population of the United States (266 million) less the number of children under one year of age (3.4 million), or 262.6 million. Per capita liquid consumption is equal to 182.5 gallons per year (from *Beverage Industry Supplement*), thus giving a potential market size of 47.9 billion gallons per year. This assumes, of course, that all beverage consumption is RTD fruit drinks. A more realistic estimate of potential uses data from Figure 2–10 (page 41). Data from *Beverage World* indicates that in 1994, fruit beverages held 12.4 percent of the beverage market, with the next largest category, beer, at 21.7 percent. We assume the potential consumption rate for RTD fruit drinks can, at best, potentially be the same as that for beer, which would imply a market potential of 10.4 billion gallons (47.9 billion times 21.7 percent) versus the 3.3 billion actually consumed in 1994. Clearly there is some untapped potential.

This method has to be used with caution for durable consumer products or expensive industrial products with long interpurchase cycles. In those cases, buyers not in the market because they recently purchased the good must be subtracted from the total. However, sometimes multiple purchases of such products occur; for example, a customer might have two or three VCRs in the home.

An example of this adjustment process for durables is from the PDA market. Two high-tech market research firms, BIS and Dataquest, estimate that the number of

[5]For more information on this approach, see William E. Cox, *Industrial Marketing Research* (New York: John Wiley & sons, 1979), Chapter 7.

mobile professionals in the United States in 1994 was 27.3 million and 30 million, respectively. Further, Dataquest reports that the proportion of mobile workers to the entire labor force is roughly constant and that the entire labor force is growing at an annual rate of 1.6 percent. Combining this growth rate and the average of the two mobile professional estimates, the number of mobile professionals in the Unitied States in 1996 is estimated as 29.6 million. This is one estimate of potential, the total market size. However, to compute the sales potential for 1996, the market potential must be adjusted downward to account for those who recently purchased PDAs. Assuming the average length of service is four years and that a given user is not likely to purchase multiple PDAs, the number of users who purchased PDAs from 1992 to 1995, 678,000 (source: Dataquest), must be subtracted from 29.6 million, leaving 28.9 million potential units if every potential customer bought one in 1996. Using a similar penetration rate from cellular phones at a similar stage in the product life cycle (2 to 3 percent of all households), the estimated sales potential is about 600,000 to 700,000 units.

This approach to estimating market potential has implications for increasing the sales volume in a category or for a brand. There are two ways to increase sales. First, the product manager can increase the number of customers—by pursuing new segments, developing new products, or just getting more customers in existing segments (see Chapter 8 for more discussion). Second, the purchase rate can be increased; that is, the product manager can attempt to get customers to buy more through promotions, package size changes, and other tactics. Both of these approaches have been used successfully at General Mills, which has a large stable of mature products (e.g., Hamburger Helper, Betty Crocker cake mixes).[6]

Area Potential

Area potential is often derived by breaking down total sales by area. When sales data are available for a variety of regions, along with some data on the characteristics of the regions, it is common to use a weighted index that combines these characteristics to indicate the relative potential in the area. Many consumer goods companies use the general *Sales and Marketing Management* buying power index, which is 0.2 × (percentage of the population of the area compared to the United States) + 0.3 × (percentage of retail sales of the area of the U.S. total) + 0.5 × (percentage of disposable income of the area of the U.S. total). When population, retail sales, and disposable income are input as a percentage of the total United States, this index projects the percentage of the product sold in the various regions. For established products, these weights may be estimated from the actual sales data by, for example, running a regression of sales versus various factors such as the number of schools in the region. Product-related data, such as sales of analogous products, might also be used. In fact, as noted earlier in this chapter, sales of truly analogous products are often the best indicators of potential. An index approach for a hypothetical new copying system might be as follows:

---

[6]Patricia Sellers, "A Boring Brand Can Be Beautiful," *Fortune,* November 18, 1991, p. 169.

Bases:	Percent population in the region (P)
	Percent schools in the region (S)
	Percent retail businesses in the region (RB)
	Percent banks in the region (B)
	Percent offices in the region (O)
	Percent warehouses in the region (WH)
	Percent manuracturing facilities in the region (MF)
	Percent other businesses in the region (OB)
	Percent Xeros sales in the region (XS)
	Percent other copier sales in the region (CS)

$$Index = W_1P + W_2S + W_3RB + W_4B + W_5O + W_6WH + W_7MF + W_8OB + W_9XS + W_{10}CS$$

Here the *W*s are the appropriate weights assigned to each factor.

Another example of area potential estimation deals with the potential cargo volume for trucks between Atlanta and Los Angeles. One potential source of business would be beverages (SIC code 208). In the 1972 Census of Transportation, the amount of beverages shipped from California to the Southeast was 87,000 tons. Assuming we are estimating potential for 1975, this figure must be updated. The *Census of Manufacturers* indicates a 35.8 percent increase in dollar sales. Deflating by the cost-of-living increase of 23.2 percent, this suggests 1975 tons = (87,000)(1.358)(1/1.232) = 95,900. Now we must convert general region-to-region shipment data into SMSA (Standard Metropolitan Statistical Area)-to-SMSA shipment data. This could be done in several ways, including using the *Census of Manufacturers* data on value added and taking the ratio of the Los Angeles SMSA to California and the Atlanta SMSA to the Southeast. The resulting market potential estimate is then (95,000 tons)(source ratio)(destination ratio) = 9,050 tons.

Sales Potential

Sales potential is the firm-level analogy to market potential. An obvious approach to calculating sales potential is to multiply the estimated potential of the market by some market share figure. This share figure should represent potential share, which the firm could achieve under optimal conditions (usually not 100 percent).

Forecasting: Basics

Overview

As noted earlier in this chapter, forecasting deals with expectations of the future, that is, what the product manager thinks will happen during the next planning year. There are a large number of different things to forecast. The most obvious, and the focus of this chapter, are results such as sales, market share, and profits. Forecasts are used in the following ways.

1. *Forecasts answer "what if" questions.* In considering which strategy and tactics to follow, the key information is an estimate of the outcomes of the various strategies and tactics, typically the sales and profit levels. The simplest "what if" question is what will happen next year if everything remains as it has been in the past, which makes the forecast basically an extrapolation.
2. *Forecasts help set budgets.* Sales forecasts become the basis of a budget because they specify both sales levels to be attained and, by implication, the resources needed. All pro forma income statements are based on a sales forecast.
3. *Forecasts provide a basis for a monitoring system.* Deviations from forecasts serve as warnings to product management to reexamine a market and their strategy in it. Both positive and negative deviations from forecasts can lead to a better understanding of the marketplace through an examination of the underlying causal factors.
4. *Forecasts aid in production planning.* With more companies and their channels moving to just-in-time production and distribution systems with low levels of inventory, accurate forecasting is becoming even more critical. This is particularly important in the personal computer industry. Mistakes in forecasting demand for personal computers cost Compaq $50 million and IBM much more in 1994.[7] Apple Computer has consistently underestimated the demand for its Powerbook laptop computers, which has exacerbated its financial problems.

Other quantities are important to forecast as well. *Resources* used as a factor of production must be forecast (note the earlier discussion about general planning assumptions). Sometimes the key resources are human, making it important to forecast the needed labor pool. *Costs* are also an important factor to forecast. If the product is manufactured and follows the experience curve, costs are somewhat more predictable than in other situations. For many product managers, accurate forecasts of the rate of change of *technology* are critical to keeping an edge on competitors. General *economic conditions* have important effects on many types of businesses. Finally, in global businesses currency exchange rates have a major impact on profits.

A good forecast takes into account four major categories of variables, all of which either have been or will be discussed in this book: customer behavior (Chapter 6), past and planned product strategies (Chapter 8), competitor actions (Chapter 5), and the environment (Chapter 4). Company actions are assumed to be predictable or at least under the control of the product manager, although, as noted in Chapter 1, many decisions such as pricing and advertising may be made in other parts of the company. In contrast, customer and competitive actions are much harder to forecast. In any event, the forecasts of customer and competitor actions are parts of the background assessment. The general environment consists of such elements as the state of the economy, key industries in it, demographic changes in the population, and costs of basic resources. Although, as noted above, some of these elements can be forecast by

[7]Gary McWilliams, "At Compaq, a Desktop Crystal Ball," *Business Week,* March 20, 1995, p. 96.

FIGURE 7–4 Format for Forecasts

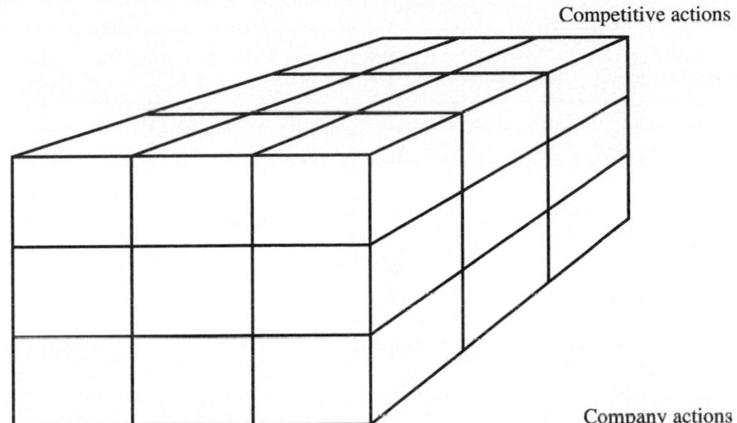

the product manager, they are generally derived from secondary sources, such as government projections, and appear in the category analysis or the planning assumptions section of the plan. While environmental changes affect the plan mainly through their impact on competitor and customer behavior, they can be so crucial that we treat them separately here.

The forecasting phase of the planning process ideally can be thought of as the process of assessing the possible outcomes under all reasonably likely combinations of the four basic determinants of outcome. This suggests that achieving forecasts by varying company decisions without considering competitive reactions is, unless the competitors are asleep, insufficient. The forecasting process can be viewed as a process of filling out a three-dimensional grid such as that shown in Figure 7–4, with the likely outcomes contingent on values of the three sets of independent variables.

We must emphasize that the forecast in each cell should not be a single number but a range of possible outcomes. While a forecast of 787.51 may sound better than 800 ± 50, it may be misleading and an example of foolish precision (which puts you out on a limb with your boss). Do not expect forecasts to six decimal places, especially when such precision is not crucial to making a sound decision.

While a best-guess forecast is useful, so is a forecast of the upper and lower bounds of the outcome. Knowing the range of likely results is crucial for strategy selection. A product manager may be unwilling to undertake a strategy with a high expected result (e.g., a profit of $8 million) that also has a reasonably likely disastrous result (e.g., a loss of $5 million). Conversely, a product manager may be willing to gamble on a possible large return even if the likely result is a small profit or even a loss. It is also useful to know the likely range of outcomes for purposes of monitoring and control. For example, in one situation, a drop of 30 percent below the forecast may be well within the expected range and therefore not necessarily cause for a major reanalysis, whereas in a different situation, a 15 percent drop below the forecast may signal a serious problem.

Figure 7–5 Summary of Forecasting Methods

	Judgment				Counting	
Dimensions	*Naive Extrapolation*	*Sales Force*	*Executive Opinion*	*Delphi*	*Market Testing*	*Market Survey*
1. Time span	Short/medium term	Short/medium term	Short/medium term	Medium/long	Medium	Medium
2. Urgency	Rapid turnaround	Fast turnaround	Depends on whether inside or outside company	Needs time	Needs time	Needs time
3. Quantitative skills needed	Minimal	Minimal	Minimal	Minimal	Moderate level	Yes
4. Financial resources needed	Very low	Low	Could be high if outside experts used	Could get high	High	High
5. Past data needed	Some	Not necessary	Not necessary	Not necessary	Not necessary	Not necessary
6. Accuracy	Limited	Highly variable	Poor if one individual; better if a group	Best under dynamic conditions	Good for new products	Limited

Source: David M. Georgoff and Robert G. Murdick, "Manager's Guide to Forecasting," *Harvard Business Review,* January–February, 1986, pp. 110–20.

At this point, it should be clear that producing a forecast for each possible combination of factors is a tedious task at best. Consequently, it is desirable to limit the task to, say, three environments (expected, benign, and hostile) and a limited number of competitive postures (e.g., status quo, more/less aggressive). This limitation should, however, be made with two points in mind. First, the initial forecasts may suggest a promising avenue or a potential disaster that may lead to refining the scenarios. Second, the assumptions made in forecasting are crucial; therefore, it is desirable to designate them formally as *planning assumptions.*

Sales Forecasting Methods

A large number of methods have been developed for forecasting, and many articles have been written comparing them on a variety of dimensions.[8] Figure 7–5 compares a selected number of methods on the following dimensions:

---

[8]See, for example, John C. Chambers, Satinder K. Mullick, and Donald D. Smith, "How to Choose the Right Forecasting Technique," *Harvard Business Review,* July–August 1971; David M. Georgoff and Robert G. Murdick, "Manager's Guide to Forecasting," *Harvard Business Review,* January–February 1986; and Steven C. Wheelwright and Spyros Makridakis, *Forecasting Methods for Management* (New York: John Wiley & Sons, 1985).

Time Series			Association/Causal			
Moving Average	*Exponential Smoothing*	*Extrapolation*	*Correlation*	*Regression*	*Leading Indicators*	*Econometric*
Short/medium	Short/medium	Short/medium/ long	Short/medium/ long	Short/medium/ long	Short/medium/ long	Short/medium/ long
Fast turnaround	Fast turnaround	Fast turnaround	Fast turnaround	Moderately fast	Moderately fast	Needs time
Minimal	Minimal	Basic skills	Basic skills	Basic skills	Basic skills	High level
Low	Low	Low	Moderate	Moderate/high	Moderate	High
Necessary	Necessary	Necessary	Necessary	Necessary	Necessary	Necessary
Good only in stable environment	Good in short run	Good for trends, stable time series	Highly variable	Can be accurate if explained variance is high	Moderately accurate at best	Best in stable environment

1. Time span for which the method is most appropriate. Time spans can be short term (zero to six months), medium term (six months to two years), or long term (more than two years).
2. Urgency with which the method can be applied. Some methods take longer than others to create forecasts.
3. Level of quantitative skills needed to apply the method.
4. Cost of the method to implement.
5. The importance of having past sales data. Some methods require past sales data, and some do not need it at all.
6. The level of accuracy.

The first set of methods is referred to as *judgment-based* methods because they rely solely on the judgments of the product manager.

Naive Extrapolation. One method of naive extrapolation uses the last-period sales level and adds x percent, the estimated percentage change in sales. For example, dishwasher sales could be forecast to be last year's plus 6 percent. Another approach might be termed "graphical eyeball." This requires plotting the past sales series and then "eyeballing" the next value to match the past pattern (see Figure 7–6).

FIGURE 7–6 Graphical Eyeball Forecasting

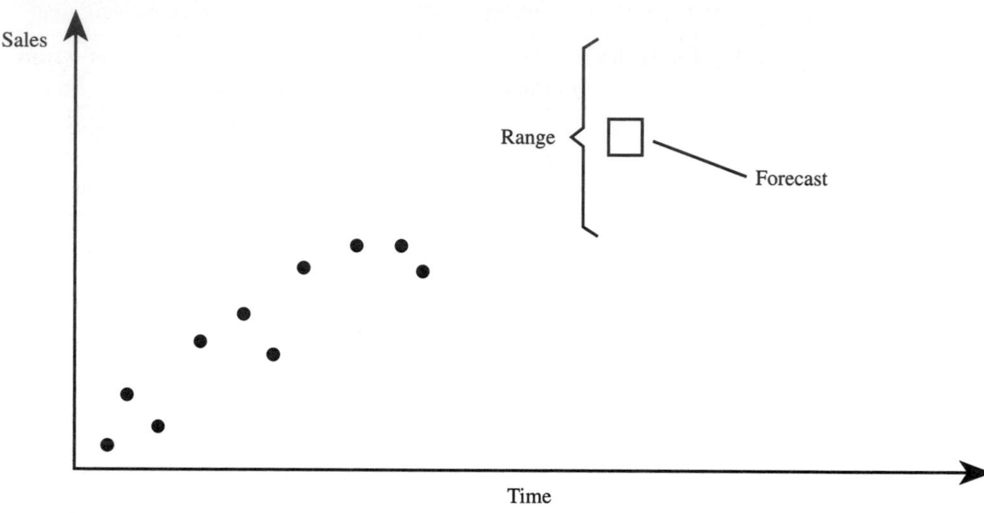

Sales Force Composite. Salespeople are often asked to make sales forecasts. Their forecasts can then be aggregated to create a sales forecast for the product or product line. The advantage of this approach is that salespeople are closest to the customers and are thus in an excellent position to understand their purchasing plans. Unfortunately, when the forecast is used to set quotas, such forecasts are naturally on the low side. Alternatively, salespeople can be overly optimistic in an attempt to impress the sales manager.

Jury of Expert Opinion. An extreme example of this method relies on one individual's expert opinion. If the expert happens to know the Delphic oracle or be a mystic, the forecast can be excellent. Unfortunately, it is hard to know ahead of time whether someone can predict the future.

Many studies have been published deriding expert forecasts. Consider the following business-related predictions made by "experts":[9]

> With over 50 foreign cars already on sale here, the Japanese auto industry isn't likely to carve out a big slice of the U.S. market for itself. (*Business Week*, August 2, 1968).
>
> A severe depression like that of 1920–1921 is outside the range of probability. (Harvard Economic Society, November 16, 1929).
>
> The phonograph . . . is not of any commercial value. (Thomas Edison, ca. 1880).

TRW sponsored a major technological forecasting project back in the mid-1960s. Some of their predictions were

[9]C. Cerf and V. Navasky, *The Experts Speak* (New York: Pantheon Books, 1984).

- A manned lunar base by 1977.
- Commercial passenger rockets by 1980.
- Undersea mining and farming by 1981.

Of 401 technological forecasts, nearly every prediction was wrong.

Despite many examples like these, expert forecasts can be useful. The key to the value of expert judgment is the ability of the expert to recall and assimilate relevant data in making a guess. While judgment is often unsystematic, it is an important supplement to other methods and can overcome some of the limitations of quantitative techniques.

The jury approach collects forecasts from a number of experts. The forecasts are then combined in a particular manner, such as a simple average or a weighted average, in which the weights can be assigned by the level of expertise. A variant of the jury approach is the panel consensus method, in which a group of experts is put in a room where they attempt to develop a forecast. Unfortunately the result is often driven by a strong, vocal member of the group.

An example of the jury approach is provided every month by *Wired* magazine. In each issue, a group of experts in an area are asked for the year in which certain phenomena are likely to occur. The forecasted year is the average across the experts. For example, five experts were asked about the year in which we could expect to be able to purchase custom clothing overnight. The average of the experts was 1999.[10]

Delphi Method. A variety of the panel consensus is called the *Delphi* method. The process begins by asking a number of individuals to independently produce a forecast. An outside person then collects the forecasts and calculates the average. Next, the outside person returns to each participant both the original forecast and the average and asks the participants to reconsider their initial forecasts. Typically, the participants then change their forecasts to more nearly conform to the average. If the process is repeated several times, consensus is generally achieved. Delphi panels are often established to forecast sales of new technologies (e.g., videotext) for which historical data do not exist.

A second set of methods relies on customer data and is referred to as *counting* methods:

Market Testing. This category includes a large set of methods involving primary market research. The methods usually involve personal interviews in mall intercept, focus group, or at-home situations in which potential customers are asked to respond to a product concept. Methods such as conjoint analysis, discussed in Chapter 6, are heavily used to assess desired product features and ultimate market share.

Market Surveys. Market surveys are a specific form of primary market research in which potential customers are asked to give some indication of their likelihood of purchasing the product. A common approach is to use a 1 to 10 scale, with a 10 implying almost certainty of purchase. Customers frequently overstate their likelihood

[10] *Wired,* November 1995, p. 76.

of purchase (although for really new products they tend to understimate their eventual purchase likelihood). Researchers often use either a "top box" approach (i.e., count only the 10s as purchasing) or some other method based on the past relation between intent and purchase as the basis for the forecast. Alternatively, respondents are asked to indicate the quantity of a product they expect to purchase. These purchase intention surveys are then extrapolated to the population to form the demand forecasts. Purchasing agents, for example, are often surveyed to determine the demand for industrial products. Many of the problems typical with surveys, such as nonresponse bias (are the people who do not respond to the survey different from those who do?) and inaccurate responses, exist with this method.

A third set of methods utilizes only historical sales data and is referred to as *time-series* methods.

Moving Averages. Moving averages, an old forecasting standby, are widely used to reduce the "noise" in data to uncover the underlying pattern. In doing so, it is important to recognize that past data have at least four major components:

1. Base value
2. Trend
3. Cycle(s) (seasonality)
4. Random

Moving averages essentially smooth out random variations to make the patterns (trends and cycles) more apparent.

Complex moving-average models are available for estimating trends and cycles. For purposes of introduction, however, we consider only the simple moving-average approach. A three-period moving average of sales at time t is given by

$$\overline{S}_t = (S_{t-1} + S_t + S_{t+1})/3.$$

Note that (1) each data point used is weighted equally and (2) no trend or cycle is accounted for. To see how this method works, consider the three-month moving average for the eight periods of sales given in Figure 7–7. The moving average for the first three periods of data is 105, the simple average of 100, 110, and 105. The moving average for periods 2 through 4 is 115, the average of 110, 105, and 130. As can be readily seen by comparing the moving averages to the "Raw Changes" column, the fluctuation in values is much less in moving averages than in the raw data, and a consistent trend of increase of about 10 units per period becomes quite apparent. Forecasts can now be based on the pattern of moving averages rather than on the raw data.

The basic moving-average method just described can be extended to track trends and seasonal patterns as well. For example, to smooth a trend, simply calculate the period-to-period changes and average them as in Figure 7–7. While other methods, such as regression, are more sophisticated means of developing forecasts, moving averages remain a popular approach.

Exponential Smoothing. A second time-series approach is called *exponential smoothing*. The formula for a simple exponentially smoothed forecast is

FIGURE 7–7 Sample Data

Period	*Sales*	*Three-Period Moving Average*	*Raw Changes*
1	100	—	—
2	110	105	+10
3	105	115	-5
4	130	125	+25
5	140	130	+10
6	120	140	-20
7	160	152	+40
8	175	—	+15

$$\hat{S}_{t+1} = aS_t + (1 - a)\hat{S}_t, \text{ where "^" refers to a forecast.}$$

In other words, an exponentially smoothed forecast for period $t + 1$ is a combination of the current period's sales and the current period's forecast. The parameter a is between 0 and 1 and can be determined from historical sales data. In reality, exponentially smoothed forecasts are close relatives to moving-average forecasts in that the former weight past sales using exponentially declining weights.[11] As in the case of moving averages, this approach literally smooths out the random variation in period-to-period values. Trends and cycles are estimated separately.

Extrapolation. The simplest form of extrapolation is to use regression analysis with time (period) as the independent variable. Time-series regression produces estimates of the base level (intercept) and the trend (slope). Seasonal patterns can either be removed a priori from the data or estimated in the model using dummy variables (see Chapter 6). Ignoring seasonality, the model is simply

$$\text{Sales} = a + b(\text{time}).$$

Addressing the same eight-period example from Figure 7–7 produces the graph in Figure 7–8 and the predicted results in Figure 7–9. The forecast for period 9 based on this model would be

$$S_9 = 85.4 + 9.9(9) = 174.5.$$

This is represented by the dotted extension to the fitted line in Figure 7–8. Two other useful statistics produced are the R^2, a measure of fit that is the percentage variance in the dependent variable (sales) explained by the independent variable (time), and the standard error of the estimate, which is a measure of the variance of the errors (the differences between the predicted values of sales based on the preceding equation and the actual values) about the line. Rather than just using the point forecast, 174.5, a confidence interval or a range of likely outcomes should be placed around it. This can

[11]To see this, simply rewrite the equation in terms of period t, that is, $\hat{S}_t = aS_{t-1} + (1-a)\hat{S}_{t-1}$, and substitute repeatedly for S_t in the equation in the text.

Figure 7–8 Times-Series Extrapolation

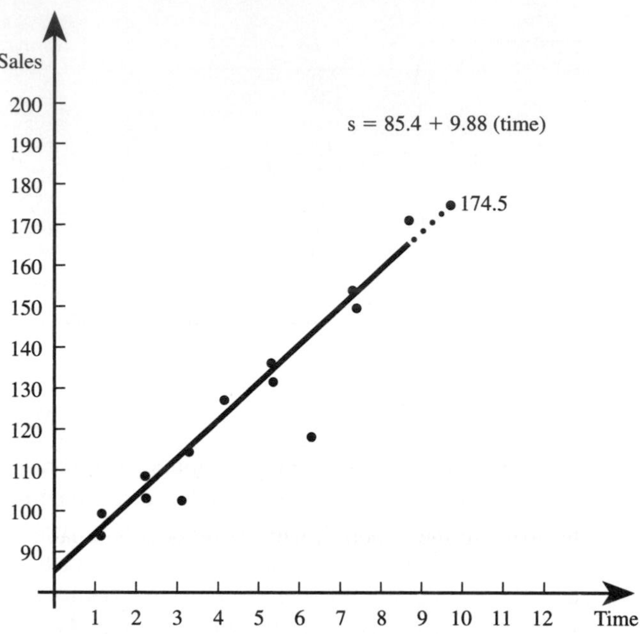

be done by multiplying the standard error of the estimate (in this case, 12.3) by 2 to approximate a 95 percent confidence interval. The forecast then becomes 174.5 ± 24.6. In addition, longer-term forecasts can be developed simply by plugging in values for time periods later than 9, extending the line farther out in time.

Sometimes sales data are highly nonlinear, as in Figure 7–10. This product life cycle curve clearly would not fit well with a straight regression line. Figure 7–10 is the classic epidemiological curve that can be estimated using a variety of functional forms, such as sine or cosine, or using models developed to handle such a time series in a marketing context.[12] Curve-fitting computer programs can fit the best functional form (quadratic, cubic, sine, etc.) to a time series using only time as the independent variable.

The fourth category of forecasting methods is termed *association* or *causal* because the techniques utilize one or more variables other than time to predict sales (e.g., advertising).

Correlation. A (zero order) correlation coefficient is a number between −1 and +1 indicating the relationship between two variables. Given that one variable is sales, the number would indicate the strength of the association between sales and the other variable chosen. A high positive correlation value indicates that as the variable (e.g.,

[12]See, for example, Frank M. Bass, "A New Product Growth Model for Consumer Durables," *Management Science,* January 1969, pp. 215–27. This model is described in more detail later in the chapter.

FIGURE 7–9 Time-Series Regression Example

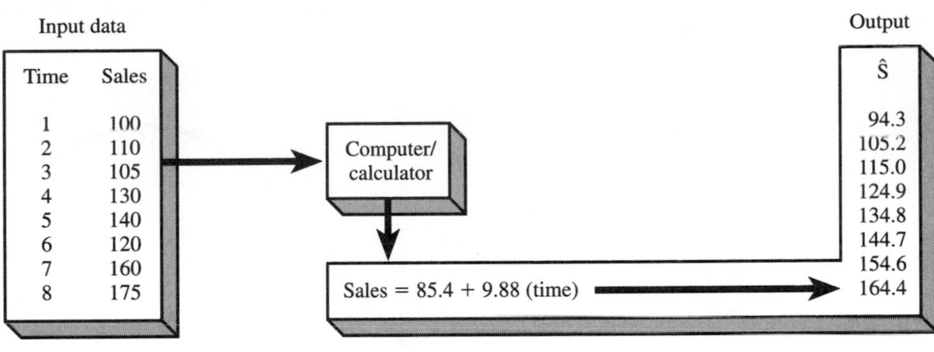

advertising) increases (decreases), sales increase (decrease). The opposite is true for a high negative correlation. The correlation coefficient itself does not produce a forecast; however, the size of the correlation between sales and the other variable chosen helps to estimate the general response of sales to changes in the variable.[13]

Regression Analysis. This method is explained in more detail later in the chapter. Basically it is a generalization of the time-series model: Instead of having only time as the independent variable, other variables that could affect sales are also included. For example, a regression model to predict sales of Pepsi might be the following:

$$\text{Sales} = a + b(\text{advertising}) + c(\text{price}) + d(\text{population age } 13\text{–}25).$$

Given historical data on sales, advertising, price, and population, the coefficients a, b, c, and d can be estimated and used to develop a forecast.

Leading Indicators. Economists use certain macroeconomic variables to forecast changes in the economy. When changes in these variables occur before changes in the economy and they are thought to be linked, they are termed *leading indicators*. For example, changes in employment, housing starts, interest rates, and retail sales often are associated with changes in the economy. The construction and real estate industries use leading indicators to forecast demand. Industry-specific leading indicators also exist, such as retail auto dealer inventories for the automobile industry.

Econometric Models. These are essentially large-scale, multiple-equation regression models. During the 1970s they were extremely popular, and companies such as Data Resources, Inc. (now owned by McGraw-Hill), sold these expensive models to companies seeking to develop better forecasts of industry sales. They are less popular

[13]Actually, a simple regression with sales as the dependent variable and, say, advertising, as the independent variable is superior to the correlation coefficient because it produces the same underlying information about the relationship between the two variables *and* provides an equation for forecasting.

Figure 7–10 Trial over Time for a New Product

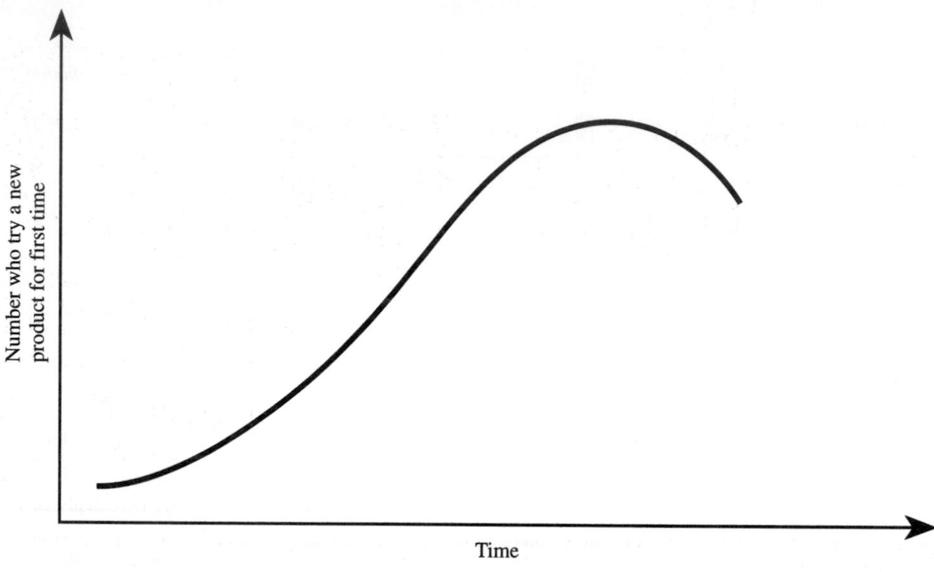

today as companies seek to keep their expenditures down in all areas. In addition, they never forecasted as well as advertised. A noteworthy failure came during the Arab oil embargo of the early 1970s when the models predicted less damage to the U.S. economy than actually occurred.

What Methods Are Used?

Figure 7–11 shows the results of a survey of 96 companies examining which forecasting methods are actually used in practice.[14] The table shows the percentage of managers who reported using various techniques for different time horizons. Clearly, for the short and medium term (as defined by the authors), judgmental approaches are heavily used. The most frequently used quantitative method is a moving average. This is rather discouraging given the length of time more sophisticated methods have been available. However, regression is used quite frequently, particularly for long-run forecasts.

Using Regression Models for Forecasting

Given the results from Figure 7–11 and the wide applicability of regression to other marketing contexts (see the application to segmentation research in Chapter 6), we devote significant space in this chapter to show how it is used in forecasting

[14]Nada R. Sanders and Karl B. Manrodt, "Forecasting Practices in US Corporations: Survey Results," *INTERFACES,* March–April 1994, pp. 92–100.

FIGURE 7–11 Incidence of Forecasting Method Usage

Forecasting Technique	Forecast Period			
	Immediate (<1 month)	*Short (1 month–<6 months)*	*Medium (6 months–1 year)*	*Long (>1 year)*
Judgmental				
Manager's opinion	27.9%	39.8	37.1	9.3
Jury of executive opinion	17.5	28.9	40.1	26.2
Sales force composite	28.6	17.5	33.1	8.7
Quantitative				
Moving average	17.7	33.5	28.3	8.7
Straight-line projection	7.6	13.2	12.5	8.2
Naive	16.0	18.5	13.8	0
Exponential smoothing	12.9	19.6	16.8	4.2
Regression	13.4	25.1	26.4	16.5
Simulation	3.4	7.8	11.2	8.3
Classical decomposition	0	6.8	11.9	9.3
Box-Jenkins	2.4	2.4	4.9	3.4

Source: Reprinted by permission, Nada R. Sanders and Karl B. Manrodt, "Forecasting Practices in the U.S. Corporations: Survey Results," INTERFACES, March-April, 1994. Copyright 1994, The Institute of Management Sciences and the Operations Research Society of America (currently INFORMS), 2 Charles Street, Suite 300, Providence, RI 02904 USA.

contexts.[15] These models are generally developed in three stages. First, the variables assumed to affect dependent variables are specified. The variables selected might be

Sales = f(our price, competitors' prices, our advertising, competitors' advertising, disposable income).

Next, a model is specified indicating the form of the relation between the independent variables and sales. Most often the nature of the relationship is linear, such as

Sales = $b_0 + b_1$ (our price)) + b_2(competitors' prices) + b_3(our advertising) + b_4 (competitors' advertising) + b_5 (disposable income).

Finally, the model is estimated by means of regression analysis, usually using commonly available computer programs:

Sales = 1.2 − .3 (our price) + .4 (competitors' prices) + 1.1 (our advertising) − .3 (competitors' advertising) + .2 (disposable income).

This estimated model serves two useful purposes. First, a regression model can be used to forecast sales. Notice that to use regression models to forecast, one must first forecast the values of the independent variables. This is because all the variables are *contemporaneous*; that is, current (say, 1996) sales are determined by current (1996) prices, advertising, and disposable income. We use data from some point in the past through 1996 to estimate the model. However, to forecast sales for 1997, we need 1997 values for the independent variables. While some of the variables are usually

[15]Regression models can also be used to help determine optimal levels of marketing mix variables, such as advertising to achieve product objectives. We illustrate this in Chapter 11.

under the product manager's control (price, advertising), several must be forecasted. If this is difficult, regression becomes less useful as a forecasting device.

Second, a regression model can answer "what if" questions. In the preceding example, b_1 is the marginal effect of changing our price and b_3 is the marginal effect of changing our advertising. If we are willing to assume the relationships between price and advertising and sales are causal rather than just correlational, the product manager can answer a question such as "What if I increase my price by $5?" In this case, based on the model, an increase in price would be predicted to lead to a decrease in sales of 1.5 (5 times the coefficient −.3).

Developing Regression Forecasting Models

While developing regression forecasting models is largely a trial-and-error process, certain steps can make the process more systematic and efficient.

1. *Plot the sales data over time.* It is useful to get a feel for the sales series by simply plotting sales versus time. An important use of this plot is as an aid for identifying key variables that might be useful in predicting changes in sales. Any peaks or valleys in the sales series can prompt the product manager to try to uncover the factor that may have caused that sharp change.

As an illustration, Figure 7–12 shows the (deseasonalized) monthly sales series from 1973 to 1975 of presweetened breakfast cereal purchases made by a sample of households on a diary panel.[16] A significant price increase for sugar occurred during 1974 and resulted in a sharp increase in cereal prices. It is difficult to pick out the effect of price alone from the graph. However, it is clear that an overall positive trend in purchases occurred over the three-year period. Thus, some variable accounting for that trend must be included in the regression model.

2. *Consider the variables that are relevant to predicting sales.* The product manager or a team of managers familiar with the product category should brainstorm to develop a set of factors that affect sales. At this stage, the list of variables should be long, allowing for as much creativity as possible. In addition, when a factor is specified, a hypothesis should be developed indicating the direction of the effect of that variable on sales, that is, whether an increase in this factor causes sales to increase or decrease.

In the case of presweetened cereals, the major factors affecting sales are price and advertising. As noted above, the data are already deseasonalized, so any winter versus summer consumption factors for cold cereals have already been eliminated from the sales series. For simplicity, the upward trend of the data can be accounted for by a trend variable that assumes the values 1 through 36. Finally, it is possible that advertising has what is called a lagged effect on sales. In other words, not only may current advertising affect current sales but last month's advertising may also affect current sales through consumer recall. Thus, the general form of the model is

---

[16]The source of these data is Scott A. Neslin and Robert W. Shoemaker, "Using a Natural Experiment to Estimate Price Elasticity: the 1974 Sugar Shortage and the Ready-to-Eat Cereal Market," *Journal of Marketing,* Winter 1983, pp. 44–57.

FIGURE 7–12 Plot of Cereal Sales Data (monthly)

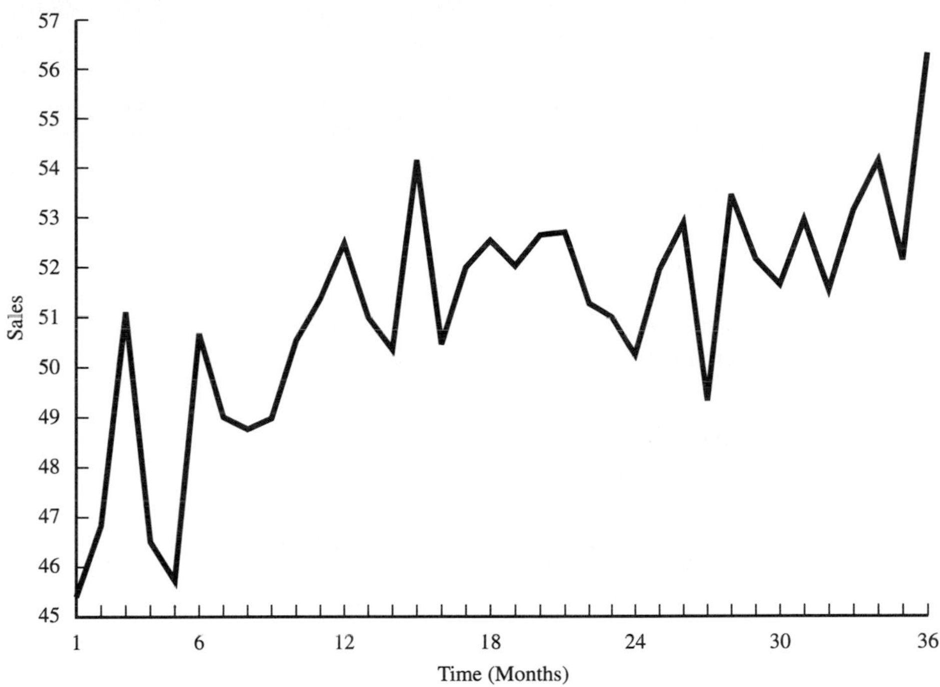

Source: Scott A. Neslin and Robert W. Shoemaker, "Using a Natural Experiment to Estimate Price Elasticity: the 1974 Sugar Shortage and the Ready-to-Eat Cereal Market," *Journal of Marketing*, Winter 1983, pp. 44–57.

$$\text{Cereal sales} = f(\text{price, advertising, lagged advertising, trend}).$$

3. *Collect the data where feasible.* Once the variables have been specified, the product manager or research analyst must collect the historical values for those variables. There must be as many historical values for the independent variables as there are for the sales variable. Thus, since there are 36 observations on cereal sales, the analyst needs 36 observations on price and advertising (lagged advertising can be computed directly from the advertising series). Figure 7–13 shows the data matrix for this example.

4. *Analyze the data.* There are several aspects to the data analysis step of the model-building process.

First, it is important to examine the correlations among the independent variables. Many time series variables are highly correlated because they tend to change over time at the same rate. For example, if the economy is expanding, employment and GDP are highly correlated. If a product is being rolled out nationally, the number of distribution outlets and advertising may be highly correlated. If two or more independent variables are highly correlated, computational problems can arise for the regression program, as well as other interpretational problems. Therefore, an important first step after the data

FIGURE 7–13 Data Matrix for Cereal Data

Sales	*Price*	*Advertising*	*Time*	*Lagged Advertising*
45.4	29.0	6803	1	—
46.8	28.7	6136	2	6803
51.1	28.1	8850	3	6136
46.5	27.9	6689	4	8850
45.7	27.9	7004	5	6689
50.7	27.6	7801	6	7004
49.0	27.0	7091	7	7801
48.8	26.7	6958	8	7091
49.0	26.6	7357	9	6958
50.6	26.7	7010	10	7357
51.4	26.7	6627	11	7010
52.5	26.7	7350	12	6627
51.0	26.6	6952	13	7350
50.4	26.6	7441	14	6952
54.2	26.8	7519	15	7441
50.5	27.1	8409	16	7519
52.0	27.6	8084	17	8409
52.6	28.3	7830	18	8084
52.1	28.6	7399	19	7830
52.7	28.9	7566	20	7399
52.7	29.3	7076	21	7566
51.3	29.8	7310	22	7076
51.0	30.9	7604	23	7310
50.3	31.6	6793	24	7604
52.0	31.6	7038	25	6793
52.9	31.6	6514	26	7038
49.4	31.7	6439	27	6514
53.5	31.7	6056	28	6439
52.2	31.7	6148	29	6056
51.7	31.1	5787	30	6148
53.0	30.9	6043	31	5787
51.6	30.5	6191	32	6043
53.2	30.3	8034	33	6191
54.2	29.7	8404	34	8034
52.2	29.8	9524	35	8404
56.4	29.9	8973	36	9524

have been collected is to construct a correlation matrix among the *independent* variables (remember, we want high correlations between the independent variables and sales, the dependent variable). The correlation matrix for the cereal data appears in Figure 7–14. This was constructed using Microsoft's Excel (the data analysis programs). Note that the diagonal of the matrix contains 1s; this is because the correlation of a variable with itself is obviously 1. The matrix is also symmetric; that is, the correlation between price and advertising is the same as the correlation between advertising and price. The analyst should be on guard against any correlations with absolute values higher than .90 or .95 (high negative correlations are as harmful as

Figure 7–14 Cereal Data Correlation Matrix*

	Price	*Advertising*	*Time*	*Lagged Advertising*
Price	1.0	−.28	.76	−.26
	(35)	(35)	(35)	(35)
	.00	.10	.00	.13
Advertising	−.28	1.00	.05	.55
	(35)	(35)	(35)	(35)
	.10	.00	.76	.00
Time	.76	.05	1.00	−.02
	(35)	(35)	(35)	(35)
	.00	.76	.00	.90
Lagged advertising	−.26	.55	−.02	1.00
	(35)	(35)	(35)	(35)
	.13	.00	.90	.00

*The numbers in each cell are presented as: correlation
(sample size)
significant level.

positive ones), although this number should not be considered a rigid threshold.[17] In this case, high correlations are not a problem.

Second, run smaller regressions. If any pair of variables is highly correlated, one of the variables may be eliminated from consideration. Although it is irrelevant which one is dropped from a statistical perspective, there may be a difference between the two variables from a managerial perspective; for example, one may be under the control of the product manager but the other may not be. Alternatively, one may be measured more accurately than the other. No matter which of a pair is retained, the one that is dropped need not be considered further.[18] As a result, the manager is usually left with a subset of the original variables for the regression. The regression results from the cereal illustration are shown in Figure 7–15, assuming the simple linear form of the model.

Third, determine the significant predictors of the dependent variable, sales. Even when care is taken to choose only those variables thought to be excellent predictors of sales, some often turn out to have little effect. To assess the strength of the effect of an independent variable on sales, the product manager looks at the ratio of the absolute value of the regression coefficient to its standard error (given on all regression printouts), otherwise known as the t statistic. Generally speaking, if this ratio is greater than 2, the variable is referred to as a significant predictor of sales. Examining the first cereal regression results in Figure 7–15, we can see that price is marginally significant (t = 1.92), advertising is insignificant (t = 1.21), time is very significant (t = 5.02), and lagged advertising is very insignificant (t = .41).

[17]Actually, this is a complex area of econometrics in which academics are continually searching for a simple rule to determine when the correlation problem, termed *multicollinearity,* is severe.

[18]Dropping a variable should be done with extreme caution, and only if the intercorrelation with another variable is very high, because model specification error could result.

FIGURE 7–15 Regression Results: Cereal Data*

1. Model: Sales = 58.528 − .461(price) + .00044 (advertising) − .00015 (lagged advertising) + .211 (time)
   (.242) (.00037) (.00037) (.042)
   Standard error of the estimate = 1.479
   Adjusted R^2 = .60

2. Model: Sales = 60.041 − .538 (price) + .00033 (advertising) + .230 (time)
   (.244) (.00032) (.038)
   Standard error of the estimate = 1.468
   Adjusted R^2 = .65

3. Model: ln Sales = 3.193 − .053 (ln price) + .090 (ln advertising) + .044 (ln time)
   (.095) (.043) (.007)
   Standard error of the estimate = .028
   Adjusted R^2 = .68

*Numbers in parentheses are standard errors.

A decision to be made here is whether to rerun the regression after dropping insignificant variables. Parsimony is important in forecasting models, because fewer independent variables must be predicted to develop the ultimate forecast for a "smaller" model, that is, one with fewer independent variables. In addition, the statistical properties of the equation are better with fewer independent variables. Since lagged advertising is clearly unimportant, regression 2 in Figure 7–15 is the same model with that variable eliminated. Price is now firmly significant (t = 2.45), as is the time trend, but advertising is still insignificant.

Fourth, check the signs of the significant independent variables. This is a logic check on the model and is perhaps the most important test of all. The product manager *must* ensure that the signs on the regression coefficients conform to the hypotheses developed earlier in the process, that is, that they make sense. For example, a significant positive sign on a price coefficient is a problem; most of the time, these kinds of sign flip-flops are due to what is called *specification error,* the omission of one or more key variables from the model. In the breakfast cereal example, the signs are all in the appropriate direction for the significant variables.

Finally, check the R^2 of the equation. This is what most analysts gravitate toward first; most people believe that a high degree of fit ensures that the forecasting model is a good one. However, that is not the case. A good forecasting model must have a high R^2, but a high R^2 does not guarantee a good forecasting model. This is due to the fact that regression is basically a correlational procedure and it is possible to choose variables that are nonsensical but do explain variance in sales. That is why we stress the combination of spending time a priori in choosing independent variables, checking the signs on the coefficients, *and* looking at the R^2. The R^2 of the breakfast cereal model is .65, as shown in Figure 7–15. This is not particularly high for a time-series model and implies that the forecast confidence interval will be relatively wide.

5. *Develop the forecast and confidence interval.* As noted earlier, the forecast is developed by plugging in the appropriate values of the independent variables. In

addition, a confidence interval can be constructed using the standard error of the estimate. This produces three forecasts: best guess (the point forecast), optimistic (the high end of the confidence interval), and pessimistic (the low end of the confidence interval).

Thus, taking the results of the second cereal regression from Figure 7–15, we can develop a forecast for the first out-of-sample period, January 1976. If we assume the price will be 30 cents per 10 ounces (remember, this is nearly 20 years ago) and category advertising will be $9 million, then, given that the value of the time trend is 37, the forecast is 55,400 ounces purchased for the panel members (55.4 in the units of Figure 7–13). Given a standard error of the estimate of 1.47, a 95 percent confidence interval around the forecast is ± 2,940 ounces, or a range of 52,460 to 58,340 ounces. Thus, 55,400 becomes the best guess, 52,460 the pessimistic scenerio and 58,340 the optimistic forecast.

RTD Fruit Drink Illustration

There are several key variables in a sales forecasting model for the RTD fruit drink category. Since demand for the category is heavily driven by image and awareness, advertising is a key independent variable. Demand is also driven by health consciousness. Moreover, category demand is affected by income since Snapple, Arizona, Ocean Spray, and other brands have become particularly popular in upper-income groups. As a result, gross domestic product (GDP) per capita is hypothesized as another causal factor. Finally, price, as usual, should have an impact.

As a result, a model for forecasting RTD fruit drink demand is the following:

$$\text{Sales} = f(\text{advertising, GDP per capita, price}).$$

Based on data through 1994, the model produced a forecast of 3.35 billion gallons for 1995 and 3.39 billion gallons for 1996. These were 1.5 and 2.7 percent increases over actual 1994 sales and still well below the 10.4 billion gallons of market potential estimated earlier in this chapter.

Nonlinear Relations

Most regression forecasting models are linear; that is, they are of the form

$$\text{Sales} = b_0 + b_1X_1 + b_2X_2 + \ldots,$$

where X_1 and X_2 are the independent or predictor variables and sales is the dependent variable.

In some cases, the product manager may face a nonlinear relationship between the Xs and sales. For example, there may be diminishing returns to advertising. In the linear framework, each dollar of advertising has equal effectiveness. If there are diminishing returns to advertising, the impact of the millionth dollar may be different (usually less) than the tenth. This can be handled in the linear framework by, for example, using a logarithmic function:

$$\text{Sales} = b_0 + b_1 \text{ (log advertising)}.$$

One model, which has been used fairly extensively, is a multiplicative model (in economics, referred to as a Cobb-Douglas function):

$$\text{Sales} = b_0 X_1^{b1} X_2^{b2},$$

which can be written and estimated with a standard regression program by using a logarithmic transformation of the *X*s:

$$\log \text{Sales} = b_0 + b_1(\log X_1) + b_2(\log X_2).$$

An interesting implication of this formula is that the coefficients are interpreted as *elasticities* rather than slopes. Thus, b_1 would be interpreted as the percentage change in sales due to a 1 percent change in X_1. Note that to forecast sales using this model, the antilogarithm of the predicted dependent variable needs to be computed.

The results of a logarithmic model of the breakfast cereal data appear in Figure 7–15 (regression number 3). It is interesting that the results differ from those of the linear model. Here the price elasticity is insignificant ($t = .56$), whereas the advertising elasticity is significant ($t = 2.09$), as is the trend. The slope results for price and advertising from the linear model were the opposite. This can happen when two completely different theories about how sales are created are specified.

Forecasting Innovations

For many products, the requirement that regression models have a large number of years (or other time period) of data simply is unrealistic. This is particularly the case for technological innovations or new durable goods. In addition, the demand in the early stages of the product life cycle does not necessarily look very linear. Figure 7–10 demonstrates such demand as a sales curve. For example, the product manager for a PDA does not face the same forecasting environment as the Snapple product manager does. PDAs have not been for sale for many years (mainly since 1992, as shown in Figure 2–13 on page 43), and they are in the early growth stage of the product life cycle.

To handle these situations, models of the diffusion of an innovation have been developed to forecast first purchases of these kinds of products. The most popular model is the Bass model.[19] The model assumes two kinds of customers for a durable good: innovators, who purchase the product early in the life cycle, and imitators, who rely on word of mouth from other purchasers. This results in what is called a *diffusion* process. The model used by Bass has the following form:

$$p(t) = p + [q/M]Y(t),$$

where

$p(t)$ = Probability of purchase given no previous purchase.
$Y(t)$ = Total number who have purchased the product.
M = The market potential (saturation level).
q = Parameter representing the rate of diffusion of the product (also called the *coefficient of imitation*).
p = Initial probability of purchase (also called the *coefficient of innovation*).

[19]See Bass, "A New Product Growth Model," pp. 215–27.

Sales is

$$S(t) = [M - Y(t)]\, p(t),$$

and, substituting $p(t)$ from the first equation into the sales equation, we obtain

$$S(t) = pM + [q - p]Y(t) - q/M[Y(t)]^2.$$

If q is greater than p (the rate of imitation is greater than the rate of innovation), the sales curve will rise and then fall. If q is less than p (the rate of imitation is less than the rate of innovation), the sales curve will fall from its initial level.

The model can be estimated running a regression of the form

$$\text{Sales} = c_0 + c_1 Y(t) + c_2[Y(t)]^2,$$

or simply using sales as the dependent variable, with the independent variable being the cumulative number of adopters and that quantity squared. In other words, all that is needed are historical sales data. Once the c coefficients are estimated, the quantities p, q, and M can be solved for by the following identities:

$$c_0 = pM,\ c_1 = [q - p];\ \text{and}\ c_2 = -q/M.$$

There are three equations and three unknowns, so p, q, and M have unique solutions.[20] Forecasts of sales can be developed directly from the sales equation, if desired.

The Bass model has fit past adoption patterns well. For example, it correctly forecast a downturn in sales of color TVs in the late 1960s, something the "expert" forecasts at the major manufacturers failed to do because they used essentially linear extrapolation. Unfortunately, the model is sensitive to the number of periods of data available and can be unreliable when only four or five years of data exist.[21] The preceding model also includes no marketing variables. For example, the market saturation level, M, is probably affected by price, and the imitation parameter, q, is affected by advertising.[22]

PDA Illustration

The four years of data available for the PDA category provide a limited basis for illustrating the basic Bass model. The data are from Figure 2–13. The results of running the model are

$$\text{Sales} = 78.123 + .783Y(t) - .0007Y(t)^2.$$

[20]If c_2 is less than zero, p must be solved for using the quadratic formula. It has two solutions, one negative and the positive one that is used.

[21]Reasonable forecasts are obtainable when the results of past studies—essentially the average values of p and q—are combined with model estimates. See Fareena Sultan, John U. Farley, and Donald R. Lehmann, "A Meta-Analysis of Applications of Diffusion Models," *Journal of Marketing Research,* February 1990, pp. 70–77.

[22]For incorporating advertising into the Bass model, see Dan Horsky and Leonard S. Simon, "Advertising and the Diffusion of New Products," *Marketing Science,* Winter 1983, pp. 1–18. For adding distribution, see J. Morgan Jones and Christopher J. Ritz, "Incorporating Distribution into New Product Diffusion Models," *International Journal of Research in Marketing,* June 1991, pp. 91–112.

Figure 7–16 Bass Model: PDA Actual versus Predicted

Year	PDA Sales (000s)	Predicted	Percent Error
1992	63	78.123	24.0%
1993	150	124.674	16.9
1994	200	213.144	6.6
1995	285	282.104	1.1
1996	?	283.614	?

Figure 7–16 shows the predicted sales and the degree of forecasting error (where it can be calculated). As can be seen, the model predicts historical sales quite well. In addition, estimates of q and p show q greater than p ($q = .798$ and $p = .065$), indicating that the product has demonstrated favorable word of mouth.

The forecast for 1996 is for 284,000 units, or flat growth. Whether this is correct will not be known until after this book is published. However, the model does not explicitly account for price, and rapid price decreases in these kinds of product categories are common. Thus, more category sales growth could occur.

Presentation of Forecasts

Forecasting Methods

As noted earlier in this chapter, it is generally difficult to say which techniques are good and which are bad because success often depends on the circumstances. Accuracy depends on factors such as time horizon, how much money is spent on the forecast, how much time was spent developing the forecast, the volatility of the category, and the like.

While using quantitative procedures may at times seem tedious, two major reasons encourage their use: (1) they simplify routine, repetitive situations, and (2) they force explicit statements of assumptions. When using quantitative methods, it is best to take the following supplementary steps:

1. *Do sensitivity analysis.* Only when a result seems to be stable over method and data points (e.g., drop one or two years of data and rerun the analysis) can the forecast be advanced with much conviction.

2. *Examine large residuals.* The residuals are individual forecasting errors made for each period. By examining the characteristics of those periods when the forecast was bad, omitted variables can often be uncovered.

3. *Avoid silly precision.* This means round off the forecast and give an honest plus or minus range.

4. *Be tolerant of errors.* Expect the methods to improve one's odds of making a good forecast, not guarantee them. Be suspicious of forecasts with very narrow ranges.

5. *Remember that you will generally miss the turning points.* Quantitative (as well as qualitative) forecasting methods work well as long as the patterns that occurred in

FIGURE 7–17 Sample Format for Summarizing Forecasts

	Forecast		
Method	*Pessimistic*	*Best Guess*	*Optimistic*
1. Time series extrapolation			
2. Regression model:			
Version A			
Version B			
3. Expert judgment:			
Expert A			
Expert B			
4. Own judgment			
5. Bottom-up forecast			
Average			

the past extend into the future. Whenever a major change occurs, however, most forecasts will be way off. Stated another way, most forecasting methods are generally useless for predicting major changes in the way the world operates, and consequently most forecasts do not include the effects of these changes.

Combining Forecasts

So far this chapter has described a number of forecasting methods and their strengths and weaknesses. When making an important forecast, it is both common and prudent to make several forecasts and then combine them, perhaps using some averaging method. An average of a set of forecasts using disparate methods will tend to be better than a forecast using only one method that is susceptible to its own particular weaknesses.

The results of several methods can be summarized in a table such as that in Figure 7–17. The range of these forecasts provides a useful indication of the uncertainty faced. Moreover, deciding how to combine these forecasts forces one to make explicit assumptions. In Figure 7–17, a simple average is used as the combination rule (that is, equal weighting), but weights could also be assigned, for example, in inverse proportion to the size of the confidence interval.[23]

For example, the forecasts for RTD fruit drinks for 1995 and 1996 from the multiple regression analysis were 3.35 and 3.39 billion gallons, respectively. A simple linear model with a time trend as the only independent variable predicts sales of 3.30 and 3.37 billion gallons. The average of the two approaches, 3.325 and 3.380 billion gallons, is likely to be a better forecast than the results of either method alone.

[23]See Peter C. Wilton and Sunil Gupta, "Combination of Forecasts: An Extension," *Management Science,* March 1987, pp. 356–72, for a description of common combination methods.

Gaining Agreement

The previous sections imply that only one person, such as a staff person or a product manager, is involved with developing a forecast. Sometimes forecasts are "top down": The product manager develops a forecast for her or his product's sales. Alternatively, forecasts can be "bottom up," an aggregation of several forecasts made by regional salespeople, country managers, or others. Unfortunately, top-down and bottom-up forecasts rarely agree. The process of reaching agreement is both useful and frustrating.

In understanding bottom-up forecasts, it is useful to recognize that both personal incomes and budgets depend on the forecast. Personal incomes, especially salespeople's, are tied to quotas, which in turn are derived from forecasts. Therefore, a salesperson will tend to be conservative in his or her forecast to make the sales goal or quota easier to attain. In contrast, certain managers may overstate sales potential to gain a larger budget. Thus, the bottom-up process, though based on the knowledge of those closest to the customer, may well produce a biased estimate. Therefore, total reliance on either bottom-up or top-down methods is generally a mistake.

Summary

Forecasting is one of the most important jobs facing the product manager. The forecast is an input to aspects of the marketing strategy such as the objectives and strategies. It is also critical to production planning. When forecasts are substantially off on the high side, objectives are overly ambitious, inventories are too large, and senior managers, production personnel, and channel members become upset. When the forecast is much lower than actual, the losses are opportunity costs: lost sales.

Market potential is generally poorly understood yet very important for different reasons. Low estimates of market potential result in marketing managers declaring categories mature too soon. This tends to create opportunities for ambitious competitors who have different views on the amount of untapped potential. The mere act of trying to calculate potential market size often gives the product manager ideas about how to extend the product or service into new segments, a topic we consider further in the next chapter.

C H A P T E R

8 Developing Product Strategy

Overview

The previous five chapters gave a detailed view of the background analysis necessary to develop a marketing plan. We described the analysis as the homework part of the plan, that is, the research and information assessment necessary to begin the planning process for a product. The motivation for the background analysis is, of course, the development of a marketing strategy for the product of interest. This is the true raison d'être for the plan. In this chapter, we show how to integrate the construction of a situation analysis with the development of product strategy.[1]

Function of a Strategy

The primary purpose of a strategy is to provide the product manager with the direction to follow in managing a business over the planning period. A successful strategy should satisfy three requirements.

1. First, a strategy must help to *achieve coordination* among various functional areas of the organization. Different areas of the organization have different perspectives on how to make a product successful. The product manager would like to increase advertising spending. The sales manager would like more flexible pricing policies. Production personnel would like longer production runs and fewer products. Financial/accounting analysts require quantitative justification of all expenditures.

For example, suppose a computer manufacturer wishes to target a specific industry with unique product features. The image or "positioning" of the product is clearly high quality and technological superiority. In such a case, a sales manager's

[1]Much of our thinking about marketing strategy has been influenced by James "Mac" Hulbert, Columbia Business School; William Brandt, Impact Planning Group; and the late Abraham Schuchman, long-time marketing professor at Columbia.

flexible pricing orientation is inconsistent with the strategy. The production people may be upset with the segmentation approach because it means lower volume and more customization. The image-building activities of the advertising agency are difficult to evaluate in financial terms for the accounting personnel.

Clearly, a strategy that is not accepted, poorly articulated, or not well understood cannot provide the necessary coordination. One purpose of strategy is to ensure that all members of the team are working together to achieve success for the product.

2. Second, strategy must *clearly define how resources are to be allocated*. At any level of the organization, resources are limited. Strategy entails allocating resources to achieve the goals set for the product. Very often some resources, such as manufacturing or service capacity, sales force, time, money and so forth, will be more limited than others. In addition, these resources are often shared. For example, a single sales force often sells many different products. The lower the level of the organization, the more resources are typically shared. Therefore, at the product level it is essential that the strategy provide clear guidance for the allocation of resources across activities and other products.

3. Third, strategy must *show how it can lead to a superior market position*. In Chapter 3, we showed how the definition of competitors is critical to market success. A good strategy takes cognizance of existing and potential competitors and their strengths and weaknesses (see Chapter 5).

A marketing strategy can be *competitively sensible* in four ways.

a) It is competitively sensible when a competitor *cannot* do it. A competitor's inability could be based on patent protection (e.g., the pharmaceutical industry), extra capacity, or some other proprietary or technological advantage. For example, until the release of Windows 95, Apple Computer was the only personal computer supplier with a truly easy-to-use graphical user interface. Other competitor operating systems, notably DOS and earlier versions of Windows, could not match the Apple interface.

b) A competitively sensible strategy is one a competitor *will choose not to do*. Often smaller companies pursue small segments of the market in the hope that large companies will ignore them due to financial criteria. For example, Silicon Graphics, Inc., a manufacturer of computer workstations, specializes in computers that manipulate three-dimensional images onscreen for jet design, movie special effects, and other applications. The other major suppliers of workstations, Sun, IBM, and Hewlett-Packard, have built more general-purpose computers that do not perform as well as those made by Silicon Graphics for the segment's needs.

c) A strategy is competitively successful if competitors *would be at a disadvantage if they chose to do it*. Sears's marketing strategy of "everyday low pricing" (see Chapter 10) was an unsuccessful attempt to emulate the success of Wal-Mart and Kmart because the company was not prepared to fully integrate a low-cost and low-price orientation into the entire organization.

d) A competitively sensible strategy *would cause us to gain if the competitor chose to do it*. Campbell Soup Company ran an advertising campaign around the theme "Soup is good food." Such a theme is clearly generic and is aimed at increasing soup consumption in general. Since Campbell has such a dominant position in the market, it benefits from such generic promotion. However, Heinz or Lipton could not afford such a strategy because it would likely cause primarily Campbell's sales to increase.

In sum, a good marketing strategy coordinates functional areas of the organization, helps allocate resources efficiently, and helps the product attain the market position management desires. It is also competitive; that is, it is a course of action that provides an advantage over the other products and services pursuing the same customers.

Elements of a Product Strategy

A complete statement of a marketing strategy for a product consists of seven parts:[2]

1. A statement of the objective(s) the product should attain.
2. Selection of strategic alternative(s).
3. Selection of customer targets.
4. Choice of competitor targets.
5. Statement of the core strategy.
6. Description of the supporting marketing mix.
7. Description of the supporting functional programs.

Often parts 3 and 5, the customer targeting and the core strategy or positioning, are considered to be the marketing strategy.[3] However, we believe all seven steps more completely describe decisions the product manager must make.

The first two elements, the objectives and the strategic alternatives, establish the general direction of the strategy. The next three elements, the selection of customer and competitor targets and a description of the core strategy, are really the essence of the strategy. Taken together, they are often referred to as positioning, that is, how the product is to be differentiated from the competition in the minds of the target segments. Finally, the supporting marketing mix and functional programs relate to the implementation of the strategy.

A systematic approach to developing strategy helps to achieve the coordination and integration referred to earlier. There is a logical order to the aspects of the strategy: It is clear that marketing mix decisions such as price and advertising logically depend on the basic strategy. For example, the strategy of a high-quality positioning to upscale customers, such as that pursued by Ralph Lauren's Polo clothing line, must be implemented by high price, exclusive distribution, and classy advertising to obtain consistency between the strategy and implementation.

[2]See James M. Hulbert, *Marketing: A Strategic Perspective* (Katonah, N.Y.: Impact Planning Group, 1985).

[3]Actually, product selection is usually considered part of the marketing strategy as well, that is, "which products" to "which markets?" However, because we assume the role of a product manager in this book, the product choice is taken as given. Modifications of the product necessary to appeal to particular customer segments can be done through step 6, the supporting marketing mix.

Figure 8–1 Hierarchy of Objectives

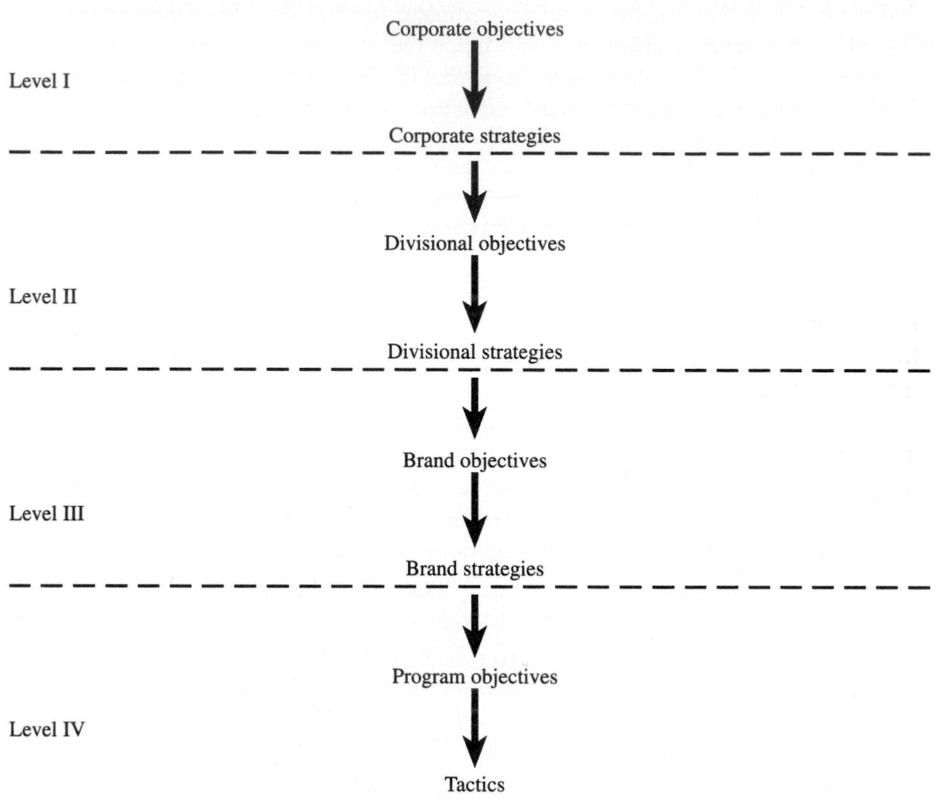

Setting Objectives

An organization has a variety of objectives, ranging from corporate to product to human resource objectives. The type of objective that is our concern addresses the question "Where do we want to go?" Clearly, the answer to such a question will differ depending on the level of the organization. At the corporate level, objectives related to return on investment, stock share price growth, and business mix are common. However, they are not very useful for the marketing manager because they give little guidance at the product level for how to proceed.

Figure 8–1 represents the different levels of objectives and strategies in an organization, referred to as a *hierarchy of objectives.* Objectives at different levels of the organization must mesh to achieve the overall corporate objectives. The job of ensuring that individual product objectives add up to the organization objective usually falls to corporate personnel who are responsibile for negotiating both business unit and product objectives to achieve the overall objective.

In this book, we are concerned primarily with level III, the product objectives. The two areas in which objectives are most commonly set for specific products or services are growth—in terms of sales revenues or market share—and profitability. This is an easy dichotomy to conceptualize because it is usually not possible to optimize both simultaneously during the time span of an annual marketing plan. The kinds of activities necessary to achieve an ambitious market share objective work against satisfying an ambitious profit objective.

For example, to reach a market share objective, the usual actions include price reductions, increased spending on advertising, increasing the size of the sales force, and so forth. Significant growth in share is, at the margin, achievable only by increasing expenditures or lowering profit margins per unit. This trade-off between profits and share is exemplified by Japanese auto manufacturers that have shifted to a profit orientation from a share objective due to losses suffered when the yen rose to 80 to the dollar in 1995. While Toyota, Nissan, and Honda are still introducing new models, there is no frenzied attempt to gain market share as there was in the 1970s.[4]

One can look at the issue of conflicting annual objectives as a mathematical programming problem. In such problems, there is some quantity to be optimized (maximized or minimized), subject to some constraints. Setting product objectives is analogous; the manager chooses whether share/sales or profits should be maximized subject to some constraint or the other. Few senior managers would permit a growth objective without some consideration of its impact on the product's profits. Likewise, profitability may be the main goal but subject to share maintenance or controlled decline (i.e., harvesting). The objective to be maximized might be called the *primary* objective and the objective acting as the constraint the *secondary* objective.

A third objective that can be set for a product is cash flow. When a company is bought through a leveraged buyout (as was the rage in the 1980s), cash flow to pay down debt is a primary concern, and thus the company's products are often charged with generating cash.

Besides choosing which objective to pursue, other characteristics of good statements of objectives are the following:

1. They should have quantified standards of performance. In other words, every objective statement should include language such as "increase market share 2 share points."

2. They should be ambitious enough to be challenging, subject to internal and external constraints. Objectives act as motivators. If regularly set too high, managers scorn them as meaningless. If set too low, the organization does not achieve its potential. For example, Floating Point Systems, a manufacturer of scientific computers, consistently disappointed stock analysts with earnings that did not reach projections. As a result, the CEO set objectives so low that they could not be missed.[5] Clearly, such an objective-setting mechanism is inconsistent with what objectives are supposed to accomplish for an organization.

---

[4]"Japan Turns a Corner," *Business Week*, February 26, 1996, pp. 108–9.

[5]J. B. Levine and M. A. Anderson, "Floating Point Sets Its Sights—Downward," *Business Week*, September 8, 1986, pp. 30–31.

3. They should have a time frame within which to achieve the objectives. Objectives are not open-ended; for proper motivation and evaluation, a time frame must be set. For annual planning purposes, the planning period serves as an adequate time frame, with perhaps quarterly checkpoints.

Thus, the two key questions for the product manager with respect to objectives are (1) which one should be pursued and (2) how much should we go for?

To answer the first question, it is clear that product managers must seek information from prior analyses and blend it with the company's current and anticipated financial resources that can be devoted to the product. For growth objectives, whether share or volume, to be feasible, there must be some competitor vulnerabilities that can be exploited (competitor analysis), a customer segment with remaining potential (customer analysis, forecasting/potential analysis), or general category growth anticipated.

Some industries have traditional views on product objectives. For example, in consumer products, the focus for many years has been market share and sales volume. Brand managers have been under constant pressure to "move cases" of products. However, as noted in the survey of product managers in Chapter 1, a recent trend in brand management is to emphasize profits more heavily over traditional volume targets. This will probably be difficult to implement, for two reasons. First, information systems at most companies do a good job of measuring share and sales volume on a regular basis but not of measuring profits. Second, and perhaps more important, these companies do not reward product managers on the basis of profits; the key to fast-track careers has always been to increase volume and share.

The second issue, then, is how much to go for in the objective: If the product manager is pursuing an increase in market share, how much is appropriate? Remember, the objective should be challenging. In some cases, no growth in share is challenging enough: If the brand has had declining share, halting the decline could be considered ambitious. Clearly, the size of the gain to be expected is built on the market size forecasts and the anticipated activities of competitors. If the competitors are predicted to be going for profits, it can be a good time to gain significant share. If the market is predicted to increase by 10 percent, a 10 percent increase in sales will only maintain share.

A number of noneconomic or nonquantitative objectives are also followed, although not necessarily as primary product objectives. For example, it is difficult to find a U.S. company that has not made a major push for quality. Many firms have set customer satisfaction objectives (e.g., to increase satisfaction from 70 to 75 on a 100-point scale) as a result. Similarly maintenance of brand equity is a concern in a growing number of companies. However, there is an obvious link between these "enabling" objectives and economic objectives: Achieving the former should eventually lead to reaching the latter.

In sum, the task of setting objectives involves choosing the appropriate objective, quantifying the objective with an amount, and setting a time frame for its achievement. It relies on the analysis that provides the background for the marketing plan.

Selection of Strategic Alternatives

The choice of strategic alternatives follows the selection of the primary objective. This is really the first step in developing the marketing strategy for the product or service

FIGURE 8–2 Strategic Alternatives

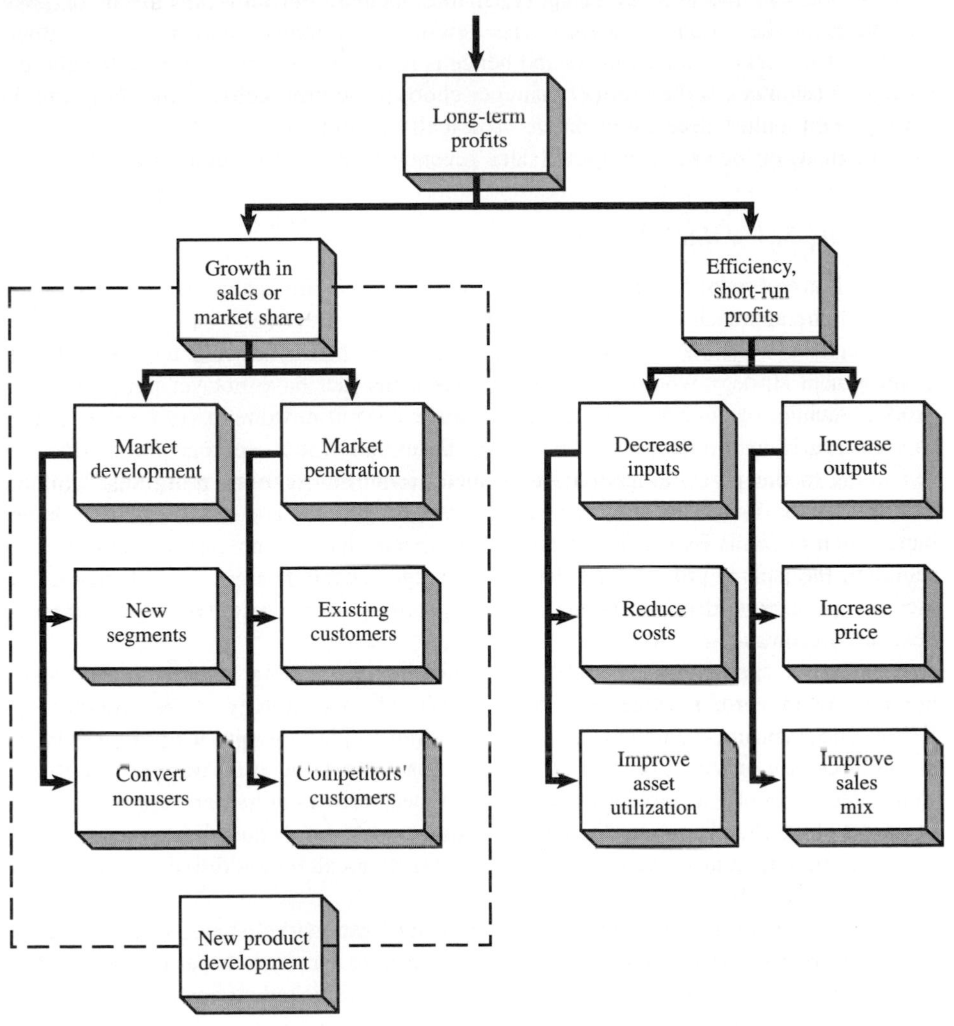

because it provides the broad guidelines for the ultimate strategy selected. Figure 8–2 provides a way to conceptualize the alternatives available to the marketing manager at a given point in time that can clarify thinking about the strategy. It presents the alternatives in a treelike structure emanating from a box labeled "long-term profits." In other words, the diagram assumes the long-run objective of any product manager is to maximize the product's profits. Given that assumption, we link the description of the alternatives to the selection of whether the primary annual planning objective is growth in sales/share and hence long-run profits or short-term profitability. The options available to the product manager depend on the objective selection. If a manager chooses growth, the three main ways to achieve it are market development, market penetration strategies, and the introduction of new products or extensions. Market development strategies are directed toward selling the current product to current noncustomers of the product category; market penetration aims at current or past customers of the product category. The new-product strategy may focus on either current customers or noncustomers and hence is related to but separate from the choice of target customers. If the product manager chooses the profitability path, the primary focus is on either decreasing inputs (basically cutting costs, a.k.a. denominator management) or increasing outputs (sales revenue from existing units sold).

Increasing Sales/Market Share

Market Development Strategies. These strategies are aimed at noncustomers of the product. One approach is to pursue nonusers in segments already being targeted. For example, if a word processing software package is being targeted to law firms, a development strategy would pursue those law firms that have not yet purchased the product (while, of course, continuing to pursue current customers with value-added services such as productivity seminars). Essentially, this approach tries to tap remaining market potential from those segments identified as prime prospects. Another example is the increased attention small business owners are receiving from large banks such as Wells Fargo. While the banks already have some customers from that segment, the lack of growth from lending to larger clients has given the banks more incentive to expand their marketing efforts by getting more customers from entrepreneurial companies.

A second approach is to enter new markets, developing segments previously ignored by the product category. An example of this strategy is the attempt by Kodak and Fuji film companies to attract children to photography using a variety of promotions and special programs.[6] Another example is the seed company that put small containers of vegetable seeds in plastic wheelbarrows at garden supply stores to try to get children to begin gardening at a young age. Antacids have been positioned as not only solving stomach acid problems but also as a calcium additive for the diet.

Market Penetration Strategies. One way to increase market share or sales volume by targeting customers of the product or service is to increase the usage rate of the brand's existing customers. This is one of the most overlooked strategies: The biggest asset the product manager owns is the customer base, and it should be leveraged as much as possible. Product managers can obtain more volume from existing customers by, for example, using larger package sizes, promoting more frequent consumption, or getting a larger share of the business if the customer uses several vendors.

Many firms have successfully taken this tack. The classic example is Arm & Hammer baking soda, which has been marketed as useful for several purposes. Banks try to get a larger share of commercial customers' business by selling other services, such as cash management and annuities. Coupons are often used to induce customers to buy larger package sizes in the hope of increasing the consumption rate. In the spirit

---

[6]Wendy Bounds, "Photography Companies Try to Click with Children," *The Wall Street Journal*, January 31, 1994, p. B-1.

of the discussion on market potential in Chapter 7, product managers should always ask themselves: Is the actual consumption rate equal to the *potential* rate?

A second route to increasing sales or market share is to try to attract competitors' customers, that is, to induce brand switching. This is not a feasible strategy in some instances in which the switching costs are just too high (e.g., mainframe computers, nuclear generators). In addition, the strategy could be risky. First, it can incur the wrath of a larger, more formidable competitor. Second, it may involve substantial use of sales promotion, which could make the strategy unprofitable. Third, a strategy inducing brand switching may call for comparative advertising, which is not only expensive but also risky; if poorly executed, it may call attention to the competitor's brand, particularly if the brand is the market leader. Because of the increase in credit card issuers (e.g., AT&T, General Electric, "affinity" cards), category participants resorted to stealing the best customers from one another.[7] AT&T is also heavily involved in defending its long-distance phone calling business from MCI, which is constantly developing new services (e.g., "Friends and Family") and launching price comparison ads to steal AT&T customers.

Increasing Profitability

Decreasing the Inputs. One way to decrease inputs is through cost reduction. Obvious candidates for reduction are fixed costs of marketing such as advertising, promotion, selling expenses, marketing research, and so forth. Unfortunately, reducing these inputs may have adverse long-run effects. A possible danger in stressing variable cost reduction is that a reduction in the inputs can cause a commensurate reduction in the outputs if some of the variable cost reduction affects product quality sufficiently. Aluminum Company of America (Alcoa) restructured its operations in 1992 and reduced its workforce; the result was a rejection rate at one of its can manufacturing facilities of 25 percent and a drop in customer satisfaction to below 50 percent.[8] At the same time, some minor product changes can save a substantial amount of money. For example, Ford reduced its costs 8-9 million dollars per year by decreasing the number of carpeting options from nine to three and saved $750,000 by using black screws rather than color-matched screws on Mustang side mirrors.[9]

A second way to decrease the inputs is to improve the utilization of the assets at the disposal of the product manager. This might mean keeping down accounts receivable and, for a manufactured product, the costs of inventories. Other, related activities could be running production equipment more efficiently and, at a more aggregate level, investing idle cash on hand in overnight interest-bearing securities.

Product managers choosing the profit branch of the tree must, of course, also choose customer targets. The probable approach for this objective would be to pursue current customers only.

---

[7]Peter Pae, "Card Issuers Turn to Stealing Customers," *The Wall Street Journal*, August 18, 1992, p. B-1.

[8]Dana Milbank, "Restructured Alcoa Seeks to Juggle Cost and Quality," *The Wall Street Journal*, August 25, 1992, p. B-4.

[9]Karen Schwartz, "Pennies Saved, Millions Earned," San Francisco *Chronicle*, March 24, 1996, p. D-1.

Increasing the Outputs. The easiest way to increase revenues from existing unit sales is to improve prices. This can be done in a variety of ways, including increasing the list price, reducing discounts, reducing trade allowances, and so forth. One must be careful to do this, however, only within a range in which the customer is relatively insensitive to price, or total revenues can actually fall.

The other way to increase revenues is to improve the sales mix. The 80/20 rule of marketing a mix of products often holds: 20 percent of the product variants (sizes, colors, etc.) produce 80 percent of the sales or profits. In such an instance, it may make sense to reduce the product line to emphasize selling more of the profitable items. Alternatively, if we apply the rule to customers, the product manager may want to deemphasize the unprofitable customers and concentrate resources on those producing 80 percent of the profits.

Summary

We have presented the broad strategic options available to a marketing manager in terms of strategic alternatives.[10] This does not mean that a manager is limited to either growth or profits. For example, it is common to seek reductions in variable costs while pursuing market share gains. In addition, a product manager may choose both to increase the consumption rate of current customers and to introduce product-line extensions.

The marketing manager's dilemma is that several of the options may appear to be equally attractive, but it is very difficult and expensive to successfully implement multiple strategic alternatives. The difficulty arises from the multiple positionings different alternatives may require. For example, to simultaneously obtain new customers and get current customers to buy more, different advertising campaigns may have to be run, projecting different images and confusing customers. Multiple strategies prevent economies of scale from advertising copy, increase the use of more expensive (in aggregate) spot TV versus national TV, and so forth, thus increasing expenses. Hence there is pressure on the product manager to select a subset of the options available and concentrate resources on them.

Positioning: Choice of Customer Targets

As mentioned earlier, positioning entails a specific statement of how the product differs from the competition in the minds of a specific set of customers. Therefore, positioning encompasses (1) customer targets, (2) competitor targets, and (3) some product attribute(s) by which the differentiation will occur.

The choice of which customer group(s) to target follows immediately from specification of the strategic alternatives and the customer analysis of Chapter 6. If the profit route is taken, the customer targets are those of the current strategy, for

[10]A similar view of the alternatives in a high-tech context is provided by Marcia Kadanoff, "Customers Who Are Ripe for the Picking," *Marketing Computers*, December 1995, pp. 24–26. She labels current customers in the installed base as "Low-hanging fruit," new customers in current segments as "Juicy fruit," new customers in "adjacent" markets as "Ripe fruit," new customers in new segments as "Fruit on the vine," and new customers in developing segments as "Seedlings."

example, "men 18 to 25" or "banks with assets between $100 million and $1 billion." The task is similar for any of the growth alternatives. For the market penetration strategy aimed at the product's own customers and the market development strategy aimed at nonusers, the customers of the current strategy would again be selected. For the market penetration strategy aimed at stealing competitors' customers, the specific descriptors of those customers would be used. Finally, for the market development strategy aimed at new segments, the descriptors from the new segments chosen would be specified.

Positioning: Choice of Competitor Targets

Even if the competition is not explicitly mentioned in any of the product's communications programs, it is still important to consider which competitors are the primary targets of the strategy. For a penetration strategy that involves stealing competitors' customers, identifying competitors should be a straightforward result of the strategy; the decision to pursue that strategic alternative should be made in conjunction with the analysis of which competitor's customers are the most easily pried away. However, all strategic alternatives at least implicitly involve competition because of the necessity to position the product *against* major competitors.

Positioning involves some prioritization of the competitors, both direct and indirect. Again, the chief source of information about this choice is the situation analysis, which details the strengths and weaknesses of the competition. Additional insight can be gained from the literature on marketing "warfare."[11] Market leaders often take defensive steps and therefore focus on the strong second competitor and perhaps the third one. The followers in the market take different competitor stances depending on their market share relative to the leader. A strong second might focus on offensive warfare and target the leader. Weak followers often try to avoid the major competitors and seek market niches that have either few or weak rivals. For example, a recent trend in banking is to avoid trying to be a full-service financial institution and instead compete with the large money center banks by being a banking "boutique" and offering customized services to high-net-worth individuals.

Positioning: The Core Strategy

The core strategy defines the differential advantage to be communicated to the target customers. It is often referred to as *product positioning*. The types of advantages that can be employed fall into two basic categories: (1) cost/price differential advantage and (2) differentiation based on product offering/service features.[12] (Note this can include psychological as well as functional benefits.) In other words, you either have to

[11]See Al Ries and Jack Trout, *Marketing Warfare* (New York: McGraw-Hill, 1986); also, see John A. Czepiel, *Competitive Marketing Strategy* (Englewood Cliffs, N.J.: Prentice Hall, 1992), Chapter 1.

[12]See, for example, Michael E. Porter, *Competitive Advantage* (New York: Free Press, 1985). Porter actually advocates a third basic strategy, market segmentation. However, we believe market segmentation is a necessary part of any strategy developed by product managers in the 1990s.

have a lower price that can be supported in the long run only with lower costs or be better on some element of the product offering customers recognize as a benefit.

As several examples will show, being "stuck in the middle" can be disastrous. In 1991, Compaq Computer was in deep trouble. The previously high-flying computer company, known for its high-priced, high-quality personal computers, showed its first-ever quarterly loss. This arose because it was neither the low-price nor the quality/performance leader in an increasingly competitive market. United Airlines' Shuttle service has failed to significantly affect Southwest Airlines in the large California market since it is not lower priced and is not perceived to be of any higher quality.

In general, the positioning decision has four steps:[13]

1. Identify alternative positioning themes. The product manager should consult the advertising account team, the product team, and past marketing plans.
2. Screen the alternatives according to whether each is (a) meaningful to customers, (b) feasible given the firm and product resources and customer perceptions, (c) competitive (see the definition in the overview of this chapter), or (d) helpful for meeting the product objective.
3. Select the position that best satisfies these criteria and is accepted by the marketing organization.
4. Implement the programs (e.g., advertising) consistent with the product position selected.

This systematic approach ensures that alternative positionings are considered and diverse constituents are consulted about the selection process.

The core strategy should be easy to summarize and communicate in paragraph form. Sometimes this statement of the core strategy is referred to as the *value proposition*. The value proposition for Southwest Airlines, for example, would be the following:

> To provide travelers with the lowest-cost air transportation with an enjoyable, fun atmosphere.

This clearly states that Southwest's differential advantage is price and fun, not food, frills, and nonstop routes.

Cost/Price Strategy

A low-price differentiation strategy can be very successful. Almost every product category has a competitor that focuses on price or "value," as opposed to product features, or on some aspect of the product other than price. Wal-Mart made Sam Walton the richest man in the United States. Charles Schwab invented the discount brokerage business. Private labels have become very popular in many supermarket product categories, often being the number one brands in the categories. Frozen juices/drinks and cookies are two examples of product categories in which private labels outsell national brands. Mail-order personal computers stressing price constitute a huge business; and Packard-Bell (now aligned with NEC) became the largest vendor

[13]See George S. Day, *Market Driven Strategy* (New York: The Free Press, 1990), Chapter 7.

FIGURE 8–3 Setting Cost Improvement Priorities

		Significance of activity: High	Significance of activity: Low
Cost of activity relative to competition	Higher	Highest priority for action	Monitor cost position
	Lower	Manage for continuous improvement	No action needed

Source: Reprinted with the permission of The Free Press, a Division of Simon & Schuster, from *Market Driven Strategy: Processing for Creating Value* by George S. Day. Copyright © 1990 by George S. Day.

of personal computers in the United States largely through its low-price, mass distribution channel approach.

However, not all products can be the low-price leader in a product category because many lack the size, capital, or other resources needed to be the low-cost manufacturer or service provider. As a result, most product managers must constantly seek that point of difference that will induce customers to purchase when comparing the product to competitors'.

To successfully implement the low-cost/low-price core strategy, several activities must be pursued that are consistent with the experience curve phenomenon. First, a high volume of a single product or family of products should be produced or sold. Focused production (also true for many service businesses) hastens cost reduction, which must be continuously pursued. Second, investment should focus on efficient facilities and market share. Again, efficiency does not apply just to production equipment. The lowest-cost companies pay strict attention to all corporate overhead, including size of staff, perks such as jets and limousines, fancy offices, and so on. Finally, control should focus on cost, in manufacturing products, delivering services, or implementing activities such as advertising and promotion.

Figure 8–3 shows a framework for thinking about cost cutting.[14] The major point of this figure is that the product manager should focus on important activities in which the cost competitiveness is low (the upper left box). The costs involved can vary widely over different products. For a personal computer, the decreased cost of semiconductors, microchip boards, video screens, cooling fans, and the like can all bring the cost of the product down significantly (and they have in recent years). However, for a laundry detergent, the major cost items might be the thickness of the plastic package and the size of the label.

The low-price core strategy poses certain risks. One is that customer tastes shift, and the product being produced in large quantities may no longer be desired (e.g.,

[14]Ibid.

Atari and other video games before the Nintendo era). A second is that technological shifts either make it easier for competitors to have the same costs or make the product obsolete. Competitors can also leapfrog in cost cutting, which eliminates the cost differential advantage. An advantage of this strategy is that there is probably always room in a product category for a low-priced, "value" option because some segment of customers will always be price sensitive. The key question, of course, is how large the price-sensitive segment is and therefore whether it is worth the investments necessary to be a cost leader.

Nonprice Strategy

One way to think about the nonprice differential advantage is as a product characteristic, not necessarily tangible, that allows the product manager to obtain a price higher than the price that would be allowed under perfect competition. As every student of microeconomics (and, it is assumed, every reader of this book) knows, with many suppliers of undifferentiated commodities, the market price is marginal cost. Therefore, the differential advantage is intended to create added value in the minds of customers that enables the producer to obtain a higher price than the pure competition case; with a significant differential advantage, customers focus on product benefits other than price.

From where can a differential advantage be obtained? We can use Figure 8–4 to structure our thinking about this issue.[15] The figure uses what is called the *total product concept* as the core idea. The *generic* product is the bundle of characteristics—the functional aspects of a product. For example, an automobile could be described by quality of tires, miles per gallon, engine size, and so forth. The *expected* product is described by other benefits delivered by the product that customers have come to take as routine. Using the car example, the expected product includes some degree of reliability and warranty coverage. The *augmented* and *potential* products are what give rise to differential advantage. The augmented product includes features or benefits that can be delivered now to go beyond expectations. The potential product contains features or benefits that can be added to a product or service some time in the future. Customers remember restaurants that offer free meals when a customer is dissatisfied or the retail clerk who pays special attention to a customer when the store is busy, and these actions lead to repeat buying.

The point here is that differential advantages are obtained by going beyond what customers expect to provide unanticipated product benefits. It may take some creative thinking, but the most important aspect of providing differential advantages is to move away from asking, "How can I make this product different?" to asking, "What am I selling?" By focusing on what customers are buying—that is, benefits—product managers can better determine how to make their products or services different from the competition.

Product managers typically use five areas for differentiation.[16]

---

[15] Theodore Levitt, *The Marketing Imagination* (New York: The Free Press, 1986).

[16] Steven P. Schnaars, *Marketing Strategy: A Customer-Driven Approach* (New York: The Free Press, 1991).

FIGURE 8–4 Total Product Concept

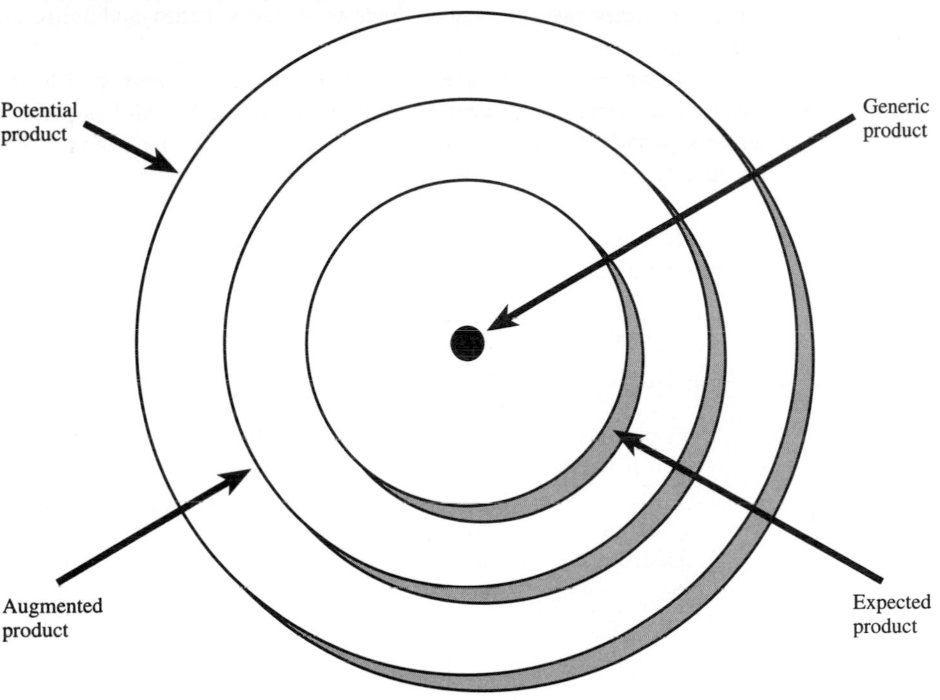

1. *Quality.* In general, product quality is very important in business today.[17] However, product quality has many dimensions. For example, particularly for technologically based products, enhanced quality can mean improved performance. Intel differentiates its products by being technologically ahead of other semiconductor companies. Quality can also mean superior design. Automobile brands such as Lexus and Taurus, computers such as Apple, stereo manufacturer Bang & Olufsen, and consumer product companies such as Sony emphasize superior design in their products. Customer service is also an area for differentiation based on quality (we expand on this area in Chapter 14). Manufacturers such as Timken (bearings) and Caterpillar (farm equipment) are well known for their customer service. For service businesses, product quality and customer service are virtually synonymous. Airlines such as Singapore and retailers such as Nordstrom differentiate on this basis. For manufactured products, quality can also mean reliability and durability. Brands marketed by the appliance manufacturer Maytag, for example, are advertised on this dimension (the "lonely repairman").

[17]Because quality issues pervade the organization and are not unique to product/marketing management, we do not get into details about such programs as total quality management (TQM) in this book.

2. *Status and image.* The bottled water category has two brands, Evian and Perrier, that have claimed this point of differentiation from other bottled waters. Many other consumer fashion brands, such as Rolex watches and Polo clothing, use this approach.

3. *Branding.* Brand names and their values communicated to customers, brand equity, can serve as a point of differentiation. IBM, McDonald's, and Nestlé are leading brands worldwide. It is particularly interesting when a product that had previously been considered a commodity is differentiated and becomes successful after branding, as Perdue chickens did. A recent illustration is the attempt by personal computer manufacturers that use Intel microprocessors to highlight this point in their ads by claiming "Intel Inside."

4. *Convenience.* Particularly in the 1990s given the demographic trends pointed out in Chapter 4, many consumer products are differentiated on the basis of convenience. Two Japanese luxury car brands, Lexus and Infiniti, differentiate themselves from other luxury car brands by making it easier for customers to have their cars serviced, giving free loaner cars and sometimes making arrangements to pick up the car at the customer's home. The grocery home shopping service, Peapod, is focusing on convenience to entice people with home computers and modems to change their buying habits and purchase their weekly supermarket orders from home.

5. *Distribution channels.* The product manager can sometimes gain differential advantage by reaching customers more efficiently and effectively than competitors (see Chapter 13 for more discussion on this topic). Federal Express, through its Powership terminals, allows its customers to determine for themselves where their packages are in the system and to order the "product." Thus Federal Express becomes, in effect, the customers' own shipping department.

As noted earlier, differential advantages are not always based on actual, physical product differences; often they are based on perceptions. The research technique of perceptual mapping, described in Chapter 6, has been extensively used by product managers to assess the current perceptual positions of brands among customer and competitor targets and to help determine if the current positioning is effective or whether repositioning can help. Figure 8–5 shows what is called a *joint space* because it not only indicates brand locations versus competition but also displays *ideal points,* the estimated preferred bundle of attributes on the two axes of clusters of households. Note that the map incorporates all three aspects of positioning. Customers are represented by the ideal points (the segments are numbered according to size), competitors are located on the map, and the differential advantage can be assessed using the brand attributes represented by the axes.

Consider the joint space figure from the perspective of RC Cola. RC is perceived as a nondiet cola, but it is equidistant from segment 1, which is close to Coke and Pepsi, and segment 3, which seems to want a lower-calorie cola. RC can position itself more within the mainstream, where it would encounter heavy competition from Coke and Pepsi, or it can pursue segment 3 with a "lighter" image where it would find fewer competitors. However, this latter group is also the smallest. Thus, the joint space method helps product managers assess a differential advantage, particularly one that focuses on perceptions.

FIGURE 8–5 Joint Space for Colas

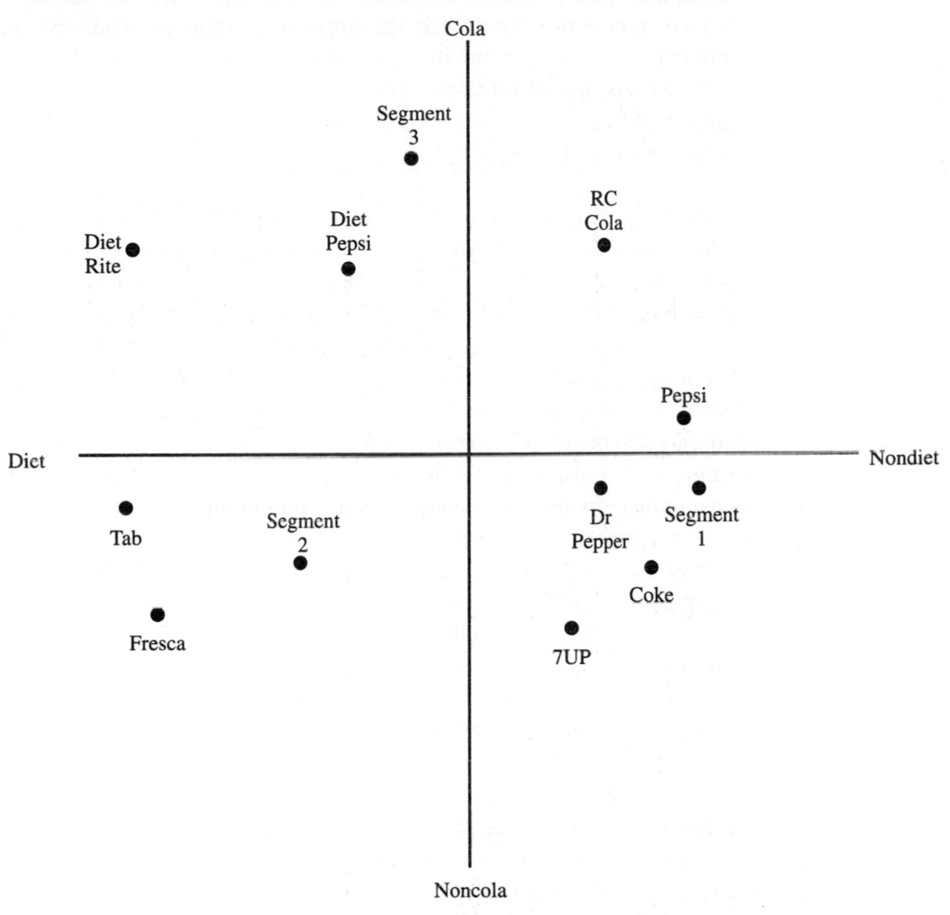

The requirements for a nonprice differential advantage core strategy are naturally quite different from those for a cost/price strategy. First, the strategy implies searching for continuous product improvements (or improvements in perceptions) to maintain the differential advantage. Second, a differential advantage core strategy requires flexibility in both production and management to keep up with changes in customer tastes and competition.

Risks are involved in the differential advantage core strategy. First, the cost/price differential may become so great that customers are willing to pay less to get less. Perhaps the biggest problem is that the differential often can disappear due to imitation. Witness the quick adoption of frequent-flier programs by almost all the major airlines. Who remembers—or cares—that American was the first with such a program?

Product Strategy over the Life Cycle

We have repeatedly mentioned the importance (and weaknesses) of the product life cycle concept. One way the life cycle can be used is to conceptualize different general approaches to developing core strategies and tactics.

Strategies for the Introduction Phase

Up to this point, this book has focused mainly on existing products, but the introductory phase of the life cycle is a useful place to begin this analysis (more will be said about new products in the next chapter). This stage in the life cycle has several characteristics. First, there are very few competitors, perhaps only one. Second, sales volume increases slowly due to the small number of firms marketing the product and the reluctance on the part of customers to purchase it. In the introductory phase of the life cycle, selling and advertising focus on selling the generic product; the effort is on product form benefits. Distributors also have the power in the relationship because the product is still unproven with customers. Prices can be high or low depending on the entry strategy of the firm(s) marketing the product.

What are the core strategy options at this stage? There are two well-known options: *skimming* and *penetration*. The skimming strategy assumes a product feature–based differential advantage that allows the product manager to enter and stay in the market during the introductory period with a high price. Market segments are narrowly defined to be those customers that are least price sensitive, that is, the pioneers or early adopters of the product. The penetration strategy is just the opposite: The product manager uses a low-price core strategy and attempts to get as many customers and establish a significant market share position as quickly as possible.

The skimming strategy is useful when the cost structure of the product is largely variable costs, usually the case when the product is a manufactured good. The ensuing high margin can be sustained because the product manager is not under intense pressure to cover large fixed costs. The distribution outlets should be limited to protect the high price. This strategy is most effective when high entry barriers exist because the high price and high margins make the category very attractive to potential competitors. The margins can then be used to fund investment in research and development.

A penetration strategy is more appropriate when fixed costs are high (e.g., many services). Since a broad segment is being pursued, it is important to obtain wide distribution and thus spend heavily on trade-oriented promotion. The product manager is also under pressure to make the market as wide as possible, which involves generic or product category marketing. This is the more expensive strategy due to the lower margins and higher marketing costs. The product manager should use a penetration strategy when the lead in the market will likely be short-lived.

There are strategic advantages to being first in the market and establishing a strong position, a situation consistent with a penetration strategy. Much empirical research shows that the first "mover" in a category has an advantage (called, not surprisingly, the *first-mover advantage*) in that it tends to maintain its lead through the product life cycle.[18] Some of this advantage is obvious: Early movers get first access to distribution channels, establish awareness, and have the first opportunity to establish brand loyalty and create preferences.[19]

Several examples of this introductory phase illustrate the different core strategies available. Consumer electronics and industrial product companies almost always pursue a skimming strategy. When VCRs, camcorders, digital tape players, and similar products were introduced, they were priced high initially and then fell in price over time. Since only one brand was usually on the market for some months and the early customers for such products (electronics nuts) are very price insensitive, there was little rationale for pricing low initially. In addition, the products needed word of mouth to help spread information about their utility. Alternatively, penetration pricing is often used for consumer packaged goods because market share is very important for retaining shelf space in supermarkets.

Strategies for the Growth Phase

The growth phase of the product life cycle actually encompasses two different kinds of market behavior: early growth—the phase just following the introductory phase—and late growth—the phase in which the rapid increase in sales begins to flatten out. In general, however, the growth phase has several features beyond the obvious fact that product category sales are still growing. First, the number of competitors is increasing. This puts pressure on product managers to keep distribution channels and changes the focus of sales and communications to the superiority of the product over others in the category. As customers become more knowledgeable about the product and the available options, this puts pressure on price. Finally, with the increased competition, market segmentation begins to be a key issue facing product managers.

The general strategic options relate to the product's position in the market: whether it is a leader (the brand with the leading market share) or a follower (the second or later entrant in the market). Figures 8–6 and 8–7 show these options. The leader can choose either to fight, that is, keep the leadership position, or to flee, which cedes market leadership to another product. If the leader chooses to fight, the product manager can attempt to either simply maintain the current position (a dangerous approach, since it is difficult to know exactly what it takes to maintain the position) or keep enhancing the product or service. Why would the leader choose a flight path? It is possible that the new entrants in the market are just too strong (as indicated by the competitive analysis) and raise the stakes for competing to a level the incumbent cannot sustain. Witness Minnetonka, which established the liquid soap category. When Lever Brothers and Procter & Gamble jumped in, Minnetonka sold out. Thus, exit is always an option. The other option implies an attempt to reposition the product so it

---

[18]See, for example, Glen L. Urban, Theresa Carter, Steven Gaskin, and Zofia Mucha, "Market Share Rewards to Pioneering Brands: An Empirical Analysis and Strategic Implications," *Management Science*, June 1986, pp. 645–659.

[19]See Gregory S. Carpenter and Kent Nakamoto, "Consumer Preference Formation and Pioneering Advantage," *Journal of Marketing Research*, August 1989, pp. 285–298.

FIGURE 8–6 Growth Strategies: Leader Options

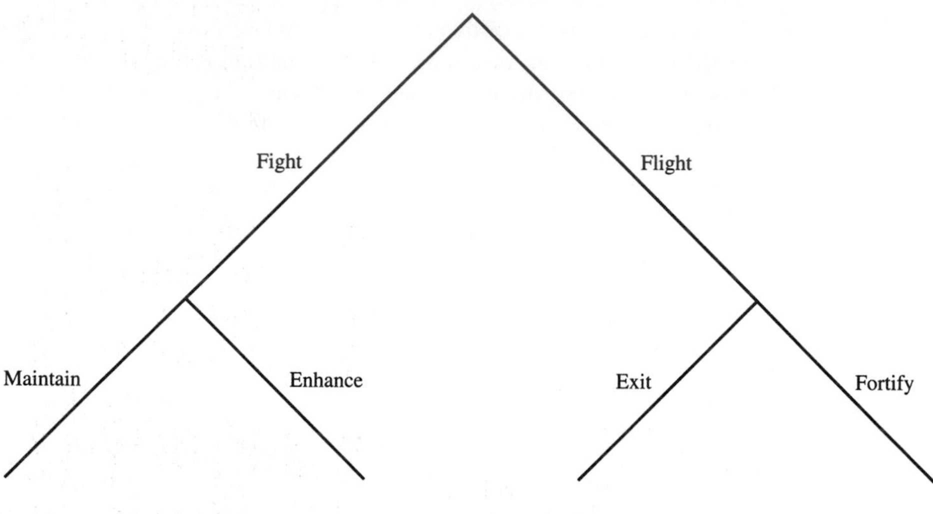

can be a strong number two or three brand, which can be accomplished through resegmenting the market.

As Figure 8–7 shows, the follower has a number of options depending on the strength of the leader, its own strength, and market conditions. One option is to simply exit quickly and invest in some product that has better long-term potential. The follower can also be content to be a strong number two or three by fortifying its position. Finally, the riskiest move is to try to leapfrog the competition. Some companies do this successfully through pure marketing muscle and an imitative product. For example, Johnson & Johnson often allows another company to establish the market and then becomes number one through its superior marketing. One example is in over-the-counter yeast infection drugs: Schering-Plough established the market and J&J followed with its Monistat 7 brand, which quickly obtained more than half of the market.[20] Other companies leapfrog through technological innovation. Although Yahoo was the first "spider" on the World Wide Web, Lycos and Digital Equipment Company's AltaVista are improved versions that gained usage share.

A good example of the growth situation shown in Figures 8–6 and 8–7 was faced by Docutel Corporation in the 1970s.[21] Docutel was the first company to develop and market automated teller machines (ATMs) to banks in the United States. The company was very small at the time, with only $25 million in sales in 1974. The market for ATMs grew rapidly during the 1970s as banks discovered they could use ATMs to differentiate themselves from other banks in a geographical area. However, new competitors entered

[20]Joseph Weber, "A Big Company That Works," *Business Week*, May 4, 1992, pp. 124–129.

[21]See Derek F. Abel, "Docutel Corporation," Harvard Business School case study 9-578-073, 1977, for further information.

FIGURE 8–7 Growth Strategies: Follower Options

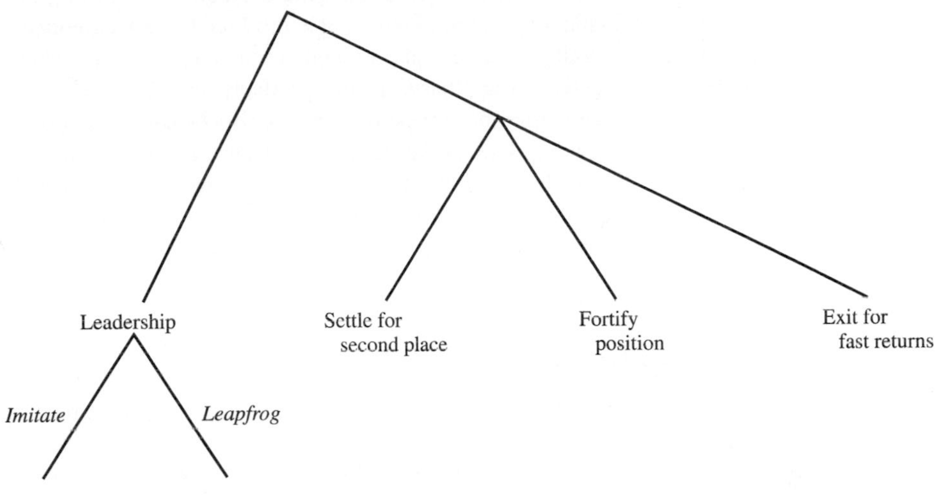

the market, including mainframe computer manufacturers IBM, Burroughs, and NCR, as well as two firms in the bank vault and security information business, Diebold and Mosler. In addition, customers became more concerned about cost savings from the machines as opposed to marketing advantages. Thus, Docutel, the market leader, had to make a fight-or-flight decision. Fighting would mean making substantial investments in marketing and product development, particularly in developing software to fit with banks' computer systems. In addition, the company would have to decide which market segments (defined geographically, by type and size of bank, etc.) it would target. Alternatively, the company could be a strong number two or three given the potential size of the market. Unfortunately, Docutel did not make a clear decision to pursue any strategy and was ultimately surpassed in the market by Diebold.

Strategies for Maturity

The maturity stage of the life cycle, of course, is characteristic of most products, particularly consumer products. Product categories exhibiting fierce battles for market share, access to distribution channels, large amounts of money spent on trade and customer promotion, and competitive pricing policies are probably in this stage of the product life cycle.

In the maturity phase of the life cycle, the sales curve has flattened out and relatively few new buyers are in the market. Market potential usually remains, but it is either very difficult or expensive to reach. Buyers are sophisticated and well versed in product features and benefits. Where differential advantage can be obtained, it is usually through intangible benefits such as image or through the extended product concept discussed earlier (e.g., service, distribution). Market segments are also well defined, and finding new ones that are untapped is a struggle.

The general strategies in mature markets are similar to those in growth markets: They depend on the relative market position of the product in question. In this case, however, leaders sometimes look at the time horizon for "cashing out" the product. If the product manager is committed to the product for an extended time period, the objective is usually to invest just enough money to maintain share. An alternative short-term objective is to "harvest" the product, that is, set an objective of gradual share decline with minimal investment to maximize short-run profits. The followers have some interesting alternatives that depend on the leader's strategy. If the leader is harvesting the product, the number one position may be left open for an aggressive number two brand. If the leader is intent on maintaining that position for a long time (many leading consumer packaged goods brands have been number one for over 50 years!), the follower may choose to be a profitable number two or to exit the category.

Strategies for the Decline Stage

In the decline stage of the life cycle, sales of the category are dropping. So is the number of competitors. Markets reach the decline stage for a variety of reasons. Perhaps the most obvious is technological obsolescence. The demise of the buggy whip is such a case. However, shifts in customer tastes also can create declining categories. The decline of brown alcohol consumption can be related to the changing tastes for "white" alcohol such as gin and vodka.

Perhaps the clearest strategy is to try to be the last in the market. By being last, a product gains monopoly rights to the few customers left. This, of course, results in the ability to charge commensurately high prices. For example, Lansdale Semiconductor is the last firm making the 8080 computer chip introduced by Intel in 1974. While most applications of computer chips are well beyond the 8080, the 8080 is still used in military systems that are typically built to last 20 to 25 years, such as the Hellfire and Pershing 2 missiles and the Aegis radar system for battleships. Where does the Department of Defense go when it needs 8080s? There is only one supplier: Lansdale.

Summary

One way to structure thinking about these strategic issues over the life cycle is to use a table such as the one in Figure 8–8. This audit of the life cycle is particularly useful in the latter stages of the cycle, because it permits the product manager to track changes in strategy over time. After having done this for several products, some similarities can be detected and general approaches to dealing with the diverse life cycle stages can be developed. It is particularly helpful to use Figure 8–8 to anticipate changes in strategy that are likely to occur as a result of changes in product category sales.

Managing Brand Equity

In several chapters of this book we refer to a concept called *brand equity,* the value of a brand name. Managing a product's brand name is one of the most important strategic

FIGURE 8–8 Life Cycle Audit

	Introduction	*Growth*	*Maturity*	*Decline*
Competitive position: leader/follower				
Objective				
Customer targets				
Competitor targets				
Product				
Price				
Distribution				
Communications				

jobs facing the product manager. Like other objects owned by a firm such as manufacturing equipment, buildings, and the like, a brand name is an asset, and a potentially valuable one.

For several years, the increased growth rates of private label brands and higher spending on price-oriented promotions led pundits to predict the "death" of national and international brands. This belief was given further credence when "Marlboro Friday," the Friday in April 1993 on which Philip Morris reduced the price of its venerable Marlboro brand by 40 cents per pack to combat private label cigarettes, caused sharp drops in the stock prices of manufacturers of national brands. This action was replicated by the cereal manufacturers, led by Post (also owned by Philip Morris) and Kellogg's in April 1996.

Since that date, however, companies have seen that the only way to combat lower-priced competitors, whether private labels for supermarket products or clones for computers, is to reemphasize their brand names. Companies such as Coca Cola, Hewlett-Packard, and Gillette are investing in advertising and attempting to reduce harmful price-oriented promotions. These efforts have caused the sales of private labels to plateau and have made 12 out of the 15 *Fortune* most admired companies household brand names.[22]

Brand names are also important in the global warfare against counterfeiters and "knockoffs," products that are made almost identical to the originals with very similar brand names and packaging but substantially lower prices. Knockoffs often mislead customers into thinking that the product is the well-known global brand. Counterfeiting is particularly prevalent in the music CD, computer software, and clothing industries and has been closely linked to China; the U.S. government has sent many trade missions to China to persuade them to crack down on these illegal activities. The problem is not just the lost revenues but the potential for the reputations of the global brands to be damaged by fraudulent poorly made substitutes.

Brand equity can be defined as follows:[23]

[22]Betsy Morris, "The Brand's the Thing," *Fortune*, March 4, 1996, pp. 72–86.

[23]The discussion in this section is based on David A. Aaker, *Brand Equity* (New York: The Free Press, 1991), and David A. Aaker, *Building Strong Brands* (New York: The Free Press, 1996).

> Brand equity is a set of assets (and liabilities) linked to a brand's name and symbol that adds to (or subtracts from) the value provided by a product or service to a firm and/or that firm's customers.

The assets and liabilities underlying brand value fall into five categories (see Figure 8–9):

1. *Brand loyalty.* The strongest measure of a brand's value is the loyalty (repeat buying, word of mouth) it engenders among customers. Sometimes the loyalty is circumstantial: Repeat buying comes from a lack of reasonable alternatives. Circumstantial loyalty includes what are called *proprietary* assets (e.g., patents, copyrights, trademarks) that give a firm at least a temporary monopoly position (the impact of generic drugs when an ethical drug comes off patent suggests that much of the advantage is in fact circumstantial and hence temporary). In other situations, loyalty reflects an *efficiency* motive: The brand is good, so we automatically select it to minimize effort. Notice that an important special case of efficiency loyalty occurs when a customer relies on an "expert" (e.g., a dealer) to make the choice for her or him and the expert has a preferred alternative. In this case, loyalty is really channel-created loyalty.

   The strongest form of loyalty is *attachment.* In this case, the customer doggedly seeks out a product, often out of deference to its role in a previous situation (e.g., "they were there when I needed them") and sometimes in an almost ritualistic manner (e.g., stopping at a certain ice cream store as a rite of summer). This level of loyalty insulates a brand from competitive pressures such as advertising and price promotion and leads to high margins and profits.
2. *Brand awareness.* The simplest form of brand equity is familiarity. A familiar brand gives the customer a feeling of *confidence* (risk reduction), and hence it is more likely to be both considered and chosen. There is also convincing evidence that, on average, customers *prefer* brands with which they are familiar. Finally, choosing a known brand gives the customer a *justification* for the decision, an explanation for his or her actions. This justification also serves a *social* role, indicating that the person has bought something of value.
3. *Perceived quality.* A known brand often conveys an aura of quality (either good or bad). A quality association can be of the general halo type; for example, Levi Strauss has an outstanding reputation both for its products and as a place to work. The associations can also be attribute or category specific: Gillette makes fine-quality razors, Apple produces user-friendly products, and Samsonite products last forever. In some cases, a brand becomes synonymous with a category (e.g., Xerox, Kleenex, FedEx). Further, a brand often has strong price associations that influence quality perceptions (e.g., a Kmart brand product is expected to be low in price and probably low in quality as well). Thus, strong quality associations exist for many products and brands.
4. *Brand association.* While quality associations are very important, other, more subjective and emotional associations are also an important part of brand value. These include *personal* associations; Gatorades' "Be Like Mike" campaign was a blatant example, but every celebrity endorsement contains elements of it.

FIGURE 8–9 Brand Equity

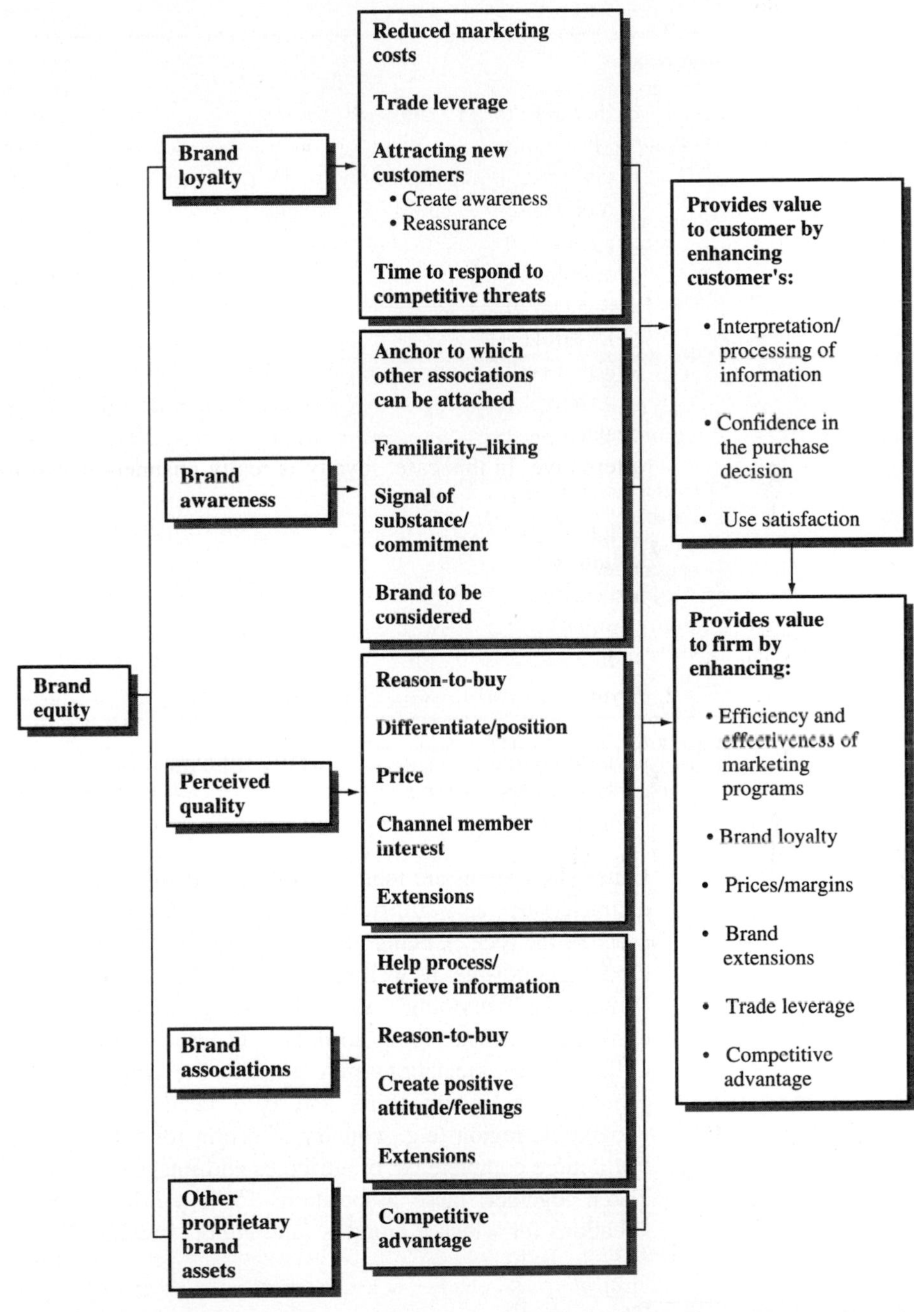

Source: Reprinted with permission of the Free Press, a division of Simon & Schuster from *Building Strong Brands* by David A. Aaker. Copyright 1996 by David A. Aaker.

FIGURE 8–10 Some Brand Attribute and Image Dimensions

Attributes	*Image Dimensions*
Flavor/taste	Reliable—unreliable
Caffeine content	Old—young
Price	Technical—nontechnical
Packaging	Sensible—rash
Size	Interesting—boring
Calories	Creative—noncreative
Brand name	Sentimental—nonsentimental
Sweetness	Impulsive—deliberate
Weight	Trustworthy—untrustworthy
Warranty	Conforming—rebellious
Durability	Daring—cautious
Convenience	Forceful—submissive
Color	Bold—timid
Style	Sociable—unsociable
Comfort	
Freshness	
Construction material	
Availability	
Serviceability	
Compatibility	
Energy efficiency	
Instructions	
Automation	
Ease of use	

Source: Rajeev Batra, Donald R. Lehmann, and Dipinder Singh, "The Brand Personality Component of Brand Goodwill: Some Antecedents and Consequences," in David A. Aaker and Alexander L. Biel, eds., *Brand Equity and Advertising: Advertising's Role in Building Strong Brands* (Hillsdale, N.J.: Lawrence Erlbaum Associates, 1993), pp. 83–96.

Other associations are more emotional, relating to such lifestyle or personality characteristics as *stability* (see many Kodak ads, as well as Prudential's "A piece of the rock"), being *"hip"* or *"with it"* (a standard appeal of fashionable clothing companies as well as soft drinks, beer, and liquor; e.g., Andre Agassi's "Image is Everything" ads), and being *responsible* (e.g., environmentally conscious, currently both an important issue and the subject of much hype). Other strong associations may be with the type of customer or user of the product (e.g., white shirts and bald heads with business executives) or geographic region (e.g., country of origin for Japanese cars, Swiss watches). For a more complete list of attributes and image dimensions, see Figure 8–10. Taken together, these associations form a *brand personality* that suggests situations for which a brand is (and is not) suitable.[24]

[24]Rajeev Batra, Donald R. Lehmann, and Dipinder Singh, "The Brand Personality Component of Brand Goodwill: Some Antecedents and Consequences," in David A. Aaker and Alexander L. Biel, eds., *Brand Equity and Advertising: Advertising's Role in Building Strong Brands* (Hillsdale, N.J.: Lawrence Erlbaum Associates, 1993), pp. 83–96.

5. *Other brand assets.* Other assets, such as patents and trademarks, are valuable to products.

Brand equity creates value for both customers and the firm. Customers can use brand names as simplifying heuristics for processing large amounts of information: awareness of the brand name Lexus and the brand associations generated can act as a substitute for reading *Consumer Reports,* talking to friends, and other methods of getting information. Dannon chose to market its new brand of bottled water under the assumption that consumers who view its yogurt positively will transfer that good feeling to the new product. Over-the-counter cold and headache remedies by well-known companies such as Bayer and Johnson & Johnson command significantly higher prices than their private label counterparts because of the trust consumers have in those companies. Thus, firms benefit enormously from having strong brand names. Investment in a brand name can be leveraged through brand extensions and increased distribution. High brand equity often allows higher prices to be charged and is therefore a significant competitive advantage.

An example of the power of brand names is the ill-fated Audi 5000, which was accused on a widely viewed edition of TV's "60 Minutes" of having a problem with sudden acceleration. The program claimed the car suddenly lurched forward without the driver's foot being on the gas pedal. Audi failed to view one of its chief marketing jobs as protecting the brand name. As a result, the company handled the problem by accusing U.S. drivers of making mistakes and stepping on the accelerator rather than the brake. Regardless of the truth (it was eventually concluded that the cars did not have a problem), protecting the asset—the company's brand name—should have been Audi's priority. The sales of *all* Audi products dropped two-thirds between 1985 and 1989. Later the manufacturer introduced new models (Quattro, 100, etc.) and eliminated the problem-ridden 4000 and 5000 lines.[25]

The concept of brand equity raises three important issues for product managers. First, it is critical to the long-term success of a product to build brand equity by paying attention to the five dimensions cited earlier. This is particularly important for packaged goods manufacturers that face increasing competition from supermarkets' "own label" brands. The price difference a national brand can support relative to a private label is a direct function of the level of brand equity of the national brand. Second, the question of product-line extensions becomes pertinent: How far can a successful brand name be stretched? Clearly Toyota, Nissan, and Honda believed luxury cars could not be sold with cars with a cheaper image; hence the development of Lexus, Infiniti, and Acura, respectively. The brand names not only are different but are sold in entirely different dealerships. However, Mitsubishi believed otherwise. It marketed its new luxury coupe, the Diamante, along with the rest of its product line.

The third issue is that the product manager must view the management and sustenance of brand equity as an important task. David Aaker[26] provides 10 guidelines for building strong brands:

---

[25]This problem of how to handle disasters and their impact on the brand name continues to surface. Witness the recent problem with British beef and its perceived link to "mad cow" disease. At the time of this writing, no country in the world would import British beef, a multibillion-dollar industry.

[26]Aaker, *Building Strong Brands.*

1. *Brand identity.* Each brand should have an identity, a personality. It can be modified for different segments.
2. *Value proposition.* Each brand should have a unique value proposition.
3. *Brand position.* The brand's position should provide clear guidance to those implementing a communications program.
4. *Execution.* The communications program needs to be executed to implement the identity and position, and should be durable as well.
5. *Consistency over time.* Product managers should have a goal of maintaining a consistent identity, position, and execution over time. Changes should be resisted.
6. *Brand system.* The brands in the portfolio should be consistent and synergistic.
7. *Brand leverage.* Extend brands and develop cobranding opportunities only if the brand identity will be both used and reinforced.
8. *Tracking.* The brand's equity should be tracked over time, including awareness, perceived quality, brand loyalty, and brand associations.
9. *Brand responsibility.* Someone should be in charge of the brand who will create the identity and positions and coordinate the execution.
10. *Invest.* Continue investing in brands even when the financial goals are not being met.

Measuring Brand Value

Product managers can measure overall brand value through a variety of means. Basically, measuring brand value requires answering the question "How much more value does the product have with the brand name attached?" Most of the methods we discuss in Chapter 10 on determining customer value can be used to do this. One other method already discussed, conjoint analysis, can also be used. By simply using brand name as an attribute and using the different brand names in the market or fictitious brand names being considered for a new product, the part-worths estimated are quantitative measures of the value of a brand name relative to the others used in the experimental design. (Recall in the example in Chapter 6, we found different values for Compaq and Gateway.)

A related method relies on so-called hedonic regression. This technique combines actual product features and prices to regress market price (or the amount customers say they are willing to pay for various products) against product features and brand name:

$$Price = B_0 + B_1(\text{Feature 1}) + B_2(\text{Feature 2}) + \ldots + C_1(\text{Brand A}) + C_2(\text{Brand B}) + \ldots$$

The output gives a dollar value for each brand. (Of course, when actual prices are used, this analysis ignores the sales volume of each brand, so it may present a somewhat distorted view of the value to those customers who choose to buy each product.)

The various components of brand value can also be assessed in relatively straightforward ways. Different levels of awareness measurement (e.g., aided or unaided) are possible. Quality associations can be directly assessed ("If ABC Inc.

made a product with X amount of attribute A, how much of attribute B would you expect it to have?").

Given the large amount of attention paid to brand equity in the last few years, it is not surprising that a variety of consulting firms, advertising agencies, and other interested parties have developed their own approaches to measuring the value of brands and, as a result, some rankings of relative brand equities. The board of governors of the United Kingdom's Accounting Standards Board held public hearings on new rules that may require all companies to value their brands. Some companies in the United Kingdom and the United States are starting to carry brands on their balance sheets. Grand Metropolitan, for example, carries specific brand equities for Smirnoff, Pillsbury, and Burger King.

One approach called Valmatrix analysis, by Trademark and Licensing Associates (TLA), values a brand by the amount another party will pay to rent or buy the brand name. TLA bases its valuation on comparable sales, licensing, and royalty agreements, as well as on 20 key descriptors of brand strength such as margins, life cycle position, extension potential, and others. The rank order of brand names in Health and Beauty Aids is Gillette, Johnson & Johnson, Estée Lauder, Chanel, and Avon; for Apparel/Fashion it is Nike, Adidas, Reebok, Dior, and Yves Saint Laurent.[27]

An example of a survey approach is Total Research's EquiTrend, in which 2,000 households are polled by telephone. Consumers are asked to rate brands on a scale from 0 to 10 where 10 represents extraordinary quality and 0 poor or unacceptable quality. In its 1996 survey, the top five brand names were Kodak, Disney World, National Geographic, The Discovery Channel, and Mercedez-Benz; the bottom five (out of the top 100) were Wal-Mart, Apple Macintosh, The Disney Store, Toyota Landcruiser, and Universal Studios.[28]

An example from the technology area is a quarterly survey conducted by Techtel Corporation. The firm surveys business buyers of computer equipment including software and hardware on behavioral measures such as awareness, trial, purchase, and repurchase intention. The survey also measures the percentage of the buyers who have a positive opinion about a brand. An illustration of the results is shown in Figure 8–11 for IBM notebook computers. The squares represent the opinion measure while the vertical bars represent those who bought recently (within the previous quarter). While the opinion measure itself is a measure of brand strength, the obviously high correlation between the positive opinion and purchasing measures gives some assurance that the brand strength is being converted into actual buying behavior.

Illustrations

RTD Fruit Drinks: Snapple

As described in earlier analyses, the ready-to-drink fruit drink category is currently a $12.2 billion (retail) market that is growing at roughly 3 percent per year. The category

[27]Terry Lefton and Weston Anson, "How Much Is Your Brand Worth?" *Brandweek*, January 29, 1996, pp. 43–44.

[28]Sean Mehegan, "A Picture of Quality," *Brandweek*, April 8, 1996, pp. 38–40.

FIGURE 8–11 IBM Notebook: Purchase versus Positive Opinion

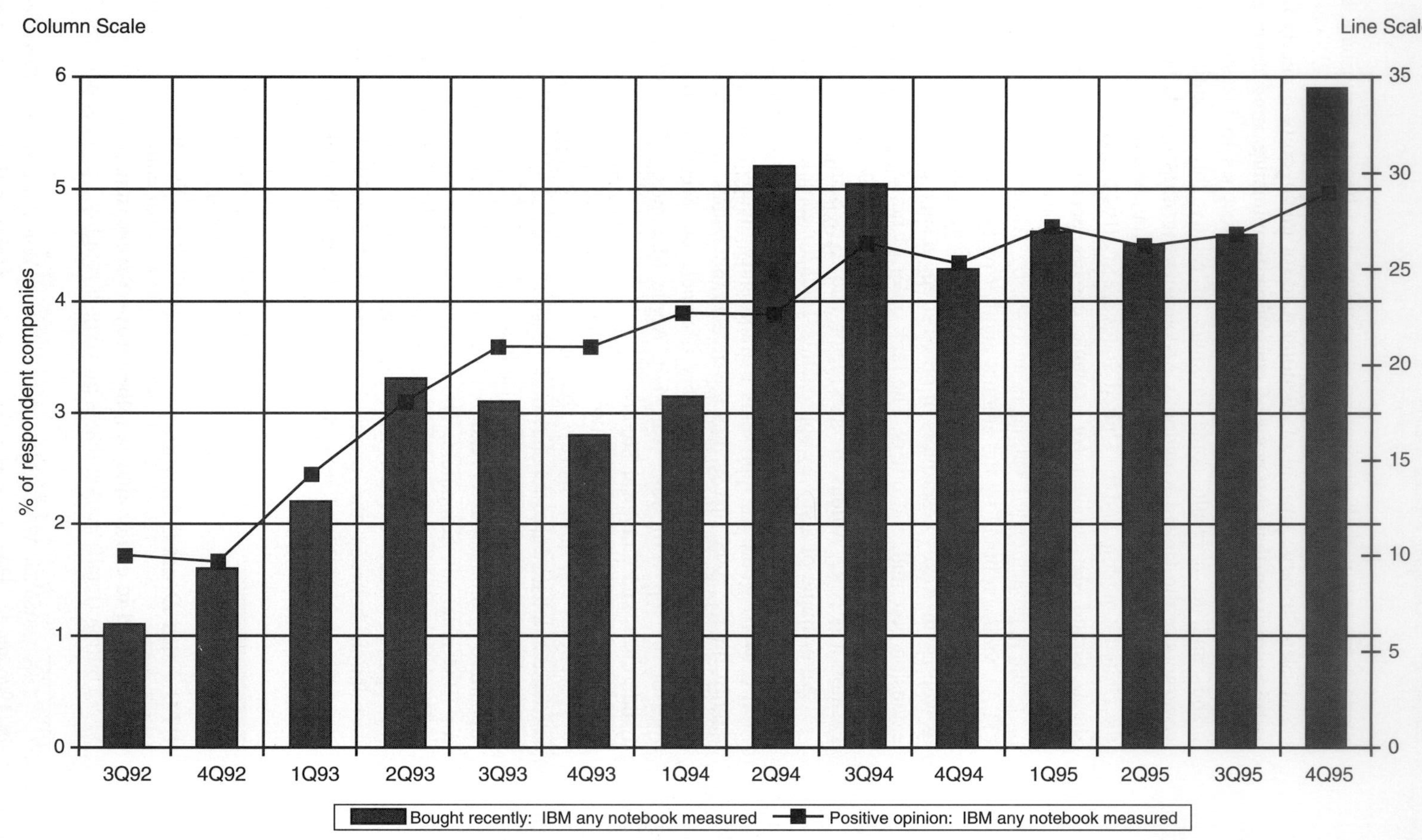

Techtel Corporation, Emeryville, CA.

Source: Developed by Techtel Corp. T-MAS™ © 1992-1996 and data © 1987-1996 by Techtel Corp. and others.

is in the late growth stage. Forecasts described in Chapter 7 predict growth slightly below this level for 1996. Snapple's current market share is about 25 percent, but the brand has experienced problems with the Quaker takeover, particularly in the area of distribution. The CEO of Quaker Oats, William Smithburg, is under intense pressure from stock analysts to turn the situation around.

Objective. Given Snapple's current market share of 25 percent and the need to be aggressive, the objective for 1996 is to achieve a 30 percent share of the RTD fruit drink category. This is still down from Snapple's 1993 share of 34 percent, but it is attempting to regain lost ground in a more competitive environment. Based on a category sales forecast for 1996 of 3.39 billion gallons, this translates into just over 1 billion gallons of volume for Snapple.

Strategic Alternatives. The data in Figures 6–20 and 6–21 (pages 172 and 174) help determine the strategic objectives. For growth, the three main options for Snapple are to get its current customers to consume more (market penetration), get more customers to buy in its current segments (market development), and explore new segments (market development). Clearly potential exists in the current segments. (See Figure 6-21.) Expanding to new segments by pursuing other demographic groups also could be tried. Stealing competitors' customers is expensive, but might be considered since any generic advertising Snapple does that benefits the category would also benefit Snapple as the market leader.

Customer Targets. The major customer targets for current customers and nonusers in current segments are described in Chapter 6: educated, 18 to 54 years old, has an employed female homemaker, has a male spouse who is an executive/professional, upper income, Middle Atlantic/Pacific resident, urban, and single. Clearly, Snapple has room to grow geographically as well, so targeting the East Central and South West, the next two best Snapple segments (see Figure 6–21), is also warranted.

Competitor Targets. The major competitors are Ocean Spray and Fruitopia.

Core Strategy. Since the segment is still growing, albeit more slowly, a price/cost–based positioning/value proposition does not make sense and is inconsistent with prior strategy. Snapple built its popularity by emphasizing fun and friendly people. Now that it is part of a larger company, the challenge is to continue to deliver that message convincingly, that it is the same brand it used to be. Thus, Snapple should position itself as the best "New Age" beverage on the market, delivering consistently high-quality refreshment with many flavor options. The brand has substantial brand equity, and the product manager needs to manage that equity carefully by continuing to build positive associations with the brand for consumers.

Personal Digital Assistants: The Sharp Wiz

This marketing strategy is for one of the two Sharp products described earlier in this book, the Wiz (the other being the Zaurus). The product is new to the United States, so the strategy can be viewed as the introductory one since the Japanese market where it has been marketed differs substantially.

Objective. The product category is in the growth stage of the product life cycle (see the category analysis in Chapter 4). Because it is a new entrant, profits are not a logical objective since the product needs to establish a beachhead in the market. Our market forecast was for flat growth in 1996, or 284,000 units (see the application of the Bass model in Chapter 7). Allowing for some conservatism in the forecast due to possible price decreases for which we do not account in the simple form of the Bass model, the market is more likely to be around 300,000 in size. A new product in this disorganized category should be able to gain 10 percent of the market, or 30,000 units, by the end of 1996.

Strategic Alternatives. The only options available involve market development, since there are few current customers. The two available options therefore are to pursue new customers in segments being targeted by competing products and pursue new segments altogether.

Customer Targets. The key customer targets can be described by the demographics shown in Figure 6–22 (page 176): mobile professionals, usually well-educated men. These can be "Wide Area Travelers" or "Local Area Travelers" who have some need for mobile devices that collect and store important information and display that information when needed. A new segment that can be pursued is professional women, as the Wiz's size and styling may appeal to that group.

Competitor Targets. The closest competitors in terms of features and price are the OmniGo and the Psion 3a.

Core Strategy. The value proposition/position for the Wiz is low price. The product is positioned as the lowest-cost PDA that offers significant feature advantages over the low-end personal organizers. This will attract those customers who are interested in more features with little sacrifice in price and those who are generally interested in PDAs but have been turned off by their high prices.

Summary

This chapter provides the reason for doing the background analyses described in Chapters 3 through 7. The major results of the marketing plan are objectives and strategies for the product that synthesize the current market situation into a recommended plan of action. The strategy then leads to specific recommendations for marketing programs, such as pricing and advertising. Thus, the strategy acts as a focal point: The drawing on data and the situation analysis leading to specific marketing programs. The success of a strategy is largely dependent on the integration of analysis and programs in providing a coherent direction for the product.

C H A P T E R

9 NEW PRODUCTS

Overview

New products are the subject of considerable interest and study. This book has intentionally focused on existing products, partly because unless they are successful, an organization will have no resources to develop and launch new products. In addition, as you will see, much of the same logic behind marketing existing products applies to new products. However, because of their importance, we briefly introduce new products in this chapter. Readers interested in a more in-depth treatment should consult one of the many excellent books on the subject.[1]

In 1995, over 22,000 new products were introduced in U.S. supermarkets. Most were not very new, however; rather, the "slightly new" products consisted of minor variations on existing products through (1) changing ingredients (e.g., to reduce the fat content of foods), (2) adding features, or (3) "me-too" entrants that closely resemble existing (competitors') products. These products account for substantial sales and profits and for that reason are very important. Further, the production process involved may be quite sophisticated. Still, these are essentially "lemon-scented" products (named for the first new product, a lemon-scented soap, studied by one of the authors) also known as *continuous innovations.* Most of their sales are drawn from existing products in the category. In general, customers readily understand what these products are used for and what they compete with (e.g., lemon-scented soap competes with lime-scented soap). These products contrast markedly with "really new" products (e.g., xerography), which create or greatly expand a product. While really new products are rare (one consumer packaged goods company has a database of over 5,000 new products of which none may be really new), their impact can be substantial (e.g., Netscape).

[1]See, for example, Robert G. Cooper, *Winning New Products,* 2nd ed. (Reading, Mass.: Addison-Wesley, 1993); William L. Moore and Edgar A. Pessemier, *Product Planning and Management* (New York: McGraw-Hill, 1993); and Glen L. Urban and John R. Hauser, *Design and Marketing of New Products,* 2nd ed. (Englewood Cliffs, N.J.: Prentice Hall, 1993).

The development of new products typically occurs in stages. At each stage, the product is evaluated to determine whether it makes sense to proceed to the next stage. Most products follow a pattern such as the following:

1. Idea generation
2. Concept development
3. Initial feasibility screening
4. Concept testing
5. Product development
6. Product testing
7. Market testing
8. Go–no go decision

While this approach works fairly well for slightly new products, it is difficult to apply to really new ones. Not surprisingly, the development and marketing of lemon-scented and really new products differ markedly. For that reason, we discuss these processes separately.

Getting Ideas for Slightly New Products

Ideas for product modifications and extensions come from many sources, both proactive and reactive, and are discussed extensively in books focusing on new-product development. Sources that rely on active efforts of the company include many aspects of the situation analysis:

1. *Customer analysis,* in particular usage/needs analyses and surveys of attitudes and attribute importance, including both unstructured (e.g., focus groups) and structured (e.g., conjoint analysis) approaches. Also, many companies maintain facilities where customers are less obtrusively observed using company products or product mock-ups (e.g., Sony on Michigan Avenue in Chicago, Whirlpool at its headquarters).
2. *Competitor analysis,* specifically studying what competitors sell or are working on. Most new products are copies of competitors' products (e.g., RC Cola first introduced diet cola).
3. *Active search,* particularly of new products and processes in other areas with an eye toward incorporating them in the company's own product.
4. *Category analysis,* typically examining changing social trends and technologies (often through various media and trade associations).

In addition, a number of sources often present ideas, suggestions, and complaints that lead to new products. The company needs to react to complaints and suggestions from the following:

1. Customers and noncustomers who reject its current products.
2. Company employees, especially the sales force.
3. Suppliers, who are also a good source of information about competitors.

4. Distribution channels.
5. Operations people, who often suggest ways to simplify a process.
6. Internal R&D.
7. Entrepreneurs, who often approach larger companies with ideas or products. (Of course, this can raise a number of legal and ethical issues about ownership of the idea.)

When such sources are combined with intuition (managerial judgment), there is no shortage of sources for new-product ideas. The real issue is how to recognize a good idea when confronted with it. Remember, Teflon and Post-it Notes were basically mistakes that a "prepared mind" saw as having value.

Product Modification

Phrases such as *continuous quality improvement, cost containment,* and *updated styling* all point toward modifying the product. Such modification can be of three types: clearly better (e.g., an upgrade), different (e.g., a styling or ingredient change that is likely to appeal more to some customers and less to others), and inferior (e.g., the substitution of a less expensive ingredient or aspect of the offering). In assessing the desirability of a product change, the reactions of three groups are crucial: loyal customers, occasional customers, and current noncustomers. Obviously, the ideal situation is for all three groups to try the new version, prefer it, and buy it more often. Because this almost never occurs, however, real decisions involve assessing the likely changes in behavior in different groups and then, based on demand and cost considerations, making a decision.

The basic modification dilemma can be considered by using the typology in Figure 9–1. The task begins by assessing the number of loyal customers, occasional customers, and noncustomers who might consider trying a new version of a product. Next, the trial rates for each group must be assessed. Consider the now famous New Coke introduction. One unforeseen problem with the introduction was that loyal Coke buyers would not even try the new version: Coke was a prisoner of its past success and brand equity to the point where many loyal Coke drinkers viewed any change as undesirable. Thus, an interesting trade-off appears at the trial stage: Big changes may induce noncustomers to try but cost you loyal customers; small changes may retain loyals but not attract new customers. Consequently, we could expect more dramatic changes from smaller-share products that risk losing fewer loyal customers.

After trial, the product manager must ascertain the reaction. Here we (somewhat arbitrarily) divide reaction into three categories: prefer the new version, like the new version about the same as the old (essentially indifference), or not like the new version (prefer the old).

The final information needed is the profit implications of each combination of customer type, decision to try or not try, and reaction to trial. Some profit implications are relatively clear: Nontrial by loyal or occasional customers means the loss of these customers and hence whatever lifetime value they represent. Similarly, if loyal or occasional customers try the new product and are indifferent between the new and old

FIGURE 9–1 Assessing the Impact of Product Redesign on Customers

Current Customers	*Reaction*	*Response after Trial*	*Impact on Sales/Profits*
1. Loyal	A. Try	1) Prefer	Gain
		2) Like	Neutral
		3) Not like	Loss
	B. Not try		Loss
2. Occasional	A. Try	1) Prefer	Gain
		2) Like	Trial sales gain
		3) Not like	Loss
	B. Not try		Loss
3. Noncustomers	A. Try	1) Prefer	Gain
		2) Like	Trial sales gain
		3) Not like	Trial sales gain
	B. Not try		Neutral

versions, there is no profit implication other than the change in margin resulting from price and cost differences between the new and old formulations (which affects all categories of customers). Triers among either occasional customers or noncustomers who find the product "good but not great" essentially contribute whatever profits (or losses) result from their trial sale and then return to their traditional buying patterns. In considering new variants, then, the impact of customers can be structured via a decision tree, which shows that the big plus is occasional users or nonusers who increase their usage and the big minus is loyal customers who decrease or cease usage.

Of course, noncustomer considerations are also relevant. The most obvious is cost. This includes both the raw material cost and any other costs of the offering (e.g., the amount of the deductible on insurance policies, the interest rate on money market accounts, the amount of training offered). Other considerations include the impact on employees (in terms of morale) and the overall image of the company.

It is important to recognize that modifications can occur not just in the physical product but in any aspect of the offering. Changing channels of distribution (e.g., by selling a product previously available in specialty stores through discount stores) can either increase or decrease the potential market and can also affect the quality image of the product and hence its brand equity and sales. Similarly, lowering price or changing the advertising focus can both open new markets (customer segments) and reduce or cut off old ones. Perhaps the most interesting type of product modification involves service. A fairly ordinary flower becomes special when it is personally delivered; a simple oil change for a car becomes an event if the garage provides a comfortable waiting area.

For many products, packaging is an integral part of the product (e.g., styling in cars). For others, the package is also a dispensing mechanism with appeal of its own (e.g., Smuckers wide-mouth jam jars, squeezable ketchup bottles, pump toothpaste, liquid soap containers). For some, the container is merely a covering. Even for mere coverings, however, the package presents an opportunity for advertising and image building. McDonald's change in packaging from plastic to biodegradable paper earned the company many positive reactions. Packaging changes have contributed to a surge in sales for many products, including Kaytee bird seed and Ray-O-Vac batteries.[2] Sutter Home's white zinfandel wine sales were reported to have increased 15 percent in six weeks following a label redesign. Of course, not all packaging innovations are successful (e.g., Benedicta's mayonnaise in a tube).

Changing a package is not cheap; often a few hundred thousand dollars are spent on design and retooling for a simple label change. Relative to advertising and promotion, however, package change is fairly inexpensive. Remember that packaging is inherently part of the product and should be treated—and potentially altered—as any other attribute would be.

Although all these modifications have specialized aspects, they can be evaluated using a version of the customer analysis framework in Figure 9–1, combined with cost and profit data. Notice that many modifications have both a fixed-cost component (the cost of the changeover) and a variable-cost-per-unit impact.

Product Variants

Product variants, also known as line extensions, are a popular way to create new products and capitalize on the original brand's equity. Many products actually are product families with a number of close relatives designed to appeal to various segments. Lemon-scented soaps and carbide-tipped drill bits are variations on a basic product. Some variants that simply add a small amount of a new ingredient to a basic product have been wildly successful (e.g., seltzer with fruit flavor); others have been flops (e.g., Clairol's Touch of Yogurt Shampoo). A question that arises, then, is how many different Tides, Jell-Os, Mazda 626s, or Compaq computers there should be.

The reason for using multiple versions is simple: They can appeal to multiple segments, either increasing potential sales (the customer base) or allowing for price discrimination among users with slightly different needs and preferences (e.g., the multiple fares and conditions for airline seats). The reason for not using multiple versions is likewise straightforward: Efficiency of operation (production, inventory, distribution) is enhanced when there are fewer versions to worry about, and overuse of a brand may dilute and weaken brand equity. Basically, the choice of number of product variations involves the trade-off between two strategies that have both at times been highly successful: Henry Ford's Model T ("any color as long as it is black") and Alfred Sloan's multiple nameplates (Chevy, Pontiac, Oldsmobile, Buick, Cadillac). The efficient (Model T) strategy failed when the market began to develop distinct segments. The multiple nameplate strategy proved unsuccessful when model proliferation and overlap (including the now infamous use of Chevy engines in Cadillacs) created customer confusion and the lack of an integrated manufacturing strategy (i.e., a common "platform" across models, which had successfully been implemented by Japanese automakers) led to increased costs. The choice of number of versions of a basic product to offer follows the "Goldilocks" principle: not too few, not too many, but just the right number. The car example also points out another fundamental

---

[2]Gretchen Morgenson, "Is Your Product Your Advocate?" *Forbes,* September 14, 1992, p. 468.

FIGURE 9–2 **Considerations in Adding or Dropping a Variant**

Adding	*Dropping*
Customer based	
New customers attracted	Old customers lost
Old customer cannibalization	Customer switching
Confusion and dilution of brand equity	Signal of weakness
Operations based	
Loss of economies of scale	Impaired efficiency
Problems in gaining additional distribution	Maintaining distribution
Additional servicing needs	Servicing old versions

principle: Involving operations thinking in designing variants, not just bringing them in after the product is designed, will save money and potentially improve customer acceptance.

Assuming a certain number of versions exist, the more relevant question is whether to increase or decrease the number on the margin. Should a variant be added or deleted? Beyond saying it depends on the long-run incremental profit, it is often useful to break down the consideration of adding or dropping a variant into customer-oriented and operations-oriented concerns (see Figure 9–2).

Adding a Product Variant

One reason to add a product variant is to attract new customers, from either a market development or a penetration perspective (see Chapter 8). One concern in doing so is current customer switching (cannibalization), which can be either beneficial (e.g., going from a lower-margin to a higher-margin version) or detrimental. Both of these possibilities require good estimates of profit implications, which in this case place a value on a new customer, typically a value much greater than that of the initial sale and the contribution margins of the different versions before and after addition of the new version. In other words, you need both customer and cost data to evaluate the effect of adding a product variant. A final, and unfortunately, even harder to assess, aspect of adding versions is customer confusion and dilution of brand equity. Customer confusion is a special problem when the new version differs not in aesthetics (e.g., flavor or color), but in quality level. In the automobile industry, levels of options (DE/DX, LE/LX) are essentially appended to the same basic vehicle and seem to be well received and understood. However, when the intended quality spread gets wide enough, even car manufacturers tend to create a new name (e.g., Honda introduced the Acura). Black & Decker essentially gave up trying to sell its regular line of power tools to professional users; instead, it bought and promoted a line, DeWalt, to the professional market.

It is generally easier to gain customer acceptance by producing a variant of similar quality than to create one of substantially higher quality. Of course, it is relatively easy to sell a lower-quality (or at least lower-priced) version of a product, but doing so tends to decrease loyalty and equity, sometimes dramatically.

There is also something to be said for maintaining a relatively streamlined set of product variants from the customer's viewpoint. Assuming customers do not view choosing a product as their life's work, they may appreciate a limited choice with clear distinctions among versions. As a corollary, customers may avoid products for which an overabundance of versions makes choosing the best one more trouble than it is worth. The information overload facing a purchaser of snow skis or tennis rackets sometimes makes customers postpone a decision because of confusion and the desire not to make the wrong decision.

In addition to customer considerations, operational issues influence the decision to add a variant. The most obvious impact is on efficiency through economies of scale. Although flexible manufacturing can cut the cost penalty for offering different versions, labeling, stocking and inventory, and demand forecasting still add costs. Each version has the potential to be misforecast, leading to problems of understocking (and hence customer disenchantment) or overstocking (which results in additional carrying costs and distress sales). Another issue is distribution. Many distribution channels (or customers in the case of direct sales) like to be able to obtain multiple items from the same supplier (which argues for a large number of variants), but not so many that their own inventory and sales tasks become too complicated (which argues for a limited number of versions). A manufacturing company may be given a fixed amount of product space (shelf facings) for its products, meaning any increase in one version (e.g., cherry flavored) means a decrease in the retail support of another (e.g., lemon-lime). The sales staff must also be able to allocate time and effort across variants. In other words, constraints often make it inappropriate to consider a product variant independently of the existing product.

Dropping a Product Variant

The decision to drop a variant (product deletion), typically one with slow sales or low profits, is in many ways just the opposite of the decision to add a variant. Considerations include how customers of the old version will react, as well as cost and operational issues. One difference is that dropping a variant means there is one less product version to contribute to (absorb) overhead costs. If any type of burdened costing system is used, dropping a version will adversely affect the costs, and hence the profits, of other versions. Another and more important consideration is the signal that dropping a version can send. Dropping a variant is an admission of failure and may be seen by customers or distribution channels as an indication of reduced commitment to the product category.

Formal Testing of Slightly New Products

While general guidelines exist for new-product success,[3] it is prudent to test each new product separately. This section discusses some of the most common tests.

[3]Robert G. Cooper, "New Products: The Factors That Drive Success," *International Marketing Review* 11 (March 1994), pp. 60–76; Mitzi M. Montoya-Weiss and Roger Calantone, "Determinants of New Product Performance: A Review and Meta Analysis," *Journal of Product Innovation Management* 11 (December 1994), pp. 397–417.

Concept Testing

The initial test for most new products involves getting customer reactions to the product concept. The main purposes of a concept test are to (1) choose the most promising from a set of alternatives, (2) get an initial notion of the commercial prospects of a concept, (3) find out who is most interested in the concept, and (4) indicate what direction further development work should take. Samples are often convenience oriented. Common sample sources include community groups, employees, and central locations (e.g., shopping centers).

The most common approach is to present consumers with a verbal or written statement of the product idea and then record their reactions. Recently many researchers have chosen to include physical mock-ups and advertising statements in the concept test. (These are really prototype or prototype/concept tests.) The data gathered are both diagnostic (why do you like/not like the product?) and predictive (would you buy it if it cost $____?). Including a concrete "would you buy" question is crucial if the results are to be at all useful predictively. The data collection procedures fall into the following three major categories.

Surveys. Surveys are useful for getting large samples for projection purposes. On the other hand, it is often difficult to effectively convey a concept in a survey, especially an impersonal one. The appendix to this chapter shows some different mail concept tests taken from an NFO brochure.

Focus Groups. The strength of focus groups is their diagnostic power in that they can be used to get detailed discussions of various aspects of the concept. As predictors of actual sales, they are fairly inaccurate due to their small sample sizes.

Demonstrations. A popular way to present a concept is to gather a group of consumers, present them with a "story" about the new product, and record their reactions. Questions asked typically relate to the following:

1. Do they understand the concept?
2. Do they believe the concept?
3. Is the concept different from other products in an important way?
4. If different, is the difference beneficial?
5. Do they like or dislike the concept? Why?
6. What could be done to make the product more acceptable?
7. How would they like to see the product (color, size, etc.)?
8. Would they buy it?
9. What price would they expect to pay for it?
10. What would their usage be in terms of volume, purpose, source of purchase, and so forth?

Actually, concept tests themselves vary. The most basic concept test is a concept screening test that describes several concepts briefly and asks subjects for an overall evaluation (e.g., intention to buy). Screening tests are used to reduce the concepts under consideration to a manageable number. Next, concept generation tests (often involving focus groups) are used to refine the concept statements. This is typically followed by concept evaluation tests. These tests are based on larger samples and attempt to quantitatively assess demand for the concept based on samples of 200 to 300. Such tests are typically done competitively in the sense that other new concepts and/or existing products are evaluated at the same time.[4]

Product Use Tests

This type of research consists of physically producing the product[5] and then getting consumers to use it. The purpose of a product test is to (1) uncover product shortcomings, (2) evaluate commercial prospects, (3) evaluate alternative formulations, (4) uncover the appeal of the product to various market segments, and (5) if lucky, gain ideas for other elements of the marketing program. Such tests may be either branded (best for estimating sales) or unbranded/blind (best for focusing directly on physical formulation).

There are three major types of product use tests. Initially such tests are usually conducted with small samples (often using convenience samples, such as employees). These initial tests are diagnostic and are directed toward eliminating serious problems with the product (e.g., the jar won't fit in the door of a refrigerator), as well as getting a rough idea of how good it is vis-à-vis competitive products. This phase also allows the company to find out how the product is actually used and, potentially, to change the target appeal. Employee testing is commonly used in connection with food products.

The second type of use test includes a limited time horizon forced-trial situation where customers are given the product to use and asked for their reactions to it. At the end, a simulated purchase occasion is also used. This may consist of a hypothetical "would you buy" type of question or, better, an actual choice situation where the customer either chooses one of a set of products, including the new product (usually at a reduced price), or simply chooses to "buy" or not buy the new product. To get a meaningful result, many researchers use a stratified sample. The strata are usually either product category usage rate (heavy, medium, light, none) or brand usually used. This stratification ensures adequate sample size to predict the effect of the product on the key market segments.

The most elaborate form of product use test requires placement of the product in homes (or business settings for industrial products) for an extended period. For packaged goods, this period is usually about two months. The advantage of this extended period is that the results allow for both the wear-out of initial expectations and the development of problems that manifest themselves only over time (e.g., food that goes stale). Subjects complete "before" and "after" questionnaires, as well as maintain a diary of actual use of the new and competitive products over the period of

---

[4]For a more complete discussion of concept tests, see William L. Moore, "Concept Testing," *Journal of Business Research* 10 (June 1982), pp. 279–94.

[5]Note that the product used in this phase is typically specially produced and may not match the quality of the product under mass production. For example, Knorr soup product test samples were produced in Europe, while the actual mass-produced product was made in a new, computerized plant in Argo, Illinois, which produced a product of different quality. Hence the success or failure of the test product does not necessarily imply success or failure of the actual product.

the test. Here again, the inclusion at the end of the test of an actual choice situation helps give the results a bottom-line orientation.

Discrimination and Preference Testing

When a product formulation is changed, a crucial issue is the customer reaction (see Figure 9–1). Reaction has three aspects: discrimination (can they tell the difference?), preference (which version do they prefer, and by how much?), and reaction to change per se (are they basically pro change, or is any change upsetting?). The previous sections presented a framework for analyzing preferences and reactions. Here we focus on the ability of customers to actually tell the differences among products.

Discrimination is the ability to correctly identify differences from the product alone, without cues such as brand name and ingredients. Industrial goods sold to or given to engineers and chemists are often subjected to testing to determine their makeup, which makes discrimination fairly precise. In many cases, however, customers cannot distinguish among alternative versions of a product without labels attached. Most people cannot distinguish among brands of beer, soda, or wine based on taste alone or among insurance policies based on the fine print.

The inability to discriminate has two main consequences. First, it suggests that within a range it is possible to alter a product without customers noticing the difference. This ability often disappears when labels are included, however. For example, when some ingredients in food are assumed to be good (e.g., soluble fiber) or bad (e.g., cholesterol, nonbiodegradable ingredients, or toxic components), including the good ones becomes a plus whereas including the bad ones may disqualify a product from further consideration, even when the foods are indistinguishable in taste and appearance.

The second consequence of customers' inability to discriminate is its impact on the interpretation of preference judgments. Stated preference can be the result of true discrimination or of random guessing. This means single preference judgments cannot be unambiguously interpreted. Assume, for example, that 60 percent of a sample say they prefer brand A over brand B. This result could be because all subjects could discriminate and 60 percent actually prefer brand A. On the other hand, perhaps only 20 percent could discriminate and preferred brand A and 80 percent randomly guessed to arrive at their preference (20% + ½ [80%] = 60%). Or it could mean that 50 percent could discriminate and among them 35 percent preferred A and 15 percent preferred B (35% + ½ [50%] = 60%).

Three approaches can get around the problem of guessing. One approach allows for *indifferences*; that is, it allows subjects to indicate that they cannot tell the difference. Unfortunately, because being unable to discriminate is generally not seen as desirable, response to this option often contains considerable error. A more subtle version of allowing for indifference asks, in addition to discrimination and preference judgments, for a rating of confidence in the judgment, thus allowing for low weighting of subjects with low confidence and vice versa.

A second approach to disentangling guessing from true preference involves *multiple preference judgments.* In a single paired comparison, it is impossible to disentangle lucky guessing from true preference. To get a better fix on consumers' ability to discriminate and their preferences, it is common to replicate the paired test. It is also possible to use groups of three products (called *triangles* or *triads,* in which two of the products are identical) to better estimate the ability of consumers to discriminate. To see why a replicated test is useful, consider the following situation.[6]

A set of subjects are presented with a pair of products (A and B) on two different occasions. We assume there are three kinds of consumers:

1. Those who can tell the difference and prefer A.
2. Those who can tell the difference and prefer B.
3. Those who cannot distinguish between A and B and indicate preference randomly.

The key is to estimate these three fractions. First, we must observe the actual reported preference table:

	First Preference	
Second Preference	A	B
A	48%	15%
B	13%	24%

The naive interpretation is that 48 percent prefer A (because they consistently choose it) and 24 percent prefer B. As we will see, however, this is a bad estimate. Consider the conditional probabilities of test results given true consumer preference shown in Figure 9–3. Hence the expressed percentage is a function of true preference as follows:

$$\%\text{AA}e = \%\text{A}t + \tfrac{1}{4}\,(\%\text{ neither } t)$$
$$\%\text{BB}e = \%\text{B}t + \tfrac{1}{4}\,(\%\text{ neither } t)$$
$$\%\text{neither } e = \tfrac{1}{2}\,(\%\text{ neither } t)$$

where

$\%\text{AA}e$ = Expressed percentage who choose A both times.
$\%\text{A}t$ = True percentage who prefer A.
$\%\text{ neither } t$ = True percentage of subjects who cannot tell the difference.

Solving this for the true fractions gives

$$\%\text{ neither } t = 2\,(\%\text{ neither } e)$$
$$\%\text{A}t = \%\text{AA}e - \tfrac{1}{4}\,(\%\text{ neither } t)$$
$$\%\text{B}t = \%\text{BB}e - \tfrac{1}{4}\,(\%\text{ neither } t).$$

For our example, we get

$$\%\text{ neither } t = 2(13\% + 15\%) = 56\%$$
$$\%\text{A}t = 48\% - \tfrac{1}{4}(56\%) = 34\%$$
$$\%\text{B}t = 24\% - \tfrac{1}{4}(56\%) = 10\%.$$

Thus, the correct interpretation of the results is that most people do not perceive a difference and that B is in trouble.

---

[6]Richard M. Johnson, *Simultaneous Measurement of Discrimination and Preference* (Chicago: Market Facts, Inc., no date).

FIGURE 9–3 Probability of Expressed Preference Given True Preference

	Expressed Preference		
"True" consumer preference	AA	BB	AB, BA (neither)
A	1	0	0
B	0	1	0
Neither	1/4	1/4	1/2

Paired comparison testing involves a number of concerns. An *order effect* favors the first alternative.[7] When letters are used to represent brands, the *letters* may not be equally appealing, which can also affect the results. Although this may sound a bit farfetched, letter preference was once a basis for a lawsuit claiming that ads reporting preference for one beverage over another were unsubstantiated and misleading. Sequential trials also offer the strong possibility of a *carryover effect.* Food tests traditionally involve an intermediate task, such as drinking water or eating a cracker to "cleanse the palate," and reduce the carryover effect.

Another, and in many ways preferable, approach involves comparing more than two alternatives at a time. For example, triangle tests (tests among three alternatives) are a common approach.[8] Using more alternatives makes it less likely that someone can make consistent identification or preference judgments by chance. Someone could make the same (correct) selection in two paired comparisons 25 percent of the time, but only 11 percent if three alternatives are used and only one of the three is the correct choice.

A third approach for dealing with limited discriminatory ability is to *separately assess discrimination and preference* and then weigh the preferences by the customer's discrimination ability. The probability that an individual will correctly identify the different member of a triad containing two identical samples of one brand and one sample of another is assumed to vary. Data on average discriminating ability and individual discrimination performance are used to produce estimates of individual discriminating ability.[9]

The procedures just mentioned generally improve understanding, but at a cost of both respondent effort (which can diminish discriminatory ability and response quality) and dollars. As a consequence, many studies rely on a single comparison. When multiple comparisons are used, they are generally few in number (e.g., three paired comparisons or two triangle tests). A reader interested in the specifics of different forms of comparative product testing should consult other sources.

---

[7]Ralph Day, "Systematic Paired Comparisons in Preference Analysis," *Journal of Marketing Research* 2 (November 1965), pp. 406–12.

[8]Donald G. Morrison, "Triangle Tests: Are the Subjects Who Respond Correctly Lucky or Good?" *Journal of Marketing* 45 (Summer 1981), pp. 111–19.

[9]The process, formally known as *empirical Bayes estimation,* increases the estimate of mean ability for individuals who correctly discriminate a substantial portion of the time and decreases it for individuals who fail to correctly discriminate a large portion of the time. See Bruce S. Buchanan and Pamela W. Henderson, "Assessing the Bias of Preference, Detection, and Identification Measures of Discrimination Ability in Product Design," *Marketing Science* 11 (Winter 1992), pp. 64–75.

Market Tests

The ultimate in realism is a market test. The purpose of such a test is to (1) predict sales and profits from a major product launch and (2) "practice up" so that marketing, distribution, and production skills are developed before entering full-scale operations. Projections are typically made for both share and actual sales, appropriately adjusted to national levels. The major sources of concern are as follows:

1. Trial rate.
2. Repeat rate (for frequently purchased goods).
3. Usage rate/number bought per customer.

In addition, awareness, attitudes, and distribution are usually monitored. Given these measures, a projected sales estimate can be made.

In designing a market test, it is important to clearly delineate what information is to be gathered and why before proceeding. Several decisions must be made.

Action Standards. Standards for evaluating the results should be set up in advance. These standards should specify when the various possible decisions (e.g., stop the test, continue the test, revamp the product, go national) will be implemented.

Where. The choice of where to test market is a serious problem. For consumer products, most market tests are done in two to three cities. (This further emphasizes that the "test" is not designed to try out numerous strategies; at most, two to three alternatives can be used.) Cities are chosen on the basis of representativeness of the population, the ability of the firm to gain distribution and media exposure in the area, and availability of good research suppliers in the area. Also, areas that are self-contained in terms of media (especially TV) are preferred. The result is that certain medium-size cities are often chosen, such as Syracuse, New York; Fresno, California; and Fort Wayne, Indiana.

What to Do? The best test market designers are careful to make the effort in the area proportional to what would reasonably be expected in a national launch. Notice that here we mean effort, not budget. If a city has particularly expensive (the former being the usual case when buying spot TV ads) or inexpensive media cost, allocating budget on a population basis would result in a media schedule with either too few or too many exposures. The goal is to make distribution, price to consumers (price breaks to retailers and wholesalers are needed to gain distribution), and so forth as representative as possible. What typically happens, however, is that the effort afforded the product (including the human talent) is somewhat greater than the comparable national effort.

How Long? The question of how long to run a test is not easily answered. Obviously, a longer run gives more information, but it also costs more and gives competitors more time to formulate a counterattack. Consumer packaged goods may stay in test markets between 6 and 12 months in order to include several purchase cycles, so repeat usage as well as trial can be accurately assessed. (It is not uncommon for a product to gain a big initial share, due to trial, and then lose share as repeat business fails to live up to trial.)

How Much? For a consumer packaged good, test marketing costs run over $1 million. Advertising and promotion typically account for 65 to 70 percent of the budget, with the rest of the budget divided between information gathering and analysis and miscellaneous administrative and other expenses.

Information Gathering. During a test market, a variety of information is gathered, most of it related to actual sales. In monitoring sales, it is important to recognize that a large percentage of first-year factory sales (e.g., 30 percent) represent a one-time stocking up by the channels of distribution, not sales to final consumers. The three major data sources are (1) actual sales (typically at least 40 stores per area) plus distribution, promotion, and so forth; (2) surveys that measure awareness, attitude, and so forth; and (3) panels that report actual purchase and allow monitoring of trial and repeat rates.

Sales Forecasting

Forecasting sales from a test market is always difficult. (If it weren't, all products that went national after test marketing would succeed.) However, at least for frequently purchased consumer products, some fairly widely used procedures have been developed. It is possible to simply wait and see at what levels sales stabilize. Unfortunately, this takes a fairly long period (up to two years) and hence a lot of money. What is really desired is an early warning system that forecasts the eventual sales level of a new product before it is attained. Four basic factors are the keys to eventual sales:

1. Awareness.
2. The eventual proportion of consumers who will try the product (trial).
3. The proportion of triers who remain with the brand (repeat).
4. The usage rate of the product category among the eventual users.

Notice that for durable goods, trial is basically first purchase, which may be the only purchase for several years (e.g., a household's car, a company's computer system). For frequently purchased products for which trial is relatively easy to induce, repeat rates are the key to success (see Figure 9–4).

Many models exist that attempt to project these factors early in the introduction. Models continue to be developed for forecasting new product sales,[10] and most research suppliers have their own versions. Still, the models follow a structure that has been around for at least 40 years.

Awareness. As in all the stages of the model, one can simply introduce the product, monitor awareness, and, by plotting awareness versus time, observe (or formally forecast) where the product is headed. Alternatively, one can relate awareness to its

[10]Glen L. Urban, John S. Hulland, and Bruce Weinberg, "Pre-Market Forecasting of New Consumer Durables: Categorization, Elimination, and Consideration Phenomena," *Journal of Marketing* 57 (April 1993), pp. 47–63.

FIGURE 9–4 Typical Penetration for New Brand over Time

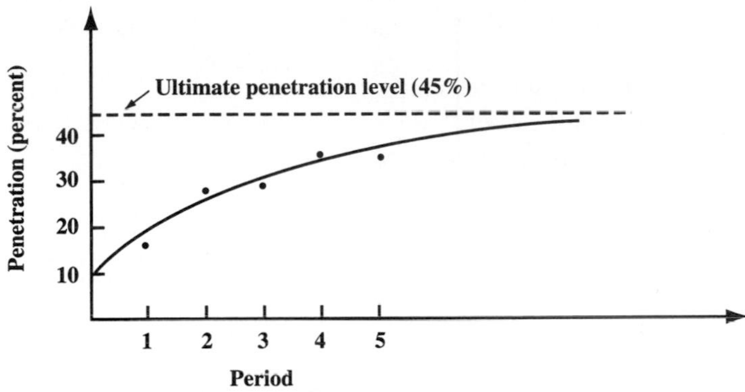

underlying causes. Awareness is usually modeled as a function of advertising. For example, the awareness stage of Blattberg and Golanty's TRACKER model[11] is as follows:

Awareness:

$$\ln\left(\frac{1-A_t}{1-A_{t-1}}\right) = a - bG_t.$$

where

A_t = Cumulative awareness in period t.
G_t = Gross rating points in period t.

N. W. Ayer[12] (an ad agency that subsequently became "consolidated") studied several introductions and, based on this research, modeled awareness in a more complex fashion as follows:

$$\begin{aligned}\text{Awareness} = a_1 &+ b_1 \text{ (product positioning)} \\ &+ b_2 \text{ (media impressions) (copy execution)} \\ &+ b_3 \text{ (ad messages containing consumer promotions)} \\ &+ b_4 \text{ (category interest)} + e_1\end{aligned}$$

Trial. Like awareness, initial purchase is often tracked across time, with the objective of forecasting its eventual level. This can be done graphically as in Figure

[11]Robert Blattberg and John Golanty, "TRACKER: An Early Test Market Forecasting and Diagnostic Model for New Product Planning," *Journal of Marketing Research* 15 (May 1978), pp. 192–202.

[12]Adapted from Henry Claycamp and Lucien Liddy, "Prediction of New Product Performance: An Analytical Approach," *Journal of Marketing Research* 4 (November 1969), p. 416.

FIGURE 9–5 Typical Repeat Rate for New Brand over Time

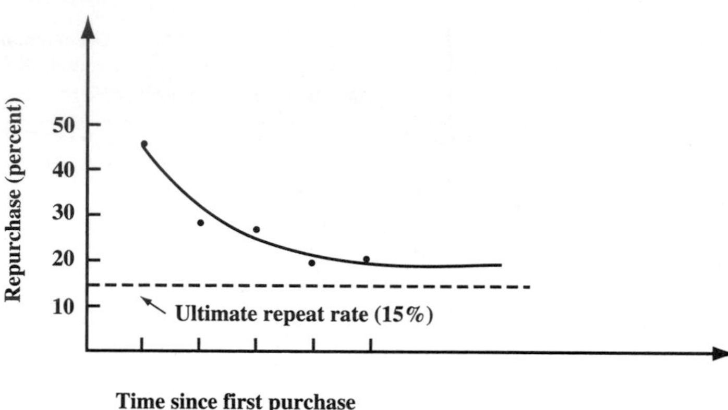

9–4. Alternatively, the saturation level can be estimated by running a regression of cumulative trial versus exp $(-t)$:

$$Cumulative\ trial\ (t) = S(f) = a + be^{-t}$$

Here a is the eventual penetration level.

When trial is forecast based on market factors, advertising, distribution, and promotion are often used. The Ayer model was as follows:

Initial purchase $= a_2 + b_1$ (estimated awareness)

$+c_2$ {(distribution) (packaging)}

$+c_3$ (if a family brand)

$+c_4$ (consumer promotion)

$+c_5$ (satisfaction with product samples)

$+c_6$ (category usage) $+ e_2$

Similarly, the trial stage of the TRACKER model is as follows:

$$T_t - T_{t-1} = \alpha(A_t - A_{t-1}) + \beta(A_{-t} - T_{t-1})$$

where

T_t = Cumulative trial in period t.

Repeat Rate. The eventual repeat rate can be deduced graphically by plotting repeat versus either time (Figure 9–5) or purchase occasion. As Figure 9–6, based on 120 products studied by NPD Research, demonstrates, repeat rate is often a good predictor of success.

Figure 9–6 Repeat Rates and Product Performance

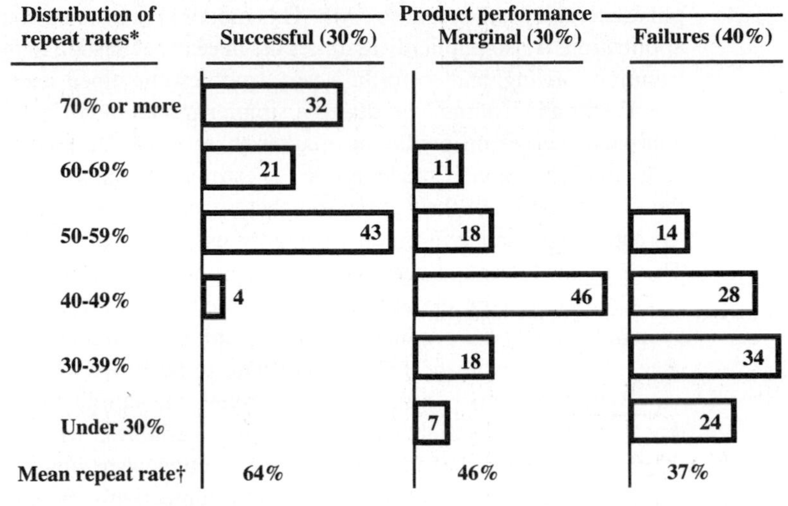

* Based upon 120 new products.
† Percent of triers who will ever repeat.

Source: "We Make the Answers to Your Marketing Questions Perfectly Clear" (New York: NPD Research, 1982).

Usage Rate. The usage rate is calculated as follows:

$$\textit{Repeat purchase} = f\,(\text{initial purchase, relative price, product satisfaction, purchase frequency})$$

The relative product category usage rate of buyers of the new brand is obtained either by using purchase panel data to estimate it (the usual way) or judgmentally.

Other Models. The earliest of the new-product models that attained widespread interest was that of Fourt and Woodlock.[13] This model was intended to predict the market success of grocery products.

The first stage of the model attempts to predict penetration (eventual level of trial). It assumes (1) there is an eventual penetration level (P) and (2) each period some percentage of the nonbuyers who eventually will buy the product buy it. The second stage of the model focuses on repeat purchase. Specifically, it focuses on the repeat ratios, the

[13]Louis A. Fourt and Joseph W. Woodlock, "Early Prediction of Market Success for New Grocery Products," *Journal of Marketing* 25 (October 1960), pp. 31–38; Frank M. Bass, Trichy V. Krishnan, and Deepak C. Jain, "Why the Bass Model Fits without Decision Variables," *Marketing Science* 13 (Summer 1994), pp. 203–23.

portion of initial buyers who repeat purchase once (N_1 / N_0), the portion of first repeat purchasers who repeat purchase a second time (N_2 / N_1), and so forth. This stage is used for forecasting sales in the next period as the sum of new buyers, plus first repeaters, plus second repeaters, and so forth. This model proved to be somewhat cumbersome in application. It also implicitly assumes the market is constant in terms of advertising, distribution, pricing, and so forth, a very troublesome albeit useful assumption.

Parfitt and Collins[14] produced a simpler model than Fourt and Woodlock's. Their approach focuses on predicting market share rather than actual sales. The three key elements in using their model are to (1) estimate eventual penetration (P), (2) estimate the ultimate share of their purchases that buyers will make of the new brand (M), and (3) estimate the relative product category usage rate of buyers of the new brand (U). The estimated eventual share is thus simply the product of P·M·U.

Continuing with the example represented in Figures 9–5 and 9–6 and assuming eventual users of the product buy 80 percent as much as an average product category user, we would estimate the ultimate share to be P·M·U = (45%) (15%) (.8) = 5.4%.

By inputting data to the estimated model, sales projections can be derived. Notice that many of the variables are marketing variables, which is, in some sense, an improvement over the previous models. Notice also, however, that many of these variables (e.g., copy execution) are often subjectively estimated, hence making the results potentially more subject to researcher bias.[15]

Numerous other models also exist, such as ESP, the NEWS Model[16] used by the ad agency BBD&O, and Assmus's NEWPROD.[17] Experience with these models has been quite good, with predicted share within 1 percent of actual share when test market data are used as input and within 2 percent when only pretest market data are used.

Laboratory Experiment–Based models. Silk and Urban's ASSESOR,[18] BASES, and Blackburn and Clancy's LITMUS[19] models use pretest market data to estimate sales. Specifically, ASSESOR uses a simulated shopping trip following advertising exposure and an in-home use period. In most cases, the market share estimates are within one share point of the share observed in the market. With LITMUS, movement from awareness to trial and trial to repeat is estimated based on a laboratory experiment. These are, not surprisingly, both less expensive and somewhat less reliable than models based on actual market experience. Nevertheless, they grew substantially in popularity during the 1980s and continue to do so in the 1990s.

---

[14]J. H. Parfitt and B. J. K. Collins, "Use of Consumer Panels for Brand-Share Prediction," *Journal of Marketing Research* 5 (May 1968), pp. 131–45.

[15]Henry Claycamp and Lucien Liddy, "Prediction of New Product Performance: An Analytical Approach," *Journal of Marketing Research* 4 (November 1969), pp. 414–20.

[16]Lewis R. Pringle, R. Dale Wilson, and Edward I. Brody, "NEWS: A Decision-Oriented Model for New Product Analysis and Forecasting," *Marketing Science* 1 (Winter 1982), pp. 1–29.

[17]Gert Assmus, "NEWPROD: The Design and Implementation of a New Product Model," *Journal of Marketing* 39 (January 1975), pp. 16–23.

[18]Alvin J. Silk and Glen L. Urban, "Pre-Test Market Evaluation of New Packaged Goods: A Model and Measurement Methodology," *Journal of Marketing Research* 15 (May 1978), pp. 171–91.

[19]Joseph D. Blackburn and Kevin J. Clancy, "LITMUS: A New Product Planning Model," in Robert P. Leone, ed. *Proceedings: Market Measurement and Analysis* (Providence, R.I.: Institute of Management Sciences, 1980), pp. 182–93.

Beyond Category Brand Extension

Brand extension involves extending brands beyond their original category (e.g., Levi's into dress clothing, Nike into sportswear). These decisions are generally both much riskier than adding variants (line extensions) and beyond the control of a product manager. Nonetheless, because they both are likely to influence the original brand and are interesting to consider, we discuss them briefly.

A considerable amount of attention has been paid to brand extensions across categories.[20] Consider the following five possible brand extensions:

H & R Block estate settlements.

Pepsi tofu patties.

Minute Maid cranberry juice.

IBM pens.

Levi's suits.

If you are "typical" (that is, similar to others to whom we have shown this list), your reaction may be something like the following:

H & R Block estate settlements: Sounds reasonable; they're pretty good at preparing tax forms (a big part of estate work).

Pepsi tofu patties: Pepsi can sure market food products, but somehow a dark, sugar-filled drink doesn't seem to go with a natural food.

Minute Maid cranberry juice: An obvious extension; don't they do this already?

IBM pens: Why would they bother? Besides, what do they know about making pens?

Levi's suits: I remember this—it didn't work, did it?

From these kinds of reactions, plus more extensive survey research,[21] it appears that brand extension value depends on the value of the original brand (e.g., the extension value of Lehmann-Winer Garage Shop, Inc., is pretty limited) and the fit in the new category. Fit, in turn, focuses heavily on two issues:

1. Technical competence sharing or transfer: Do the skills and quality and service levels of the original brand seem to transfer productively to the extension category?
2. Personality match: Are the products consistent in terms of image on such dimensions as young-old, serious-fun, and the like?[22]

---

[20]David A. Aaker and Kevin L. Keller, "Consumer Evaluations of Brand Extensions," *Journal of Marketing* 54 (January 1990), pp. 27–41; Edward M. Tauber, "Brand Leverage: Strategy for Growth in a Cost-Control World," *Journal of Advertising Research* 28 (August 1988), pp. 26–30.

[21]C. Whan Park, Sandra Milberg, and Robert Lawson, "Evaluation of Brand Extensions: The Role of Product Feature Similarity and Brand Concept Consistency," *Journal of Consumer Research* 19 (September 1991), pp. 185–93.

[22]Rajeev Batra, Donald R. Lehmann, and Dipinder Singh, "The Brand Personality Component of Brand Goodwill," in David A. Aaker and Alexander L. Biel, eds., *Brand Equity and Advertising* (Hillsdale, N.J.: Lawrence Erlbaum, 1992), pp. 83–96.

Based on these considerations, the H & R Block estate settlement concept seems to match on both, as does Minute Maid cranberry juice. But Minute Maid cranberry juice, unfortunately, is less matched operationally. Because oranges grow on trees in Florida and cranberries in bogs in Massachusetts, different machines are needed to extract the juice, and so on. The issue of operational efficiency is important but separate from the issue of how well brand value (equity) transfers from the customer's perspective. In contrast, Pepsi tofu patties and Levi's suits fail to match in terms of image and personality, and IBM pens seem not to involve technology sharing.

The success of an extension also seems to depend on the order in which extensions occur.[23] A study found that brand extensions work best in more mature markets (that is, as a later entrant) for frequently purchased consumer goods and generally outperform new products.[24]

Another interesting study evaluated the impact of brand extensions on market share and advertising efficiency as measured by the advertising/sales ratio. Smith and Park[25] collected data from 188 product/brand managers in consumer goods companies and from 1,383 consumers. The managers provided data on

1. Products offered ("focal" products) and whether or not they were extensions.
2. Other products using the same brand name or company logo as the focal product.
3. Age of the focal product.
4. Number of competitors of the focal products and extensions.
5. Advertising/sales ratio of the focal products and extensions.
6. Market shares of the focal products and extensions.

Consumers provided measures of brand strength (the average of 7-point quality and value scales), extension similarity to focal product (both extrinsic and intrinsic), whether the product could be evaluated through inspection as opposed to actual use, and general product class knowledge. Analysis produced several interesting results. Not surprisingly, parent brand strength related to extension brand share but not to the advertising/sales ratio. Neither extension share nor the advertising/sales ratio was related to the number of products associated with a brand. Similarity of the extension, extensions that are experience goods, and the presence of few competitors increase the market share effect. These effects decrease as the extension ages or when customers have considerable product knowledge.

Although our focus has been mainly on the success of the new product, a key issue regarding extensions is the impact of the extension on the original brand. One study examined the impact of extensions on beliefs about the original brand.[26] Dilution

---

[23]Kevin L. Keller and David A. Aaker, "The Effects of Sequential Introductions of Brand Extensions," *Journal of Marketing Research* 29 (February 1992), pp. 35–50.

[24]Mary W. Sullivan, "Brand Extensions: When to Use Them," *Management Science* 38 (June 1992), pp. 793–806.

[25]Daniel C. Smith and C. Whan Park, "The Effects of Brand Extensions on Market Share and Advertising Efficiency," *Journal of Marketing Research* 29 (August 1992), pp. 296–313.

[26]Barbara Loken and Deborah Roedder-John, "Diluting Brand Beliefs When Brand Extensions Have a Negative Impact," *Journal of Marketing* 57 (July 1993), pp. 71–84.

FIGURE 9–7 Examples of Really New Products

Packaged goods	Bottled tea
	Light beer
	Frozen vegetables
	Frozen yogurt
	Sports drinks (Gatorade)
Services	Overnight air delivery
	ATMs
	Credit cards
	IRAs, annuities
	Internet
Durables	Microwave ovens
	Room air conditioners
	Dishwashers
	Black-and-white TVs
Industrial products	Nylon
	Semiconductors
	Nuclear power reactors
	Printing presses

effects occurred for both within-category extensions (i.e., adding product variants) and across-category extensions. The study found dilutions to be greater for specific attributes (e.g., gentleness) rather than for more general attributes (e.g., quality). Perhaps most interesting, it found that dilution was greater for moderately consistent extensions than for clearly different extensions. Hence even a successful new product may have adverse effects on the original product.

Really New Products

Really new products are those that:

1. Create or expand a new category, thereby making cross-category competition the key (e.g., fruit teas versus soft drinks).
2. Are new to customers for whom substantial learning is often required (i.e., what it can be used for, what it competes with, why it is useful).
3. Raise broad issues such as the appropriate channels of distribution and organizational responsibility.
4. Create (sometimes) a need for infrastructure, software, and add-ons.

Figure 9–7 gives some examples of really new products. While slightly to really new products form a continuum, notice how these differ from lemon-scented soaps or printers that produce six instead of five pages of output per minute.

One way to examine new products is to see how the material covered earlier in the book applies to new products. Clearly, the less new the new product, the more analysis of and decisions for it resemble those for existing products. Therefore, to highlight the

FIGURE 9–8 Analysis and Programs for New versus Old Products

Market Analysis	*Existing Product, Mature Market*	*Existing Product, Dynamic Growing Market*	*Slightly New Product*	*Quite/Really New Product*
Competitor identification and focus	Current (same as last year) (Product form, category)	Current plus likely entrants (Category, generic)	Current producers of product category (Category)	Possible entrants with similar products and competing technologies (Generic, budget)
Industry analysis	Known	Partly known	Known	Undetermined
Customer analysis	Current customers Competitors' customers	Current customers Potential new customers Competitor's customers	Competitors' customers Current customers (cannibalization, upgrading)	Potential new customers Users of alternative technologies
Potential and forecasting	Extrapolation from past results	New uses and users	Survey data; controlled experiments	Potential analysis Epidemic models (e.g., Bass)
Objective	Profit Share	Sales	Share Profit	Sales Learning Keeping options open
Marketing Programs				
Price	Competitively based	Competition Experience curve	Competitively based Value for added feature (lemon scent)	EVC* based Portion of value—cost difference to give to customers to cover risk, dislocation (incompatibility)
Advertising strategy	Reminder/repeat Comparative	New uses	New feature	Awareness and trial Information on use
Promotions	Retain current users Induce switching	Increase use New users	Trial	Trial Awareness/interest
Sales and service	Delivery	Gaining distribution	Gaining distribution	Technical support Training Gaining distribution

*EVC is Economic value to the customer.

differences, we contrast the likely focus of various analyses and programs for four situations: (1) existing product, mature market; (2) existing product, dynamic/growing market (basically a new product that has been around for awhile); (3) a slightly new product; and (4) a really new product.

As Figure 9–8 shows, the task becomes increasingly complex as product newness increases. For a really new product there is no industry to analyze other than generic usage situations, and the competitive set is undefined. Only potential customers exist, and while they can indicate their satisfaction level with current offerings, it is often hard to directly assess the likelihood that they will buy a new offering.

While more mature products tend to be managed to maximize some combination of profits and shares, really new ones can be pursued to learn from the experience and/or keep the option open to participate in a potentially large market. In terms of marketing programs, less emphasis is placed on competitors and gaining share and more on primary demand (sales). Advertising and sales shift from an emphasis on current customers and customers of similar products to new customers and increased awareness, trial, and eventual use by noncustomers.

Economic Value. An important influence on the adoption and pricing of a product, especially a new one, is the product's long-run costs and benefits versus the product it might replace (that is, the one a customer currently uses). This type of analysis is typically performed by highly involved buyers, especially in industrial markets, and used by salespeople to generate new business.

We illustrate this concept with an example. Consider Snidlaps. Snidlaps contain a transmission. Really New, Inc., has created a new part for the transmission. The new part, which also makes the transmission run more smoothly, compares to the old one as follows:

	Old Part	*New Part (Really New)*
Price	$10	?
Useful life	2,000 hours	5,000 hours
Time to change	1 hour	2 hours

Parts were changed by a mechanic, who was paid $40 per hour. The machine used three operators who get paid $200 per hour (total salary and fringes). The opportunity cost (lost business) of having the machine down was estimated to be $1,000 per hour.

To figure the economic value, we compare the cost of using the old and new parts for 5,000 hours (the time to use one new part):

	Old (2.5 needed)	*New (1 needed)*
Cost of parts	(2.5)($10) = $25	—
Mechanic time	(2.5)(1)($40) = $100	(1)(2)($40) = $80
Operator time	(2.5)(1)($200) = $500	(1)(2)($200) = $400
Operator cost	(25)(1)($1,000) = $2,500	(1)(2)($1,000) = $2,000
	$3,125	$2,480

Therefore, the economic value of the new product (part) is $3,125 – $2,480 = $645.

Clearly, economic value is an important determinant of price. However, so is cost: If the part costs $1,000 apiece to produce, you probably don't want to sell it unless you expect cost to fall substantially over time. Further, you need to consider price expectations. If customers are used to paying $10 for a part, will they pay $600? (Even though many cars now recommend changing oil infrequently, many owners still change it every 3,000 miles.) Also, if customers were used to changing a part every 2,000 hours, would they continue to do so? Finally, the newer the product's technology and the less well known and respected Really New is, the greater the risk and, generally, the more change is required to use it. Hence, if the cost were $30, you would probably price it closer to $30 than $645 to give the customer an inducement to switch.

Getting Ideas for Really New Products

Ideas for really new products can come from the same sources product variants do. However, really new products have a certain radical quality. Thus, the emphasis may be on

1. Asking (or listening to) *dis*satisfied customers.
2. Asking *non*representative customers.
3. Using open-ended, qualitative (versus structured survey) procedures.
4. Involving customers as codevelopers (especially for industrial products).
5. Listening to scientists and newcomers rather than engineers and experts.
6. Scanning the literature (e.g., technology) for interesting possibilities.

Further, the style of search is likely to differ. For lemon-scented new products, the emphasis is on fixing or improving existing products, methodical continuous improvement, and project completion. In contrast, the mindset for really new products involves taking an outsider's view, doing things differently, disrupting current behavior, and using different technologies. In contrast to well-defined project completion, process reengineering and discovery (à la Franklin, Bell, and Edison) are the models.

Evaluating Really New Products

Really new products tend to take a long time (e.g., 20 years). from conception to development and from initial development to mass sales. Hence one of the main requirements is patience, something that is in short supply in most corporations.

In considering a new product, it is useful to analyze a set of characteristics defined by Rogers[27] plus the perceived risk dimension of Bauer.[28] These are:

1. *Relative advantage.* Essentially, is it a "better mousetrap"? (that is, the benefit versus the product it replaces).
2. *Compatibility.* The ability of the consumer to use it in a way consistent with past behavior, which increases the chances of adoption. This includes (1) the procedures the user employs (Hint: don't try to change the location of keys on a keyboard) and (2) the ability to use existing "software" and complementary

---

[27]Everett M. Rogers, *Diffusion Innovations* (New York: The Free Press, 1983).

[28]R. A. Bauer, "Consumer Behavior as Risk Taking," in R. S. Hancock, ed., *Dynamic Marketing for a Changing World* (Chicago: American Marketing Association, 1960), pp. 389–98.

FIGURE 9–9 Evaluating New Products

	Constituency				
Aspect	*Customers*	*Within Company*	*Suppliers*	*Channels*	*Public/ Regulators*
Relative advantage					
Compatibility					
Risk					
Complexity					
Communicability					
Trialability					

products (e.g., bobbins on sewing machines). Incompatibility is often the major deterrent to adoption.

3. *Risk.* Perceived risk can be broken down into several categories (e.g., financial, physical/health, psychic/social), all of which work against adoption.

Three other dimensions also affect adoption, although generally indirectly:[29]

4. *Complexity.*
5. *Observability/communicability.* The ability to explain and see the benefits in simple, clear terms.
6. *Trialability/divisibility.* The ability to sample the product without a major commitment.

In general, complexity works against adoption and observability and trialability work for it.

For slightly new products, the basic emphasis is on relative advantage (e.g., the lemon scent) versus financial risk (cost) as emphasized by economic value calculations. In contrast, for really new products compatibility and social risk become much more crucial. Human beings, unless desperate, generally resist innovation and change. Incompatibility and social risk thus are major impediments to adoption. While some delay in adoption can be traced to customers waiting for the (inevitable?) (1) price to drop and (2) quality (features, reliability, availability of complementary products) to increase, incompatibility accounts for more of the delay.

Also, for a really new product to succeed, a variety of parties must adopt it (e.g., customers, channels, and suppliers plus within the firm both superiors and vital functions such as production and sales). Hence evaluating the likelihood of success of a really new product requires considerations such as those in Figure 9–9.

As an example of resistance to innovation, consider plastic plumbing. Lighter in weight and less toxic than metal plumbing (no lead in the solder), it seemed like a

[29]Susan Holak and Donald R. Lehmann, "Purchase Intentions and the Dimensions of Innovation: An Exploratory Model," *Journal of Product Innovation Management* 7 (March 1990), pp. 59–73.

natural improvement. Yet it took over 20 years to make major inroads in the U.S. home market. Part of the delay can be traced to resistance by plumbers. Their livelihood was based partly on the skill of sweating joints (joining copper pipe together using flux, solder, and a torch). They also had considerable influence on local building codes, which set standards for construction. As a result, the first widespread use of plastic plumbing was in mobile homes, which were not subject to local building codes.

Perhaps the ultimate examples of resistance to change occur in the military. In spite of the clear objective function and reliable data, tradition has overwhelmed data time after time. From the tradition of marching in close formation through the woods (General Braddock and the Red Coats) through repeating rifles in the U.S. Civil War, continuous arm firing gunnery in the Navy, and air power (General Billy Mitchell), clearly superior technology was actively resisted. Given the life-or-death nature of the consequences, it is less surprising that profits (for industrial firms) or inconvenience or social pressure (for individuals) are insufficient to induce immediate adoption of new things.

For any new product, it is important to consider where sales will come from. The potential sources are as follows:

1. Within category
   a. Own company/same brand
   b. Own company/different brands
   c. Competition
2. Other, related categories (generic competition)
   a. Own company
   b. Competitors
3. Unrelated categories (budget competition)

Same brands and other company brands are a major source of sales of slightly new products (e.g., Dannon raspberry versus blueberry yogurt). Failure to consider this cannibalization leads to bad decisions. On the other hand, the attention-getting "shopping center" effect may increase sales of other company products by drawing attention to them and needs to be considered as well. For really new products, cannibalization (if it exists) is likely to be cross-category (e.g., IBM word processors and later personal computers drew from electric typewriters).

Adoption and Expansion

First purchases of a new product are crucial. Still, adoption implies something different, a commitment to using the product in the long run. Basements are full of exercise equipment and other items that are used briefly and then stored (or used as clothes hangers). For that reason, frequently purchased products are considered to be adopted on second repeat (to exclude novelty-based trial). Other signs of true adoption are (1) "automated" replacement when a product fails ("I never thought I needed a VCR or microwave oven, but now, when mine breaks, I go directly to the store to buy another"), (2) upgrades to better models, and (3) purchases of accessories and complementary products (which also provide an opportunity to increase profits, as sellers of cameras and snowmobiles well know).

Forecasting Really New Products

Forecasting sales of really new products is hazardous at best. Mechanistically, one can apply the Bass model[30] to develop category-level first-purchase estimates, combining past patterns with actual sales data.[31] In terms of customer input, direct structured questioning either in straight concept evaluation form or through devices such as conjoint analysis is less useful.

First, the product itself often is not available, so product tests are not possible. Further, the product often requires a major shift in behavior and may service a need that is latent (unknown) rather than active (when the customer is actively searching for such a product) or even passive (the customer wasn't searching for it but responds, "Now that you mention it, . . ."). Hence standard concept tests are not easily used.

Therefore, methods such as "information acceleration" (developed by Glen Urban at MIT and now offered by Mercer Management Consultants[32]) have been developed. In essence, these methods attempt to place subjects in a future world and familiarize them with a product (often using multimedia technology) to improve the quality of their responses. However, it remains extremely difficult to have people imagine both a radically new product and the world in 20 to 30 years and then accurately assess likelihood of their using it. Put differently, to forecast you need a really big—and lucky—coin.

Summary

New products are the lifeblood of many companies. Indeed, many companies (e.g., 3M, Gillette) set goals for sales based on new products (e.g., 35 percent from products introduced in the last five years). Like any metric, however, these goals may distort behavior. One suspects the reason life cycles are often thought to be shortening is the increasing number of lemon-scented products and the decreasing fraction of really new ones.

Little evidence exists that really new products are being adopted faster. Humans' inherent tolerance for innovation is largely unchanged. Indeed, considering the risk taken by those who set out in small wooden boats across a sea and were predicted to fall off the edge of the world, our reluctance to try new things seems almost laughable.

Lemon-scented, slightly new products are relatively easy to forecast and low in risk. Further, they rarely raise messy issues about channels and organization structure. They are also often profitable.

Really new products, in contrast, are hard to forecast, raise numerous tough organizational issues, take a long time to develop (see Figure 9–10), and frequently produce profits for later entrants but not for pioneers (or none at all, if a subsequent technology makes them obsolete). Because of the time it takes them to reach a mass

---

[30]Frank M. Bass, "A New Product Growth Model for Consumer Durables," *Management Science* 15 (January 1969), pp. 215–27.

[31]Fareena Sultan, John U. Farley, and Donald R. Lehmann, "A Meta-Analysis of Applications of Diffusion Models," *Journal of Marketing Research* 27 (February 1990), pp. 70–77.

[32]Glen L. Urban, Bruce D. Weinberg, and John R. Hauser, "Pre-Market Forecasting of Really-New Products," *Journal of Marketing* 60 (January 1996), pp. 47–60.

FIGURE 9–10 Sales Patterns for Levels of Product Newness

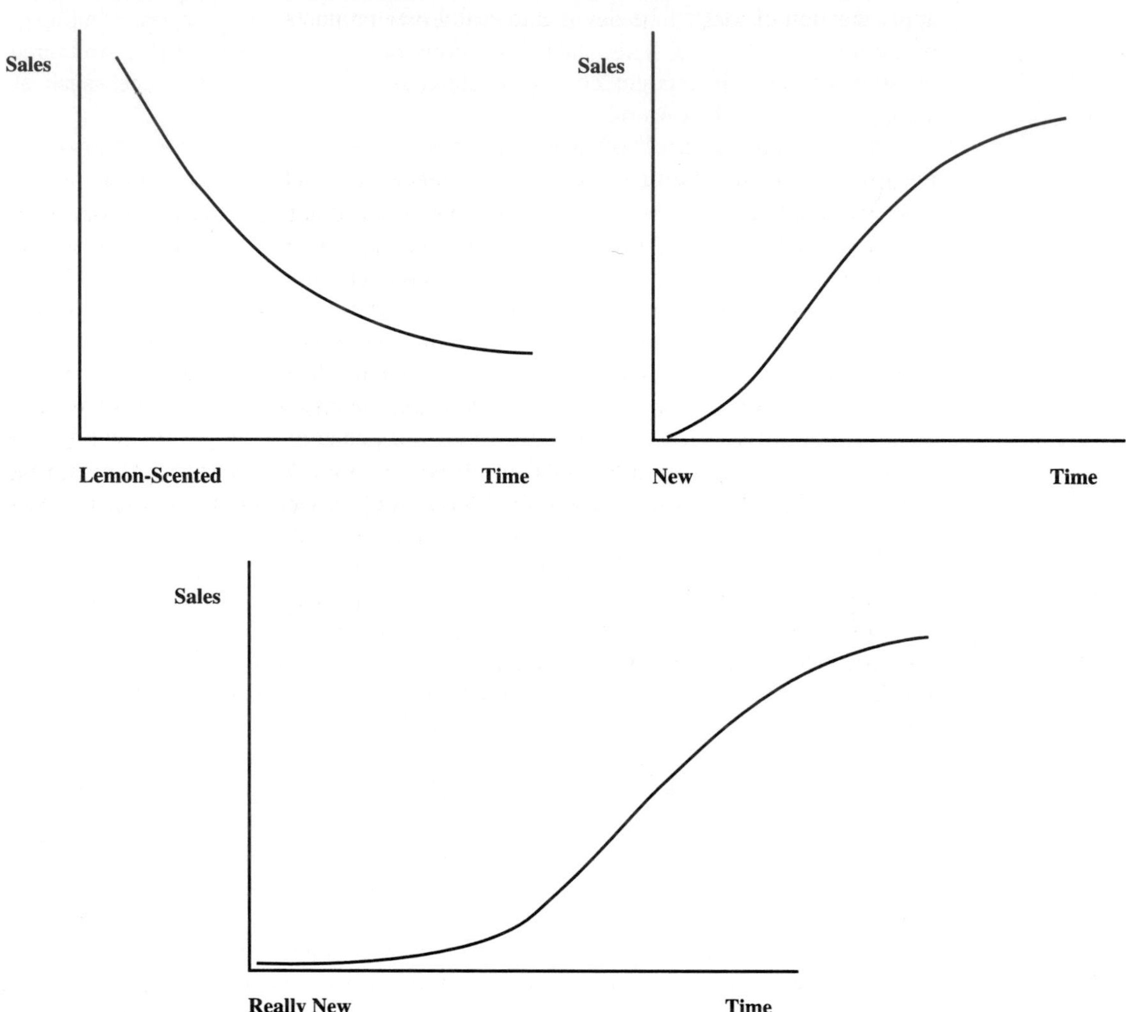

market (often 20 years or more), really new products require a level of patience unusual for businesses driven by quarterly profits. They are probably the equivalent of a lottery ticket or an option: Typically you lose a little, but if you win, you can win big.

This book has focused on managing existing brands and marginal improvements. Really new products, however, involve quantum improvements. The riskiness of new products increases as both the *newness to the company* (in terms of both customer and process knowledge) and *newness to the customer* increase, as does the likelihood that success will disrupt the current organization. It is therefore not surprising that really new products are viewed with suspicion. Still, both for the potential they offer and for the invigorating effect radical change has on an organization, we recommend that some fraction of activity be devoted to really new products.

Summary

In this chapter, we focused on product modification and the addition of product variants. Marketing the same product for a new use (often to current customers) or to new users (often to noncustomers, as in expanding distribution to a different region or country) does not physically involve a new product. However, since it involves a change in the product offering, it shares many of the characteristics of a product modification or variant. Hence strategic decisions to increase sales by expanding the market can be evaluated using many of the techniques discussed here.

Most product managers have limited flexibility in changing product composition. Still, small changes can have a major impact. This chapter gave a brief overview of some considerations in deciding whether to change a product, with emphasis on the long-run effects (the impact on brand value/equity) as well as the immediate sales impact on current customers, occasional customers, and noncustomers. Although change (even in product labels) can have important and even dramatic positive effects, it has downside risks in terms of costs and potential customer confusion and alienation. Hence, as in the case of any mix decision, analysis must be added to general principles before a product change is implemented.

Appendix
Sample Concept Test Formats*

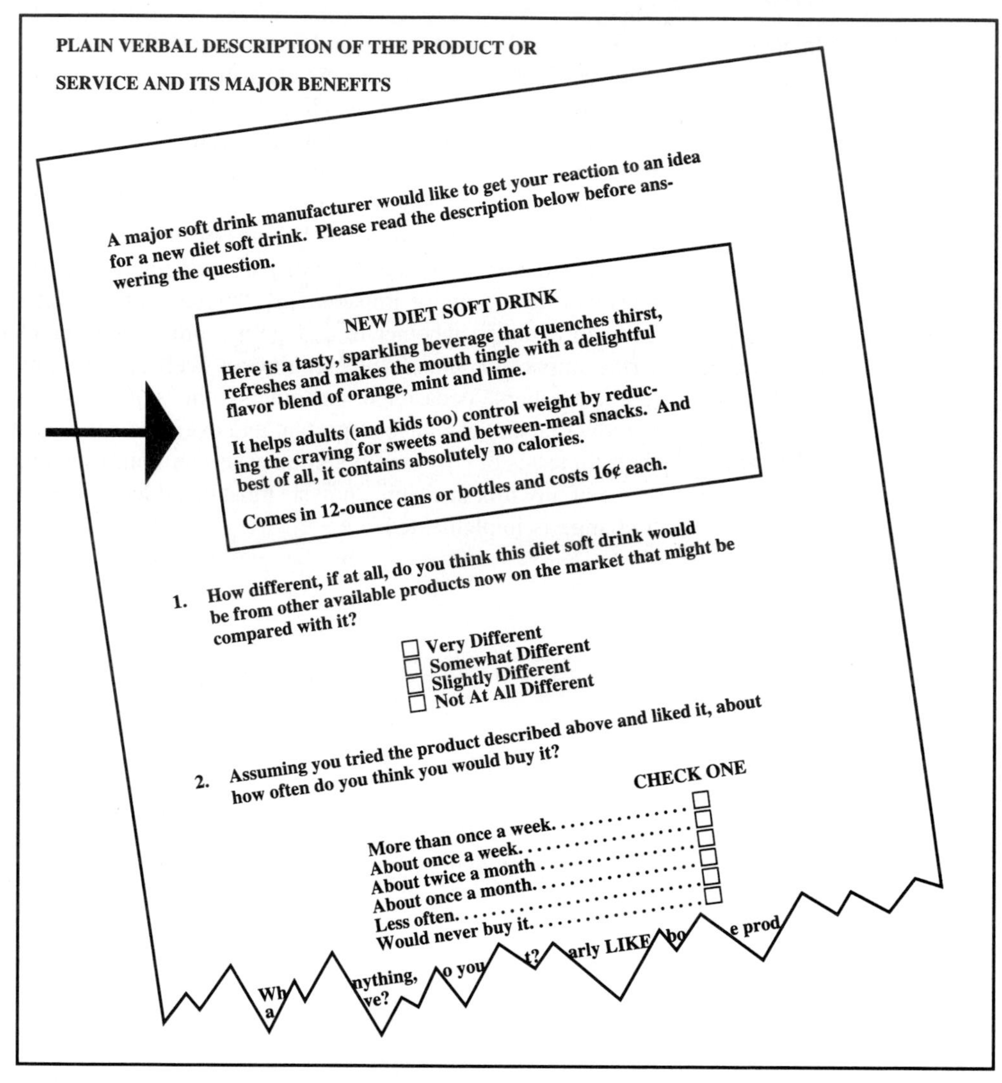
PLAIN VERBAL DESCRIPTION OF THE PRODUCT OR SERVICE AND ITS MAJOR BENEFITS

A major soft drink manufacturer would like to get your reaction to an idea for a new diet soft drink. Please read the description below before answering the question.

NEW DIET SOFT DRINK

Here is a tasty, sparkling beverage that quenches thirst, refreshes and makes the mouth tingle with a delightful flavor blend of orange, mint and lime.

It helps adults (and kids too) control weight by reducing the craving for sweets and between-meal snacks. And best of all, it contains absolutely no calories.

Comes in 12-ounce cans or bottles and costs 16¢ each.

1. How different, if at all, do you think this diet soft drink would be from other available products now on the market that might be compared with it?

☐ Very Different
☐ Somewhat Different
☐ Slightly Different
☐ Not At All Different

2. Assuming you tried the product described above and liked it, about how often do you think you would buy it?

CHECK ONE

More than once a week. . . . . ☐
About once a week. . . . . ☐
About twice a month . . . . ☐
About once a month. . . . . ☐
Less often. . . . . ☐
Would never buy it. . . . . ☐

Wh a nything, o you ve? t? arly LIKE bo e prod

*Source: National Family Opinion, Inc., *Concept Testing* (New York, 1975).

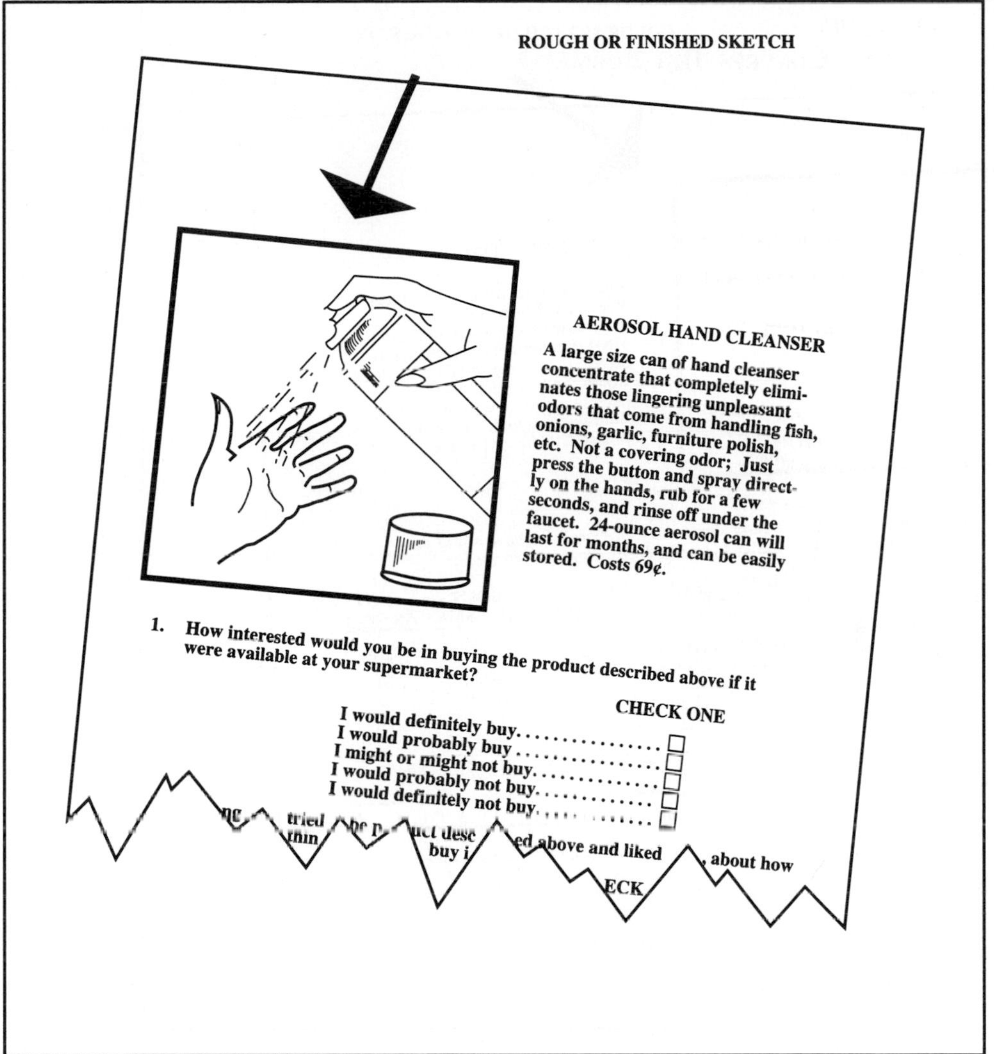

ROUGH OR FINISHED SKETCH

AEROSOL HAND CLEANSER

A large size can of hand cleanser concentrate that completely eliminates those lingering unpleasant odors that come from handling fish, onions, garlic, furniture polish, etc. Not a covering odor; Just press the button and spray directly on the hands, rub for a few seconds, and rinse off under the faucet. 24-ounce aerosol can will last for months, and can be easily stored. Costs 69¢.

1. How interested would you be in buying the product described above if it were available at your supermarket?

CHECK ONE

I would definitely buy. . . . . ☐
I would probably buy . . . . ☐
I might or might not buy. . . . . ☐
I would probably not buy. . . . . ☐
I would definitely not buy. . . . . ☐

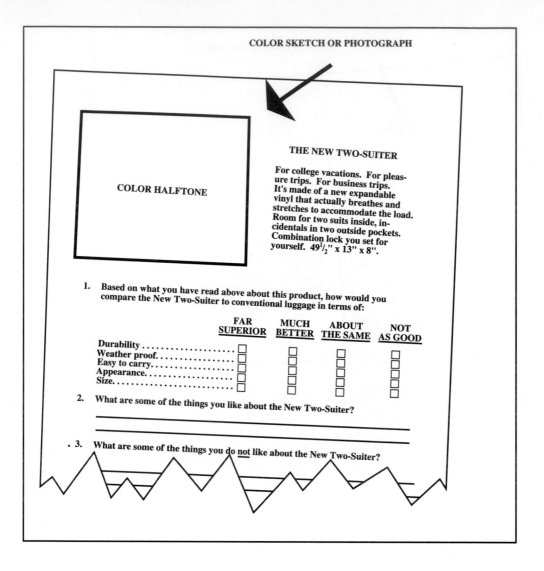

COLOR SKETCH OR PHOTOGRAPH

COLOR HALFTONE

THE NEW TWO-SUITER

For college vacations. For pleasure trips. For business trips. It's made of a new expandable vinyl that actually breathes and stretches to accommodate the load. Room for two suits inside, incidentals in two outside pockets. Combination lock you set for yourself. 49½" x 13" x 8".

1. **Based on what you have read above about this product, how would you compare the New Two-Suiter to conventional luggage in terms of:**

	FAR SUPERIOR	MUCH BETTER	ABOUT THE SAME	NOT AS GOOD
Durability	☐	☐	☐	☐
Weather proof	☐	☐	☐	☐
Easy to carry	☐	☐	☐	☐
Appearance	☐	☐	☐	☐
Size	☐	☐	☐	☐

2. **What are some of the things you like about the New Two-Suiter?**

____

____

3. **What are some of the things you do not like about the New Two-Suiter?**

C H A P T E R

10 Pricing Decisions

Overview

No decision worries a product manager more than the appropriate price to charge customers because, for most product categories, price is the marketing variable customers react to more than any other. Price is an observable component of the product that results in consumers purchasing or not purchasing it and at the same time directly affects margin per unit sold. Other components of the marketing mix are important, of course, since they must work together to create a unified brand image and produce sales. However, price is the marketing variable that most often makes or breaks the transaction.[1]

If price is such an important decision variable, why does so little science underlie the decision? Many writers have noted that, when compared to the other marketing elements, pricing decisions are often made more quickly after less analysis. Product managers make decisions about what prices to charge intuitively and routinely, usually based on cost.[2]

This focus on costs as the basis for pricing decisions results because traditionally accountants or financial analysts have done most of the analyses for determining price. It is easy to see why many pricing decisions are cost based. First, adding some kind of markup or profit target to the actual cost reduces setting price to a formula and produces a usable number. Second, it makes intuitive sense that a product manager cannot charge a price lower than what it costs to make the product or deliver the service. Third, such a pricing mechanism can be implemented quickly because it is generated internally and the only data needed are available within the firm.

[1]Because the focus of this book is largely on existing products, we will ignore the issues involved in pricing new products.

[2]See, for example, Kent B. Monroe, *Pricing: Making Profitable Decisions,* 2nd ed. (New York: McGraw-Hill, 1990); and Thomas T. Nagle and Reed K. Holden, *The Strategy and Tactics of Pricing,* 2nd ed. (Englewood Cliffs, N.J.: Prentice Hall, 1995).

Costs, of course do matter in setting price. However, the customer is much more important, specifically what we will refer to as *customer value*: what a product or service is worth to the customer in dollars. As a product manager, you must remember that the customer generally does not know or care what your costs are; what is important is whether or not the product delivers an appropriate amount of value for the price being paid. Cost-based pricing mechanisms can produce prices lower than value so the product manager is "leaving money on the table." More often, they result in prices higher than value, producing lost sales and eventual adjustment downward.

> Thus, the purpose of price is not to recover costs, but to capture the perceived value of product in the mind of the customer.[3]

This short statement represents a totally different approach to pricing than the cost-based methods. It recognizes that price is determined not by internal company factors alone but also by customers. The often-heard statement "price what the market will bear" is not market-based pricing or useful; different prices produce different levels of demand. What *is* useful is to continuously look at the customer for cues to what prices to set. This chapter therefore places a special emphasis on the role of customer research in making decisions about price.

However, prices are not determined by customer value and costs alone. Other elements include the marketing strategy and competitors' prices. In this chapter, we go into more depth about these four factors and other issues that enter into the product manager's pricing decision.

The Role of Marketing Strategy in Pricing

As discussed in Chapter 8, marketing strategy is first designed and *then* the implementation of that strategy, the marketing mix, is set. Thus, a key point is that the price must be consistent with the marketing strategy that is developed. As noted in Chapter 8, the marketing strategy consists primarily of the market segmentation and core strategy or product positioning decisions. Strategy decisions do not lead to a specific price-setting rule; rather, they give general guidelines for whether a price should be low or high.

For example, a number of years ago, the short-sleeved sport shirts sold under the Izod label (i.e., the "crocodile"—not alligator) were very popular. They were sold in many colors and were extensively distributed in the best department stores, such as Macy's. The marketing strategy and mix were consistent: The target segments were upscale consumers, the product positioning emphasized fashion and color, and the marketing mix supported the strategy through classy advertising, limited distribution, and, of course, high price.

Izod was subsequently bought by the packaged goods marketer General Mills. The company believed the brand had substantial growth opportunities beyond the targeted segments. In the words of the strategic framework developed in Chapter 8, it believed there were considerable market development opportunities available. To

[3]This quote is adapted from pricing consultant Daniel A. Nimer.

reach these other segments, the channels of distribution were widened and the price reduced; discount stores began selling the Izod sport shirts. Unfortunately, reaching new market segments produced a mismatch between the strategy (fashion, color, exclusivity) and the marketing mix (discount stores, low price). The upscale segment simply stopped buying the shirts and fled to competitors such as Polo. Eventually, General Mills divested Izod and it recently has begun to go back to its former successful strategy, including opening up its own exclusive retail stores.

The market segmentation decision affects price because prices can vary widely over segments. Economists refer to this as *price discrimination,* that is, charging different prices to segments according to their price elasticity or sensitivity. The brand offerings in most product categories vary in price among market segments, often based on order quantity. Airline ticket prices vary based not just on class of service (first, business, tourist), but time of travel and when the ticket is purchased (e.g., 21-day advanced). Industrial products often have multi-tiered pricing depending on whether or not a service contract is purchased, speed of delivery required, and so forth.

Of course, substantial price variation can exist even within a targeted segment. These variations have been referred to as price *bands.*[4] Figure 10–1 shows the price band within market segments and price discrimination among segments for the ice cream market. As the movement of the price distributions shows, there is a positive relationship between price and perceived quality. The curves in Figure 10–1 represent distributions of prices within each segment so that the greater the spread in the distribution, the wider the variation in price. The higher perceived quality segments also exhibit greater price variation among brands.

Why do such variations exist even within segments? For both industrial and consumer products, there seem to be several reasons. First, customers become brand loyal to certain products or suppliers; they tend to rate price relatively low compared to other factors such as reliability, speed of delivery, and the like. Second, in some industries, price visibility is low; that is, the price charged is less obvious than it is at supermarkets or other retailers where the price is marked on the item. For many industrial products, the list price is only the basis from which discounts that vary among customers are given. Third, competitive intensity can vary among segments; the larger the number of suppliers, the narrower the price band, because more competition implies greater convergence on a standard price.

The implication for the product manager is that it is critical to understand the price sensitivity of the different market segments and, further, how much price flexibility (i.e., the width of the price band) exists in the segments actively targeted by the marketing strategy. Thus, the marketing strategy dictates the kind of pricing policies that can be employed at any given point in time.

Along with understanding customers' price sensitivity, the product manager should ask other questions that relate to price (see also the discussion on customer analysis in Chapter 6). A key question is how customers make purchase decisions.

---

[4]Elliot B. Ross, "Making Money with Proactive Pricing," *Harvard Business Review,* November–December 1984, pp. 145–155.

FIGURE 10–1 The Price Band in Ice Cream

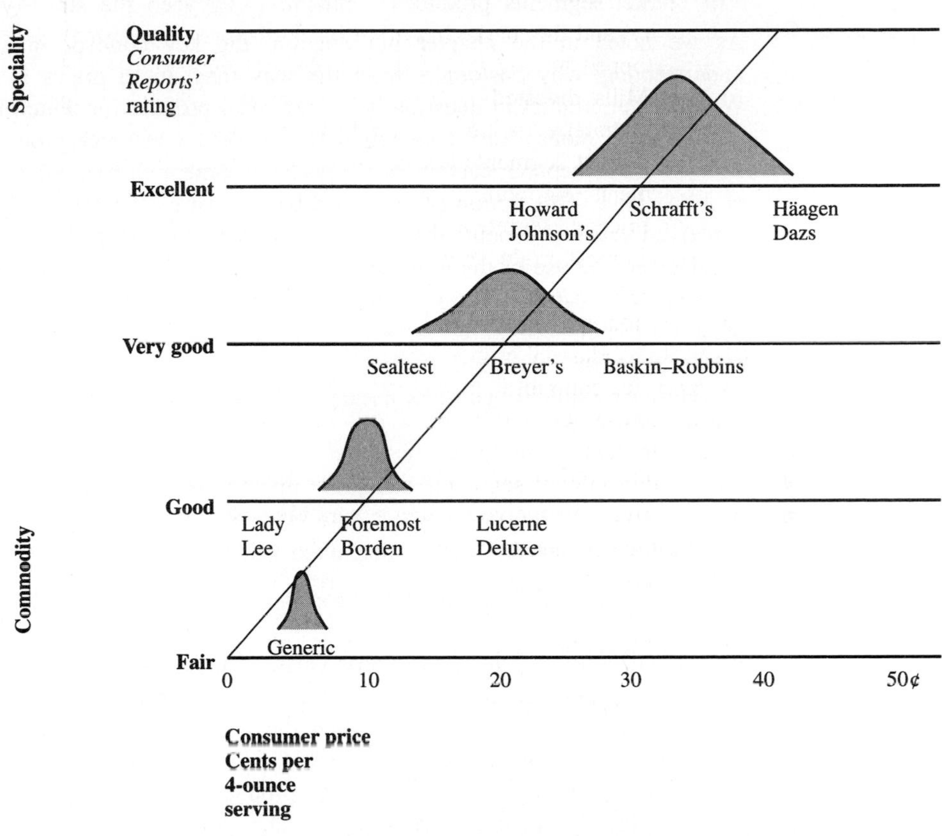

Source: Reprinted by permission of *Harvard Business Review.* An exhibit from "Making Money with Proactive Pricing," by Elliott B. Ross, November–December 1984.

How important is price in the overall decision, and how important is it to different individuals in the purchase decision process? Simple surveys will not suffice since respondents often claim price is more important than it really is. Finding out the importance of price takes in-depth knowledge of the customers and perhaps some auxiliary marketing research such as conjoint analysis. For example, a study of buyers of local area networks (software and hardware used to link personal computers) showed that in terms of importance, price was behind service, the supplier's reputation and technical ability, and product availability. Another aspect of understanding price is determining how important your product is to the customer, who will be less price sensitive for a key component in a high-quality product. For example, Rolls-Royce does not quibble about the cost of the leather it uses for its car interiors.

Measuring Perceived Value

Customer Value

As we noted in the chapter introduction, the key concept in setting price and understanding why customers react the way they do to prices is perceived value. Whether the product in question is an industrial product for which the customer can calculate the money saved by purchasing it or a consumer product for which the benefits are perceptual, customers always have some notion of what constitutes a good or a bad price. This notion is developed by comparing the price being charged to the perceived value or benefits that would be derived through purchasing.

Despite the use of the term *perceived value,* no such single quantity exists in the marketplace; customer value is idiosyncratic to the individual customer. Therefore, when we use the term *perceived value,* we refer to an "average" value for a particular market segment.

Here we explicitly consider three possible relations among perceived value, price, and variable cost:

1. Perceived value > price > variable cost.
2. Price > perceived value > variable cost.
3. Price > variable cost > perceived value.

Note that in all three situations, we assume price is greater than variable cost.

Perceived Value > Price > Variable Cost. This represents a situation in which the product manager has set a price that covers the cost of making the product (or delivering the service) but is less than the customers' true perceived value.[5] This "leaving money on the table" scenario sacrifices profits (either knowingly or unknowingly) by charging less than the producer could obtain. The amount of lost profit is directly related to the dollar value the customer places on the product. Customers react to this by thinking they are getting a "bargain." Interestingly, customers do not usually write letters to the company complaining they are not paying enough. Thus, except for the extreme case of such insufficient production that shortages occur, this situation is difficult for the product manager to discover without using the marketing research methods described later in this chapter.[6] Of course product managers may purposely price below value. This notion of "value pricing" (to be distinguished from "pricing to value," which is a price set equal to customer value) is common in today's price-sensitive marketplace and is discussed later in this chapter.

---

[5]Again, we emphasize that although we refer to a "customer," in applying the perceived value concept we assume the product manager is interested in the average perceived value of a market segment.

[6] This is sometimes referred to as "seller's remorse." For example, a person selling a house who receives several offers immediately at the listing price always believes he or she should have set a higher price.

A good example of value pricing is the Mazda Miata, introduced in 1990. Mazda's objective was to introduce a two-seat convertible with few power options and luxurious details. This throwback to the 1950s is just a simple car with a sporting feel and was introduced at a low price of $16,000 to $18,000. However, demand for the Miata was so high during the first few months after it was introduced that prices of $25,000 in the used-car sections of newspapers were common. Customers were buying the cars and quickly reselling them to make a significant arbitrage profit. Clearly, Mazda could have charged more for the Miata. Perhaps company managers underestimated the demand for the car. However, they probably knew this craze was a short-term aberration and believed the original price was more consistent with their long-term marketing strategy for the car. Also, high initial prices that are later reduced play havoc with the used-car market. Customers who paid the high price and tried to sell the cars later would find no demand for them because people could buy a new car for less than a used one. Interestingly, this low entry price relative to customer value strategy was copied by Porsche and BMW with their own roadster entries, the Boxster and the Z3.

Price > Perceived Value > Variable Cost. This represents an unfortunate situation: The price is set higher than the costs *and* higher than the customer's perceived value. In this case, the customer thinks purchasing the product is a "bad deal." Unlike in the first scenario, customers *do* let you know when the price is higher than their perceived value; they simply do not buy the product. Waiting for customer reaction is an expensive form of marketing research, however, because the customers may have bought another brand and be out of the market for some time. The cure for customers' failure to buy is obvious: Some kind of downward price adjustment or increase in customer value is necessary. However, without knowing what the perceived value is, the product manager does not know how far to lower price and usually uses the competition as the reference point.

Reduction in price due to lower perceived value is very common today. For example, with Microsoft's introduction of the Windows 95 operating system, the relative advantage held by Apple's operating system has diminished considerably. As a result, Apple has had to reduce prices on its Macintosh desktop and laptop computers to adjust for this decline in perceived advantage over the Windows-based computers. Even companies that might be thought to be impervious to price reductions, such as Disney, are susceptible to the problem of decreasing perceived value relative to price. In 1991, Disneyland began offering discounts to Los Angeles–area residents (proof of residence is required). Given the other recreational options in the Los Angeles area plus the fact that the novelty of going to Disneyland had worn off, local residents were showing by reduced attendance that a gap existed between the admissions price and perceived quality relative to other options. This is, of course, not the case for out-of-town tourists, who are still happy or at least willing to pay the full price.

Price > Variable Cost > Perceived Value. The final scenario represents the case in which price is higher than cost but the perceived value is even lower than the cost. This is clearly a failure scenario. Usually such products are weeded out in the new-product development process. If not, they are ultimately withdrawn from the market. For example, the Yugoslavian-made car, the Yugo, was withdrawn from the U.S. market

FIGURE 10–2 A Taxonomy of Methods for Calculating Customer Value

1. Industrial engineering methods
   Internal engineering assessment: Physical laboratory tests within the firm.
   Field value-in-use assessments: Customer interviews determining economic benefits to using the product.
   Indirect survey questions: Customer estimates of the effects of product changes on firm operations used to infer the value of product attributes.
2. Overall estimates of customer value
   Focus group value assessment: willingness-to-pay questions in a small-group setting.
   Direct survey questions: willingness-to-pay questions in a survey format.
3. Decomposition approaches
   Conjoint analysis: A method for estimating customer trade-offs of product attributes.
   Benchmarks: Customer indication of willingness to pay for incremental (or fewer) attributes that can be compared to an example from the product category.
4. Compositional approach: Direct customer questions about the value of product attributes.
5. Importance ratings: Customer rank ordering or rating of the importance of product attributes as well as comparisons among competitors.

because it received such negative press in publications such as *Consumer Reports* that consumer value fell even below the manufacturing and marketing costs.

Optimally, the product manager seeks the following relationship:

$$\text{Price} = \text{perceived value} > \text{variable cost.}$$

In other words, in most circumstances, we would like price to fully capture the perceived value customers place on the product. The product manager would be happy (no profits are being forgone), and customers would be satisfied (the price is no higher than the value they place on the product). However, this equality rarely occurs. As we will show in the next section of this chapter, it is difficult to precisely estimate perceived value. In addition, many product managers wish to leave some money on the table to provide the feeling of a bargain for the customer. When the product manager understands customer value, the pricing decision becomes clear: The product manager decides how much value to give to the customer and how much to keep. The maximum price the manager can charge is the customer value; the minimum is the variable cost. Anything in between represents sharing value between the product manager and the customer.

Methods

Figure 10–2 shows the general types of methods that can be used to estimate customer value.[7] The following sections indicate how to use them.

[7] See James C. Anderson, Dipak C. Jain, and Pradeep K. Chintagunta, "Customer Value Assessment in Business Markets: A State-of-Practice Study," *Journal of Business-to-Business Marketing,* Vol. 1, 1993.

FIGURE 10–3 The Economic Value Concept

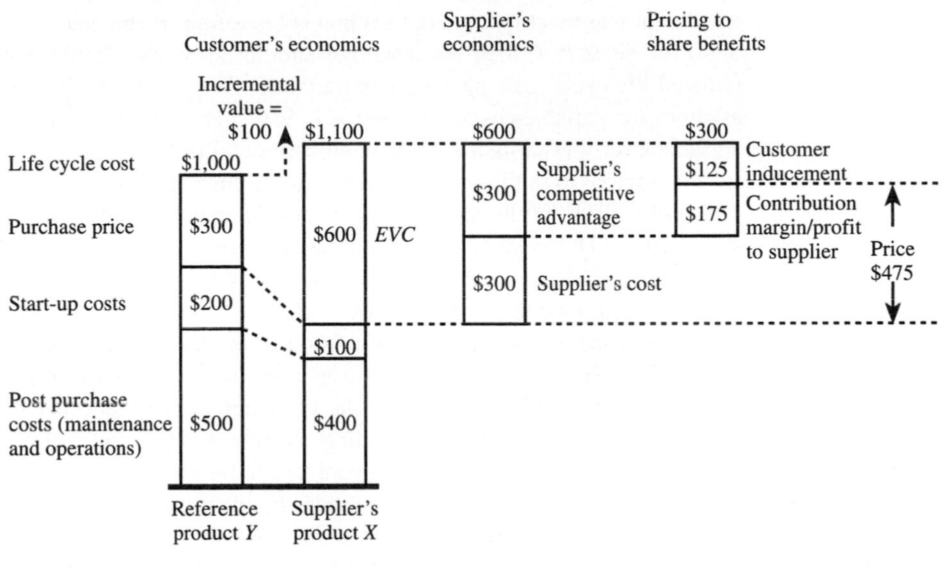

Calculating Value-in-Use

Particularly for industrial products, a useful way to estimate customer value is through a method called *value-in-use* (referred to as *field value-in-use* in Figure 10–2). The approach is basically the same as the economic value calculation discussed in Chapter 9. First, the product manager selects a reference product, usually either the product the customer is currently using or a competitor's product. Second, the product manager calculates the *incremental* economic (dollar) benefit to the customer of using the product or brand in question. Assuming it is positive, this incremental economic benefit describes the range of prices obtainable: Pricing to the limit of the incremental benefit gives all the value to the product manager, pricing to capture none of the incremental benefit gives it all to the customer, and in-between prices share the economic benefit.

Figure 10–3 shows one approach to the value-in-use calculation.[8] The bar on the far left is the reference product, Y. Assume the reference product cost (i.e., the initial price) is $300. Also assume that the company that produces it incurs start-up costs of $200 (e.g., training) and postpurchase costs of $500 (e.g., maintenance). Together these costs are referred to as *life cycle costs* and recognize that the cost of buying a product often goes far beyond the acquisition cost.

[8] See John L. Forbis and Nitin T. Mehta, "Value-Based Strategies for Industrial Products," *Business Horizons,* May–June 1981, pp. 32–42.

The product manager's product, X, is represented in the next bar on the right. It is assumed product X has $100 less in both start-up and postpurchase costs. It is also assumed the product offers approximately $100 more in "value" through some additional features (e.g., energy savings). Therefore, if the customer is willing to pay $300 for product Y, then the customer should be willing to pay $300 more ($200 in reduced life cycle costs plus $100 extra value) for product X. The third bar to the right assumes the variable cost of product X is $300. Thus, we know our pricing range: The variable cost of $300 is the floor; the incremental dollar value to the customer is $600 (this is referred to as the *economic value* to the customer, or EVC, in Figure 10–3). The difference, $300, is the amount the product manager has to "play with" in terms of setting price. This is labeled the "supplier's competitive advantage." The last bar to the right shows one hypothetical split of the $300 pricing range (incremental to the $300 variable cost). One such split leaves $125 for the customer and $175 for product X.

An attractive feature of this approach is that the analysis provides valuable information for the salesperson to use in trying to close the sale. In this case, the salesperson can explicitly quantify the incremental economic benefit to the customer and show that the company is willing to give a "discount" of $125 from the true economic value. Since industrial buyers like to be shown how they can make a greater profit buying one product versus another, this information should be quite persuasive.

It is possible, of course, to apply this method to a case in which the incremental value is lower than the reference product but the customer would be compensated by a lower price. Suppose the reference product is again product Y in Figure 10–3. However, let product X have $50 higher start-up costs and $75 higher postpurchase costs with no incremental value characteristics. This puts product X at a $125 deficit for the EVC. However, if the cost of making this new product is only $50, the product manager still has a $75 pricing decision range.

Of interest in the first illustration is how the $100 worth of incremental value is calculated. The value-in-use approach attempts to break down the advantages of the product into its components and thus has a decompositional aspect. That is, if the product has advantages over the reference product, these advantages must be quantified in terms of each way the product benefits the customer economically.

Animalens, Inc., which makes vision-blurring lenses for chickens,[9] is an effective if unusual example of this approach. The lenses were developed to reduce cannibalism in egg-laying chickens; reducing their vision makes them less able and willing to fight, thereby increasing their productivity. The reference "product" in this case is debeaking, that is, shortening the chickens' beaks to make it difficult to use them as a weapon. The contact lenses have four main advantages that produce economic benefits to chicken farmers: (1) reduced cannibalism, (2) increased egg production, (3) reduced feed consumption, and (4) eliminating of debeaking. Actual data have shown that the costs of lens insertion and debeaking are about the same; therefore, the economic benefits are the sum of the first three. The economic benefits can be quantified by

---

[9]A description of this company's early history as well as more background on the product appears in "Optical Distortion, Inc.," Harvard Business School case study 9-575-072.

studying the behavior of two flocks, one using the lenses and the other using debeaking. The comparison establishes the range of prices: The lower limit is the variable cost of producing the lenses, and the upper limit is the sum of the economic benefits of the three components of cost saving or improved productivity.

The method shown in Figure 10–3 can be applied to both products and services. A trend in business is to purchase a service from an outside vendor to replace the company's operation. For example, rather than operating copying machines and worrying about how to use them properly, many companies subcontract their copying operations to third parties that assume responsibility for the work. University bookstores are subcontracting their bookstore operations to national companies with more efficient operations. Other examples include General Motors paying PPG Industries to operate its automobile painting facilities and IBM contracting with Federal Express to act as a warehousing agent around the world. In these cases, the agents whose services are purchased can use the cost of the company providing the service itself as a reference product. Even if it is more expensive to pay other companies for these services, benefits such as better utilization of employee time and company capital, increased productivity, and better technology can be quantified and shown to produce value to potential customers.

As you have probably discerned, the value-in-use method works particularly well with industrial products and services but not as well for consumer products, whose benefits are usually very difficult to quantify in dollar terms. The methods described next are primary research methods that can be applied to all kinds of product categories.

Simulating the Buying Experience

A common approach to understanding how customers react to new-product concepts or product modifications involves simulating the shopping experience, a form of benchmarking (see Figure 10–2). Marketing research companies often set up laboratories at or near shopping malls where customers are asked to select brands, watch commercials, and the like in what looks like an actual store (e.g. supermarket) setting. In such experimental settings, marketing mix variables such as price can be manipulated to see if reactions vary to different possible prices for a brand. The reactions are usually measured by purchase intention or selection from a set of choices rather than actual purchase.

Industrial product companies also have used such a research design. For example, Hewlett-Packard (HP) developed a new test instrument and wanted to find an appropriate pricing level. The company realized that asking direct questions about willingness to pay was not likely to produce accurate responses. So it developed a catalog that included competing products and the new product. HP then hired a marketing research firm to conduct the study and disguise who was collecting the data to avoid biasing responses. Potential customers were randomly assigned to different groups, and each group received the same brochure, except that the price for the HP instrument varied. By controlling all other factors, the only difference in response had to be due to price. The customers were then asked to indicate which testing machine they would choose, thus simulating the buying experience. Interestingly, HP managers

Figure 10–4 What Buyers Will Pay For PC Brands

Question: "How much more are you willing to pay for Brand X compared to a no-name clone?"

Brand	1993	1995
IBM	$364	$339
Compaq	301	318
Apple	264	182
DEC	198	10
AST	176	17
Dell	161	230
Hewlett-Packard	145	260

Source: Reprinted by permission of *The Wall Street Journal,*

found that as they increased price, demand went up. They subsequently priced the instrument thousands of dollars higher than they had planned.[10]

Estimating Brand Equity

The concept of brand equity, discussed in Chapter 8, can be used to estimate the value a customer might place on one brand versus another. We mentioned in Chapter 8 how conjoint analysis can give the product manager some idea about the relative utility customers have for brands in a category. However, the examples given there did not give results in explicit dollar terms.

Figure 10–4 gives an example of a 1995 study that asked the following question of business customers of personal computers: "How much more are you willing to pay for Brand X compared to a no-name clone?"[11] These results were compared to a similar study done in 1993. As can be seen, the survey results are striking in that they not only estimate how much more or less one manufacturer can price its line relative to competitors but also show how some brands have increased and some have decreased in terms of their customer value in a relatively short period of time. IBM and Compaq can charge roughly $300 more than DEC and AST. Moreover, the latter two companies should be alarmed about how far their customer value has fallen. In fact shortly after the survey, DEC pulled out of the personal computer market.

Using Price Thresholds

Another approach that requires primary marketing research involves customer price thresholds. This approach provides an overall estimate of customer value (Figure 10–2). One important threshold is called the *reservation* price. This is the highest price a customer would pay for a product or service. A second price threshold is a

[10]Ted Kendall, "And the Survey Says . . . ," *The Marketer,* September 1990, pp. 47–48.
[11]"What Buyers Will Pay for PC Brands," *The Wall Street Journal,* October 16, 1995.

lower boundary, the lowest price someone would pay for a product. It may appear to be common sense that one would pay as little as possible in all instances. However, many products are such that customers associate low price with low quality. This relationship between price and perceived quality has been found in many (but not all) product categories.[12] Thus, a price level can exist below which a customer would not purchase due to suspicions about the product's quality.

These two thresholds can be used as follows. First, the product manager identifies customers most likely to buy the product category. These respondents are then shown a card with a range of specific prices. For example, if the product is a low-priced good that normally sells for around \$5, the range might be from \$2 to \$8 in 25 cent or 50 cent increments. The respondents are then asked to identify their two price thresholds with the following questions: (1) "Above which price on this card would you not buy this product?" and (2) "Below which price on this card would you not buy this product from suspicions that the quality is poor?" The product manager can then determine the price to charge by identifying the price most often mentioned as acceptable.

Dollarmetric Scales

Conventional rating scales are often used to assess willingness to pay for a product. For example, a typical survey question offers a series of prices and then asks potential customers to indicate how likely they are to purchase the product on a 1 to 7 scale, with 1 being very unlikely and 7 representing very likely. Among other problems with such an approach, the 1 to 7 ratings give the product manager little information on which to base a pricing decision; it is difficult to know whether a 6 should be counted as a likely buyer or whether only 7s should be used.

An alternative scale puts responses in dollar or other currency terms. Figure 10–5 applies and analyzes a dollarmetric scale for soft drinks. This example includes five brands: Coke, Pepsi, 7UP, Dr Pepper, and Fresca. The question is: What should be the relative prices of the four brands? The respondent first chooses which of two brands she or he prefers. Next, the respondent indicates in dollars and cents how much extra he or she would be willing to pay to get a six-pack of the preferred brand.[13] The product manager then analyzes the data by summing the differences, positive and negative, between each brand compared to each of the others. As the bottom of Figure 10–5 shows, for this customer a six-pack of Coke is worth 2 cents more than Pepsi, 8 cents more than 7UP, 5 cents more than Dr Pepper, and 12 cents more than Fresca. If these results held up over a national sample, they would give some indication of the price differences Coke could maintain over the competing brands (such as the survey results shown in Figure 10–4).

---

[12]See, for example, Valerie A. Zeithaml, "Consumer Perceptions of Price, Quality, and Value: A Means-End Model and Synthesis of Evidence," *Journal of Marketing,* July 1988, pp. 2–22.

[13]An alternative way to phrase the question is to ask how much the respondent would have to be paid to be indifferent between the preferred brand and the other brand.

FIGURE 10–5 Dollarmetric Example

Data

Pair of Brands (more preferred brand underlined)	*Amount Extra Willing to Pay to Get a Six-Pack of the More Preferred Brand (cents)*
Coke, Pepsi	2
Coke, 7UP	8
Coke, Dr Pepper	5
Coke, Fresca	12
Pepsi, 7UP	6
Pepsi, Dr Pepper	3
Pepsi, Fresca	10
7UP, Dr Pepper	3
7UP, Fresca	4
Dr Pepper, Fresca	7

Analysis

Coke:	+ 2 (versus Pepsi) + 8 (versus 7UP) + 5 (versus Dr Pepper) + 12 (versus Fresca)	= 27
Pepsi:	−2 + 6 + 3 + 10	= 17
7UP:	− 8 − 6 − 3 + 4	= −13
Dr Pepper:	− 5 − 3 + 3 + 7	= 2
Fresca:	− 12 − 10 − 4 − 7	= −33

Using the Perceived Value Concept

Managers can use the concept of perceived value by considering a functional relationship among market share, perceived value, and price:

$$\text{Market share} = f[\text{ perceived value/price }].$$

As an application of this relationship, take an observed decline in the market share of a product. How can this trend be reversed? Usually the immediate response is a decrease in the denominator, that is, a price cut either through list price or a price promotion. Cutting price is certainly one way to bring the relationship between perceived value and price back into balance. However, there is another way: The product manager could also choose to increase the perceived value of the product.

This increase in perceived value can be accomplished in a variety of ways, including the following:

- Improve the product itself by increasing actual quality or offering better service or a longer warranty period.
- Advertise to enhance the product's image.
- Institute value-added services, such as technical support or financing, in the distribution channels.
- Improve the sales effort by training the sales force to sell value rather than price.

These are only a sampling of the kinds of things product managers can do to improve value rather than cut price.[14]

Interestingly, although reducing price is a more common way to regain share losses, it is actually much more expensive than adding value since the lower resulting profit margin must be multiplied by the old number of units sold to estimate the "investment" that may or may not be recovered by increased sales volume. A 3 percent price cut by the average Standard & Poor's 1,000 company reduces profits from 8.1 percent to 5.1 percent, a reduction of 37 percent. In addition, McKinsey consultants estimate that the average S&P 1,000 company would need a 12 percent increase in sales volume to offset the 3 percent price cut.[15] Note that the activities designed to raise perceived value can cost considerably less. How much does it cost to improve sales training procedures? How expensive is it to offer improved customer service? Value-enhancing activities are not free, but they are usually fixed costs that can be spread over a large volume as opposed to per-unit reductions in margins.

A good example of this value-adding approach to pricing was provided by the biotechnology firm Genentech in 1990. In 1987, the firm introduced a drug called TPA that clears blood clots that cause heart attacks. At $2,220 per dose, the product was (and still is) quite important to the company. However, in March 1990, a study was released showing the drug was no more effective than an alternative, streptokinase, that sold for only $200 per dose. However, months later, Genentech was still selling TPA for $2,220 per dose. How? First, it trained its sales force to aggressively point out some of the limitations of the damaging study. Second, it temporarily gave hospital pharmacies a longer period in which to pay for TPA, thus encouraging them to stock up on the drug. Clearly, the costs of these two moves were far less than the cost of dropping the price of the product.[16]

Thus, a key point is that product managers can get considerable leverage from first increasing the perceived value of products rather than immediately reducing price. Although reducing price is usually the gut reaction to a drop in market share, it is worth thinking about the numerator in the value/price relationship. Companies know this: In the automobile industry, executives say they want to stop focusing on price and break the habit of rebates and instead build brand equity—add value.[17] However, with few exceptions, such as Saturn, the price/promotion wars continue, even for new, highly touted models such as Ford's restyled Taurus.

Competition and Pricing

So far our discussion about setting price has described two key elements of the product manager's thinking: the marketing strategy and the value customers place on the

[14]Since price and perceived value are often correlated, some readers may argue that one way to increase perceived value is to raise price. However, this works only if there is additional investment in the product that also raises value, such as packaging and advertising, and if an appropriate market segment exists that will respond to such a strategy.

[15]Andrew E. Serwer, "How to Escape a Price War," *Fortune,* June 13, 1994, pp. 82–90.

[16]Joan O' C. Hamilton, "Genentech: A Textbook Case of Medical Marketing," *Business Week,* August 13, 1990, pp. 96–97.

[17]Bill Saporito, "Why the Price Wars Never End," *Business Week,* March 23, 1992, pp. 68–78.

product relative to other available options. The first is obviously an internal factor because the product manager has control over the marketing strategy. The second dimension accounts for one of the external elements affecting all decisions: the customers.

A third critical element in pricing decisions is the competition. The competitors' prices act as a reference point, either explicitly as shown in the value computations earlier, or implicitly as a way to assess the price of the product in question. Competitors' prices do not necessarily represent willingness to pay because the set of possible prices or marketing strategies may have been limited. In other words, just because the major competitors' prices hover around 50 cents does not mean customers would not pay more for a product delivering superior value, either real or perceived. However, the 50 cent price level does represent a reference point; a price of $1 may appear to customers to be out of the reasonable range, even when the product manager believes it is reasonable from a value perspective.[18]

The two factors that are key to understanding the role of competition in the pricing decision are the competitors' costs and the historical pricing behavior in the category.

Competitors' Costs

In Chapter 5, we discussed the importance of studying the competition to make better strategic decisions. Product managers cannot make intelligent pricing decisions without having some estimate of the relative cost positions held by competitors in the product category. Even better are estimates of the actual costs. An understanding of the cost structure of the category provides at least two types of guidance. First, assuming no brand would be priced below variable cost, cost estimates provide the product manager with an idea of how low some competitors can price. This can be very useful in a price battle in which prices are going down. Second, cost estimates give the product manager some idea of the margins in the category. Coupled with data on sales volume, which are usually relatively easy to obtain, and information on marketing program costs, total profits can then be estimated. This can be important information in forecasting the likelihood that a product will stay in the market or the amount of money a competitor has to put behind the brand strategy.

Costs can be estimated in several ways. A common approach for manufactured products, described in Chapter 5, is to use reverse engineering for a detailed analysis of the cost structure. Product managers should purchase competitors' products and take them apart, studying the costs of the components and packaging. For many products, managers can readily identify components and their costs in the market. If a component is proprietary, such as a custom microprocessor in a computer, the cost can be estimated by engineers or other personnel.

Another way to estimate costs, or at least margins, is to use publicly available data on the competitors. Based on annual reports, 10Ks, and the like, average margins can be ascertained. These can be assumed to directly apply, especially if the product is a big

---

[18]We discuss the notion of a customer's reference point later in the chapter when we address psychological aspects of price.

FIGURE 10–6 Market Share versus Price/Costs

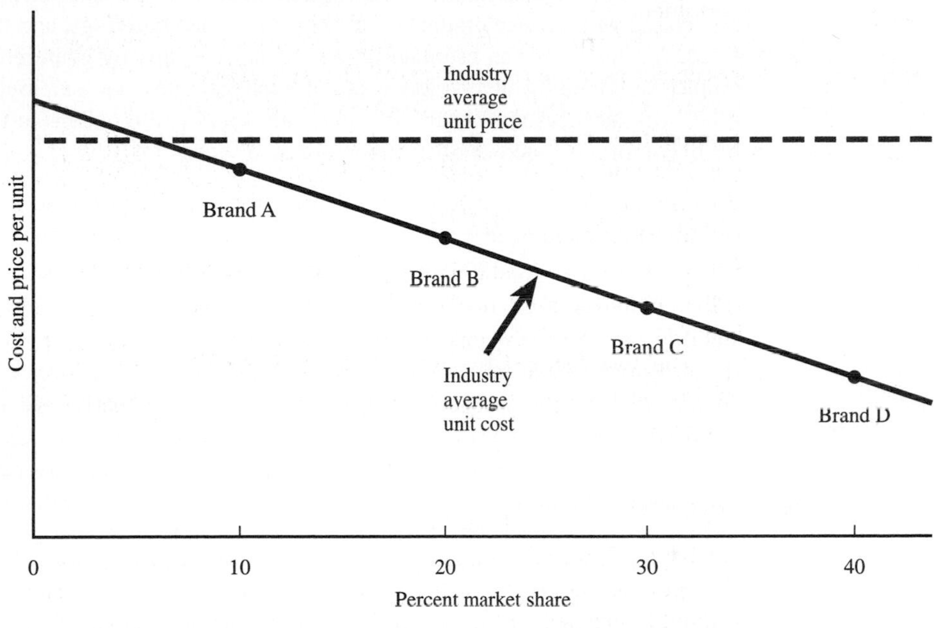

component of total sales or if, as is often the case, the company tends to follow a cost plus percent markup strategy. Alternatively, the overall average can be adjusted (either subjectively or via analysis) to account for such factors as the category average, the relative number and strength of competitors in the category, and production experience

Particularly for manufactured products, it is possible to both understand current costs and forecast future costs through the use of the experience curve.[19] The experience curve phenomenon applies to certain products for which repetitive production of larger and larger amounts and concomitant investment in new manufacturing equipment systematically reduce costs over time. The conventional functional relationship assumed in experience curve economics is that costs (adjusted for inflation) are a decreasing function of accumulated "experience" or production volume. Figure 10–6 shows an example of the experience curve phenomenon. In this case, experience is approximated by market share. Costs (and concomitant prices) are shown to be correlated with market share: The larger the share, the lower the costs.[20] If the product manager can construct a plot such as that in Figure 10–6 and

[19]See Derek F. Abell and John S. Hammond, *Strategic Market Planning* (Englewood Cliffs, N.J.: Prentice Hall, 1979), Chapter 3.

[20]This is discussed at length in Robert D. Buzzell and Bradley T. Gale, *The PIMS Principles* (New York: The Free Press, 1987), Chapter 5. Their analysis is based on the PIMS (Profit Impact of Market Strategies) database composed of cross-sectional time-series data across different firms and industries. The difference between using experience and share is that the former measures volume over time whereas the latter is more closely related to economies of scale or current production values.

statistically estimate the implied relationship between share and costs, she or he can forecast future relative cost positions under different assumptions of the brand shares.

The costs of delivering services are more difficult to estimate. Because the costs associated with service products such as labor, office buildings, and the like are largely fixed, the manager can estimate relative cost positions by examining the number of employees, looking at efficiency ratios such as sales per employee, and assessing other, similar measures. Again, it is particularly useful to understand the cost structure by becoming a customer of a competitor's service.

Historical Pricing Behavior

As noted at the beginning of the chapter, the product manager makes pricing decisions in two contexts. First, the decision can be *proactive:* During a period of relative price stability, the product manager can choose to be the first to either raise or lower price. In this situation, the product manager wonders what the reaction will be to the price change. Second, the decision can be *reactive* when a competitor has taken the lead and the product manager has to decide whether to match the price, keep it the same, or reduce the price more or less than the competitors. If prices are being adjusted in a category, most product managers prefer to be proactive because that forces competitors to make difficult decisions at a time and in circumstances not of their choosing; in other words, the product manager is setting the rules of the game.

To understand these patterns of price change, it is useful to examine the historical behavior of the products in the category. Individual product managers may change over time, but there are often companywide or institutional reasons certain brands consistently tend to be proactive and others reactive. For example, U.S. Steel (before it was USX) was consistently the price leader in the U.S. steel industry: It would change prices first and competitors would follow. Similarly, predicting future reactions of competitors can be partially related to historical price competition in the category for many products.

More important, the competitor analysis gives clues to the pricing behavior in the product category. What are some noncost characteristics to look for? The most important is the competitor's operating objective. Clearly, if the objective seems to be profit oriented, that brand will not be an aggressive price cutter. Alternatively, if the objective is to increase market share, lower price might be used as a weapon. Thus, as noted in Chapter 5, understanding competitors' objectives is key to anticipating pricing moves in the category. Other factors are the financial health of the product or parent company, its capacity (undercapacity is a warning that price might be cut), and a new product's or a senior manager's historical behavior in other markets.

The Role of Costs

We suggested earlier in this chapter that costs should have little to do with the pricing decision other than to act as a floor or lower limit for price.[21] In a non-market-driven

[21] In fact, Peter Drucker refers to cost-driven pricing as a "deadly sin." See his article "The Five Deadly Business Sins," *The Wall Street Journal,* October 21, 1993, A-16.

firm, full costs (variable costs plus some allocation for overhead) plus some target margin is used to set price. This approach totally ignores the customer: The resulting price may be either above or below what the customer is willing to pay for the product. Yet this is a very common approach to setting price.

Other problems exist with using costs to set price. First, there are at least four different kinds of costs to consider.[22] Development costs are expenses involved in bringing new products to market. Often these costs are spread out over many years and sometimes products. Should price be set to recover these costs and if so, in what time period? In some industries, such as pharmaceuticals, patent protection allows setting the prices of prescription drugs high initially to recover development costs and then reducing them when the drugs come off patent and the generics enter the category. However, if there is no legal way to keep competitors out, these costs must be viewed as sunk costs that do not affect decision making after the product is introduced into the market. A second kind of costs is overhead costs such as the president's salary, the corporate jet, and the exercise club at headquarters. These costs must ultimately be covered by revenues from individual products, but they are not associated with any one product. Often the mechanism used to allocate these overhead costs among products is arbitrary and bears no relationship to how individual products utilize overhead or whether they would change if the product were not produced. A third kind of costs is direct fixed. These costs, such as the product manager's salary, product advertising and promotion, and so on, are associated with individual products but do not vary with volume. Finally, there are variable costs, the per-unit costs of making the product or delivering the service. These, of course, must be recovered with price. Therefore, one problem with using "costs" to set price is that several kinds of costs are related in different ways to an individual product. Included in this category are the costs of plant, inventory, receivables, etc., tied to the product. Many companies now attempt to account for these by calculating the opportunity cost of the resources committed to the product by multiplying the amount of resources by either the firm's average cost of capital or return on investment. By subtracting these from revenues, the so-called direct product profitability (DPP) is calculated.

A second problem with using costs to set price, particularly variable or unit costs, is that they may be a function of volume and therefore difficult to know in advance when developing marketing plans. Even if this is not the case, unit costs may be related to the utilization of capacity. Therefore, when developing marketing plans, product managers should simulate profits and sales volume using a number of possible prices and costs.

Ultimately, in most instances customers do not really care what the firm's costs are; as Drucker puts it, "Customers do not see it as their job to ensure manufacturers a profit."[23] Using cost increases to justify raising price generates little sympathy (which of course is better than none in the case of increases that appear to be opportunistic gouging) from customers, particularly industrial customers, because the price increase (justified by a cost increase) has just raised their costs, which they may

---

[22] We will cover this area of financial analysis for product management more completely in Chapter 15.

[23] Drucker, "The Five Deadly Business Sins."

not be able to pass along in their market segments. The price increase may stick, but only if there is value behind the product that substantiates the price.

Costs play other important roles in marketing management besides acting as a floor to the price the product manager can charge. They are particularly important in the new-product development process. One role costs play is that they determine which products under development are eventually introduced. Typically, in the new-product development process, managers estimate the eventual cost and compare it to the approximate price they can obtain. If the cost is too high, the product concept is scrapped. Similarly, managers can calculate the profit potential of a product concept by forecasting the margins they can obtain. This potential is then matched against other new-product concepts to help prioritize products being developed.

Interestingly, many Japanese companies have developed a very different approach whereby the product team first attempts to understand what price can be charged for the product by talking to customers and then works backward to figure out what the product has to cost to allow the company to make an acceptable margin. This approach has been termed *target costing*.[24] The company then works with suppliers to reach appropriate target costs to keep components within an overall cost budget.

For example, the camera company Olympus first determined what features future customers would value in families of new products. Marketing research included focus groups, interviews at fashion centers, interviews with photographers, and a complete competitor analysis, including capabilities, price points, and filed patents. The company then set a target price point for a new, compact camera at $100. After subtracting margins for dealers, import costs, and its own margin, Olympus arrived at a preliminary target cost for the new product. This target cost forced company scientists to develop a new technology to meet the cost target.

Deciding How Much of the Value-Cost Gap to Capture

The pricing structure just described leans heavily on estimating customer value to understand the maximum price to charge to a market segment. The cost of producing the product or delivering the service is the minimum that can be charged. Often there is a great deal of flexibility for setting price within this range. This framework can also be used to assess whether a current price is appropriate or at what level to set a new price.

The decision about how much of the value to keep or give away is manifested first in the general pricing policy being pursued by the product manager. This setting of the pricing policy or objective(s) is captured by Figure 10–7. In this figure, it is shown that the general pricing objectives are set after the three major background analyses described earlier in the book, category, customer, and competitor, are performed and the marketing strategy is determined. Like brand or product objectives, a price objective is a guide for more precise decision-making. For example, if a penetration or low price objective is selected, the product manager considers a range of prices at the low end of the cost-value gap.

---

[24]Robin Cooper and W. Bruce Chew, "Control Tomorrow's Costs Through Today's Designs," *Harvard Business Review,* January-February 1996, pp. 88–97.

FIGURE 10–7 Influences on the Product Manager's Pricing Decisions

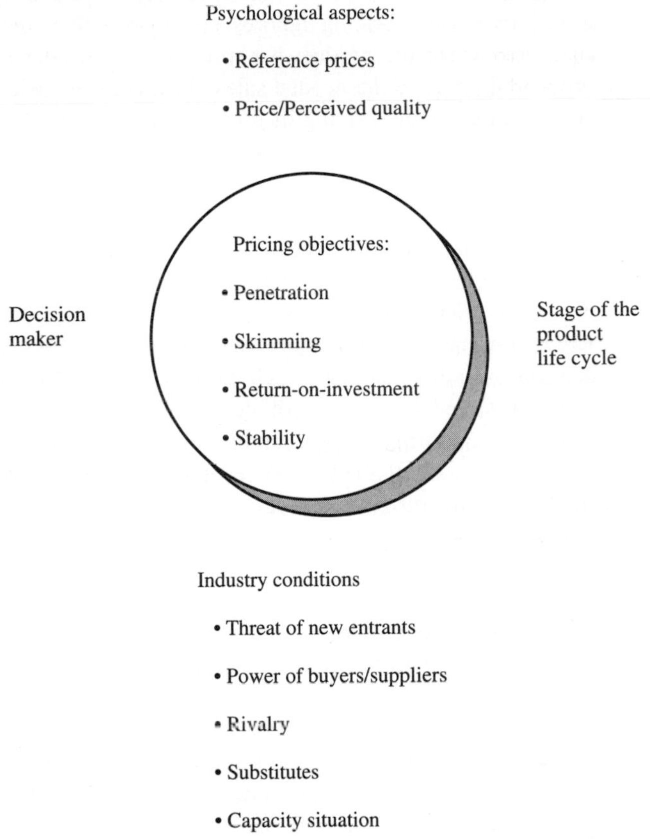

Penetration Pricing

Penetration or market share pricing is employed when the product manager purposely gives most of the value to the customer and keeps a small margin. It is often used as an entry strategy for a new product and is particularly useful for preventing competitive entry. The objective of penetration pricing is to build or keep market share. It is appropriate when experience or scale effects lead to a volume-cost relationship, and it is necessary for price-sensitive market segments. Penetration pricing generally should not be used with products or services subject to a price-perceived quality relationship (see the further discussion that follows) or when the product has a strong competitive advantage. Another limitation of penetration pricing is that it is always more acceptable to customers to drop price than it is to raise it, which limits the flexibility of penetration pricing for some situations.[25]

[25]For some examples concerning the difficulty of raising prices, especially in periods of low inflation, see Christopher Farrell and Zachary Schiller, "Stuck! How Companies Cope When They Can't Raise Prices," *Business Week,* November 15, 1993, pp. 146–155.

Return on Sales/Investment Pricing

This objective has fairly limited use. It implies that the product manager can set a price that delivers the rate of return demanded by the senior managers in the company. Of course, investment pricing ignores customer value and competition. It is therefore useful only when the product has a monopoly or near-monopoly position so that the market will produce the needed sales volume at the price set by the product manager. This is typical of the pricing of regulated utilities such as gas and electricity.

Pricing for Stability

Sometimes customers for industrial products are more concerned about price stability than levels. This is because it is difficult to develop profit forecasts and long-range plans when prices for products that make up a substantial portion of the buyer's costs fluctuate dramatically. Telephone rates for large users such as telemarketing firms and banks fall into this category. Such customers expect rates to rise over time. However, significant price hikes at random intervals play havoc with their planning processes. As a result, these firms would rather pay a somewhat higher average rate than be subjected to constant fluctuations. Forward contracts on raw materials play this role in many manufacturing industries.

Skimming

The opposite of penetration pricing is skimming or prestige pricing. Skimming returns more of the value to the producer rather than the customer. This is appropriate in a variety of situations. If there is a strong price–perceived quality relationship (e.g., wine) and the core strategy is to position the product at the high end of the market, this objective makes sense. It is also a reasonable objective when there is little chance of competition in the near future; however, the higher the price, the higher the margins and thus the greater the chance that competition will enter. Skimming is also a good objective when costs are not related to volume and managers thus are less concerned about building significant market share.

Competitive Pricing

Competitive pricing describes a situation in which the product manager tries to maintain a "competitive" price by either pricing at the category average or mimicking a particular brand. This is appropriate when customers have not been persuaded that significant differences exist among the competitors and view the market as a commodity category. It may also be necessary in a product category with high fixed costs.

Other Factors Affecting Price

The previous section focused on pricing objectives, implying that the product manager has full discretion about how much of the value-variable cost gap she or he could obtain at any given point in time. However, other factors outside the control of the product manager also affect available pricing flexibility.

Psychological Aspects of Price

Many customers actively process price information; that is, they are not just price "takers" (to use the conventional term from microeconomics). Customers continually assess the prices charged for products based on prior purchasing experience, formal communications (e.g., advertising) and informal communications (e.g., friends and neighbors), and point-of-purchase listings of prices and use those assessments in the ultimate purchase decision. Two key concepts relating to the psychological aspects of pricing are reference prices and the price–perceived quality relationship.

Reference Prices. A reference price is any standard of comparison against which an observed price is compared. Usually the reference price is compared against some discounted price. There are two kinds of reference prices: internal and external, also sometimes referred to as *temporal* and *contextual* respectively.[26] External reference prices are usually observed prices that, in a retailing setting, are typically posted at the point of purchase as the "regular retail price." Internal reference prices are mental prices used to assess an observed price. Since the product manager cannot easily manipulate internal reference prices yet they have a strong effect on buying behavior, we will discuss them in more detail.

A large number of internal reference prices have been proposed,[27] including

- The "fair" price, or what the product ought to cost the customer.
- The price frequently charged.
- The last price paid.
- The upper amount someone would pay (reservation price).
- The lower threshold or lowest amount a customer would pay.
- The price of the brand usually bought.
- The average price charged for similar products.
- The expected future price.

Many of these considerations contribute to the concept we will call the *perceived* price, the price the customer thinks is the current actual price of the product.

Reference price defined in this way has a significant impact on brand choice of both durable and nondurable goods.[28] In particular, when the observed price is higher than the reference price, it can negatively affect purchasing because the consumer

---

[26] See K. N. Rajendran and Gerard J. Tellis, "Contextual and Temporal Components of Reference Price," *Journal of Marketing,* January 1994, pp. 22–34.

[27] See Russell S. Winer, "Behavioral Perspectives on Pricing," in Timothy M. Devinney, ed., *Issues in Pricing: Theory and Research* (Lexington, Mass.: Lexington Books, 1988), Chapter 2.

[28] For a literature review in this area, see Gurumurthy Kalyanaram and Russell S. Winer, "Empirical Generalizations from Reference Price Research," *Marketing Science* 14, no.3, part 2 of 2 (1995), pp. G161–G169.

perceives this situation as an unpleasant surprise. For example, the large price increases for cars in the 1970s created what became known as a "sticker shock" effect when consumer reference or perceived prices for cars were significantly lower than the prices they saw in the showroom. A happier situation occurs when the observed price is either at or below the reference price. This happens when a brand a consumer might buy anyway is being promoted at a lower price. Interestingly, several studies have found that the unpleasant surprises have a greater impact on purchasing probabilities than the pleasant surprises.

This concept of reference price has important implications for product managers. Consider the situation in which a brand has been on price promotion for several weeks. The customer will begin to replace the normal price with the promoted price as the reference point. Then, when the brand comes off deal and returns to the regular price, the customer may perceive the change as an increase in price, with a resulting positive difference between observed price and reference price, and at least temporarily stop purchasing it.

A second important concept of reference price is expected future price. This is a particularly important concept for any product category that experiences significant price changes over time. Several examples will highlight how customers use future price expectations. The airline industry has had protracted fare wars in which the prices of some flights fell rapidly in short periods of time. Some segments of fliers, such as business travelers, are unaffected by changes in fares because they do not have discretion concerning when they fly. However, fliers who do have discretion, such as people wishing to visit relatives or having otherwise flexible schedules, simply wait for prices to drop further before booking. Price cutting merely exacerbates the airlines' problems because sales are low while discretionary travelers wait for the fares to drop even further. The same situation results from rebate programs in the automobile industry. Why purchase a car while a rebate war is in progress? Why not wait to see if further price cuts are possible? Finally, new consumer durables are also subject to this phenomenon. The prices of Pentium-based computers with CD-ROM drives are falling so rapidly that customers are worried they will overpay. Again, discretionary purchasers can simply wait until the prices decrease further. The problem is predictability: Product managers who create predictable pricing patterns underestimate customers' abilities to process the information and make decisions based on their personal forecasts of future prices.

The Relationship between Price and Perceived Quality. In some situations, contrary to standard microeconomics, a higher price can lead to higher rather than lower demand. This occurs when price is used as a signal that the product in question is of high quality.

One reason such a relationship exists is for exclusivity or prestige. Pricing a product high means fewer customers can afford it. It is likely that Rolex could charge substantially less for its watches and still make a profit. However, because few consumers can afford thousands of dollars for a watch, few will own a Rolex, imparting a feeling of prestige to the owner.

A second example of a strong price–perceived quality relationship occurs when a product's quality is either difficult to assess before purchasing (sometimes these

FIGURE 10–8 DuPont Pricing over the Product Life Cycle

Competitive Cycle Stage	*Focus of Attention*	*Pricing Method*
Sole supplier	Customers	Value-in-use Perceived value
Competitive penetration	Customers Competitors	Reaction analysis
Shared stability Commodity competition Withdrawal	Competition and costs	Profitability analysis

products are referred to as *experience* goods because you have to actually try the product to know how good it is) or difficult to assess at all. Good examples include wine, perfume, and many professional services such as consulting and legal advice. Perhaps the ultimate example is life insurance; no matter what you pay, you will never use the product.

The major implication for the product manager was stated earlier in this chapter: The price must be consistent with the marketing strategy. If customer research shows a significant correlation between price and perceived quality, a core strategy stressing quality or value-added features requires a consistent price. An exotic vodka supported with highly creative advertising stressing exclusivity and prestige cannot be priced at $1.99 a bottle without striking a discordant feeling in the (presumably) upscale consumer.

Stage of the Product Life Cycle

As with many decisions discussed in this book, the way prices are set also changes over the product life cycle. Figure 10–8 illustrates how DuPont approaches pricing with the life cycle in mind. As can be seen, DuPont simplifies the life cycle to three generic stages: sole supplier (introductory phase); competitive penetration (early and late growth); and shared stability, commodity competition, and withdrawal (maturity and decline). Particularly interesting is the focus for pricing decisions over the life cycle. When little competition exists, focus is on the customer and value is stressed. Notice that there is no mention of either variable or investment costs that must be recovered. When competition enters, the focus is on both customers and competitors. Customer value is still important but, as discussed earlier in this chapter, how competitors will react is also addressed. Finally, in the late stages of the product category, the focus shifts toward competitors and costs to determine whether remaining in the market makes economic sense. There profitability analysis is the key.

Another way to look at the life cycle impact is through experience curve pricing. Product managers have flexibility in pricing decisions when the product tends to adhere to the experience curve. Figure 10–9 shows three different pricing scenarios. Increases in industry cumulative volume represent movement along the product life cycle. One possible pricing pattern, C, acknowledges little competition and assumes increased customer value through consistent lowering of prices over time. In pattern B,

FIGURE 10–9 Experience Curve–Based Pricing Patterns over the Product Life Cycle

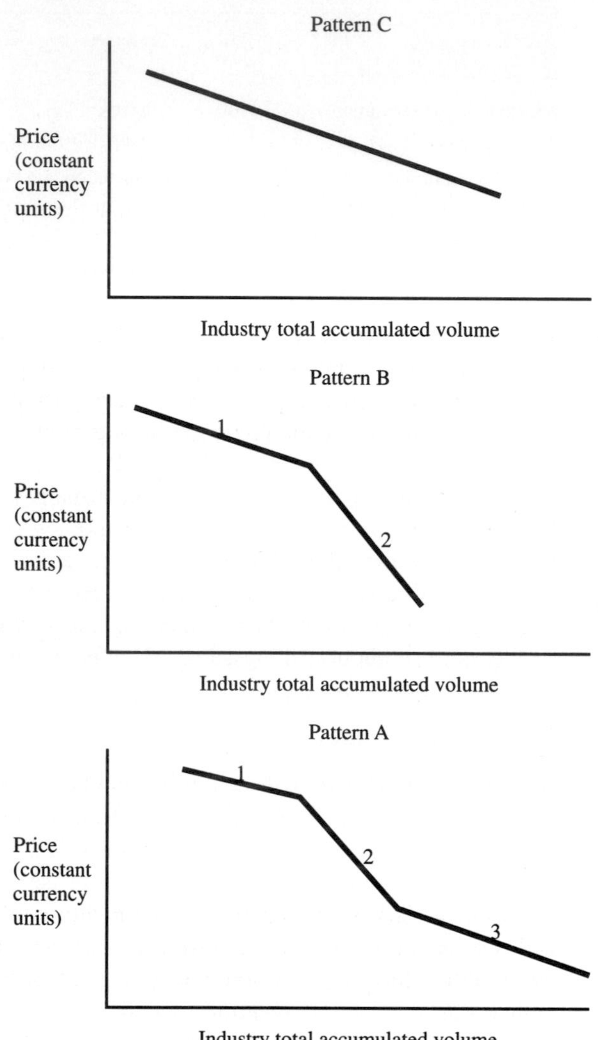

the product manager keeps margins up for a period of time because there is little competition (segment 1 of the curve is flatter than segment 2) and then drops price more rapidly as competition enters later in the life cycle. In pattern A, the product manager reacts twice: first when competition enters (segment 2 is again steeper than segment 1) and again when competition drops out (segment 3 is flatter than segment 2). Thus, under this last pricing pattern, margins are high in the early phase of the life cycle, drop due to competition, and then rise again when after a category shakeout occurs.

Category Conditions

The category factors discussed in Chapter 4 also apply to pricing decisions. These factors give product managers some ideas about the kind of pricing environment in the product category.

Threat of New Entrants. The likelihood of new entrants into a category has an important effect on price. If the likelihood is low (barriers to entry are high), higher price levels can be sustained. If new entrants are possible either from within the industry or from outside, lower prices help to protect the market position from potential erosion and make the profit potential of the market look worse for new product entries.

Power of Buyers/Suppliers. High buyer power obviously tends to depress prices, as it puts more pressure on the product to deliver a good value/price ratio. If suppliers have high power, they will often charge higher prices for goods or services supplied, whether raw materials, labor, or anything else. High supplier power thus raises the floor beneath which prices cannot be set.

Rivalry. This concept is also relatively straightforward: High industry rivalry tends to be manifested in strong price competition. One industry factor that should be examined in this context is the level of exit barriers, that is, how difficult it is to withdraw a product from the market. Substantial investment in plant and equipment is one example of an exit barrier. Sometimes the exit barrier is emotional, such as when the product has a long history in the company. When exit barriers are high for some or all of the category participants, price competition is likely to be fierce.

Pressure from Substitutes. As with the threat of entry, the more potential substitute technologies or solutions to customer problems are available and the more value they offer, the greater the chance that price competition will exist.

Unused Capacity. This concept is particularly important in a high fixed cost, high contribution margin (price less variable cost) product category. These markets are characterized by some of the most vicious price battles (e.g., airlines) because there is plenty of margin to give and the products need to generate revenues to cover fixed costs. When economies of scale are important (e.g., in automobile manufacturing), overcapacity also leads to price wars because the degree of capacity utilization directly affects unit costs.

Who Is the Decision Maker?

In industrial product categories, product managers must make sure the price eventually set is consistent with the needs of the people in the buying organization who influence the purchasing decision.[29] In Chapter 6, we discussed the importance of understanding

[29]See Ross, "Making Money with Proactive Pricing," pp. 145–155.

the roles different people play in the purchasing process and of recognizing that their needs differ. This is important for making pricing decisions. For example, a gatekeeper for the sale of a product may be someone in R&D. This person has to be convinced that the value offered is favorable relative to the benefit for the product that will use the component. The price itself is somewhat less important than the benefit or value. The people involved in developing specifications for the new product may be more interested in life cycle costs if they are being judged on the profitability of the product over, say, a 10-year period. Purchasing managers are evaluated on their abilities to keep cost variances down and may pass by suppliers who try to raise prices at a rate greater than inflation.

Some Specific Pricing Tactics

Product Line Pricing

One common pricing task facing product managers is setting prices for a closely related set of products or for a product line. The products can differ in small ways, such as features (e.g., a 17-inch versus a 21-inch color TV), or they can be complementary (e.g., razors and blades). We assume that one product manager has the authority to price the line or that the decision is made in tandem with another manager.

Price Bundling. One approach is price bundling, which takes a set of products, offers them to customers in a package, and then usually prices the package lower than the sum of the individual components. For example, home stereo systems are commonly offered in a "rack" system consisting of a turntable, an amplifier, a cassette player, a tuner, and perhaps a CD player in an attractive case. This bundle of items, often consisting of models that are slow sellers, is usually specially priced to eliminate inventory. A similar example is packages of options in automobiles.

An alternative approach takes the opposite view: Sometimes the bundle can be priced *higher* than the sum of the components because it is attractive or convenient. A good example is McDonald's Happy Meals, which are targeted toward children. Any parent who computed the sum of the hamburger, french fries, and drink would find that he or she is paying a considerable sum for the toy and the package. Clearly, such a bundle provides extra value to customers and can be priced accordingly.

A different way to look at the issue is by unbundling. Some companies offer predesigned packages of features and services that include components some market segments do not need. For example, a telecommunications system might come with a standard service contract some customers may not find attractive because they already have considerable on-site technical help or a value meal may come with unwanted fries. In such cases, the product manager could seek ways to unbundle the product package to allow customers to choose what they want to pay for.

For example, San Luis Sourdough Company sells one-pound loaves of sourdough bread to supermarkets using a three-tier pricing policy.[30] Level 1 prices the bread at 97 cents per loaf for supermarkets that are happy to have the bread simply dropped off. If

[30]Paul B. Brown, "You Get What You Pay For," *Inc.*, October 1990, p. 155.

the store wants to be able to return day-old bread for credit—level 2—the cost is $1.02 per loaf. If the store wants the company to accept returns, stock the shelves, and place bar codes on the packages, this level 3 service costs $1.05 per loaf. Thus, the company has cleverly unbundled its service levels so customers can choose the level that fits their needs.[31]

Line Pricing. A second product-line pricing approach involves offering both a high-priced and a lower-priced brand. This is a classic strategy employed by Procter & Gamble. The objective is to have brands at multiple price tiers: at the premium level (e.g., Crest toothpaste) and at a lower level (e.g., Gleem). This strategy can reach both the price-sensitive customers *and* the ones desiring the premium brand.

Complementary Pricing. This pricing policy applies to products that are used together when one of the products fills a sustainable need. Two good examples are razors and blades and cameras and film. Gillette prices razors rather modestly but makes huge margins on the blades. Similarly, the prices for Polaroid instant cameras are rather low compared to those for 35mm cameras. However, the film for Polaroids is more expensive. This kind of pricing is useful only when there is limited competition for the sustainable component. For example, it does not apply to autos and replacement parts because of the huge aftermarket composed of companies that do not manufacture the cars themselves.

Complementary pricing is also used for services that have fixed and variable components to price. Two examples are private golf clubs and telephone service. Both have a fixed monthly fee and a variable usage fee. Such complementary pricing can be a creative way to keep the marginal costs to customers low ("pennies per day") and retain a continuous stream of revenue.

Value Pricing

Value pricing has been a key phrase in pricing during the 1990s. Although the term has never really been defined, it has been used by airlines, hotels, rental cars, supermarkets, and various other (usually consumer) categories. The originator of the concept may have been Taco Bell. In 1990, Taco Bell developed a value menu that offered several entries, such as tacos, for very low prices, around 29 to 39 cents. The company was very successful in making inroads against other fast-food chains, which subsequently caused McDonald's and others to offer value-priced menu entries (which they still offer today). The sustained recession of the early 1990s caused other products to pick up the concept.

It is important to clarify the distinction between value pricing and pricing to value. Pricing to value relies on estimates of the dollar value customers place on products and, when coupled with an estimate of the variable costs of producing a product or delivering a service, determines the range of possible prices that can be charged. Value pricing gives the customer most of the value-cost difference, that is, a "good deal."

[31]For a good review of bundling, see Hermann Simon, Marin Fassnacht, and Georg Wubker, "Price Bundling," *Pricing Strategy & Practice,* 3, No. 1, (1995), pp. 34–44.

However, the term *value pricing* is not the same as penetration pricing, described earlier. Penetration pricing implies low price alone. Value pricing is related to customer expectations: It gives customers more than they expect for the price paid. This does *not* necessarily imply low price. Thus, value pricing is consistent with pricing at less than customer value, but it is accompanied by communications, packaging, and other elements of the marketing mix that indicate a reasonably high level of quality.

A good example of a product that was value priced when introduced is the Lexus 400. The car cost around $40,000, which is not at the low end of the market. However, the brand was very successful because it offered the kinds of luxury, features, and service for which some European manufacturers charged much more. Again, value pricing does not imply inexpensive, only that what you get represents more net value than other available options. At about $50,000 today, the Lexus is less value priced and represents Toyota's ability to capture more of the customer value due to its prior success in the market.

There are several other good examples of successful value pricing.[32] Seagram's gin has 30 percent of the gin category and is the third-place spirit brand because the product is priced at half the level of the premium brands such as Beefeater and Tanqueray. However, the product is not "cheap"; the Seagram name connotes quality, and the bottle has an upscale look. Sara Lee Corporation markets L'Eggs hosiery, a brand with a well-established quality reputation and a relatively low price. Southwest Airlines has low prices but an excellent on-time record.

Everyday Low Pricing

At the time the first edition of this book was written, an important phenomenon in retailing was everyday low pricing, or EDLP. Both consumers and regulators had become more suspicious of high "regular" prices and frequent "sales" sponsored by retailers, sometimes referred to as "high-low" pricing. In addition, many companies were tiring of the enormous levels of spending required for promotions to get retailers to stock and promote products and get customers to buy and the effect of uneven demand on the costs of producing and distributing the product. Therefore, a simpler approach was advanced that would lower prices permanently and significantly reduce both trade and consumer promotions. EDLP has, in fact, been adopted by very successful chains such as Wal-Mart, Home Depot, and Toys "R" Us. In a well-publicized move, Sears attempted an EDLP policy in 1989, although it was ultimately unsuccessful and rescinded. By late 1992, as many as 6 out of 10 consumer product companies were either testing or putting EDLP policies in place, and another 16 percent were planning to test the strategy.[33]

Sears's experience showed there are risks in switching to an EDLP policy. Some of the problems are peculiar to Sears. Given its high cost structure, its price reductions were not sufficiently significant to produce a large consumer response, particularly

---

[32]For an excellent description of this value pricing environment, see Stratford Sherman, "How to Prosper in the Value Decade," *Fortune,* November 30, 1992, pp. 90–103.

[33]Jon Berry, "It's Closer Than You Think," *Brandweek,* October 26, 1992, pp. 26–28.

when compared with its competitors. Because the prices were not low enough, Sears continued to run sales, thus confusing customers. Two other problems exist in shifting abruptly to EDLP policies. First, reference prices and pricing policies are conditioned by past prices and are hard to change in the short run. Second, an aggressive adoption of EDLP can create a pricing environment in which competitors engage in cutthroat pricing. EDLP is also unstable in terms of competitive reaction; if all but one firm is EDLP, then the firm which prices High-Low will capture a substantial share of the market.

Extremely damaging to EDLP prospects was an extensive field experiment conducted in the Chicago area in a supermarket environment across 19 very disparate product categories. The experiment showed that while retail EDLP policies increased sales volume relative to high-low pricing, the increased volume did not nearly compensate for the lower margins. The result was lost profits in every category.[34] The problem is one alluded to earlier in the chapter: The price elasticities of demand at the retail level in most supermarket categories (and probably many other consumer product categories) are simply too small to support significant price cuts. Despite these problems, some large companies, such as Procter & Gamble, are still looking to change pricing strategies from high-low with extensive use of coupons to EDLP.[35]

Differential Pricing

The key strategic decision of which customers to target recognizes that potential customers' behavior is heterogeneous. This heterogeneity can be reflected in price in various ways.

Direct Price Discrimination. Price discrimination to end customers, while unpopular with consumer advocacy groups, is not always illegal, and it is done all the time.[36] Witness the senior citizen discounts given at movie theaters or the quantity discounts on personal computers given to large customers. The theory is that price discrimination maximizes products' profits by charging each market segment the price that maximizes profit from that segment because of different price elasticities of demand. However, in practice, it is difficult to implement a price discrimination policy, particularly in consumer markets, due to the fragmentation of the customer base and the existence of firms that buy at one segment's low prices and resell to others (such as consolidators in airline tickets).

One way to implement price discrimination is through target delivery of coupons or other discount mechanisms. Given the quality of databases available today, it is relatively easy to determine those households that have the highest probability of buying the product *and* need a price inducement. These households can then be

[34] Stephen J. Hoch, Xavier Drèze, and Mary E. Purk, "EDLP, Hi-Lo, and Margin Arithmetic," *Journal of Marketing,* October 1994, pp. 16–27.

[35] Raju Narisetti, "P&G Bets on Low Prices Every Day to Cut Out Need for Company Coupons," *The Wall Street Journal,* January 8, 1996, p. A-9B.

[36] See Nagle and Holden, *The Strategy and Tactics of Pricing,* Chapter 14, for a good discussion of the legal aspects of pricing.

targeted by direct mail or magazine delivery of coupons. In fact, the amount of the discount can be varied if managers find multiple levels of price sensitivity. Customers who are brand loyal apparently should receive no inducement, because that would merely give them a discount for a product they would have purchased at full price. Still great disparity in price erodes brand equity and loyalty. For example, many magazine subscribers realize they should not renew early since better offers follow.

Second-Market Discounting. A useful pricing strategy when excess production exists is called *second-market discounting.* This policy sells the extra production at a discount to a market separate from the main market. As long as the product is sold at a price greater than variable cost, the contribution margin produced can help cover corporate overhead. Some examples of secondary markets are generic drugs, private label brands, and foreign markets. The difficulty with generics and private labels, however, is that you go into competition against yourself if the target customers are not completely different than your main segments or if the equivalence of the products is widely recognized.

Periodic Discounting. This pricing strategy varies price over time. It is appropriate when some customers are willing to pay a higher price to have the product or service during a particular time period. For example, utilities such as electricity and telephone service use peak load pricing policies that charge more during the heaviest usage periods, partly to encourage off-peak usage. Clothing retailers mark down items that are slow sellers; those who want an item when it is first introduced pay a higher price. Theater tickets are more expensive on weekends, and movie tickets cost more in the evenings.

Competing against Private Labels

Private labels—or "own" brands, as they are sometimes called, as they are often a retailer's captive brand name—and the threat they pose to national brand manufacturers have been mentioned a number of times in this book. Private labels are ubiquitous and not limited to supermarkets. For example, Sears has a large number of private labels: Kenmore appliances, Craftsman tools, DieHard car batteries, Fieldmaster outdoor apparel, Laura Scott women's clothes, Nice Touch Promise pantyhose, and Freeze Frame junior clothing, among others. Large personal computer retailers such as CompUSA sell their own brands.

Although doing battle with private labels clearly is a strategic issue, it is also a pricing issue since a major justification for private labels' existence is to produce a lower-priced competitor to national brands.[37] Product categories that private labels have successfully penetrated usually have two characteristics: (1) there is a large price-sensitive segment, and (2) no lower-priced entries exist in the category, except perhaps for a no-name generic option; thus, consumers pay a large premium for buying

[37]This is not always the case. The Canadian retailer Loblaw has a private label brand, President's Choice, that is fully competitive with national brands in quality and only slightly lower in price. The same is true of the British firm Marks & Spencer.

national brands. Generally this means that national brand product managers have made pricing decisions that keep much of the difference between variable cost and customer value for themselves. Supermarket categories experiencing significant recent private label growth include cold cereal, bottled water, dog food, coffee, chewing gum, and condensed soup. These categories historically have had high prices and fat profit margins (an exception is coffee, which usually has only high prices).

How should product managers defend their brands against the incursion of private labels? One obvious way is to reduce the price gap to the point where consumers are willing to pay and therefore value the brand name. However, as we already said, this is an expensive solution and one to which the product manager should not immediately gravitate. Product managers can battle back in the following ways:[38]

- Add value in ways discussed earlier in this chapter.
- Develop new market segments that are less price sensitive.
- Build stronger relationships with the trade.
- Prune product lines of sizes/flavors that are not generating profits for the retailer.
- Raise the barriers to entry for private labels by investing in better customer databases and retention programs (information technology).

Again, the key to fighting the price-oriented private labels is not making a knee-jerk reaction to compete on price but exploring other options such as those just discussed, as well as understanding relative customer value for your brand.

Ethical Issues

For certain kinds of products, the pricing decision can have implications far beyond generating revenue (or recovering value). A good example of this is the high-priced basketball shoes produced by Nike, Reebok, and other manufacturers and endorsed by NBA stars such as Michael Jordan. Most of these shoes are priced over $125, and their desirability due to exclusivity and peer pressure has led to several highly publicized incidents in public schools in which owners of the shoes were assaulted and the shoes stolen. One can argue that Nike bears no responsibility for what is essentially a U.S. social problem. However, the fact that the high price and resulting image of exclusivity may have had some influence on the school incidents cannot be easily dismissed.

A somewhat different ethical problem involved the pricing of the Wellcome PLC drug AZT, a treatment for AIDS. When the drug was introduced, a year-long treatment cost $10,000. The company argued that the investment in such a drug, which had a relatively small market, required a high price. In addition, the analysis provided earlier in this chapter shows that the customer value for a drug that could substantially ameliorate AIDS symptoms would be enormous. However, the reaction to AZT's price was so negative that the company eventually reduced it to a more reasonable level. Despite the price reduction, the company's image and reputation suffered some damage.

[38] See John A. Quelch and David Harding, "Brands versus Private Labels: Fighting to Win," *Harvard Business Review,* January–February 1996, pp. 99–109.

As a result, in addition to the aspects involved in setting price discussed in this chapter, price may have some social implications far beyond what is expected. Furthur, this issue is not relevant only to products such as drugs that clearly can generate negative public reaction if priced too high.

Summary

In this chapter, we have argued that, as shown in Figure 10–7, the price objective and subsequent decision cannot be made without adequate analysis of the market and a consideration of the marketing strategy being employed. Customers (e.g., their value for the product and your brand), competitors/your company (e.g., costs, their pricing actions), and category conditions (e.g., stage of the product life cycle) all impact the product manager's selection of what price to charge. We particularly emphasized the importance of customers, as past pricing practices have focused on the other factors without paying sufficient attention to measuring how much customers are willing to pay. The product manager's job is to decide where the price should be in the range between cost and value.

C H A P T E R

11 Advertising Decisions

Overview

Customers generally become aware of a product and are persuaded to purchase it through some form of communications from the company. Therefore a major job of the product manager is to develop a communications program for the product.

Figure 11-1 shows the typical communications mix a company uses. As the figure indicates, the different elements of the mix are advertising, public relations (PR), sales promotion, direct marketing, and packaging and graphics.[1] One would hope that these elements work together to effectively communicate the product's features and benefits to the target customers. However, the vertical lines imply that the different decisions about these communications mix elements are often made independently by different people and organizations, that they are often like "silos" in the company. Under this silo-type communications organization, advertising is handled largely by the advertising agency, public relations by the PR department or agency, direct marketing by an outside agent, and packaging and graphics by either in-house specialists or consultants. Only sales promotion would be handled by the product manager.

Our concept of the product manager, however, is more consistent with the current notion of a coherent communications mix, usually referred to as *integrated communications.*[2] In an integrated marketing communications approach, the manager emphasizes the problem to be solved (e.g., increase the repeat purchasing rate) and coordinates the communications tasks necessary to solve the problem rather than using a predetermined set of communications tools (i.e. those that the company always uses). An integrated approach also assumes that a combination of activities does better than any one alone: Each element brings unique strengths to the communications problem.

[1]Personal selling obviously has an important communications role. However, it is usually considered separately or as part of distribution channels decision making.

[2]See, for example, Don E. Schultz, *Strategic Advertising Campaigns,* 3rd ed. (Lincolnwood, Ill.: NTC Business Books, 1990).

FIGURE 11–1 The Communications Mix

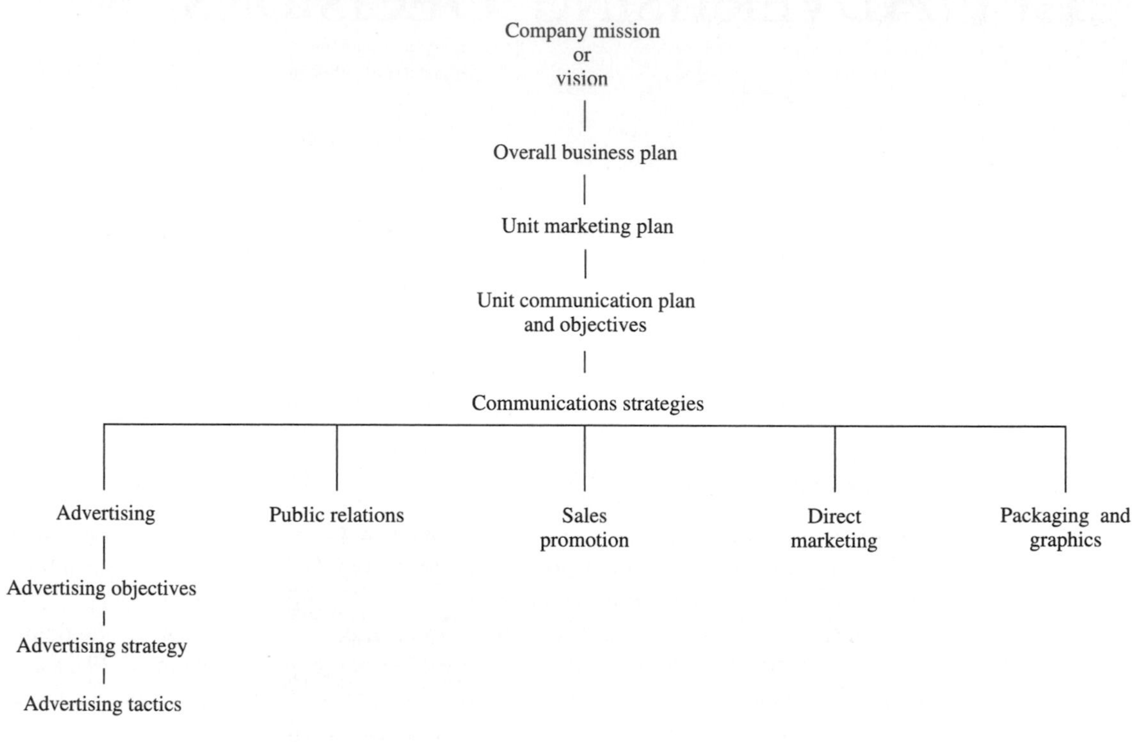

Source: Don E. Schultz, *Strategic Advertising Campaigns,* 3rd ed (Lincolnwood, Ill.: NTC Business Books, 1990).

This also implies that they are planned to work together. For example, in an integrated communications campaign, a point-of-purchase (POP) display might use the same display theme or a character used in a TV ad. Figure 11–2 shows an illustration of an integrated communications program. As can be seen, the objective of the communications—in this case to encourage the target audience to avoid sunburn—is common to all the elements of the possible programs that can be used. The targets might vary over the different programs depending on how the marketing manager viewed the different strengths and weaknesses of, say, advertising versus promotion for this particular campaign. Still, the communications themes and personality the campaign will exhibit are common across the mix elements.

Figure 11–3 shows how the allocations for specific communications mix elements vary between consumer and industrial or business-to-business products.[3] Not

[3] Cyndee Miller, "Marketing Industry Report: Who's Spending What on Biz-to-Biz Marketing," *Marketing News,* January 1, 1996, p.1; Cyndee Miller, "Marketing Industry Report: Consumer Marketers Spend Most of Their Money on Communications," *Marketing News,* March 11, 1996, p. 1.

Figure 11–2 American Cancer Society Integrated Communications Strategy

Health objective	To encourage the target to avoid sunburn			
Purpose	To encourage the target to protect their skin from the cancer-causing rays of the sun by using a sunscreen with a sun protection factor (SPF) of 15+ instead of other tanning lotions or oils			
Target	Adult "sun worshippers"	*Primary* Adult "sun worshippers"	*Secondary* Cosmetic, Toiletry and Fragrance Association Physicians Pharmacists	
Promise	When I use a sunscreen with an SPF of 15+, I will feel in control of my health because sunscreen with SPF 15+ helps protect me from the deadly, cancer-causing rays of the sun while allowing me to obtain an attractive "light" tan.	*Primary* Same as for advertising	*Secondary* CTF Assn.: "I will feel satisfied that I am helping to create a favorable sales environment." Physicians, pharmacists: "I will feel satisfied that I am doing the best job possible for my patients'/customers' preventive health maintenance."	
Support	Studies show that unprotected sun exposure is closely related to all types of skin cancer, including those that can kill you. Doctors advise moderate exposure to sun and to use sunscreen. Sunscreen with SPF of 15+ gives 15 times your natural defenses against the sun's rays.			
Personality	Warm; caring; foremost authority; professional; renowned;			
	General Advertising	*Public Relations*	*Sales Promotion*	*Direct Response*
Media	National TV MTV (cooperative program) Pop radio Print magazine ads Billboards	Program with CTF Assn. to help with visibility, reach, materials distribution, and costs Collateral materials: educational brochure (with coupon to purchase any SPF 15+ product) Poster (professionals only) Spokesperson	Work with CTF to develop and implement system to code (via symbols and/or colors) grades of protection for sunscreen products to include packaging and POP chart coordinated with packaging Coupon	Direct-response offer

Source: Don E. Schultz, *Strategic Advertising Campaigns*, 3rd ed. (Lincolnwood, Ill.: NTC Business Books, 1990).

FIGURE 11–3 Marketing Communications Expenditures: Consumer versus Business-to-Business Products

	Percentage of Communications Budget	
Category of Expenditures	*Consumer*	*Business-to-Business*
Television	45.1%	2.7%
Print advertising	14.5	27.4
Literature, coupons, POP	16.2	9.3
Direct Mail	6.4	27.1
Radio	5.6	0.8
Catalogs	4.1	10.7
Public relations	3.1	5.3
Trade shows	2.0	12.9
Out-of-home media	1.7	0.5
Dealer/distributor materials	1.3	3.3

Source: Cyndee Miller, "Marketing Industry Report: Who's Spending What on Biz-to-Biz Marketing?" *Marketing News,* January 1, 1996, p. 1, "Marketing Industry Report: Consumer Marketers Spend Most of Their Money on Communications" *Marketing News,* March 11, 1996, p. 1.

surprisingly, consumer product managers emphasize the use of television, print advertising, and promotional events while industrial product managers use print advertising, direct mail, catalogs, and trade shows. While we do not show any trend data, the large amounts industrial product managers spend on direct mail has definitely been increasing with the overall trend toward greater use of direct marketing. Industrial product managers find that direct mail is an excellent support program to aid the direct sales force as well as to sell lower-priced items and aid in customer retention.

In this book, we emphasize the three elements of the integrated mix that are most often the responsibility of the product manager: advertising (this chapter), sales promotion (Chapter 12), and direct marketing (Chapter 13). Much of PR involves divisional or corporate-level promotions designed to improve the general image or equity of the company and hence is not within the control of the product manager. As a consequence, we have chosen not to focus on public relations in this book. Still, some elements of public relations, such as event sponsorship, are product or product-line focused, and as a result product managers should prepare a budget to account for these activities. Packaging and graphics are specialized activities best left to experts, although the product manager would be the final decision maker about what is and is not appropriate.

Advertising is in many ways the most visible form of marketing, perhaps because U.S. advertisers are expected to spend nearly $200 billion on advertising in 1996. The high visibility of advertising is somewhat unfortunate, however, because it diverts attention from the many other roles marketing plays (e.g., development of quality products, distribution, and service) that are important in terms of both their impact and their budget levels. Advertising cannot be considered separately from other aspects of the product offering and from other programs because, as argued in the case of price in Chapter 10, advertising is an embodiment of product strategy and not vice versa.

Figure 11–4 shows the typical advertising planning process and the product manager's role in it.[4] While we do not necessarily advocate this ordering of the steps of the

FIGURE 11–4 The Advertising Planning Process

Stage	*Primary Players*	*End Product*
Developing the marketing plan and budget	Product manager	Budget Spending guidelines Profit projections
Planning the advertising	Product manager Advertising manager Ad agency Corporate advertising department	Identification of target market Allocation of spending Statement of advertising strategy and message
Copy development and approval	Ad agency Copy research company Product manager Advertising manager Senior management	Finished copy Media plan (with reach and frequency projections)
Execution	Ad agency or media buying company	Actual placement
Monitoring response	Market research manager Product manager Ad agency (research)	Awareness, recognition, and perception tracking Perceptual maps Sales/share tracking

Source: Naras V. Eechembadi, "Does Advertising Work?" *The McKinsey Quarterly,* no. 3 (1994), pp. 117–29.

process, particularly setting the advertising budget as the first step, the figure does highlight the important points of contact the product manager has with the advertising campaign. Besides the development of the overall marketing plan that drives the marketing mix, the product manager's major responsibilities include setting the budget, planning the advertising (identifying the target audience, developing the general advertising strategy and message), working with the ad agency to test different advertising copy and the media plan, and monitoring the response to the advertising. The product manager typically does not develop advertising copy, nor does he or she execute the media plan by buying specific media for placing the advertising. Thus, in this chapter we focus on those areas that are most critical for a product manager to manage. We also discuss some of the current issues regarding how the advertising agency should be compensated. Finally, we present and illustrate a format for presenting an advertising plan.

The Target Audience

In deciding who the target audience is (sometimes divided into primary and secondary audiences), the obvious starting point is the target customers in the overall marketing

[4] Naras V. Eechembadi, "Does Advertising Work?" *The McKinsey Quarterly,* no. 3 (1994) pp. 117–29.

FIGURE 11–5 Educational Toy: Advertising Choices

Target Audience	*Objective*	*Copy Focus*
Children	Buy on their own	Fun
	Ask for it by name	Popular
Parents	Buy it for their children	Educational benefits
Friends, other relatives	Buy it as "just the right gift"	Fun to play
	Sample "Logical" Media	
	Print	*TV*
Children	*Scholastic Magazine*	"The Simpsons"
Parents	*Better Homes & Gardens*	"60 Minutes"
Friends, other relatives	*U.S. News and World Report*	"Murder, She Wrote"

strategy (see Chapter 8). That strategy provides a clear statement about who the likely buyers are for the product, and these buyers will be the central focus of communications. Consider a company selling a CD-ROM software product that is targeted toward children and has both play value and some educational value. In this case, several decision makers and possible influencers may be relevant, including children, parents, and other friends or relatives searching for gift ideas. The choice of the primary target audience (see Figure 11–5) depends to a large extent on who is most influential in the decision process. You can focus on the children and hope they will use their own financial resources, which in the United States are substantial, or they will "pull" the purchase through the channels of parents, friends, and relatives, at which they tend to be very effective. On the other hand, you may want to address the parents, possibly trying to convince them that their children will be at a disadvantage if they do not have the software.

The "kids versus parents" issue arises in many product categories, illustrating the "buying center" concept developed in Chapter 6, that shows multiple individuals involved in the purchasing decision. Industrial goods offer even more cases of multiple parties involved in decisions. Most technical products can be directed to either technical people (e.g., engineers, who tend to set specifications), operational people (e.g., production supervisors or workers), or managers (who tend to focus more on some bottom line or, in the case of product managers, on the top line, than on operational details). Thus, the advertising target audience could in fact be broader than the target markets or market segments identified by the product manager in the product strategy, and identifying the target audience becomes an important task.

Of course, it is perfectly reasonable, albeit expensive, to target all relevant groups, but it is generally best to have one primary focus. Figure 11–6 shows a generic example of this choice: selecting a target audience for a new microprocessor for a personal computer. In this case, there are at least four target audiences: the engineers, who probably have the final say because they must write the PC specifications; the production supervisors, who are responsible for efficient production; the production workers, who install the new microprocessor; and the managers, who are responsible for sales of the end product. (Note we are ignoring for the present final customers who are addressed with "Intel inside" style promotions.) The product manager for the

Figure 11–6 New Personal Computer Microprocessor: Advertising Choices

Target Audience	*Objective*	*Copy Focus*
Engineers	Get them to write it into specifications	Improved performance
Production supervisors	Get them to put/request it in their budget	No downtime problems
Production workers	Get them to lobby for it	Easy to install
Managers	Get them to pressure operations to include it in their budget	Improved profit

microprocessor has different objectives for each party to the decision and focuses the sales message differently for each. The manager also chooses different media to present the message because the groups may read different magazines.

In summary, if multiple parties are involved, it is important to specify the primary target audience. This decision depends mainly on an assessment of the relative importance of the different target audiences, the relative susceptibility of the audiences to advertising, and the relative cost of reaching them.

Often the target audience is described in product category terms (e.g., heavy users, nonusers) or in terms of current product usage (e.g., users of product X, users of our product). This type of focus is strategically sound, but it is often less useful for selecting media vehicles that tend to be described in terms of demographic characteristics. Consequently, in describing target audiences, it is useful to consider and define primary and secondary targets and to describe segments both generally and in specific terms that facilitate media planning.

Setting Advertising Objectives

As in the development of marketing strategy described in Chapter 8, advertising decision making requires setting objectives that act as ultimate advertising goals. The product manager can choose from several types of objectives.

Customer-Oriented Objectives

The most obvious objective, of course, is to increase sales and profits. For industrial products, an alternative measure is leads generated for the sales force. Advertisers pay advertising agencies large amounts of money and expect to get a return of increased customer demand. Using sales-related measures as objectives, however, causes problems for most forms of advertising.[5] Two common difficulties are the following:

- Most advertising takes a certain period of time to create an effect; thus, setting annual sales goals is often inappropriate for a particular campaign.

[5]We exclude direct-response advertising from this discussion because we cover it in Chapter 13. Such advertising would normally be expected to deliver a good response in terms of sales.

FIGURE 11–7 Strategic Advertising Objectives (impact based)

Central/High Involvement/Thinking Route	*Peripheral/Low Involvement/Feeling Route*
Awareness/recall	Awareness
(Emotional) arousal/interest	Arousal
Information search	
Comprehension	
Attitude	
Intention	Intention
Trial/purchase	Purchase
Reevaluation	Evaluation

- It is difficult to separate the effects of advertising from the other marketing mix variables or the quality of the strategy. The advertising could be great, but the strategy or price could be inappropriate.

Thus, the objective of advertising is usually to make the customer aware of the product and create interest, positive attitudes, or intention to buy the product since other marketing and communications mix elements (e.g., price, channels, promotion, and sales force) actually close the deal.

A crucial distinction in customer decision processes is made between so-called high-involvement and low-involvement decisions. High-involvement decisions involve thought ("cognitive effort") to evaluate the pluses and minuses of a product and their net benefit. This evaluation then either leads or does not lead to a positive decision (purchase). In the low-involvement situation, exposure to an ad or a product leads more or less directly to purchase, with evaluation occurring only after use. These two different approaches have been called the central and peripheral routes to persuasion.[6] Foote, Cone, and Belding (FCB), a major advertising agency, adds to this distinction by further classifying products into "thinking" and "feeling" products and then uses a 2 × 2 table (high versus low involvement, feeling versus thinking) to help direct advertising design.[7]

Figure 11–7 presents an abbreviated hierarchical model of the central route decision process (which is more prevalent for high-involvement, "thinking" products). A basic implication of the high-involvement hierarchy is that in many cases individuals proceed through the stages sequentially. For an unknown product, it may be important to first establish awareness and interest, then convey specific information (e.g., product benefits), and finally convert the benefits into attitude, action plans (intention), and actual behavior. Hence awareness objectives are often appropriate. In contrast, for a well-established product (assuming major repositioning is under way), it may be more appropriate to define objectives in terms of attitude, shopping, or purchase. Some research suggests that mere exposure to ads is enough to improve

[6]See Richard E. Petty, John T. Cacioppo, and David W. Schumann, "Central and Peripheral Routes to Advertising Effectiveness: The Moderating Role of Involvement," *Journal of Consumer Research* 10 (1983), pp. 134–48.

[7]See Richard Vaughn, "How Advertising Works—a Planning Model," *Journal of Advertising Research* 20 (October 1980), pp. 27–33.

attitude. Interestingly, research has also found that a relation may exist between exposure and perceived quality, suggesting that awareness leads to better quality ratings as consumers infer quality from advertising expenditures. Also a long delay (several months) often occurs between deciding to buy a particular consumer good and actually making a purchase. As a consequence, shortening this cycle might be a reasonable objective.[8]

On the other hand, sometimes (e.g., in the case of new food products) the process is almost reversed: The decision to try precedes "formal" consideration of benefits. In these situations, objectives tend to focus on either generating awareness and interest (and hence trial) *or* increasing positive reinforcement. Reinforcement can be especially important in the case of products such as life insurance, which has annual premiums (and hence requires renewed commitment on the part of the customer) but no feedback to indicate whether the choice of policy was a good one.

Also relevant to the selection of advertising objectives is the question of who is the target. As discussed earlier, you can focus on your current customers, your competitors' customers, or noncustomers. Not surprisingly, these different customer targets have an impact on objectives chosen.

Exposure-Oriented Objectives (Media Planning)

Exposure-oriented objectives are generally quantitative measures of exposure, typically in terms of reach (the number or percentage who receive at least one exposure), frequency (the average number of exposures a potential customer receives), or gross rating points (GRPs, or the total number of advertising exposures received [reach × frequency]). When feasible, these objectives should be defined in terms of a target audience rather than just customers or people in general. One intriguing rule of thumb, developed many years ago, suggests that customers need three exposures for an ad to have an impact.[9]

The choice between reach and frequency depends on the assessment of how many exposures are needed for the advertising to be effective. In general, the clearer the message in the ad and the more involved the customer, the fewer ad impressions are needed before a customer responds. Thus, an industrial product advertising a new feature that increases output 30 percent probably needs fewer exposures than a laundry detergent with no obvious distinguishing feature.

Because these operational objectives have such direct budget implications, we turn to a discussion of budget setting, leaving the choice of exact reach, frequency, and GRP objectives to be constrained by the overall budget decision.

Specific Objectives

Like product objectives, advertising objectives are operational and hence specific in nature. Examples of advertising objectives include increasing awareness from 45 to 60

---

[8]For some research in this area, see Eric Greenleaf and Donald R. Lehmann, "Causes of Delay in Consumer Decision-Making," *Advances in Consumer Research* 18 (1991), pp. 470–75.

[9]Herbert Krugman, "The Impact of Television Advertising: Learning without Involvement," *Public Opinion Quarterly* 29 (1965), pp. 349–356.

Figure 11–8 Leading Consumer Product Advertisers in 1995

Product	*Spending (thousands of dollars)*
AT&T Telephone Services	$673,387
Ford cars and trucks	564,866
Sears stores	540,053
McDonald's restaurants	490,550
Kellogg's breakfast foods	488,205
Chevrolet cars and trucks	477,600
Dodge cars and trucks	414,531
Toyota cars and trucks	384,074
MCI telephone services	320,956
Warner Bros. movies	294,004

Source: *Advertising Age,* May 6, 1996, p. 36. Reprinted with permission.

percent, improving attitude toward a brand 1 point on a 7-point scale, increasing average usage from 1.7 to 2 units per household per year,[10] and generating 6,000 shopping visits or inquiries from potential customers. Exposure objectives are more removed from actual purchase and hence are used partly because they are easier to assess and partly because other measures, such as awareness, attitude, and store visits, are influenced by a number of factors, so the impact of advertising on them is not clear. A reasonable exposure objective might be to reach 80 percent of a target audience (e.g., females age 13 to 30) at least once during a three-month period and to reach 30 percent of them at least three times. In many cases, it makes sense to have both exposure objectives (to guide media selection) and customer objectives (to aid in the development and evaluation of copy).

Setting Advertising Budgets

As noted earlier in this chapter, advertising is a big business. To give the reader some idea of how large advertising budgets are, Figure 11–8 shows the 10 largest consumer product advertising spenders for 1995 and Figure 11–9 shows the 10 largest industrial product advertisers for 1994.[11] The numbers, particularly those for the consumer products and services, are enormous. Even relatively small brands, such as Philip Morris's Red Dog beer, received over $57 million in advertising support in 1995.

Because of the large amounts involved and the importance of advertising to the success of many products, one of the most important jobs of the product manager is to

[10]For some recent research on the importance of usage-based advertising objectives, see Brian Wansink and Michael L. Ray, "Advertising Strategies to Increase Usage Frequency," *Journal of Marketing,* 60 (1996), pp. 31–46.

[11]Note that AT&T and MCI are on both lists. Although the publications from which we obtained these data do not detail how the advertising is measured, there could be some overlap in the data; in particular, the Figure 11–8 numbers probably contain some advertising targeted toward business users.

FIGURE 11–9 Leading Industrial Product Advertisers: 1994

Company	*Spending (millions of dollars)*
AT&T Corporation	$258.6
IBM Corporation	154.9
MCI Communications Corporation	111.6
Hewlett-Packard Company	67.9
Microsoft Corporation	66.6
Compaq Computer Corporation	65.3
Sprint Corporation	62.7
United Parcel Service of America Inc.	62.1
American Express Company	60.2
Digital Equipment Corporation	60.0

Source: *Business Marketing,* October 1995, p. 12. Reprinted with permission. © Crain Communications, Inc.

determine how much to spend on advertising. Setting advertising budgets has an immediate impact on costs and longer-term effects on sales. Consequently, advertising is in many ways an investment (sometimes called "consumer franchise building") in much the same way spending on R&D is, albeit with both a less distant and, at least in a technical sense, a less dramatic breakthrough potential. Like spending on R&D, spending on advertising has a long history and a relatively weak record for measuring effectiveness precisely.

A crucial distinction exists between viewing advertising spending as an investment versus an expense. Investments are expected to generate returns over a long period of time. Often, when advertising is used as an expense, the budget is cut near the end of the quarter or fiscal year to achieve a profit target. In contrast, marketing-oriented firms view advertising as a long-term investment in the brand.[12]

Figure 11–10 shows examples of successful investments in brands. The two graphs show a positive relationship between advertising investment measured as cumulative advertising spending and market share for the tobacco and antiulcer drug categories. The general point is that consistent investment in advertising for products can lead to a superior market position.

Clearly the "right" way to set budgets is to first develop a model that quantitatively estimates the impact of advertising (as well as the rest of the product offering *and* the impact of competitors and environmental changes) on sales and profits. Then the product manager need only determine optimal spending levels either analytically for a simple model or, for more complicated models, numerically or by trial and error. Unfortunately, though later in this chapter we briefly discuss some promising model-building and data analysis methods for improving advertising effectiveness, current models neither have been perfected nor are universally used. The most widely considered methods are described next.

---

[12]For a good discussion on this topic, see Adrian J. Slywotzky and Benson P. Shapiro, "Leveraging to Beat the Odds: The New Marketing Mind-Set," *Harvard Business Review,* September–October 1993, pp. 97–107.

FIGURE 11–10 The Relationship between Cumulative Advertising Spending and Market Share

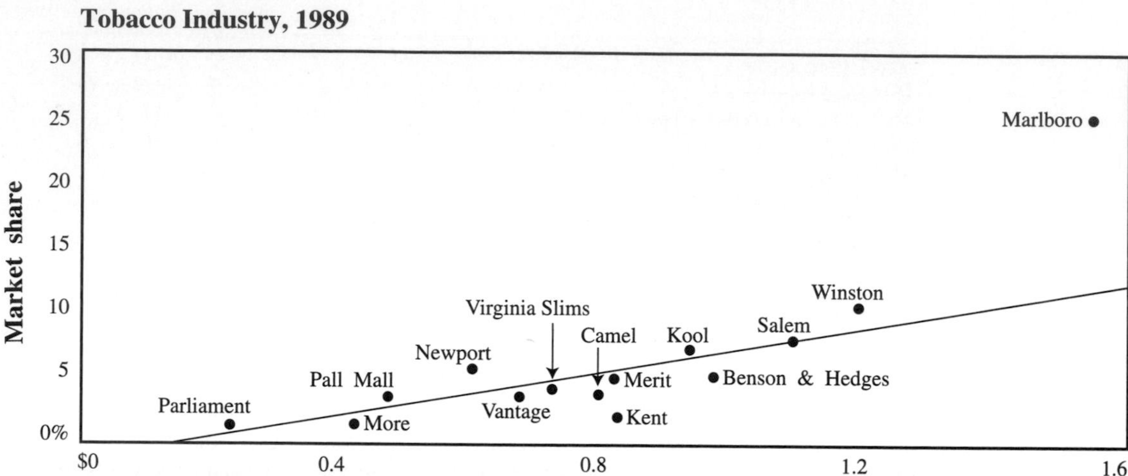

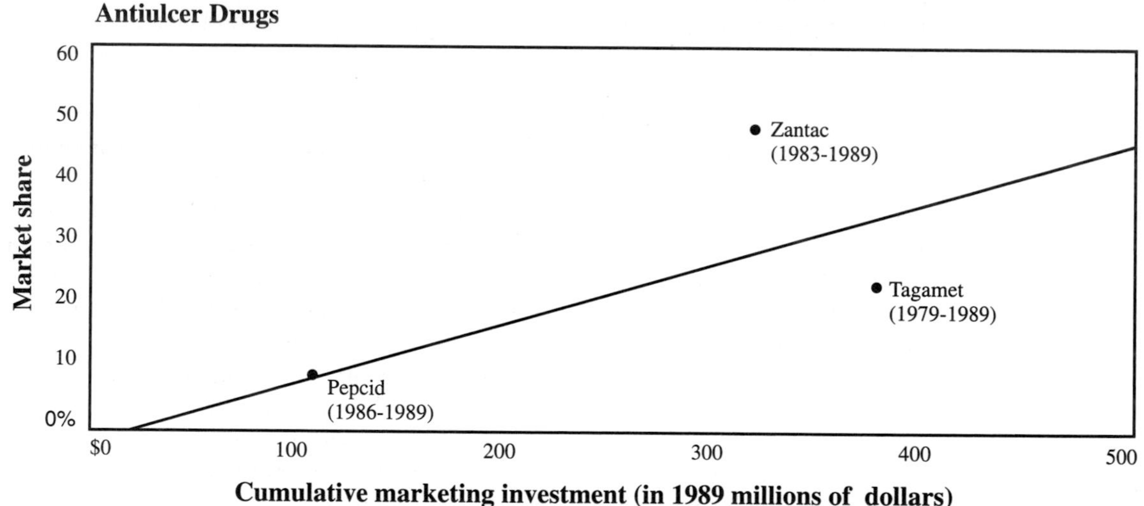

Source: IMS America, Ltd, and CDI estimates.

FIGURE 11–11 Advertising Budget Methods

	1982	1987
1. Objective and task	40%	50%
2. Percentage of sales	38	25
3. Competition/competitive parity	8	8
4. Affordable	49	50
5. Experimentation	14	20

Source: James E. Lynch and Graham Hooley, "Increasing Sophistication in Advertising Budget Setting," *Journal of Advertising Research* 30 (1990), pp. 67–75.

Objective and Task

While not a global optimizing method, budgeting by objectives and tasks is a logically appealing approach in which the product manager first determines the advertising objectives (e.g., target audience, reach, and frequency goals), and then chooses an advertising plan (and consequently budget) to achieve the objectives. One study showed that by 1987, 50 percent of surveyed firms reported using this method, an increase of 10 percent over 1982.[13] (See Figure 11–11 for the incidence of use of budget-setting methods.) When following the objective and task method, objectives lead to a budget and determine reach and frequency. However, given limited budgets, criteria such as reach and frequency are more often objectives within budget constraints. For example, an objective might be to maximize reach subject to a $10 million budget cap.

Percentage-of-Sales

The percentage-of-sales method approaches advertising as a cost to be borne and selects a percentage of sales to devote to advertising. This method seems to turn normal causal thinking—that advertising causes sales—on its head. One argument for this approach is based on a form of the efficient market hypothesis developed in finance: Firms that survive tend to be those with more optimal budgets, so the survivors' budgets may offer an estimate of the optimal level in a competitive market. Alternatively, you can view the ad/sales ratio as the cooperative (agreed-to) solution in a multiperson game. Basically, however, the percentage-of-sales method is used because it is convenient and is safer than committing to nontraditional spending levels. Though slipping in stated popularity, this method was still reportedly used by 25 percent of companies in 1987, and it is probably even more widely used (some industry experts estimate that perhaps as many as 50 percent use it). Figure 11–12 shows advertising-sales ratios by industry for 1995. Although this table is not meant to imply that all the companies in these industries use some kind of percentage-of-sales method for setting ad budgets, the ratio for a product's industry category or SIC code is a useful starting point for trying to put together a budget from scratch. The range of the ratios is quite large; the highest advertising to sales ratio is games and toys (18.1

[13]James E. Lynch and Graham Hooley, "Increasing Sophistication in Advertising Budget Setting," *Journal of Advertising Research* 30 (1990), pp. 67–75.

FIGURE 11–12 Advertising to Sales Ratios for the 200 Largest Ad Spending Industries: 1995

Industry	SIC no.	Ad Dollars as Percent of Sales	Ad Dollar as Percent of Margin	Annual Ad Growth Rate (%)
Abrasive, asbestos, misc minrl	3290	1.0	2.3	5.0
Adhesives and sealants	2891	5.4	8.5	8.6
Advertising	7310	5.2	13.1	17.8
Agriculture chemicals	2870	1.8	8.0	15.4
Agriculture production-crops	100	1.3	5.1	–5.9
Air cond, heating, refrig eq	3585	1.5	6.0	8.8
Air courier services	4513	1.4	9.4	4.7
Air transport, scheduled	4512	1.3	9.3	–2.7
Apparel & other finished pds	2300	5.4	13.6	6.3
Apparel and accessory stores	5600	2.4	6.7	7.8
Auto and home supply stores	5531	1.1	2.8	6.2
Auto dealers, gas stations	5500	1.3	8.4	11.6
Auto rent & lease, no drivers	7510	2.3	14.3	–0.9
Bakery products	2050	2.8	5.6	–2.6
Beverages	2080	8.2	16.3	5.0
Biological pds, ex diagnostics	2836	0.9	2.2	8.3
Blankbooks, binders, bookbind	2780	3.0	5.6	9.7
Bldg matl, hardwr, garden-retl	5200	2.9	8.5	9.0
Books: pubg, pubg & printing	2731	3.6	6.6	6.6
Brdwoven fabric mill, cotton	2211	6.0	26.8	–2.7
Btld & can soft drinks, water	2088	3.0	6.4	9.5
Cable and other pay tv svcs	4841	1.2	2.1	11.4
Calculate, acct mach, ex comp	3578	1.4	3.5	14.5
Can fruit, veg, presrv, jam, jel	2033	1.3	4.7	–12.0
Can, froznpresrv fruit & veg	2030	8.2	19.7	4.3
Catalog, mail-order houses	5961	7.7	20.7	8.9
Chemicals & allied pds-whsl	5160	2.8	6.1	11.2
Chemicals & allied prods	2800	2.6	6.0	–10.1
Cigarettes	2111	4.1	7.3	–8.0
Cmp integrated sys design	7373	1.3	3.6	–1.7
Cmp processing, data prep svc	7374	1.1	2.7	1.9
Cmp programming, data process	7370	0.3	0.8	4.3
Commercial printing	2750	2.1	7.2	14.5
Communications equip, nec	3669	3.1	7.5	18.8
Computer & office equipment	3570	0.9	2.6	–1.5
Computer communication equip	3576	2.2	3.9	20.1
Computer peripheral eq, nec	3577	2.8	7.6	13.7
Computer storage devices	3572	0.7	2.7	8.2
Computers & software-whsl	5045	1.6	12.0	33.2
Convrt papr, paprbrd, ex boxes	2670	5.6	15.4	4.7
Cutlery, hand tools, gen hrdwr	3420	9.7	17.8	7.3
Dental equipment & supplies	3843	2.0	3.8	19.5
Department stores	5311	2.5	9.6	4.5
Dolls and stuffed toys	3942	15.4	28.6	16.5
Drug & proprietary stores	5912	1.1	4.1	1.2
Eating places	5812	3.3	15.8	4.1
Educational services	8200	7.4	18.6	4.6
Elec meas & test instruments	3825	2.9	5.9	8.8
Electr, oth elec eq, ex cmp	3600	2.0	6.2	–0.2
Electric housewares and fans	3634	4.8	15.4	8.7
Electric lighting, wiring eq	3640	1.5	4.0	4.2
Electrical indl apparatus	3620	2.3	6.2	9.8
Electromedical apparatus	3845	0.8	1.4	6.3
Electronic components, nec	3679	0.9	3.0	11.5
Electronic computers	3571	1.7	5.8	10.0
Electronic parts, eq-whsl, nec	5065	3.1	15.9	18.2
Engines and turbines	3510	2.0	8.3	3.1
Engr, acc, resh, mgmt, rel svcs	8700	0.5	2.0	3.3
Equip rental & leasing, nec	7359	2.5	4.4	5.3
Fabricated rubber pds, nec	3060	2.1	7.6	2.2
Family clothing stores	5651	2.7	8.2	10.8
Farm machinery and equipment	3523	1.0	3.9	4.5
Finance-services	6199	3.0	7.8	–49.6
Fire, marine, casualty ins	6331	0.8	7.6	0.7
Food and kindred products	2000	6.5	16.7	5.4
Food stores	5400	4.3	10.5	13.46
Footwear, except rubber	3140	3.8	10.2	5.
Furniture stores	5712	6.1	13.3	5.9
Games, toys, chld veh, ex dolls	3944	18.1	34.6	8.4
Gen med & surgical hospitals	8062	1.0	4.9	30.4
General indl mach & eq, nec	3569	0.7	2.1	4.8
General industrial mach & eq	3560	2.0	6.9	9.0
Glass, glasswr-pressed, blown	3220	1.2	2.7	10.2
Grain mill products	2040	8.7	17.1	–0.3
Greeting cards	2771	5.3	7.6	9.1
Groceries & related pds-whsl	5140	3.5	24.6	10.2
Grocery stores	5411	1.1	4.7	1.2
Hardwr, plumb, heat eq-whsl	5070	2.0	31.4	7.3
Health services	8000	1.5	7.2	4.6
Help supply services	7363	0.8	3.9	2.7
Hobby, toy, and game shops	5945	1.4	4.3	10.1
Home furniture & equip store	5700	2.8	7.7	12.2
Hospitals & medical svc plans	6324	1.0	4.0	16.4
Hospitals	8060	4.1	32.2	11.0
Hotels, motels, tourist courts	7011	3.6	11.0	10.1
Household appliances	3630	2.6	8.5	–2.2
Household audio & video eq	3651	3.2	10.7	6.9
Household furniture	2510	4.5	14.0	10.6
Ice cream & frozen desserts	2024	6.8	20.4	13.4
In vitro, in vivo diagnostics	2835	2.5	6.4	17.3
Indl coml fans, blowrs, oth eq	3564	1.0	4.2	14.4
Indl trucks, tractors, trailers	3537	0.9	3.7	7.2
Industrial measurement instr	3823	0.6	1.5	9.8
Industrial organic chemicals	2860	0.8	3.0	6.3
Ins agents, brokers & service	6411	1.2	5.6	7.3
Investment advice	6282	5.1	14.3	14.3
Iron and steel foundries	3320	1.1	4.0	7.4
Jewelry stores	5944	3.9	6.3	–9.2
Jewelry precious metal	3911	4.6	9.6	1.1
Knit outerwear mills	2253	3.3	10.1	12.0
Knitting mills	2250	3.8	12.8	3.5
Lab analytical instruments	3826	1.8	3.2	-1.0
Lawn, garden tractors, equip	3524	3.2	8.4	8.4
Leather and leather products	3100	8.2	17.1	–7.9
Lumber & oth bldg matl-retl	5211	1.0	3.5	8.0
Lumber and wood pds, ex furn	2400	0.2	0.9	1.6
Machine tools, metal cutting	3541	1.1	3.3	3.7
Magnetic, optic recording media	3695	2.8	8.0	5.0
Malt beverages	2082	4.9	12.9	3.5
Management services	8741	1.8	8.7	1.5
Meas & controlling dev, nec	3829	2.0	4.1	17.4
Meat packing plants	2011	6.4	25.2	8.8
Membership sports & rec clubs	7997	8.8	12.7	7.7
Men, yth, boys frnsh, wrk clothg	2320	3.6	10.5	12.4
Metal forgings and stampings	3460	0.8	2.7	18.0
Metalworking machinery & eq	3540	3.3	8.9	4.9
Millwork, veneer, plywood	2430	1.7	7.0	12.1
Misc amusement & rec service	7990	2.3	5.7	9.2
Misc business services	7380	2.2	4.1	5.4
Misc durable goods-whsl	5090	2.4	9.1	11.2
Misc elec machny, eq, supplies	3690	1.6	5.6	7.4
Misc fabricated metal prods	3490	0.7	2.6	7.3
Misc food preps, kindred pds	2090	2.3	6.0	7.6
Misc general mdse stores	5399	3.8	15.8	9.2
Misc indl, coml, machny & eq	3590	1.6	4.4	3.0
Misc manufacturing industries	3990	2.4	5.9	8.1
Misc nondurable goods-whsl	5190	3.4	12.3	17.0
Misc plastic products	3080	1.3	5.6	9.4
Misc shopping goods stores	5940	1.9	6.9	9.2
Misc transportation equip	3790	2.8	12.5	13.5
Miscellaneous retail	5900	2.0	6.7	12.3
Mortgage bankers & loan corr	6162	2.7	4.2	20.1

Figure 11–12 (concluded)

Industry	SIC no.	Ad Dollars as Percent of Sales	Ad Dollar as Percent of Margin	Annual Ad Growth Rate (%)	Industry	SIC no.	Ad Dollars as Percent of Sales	Ad Dollar as Percent of Margin	Annual Ad Growth Rate (%)
Motion pic, videotape prdotn	7812	12.7	34.4	13.5	Pumps and pumping equipment	3561	1.9	4.7	9.7
Motion pic, videotape distr	7822	7.4	16.8	9.8	Radio broadcasting stations	4832	5.3	12.1	19.0
Motion picture theatres	7830	2.8	17.0	5.6	Radio, tv broadcast, comm eq	3663	1.0	3.0	18.1
Motor vehicle part, accessory	3714	0.8	3.3	10.4	Radio, tv, cons electr stores	5731	3.3	13.8	2.9
Motor vehicles & car bodies	3711	2.5	11.2	−0.3	Radiotelephone communication	4812	3.8	5.6	15.7
Motorcycles, bicycles & parts	3751	1.2	4.5	6.2	Real estate investment trust	6798	2.1	4.2	7.2
Newspaper; pubg, pubg & print	2711	3.8	8.3	3.6	Record and tape stores	5735	1.9	4.9	1.1
Office machines, nec	3579	1.3	3.8	1.2	Retail stores	5990	4.1	10.0	14.1
Offices of medical doctors	8011	1.6	7.5	13.1	Rubber and plastics footwear	3021	7.5	18.4	6.8
Operative builders	1531	1.2	12.1	10.7	Sausage, oth prepared meat pd	2013	5.3	28.3	5.8
Operators-nonres bldgs	6512	1.9	4.3	0.2	Security brokers & dealers	6211	1.2	3.4	12.4
Ophthalmic goods	3851	9.5	16.9	6.8	Semiconductor, related device	3674	1.8	3.6	15.3
Ortho, prosth, surg appl, suply	3842	1.3	2.6	5.3	Ship & boat bldg & repairing	3730	0.5	2.5	3.0
Paints, varnishes, lacquers	2851	2.5	6.0	4.6	Shoe stores	5661	2.4	7.4	−0.2
Paper & paper products-whsl	5110	1.2	5.0	11.2	Skilled nursing care fac	8051	1.9	12.8	9.7
Paper mills	2621	1.9	5.8	0.9	Soap, detergent, toilet preps	2840	9.7	22.1	5.1
Patent owners and lessors	6794	5.2	11.3	11.3	Special clean, polish preps	2842	17.3	29.4	4.2
Pens, pencils, oth office matl	3950	5.0	1.1	4.6	Special industry machinery	3550	4.0	13.7	7.2
Perfume, cosmetic, toilet prep	2844	8.2	14.4	4.5	Special industry machy, nec	3559	0.9	1.8	14.1
Periodical: pubg, pubg & print	2721	7.6	13.2	12.4	Sporting & athletic gds, nec	3949	6.4	15.2	14.4
Personal credit institutions	6141	1.0	2.0	8.5	Sugar & confectionery prods	2060	4.8	11.4	6.7
Personal services	7200	6.4	16.5	7.6	Surgical, med instr, apparatus	3841	1.1	2.3	2.0
Petroleum refining	2911	1.1	8.6	4.5	Svcs to dwellings, oth bldgs	7340	1.7	6.1	7.9
Pharmaceutical preparations	2834	5.3	7.6	2.0	Tele & telegraph apparatus	3661	0.9	2.1	−1.0
Phone comm ex radiotelephone	4813	1.7	4.1	8.2	Television broadcast station	4833	8.1	7.9	16.6
Phono recrds, audio tape, disk	3652	5.4	10.5	−14.3	Tires and inner tubes	3011	2.1	7.3	2.9
Photographic equip & suppl	3861	3.0	7.6	−5.9	Unsupp plastics film & sheet	3081	3.1	9.1	1.7
Plastic matl, synthetic resin	2820	0.8	2.7	−12.2	Variety stores	5331	1.6	6.8	6.4
Plastics products, nec	3089	2.6	6.7	5.9	Watches, clocks and parts	3873	8.5	17.2	8.2
Plastics, resins, elastomers	2821	0.7	2.1	−7.7	Water transportation	4400	8.2	22.7	3.7
Poultry slaughter & process	2015	2.5	13.2	10.7	Wmns, miss, chld, infnt undgrmt	2340	4.5	10.9	10.3
Prepackaged software	7372	3.3	4.4	13.9	Women	5621	2.6	6.9	2.6
Prof & coml eq & supply-whsl	5040	1.9	4.9	8.7	Womens, misses, jrs outerwear	2330	3.5	11.1	0.2
Public bldg & rel furniture	2531	0.6	3.5	14.30	Wood hshld furn, ex upholsrd	2511	2.3	8.4	8.3

Source: *Advertising Age,* August 14, 1995, p. 26. Reprinted with permission.

percent), while the smallest ones include ship and boat building and repairing (0.5 percent) and lumber and wood products (0.2 percent).

Competitive Parity

The comparative parity approach considers share of advertising dollars spent (also known as *share of voice*) rather than absolute advertising dollars to determine sales per share point and to set budgets accordingly. As Figure 11–11 shows, a relatively small number of firms (8 percent) reported using this approach.

One approach to competitive parity is to compare share of voice to actual or desired brand share. Small-share brands tend to focus on profit taking and large share brands on investing in future profits.[14] Moreover, the average share of voice tends to be higher for low-share brands and lower for high-share brands relative to their market

[14]See John Philip Jones, "Ad Spending: Maintaining Market Share," *Harvard Business Review* 68 (January–February 1990), pp. 38–48.

Figure 11–13 Market Share versus Share of Voice

Market Share	*Share of Voice – Market Share*
1–3%	+5%
4–6	+4
7–9	+2
10–12	+4
13–15	+1
16–18	+2
19–21	0
22–24	–3
25–27	–5
28–30	–5

Source: Reprinted by permission of *Harvard Business Review.* An exhibit from "Ad Spending: Maintaining Market Share," by John Phillip Jones, January–February 1990.

shares (see Figure 11–13). This suggests that large, well-known brands (products with over a 13 percent market share) can underinvest in advertising relative to their market share. In focusing on brands with at least a 13 percent market share, it was found that brands with rising trends underinvested by 1 percent on average (their share of voice was 1 percent less than their share of the market), brands with constant share had share of voice 3 percent less than their market share, and brands with declining trends had share of voice 4 percent less than their market share. While the direction of causality in these data is unclear (did they spend less on advertising because they knew share was going down, or did spending less on advertising contribute to decreasing share?), it does suggest that market share is a good starting point for choosing advertising share and hence budget.

Affordable

The affordable method is the ultimate in "advertising as a cost of doing business" thinking. It selects an advertising budget that, together with projected sales, price, and other costs, results in an "acceptable" income statement and profit level. This method has also been widely used for many years, with 50 percent of the companies reporting (admitting to?) using this approach in 1987. Unfortunately, as advertising becomes less affordable because a brand is doing poorly, the role of advertising may become more important, thus leading to a vicious cycle of poor results, less advertising money, poorer results, even less advertising money, and so on.

Experimentation

In the experimentation approach, the manager tries different levels of spending, either in different regions or in more controlled settings, and monitors the results. The manager then uses the results to select among different advertising budgets and plans. With up to 20 percent of companies reporting using this method, it is increasing in popularity and represents a step toward developing optimizing models. The case of Equal highlights the use of experimentation in helping to set advertising budgets.[15] Product managers for Equal used information from a marketing research company, Information Resources, Inc. (IRI), to determine advertising spending. IRI operates what it calls BehaviorScan markets, geographically distinct markets in which the company installs electronic scanners in all the retail outlets in the city to track purchase behavior, and "split cable," two different TV cables running through the city with some households on cable A and others on cable B, to test different advertising strategies and budget levels. Companies can run extra commercials on one cable—say, A—when public service spots run on B for comparison. The household purchasing data indicate if the extra advertising created additional purchasing in the households on cable A. In the case of Equal, when the brand was introduced, the brand manager tried two levels of media spending: $3.8 million and $5.7 million (extrapolated to national levels). After a 20-week test, there was no significant difference between Equal purchasing rates from households on the two cables; thus, the lower spending level was reasonable.

Decision Calculus

Computerized decision support systems (DSSs) such as ADBUDG[16] help structure budget decisions systematically. Managers provide subjective inputs about, for example, the impact of increasing or decreasing advertising spending by 50 percent. The computer program then estimates consumer response and solves for optimal spending. Although using solely subjective data produces results that are hard to sell to others, DSSs that combine judgment with data have facilitated decision making and promise to be more useful in the future.

Summary

Reported usage of the six budgeting methods is almost equally split between convenience/affordable methods (percent of sales, affordable, competitive parity) and the effectiveness-based methods (objective and task, experimentation). In fact, the two approaches are likely to overlap, with effectiveness-based budgets considered in light of the current P&L statements and past budgets (both the company's own and competitors') and projected profits playing an important role in setting "reasonable" objectives and spending levels. As better measures of advertising effectiveness slowly emerge, the analytical methods are gaining importance relative to rules of thumb such as percentage of sales, though allocation of "affordable" amounts remains a powerful constraint on budgets, especially in a recession.

Some reasonable guidelines to setting advertising budgets that ignore the convenience/affordable approaches are the following:[17]

---

[15]These data are from Darral G. Clarke, "G.D. Searle & Co.: Equal Low-Calorie Sweetener (A)," Harvard Business School case study 9-585-010, 1985.

[16]John D. C. Little, "Models and Managers: The Concept of a Decision Calculus," *Management Science* 16 (1970), pp. B466–485.

[17]Bob Lamons, "How to Set Politically Correct Ad Budgets," *Marketing News,* December 4, 1995, p. 5.

- Market share is important; the higher your share, the more you should spend to protect it.
- New products require higher advertising support than established ones.
- Markets growing 10 percent or more annually require a higher than average advertising investment.
- If your production is at less than two-thirds capacity, you should think about increasing the ad budget.
- Products with low unit prices (under $10,000) require higher advertising support than ones with high unit prices. Premium-priced and heavily discounted products should receive more support than those "average" priced.
- Higher-quality products generally require higher advertising spending.
- Broader product lines require more support.
- Standard, off-the-shelf products need more support than customized products.

Evaluating Message Copy

As noted earlier in this chapter, product managers get involved only infrequently with the development of the actual advertising copy; that task is delegated to either in-house or agency creative specialists. However, the product manager must be heavily involved with testing the advertising campaign before a substantial amount of money is committed to it. A large number of variables are usually testable: the spokesperson, the message itself (copy), the execution (e.g., humor versus other approaches), media, and other factors.

Laboratory Tests

Figure 11–14 is a typology of the different methods used for both pretesting and posttesting advertising.[18] Pretests are measures taken before implementation of the campaign, and a posttest is an evaluation of the advertising after it has been developed but before it has been "rolled out" nationally or internationally. Laboratory tests are run in which people are brought to a particular location where they are shown ads and asked to respond to them. The advantage of lab tests is that the researcher can carefully control the environment without distractions to the respondent and manipulate several different aspects of the advertising. The disadvantage is that the situation is not realistic; the respondent provides answers in an unnatural environment. Field tests provide real-world measures because they are conducted under natural viewing conditions. Their advantages and disadvantages are the mirror image of lab tests: The environment is realistic, but the researcher cannot absolutely control other variables that might affect the response to the ad, such as a competitor's ad, noise from children, and so on.

---

[18]George E. Belch and Michael A. Belch, *Advertising & Promotion: An Integrated Marketing Communications Perspective,* 2nd. ed. (Homewood, Ill.: Richard D. Irwin, 1993), Chapter 20. Another good reference on copy testing procedures is Rajeev Batra, John G. Myers, and David A. Aaker, *Advertising Management,* 5th ed. (Upper Saddle River, N.J.: Prentice Hall, 1996), Chapter 14.

Figure 11–14 Classification of Advertising Copy-Testing Methods

	Advertising-related test (reception or response to the message itself and its contents)	**Product-related test** (impact of message on product awareness, liking, intention to buy, or use)
Laboratory measures (respondent aware of testing and measurement process)	**Cell I** Pretesting procedures 1. Consumer jury 2. Portfolio test 3. Readability tests 4. Physiological measures Eye camera GSR/EDR	**Cell II** Pretesting procedures 1. Theater tests 2. Trailer tests 3. Laboratory stores
Real-world measures (respondent unaware of testing and measurement process)	**Cell III** Pretesting procedures 1. Dummy advertising vehicles 2. Inquiry tests 3. On-the-air tests Posttesting procedures 1. Recognition tests 2. Recall tests 3. Association measures 4. Combination measures	**Cell IV** Pretesting and posttesting procedures 1. Pre- and posttests 2. Sales tests 3. Minimarket tests

Source: *Advertising and Promotion: An Integrated Marketing Communications Perspective,* Chapter 20, p. 687.

Consumer Jury. The most common form of testing for advertising concept testing is the use of focus groups, a small group of customers who are led in a discussion of the advertising by a moderator. Advertising concepts are usually in the form of what are called *storyboards* for TV ads, rough pictures showing the idea behind the "story" that will be told (obviously for radio ads, words instead of pictures are used). For magazine or other print formats, actual executions are shown; multimedia technology allows for the the use of more realistic ads.

Portfolio Tests. In this approach, a group of respondents are shown both control and test ads. After viewing the portfolio, respondents are asked what information they recall from the ads and which they liked best. The ads with the highest recall and liking are considered to be the most effective.

Readability Tests. Readability of the copy of a print ad can be determined through the use of methods that, for example, count the number of syllables per 100 words, the length of sentences, and other structural aspects of the copy. The results are a sense of the reading skill needed to comprehend an ad that should match the target audience (you don't talk to third graders the same way you talk to Ph.D.'s, it is simpler and often more enjoyable to deal with third graders) then compared to norms obtained from successful ads.

Physiological Methods. A "weird science" approach to assessing advertisements involves a set of techniques that measure involuntary physical responses to the ad. These include

- Pupil dilation. Pupilometers measure dilation (an activity related to action or arousal) and constriction (conservation of energy).
- GSR/EDR (galvanic skin response/electrodermal response). Response to a stimulus activates sweat glands; this activity can be measured using electrodes attached to the skin.
- Eye tracking. Viewers are asked to watch or read an ad while a sensor beams infrared light at their eyes. This can measure how much of an ad is being read, what part of the ad is attracting attention, and the sequence of reading/attention.

Theater Tests. This is a widely used method for pretesting TV commercials. The service is sold by companies such as Advertising Research Services and Advertising Control for Television. Participants for theater tests are recruited by phone, shopping mall intercepts, and direct mail. A television show or some other entertainment is provided in a movie theater–like facility with commercial breaks ("trailer" tests use smaller, mobile facilities near shopping malls). The show is used so the respondents do not focus solely on the commercials; a cover story might inform them that the TV show is a pilot for a new network or cable series. After viewing the ads, the participants are asked questions about recall, attitude, interest, and other behavioral responses.

Laboratory Stores. In this testing procedure, the researcher attempts to simulate a shopping environment by setting up, for example, a supermarket-like shopping shelf with real brands. Respondents are shown advertising copy and make actual brand choices. A popular supplier of this kind of testing is Research Systems Corporation with its ARS Persuasion copy-testing system.

Real-World Measures

Dummy Advertising Vehicles. Researchers construct "dummy" magazines with regular editorial matter, regular ads, and a set of test ads. The magazines are distributed to a random sample of homes in a predetermined geographic area. After being asked to read the magazine as they normally would, the consumers in the sample are interviewed on the editorial content as well as the test ads.

Inquiry Tests. These are also used for print ads. The product manager and/or ad agency can track the number of inquiries generated from an ad that has a direct-response toll free phone number or a reader inquiry card attached. In industrial marketing, the use of "bingo" cards, response cards that have numbered holes corresponding to the numbered ads in the magazine, is very common.

On-the-Air/Recall Tests. IRI, Burke Marketing Research, ASI Market Research, Gallup & Robinson, and Nielsen all sell this kind of service. Essentially, a real TV ad (one of perhaps several executions being tested) is inserted in a TV program in one or more test markets. Consumers are then contacted and asked if they saw the ad; if so, they are asked further questions about recall of copy points, brand, and the like. The services differ somewhat in the questions asked and how the sample is recruited. Gallup & Robinson, for example, prerecruits a sample who are asked in advance to watch the particular show on which the test ad is being run.

Recognition Tests. This is the most widely used method for posttesting print ads and is closely associated with Starch INRA Hooper's "through the book" method. With this approach, a researcher interviews respondents at home by first asking if they have read a particular issue of a magazine and then going through the issue to obtain information about whether the respondents have seen the ad, how much of it they have read, and how much they recall. The Starch method and the resulting Starch "scores" are used to track and evaluate complete campaigns.

Sales/Minimarket Tests. The Information Resources, Inc. (IRI), BehaviorScan markets described in the section on advertising budgeting are also used to test ad copy. Using the split-cable methodology rather than testing a pure increase in advertising dollars, households on the two cables can receive different advertising copy being tested. By comparing the purchasing of the brand at the stores where the households shop, the product manager can determine if one copy platform is more persuasive in producing sales than the other. However, as we have noted elsewhere in this chapter, a short-term sales criterion is not necessarily appropriate for advertising.

Media Decisions

Media planning is a field in itself and typically is a specialty within advertising agencies. Therefore, as we noted earlier in this chapter, the media plan is often left up to the "experts." However, both to help product managers understand some aspects of media planning and to provide an approach to follow when no help is available, we provide a skeletal discussion of media planning. More detailed treatments are available that are well beyond the scope of this book.[19]

[19]See, for example, Jack Z. Sissors and Lincoln Bumba, eds., *Advertising Media Planning,* 4th ed. (Lincolnwood, Ill: NTC Business Books, 1993).

The basic media plan defines *where* (in what vehicles, e.g., TV, magazines, radio, the World Wide Web) and *when* (time of year, day, etc.) advertising will appear. These decisions, which effectively determine how often an ad is seen and by how many people, are in turn heavily influenced by both earlier decisions on advertising strategy, message, and target audience and issues such as the rate of ad wearout (which in turn is influenced by the amount of "clutter" anticipated in general and in competitive ads in particular). For ease of explanation, we discuss the *where* and *when* issues separately.

Where

The decision of where to advertise has three basic components: match to target audience, contextual fit, and duplication and wearout.

Efficient Audience Selection. Trying to match target audiences typically leads to a comparison of vehicles in terms of efficiency in reaching desirable audiences. Some measures, such as cost per thousand (CPM), become the yardstick for comparing different vehicles. CPM measures how much it costs the advertiser to reach 1,000 customers by using a particular medium. For example, using *Adweek's 1996 Major Media Directory,* the CPM for *Business Week* for a four-color print ad is $78.51, whereas for *People* it is $35.24.

Ratings and circulation data (such as Arbitron's radio audience ratings, Nielsen's TV ratings, Standard Rate and Data Services, Audit Bureau of Circulations, and Simmons's magazine audience measurements) are vital inputs to decisions and consequently are hotly contested measures. The focus should be (and increasingly is) on cost per thousand of "relevant" readers, listeners, or viewers, that is, the cost per thousand in the target market. This type of thinking is what leads to so many beer and car ads on sports shows, for example. All this said, much of the industry still relies on maximizing GRPs as a criterion for media selection.

It is important to recognize that CPM or GRP numbers may badly overstate actual ad readers or viewers. Most people do not read the many pages of ads that fill the fronts of magazines, study inserts in newspapers, or even stay in the room during TV ads (preferring instead to read, get food, go to the bathroom, sleep, etc.). Hence adjusting total audience to likely readership or viewership levels is very important. This is the reason A.C. Nielsen spends millions of dollars improving its TV viewing methodology, introducing "peoplemeters" so individuals can record when they are actually in the room viewing the TV.

One important aspect of targeting spending is product use. A number of services (e.g., Simmons's Guide to Media and Markets) rate media vehicles by product usage. Therefore, for strategies targeting heavy users of a product, cost per thousand can be weighted by product usage.

Another important aspect of a media plan is regional differentiation. Not only does product usage vary by region; so do features desired and cultural preferences. Therefore, even though regional vehicles may cost more in a CPM sense, it is often desirable to focus on certain regions (especially if your share or distribution level varies regionally) and use somewhat different messages and media by region.

Contextual Fit. Contextual fit falls into two subcategories, general media fit and program and ad context. The media level fit issues are fairly obvious: It is difficult to demonstrate operation of a machine on the radio, incorporate music or other sounds in print media, or provide detailed information that will be recalled in radio or TV ads.

A more subtle level of fit involves the context of the ad, including both the program and other ads. Product fit involves the interaction between the product image and the image of the vehicle. For example, even if professional wrestling delivers upscale viewers at a competitive CPM, does it make sense to advertise upscale products (e.g., Tiffany glass, imported fine wine) between bouts? This issue is magnified if a vehicle airs controversial topics that can lead to a backlash or even a boycott against advertisers (as the quick withdrawal of ads from controversial shows or shows with controversial spokespersons demonstrates).

The interaction of the image of the immediate context is also relevant. For example, a humorous ad may lose its effect if placed in the context of a comedy show or a series of eight other humorous ads. In a serious vehicle, it may even be perceived as tasteless. Although it is impossible to control or predict exactly what story will appear on the facing page for a print ad or exactly which other commercials will run during a particular TV commercial break, educated guesses are both possible and recommended. Competitive effects are serious when many products in the same category advertise close together, with the result that many consumers cannot distinguish the claims from one another. (We know after watching sports we should buy beer, sneakers, and cars, but we rarely remember why or which ones.)

The point of considering the two contextual fit levels is to assess the relative impact of an ad in the particular vehicle. While this discussion breaks contextual fit into two components, you can also assess it directly.

Duplication and Wearout. Depending on the goal, duplication (multiple exposures to the same ad) may be either desirable (e.g., for a subtle message, a complicated concept or benefit, or a message that is soon forgotten) or unwanted (e.g., for a simple message). Apparently competing vehicles commonly duplicate audiences; for example, tremendous overlap occurs among readers of *Fortune, Business Week,* and *Forbes.* There is also evidence that customers tire of exactly the same message fairly quickly, though less so for complex messages than simple ones. In contrast, some evidence suggests that varying copy slightly, though somewhat expensive due to the multiple executions necessary, slows down ad wearout.[20] Although the number of possible combinations of vehicles makes thorough analysis difficult (though not impossible given increased computer power), a reasonable sense can be achieved by estimating the unduplicated audience of each vehicle and, when reach is the objective, concentrating on vehicles with large unduplicated audiences.

---

[20]H. Rao Unnava and Robert E. Burnkrant, "Effects of Repeating Varied Ad Executions on Brand Name Memory," *Journal of Marketing Research* 28 (1991), pp. 406–16.

When

A number of issues involving when to advertise directly affect the evaluation of where to advertise. For example, readership and product consumption vary by season or issue and viewership or listenership by program, time of day, day of week, and so on. For this discussion, we assume most of these are accounted for in the *where* analysis and address here two more strategic issues: seasonality and spending pattern.

As discussed in other contexts earlier in the book, seasonality exists for many products, both consumer and industrial. The question of when to advertise is affected strongly by the target audience—for example, retail stores versus consumers for skis and dealers versus customers for industrial goods, because retailers and dealers make decisions well before most customers do. In addition, issues of immediate relevance (which suggests advertising during the buying season) and clutter (which may argue for off-season advertising) have an impact on timing. Alternatively, for some products such as cold remedies, a "leading" spending pattern is sometimes used that delivers messages prior to the major usage season (e.g., the cold/flu season) to get consumers to stock up on a brand and simultaneously take them out of the market for competing brands.

One issue in setting the spending pattern is when during the life cycle to advertise. One study found that advertising is more effective early in the life cycle and hence should be heaviest during introduction and growth.[21] Also important is the question of whether spending should be level throughout the relevant time period or heavily bunched in a short span of time. A number of studies suggest that an uneven spending pattern (pulsing) is more effective than a level pattern.

Overall Considerations

In addition to the complexities already discussed, decisions concerning media schedules are influenced by various pricing deals and promotions offered by the media. For example, large advertisers get a much better rate for TV than small advertisers because they buy large blocks of time "upfront," such as before the fall TV season begins. Consequently, as we mentioned earlier in the chapter, the media decision is typically left to specialists who have the best information on current rates and the negotiating ability to get the best media prices. Nonetheless, it is still sometimes useful to have a worksheet for evaluating various vehicles, as the product manager does not want to be totally left out of the process. The worksheet in Figure 11–15 has been found helpful in this regard.

Evaluating Advertising Effects

Given the amount of money spent on advertising, it is surprising how little effort is spent assessing whether or not it is working to achieve the stated objectives. Volumes have been written on topics such as copy testing with focus groups and in theater

[21] Leonard J. Parsons, "The Product Life Cycle and Time-Varying Advertising Elasticities," *Journal of Marketing Research* 12 (1975), pp. 476–80.

FIGURE 11–15 **Media Vehicle Evaluation Form**

		Contact			Impact			Effective CPM
Vehicle	Cost	Size of target audience	Duplication with other vehicles	Target CPM (T)	Impact/ product vehicle fit	Copy, context fit	Effective and impact (E)	(T)(E)

settings; however, as we discussed earlier in this chapter, these two methods tend to be used for making decisions about different copy strategies rather than for postimplementation assessment. In this section, we focus on quantitative assessment of the impact of advertising expenditures after the finished campaign has run through tracking studies, analysis of past sales and advertising, use of experiments, and a way to link advertising evaluation to objectives.

Tracking Studies

Conventional tracking studies are relatively simple surveys that ask respondents two kinds of questions. One type is "top of mind" or, more technically, unaided recall in which the respondent is asked if he or she can recall seeing an ad for the brand. For example, the respondent might be asked, "Have you seen the advertising campaign with famous actors and actresses with milk on their lips?" If the answer is *yes,* this technique follows up the question with a request to repeat the main copy points to determine comprehension. If the respondent indicates that the campaign is "Got Milk?," the campaign gets higher marks. Attitudinal questions might also be asked. The second type of survey uses aided recall: "Have you seen the 'Got Milk?' advertising campaign?" This method detects information not actively in memory that can be important when primed at point-of-purchase. Not surprisingly, the numbers produced by aided recall are much larger than those by unaided recall.

These studies then track the responses over time, often at constant time intervals, using either the same sample of respondents (called a panel) or a different, randomly selected group. The product manager can then view how awareness, comprehension, or interest builds, plateaus, or never gets off the ground. Often the percentages obtained from these studies are also compared to norms derived from previous advertising campaigns.

Tracking studies also use recognition tests. Starch uses what are called "through the book" methods. These aided recall situations show respondents a magazine (or other media vehicle). For each ad, they ask questions pertaining to whether the person had seen the ad, how much she or he had read, and so on. Tracking studies such as these tend not to ask questions about purchasing because the focus is more on objectives such as those shown in Figure 11–7.

Past Sales and Advertising

Most early studies of historical advertising effects were at the aggregate level (that is, they assessed the impact of annual budgets on annual sales). Essentially they involved

Figure 11–16 The Impact of Advertising Spending

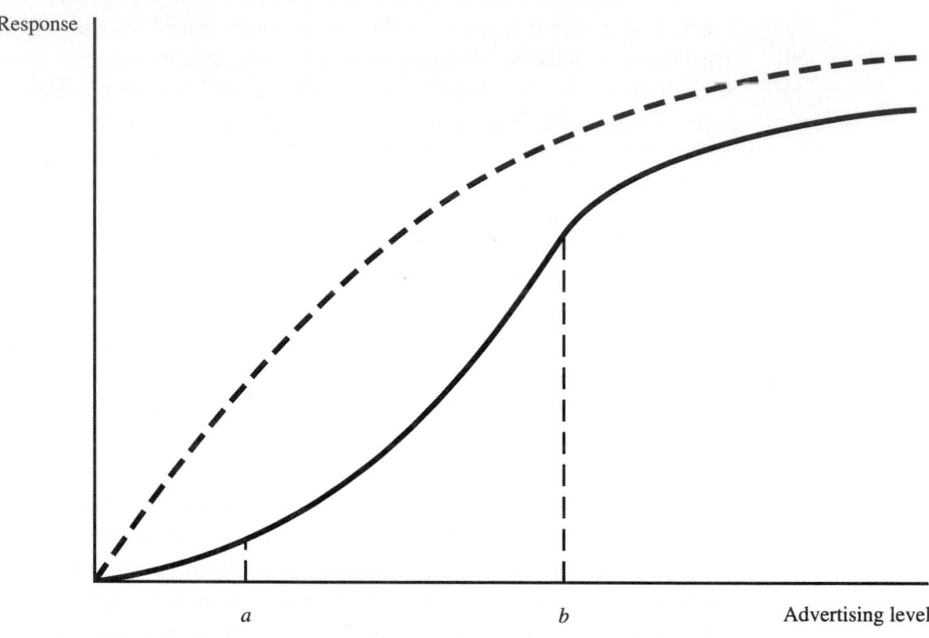

observing the relation between past advertising spending and past sales either across different geographical areas (cross-sectionally) or over different time periods. These methods continue to be used, albeit less often than the tracking studies.

Figure 11–16 shows two possible nonlinear relationships between advertising spending and market response (sales, share, etc.) The solid curve is S shaped and assumes there is an interval in which advertising delivers increasing returns: the next dollar spent is actually more effective than some previous dollars were. This occurs between points *a* and *b*. Past point *b*, advertising delivers decreasing returns. The dotted curve shows a relationship delivering decreasing returns over the whole range of advertising expenditures.

These methods involve using actual market data to assess the impact of sales on advertising: $S = f(\text{Adv})$, that is, to estimate the curves shown in Figure 11–16. Mathematically, these tend to follow three different forms:

1. Linear: $S = B_0 + B_1 \text{ Adv}$
2. Decreasing marginal returns:
   (*a*) $S = B_0 + B_1 \log(\text{Adv})$
   (*b*) $S = B_0 + B_1 \text{ Adv} - B_2 (\text{Adv})^2$
3. S shaped: $S = \exp[B_0 - B_1 \text{ Adv}]$,

where "exp" is "exponentiation," that is, raising the mathematical constant *e* to the $[B_0 - B_1 \text{ Adv}]$ power. Generally, these models are estimated using standard regression analysis programs. Though generalizations are difficult, support for the S-shaped model seems strongest.[22]

One serious problem with the previous models is that they are incomplete (technically called *misspecified*); that is, other variables that affect sales (e.g., price, quality, distribution, inertia/past sales, competition) are excluded from the model. Hence the estimates of the effects of advertising may be inaccurate (typically they are overstated) due to confounding with the effects of the other (omitted) variables. This suggests that attempts to assess the effect of advertising also need to assess simultaneously (control for) the effects of other relevant variables. For example, this converts the linear model into

$$\text{Sales} = B_0 + B_1\,\text{Adv} + B_2\,\text{Price} + B_3\,\text{Quality} + B_4\,\text{Distribution} + B_5\,\text{Past sales} + \ldots$$

Here B_5 represents the carryover effect of past sales (and hence prior advertising, etc.) on current sales. Models of this type are often referred to as *Koyck* models.

A number of studies done in this tradition have yielded some generalizable results.[23] Averaging across 128 studies, it appears the average effect (elasticity) of current advertising on current sales is about .22 (that is, a 100 percent increase in advertising leads to a 22 percent change in sales), and the carryover effect, the elasticity of impact of current advertising on future sales through the inertia effect of past sales on current sales, is about .47, indicating that the long-run impact is more important than its immediate effect. Also, small but interesting differences seem to occur across products and markets; for example, food products had slightly higher elasticities. However, other researchers suggest lower impacts for advertising. Consequently, a reasonable starting point for estimating the impact of advertising is that doubling the advertising budget (a 100 percent increase) is likely to generate between a 2 and 25 percent increase in sales, ceterus paribus.[24]

Given our earlier discussion about the investment value of advertising, it is worth describing some further results about its long-run impact. Rather than simply looking at the long-run elasticity, an interesting perspective is how long $1 of advertising lasts. Several studies have examined this issue.[25] They have found consistent evidence that 90 percent of the impact of advertising for consumer goods occurs within the first six to nine months, implying that any benefits due to "mere exposure" are gone within a year and that advertising and other communication efforts must be continually employed.

---

[22]Julian L. Simon and Johan Arndt, "The Shape of the Advertising Function," *Journal of Advertising Research* 20 (1980), pp. 11–28.

[23] Gert Assmus, John U. Farley, and Donald R. Lehmann, "How Advertising Affects Sales: Meta-Analysis of Econometric Results," *Journal of Marketing Research* 21 (1984), pp. 65–74.

[24]It should be noted that the vast majority of empirical research in this area has focused on consumer products and services. Thus, generalizing these findings to industrial products should be done with caution.

[25]The classic study is by Darral G. Clarke, "Econometric Measurement of the Duration of Advertising Effect on Sales," *Journal of Marketing Research* 13 (1976), pp. 345–57. A more recent summary of the area is by Robert P. Leone, "Generalizing What Is Known about Temporal Aggregation and Advertising Carryover," *Marketing Science* 14 (1995), pp. G141–G150.

Another weakness of these econometric models is that they ignore the effect of competition. Competition can be incorporated simply by using relative values for the predictor variables such as share of advertising, price relative to average category price, and so on. An alternative approach is to consider the following starting point, assuming a mature market with constant primary demand:

Our share = Our effort/Our effort + Sum of their efforts

Mathematically, this is typically represented by the following (logit) model:

$$\text{Market share of brand i} = \exp[B_{i0} + B_{i1}\text{ Adv} + \ldots]/\Sigma \exp[B_{j0} + B_{j1}\text{ Adv} + \ldots]$$

There is also some evidence that advertising interacts with other variables such as price. Two hypotheses suggest how advertising can affect price sensitivity. One is the *market power* hypothesis that increased levels of advertising build brand loyalty and therefore decrease price sensitivity. The other is the *advertising as information* hypothesis, which suggests that advertising provides more information about brands in a category, which consumers will then use to switch based on price and other factors; that is, advertising increases price sensitivity. Not surprisingly, the empirical evidence supports both hypotheses.[26]

This kind of analysis can be used to help set budgets as well as diagnose the effects of advertising spending. An example of the application of econometric methods to budget setting involved the General Foods powdered orange drink, Tang.[27] The model used in that application was

$$S_t = B_0 + B_1 \times L[1 - \exp^{(-bA_t)}] + B_2 P_t + B_3 S_{t-1},$$

where the dependent variable, sales, was measured over time for different sales territories; the L term shows differences in advertising effects due to distribution coverage, demographics, and existing sales levels among sales territories; P is promotion expense; and the lagged sales term shows carryover effects. The exponential advertising term creates a nonlinear response between advertising and sales with both a ceiling and a lower-bound constraint on advertising effectiveness. After estimating advertising spending effects with actual data, the parameters of the model (the Bs) were used to determine optimal spending levels of advertising.

The other main approach to estimating the impact of advertising on sales has been to use individual customer purchase data. These data have become widely available with the introduction of supermarket scanners in some categories (frequently purchased consumer goods) and are also available in many company records (e.g., utilities and phone companies). Essentially, the model forms parallel those discussed before, but the data are analyzed at the individual household (or at least segment) level. While start-up costs (e.g., getting data in good form for analysis) are high, this type of data is beginning to provide more precise estimates of the impact of advertising, especially

[26]For a good summary of the advertising-price interaction literature, see Anusree Mitra and John J. Lynch, Jr., "Toward a Reconciliation of Market Power and Information Theories of Advertising Effects on Price Elasticity," *Journal of Consumer Research* 21 (1995), pp. 644–59.

[27] F. Stewart DeBruicker, "General Foods Corporation: Tang Instant Breakfast Drink (A)," Harvard Business School case study 9-575-063, 1974.

when "single-source" data, data that also have advertising exposure at the individual level, are used.[28]

An analysis based on IRI scanner data suggests that advertising alone is fairly ineffective in influencing short-term sales unless the advertising conveys new information or benefits.[29] Figure 11–17 summarizes the results.

Experimentation

In addition to its use in setting budgets and evaluating potential advertising copy described earlier in this chapter, experimentation as a means of assessing advertising effectiveness has a long tradition in marketing. Early examples involved examining different advertising timing policies[30] and alternative amounts of advertising spending.[31] Unfortunately, field experiments—using real products in an actual setting—are costly and time consuming. Field experiments involve manipulating different levels of marketing variables in different sales territories, different stores, or to different groups of customers for an extended period of time to detect any effects of the manipulated variable. Moreover, field experiments are politically difficult, for although it is easy to get a regional manager to accept an increased advertising budget (or price cut), it is hard to obtain acceptance for a cut in advertising (or an increase in price), both at the regional and corporate levels.[32]

A popular testing vehicle for advertising is IRI's BehaviorScan markets, which use a split-cable, TV-type design described earlier in the chapter. A comprehensive analysis of 389 split-cable experiments found that the average elasticity for new products was higher than for established products, .26 versus .05. The researchers also found that an examination of successful advertising weight (i.e., spending) tests showed that about two-thirds of the original increase persisted in the year after advertising returned to normal levels and one-third persisted into the second year. They also found that most of the increase was due to increased purchases of the product per household (the purchase rate) rather than an increase in the percentage of households that buy the product (the penetration rate), suggesting that the advertising served to remind or encourage consumers to do something they were already inclined to do.[33]

---

[28]Two examples of single-source advertising studies are Gerard J. Tellis, "Advertising Exposure, Loyalty, and Brand Purchase: A Two-Stage Model of Choice, *Journal of Marketing Research* 25 (1988), pp. 134–44, and Russell S. Winer, "Using Single-Source Scanner Data as a Natural Experiment for Evaluating Advertising Effects," *Journal of Marketing Science* (Japan), 2 (1993), pp. 15–31.

[29]Magid M. Abraham and Leonard Lodish, "Getting the Most out of Advertising and Promotion," *Harvard Business Review* 68 (1990), pp. 50–60.

[30]Hubert A. Zielske, "The Remembering and Forgetting of Advertising," *Journal of Marketing* 23 (1959), pp. 239–43.

[31]Russell Ackoff and James R. Emshoff, "Advertising Research at Anheuser-Busch," *Sloan Management Review,* Winter 1975, pp. 1–15.

[32]There has been an upward trend in experimentation in general, however, in marketing and production contexts. See Rita Koselka, "The New Mantra: MVT," *Forbes,* March 11, 1996, pp. 114–17.

[33]Leonard M. Lodish, Magid Abraham, Stuart Kalmenson, Jeanne Livelsberger, Beth Lubetkin, Bruce Richardson, and Mary Ellen Stevens, "How T.V. Advertising Works: A Meta-Analysis of 389 Real World Split Cable T.V. Advertising Experiments," *Journal of Marketing Research* 32 (1995), pp. 125–39.

Figure 11–17 How Advertising "Works": Evidence from Scanner Data

Management Summary

1. **TV advertising weight alone is not enough.** There is no simple correspondence between increased advertising weight and increased sales
2. **The status quo is not enough.** TV advertising is more likely to work when there are changes in:
   - **Brand/copy strategy**
     An increase in sales effect is more likely when the brand's objective is to increase penetration, where copy strategy is new, where copy used is introductory in nature, or when copy is intended to change attitudes.
   - **Media strategy**
     Advertising plans which include an expansion of the target audience or a shift in emphasis have a better chance of generating sales increases.
   - **Category dynamics**
     Brands in categories in a growth mode or in categories with more purchase opportunities are more likely to be able to improve sales through increased TV advertising weight.
3. **TV advertising can have a significant long-term impact on sales.** When increased advertising has been successful, the cumulative incremental effect over the year in which the higher weight was delivered plus the following two years is twice that of the first year. This increase in sales is driven primarily by buying rate. That is, the brand's buyers purchase more or more often.
4. **When evaluating TV advertising response, more attention should be paid to absolute measures of volume change versus sole reliance on relative "percentage" change.** It is easier for medium to smaller size brands than for larger brands to achieve higher percentage increases in sales or share corresponding to changes in copy or increased weight. Evaluations of sales impact should thus be measured in absolute terms as well as in relative terms.
5. **Common beliefs regarding the impact of promotions on the effectiveness of TV advertising are supported by this study.** Higher levels of trade dealing appear to correspond with a reduction in the ability of TV advertising to positively affect sales. However, higher levels of couponing appear to correspond with an increase in the ability of TV advertising to positively affect sales.
6. **It is very unlikely that there is a strong relationship between standard measures of TV commercial recall and persuasion for established brands and the sales impact of the copy.** An examination of copy test scores, both recall and persuasion, shows that the relationship between scores and success at generating increased sales is tenuous at best. (The statistical significance of the relationship that was found in this study depended on one or two observations.)
7. **New brands/line extensions tend to be more responsive to alternative TV advertising plans than established products.** Among new brands/line extensions, 58% of increased weight plans resulted in stronger sales, compared with 46% for established brands. Similarly, 70% of new brand copy tests generated higher sales for one copy versus another, compared with 31% for established brands.
8. **These data support the importance of introductory weight and prime time for new products.** Higher boosts in prime time TV advertising correspond to larger increases in sales for new products. A heavy-up plan which is proportionately less front loaded than the base plan results in a reduced likelihood of increased sales.
9. **Concentration of higher TV advertising weight is related to increases in brand sales.** Weight added to either the front or back end of a media plan is more likely to result in higher sales than the same cumulative level of increased weight distributed throughout the plan. Fewer weeks added to the heavy plan is also related to stronger sales.

Source: Magid M. Abraham and Leonard Lodish, "Fact-Based Strategies for Managing Advertising and Promotion Dollars," *How Advertising Works,* vol. 1, (Chicago, Ill. Information Resources, Inc.), 1991.

FIGURE 11–18 From Objectives to Incremental Contribution

Example: Luxury Sports Sedan			
Changes in perceptions		6.7%	
Impact on consideration	× 1.5	10.0%	Increase in consideration
Conversion to showroom visits	× 0.5	5.0%	Increased probability of showroom visit
Closing rate on showroom visits	× 0.10	0.5%	Increased probability of purchase
Size of segment	× 500,000	2,500	Incremental cars sold
Marginal contribution per car	× $5,000	$12.5m	Net incremental contribution from advertising to segment

Linking Objectives to Incremental Contribution

A financially oriented approach to evaluating advertising effectiveness attempts to draw a direct link from the advertising objectives to the (hopefully) increased contribution resulting from the advertising.[34] An illustration of the approach for a luxury sports sedan appears in Figure 11–18. It assumes the product manager has set quantitative, measurable objectives for the advertising. Suppose the product manager has set goals of a 10 percent improvement in the perception of style, 5 percent in performance, and 5 percent in sportiness, for an average improvement of 6.7 percent over the three dimensions. Prior research has shown that there is a multiplier of 1.5 from perception improvement to increase in the number of buyers who will consider buying the car, hence the 10 percent increase in consideration. Also, experience tells us that 50 percent of the increase in consideration actually results in a showroom visit and 10 percent of those cases result in a sale (these assumptions can be continually monitored in the marketplace). Thus, the advertising has increased probability of purchase 0.5 percent. If the segment size is 500,000 people and the profit contribution per car is $5,000, the incremental contribution from the advertising is $12.5 million. This figure can then be compared to the cost of the advertising for evaluation purposes.

Advertising Agency Compensation Decisions

Traditionally, advertising agencies were compensated based on a straight 15 percent commission on billed media used in running the campaign. Thus, if the product had a $10 million campaign on TV and in magazines, the advertising agency received $1.5 million. Product managers, usually in conjunction with senior marketing personnel, often control the amount of money paid to the agency.

However, although simple to administer, this system has a number of drawbacks that have led many advertisers to switch to some other system. Clearly, other than facing the possibility of losing the account (i.e., fear), the agency has no incentive to

[34]Eechembadi, "Does Advertising Work?"

FIGURE 11–19 Advertising Strategy Summary

	General Description	Specific Targeting Characteristics (e.g., demographics)
1. Target audience		
Primary		
Secondary		
2. Operational objectives		
Impact		
Exposure		
3. Message/copy		
Primary		
Secondary		

achieve superior results measured against objectives under flat-rate method. There is also a clear incentive for agencies to recommend expensive media to clients. From the agencies' side, during recessionary periods it is not uncommon for product managers to pull a campaign for financial reasons. However, the advertising agency has already invested time and money in producing the advertising. Under the traditional compensation system, cutting the budget directly reduces advertising agency income.

As a result of these difficulties with the straight 15 percent commission system, a 1995 survey showed it is now the fourth most preferred system (from number one in 1992) behind commission structures paying less than 15 percent, preset fees, and performance-based fees.[35] As an example of a hybrid system, Cheesebrough-Pond's, a subsidiary of Unilever, awards a base commission rate of 13.25 percent on media billings that can rise to as high as 16.5 percent upon meeting mutually agreed-upon objectives for the advertising.

Summary

In this chapter, we delineated advertising decisions to be made, provided a set of worksheets to facilitate the process, and suggested what we have learned about the effects of advertising. Having developed the advertising plan, it is important to concisely summarize it. Here we suggest three summary charts.

The first chart, Figure 11–19, succinctly summarizes the general strategy in three parts. It defines the target audience (both primary and, when applicable, secondary), both generally (e.g., children) and in terms of specific descriptors used for selecting among media vehicles (e.g., children age 11 to 14 in homes with over $20,000 per year annual income). It specifies operational goals in terms of impact (e.g., increase awareness from 20 to 40 percent) and exposure (reach 80 percent of the target

[35]Mary Kuntz, "Now Mad Ave Realy Has to Sing for Its Supper," *Business Week,* December 18, 1995, p. 43.

FIGURE 11–20 Advertising Spending Plan and Budget

Media Category	*Specific Vehicles and Frequency*	*Production and Testing Budget*	*Space/Time Budget*	*Total Budget*
Newspaper				
National				
Regional/local				
Magazine				
National				
Regional/local				
TV				
Network				
Spot				
Regional/local				
Radio				
Network				
Regional/local				
Other				
(Billboard)				
Public relations				
Research and monitoring				

FIGURE 11–21 Detailed Monthly Advertising Spending Plan: Production and Placement

	January		**February**		. . .
Media Category	*Ads*	*Cost*	*Ads*	*Cost*	
Newspaper					
National					
Regional/local					
Magazine					
National					
Regional/local					
TV					
Network					
Spot					
Regional/local					
Radio					
Network					
Regional/local					
Other					
(Billboard)					

audience at least three times from January through March). Finally, it states the basic message (selling point in terms of benefit).

The second chart, Figure 11–20, summarizes the spending plan. Basically, it divides the budget among the costs of the media vehicles selected plus production and testing. Production costs vary widely depending on, among other things, the use of a celebrity endorser, the length of the ad (e.g., quarter page, full page, multiple page; 15 seconds, 30 seconds, 60 seconds in TV), and the general slickness of the presentation. Similarly, testing costs vary depending on the sample used (size, ease of locating), what is asked of respondents, and sampling method. The main point here is that the spending plan should include adequate resources to conduct production and testing well *and* allow for the time needed to accomplish these activities.

The third chart, Figure 11–21, provides a timetable detailing when spending will occur. This chart also provides a standard against which to compare actual spending throughout the year. Remember that production is not instantaneous; for example, TV ads often require four to six months to prepare and finalize.

Of course, a number of parties need to approve an advertising budget, including divisional and corporate managers, engineering/R&D, and the legal department. Moreover, as the year unfolds, various events may (and often do) occur that lead to a revision of the plan. Thus, the advertising plans developed, like any other plans, need to be viewed as something to be sold internally and modified as needed rather than something to be inflexibly implemented.

C H A P T E R

12 Promotion Decisions

Overview

Sales promotion (hereafter referred to as *promotion*) consists of a collection of devices aimed at generating active customer response within a short period of time. It is a topic that has generated a large amount of discussion and literature, including several books.[1] Moreover, as Figure 12–1 shows, it has been receiving an increasingly large share of the advertising/promotion budget, particularly for promotions oriented toward the trade (distribution channels). One study reported that 25 percent of sales time and 30 percent of brand management time are spent on promotions.[2]

At the same time, the use of promotions is a hotly debated topic. For example, Procter & Gamble is attempting to reduce its use of coupons due to their inefficiency

Figure 12–1 Changes in Advertising and Promotion Spending*

	1981	*1986*	*1991*	*1994*
Advertising	43%	34%	25%	26%
Consumer promotion	23	26	25	25
Trade promotion	34	40	50	49

*Expressed as percentages of the total amount of dollars spend on advertising and promotion.
Sources: "Category Management: Marketing for the 90's," *Marketing News,* September 14, 1992; Donnelly Marketing Inc., *17th Annual Survey of Promotional Practice,* 1995.

[1]See, for example, Robert C. Blattberg and Scott A. Neslin, *Sales Promotion: Concepts, Methods, and Strategies* (Englewood Cliffs, N.J.: Prentice Hall, 1990), and John C. Totten and Martin P. Block, *Analyzing Sales Promotion,* 2nd ed. (Chicago: The Dartnell Corporation, 1994).

[2]Robert D. Buzzell, John A. Quelch, and Walter J. Salmon, "The Costly Bargain of Sales Promotion," *Harvard Business Review* 68 (March–April 1990), pp. 141–49.

FIGURE 12–2 IRI Data on Instant Coffee Purchasing

Brands purchaed by 0.5% or More of All Households	Category Volume Share	Type Volume Share	% of Households Buying	Volume per Purchase	Purchase per Buyer	Purchase Cycle (days)
Category—coffee	5,647.4*	100.0%	76.1%	1.1	6.9	60
Type—soluble	9.6	100.0	31.9	0.5	3.5	81
Flavored	5.1	53.2	17.9	0.5	3.3	76
Nestlé S.A. (Switzerland)	0.7	7.7	5.6	0.4	1.9	84
Nescafé	0.2	2.5	3.0	0.3	1.5	72
Nescafé Mountain Blend	0.2	2.6	1.4	0.5	2.2	87
Tasters Choice	0.1	0.7	1.3	0.2	1.5	88
Philip Morris Co. Inc.	4.2	43.0	14.3	0.5	3.2	75
General Foods International Coffee	3.1	32.2	9.0	0.6	3.2	71
Maxwell House	1.0	10.8	7.2	0.3	2.5	75
Caffeinated	3.2	33.1	13.9	0.5	2.8	82
Nestlé S.A. (Switzerland)	0.5	5.3	2.7	0.5	2.0	85
Nescafé Classic	0.5	5.2	2.5	0.5	2.1	85
Philip Morris Co. Inc.	0.8	8.5	3.5	0.5	2.6	81
Maxwell House	0.8	8.5	3.4	0.5	2.6	81
Procter & Gamble	1.4	14.1	7.3	0.4	2.4	83
Folgers	1.4	14.1	7.3	0.4	2.4	83
Private Label	0.4	3.9	2.5	0.4	2.3	79
Private Label	0.4	3.9	2.5	0.4	2.3	79
Decaffeinated	1.3	13.7	6.8	0.5	2.4	90
Nestlé S.A. (Switzerland)	0.2	1.9	1.3	0.5	1.7	102
Nescafé Decaf	0.1	1.1	0.8	0.5	1.5	125
Philip Morris Co. Inc.	0.5	5.5	2.2	0.5	2.6	91
Sanka	0.5	5.2	2.1	0.5	2.6	91
Procter & Gamble	0.6	6.2	3.9	0.4	2.0	83
Folgers	0.6	6.2	3.9	0.4	2.0	83

(only 2 percent are redeemed) and costs of printing, distribution, and processing.[3] Similarly, Heinz, is attempting to reduce its dependence on price-focused communications activities (e.g., trade-oriented promotion), and make greater investment in advertising.[4] In general, Figure 12–1 shows that promotion expenditures are about three times greater than expenditures for advertising (mainly for consumer packaged goods) and since few studies have shown any long-term effects of promotions, it is no surprise that product managers are beginning to take a harder look at sales promotion and wondering how much to spend.

To give the reader an idea of how strongly promotions affect consumer behavior, Figure 12–2 displays some descriptive data for the soluble (instant) coffee category.

[3]Zachary Schiller, "First, Green Stamps. Now, Coupons?" *Business Week,* April 22, 1996, p. 68.

[4]Betsy Spethmann, "Heinz Moves to Balance Ads vs. Trade Spending," *Brandweek,* June 26, 1995, p. 3.

		% Volume with the Specified Deal						Average % Off on Price Deals
Share Category Requirements	Price Per Volume	Any Trade Deal	Print Ad Feature	In-Store Display	Shelf Price Reduction	Store Coupon	Manufacturer Coupon	
100%	3.75	42%	20%	17%	31%	3%	18%	24%
27	7.91	18	6	3	14	1	25	23
22	6.90	18	4	4	13	1	31	27
11	7.84	18	2	1	18	0	26	29
6	6.39	19	3	3	17	0	36	38
17	8.62	19	1	0	19	0	25	19
5	18.23	12	1	0	12	0	62	23
21	6.68	18	5	4	13	1	33	26
25	6.29	17	5	5	11	1	32	23
10	7.82	23	4	3	18	1	37	30
23	8.76	22	11	4	16	1	15	18
17	7.50	39	27	13	26	4	31	23
17	7.50	40	27	13	26	4	31	23
24	8.22	27	13	5	20	1	25	16
24	8.22	27	13	5	20	1	25	16
19	9.39	16	7	1	12	1	8	16
19	9.39	16	7	1	12	1	8	16
13	7.96	12	2	0	11	2	1	16
13	7.96	12	2	0	11	2	1	16
20	9.75	13	5	1	11	1	29	17
13	9.27	12	7	5	7	5	21	21
12	9.34	16	12	8	8	9	36	22
26	9.41	14	8	1	11	1	46	16
26	9.40	15	8	1	12	1	47	16
16	10.19	12	2	0	12	0	17	17
16	10.19	12	2	0	12	0	17	17

Data reflect grocery store purchases only.
*Category volume per 1,000 households.
Source: Marketing Fact Book, 1994 edition.

The data are from IRI's 1994 edition of *The Marketing Fact Book,* which represents purchases of 35,000 households in supermarkets where the products' UPCs (Universal Product Codes) are electronically scanned. The column definitions are as follows:

Category Volume Share: share of all coffee sales.

Type Volume Share: share of subcategory (e.g., flavored, caffeinated).

% of Households Buying: percentage of all households that purchased the category at least once during the period.

Volume per Purchase: average volume purchased on a single purchase occasion in pounds.

Purchases per Buyer: average number of times the item was purchased by each buyer.

Purchase Cycle: average interpurchase time in days between purchases of the item.

Share of Category Requirements: total proportion of category volume that the item represents among its buyers (a measure of brand loyalty).

Price per Volume: average price paid per equivalent volume (not necessarily the price per unit or package).

Any Trade Deal: percentage of volume purchased using an advertising feature (newspaper), in-store display, shelf price reduction, store coupon, manufacturer coupon, or a combination of these.

Average percent off on price deals: the average percentage price reduction obtained by the consumer when a price deal is used.

What is notable about the data in Figure 12–2 are the percentages of purchases made with some kind of promotion. Overall (the top row of the figure), 31 percent of all coffee purchases are made with some shelf price reduction, 18 percent use a manufacturer coupon, and the average price reduction is 24 percent. Interestingly, a whopping 62 percent of purchases of Tasters Choice flavored instant coffees are made with a Nestlé coupon. Also, Maxwell House uses trade deals and coupons much more than Folgers in the caffeinated subcategory; 27 percent of Maxwell House purchases are made using some kind of trade deal, and 25 percent are made using a coupon.

One way to think of promotion is to contrast it with advertising while recognizing that there is strong evidence of a synergistic effect between advertising and promotion. Not only does promotion compete with advertising for budget; it also provides a different approach to influencing sales. In the case of advertising, the basic approach is to create or increase a desire on the part of the customer for the product itself. In contrast, most promotions implicitly assume the level of desire for the product is fixed and try to "close the deal" by providing incentives to purchase. This is, of course, an oversimplification. A "get them while supplies last" ad focuses on immediate response, and promotions involving free samples aim at generating repeat business. Nonetheless, promotions, many of which involve temporary price reductions, are seen as a more aggressive and immediate results–oriented form of marketing effort. In reality, one of the few ways product managers can obtain a short-run change in sales or market share is to use sales promotion activities.

Figure 12–3 shows a simplified channel structure in which the manufacturer sells to a channel (here a retailer), which in turn sells to the final customer (the consumer). In this situation, promotion falls into three categories:

1. Customer promotion.
2. Promotion to the channels, or trade promotion.
3. Channel-originated promotion, or retailer promotion.

We do not discuss promotion targeted toward the company's own sales force, such as sales contests and other incentives.

Customer promotion comes directly to the customer from the manufacturer. Trade promotion, in contrast, is directed at intermediate channels of distribution in an attempt both to get them to buy more of a product and to commit their own efforts (e.g., sales

FIGURE 12–3 Simplified Channel and Promotion Structure

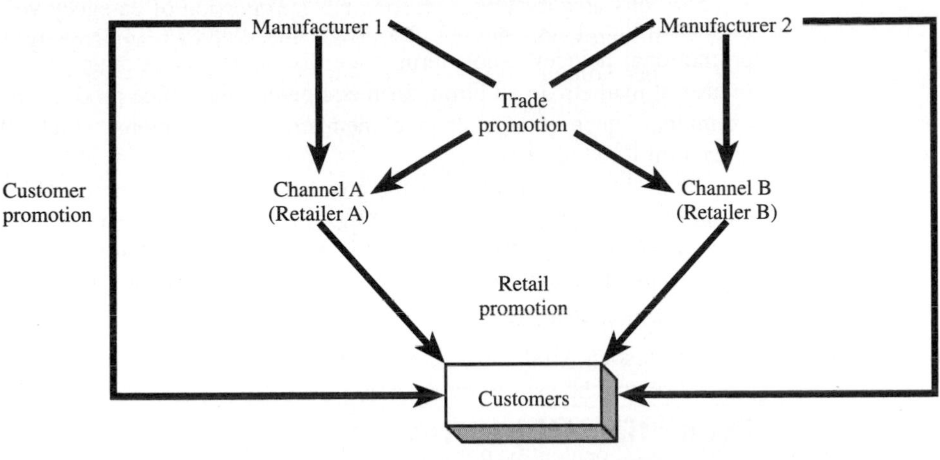

force) to "pushing" the product through the next channel and ultimately to the consumer. Channel-originated promotions are run by the channel itself to either the next channel in the distribution chain or to final customers.

Channel-originated promotions are clearly an important part of the market. For consumer packaged goods sold through supermarkets, retailer promotions are an especially visible form of promotion. Displays, feature advertising, and price deals (price cuts, free merchandise, retailer-issued coupons) all affect sales and profits and either augment or detract from manufacturers' direct customer promotions. In general, the purpose of channel promotions is to increase sales of all products to the customer. Hence a promotion of Pepsi by a retail store may be to increase store traffic and total sales or profits and not to increase Pepsi sales alone (e.g., in Figure 12–3, a promotion by retailer A is designed to increase store sales and profits, typically at the expense of retailer B). However, a manufacturer may have limited (or no) control over retail promotions; in fact, in the United States, retailers of consumer goods now have considerable control over manufacturers' trade promotions. Therefore, this chapter focuses on promotions, both direct and trade, that originate with the manufacturer while recognizing that a major goal of trade promotion is to stimulate channel-originated promotion. This focus is also consistent with a product management perspective.

Promotion objectives and programs may be either *offensive* or *defensive.* Offensive promotions attempt to gain an advantage through exclusivity: being the only company to offer a particular promotion or level of promotional support. In most markets, however, competitors are fairly quick to match (provide defensive) promotions (e.g., airline frequent flyer programs). On top of that, in some areas, notably consumer packaged goods, the channels have become sufficiently powerful to both demand and schedule promotions. The result is that companies, including those with household brand names and dominant market shares, are promoting due more to a perceived necessity to match competition and satisfy the channels than to a conviction that promotions benefit the manufacturer.

Although many of the examples and references in this chapter apply to consumer products, the reader should not infer that industrial products do not use sales promotional devices. Short-term price discounts to customers are very common in industrial markets. In addition, farm equipment and office products manufacturers, for example, frequently target channel members for promotions, which may or may not be passed on to the customers.

As in the previous chapter, the goal here is to decide on the best combinations of consumer and trade promotions. Operationally, this means producing versions of Figures 11–19, 11–20, and 11–21 that provide budget and time schedules for promotions. This chapter will make filling out these tables easier and the implied decisions more effective.

Promotion Objectives

Consumer Promotions

As we noted earlier, promotion typically takes the short-run view. Even when the focus is long run, such as to generate repeat business from trial customers based on satisfaction with product performance, the operational objective of most promotion is to generate immediate response in the form of sales. Recall the possible advertising objectives given in Figure 11–7. These objectives range from generating awareness to increasing product understanding to improving attitude toward purchase. In principle, promotion can be directed toward any of these goals as well as to those shown in Figure 12–4.

In addition, the product manager can view the objectives shown in Figure 12–4 as "problems" to be solved. Hence these objectives can be used as guides for decisions the product manager must make.

For example, if awareness is a problem, a company can run a promotion such as a game or sweepstakes designed to increase awareness of a product rather than to increase immediate sales. Similarly, a company can run a tie-in promotion (e.g., giving a certain percentage of sales revenues to a worthy cause) that may, in addition to raising current sales, have a residual positive impact on brand image. Such relationship-building motives, however, account for only a small percentage of the promotion dollar.

By far the most common objective of a consumer promotion is a short-run (transactional) goal: to generate more transactions (sales) in a short period of time. The objective is usually stated in specific terms, such as "to increase sales 20 percent in the March–April time period." This statement should be qualified in two ways. First, we need to specify from what level sales should increase. The easiest benchmark is last year or last period; the more difficult measure, but one from which the true success of the program should be gauged, is what sales would be absent the promotion. Later in the chapter we address building baselines against which to evaluate promotion. Second, we must select the target customer and define desired behavior. Basically, you

FIGURE 12–4 Customer Promotion Objectives

Objective	*Typical Programming*
I. Short-run (transactional)	
A. Current customers	
1. Buy more	Volume discount/special "value" packages
2. Be more loyal	"In pak" coupons, premiums
3. Buy now	Rebates, coupons
B. Occasional customers (deal prone; brand switchers)	
Capture next purchase	Coupons, displays, rebates
C. Noncustomers	
Trial	Trial sizes, sampling
II. Long-run (relationship building)	
A. Awareness enhancement	Sweepstakes, contests, tie-ins
B. Image enhancement	Sponsorships

can focus on getting current customers to buy more (customer expansion), capturing occasional but not loyal customers (customer retention), or generating sales from current noncustomers (customer acquisition). Many promotions focus on current customers, attempting to get them to buy more through a volume discount, to be more loyal (using coupons or frequent user programs), or to accelerate their purchases and buy sooner (rebate-type promotions). Attracting occasional customers, typically through temporary price cuts such as coupons and rebates, is effective but also expensive. This not only produces lower margins on the sales to occasional customers but may also lower margins on sales that would have been made in the absence of the promotion to either occasional or regular customers. Hence a major concern is how to target promotions to competitors' customers alone. Promotions to noncustomers are generally used when a product is new (or "new and improved") to generate trial. In a sense, targeting noncustomers implies a long-run relationship-building objective. In addition to their sales-generating role, selectively distributed promotions provide a legal means of price discrimination. Special airline fares requiring Saturday night stayovers are designed to lure pleasure travelers with the lower fares and exclude business travelers, who then pay a higher fare. Special coupons may act as price discriminators as much as sales promoters, which we discuss further later in the chapter. Different sale prices can be offered to target groups in catalogs based on their past purchasing behavior.[5]

[5]Interestingly, this ability to price discriminate though direct-mail pieces such as catalogs is being challenged. In 1996, several recipients of Victoria's Secret catalogs noticed they were being offered different discounts on merchandise and filed a lawsuit. At the time this book was being written, the case had not been decided, but legal experts opined that as long as Victoria's Secret was not discriminating on the basis of sex, race, and other groups protected by U.S. law, the case had little substance.

FIGURE 12–5 Trade Promotion Objectives

Objective	*Typical Programs*
Transactional: increase stocking levels	Volume allowances Financing terms Discounts/price cuts Slotting allowances
Transactional: increase sales efforts	Advertising allowances Display allowances Premiums Contests Sales force incentives (not all dealers allow these)
Relationship building	Free goods

Trade Promotions

The objectives of trade promotions basically fall into three main categories (Figure 12–5). The first category focuses on getting the trade to buy or stock the product in greater quantities by offering various financial incentives. The second category tries to increase the level of trade support given to the product by means other than increasing their inventories. A variety of allowances and direct incentives relate to this task. The final set of objectives involves relationship building, a longer-term objective. One example of relationship building is to give extra product to a channel with no explicit strings attached.

An interesting study examined the reasons for conducting trade and consumer promotions.[6] The survey contacted 65 brand managers, and then average importance ratings on 10-point scales were calculated. The results, shown in Figure 12–6, show that introduction of a new product was, not surprisingly, the most important reason, and neither reducing inventories nor collecting market research information was at all important.

Promotion Budgeting

Overview

Deciding on a promotion budget generally follows the same approaches discussed for setting advertising budgets (see Chapter 11). Again, the major distinction is between analytical methods (e.g., objective and task, optimization) and convenient rules of thumb (e.g., percentage of sales, competitive parity). However, two questions must be considered: (1) How much money should be spent on the total advertising and promotion budget, and (2) given the answer to the first question, how much should be spent on promotion?

[6]Chakravarti Narasimhan, "Managerial Perspectives on Trade and Consumer Promotions," *Marketing Letters* 1 (Novermber 1990), pp. 239–51.

FIGURE 12–6 Survey Results: Why Trade and Consumer Promotions Are Used

Importance Ratings: Trade Promotions*		
Variable	*Mean (standard deviation)*	*Rank*
1. Introducing a new product	8.16 (2.43)	1
2. Getting more retailer push	7.92 (1.98)	2
3. Achieving sales/contribution targets	7.58 (2.08)	3
4. Maintain shelf space	6.98 (2.50)	4
5. Meeting competition	6.78 (2.23)	5
6. Increasing consumer usage rate	6.53 (2.65)	6
7. Motivating the sales force	6.02 (2.21)	7
8. Reduce inventory	3.56 (2.43)	8

Importance Ratings: Consumer Promotions†		
Variable	*Mean (standard deviation)*	*Rank*
1. Introducing a new product	8.86 (1.83)	1
2. Increasing sales	8.12 (2.03)	2
3. Inducing brand switching	8.02 (1.68)	3
4. Increasing consumer usage rate	6.68 (2.72)	4
5. Achieving sales/contribution targets	6.51 (2.39)	5
6. Lower price to more price-sensitive consumers	6.50 (2.31)	6
7. Retaining loyal consumers	6.29 (2.34)	7
8. Meeting competition	6.28 (2.25)	8
9. Expanding category volume	4.60 (2.54)	9
10. Increasing total shelf space	4.35 (2.70)	10
11. Conducting marketing research	2.75 (1.98)	11

**N* = 64
†*N* = 65
Source: Chakravarti Narasimhan, "Managerial Perspectives on Trade and Consumer Promotions," *Marketing Letters* 1 (November 1990), p. 241.

The Advertising and Promotion Budget

Seven factors have been found to affect the total budget for advertising and sales promotion for manufactured products.[7] Companies spend more on advertising and promotion relative to sales when

1. The product is relatively standardized (as opposed to when the product is produced or supplied to order).
2. There are many end users.
3. The typical purchase amount is small.
4. Sales are made through channel intermediaries rather than directly to end users.
5. The product is premium priced.

[7]Paul W. Farris and Robert D. Buzzell, "Why Advertising and Promotional Costs Vary: Some Cross-Sectional Analyses," *Journal of Marketing* 43 (Fall 1979), pp. 112–22.

6. The product has a high contribution margin.
7. The product or service has a small market share.

Note that most of these conditions, mainly 1 through 4, are consistent with the data shown in Figure 11–3, which indicate that the managers of consumer products and services spend much more money on advertising and promotion than do their counterparts managing business-to-business products and services.

Allocating Money between Advertising and Promotion

The second important question is how to allocate dollars between advertising and sales promotion. In organizations in which the overall marketing budget is set rather than specific amounts for either advertising or promotion (or other expenditures), this may be the most important question to ask.

Several factors affect this allocation decision. First, the total amount of resources (budget) available has a major impact. If the marketing budget is small, major media advertising is usually not worthwhile unless the target market is local and can be reached by media such as radio and newspapers, because advertising usually needs a minimum or threshold amount to make any impact at all. Beneath the threshold value, the money is virtually wasted. In such cases, spending the budget on sales promotion results in a greater market impact than advertising.

Second, customer factors affect allocation decisions. Knowing the behavior of customers can give valuable insights about whether advertising or promotion makes more sense. One relevant aspect of customer behavior is the degree of brand loyalty customers exhibit. Clearly, promotion money spent on a product or service exhibiting high levels of loyalty rewards primarily existing customers. Although this may be what the product manager wants, it is usually not the best way to spend the money. If customers are not very loyal, the product manager should try to understand if their behavior is endemic to the category; if so, there may be an opportunity to attract brand switchers with promotions. It is also possible, however, that the product manager has created nonloyal customers through frequent, price-based promotions, and thus all that happens is a temporary swapping of customers.

A second relevant aspect of consumer behavior is the type of decision required of them. If the product is complex and therefore requires a fair amount of information processing, more dollars should be spent on advertising because it is a better communications device. Alternatively, most sales promotion dollars are spent on product categories in which decision making is routine and involves little processing of information about the product.

The third factor affecting allocation decisions is whether advertising and promotion dollars highlight the unique aspects of the product, *consumer franchise building* or CFB aspects.[8] CFB activities are those that build brand equity, including advertising, sampling, couponing, and product demonstrations. Non-CFB activities focus on price

[8]Robert M. Prentice, "How to Split Your Marketing Funds between Advertising and Promotion," *Advertising Age,* January 10, 1977, p. 41.

FIGURE 12–7 Consumer Promotions

I. Product based
  A. Additional volume/bonus pack
  B. Samples
    1. Central location
    2. Direct (e.g., mail)
    3. Attachment (in-/on-pack coupons)
    4. Media placed (clip-and-send coupons)
II. Price based
  A. Sale price
  B. Coupons
    1. Central location (e.g., in-store)
    2. Direct (mail)
    3. Attachment (in-/on-pack)
    4. In media
  C. Refunds/rebates
  D. Financing terms
  E. Frequent users
III. Premiums
IV. Place-based promotion (displays)
V. Games (sweepstakes, contests)

alone and include trade promotions, short-term price deals, and refunds. This approach warns the product manager to track the following ratio:

$$\text{CFB ratio} = \text{CFB \$/CFB \$} + \text{Non-CFB \$}.$$

The rule of thumb is that the CFB ratio should stay above 50 to 55 percent for the brand to remain healthy.

Types of Customer Promotions

Deciding on which promotion elements to employ is more difficult than promotion budgeting, and in many ways it parallels the media selection process in advertising. Although we discuss promotion evaluation later in this chapter, basically the product manager should attempt to calculate the return (i.e., incremental sales and profits) from various options and then select those with the biggest "bang for the buck."

This section briefly describes several types of customer promotions. The number of different promotions is limited only by the promoter's imagination. Nonetheless, it is possible to classify most customer promotions into five main categories (see Figure 12–7).

Product-Based Promotions

One obvious category of promotions is to give away the product itself. Extra volume packages are common in consumer products (e.g., "get a sixth candy bar free"). Even more dramatic are completely free products. One year Ford reportedly placed certificates good for one free month's use of a car under chairs at business meetings; of those who used the certificate, 25 percent ended up buying the car. In 1992, Pepsi planned to ship 1 million cases of Diet Pepsi to confirmed Diet Coke drinkers. Coupons for free goods show up in the mail, on or in packages of the good, or in media vehicles (e.g., newspapers, magazines). Computer hardware and software companies often give free copies of their products to select customers as "beta" test sites to help get any bugs out and stimulate (hopefully favorable) early word of mouth.

Sampling has the obvious benefit of stimulating product trial because it gives the customer the opportunity to try the product for free. However, it does have some serious shortcomings. First, it is very expensive. Second, it may not target the right potential customers; people who distribute free samples in supermarkets or on street corners are not very discriminating about to whom they give the product. (The Gatorade and Power Bars consumed at the conclusion of road races rarely go to nonusers.) This is particularly a problem for tobacco companies because trial packs could be given illegally to teenagers under 18 years old.

Price-Based Promotions

Another obvious (given the impact on margins) type of promotion involves price. The use of sale prices is understated if we describe them as being "widespread." As Figure 12–2 shows, 31 percent of the purchases in the coffee category in 1994 were accompanied by a shelf price reduction. Unfortunately, most short-term price reductions are not narrowly targeted because all buyers, including extremely brand-loyal ones, have access to in-store price reductions.

More targeted price reductions that require at least some effort on the part of the consumer involve coupons. Coupons are one of the very few ways to legally implement price discrimination, that is, charge different prices to segments with different sensitivities to price by delivering targeted coupons. In 1995, over $8 billion was spent on coupon promotions delivering nearly 300 billion coupons, many from Wednesday editions of local newspapers and others from mass mailings such as Carol Wright. The use of attachment coupons (either in or on the package of a good) allows a more focused price cut, though outright theft and trading of coupons are common. One interesting use of coupons is by Quaker Oats, which provides coupons for its products to its own shareholders.

As just noted, one advantage of coupons is that they can be delivered by mail, at the cash register, or even through the Internet to carefully targeted audiences. In addition, because they normally have to be cut out and physically carried to the point of transaction, coupons require more commitment to purchase the product, and thus they may engender more repeat purchases. They are also flexible because they can be designated for larger package sizes, a new flavor extension, and other applications. However, the redemption rates are appallingly low, around 2 percent, and discounts given for the wrong brands at checkouts are a significant misredemption problem.

Other, miscellaneous kinds of price-based consumer promotions are also options. Refunds and rebates are also common and effective, though the long-run effects may be negative. For example, car rebates may speed up sales volume initially but lead to lower profits and lower sales immediately after the rebates end. Frequent user programs such as those offered by airlines, supermarkets, hair salons, and sporting goods stores, are useful for encouraging brand loyalty and allow consumers to buy products at a discount after they have accumulated a sufficient number of "points."

Other Customer Promotions

In addition to product- and price-based promotions, other elements of the marketing mix can be used to meet company objectives. Point-of-purchase displays ("place" based) are common; notice the checkout and end-of-aisle displays at any supermarket. The L'eggs pantyhose display trees are an effective example of the power of display. One popular form of place-based promotion is the exposition at which manufacturers congregate to display and sell their wares, such as annual car shows, ski expositions, and computer expos. Another inducement to purchase is free service (e.g., free oil changes for one year). In addition, various premiums have proven effective. The use of free glasses or classic packaging to promote beverage sales (e.g., Coke's reuse of its classic glass bottle) is widespread. It is amazing how many cereal boxes have been bought for the "prize" inside or how many stupid acts have been performed for trinkets, including a large number by otherwise intelligent people who recognize how they are being manipulated. Finally, games, sweepstakes, and contests, both those that require proof of purchase and those that are open to the general public, such as Publishers' Clearing House Sweepstakes, are other types of promotions. One amazing example was *Scientific American*'s contest that gave prizes for the paper airplane that flew the farthest and longest. Not only did the contest attract both top engineers and "normal" people, it also generated substantial publicity for the magazine itself. Premiums are big business in their own right, as evidenced by the Annual Premium Incentive Show held at the massive Javits Convention Center in New York each spring.

Summary

An interesting study of many consumer packaged goods categories attempted to draw some general inferences about the use of different consumer promotions.[9] Overall, 27.1 percent of volume was purchased on deal. Also, not surprisingly, the use of newspaper features, in-store displays, price cuts, and store coupons were all highly correlated, ranging from .39 (display, store coupon) to .92 (feature, price cut), with manufacturer's coupons slightly negatively correlated to the other four variables (–.04 to –.07).

The study also grouped 331 grocery product categories into four clusters based on the percentage of volume purchased on various deals (see Figure 12–8). The first cluster contained product categories dominated by features and price cuts. This category was the second highest in purchase frequency and private label share. The second category was highest in terms of purchase frequency, private label share, and all forms of store promotion. The third cluster was dominated by manufacturer couponing. The final cluster was the most infrequently purchased and least promoted. This suggests that different types of promotions may be appropriate in different

---

[9]Peter S. Fader and Leonard M. Lodish, "A Cross-Category Analysis of Category Structure and Promotional Activity for Grocery Products," *Journal of Marketing* 54 (1990), pp. 52–65.

FIGURE 12–8 Dealing Patterns in Grocery Products

	Cluster				Overall
	1 (N = 80)	2 (28)	3 (77)	4 (146)	N = 331
Features	16.8	21.6	7.7	5.6	13.9%
Display	8.4	26.4	7.1	3.4	11.0
Manufacturer coupon	7.3	6.7	26.1	4.2	9.7
Store coupon	1.3	1.9	0.5	0.3	1.1
Price cut	20.3	25.1	10.9	7.9	17.9
Penetration	58.1	70.9	22.6	15.1	
Purchase cycle (days)	65.9	61.4	83.4	97.9	
Purchases/household	5.6	7.6	3.2	1.9	
Private label share	16.9	17.8	9.5	7.6	
Price	1.9	10	2.0	2.0	

Source: Peter S. Fader and Leonard M. Lodish, "A Cross-Category Analysis of Category Structure and Promotional Activity for Grocery Products," *Journal of Marketing* 54 (1990), 56, 60.

situations. By matching a product category with one of the clusters, a product manager can estimate the level and type of promotion necessary to achieve competitive parity.

Trade Promotions

Trade promotions are directed not to the final customer but to the channels through which the goods are sold. Like consumer promotions, they can be broken into five categories (Figure 12–9).

Product-based promotions include free goods and generous returns policies. Returns policies allow the channel to return unsold merchandise for a full or partial refund, reducing the risk of carrying the product. Price deals include various volume discounts and allowances, as well as financing terms such as a long period of time before payment is due or below-market interest rates.

Place-based allowances are especially important for consumer packaged goods. Slotting allowances, which are basically payments for placing a product on the shelf, have become increasingly important as power has shifted from manufacturers to retailers. These fees charged to manufacturers have had a negative effect on the number of competitors in many product categories and have been particularly hard on small companies, for which the fees can become prohibitive. Display allowances compensate retailers for prominent display of goods.

Other promotions involve reducing inventory and transportation costs by either warehousing the goods for the channel (as in just-in-time inventory) or paying all or part of delivery charges.

Providing selling assistance is also common. In addition to selling aids (brochures, etc.), companies often provide cooperative advertising, sharing the channel's advertising expense. One problem with this approach is the possibility of fraudulent charges, so monitoring becomes an advisable part of such arrangements. Manufacturers can also provide cooperative selling, in which their sales forces back up or refer leads to the channel's sales force.

FIGURE 12–9 Trade Promotions

I. Product based
  A. Free goods
  B. Consignment/returns policy
II. Price based
  A. Buying allowances
  B. Financial terms
III. Place based
  A. Slotting allowances
  B. Display allowances
  C. Warehousing/delivery assistance
IV. Advertising and promotion based
  A. Co-op advertising
  B. Selling aids
  C. Co-op selling
V. Sales based
  A. Bonuses and incentives
  B. Contests and prizes

Finally, there are sales-based incentives, for example, bonuses to the company for meeting or exceeding a quota. Sales incentives can also take the more controversial (and in some cases forbidden) form of direct prizes, bonuses, and the like to the channel's own sales force.

Evaluating Customer Promotions

Overview

The easiest approach to evaluating customer promotions is to simply look at incremental results (sales, share, profits) during the period of promotion. This method provides a useful starting point, but may lead to an overestimate of the benefit of promotion because it ignores both where the sales come from and the long-term consequences of promotion.

Just as with evaluating advertising effects, a standard approach to measuring the impact of a sales promotion is tracking. Figure 12–10 shows a typical tracking study with point A on the horizontal axis representing the time when the promotion—say, a price reduction—is given to end customers. Tracking studies such as these are used frequently because the effects of a sales promotion often show up quickly.

Unfortunately, product managers tend to look at the area above point A in Figurc 12–10 shaded by the diagonal lines as a measure of the impact of the promotion. This kind of simplistic analysis has many problems:

- The gain could be offset by the cross-hatched "dip" at point B representing the possibility that consumers have increased their inventories at home, thus negating the need to rebuy soon.
- The gain must be evaluated relative to a base amount: the amount of sales that would have been generated had the promotion not run. The baseline is difficult

FIGURE 12–10 **Evaluating Sales Promotions: Tracking Studies**

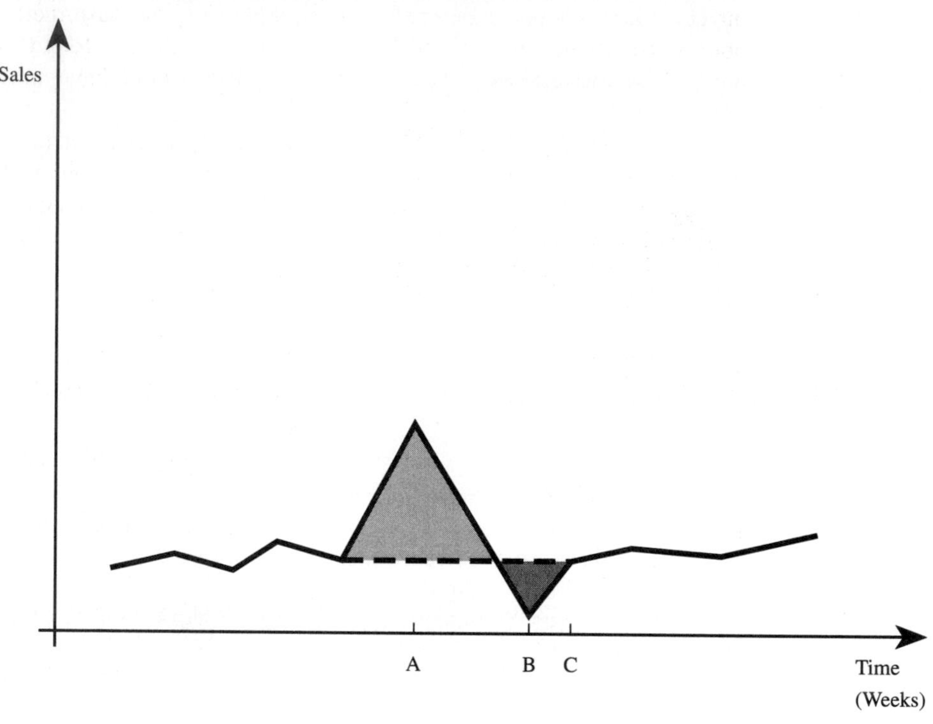

to calculate because it can change depending on time of year, competitive conditions, and so on.

- The analysis does not account for other factors in the marketplace, both by the product in question (e.g., an advertising change) and by the competition.
- Product managers must carefully examine point C in Figure 12–10, the point at which sales seem to return to "normal"; it could be higher than the base for some period of time, representing a positive long-run effect (see further discussion below).
- If products have several promotions running simultaneously, it is difficult to separate the effects of one promotion from another.

Thus, although it appears it should be easy to measure the effect on sales or share from a sales promotion, it is actually complicated.

An appropriate approach, of course, is to evaluate the promotion against its objectives (Figures 12–4 and 12–5). A price promotion that increases sales 30 percent but fails to attract a substantial number of new customers may be a failure because it basically gave a discount to current customers who may have simply stocked up, thus depressing future sales. The following section provides a more extensive approach for evaluating the sales impact of promotion.

Short-Run Evaluation

Sales increases from promotions may be generated by accelerating purchasing by loyal buyers. Many coupon redeemers, for example, may be customers who would have bought the product anyway and simply used the coupon as "found money" or, at best, bought the product somewhat sooner than they would have in the absence of a promotion.

One approach to evaluating coupon promotions looks at purchase acceleration (the moving forward in time of purchases) and brand switching as well as the impact of consumer promotions on retail purchasing.[10] Basically, a coupon can have several incremental impacts:

1. Accelerated regular purchases—that is, regular buyers of the brand simply buy sooner.
2. Accelerated captured purchases—purchasers who neither would have bought at the time nor bought the promoted brand but are persuaded to do both by the promotion.
3. Unaccelerated regular purchases—regular buyers who use the coupon as a "bonus" price cut.
4. Unaccelerated captured purchases—purchasers of other brands who switch to the promoted brand because of the promotion.

Obviously, categories 2 and 4 are pluses and category 1 also represents incremental sales, albeit borrowed ones. Category 3 is basically a negative, with the amount of the coupon (plus redemption costs) coming out of revenues. Category 1 is potentially but not necessarily negative. If subsequent sales are depressed as a result of increased inventory, there is no benefit (except a slight time value of money advantage) and a clear cost (the coupon value). Of course, one possible benefit of promotion is that "captured" buyers will remain loyal and repeat purchase the promoted brand on a subsequent purchase occasion. It is also possible that promotion increases category purchase quantity, either with or without depressing future purchase quantity. Interestingly, considerable evidence seems to suggest that increased quantity due to promotion is neither preceded nor followed by decreased quantity purchased, which is the opposite of the normally expected trough effect shown in Figure 12–10.[11]

To assess the value of a promotion, then, it is necessary to estimate both the source of additional sales (accelerated or not, increased quantity or not, loyal buyers or nonregular/captured buyers) and its overall magnitude. In addition, the profit consequences of each need to be considered. Figure 12–11 provides a framework for such an evaluation.

In Figure 12–11, the promotion decision appears to be nontrivial, as it should. Of course, some of the complication disappears if you are willing to make certain assumptions (e.g., that no share changes occur). On the other hand, this analysis does

[10]Scott A. Neslin and Robert W. Shoemaker, "A Model For Evaluating the Profitability of Coupon Promotions," *Marketing Science* 2 (1983), pp. 361–88.

[11]Scott A. Neslin and Linda G. Schneider Stone, "Consumer Inventory Sensitivity and the Postpromotion Dip," *Marketing Letters* 7 (January 1996), pp. 77–94.

FIGURE 12–11 Profit Impact of Customer Promotion

	Category Quantity		Sales Impact	
Buyer Segment	*Promotion Period*	*Subsequent Period*	*Promotion Period*	*Subsequent Period*
1. Loyal	No change	No change	0	0
2. Loyal	Increase	No change	ΔQ_P	0
3. Loyal	Increase	Decrease	ΔQ_P	ΔQ_S
4. Switchers	No change	No change	$\Delta M_P Q$	$\Delta M_S Q$
5. Switchers	Increase	No change	$\Delta M_P Q + (M + \Delta M_P)\,\Delta Q_P$	$\Delta M_S Q$
6. Switchers	Increase	Decrease	$\Delta M_P Q + (M + \Delta M_P)\,\Delta Q_P$	$(M + \Delta M_S)\,\Delta Q_S + \Delta M_S Q$
7. Nonbuyers of category	No change	No change	0	0
8. Nonbuyers of category	Increase	No change (return to 0 consumption)	$\Delta M_P \Delta Q_P$	0
9. Nonbuyers of category	Increase	Increase (continue to purchase)	$\Delta M_P \Delta Q_P$	$\Delta M_S \Delta Q_S$

Profit Impact	
Promotion Period	*Subsequent Period*
$-QDR$	0
$-QDR + \Delta Q_P(P - C - DR)$	0
$-QDR + \Delta Q_P(P - C - DR)$	$\Delta Q_S(P - C)$
$-MQDR + \Delta M_P Q(P - C - DR)$	$\Delta M_S Q(P - C)$
$-MQDR + (\Delta M_P Q + \Delta M_P \Delta Q_P + M\Delta Q_P)(P - C - DR)$	$\Delta M_S Q(P - C)$
$-MQDR + (\Delta M_P Q + \Delta M_P \Delta Q_P + M\Delta Q_P)(P - C - DR)$	$(M\Delta Q_S + \Delta M_S\, Q + \Delta M_S \Delta Q_S)(P - C)$
0	0
$\Delta M_P \Delta Q_P(P - C - DR)$	0
$\Delta M_P \Delta Q_P(P - C - DR)$	$\Delta M_S \Delta Q_S(P - C)$

(continued)

not explicitly include competitor reactions (e.g., matching promotional deals in either the promotion period or a subsequent period) or the impact of promotion on brand equity (e.g., loyal buyers could perceive their brand to be cheapened by promotion and hence become less loyal). Second, it is obvious that for many segments, promotions hurt long-run profits. This is especially true of loyal segments 1 and 3. In fact, Figure 12–11 tediously but correctly suggests that unless segments 8 and 9 and, under some circumstances, 2, 4, 5, and 6 are large, promotions hurt profits. Put differently, if promotions primarily cannibalize existing sales, they harm profits. Because segments 8 and 9 tend to be small in mature markets, this suggests that promotions need to capture a large number of switchers to make up for lost profits due to deal redemption. Notice that some promotions have lower redemption rates than others, for example, freestanding insert coupons (low) versus on-pack or register price discounts (high), which lessens their negative impact on profit margins but at the same time decreases

FIGURE 12–11 Profit Impact of Customer Promotion *(Concluded)*

Net Profit* Impact per Segment Member	*Segment Size*	*Total Impact: Size × Profit Impact*
$-QDR$	N_1	
$-(Q + \Delta Q_P)DR + \Delta Q_P (P - C)$	N_2	
$-(Q + \Delta Q_P)DR$	N_3	
$-(M + \Delta M_P)QDR + \Delta M_P Q(P - C) + \Delta M_S Q(P - C)$	N_4	
$-(M + \Delta M_P)(Q + \Delta Q_P)DR + (\Delta M_P Q + \Delta M_P \Delta Q_P + M\Delta Q_P)(P - C)$ $+ \Delta M_S Q(P - C)$	N_5	
$-(M + \Delta M_P)(Q + \Delta Q_P)DR + (\Delta M_P Q + \Delta M_P \Delta Q_P + M_P \Delta Q_P)(P - C) +$ $(\Delta M_S Q + \Delta M_S \Delta Q_S + M_S \Delta Q_S)(P - C)$	N_6	
0	N_7	
$\Delta M_P \Delta Q_P (P - C - DR)$	N_8	
$(\Delta M_P \Delta Q_P + \Delta M_S \Delta Q_S)(P - C) - \Delta M_P \Delta Q_P DR$	N_9	______

Q = Typical purchase quantity
P = Price
C = Variable cost
D = Cost of promotion (i.e., face value of coupon plus redemption cost)
R = Redemption rate of the promotion for those who buy the brand
ΔQ_P, ΔQ_S = change in quantity due to promotion in the promotion and subsequent period
M = typical share among switchers (M = 0 for nonbuyers, 1 for loyals)
ΔM_P , ΔM_S = change in share due to promotion in the promotion and subsequent periods
*This means members forward buy, stockpiling the good when it is on promotion. Since nonbuyers can't go below their current 0 level of sales, stockpiling is not considered for segments 7–9.

their impact on quantity. The main point here, then, is that it is possible to estimate the impact of a promotion through systematic analysis and that the results of such analysis are often quite sobering. Not surprisingly, small-share brands often benefit more from promotions than large-share brands, mainly because promotions cannibalize fewer sales to regular customers.

In addition to the direct effects of manufacturer promotions on customers, the promotion has an indirect impact on channel (retailer) behavior. For example, retailers may increase stocking of the good or run their own promotions in conjunction with the manufacturer. Inasmuch as these generate benefits beyond immediate customer sales, they need to be considered as well.

Notice that a major factor affecting the profitability of promotions is whether or not a good is easily stockpiled. Perishable goods and services (e.g., seats on an airplane) cannot be stockpiled; paper towels or computer chips can be. Hence paper towel promotions tend to result in stockpiling, and, if the promotion is matched by competitors, actually lead to lower profits. In contrast, promotions on underused services or perishable goods may produce increasing profits for the product manager.

Long-Run Concerns

Promotion also has two important long-run impacts. First is the impact of promotion on customer perceptions of the brand. Brands bought on promotion may be seen as lower in quality (i.e., "if they were really good, they wouldn't have to put them on sale") and, in the extreme, something it makes sense to buy only on deal. Moreover, as we mentioned in Chapter 10, customers may anticipate promotions and actually delay purchase until a deal occurs. This is particularly a problem when the deals are run at regular intervals, such as January white sales on linens and bedding. However, delaying purchases has also been a problem when the deals were frequent but irregular; for example, auto rebates and airline fare wars tend to cause discretionary buyers to wait until a better deal comes along. After a promotion ends, consumers may view the return to normal prices as a price increase and suffer "sticker shock."

There is also concern about the impact of promotions on competitors. Most markets are oligopolies, and hence decisions need to take likely competitive reactions into account. Not surprisingly, competitors often match promotions quickly, thus negating many of the possible benefits. Hence a promotion spiral can ensue with great benefit to customers and harm to companies' profits. One classic example of this occurred at the retail level when Miracle Whip was promoted at well below its cost to the retailer ($1.09 versus $1.60) after a series of reactions to competitors' promotions.

The Competitive Dilemma

Obviously, there is a question of whether it is in a company's best interest to engage in heavy promotion spending. Promotion spending is another example of the decision problem referred to as the "prisoner's dilemma." In the prisoner's dilemma, two criminals are apprehended and questioned separately, with no communication between them. Both are separately told that the law will go easier on them if they confess, which is true. They are not told, however, that the evidence is mainly circumstantial and hence if neither confesses, they may get off free or at most face a reduced charge. The dilemma is that each prisoner is always better off by confessing regardless of what the other prisoner does, but both are collectively better off if neither confesses.

The "promotion dilemma" can be similar. If category sales are fixed—that is, marketing expenditures do not increase primary demand and dropping expenditures does not cause them to decrease to the benefit of other product categories—and no objectives exist to increase market share, all companies are better off at a low level of expenditure, with the difference between a high and a low level being increased profits. Short of collusion (which is illegal in the United States), however, cooperating is risky. In fact, playing a "martyr" strategy (always keeping expenditures low) turns out to be a strategy that performs poorly. Rather, a so-called "provocable" strategy that retaliates against competitors with high promotion expenditures has often proven most effective in simulated markets.

Evaluating Trade Promotions

A major issue in determining the value of a promotion is its opportunity costs. As discussed earlier, many users of consumer promotion would have bought the product anyway, so they simply pocket the value of the promotion or stock up at the low price. For trade promotions, the issue of "gray markets" is especially crucial. Gray markets involve authorized dealers or retailers that buy the product from the producer and then resell it to other, unauthorized dealers. This practice is common when a company offers a volume discount and multiple dealers in effect pool their orders to obtain it. Gray markets often account for 20 to 30 percent of sales, so their impact is substantial. Consequently, the lost revenue due to gray market activity is an important component of calculating the effectiveness of a trade price promotion.

Evaluated as profit-enhancing devices, trade promotions are often failures. On average only 16 percent of trade promotions directed at supermarkets are profitable, according to one estimate.[12] Further, although many trade promotions involve implied cooperation on the part of the channel (e.g., to pass along at least 40 percent of the price discount to the customer and advertise the sale price), these provisions are hard to monitor and enforce. Put differently, although the manufacturer's objectives are best served when promotions are passed through to consumers, channels' profits are often increased by retaining all or a substantial amount of a promotion allowance as profit. One way to evaluate trade promotions is as a necessary cost of doing business, an explicit recognition of the growing power of mass merchandisers in consumer packaged goods marketing in the United States. Slotting allowances of over $200 per slot (shelf keeping unit or SKU) to introduce a new product indicate the power of retailers over manufacturers.

As Figure 12–1 shows, trade promotions now account for about 49 percent of the promotion budget, more than either advertising or consumer promotions. One reason is that trade support is a key to increased volume. For example, the results of IRI studies of 2,400 products show that although price reductions produced increases of 25 to 60 percent in five categories (English muffins, toilet tissue, cough drops, yogurt, and sausage), adding a newspaper feature raised the increase to between 103 and 440 percent, adding a display increased sales by 109 to 708 percent, and adding both a feature and a display increased sales by 181 to a whopping 1,008 percent.[13] Unfortunately, such strong support rarely occurs. Another study examined 992 promotions and found that only 7.3 percent were coupled with major displays and 15.2 percent with minor displays, meaning over 77 percent received no additional display. Similarly, while 827 of the 992 promoted products were advertised, most (500) received only a single line in the store ad, 29 percent received one column inch, and only 4 percent received more than two column inches.[14]

One major purpose of trade shows is to entice current and potential channel members to carry a product. Trade shows are a multibillion-dollar business in their own right. Participants have multiple objectives, including image enhancement and new-product introduction (see Figure 12–12).[15] Interestingly, immediate sales are not the top priority; competitor monitoring is more important.

---

[12]Magid M. Abraham and Leonard M. Lodish, "Getting the Most out of Advertising and Promotion," *Harvard Business Review* 68 (1990), pp. 50–60.

[13]Monci Jo Williams, "Trade Promotion Junkies," *The Marketer* (October 1990), pp. 30–33.

[14]Michel Chevalier and Ronald C. Curhan, "Retail Promotions as a Function of Trade Promotions: A Descriptive Analysis," *Sloan Management Review* 18, no. 1 (Fall 1976), pp. 19–32.

[15]Roger A. Kerin and William L. Cron, "Assessing Trade Show Functions and Performance: An Exploratory Study," *Journal of Marketing* 51 (July 1987), pp.87–94.

FIGURE 12–12 Purposes of Trade Show Participation

	Mean Importance
Enhancing corporate image	5.32
Introducing new products	5.14
Identifying new prospects	5.08
Getting competitor information	4.94
Servicing current customers	4.69
Enhancing corporate morale	3.75
Selling at the show	2.79
New-product testing	2.17

Source: Roger A. Kerin and William L. Cron, "Assessing Trade Show Functions and Performance: An Exploratory Study," *Journal of Marketing* 51 (July 1987), pp. 87–94.

One interesting approach to modeling the impact of trade promotions develops a model to trace the effects through channel inventories and retailer promotions to consumer sales.[16] The model consists of four equations:

$$\text{Manufacturer shipments } (t) = f_1(\text{channel inventory } (t-1), \text{trade promotions } (t), \text{other factors } (t))$$

$$\text{Retailer promotions } (t) = f_2 (\text{trade promotions } (t), \text{channel inventories } (t-1))$$

$$\text{Consumer sales } (t) = f_3 (\text{trade promotions } (t), \text{retailer promotions } (t-1), \text{other factors } (t), \text{other factors } (t-1))$$

$$\text{Inventories } (t) = f_4 (\text{inventories } (t-1), \text{shipments } (t), \text{consumer sales } (t)) = \text{Inventory } (t-1) + \text{Shipments } (t) - \text{ConsumerSales } (t)$$

In an application of this model, data on retailer promotions were not available, so the retailer promotion equation was dropped and the consumer sales equation was simplified to

$$\text{Consumer sales } (t) = f_3 (\text{inventories } (t-1), \text{other factors } (t))$$

Trade promotions consisted of three basic types—off-invoice discounts, sales drive discounts, and special fall premiums—and their effects were treated separately. The model included an "end-of-deal" variable to account for orders placed during the deal period but not shipped until the next period. The sales drive consisted of a percentage payment to the channel when it sold units to the retailer. The special fall premium was direct payment to the manufacturer's own sales force. To remove the impact of the direction sales were headed on their own (i.e., to establish a baseline), the model also used a time trend term.

The shipment and consumer sales equations were fit to 10 items in 10 markets. The overall fits were good, with average adjusted R^2s of .66 (range .23 to .95) and .57 (range .15 to .94) for the shipment and sales equations, respectively. The signs of the

[16]Robert C. Blattberg and Alan Levin, "Modeling the Effectiveness and Profitability of Trade Promotions," *Marketing Science* (Spring 1987), pp. 124–46.

FIGURE 12–13 Impact of Trade Promotions on Shipments and Consumer Sales

Coefficient Estimates for Two Markets and One Size

Shipments Equation

	Market 1/Size 2		Market 2/Size 2	
Variable	*Coefficient*	*t-Ratio*	*Coefficient*	*t-Ratio*
Lagged inventory	-3.29×10^{-5}	−2.94	-4.26×10^{-5}	−3.15
Trend	-5.964×10^{-3}	−0.72	7.24×10^{-3}	0.88
Off-invoice	36.9071	6.51	25.6119	4.93
End of deal	3.4142	0.75	4.2845	0.99
Sales drive	21.4402	3.27	3.4890	0.55
Price change	13.5317	2.31	4.6786	0.89
Fall premium	0.2029	1.34	0.2290	1.61
Constant	8.8366	45.32	8.7882	45.54
	$\bar{R}^2 = 0.845$ Number of observations = 35		$\bar{R}^2 = 0.611$ Number of observations = 35	
Consumer Sales Equation				
Lagged inventory	3.295×10^{-6}	2.10	4.880×10^{-7}	0.17
Seasonality	0.0127	2.69	0.0270	4.60
Trend	−0.0005	−2.01	1.737×10^{-3}	0.92
Lagged advertising	0.0005	0.33	1.990×10^{-3}	1.08
Constant	7.89	16.45	6.2365	10.65
	$\bar{R}^2 = 0.446$ Number of observations = 35		$\bar{R}^2 = 0.511$ Number of observations = 35	

Source: Robert C. Blattberg and Alan Levin, "Modeling the Effectiveness and Profitability of Trade Promotions," *Marketing Science* (Spring 1987), p. 134.

coefficients were overwhelming (over 90 percent) as expected. Figure 12–13 gives a sample result. Shipments responded significantly and positively to off-invoice price reductions in both markets and to the sales drive and price reduction in market 1 as well. Also interesting were wide swings in manufacturer shipments (up at the beginning and at the end of the promotion, then down) and little change in consumer sales. This suggests most of the impact was on channel stockpiling and relatively little led to increased sales to customers.

A different approach uses an expert system style modeling method (PROMOTER) based on the results of many past promotions.[17] This approach begins by developing a baseline sales level based on trend and seasonality plus any unusual factors that may have affected sales. Basically, a baseline estimation procedure relies on periods when promotion is zero. Incremental sales are then computed as the difference between

[17]Magid M. Abraham and Leonard M. Lodish, "PROMOTER: An Automated Promotion Evaluation System," *Marketing Science* 6 (1987), pp. 101–23.

baseline and actual sales, and this figure is used to evaluate a promotion. Thus, in contrast to the multiple-equation approach shown in Figure 12–13, PROMOTER does not assess the process by which a promotion works; rather, it concentrates on a statistical estimate of its magnitude.

The general findings from PROMOTER are the following:

- Trade deals tend to have lower "pass-through"; that is, savings by the retailer are passed along to consumers less often than manufacturers hope.
- Retailers tend to forward buy when they are offered promotions, allowing them to stock up and ultimately making the promotion unprofitable for the manufacturer.
- The effectiveness of trade deals varies greatly across sizes of products and markets.

Assessing Consumer Promotions with Scanner Data

Some Findings about Promotion Effects

The widely available electronic scanner data for supermarket and drugstore products have been used extensively to assess the effects of promotions on buying behavior. We know consumers use coupons extensively. Further, while some consumers purchase at regular intervals, many may accelerate purchases and stockpile goods. Overall, many different reactions to promotions have been identified.[18] One particularly interesting issue concerning promotions is their impact on both a brand's equity (overall evaluation) and its reservation price, that is, the most a consumer is willing to pay for it.

Given the prevalence of scanner data, it is not surprising that a large number of models have been developed to use them to assess the impact of marketing variables such as promotion. Models have attempted to separate the effects of price, advertising, and promotion on sales for nearly 15 years.[19] Assuming primary demand (market size) is constant, the models generally assess the value of each brand to an individual customer as a function of several components:

1. The inherent value of a brand-size combination (e.g., Ragu 16 ounces plain spaghetti sauce). This is either treated holistically (with a dummy variable and a unique value for each brand) or further decomposed into product attributes (plain, chunky, etc.).
2. The nonproduct marketing mix elements: price, promotion, the amount of the promotion, and advertising.
3. Carryover effects of past purchases.
4. Customer loyalty or inertia.

---

[18]See, for example, Imran S. Currim and Linda G. Schneider, "A Taxonomy of Consumer Purchase Strategies in a Promotion Intensive Environment," *Marketing Science* 10 (1991), pp. 91–110.

[19]Credit for the first published attempt to model promotion and other marketing mix effects using electronic scanner data is generally given to Peter M. Guadagni and John D. C. Little, "A Logit Model of Brand Choice Calibrated on Scanner Data," *Marketing Science* 2 (1983), pp. 203–38.

Mathematically, this becomes

$$\begin{aligned}\text{Value} = {} & B_i \text{ (if brand size } I) + B_p \text{ price} + B_{pr} \text{ (if promotion)} \\ & + B_{\text{deal}} \text{ (if promotion)(amount of promotion)} + B_A \text{ (advertising)} \\ & + B_C \text{ (Value last period)} + B_R \text{ (if same brand was} \\ & \text{brought last time)}\end{aligned}$$

Share is then typically specified via a logit model:

$$\text{Share}_i = \exp[\text{Value}_i]/\Sigma_j \exp[\text{Value}_j].$$

This model is then estimated with a procedure to maximize predictive accuracy by varying the model's parameters. An alternative model form involves a multiplicative relation among the determinants, that is, Value = (Brand) B^1 (Price) B^2, and so forth.

Scanner data are not a perfect means for assessing the impact of promotions. They generally include only household-level (as opposed to individual) data, do not cover purchases at nonscanned stores, and exclude many potential influences on sales (e.g., magazine ads). They are, however, a useful and unobtrusive means for evaluating both natural and controlled experiments (see the discussion that follows). Scanner data are increasingly being used to compare different promotions and provide directional guidance (e.g., whether to raise or lower the advertising spending level) to managers.

Most of our knowledge of the impact of promotion is based on analysis of consumer packaged goods. Following is a summary of what we have found from these analyses:[20]

1. Temporary retail price reductions substantially increase sales.
2. Higher market share brands are less deal elastic.
3. The frequency of deals changes the consumer's reference price (see also Chapter 10).
4. The greater the frequency of deals, the lower the height of the deal "spike."
5. Cross-promotional effects are asymmetric, and promoting higher-quality brands affects weaker brands (and private label products) disproportionately.
6. Retailers pass through less than 100 percent of trade deals.
7. Display and feature advertising have strong effects on item sales.
8. Advertised promotions can result in increased store traffic.
9. Promotions affect sales in complementary and competitive categories.

Some other recent findings include:

1. Past research on the demographics of coupon users has found contradictory results. While one might think that coupons would appeal mainly to low-income consumers who could benefit most from the deal, some research has found the opposite. One study found that demographics cannot explain coupon redemption rates; product managers also have to understand cost/benefit perceptions, shopping-related

[20]Robert C. Blattberg, Richard Briesch, and Edward J. Fox, "How Promotions Work," *Marketing Science* 14 (1996) no. 3, Part 2 of 2, pp. G122–G132. The interested reader can consult the many references cited in this paper for more detailed results.

person traits, and nondemographic general consumer characteristics (e.g., loyalty, psychographics).[21]

2. An important issue concerning promotions is whether or not they have any long-term effects after the promotion period. Most early studies found that deals had a negative effect on subsequent attitudes and repeat purchase rates.[22] More recent research has softened this position, suggesting that repeat purchasing depends on brand knowledge or loyalty, and the negative effect of deals decreases for knowledgeable, loyal customers.[23] Other work on the long-term effects of coupons shows that increased purchases using coupons erode brand loyalty and increase price sensitivity.[24] Promotion retraction often leads to a decreased repeat purchasing rate due to the fact that promotions attract buyers who value the brand itself less and hence are naturally less likely to repeat buy it.[25] Finally, it does appear that consumers anticipate deals[26] and hence may delay purchase until the next deal.

3. Promotional response appears to depend upon characteristics of the product category.[27] Some findings indicate that promotional response is higher for categories with fewer brands, higher category penetration, shorter interpurchase times, and higher consumer propensity to stockpile.

Test Markets

Test markets are as useful for evaluating different sales promotions as they are for advertising copy or pricing experiments. A product manager can attempt different combinations of free samples, end-of-aisle displays, coupons, and special price promotions over a period of time, using some stores as the experimental group and others with no promotional activity as the "control" group.

Figure 12–14 shows an illustrative result of a special display experiment run in a BehaviorScan market. As can be seen, a significant spike in unit sales occurred around the date when all of the special displays were installed. The dotted line is the sales volume from the control stores where there were no special displays. The figure shows an 80 percent change at the peak of the sales increase. An interesting result is that although the sales in the experimental stores were lower than those in the control

---

[21]Banwari Mittal, "An Integrated Framework for Relating Diverse Consumer Characteristics to Supermarket Coupon Redemption," *Journal of Marketing Research* 31 (1994), pp. 533–44.

[22]Joe A. Dodson, Alice M. Tybout, and Brian Sternthal, "Impact of Deals and Deal Retraction on Brand Switching," *Journal of Marketing Research* 15 (1978), pp. 72–81.

[23]Scott Davis, J. Jeffrey Inman, and Leigh McAlister, "Promotion Has a Negative Effect on Brand Evaluations—or Does It?" *Journal of Marketing Research* 29 (1992), pp. 143–48.

[24]Purushottam Papatla and Lakshman Krishnamurthi, "Measuring the Dynamic Effects of Promotions on Brand Choice," *Journal of Marketing Research* 33 (1996), pp. 20–35.

[25]Scott A. Neslin and Robert W. Shoemaker, "An Alternative Explanation for Lower Repeat Rates after Promotion Purchases," *Journal of Marketing Research* 26 (1989), pp. 205–13.

[26]Aradhna Krishna, "Effect of Dealing Patterns on Consumer Perceptions of Deal Frequency and Willingness to Pay," *Journal of Marketing Research* 28 (1991), pp. 441–51; Aradhna Krishna, "The Effect of Deal Knowledge on Consumer Purchase Behavior," *Journal of Marketing Research* 31 (1994), pp. 76–91.

[27]Chakravarthi Narasimhan, Scott A. Neslin, and Subrata K. Sen, "Promotional Elasticities and Category Characteristics," *Journal of Marketing* 60 (1996), pp. 17–30.

FIGURE 12–14 **Illustration of a BehaviorScan Display Experiment**

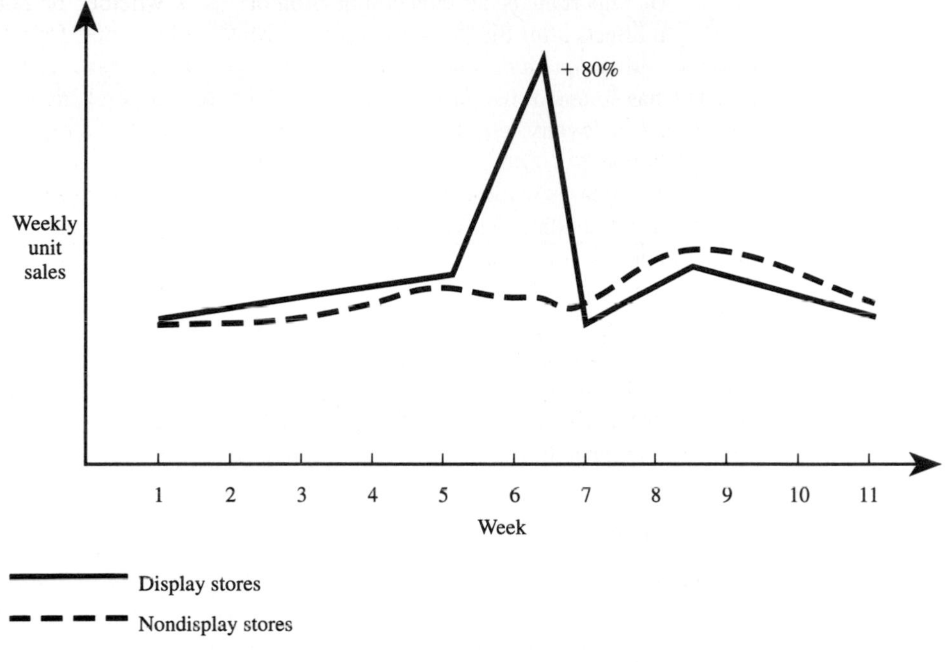

stores after the experimental period, there was no "trough," thus implying that the net effect was substantial. Notice that Figure 12–14 indicates a significant effect of the displays on sales, not necessarily profits, since the cost of the displays has not been accounted for.

The Retailer's Perspective

Although this book focuses on the product manager rather than the retailer, the effectiveness of both consumer and trade promotions clearly relies on the cooperation of the retailers involved. In addition, given the trend toward category management described in Chapter 1, the product manager should now view the retailer as an ally to work with for the profitability of the entire category. The product manager becomes successful only if the retailer is successful, that is, if the product generates sufficient contribution margin to warrant the shelf space allocated to it. When this perspective is lost, the product manager–retailer relationship becomes more adversarial than cooperative.

Why does the product manager need this cooperation? As noted earlier, many trade deals simply provide additional profit for the retailer, who forward-buys goods at a lower price without passing the lower price along to the end customer. The product manager must demonstrate that the retailer can enhance total profits over a period of time by passing the promotion through. In addition, manufacturers often need the

FIGURE 12–15 Consumer Promotional Budget

Promotion Category	*Production Cost*	*Distribution Cost*	*Redemption Cost*	*Total Cost*
Product based				
Price based				
Premiums				
Place based				
Games				

FIGURE 12–16 Trade Promotion Budget

Promotion Category	*Production Cost*	*Distribution Cost*	*Redemption Cost*	*Total Cost*
Product based				
Price based				
Place based				
Advertising and promotion based				
Sales based				

cooperation of retailers to implement various promotions. For example, "shelf talkers," signs at point of purchase indicating reduced prices, must be installed. Sometimes on-pack coupons must be physically placed on the packages by the retailer. Of course, manufacturers rely on the accurate redemption of coupons by the checkout personnel and, as noted earlier in the chapter, this can be a major problem. The important point for a product manager is that most product categories are highly competitive and consumers do not have substantial brand loyalty. It is therefore easy for a supermarket to give the space allotted to the products of an "uncooperative" product manager to a competing brand.

Summary

To summarize promotion plans, both budget and time schedule tables similar to those developed for advertising are useful. For consumer promotions (Figure 12–15), three basic cost categories are relevant: the cost of "producing" the promotion (e.g., coupon printing or premium buying), the incremental cost of distributing the promotion (e.g., mailing or newspaper ad or insert costs), and the cost of "redeeming" the promotion (e.g., sending out rebates). Also, recognize that redemption costs include the cost of misredemption. For trade promotions (Figure 12–16), redemption costs also include the cost of monitoring trade performance, for example, in the case of cooperative

FIGURE 12–17 Detailed Promotion Schedule

Promotion Category	*January*	*February*	*March*	. . .
Trade promotions				
.				
.				
.				
Consumer promotions				
.				
.				

advertising. Both trade and consumer promotions are put together into a promotion schedule or calendar as shown in Figure 12–17.

Promotions in general and price promotions in particular are the elements of the marketing mix that have the most dramatic impact on short-term sales. Used sparingly and strategically, by a weak brand or in connection with new-product introductions, they can be powerful and useful tools. When used extensively and matched by competition, however, they damage profits.[28] While "ruinous" competition may suit the objective of driving less well-capitalized competitors out of a market (or discourage entry), it does so at a high cost.

[28]John Philip Jones, "The Double Jeopardy of Sales Promotions," *Harvard Business Review* 68 (September–October 1990), pp. 145–52.

C H A P T E R

13 Channel Management, Customer Contact, and the Product Manager

Overview

In this chapter we cover distribution channels for two important reasons. First, even assuming that the product's distribution structure is difficult to change within a short time frame, it is still critical for the product manager to understand that maintaining good channel relations is a key part of the job. Even when the product uses "direct" distribution through a sales force, the product manager must depend on others in the distribution system. Second, for many product categories, the distribution system has changed dramatically due to shifts in customer behavior or innovation by one product manager. As with other aspects of the marketing mix, innovation in distribution offers opportunities for differential advantage.

The personal computer (PC) category is a good example of innovation in distribution (see Figure 13–1). Traditionally, mainframes and minicomputers were sold through direct sales via a company's own sales force or some other third party such as independent agents. Particularly for minicomputers, an additional channel evolved: the OEM (original equipment manufacturer) or VAR (value-added reseller), which was composed of companies that bought computers from major firms such as DEC, added proprietary software, and sold the resulting systems to banks, hotels, and other users with particular needs for transaction processing, reservations, and so forth. These channels continue to be used in the personal computer industry. However, new distribution channels also developed. Computer retailers became widespread, dominated by companies such as ComputerLand and Businessland. These retailers targeted both households and small businesses, sold the products as well as software, and gave service and instruction to novice users.

A critical change in the market occurred in the mid-1980s: Customer knowledge about PCs grew as the novelty factor wore off, and increased numbers of competitors made price and availability the most highly valued product attributes. The change in the market resulted in three major changes in distribution channels for PCs. First, a

FIGURE 13–1 Personal Computer Distribution Channels

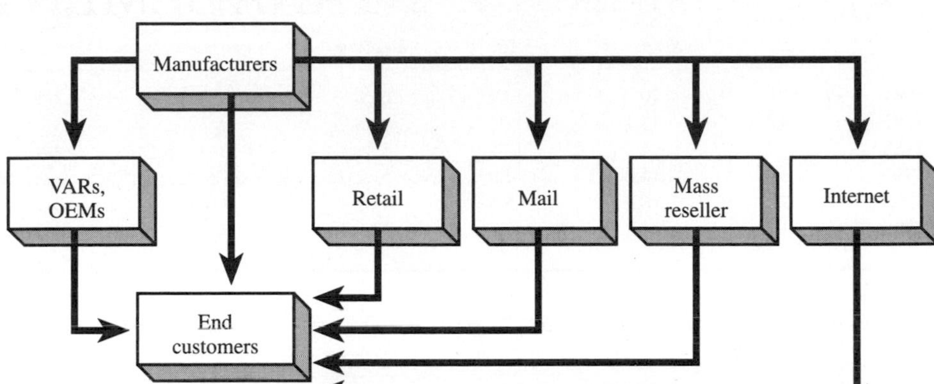

new channel developed consisting of mass resellers, companies that buy large quantities from manufacturers and resell them at quantity discounts to large companies. This channel is particularly important for companies that use many personal computers, such as Merrill Lynch. Second, mail order has become a very large and important channel. For example, Dell sold $2.9 billion worth of computers in 1995 in the U.S. mainly through direct mail. In contrast, Dell's efforts to use conventional retail channels have been unsuccessful. Third, we have seen the growth of computer "supermarkets," such as CompUSA and Soft Warehouse. Finally, the most recent phenomenon is the growth of the Internet as a retail "site" e.g., <lnet for computer equipment (see Figure 16-4). Figure 13–2 shows personal computer by distribution channels.

Is the personal computer category unique? Hardly. Witness the same shift from small stores with personalized service to large superstores such as Circuit City in consumer electronics. Likewise, large office equipment retailers such as Staples and Office Depot have grown dramatically. Many other businesses have prospered based on their use of direct marketing, including Harry and David in fruits, Calyx and Corolla in flowers, and Franklin Mint in collectibles. The key point is that for many product categories, channels change.

Direct-distribution consumer packaged goods companies, such as Avon in cosmetics and Amway in household cleaning products, have gained differentiation through the channel decision. Competitors of these companies used conventional retailers such as supermarkets and drugstores. In fact, almost any economic analysis would show how expensive it is to sell lipstick door to door. However, these companies found that some segments of the population enjoy their personal approach to selling these low-priced products, and they have created very large niches for themselves not only in the United States but in Europe, Asia, and other parts of the world as well.

Changing relationships complicate the channel issue facing product managers, particularly in consumer products. In the 1990s, retailers have gained power vis-à-vis

Figure 13-2 Break-up of PC Sales Volumes by Channel (% of units shipped)

	Direct Sales	*Direct Response*	*VARs*[1]	*Dealers*	*Computer Superstores*	*Mass Merchants*	*Consumer Electronics*
1984	15.0	10.0	10.0	60.0	0	2.0	3.0
1987	10.4	13.1	12.3	56.8	0	3.4	4.1
1988	9.5	14.2	13.4	55.1	0	3.6	4.1
1990	8.3	14.6	14.9	51.2	1.5	5.0	4.5
1992	5.1	16.1	15.5	44.7	4.9	8.6	5.1
1994	3.9	14.2	16.2	42.0	8.5	9.6	5.6

[1] Value-added resellers

Source: Das Narayandas and V. Kasturi Rangan, "Dell Computer Corporation," Harvard Business School Case #9-596-058, 1996.

Figure 13–3 Dependence of Some Manufacturers on Key Retailers

Gibson Greetings: 35% from 5 customers, 13% from Phar-Mor
Gitano: 56% from 10 retailers, 26% from Wal-Mart
Haggar: 22.6% from J.C. Penney, 10% from Wal-Mart
Hasbro: 75% from 10 customers, 17% from Toys "R" Us
Huffy: 23% from Kmart and Toys "R" Us
Mattel: 13% from Toys "R" Us
Mr Coffee: 21% from Wal-Mart, 10% from Kmart
Procter & Gamble: 11% from Wal-Mart
Rubbermaid: 11.1% from Wal-Mart
Royal Appliance: 52.6% from 5 retailers, 26.5% from Wal-Mart, 16% from Kmart
The Scotts Co.: 26% from Wal-Mart, Kmart, and Home Depot

Source: Zachary Schiller, Wendy Zellner, Ron Stodghill II, and Mark Maremont, "Clout! More and More, Retail Giants Rule the Marketplace," December 21, 1992, pp. 66–73. Reprinted from December 21, 1992 issue *Business Week* by special permission, copyright © 1992 by McGraw-Hill, Inc.

manufacturers.[1] Figures 13–3 and 13–4 show how these "power" retailers have dominated many areas of retailing.

This chapter emphasizes the two major aspects of channel decision making that are relevant for product managers: the channel selection problem and channel management.

[1]Although this statement is generally true, it is surprising that retailer profits have not grown faster than manufacturer profits. See Paul W. Farris and Kusum L. Ailawadi, "Retail Power: Monster or Mouse?" (Cambridge, Mass.: Marketing Science Institute, 1992).

FIGURE 13–4 Reliance on Wal-Mart

	Revenues	
Company/business	*Latest 12 Months ($ millions)*	*from Wal-Mart* (%)*
Newell/housewares, home furnishings	$2,498	15%
Fruit of the Loom/apparel	2,478	16
Rubbermaid/plastic and rubber products	2,329	15
Springs Industries/finished fabrics, home furnishings	2,233	12
Westpoint Stevens/linens, home furnishings	1,651	10
Sunbeam/household appliances	1,202	17
Fieldcrest Cannon/linens, home furnishings	1,095	18
First Brands/household products	1,053	12
Coleman/recreational gear	902	10+
Huffy/recreational gear	685	10+
Roadmaster Industries/recreational gear	675	28
Paragon Trade Brands/diapers	519	15
Playtex Products/personal care products	471	15
Ekco Group/housewares	278	10+
Royal Appliance Manufacturing/vacuum cleaners	270	23
Crown Crafts/textiles, home furnishings	214	16
Armor All Products/auto polishes, protectants	204	20
Toastmaster/home appliances	187	30
Windmere/personal care products	185	18
National Presto Industries/home appliances	123	35
Empire of Carolina/toys	119	17
General Housewares/household products	117	13
Safety 1st/child safety products	70	18
National Picture & Frame/frames, mirrors	61	36
Ohio Art/toys	43	20

*Based on latest fiscal year disclosure.
Source: Matthew Schifrin, "The Big Squeeze," *Forbes,* March 11, 1996, pp. 45–46.

Channel Selection

Direct versus Indirect Channels

Channel selection is often thought of as two sequential decisions (see Figure 13–5). First, the product manager has to decide whether to use direct or indirect customer contact. Then the manager must select particular channels (e.g., representatives or distributors).

The choice between direct and indirect channels, like any other decision, ultimately rests on the relative profitability of the two methods. How much is it worth (in terms of margin) to use distributors to get products and services to customers? Studies point to some general guidelines. Direct appears to be better than indirect when

1. Information needs (often due to technical complexity) are high.
2. Product customization is important.

FIGURE 13–5 Company-to-Company Contacts

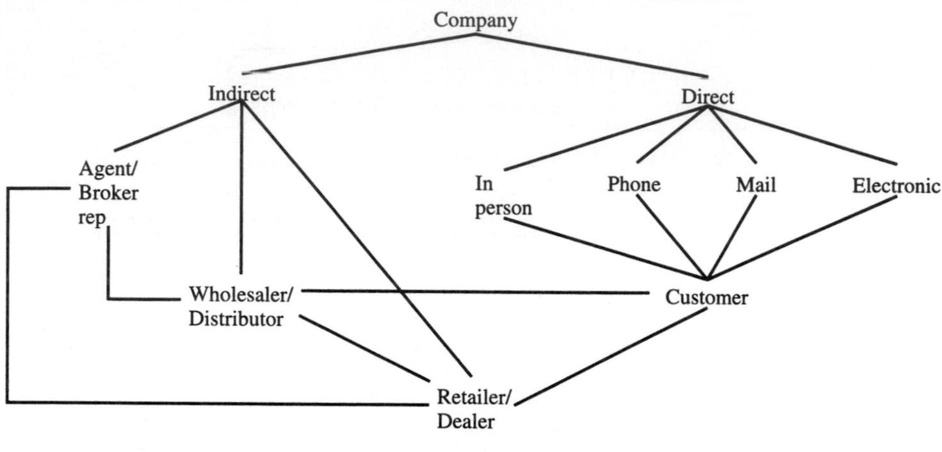

3. Quality assurance matters.
4. Purchase orders are large.
5. Transportation and storage are complex.[2]

In contrast, the following factors tend to point to indirect channels:

1. One-stop shopping for many products is important.
2. Availability is important.
3. After-sales service is important.

There are numerous counterexamples to these general guidelines. As mentioned before, Dell and Gateway have been very successful with a direct (phone) marketing strategy even though availability and service are important for PCs. Similarly Avon, Mary Kay, and Tupperware have done well with direct strategies even though information needs, customization, and purchase order levels are low. This suggests that both direct and indirect channels are often useful.

Another factor to consider in choosing between direct and indirect channels is the level of commitment from the potential intermediaries. Channel members must be motivated to sell your product when they have multiple products to sell. Figure 13–6 gives some conceptual idea of why levels of commitment can vary. From the product manager's perspective (shown in the top part of the figure), different channel entities can be utilized to get the product or deliver the service to the customer. However, from the channel member's perspective, multiple products must be distributed, some that sell better than others and some that do a better job of giving the channel services and

[2]Kasturn, Rangan, Melvyn A. J. Menezes, and E. P. Maier, "Channel Selection for New Industrial Products: A Framework, Method, and Applications," *Journal of Marketing* 56 (1992), pp. 69–82.

FIGURE 13–6 Differing Perspectives between Manufacturers and Channel Members

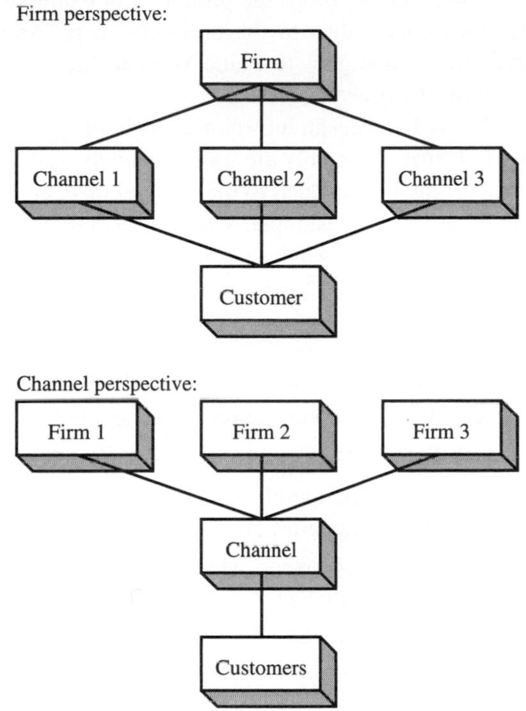

incentives to sell the product. This has led to the emphasis on "category management" by retailers, that is, trying to optimize profits from soft drinks as a whole. As a consequence, manufacturers (including big ones such as Pepsi) are required to present a plan to retailers for selling not only their own brands but competing ones as well.

The product manager can implement a variety of means to get higher levels of commitment from channel members. Of course, higher margins are important. Giving the channel member the exclusive rights to distribute or sell the product in a particular geographic area is another approach. Providing sales training programs, promotions such as cooperative advertising plans, and "pull" support through customer-targeted advertising are other ways to gain channel commitment.

Sometimes the choice between direct and indirect channels is based on the likelihood that the channel member will compete with your product. Most channel members are in business solely to act as an intermediary between firms and customers. However, sometimes channel members become competitors. Store brands or private labels are examples of channel-manufacturer competition and during the early 1990s gained share at the expense of national brands. The Gap started by selling Levi's jeans and other products. However, The Gap switched to selling its own brand of jeans and eventually dropped Levi Strauss as a supplier.

Another factor in the decision between direct and indirect channels is customer loyalty. For some kinds of products, the customer builds loyalty to the channel member rather than to the manufacturer. This loyalty can pose a long-term problem if the channel member drops the product. For example, customers are often more loyal to their stockbrokers than to the brokerage firm. As a result, if the broker leaves, say, Merrill Lynch and goes to Paine Webber, the customer will shift his or her business along with the broker.

Finally, advances in information technology are disrupting the channel structure of many industries. Not only are more channels, such as electronic shopping services and telemarketing, being added to the channel mix, but in some circumstances channels are being bypassed. For example, Wal-Mart's deliveries come directly from manufacturers rather than through a wholesaler because its suppliers are tied in directly to Wal-Mart's central computers that track sales by item.

Indirect Channels

The main choices among indirect channels are

1. Representatives/agents (reps), who sell the product or service but carry no inventory and merely refer orders back to the manufacturer. Reps are common for many industrial goods as well as for personal insurance and real estate.
2. Wholesalers/brokers, who physically take possession of the product and then resell it to retailers.
3. Retailers, who take possession of the product and resell it to final customers (who, of course, may use it as a component in their own products).

The choice of channel involves division of effort and profits. From the company's point of view, an ideal channel does all the work (incurs all the cost) at a high level of quality and incurs all the demand uncertainty while making a minimal profit. Obviously, from the channel's point of view, the opposite is true. Choice of channel therefore implies trade-offs, with the stronger party gaining the greater share of available profits.

Channel image can also have an impact on the product, and vice versa. High-quality channels enhance the appeal of a product; low-quality channels often decrease the value of a product, as Izod found out when it started selling its once-famed crocodile shirt through discounters. In other words, being featured at "blue light specials" may increase volume at the cost of brand equity and profits.

Channel Members as Value-Added Intermediaries

A distribution system can be thought of as a value-added chain (see Figure 13–7). In this system, firms supply the product manager with the raw material for the product or service in question (with services, the raw material might be limited to people and the "suppliers" would be the labor market). The channel options between the product and the end customer are intermediaries that may or may not take title to or possession of the product. For example, travel service firms usually do not buy the seats on the

FIGURE 13–7 The Distribution Value-Added Chain

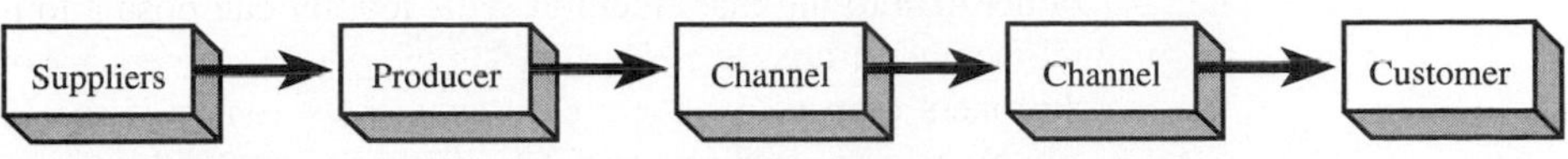

FIGURE 13–8 Services Provided by Channel Members

- *Marketing research:* Gathering information necessary for planning and facilitating interactions with customers
- *Communications:* Developing and executing communications about the product or service
- *Contact:* Seeking out and interacting with prospective customers
- *Matching:* Shaping and fitting (customizing) the product or service to the customer's requirements
- *Negotiation:* Reaching final agreement on price and other terms of the transaction
- *Physical distribution:* Transporting and storing goods (inventory)
- *Financing:* Providing credit or funds to facilitate the transaction
- *Risk taking:* Assuming risks associated with getting the product or service from firm to customer
- *Service:* Developing and executing ongoing relationships with customers, including maintenance and repair

airplanes they are selling; instead, they act as agents on behalf of the airlines.[3] Oil brokers take title to large quantities of the product but usually do not take physical possession of it.

The intermediaries in Figure 13–7 survive only if they add value to the product. These intermediaries are compensated through margins based on the value of the services delivered. If no services that add value can be delivered, there is no economic rationale for having a particular intermediary.

What kinds of services do channel members normally provide? Figure 13–8 lists some of them. Some services are particularly valuable to the product manager and are clearly worthy of compensation. Physical distribution is often very important, particularly when customers are geographically dispersed. Distributors often can also promote the product more efficiently. Auto dealers, electronics stores, and farm equipment dealers all do the actual selling. Matching customers to specific products can be particularly important for complex products. For example, the local area network supplier Novell used regional Bell operating companies to determine the exact needs of new office buildings for computer interconnections.

In designing a distribution (supply) chain, it is important to make sure all the functions in Figure 13–9 are covered. Unless you can put a "check" in each row indicating that one part of the supply chain is dealing with each activity, the supply

[3]There are, of course, travel service firms that actually buy airline seats in bulk and resell them to customers.

FIGURE 13–9 Channel Function Analysis

	Channel			Internal	
	Representative	*Wholesaler*	*Retailer*	*Sales force*	*Direct (phone, mail, Internet)*
Research information					
Communication					
Contact					
Matching/customizing					
Negotiating					
Physical distribution					
Financing					
Risk taking					
Product service					
Relationship management					
Overall attractiveness					

chain is probably inadequate. Figure 13–9 also raises the issue of whom to contact, whom to deliver to, and so on. Therefore, it should be considered on a segment-by-segment basis to make sure all key segments are covered.

The product manager can also use the services channel members provide to help identify which ones are attractive at any given point in time. For example, assume the product manager has assigned a set of weights that sum to 1 to the importance of the different functions provided. The product manager then rates each channel option on, say, a 1 to 7 scale, evaluating the ability of the option to provide the function. By multiplying the importance weight of the function by the channel evaluation and adding across all the functions, each channel receives a score that can be compared against the other options. Although you should not rely solely on a mechanical scoring procedure for making important decisions such as which channel(s) to use, the process of thinking about the importance weights and how the different channel options perform the functions shown in Figure 13–9 is very useful.

Hybrid Channels

Product managers often use combinations of channels. For example, a common approach is to use direct sales to large accounts (either final users or discounters) and a wholesaler to smaller accounts (for which direct sales are not cost effective).

Figure 13–10 shows an example of a hybrid marketing system[4] utilizing different channel options. The channels vary by the tasks they perform for the product manager. These tasks include lead generation, qualifying sales leads, presale marketing activity, closing the sale, postsales service, and account management, that is, maintaining

[4]See Rowland T. Moriarity and Ursula Moran, "Managing Hybrid Marketing Systems," *Harvard Business Review* 68 (1990), pp. 146–55.

FIGURE 13–10 A Hybrid Marketing Channel System

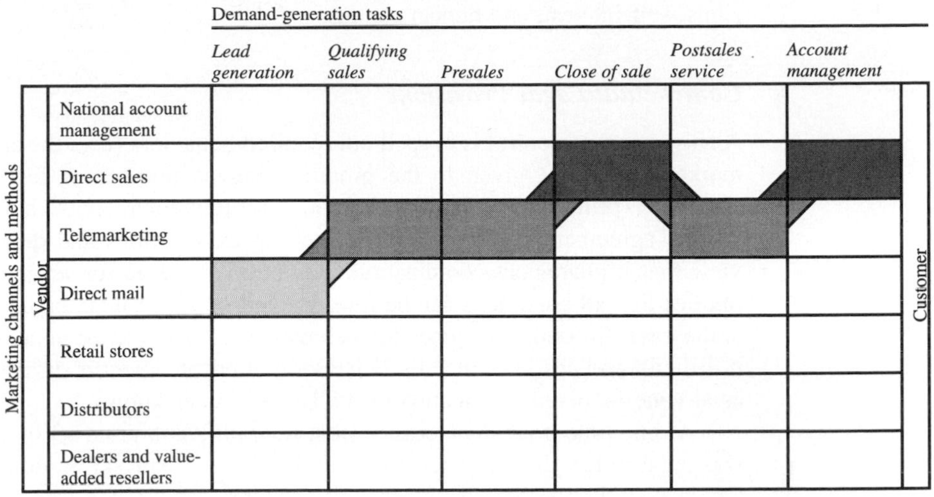

Demand-generation tasks

Marketing channels and methods (Vendor)	*Lead generation*	*Qualifying sales*	*Presales*	*Close of sale*	*Postsales service*	*Account management*	Customer
National account management							
Direct sales							
Telemarketing							
Direct mail							
Retail stores							
Distributors							
Dealers and value-added resellers							

Source: Reprinted by permission of Harvard Business Review. An exhibit from "The Hybrid Grid: The Elements of a Hybrid Marketing System," by Rowland R. Moriarity and Ursula Moran, November–December 1990. Copyright © 1990 by the President and Fellows of Harvard College; all rights reserved.

relations with an existing account. The various methods and channels that can be used to accomplish these tasks are listed down the side of the figure. In this example, direct mail is used to generate leads, telemarketing to qualify leads and for presale activity, and postsales service, and direct sales to close the deal and manage the account once the sale is made. The grid in Figure 13–10 can be useful for identifying points of overlap and conflict in a marketing system. It can also be useful for designing a system for a new target group of customers who may require a different marketing approach than prior customers.

Summary

The main problem with using multiple channels is the conflict that often results when multiple channels try to attract the same customers. At some level, then, channel selection involves selecting a portfolio of approaches that is neither too large (so that it is inefficient, gives little incentive to any channel member to promote the product, and leads to conflict among the channels) nor too small (leaving important customer segments or activities uncovered).

Channel Control

Channel management is easiest when the incentives of the manufacturer and the channel are consistent, and consistent goals are another useful basis for channel selection. At some point, however, a manufacturer generally wants to exert some direct control over the channel. The degree of control a company has through an intermediary depends on three basic components of the relationship: contractual/legal provisions, self-interest, and human contact.

Contractual/Legal Provisions

A naive view of control is to spell out required behaviors (e.g., the amount and type of marketing support given to the product such as number of feature ads run) and outcomes (primarily sales volume) through written contracts. Although some level of written agreement is often useful for setting expectations and delineating roles, the view that it guarantees coordination and control is naive for several reasons. First, it implies that all conditions can be foreseen and specified unambiguously, which rarely is the case. Second, it assumes the behavior specified will be adhered to. Not only is it difficult and costly to monitor behavior, but enforcement is difficult and expensive, as anyone involved in litigation in the United States knows.

At one time price maintenance (that is, selling at a price set by the manufacturer) was legal in the United States. In the early 1960s, Head Ski introduced the metal ski, which it sold only through specific specialty retailers, which were required to feature the skis and sell them at a set price. Head dropped retailers that did not follow the policy. The company had this degree of control largely because of its technological strength and the equity of the brand. However, as other competitors began producing skis of high quality and retailers grew larger and hence less dependent on a particular product line, manufacturer control of the channel decreased. Decreased control, coupled with the abolition of "fair trade" laws (which allowed a manufacturer to set the retail price), effectively ended Head's control over the channel.

Self-Interest

A good starting point for understanding the behavior of people or organizations is their own utility function. Put more bluntly, most people act largely, if not exclusively, in their own best interests. In business dealings, self-interest is largely coincident with economic interest. In other words, channels act to maximize their profits.

The term *agency theory,* borrowed from economics, refers to the behavior of an agent (channel) in response to the needs or demands of a principal (manufacturer). Considerable effort has been expended to relate this concept to sales force compensation, channel selection and control, and consumer promotion, and an excellent review of its use in marketing is available.[5] Basically, agency theory formalizes the explicit consideration of self-interest.

Consider the example of a manufacturer (Good Stuff, Inc.) of hardware items (hammers, screwdrivers, etc.) selling through four retailers in a concentrated geographic region (see Figure 13–11). From which channel would you like the most

[5]Mark Bergen, Shantanu Dutta, and Orville C. Walker, Jr., "Agency Relationships in Marketing: A Review of the Implications and Applications of Agency and Related Theories," *Journal of Marketing* 56 (1992), pp. 1–24.

FIGURE 13–11 Good Stuff, Inc., Sales by Channel

Channel	*Dollar Volume (000s)*	*Percent of Channel's Total Sales*
Sears	62	0.12
Home Depot	20	1.02
Cost Cutters	6	0.63
Pro Hardware	12	21.17
	100	

Source: Mark Bergen, Shantanu Dutta, and Orville C. Walker, Jr., "Agency Relationships in Marketing: A Review of the Implications and Applications of Agency and Related Theories," *Journal of Marketing* 56 (1992), pp. 1–24.

cooperation, and from which channel would you expect the most cooperation? Obviously, Sears represents the most volume (62 percent of your sales) and hence is most critical to you, followed by Home Depot and Pro Hardware. On the other hand, as a percentage of Sears's total sales (and profits), you represent very little. Hence you depend on Sears far more than it depends on you (unless, of course, your hammer has impact as a traffic builder or an image creator, which seems highly unlikely for an unknown company called Good Stuff). Consequently, you will have little control over Sears. Since it already carries Craftsman (its own brand) and Stanley Works tools, you are likely to be a price brand (and have very poor margins) at Sears. In contrast, you are somewhat more important to Pro Hardware than it is to you (at least in terms of volume), so you will tend to have more control over it. This means not only that you could enforce contract provisions with Pro Hardware for marketing support (e.g., newspaper advertising) but also that Pro Hardware will tend to display and promote your product on its own. Hence it is important to assess the (economic) importance of manufacturers to channels, and vice versa, before structuring formal arrangements and behavioral expectations.

Company policy often dictates using a shared company sales force. Using a company sales force is similar to using other channels such as representatives. The sales staff has multiple products and the attention it can pay to yours is limited. Although you can try to get management to single out your product for extra effort, other product managers are likely to be doing the same thing. Hence the best approach to getting attention is the same for any channel: Make it easy to sell the product and thus earn commissions or bonuses, provide incentives (in addition to cash, prizes and other incentives have impact), and maintain simple human contact. Put bluntly, selling the sales force is an important job of the product manager, and the company sales force is best treated as a potential channel to be encouraged rather than as a dedicated staff.

Human Contact

A final source of control in any kind of relationship is human contact. How often have you done something (given a donation, bought a product) just because someone asked you nicely? Most people respond positively to friendly, reasonable requests. Hence regular contacts by competent company personnel are likely to encourage desirable behavior above and beyond that driven by contracts and economic self-interest. In contrast, standoffish, bureaucratic treatment will decrease support. It is hard to say *please* and *thank you* too often.

Power in Channel Relationships

How different parties in a channel relationship ultimately get along relates to the balance of power among them. The party with the most power generally calls the shots and dominates the relationship. As noted earlier in this chapter, in many consumer product categories power has drifted more and more toward large retailers.

What factors affect this balance of power? Channel members are likely to have significant bargaining power with the product manager if:

- The channel's volume of sales of the product is large relative to the product's total sales volume.
- The product is not well differentiated from competitors (having brand equity leads to power over the channels).
- The channel has low switching costs; that is, it is relatively easy to find an alternative to replace the product.
- The channel poses a credible threat of backward integration or competing with the product.
- The channel member has better information than the product manager about market conditions. (Note that with scanner data, retailers now know the profitability of various products and hence are less easily influenced by manufacturer claims.)

As noted previously, the product manager–channel relationship need not be adversarial; that is, it is mutually beneficial for all parties in the channel structure to be successful. Still, the party with incremental power (or the perception of power) is often able to take aggressive actions. For example, a product manager could allocate less product to a retailer, or a channel member could drop a supplier capriciously.

Coping with Power Retailers

Figures 13–3 and 13–4 describe the rapid growth of "power" retailers in many product categories. Some ways product managers can deal with power retailers are the following:[6]

- Protect the brand name. If customers come to a store and ask for the product by brand, the retailer's power is diluted. This implies spending money on the consumer franchise building activities.
- Customize products and promotions. This involves treating each retailing chain as a separate market segment and developing a unique approach for each, such as separate brand names or model numbers.

[6]Zachary Schiller, Wendy Zellner, Ron Stodghill II, and Mark Maremont, "Clout! More and More, Retail Giants Rule the Marketplace," *Business Week,* December 21, 1992, pp. 66–73.

- Innovate constantly, since commodities are sold based on price.
- Organize around the customers, in this case the retailers, as mentioned in Chapter 1.
- Invest in technology. The large retailers are demanding that their suppliers be as sophisticated as they are in managing inventory and monitoring sales performance.
- Cut costs to keep prices down.
- Support smaller retailers as well; they may grow and help you survive sometime in the future!

Channel Arrangements

Exactly what duties channels perform and how they are compensated is open to negotiation. Many channels have patterns and hence expectations of treatments (e.g., a set markup to retail for wholesalers). Thus a practical starting point is the industry standard.

One important area of arrangement is (1) *service.* When a customer finds that a product does not perform according to expectations, he or she often returns to the place of purchase. An important issue, therefore, is who is responsible for service and at what level (e.g., replacement or repair, training, timeliness). Other issues include (2) *delivery* (timing, speed), (3) *price,* (4) *returns and allowances* policy (e.g., can the channel return unused product for a full refund up to a certain date?), and (5) *support level* given the product by the channel (e.g., display) and the channel by the company (e.g., advertising). Another important issue is (6) *the degree of exclusivity* afforded the channel and product (e.g., may an auto dealer sell multiple nameplates/brands?). Further, the (7) *compensation* expected for a sale when direct company sales effort and a channel's region and customers overlap (see Figure 13–12) is important. Even if a product manager has little control over these arrangements, the manager still benefits from a clear understanding of what they are.

Monitoring Profitability by Channel

Obviously, many aspects of a channel are worth monitoring, including effort, specific support programs (e.g., advertising), and the quality level of the channel (cleanliness, intelligence of personnel, etc.). Here we focus on one important aspect: profitability by channel, with the implicit goal of considering when to add or delete a channel. Basically, this is an exercise in cost accounting, with cost allocation being the key decision.[7] The same basic approach that applies to evaluating products (e.g., direct product profitability or DPP) or territories applies here: Assign revenues and costs to subunits (channels, products, territories) and then ask whether other considerations (e.g., future trends, image, contracts) affect current profit-based decisions.

[7]We cover more accounting-related issues in product management in Chapter 15.

FIGURE 13–12 Channel Arrangements

Inventory	Who holds it; who pays for it
Service	Who does what—repair, replacement, training—and who pays for it
	Quality expectations
	Timeliness
Delivery	Time frame
	Minimum order size
	Customization
Price	Wholesalers/brokers:
	Basic price
	Discount schedule
	Payment (e.g., terms)
	Reps/agents: Commissions/fees
Returns and allowances	What is allowed to be returned and at what price by customer, channel
Support level: channel	Sales effort
	Advertising
	Display prominence
Support level: company	Sales effort
	Advertising
	Stocking
Exclusivity	Overlapping channels
	Overlapping product lines
Credit for sales	When direct contact occurs in a channel's region or customer list, how much does the channel get

Consider the hypothetical Surefoot Company, which makes a line of running shoes. As product manager of the Master, a training shoe, you are interested in the profitability of the three channels you use:

- Specialty outdoor and running stores.
- General sporting goods stores (e.g., Sport's Authority).
- Discount stores (e.g., Kmart, Wal-Mart).

You have the following data:

1. Sales are $150,000 for specialty stores, $450,000 for general stores, and $300,000 for discount stores.
2. Gross margin is 50 percent.
3. Salaries and fringes for the people working on the Master (manager, salespeople, warehouse, clerical) are $150,000.
4. The lease on the building where offices and warehouse facilities are located is $75,000 per year.
5. Purchases of supplies total $40,000.
6. The co-op advertising budget is $90,000 per year.

Notice this example includes no fixed assets. If such assets existed, you might also consider their opportunity cost (e.g., a $1 million building in a company that earns a 10 percent return on capital has a $100,000 implicit cost to being in business, and unless

FIGURE 13–13 Overall Surefoot Master Contribution

Sales	$900,000	
Cogs	450,000	
Gross margin		$450,000
Salaries	150,000	
Lease	75,000	
Supplies	40,000	
Advertising	90,000	
		355,000
Net profit		$ 95,000

FIGURE 13–14 Allocation of Costs by Function

	Function		
	Sales	*Advertising*	*Shipping & Billing*
Salaries	$ 60,000	$ 30,000	$ 60,000
Lease	10,000	20,000	45,000
Supplies	10,000	20,000	10,000
Advertising		90,000	
	$ 80,000	$160,000	$ 115,000

you cover that you might be better off dropping the particular product/channel). Here the overall profitability, given in Figure 13–13, is $95,000, a 10.6 percent return on sales. However, as in many cases, the aggregate picture may obscure problems (or opportunities).[8] Here we assess the profitability of the three main channels (specialty, sporting goods, and discount stores). To do that, we need to allocate costs to represent activities. We could allocate costs based on percent of sales, but this approach does not recognize differential expenses and would make all channels appear profitable.

Instead we allocate costs in two steps. First, we allocate the basic expenses (salaries, etc.) to functions (selling, advertising, etc.). For salaries, allocation often is based on the percentage of time spent on the activities. For leases, allocation can be based on the amount of space allocated to each activity. For supplies, allocation can be based on purchase orders. In this case, assume the allocation was as shown in Figure 13–14.

Next, we allocate functional costs to the channels based on activity level. That is, we can allocate selling expense per sales call, advertising based on actual billings (here we use a per-ad basis that would be accurate if a fixed subsidy per ad were offered), and shipping and billing per order (which will slightly understate the cost of large orders). This leads to the breakdown given in Figure 13–15.

[8]This is referred to as the "iceberg" principle in Chapter 15.

FIGURE 13–15 Allocation of Functional Costs to Channels

Basis for Allocation	*Selling (number of sales calls)*	*Advertising (number of ads)*	*Shipping and Billing (number of orders)*
Specialty stores	5,000	800	13,000
Sporting goods stores	4,000	1,600	4,000
Discount stores	1,000	600	3,000
Total	10,000	3,000	20,000
Expense to allocate	$80,000	$150,000	$115,000
Expense per activity	$8	$53.33	$5.75

FIGURE 13–16 Profit by Channel for Master Shoes

	Channel		
	Specialty	*Sporting Goods*	*Discount*
Sales	$150,000	$450,000	$300,000
COGS	75,000	225,000	150,000
Gross margin	75,000	225,000	150,000
Selling	40,000	32,000	8,000
Advertising	42,667	85,333	32,000
Shipping and billing	74,750	23,000	17,250
	157,417	140,333	57,250
Net profit	$(82,417)	$85,667	$92,750
Return on sales	(54.9%)	19.0%	30.9%

Using the results in Figure 13–15, we now restructure the profit statement of Figure 13–13 into three separate statements in Figure 13–16. For example, allocating selling expense per call leads to a selling expense for specialty channels of 5,000 calls × $8/call = $40,000. Notice that the picture is now quite different: Discount stores appear to be most profitable, followed by sporting goods stores, with specialty stores apparently unprofitable. This analysis reflects the economies of scale in dealing with large customers.

The obvious next question is what to do about these findings. The obvious, naive, and usually incorrect answer is to drop specialty channels. This response ignores both the still aggregate (e.g., across all specialty stores) nature of the analysis and the possibility that costs would not go down as a result of dropping a channel. Hence, although channel deletion may be worth considering, a number of issues must be addressed:

1. Does appearance in specialty stores enhance brand equity? Do people see the shoes there, then look for them on sale at sporting goods or discount stores? Conversely, does the shoes' presence in discount stores detract from brand equity?

2. Is selling expense an allocated part of a shared sales force and hence fixed?
3. Is the lease breakable? Would the same space be used even if a channel (e.g., specialty) were dropped?
4. Is the shoe part of a product line that enhances the sale of other Surefoot products (e.g., the Novice, etc.)?
5. Should the company change the allocation of sales calls by channel?
6. Should the company use distributors rather than sell direct to the specialty stores (thereby decreasing both sales and shipping and handling expenses)?
7. Are there some specialty stores that are profitable (and some discount stores that are not)?

In short, the product manager should assess the profitability of channels carefully and not jump to hasty conclusions.

Direct Contact

Perhaps the strongest trend in marketing has been toward forms of direct marketing. Direct marketing includes traditional methods such as direct mail and phone (telemarketing), which have become ubiquitous. (Check your mail or see if you don't get a call during dinner this week.) It also includes the burgeoning business of Internet-based marketing via the World Wide Web, often accessed through services such as America Online, Prodigy, and CompuServe. Another trend is for consumer goods retailers to establish their own retail outlets rather than sell only through department and discount stores, creating numerous discount shopping malls featuring "factory outlet" stores. As an example, Niketown, a three-story store owned and run by Nike on Chicago's Michigan Avenue, sells only Nike products separated by activities (e.g., basketball, tennis). Niketown is a minimall in itself. Not only does the store expose shoppers to the entire Nike line; it also does a fairly good retail business. Also, by selling at full price, the store establishes a reference point that makes purchases at discount seem like a great deal, thus increasing their likelihood. Perhaps most fascinating is a room where Nike TV commercials are shown continuously on a wide screen. The room always seems to contain at least 10 to 15 people, which is perhaps the ultimate compliment: People come to your store to watch your ads. Looming on the horizon is increased use of computerized contact, already apparent in TV simulated-auction shows such as the Home Shopping Network.

Direct Marketing

The scope of direct marketing is huge, as documented by the Direct Market Association's *Statistical Fact Book.* Its use goes far beyond catalog sales of clothing epitomized by L. L. Bean and Lands' End. For example, by 1995, 37 percent of mutual funds were sold by direct marketing. In 1990 companies spent over $23 billion in the United States on direct-mail advertising, and a typical family received 12 pieces of third-class mail a day, with high-income families receiving much more. (Of course a substantial percentage, 20 percent or more, is thrown away without being opened.) A trade association (the Direct Marketing Association), the *Journal of Direct Marketing,* and numerous books are devoted to the subject.[9] According to a study done for the Direct Marketing Association, $1 in every $15 in sales comes from direct marketing.[10]

The response to direct solicitation varies widely, depending on the product category, perceived product quality, price, presentation method (including what page a product appears on in a catalog), perceived risk,[11] and copy.[12] It also depends heavily on characteristics of the "in-home" shopper.[13]

Customer Acquisition

Much of the literature and popular press focuses on one-shot attempts to get prospects to buy something. The process has two stages: target (list) identification and actual solicitation.

Customer targeting follows the basic principles of Chapter 6; that is, you look for high potential customers (e.g., those with high income). For ongoing businesses, this is typically done by gathering data on current customers and then targeting similar individuals or businesses. If your current customers are primarily young urban professionals (people in certain ZIP codes), they are probably the best target.

In general, samples are used to determine or predict response rates in different segments. One approach links sample response to individual characteristics (e.g., income, education, age) by a statistical procedure such as regression analysis or variations such as discriminant analysis, log linear models, and AID (automatic interaction detector). Basically, these techniques use samples of customers to predict response (e.g., response rate to an offering) based on income and other variables. For example, assume you ran a regression based on 2,000 people similar to model A in Figure 13–17. The advantage of this approach is that it generates a predicted response rate for each segment (i.e., age by income by education category).

The break-even response rate a solicitation needs to be profitable is

$$\text{Break-even response rate} = \frac{\text{Cost of solicitation}}{\text{Expected net revenue from a respondent.}}$$

Hence, one rule is to solicit only those segments whose expected response rates are above the break-even rate.

---

[9]Some good books on this subject are E. L. Nash, ed., *The Direct Marketer's Handbook* (New York: McGraw-Hill, 1992); Mary Lou Roberts and Paul D. Berger, *Direct Marketing Management* (Englewood Cliffs, N.J.: Prentice Hall, 1989); and David Shepard, *The New Direct Marketing* (Homewood, Ill.: Dow Jones-Irwin, 1990).

[10]The WEFA Group, Inc., *Economic Impact: US Direct Marketing Today,* a landmark study (1995) conducted for the Direct Marketing Association.

[11]Dennis E. McCorkle, "The Role of Perceived Risk in Mail Order Shopping," *Journal of Direct Marketing* 4 (Autumn 1990), pp. 26–35.

[12]David L. Williams, John D. Beard, and J. Patrick Kelly, "The Readability of Direct-Mail Copy: A Test of Its Effect on Response Rates," *Journal of Direct Marketing* 5 (1991), pp. 27–34.

[13]Kenneth C. Gehrt and Kent Carter, "An Exploratory Assessment of Catalog Shopping Orientations: The Existence of Convenience and Recreational Segments," *Journal of Direct Marketing* 6 (Winter 1992), pp. 29–39; Dennis E. McCorkle, John M. Planchon, and William L. James, "In-Home Shopping: A Critical Review and Research Agenda," *Journal of Direct Marketing* 1 (Spring 1987), pp. 5–21.

FIGURE 13–17 Basic Models for Analyzing Direct Response

A. *From a one-time sample:*
Response rate = Constant + B_1 (Income) + B_2 (If Age < 30) + B_3 (If $30 <$ Age < 50) + B_4 (If college education)

B. *From a customer response data base:*
Response rate = Constant + B_1 (if purchased within 6 months) + B_2 (Number of purchases made in the past year) + B_3 (Dollar amount)

FIGURE 13–18 Determining Profitable Segments and Number of Contacts

	Contact/Solicitation Attempt			
Segment	*A*	*B*	*C*	*D*
1 (highest potential)	5.32	4.02	3.18	2.14
2		4.61	2.70	
3			3.98	2.02
4				2.51
5				
6 (lowest potential)				

Another approach involves doing repeat mailings until the mailings stop being profitable. Typically the response rate decreases as one moves from higher potential segments to lower ones. Assume there were six segments arranged from high to low potential. Given that the break-even response rate is 3 percent, you would first contact some members of the first (highest-potential) segment. If the response was 5.32 percent, you would mail to this entire segment and proceed to sample segments 2 (4.61 percent) and then 3 (3.98 percent). When you contacted segment 4 (2.51 percent), however, you would find it to be unprofitable. Hence you would restrict your mass solicitation to segments 1, 2, and 3.

This same logic applies to subsequent contacts to the same target segment. If the first contact generated a 5.32 percent response, you would contact them again (4.02 percent) and again (3.18 percent) until it was no longer profitable to do so (2.14 percent). This would lead to Figure 13–18, which suggests it is worth three tries to attract business from segment 1, one try each for segments 2 and 3, and no tries for segments 4 (and, by implication, 5 and 6).

Of course, if you had a panel of people who had received several direct solicitations, you could use a model based on actual experience with these customers (model B in Figure 13–17) and eliminate the so-called list-processing and segmentation problems.[14] This approach, called *database marketing,* relies on a customer database that is updated with each contact. Firms such as L. L. Bean in clothing and

[14]Arthur Blumenfeld, "List Processing," and Barry Hauser, "List Segmentation," in E. L. Nash, *The Direct Marketer's Handbook.*

USAA in insurance and other financial products have capitalized as much as or more on their customer information systems than they have on their products.

Customer Relationship Management

Once a customer base is established, two types of communication exist: customer initiated and company initiated. Customer-initiated communication benefits from easy access (e.g., 800 numbers or Internet sites) and provides both an opportunity to sell and a chance to learn about problems and preferences. Ford receives over 19,000 calls a day from customers and, having an operating system for dealing with them (i.e., requiring a person to respond within 30 seconds) is a major task. Likewise, capturing the information requires a well-designed system.

Company-initiated contact is of two types. One basically aims at enhancing the relationship. These include periodic mailings with information about the company or product (e.g., service interval reminders), special mailings (e.g., birthday greetings), and, for first-time buyers or buyers of expensive products, information to justify the decisions already made. The other type of contact is for the express purpose of selling more.

When a customer database exists, consumer response to direct-mail solicitations has traditionally been described in terms of *recency* (how recently they responded), *frequency* (how often they respond), and *amount spent,* referred to in the industry as *RFM.* In predicting recency, frequency, or amount spent from a customer response database, one approach uses the records of each customer directly. If someone responded two of four times, you could assume that person has a 50 percent response rate. Note, however, that this is a very small sample ($n = 4$) on which to base an estimate. Hence you might want to take into account either what the general response rate is (e.g., 5 percent) or what the response rates of similar people (in terms of age, income, and education) have been (e.g., 10 percent). In this case, the other information suggests that 50 percent may be too high an estimate. As a result, you may want to decrease the 50 percent by averaging it with the 5 percent or 10 percent figures in some manner.

The process of combining base rates (the 5 percent or 10 percent) with specific case information (the 50 percent) is formally done statistically using Bayes' theorem, which weights the base and case information by their accuracy. Therefore, if similar people were almost always close to 10 percent (i.e., in a range of 5 to 15 percent), you would tend to weight the 10 percent high. Conversely, if the case information had been based on a sample of not 4 but 400 solicitations, you would be reasonably confident that the 50 percent was correct and make your estimate accordingly.

In spite of the relatively low historic profile of direct marketing vis-à-vis advertising and promotion, it has probably generated better statistical work than most other areas, largely due to the volume of data direct-mail solicitations produce.[15]

---

[15]Amiya K. Basu, Atasi Basu, and Rajeev Batra, "Modeling the Response Pattern to Direct Marketing Campaigns," *Journal of Marketing Research* 32 (May 1995), pp. 204–12; Jan Roelf Bult and Tom Wansbeek, "Optimal Selection for Direct Mail," *Marketing Science* 14 (Winter 1995), pp. 378–94.

Mailings in the tens of thousands or even millions are common for consumer products. Recently so-called empirical Bayes methods have been applied to customer response data.

One approach[16] assumes individuals differ in their true (average, long-run) response rates according to the beta distribution (a flexible distribution bounded by 0 and 1 that can have a single peak at, say, 20 percent or be bimodal with segments clustered around zero and 100 percent response rates). The beta distribution describing the probability, *p,* of responding to a solicitation is given by

$$f(p) = \frac{g(a+b)}{g(a)g(b)} p^{(a-1)}(1-p)^{b-1}$$

where $g(\ )$ is the gamma function. The expected value of p is $a(a + b)$.

Assume a and b are related to descriptor variables (e.g., age) as follows:

$$a = A_0 + A_1X_1 + A_2X_2 + \ldots$$
$$b = B_0 + B_1X_1 + B_2X_2 + \ldots$$

Then the *A*s and *B*s (the unknown parameters) can be estimated based on sample data. Given *A*s and *B*s, each person has a base (estimated) purchase probability described by a and b.

We can update a person's average response rate based on his or her specific response to previous solicitations. For example, if a person has responded to three of eight solicitations, the new mean becomes

$$\text{Person A's estimated response rate} = \frac{a + 3}{a + b + 8}$$

Hence, as the number of solicitations increases, the expected response rate approaches the rate of the individual customer. In essence, this approach combines the response factors in model B with the general background factors in model A in predicting response. Based on the submissions to the Marketing Science Institute and Direct Marketing Association's Research Competitions on Understanding and Measuring the Effects of Direct Marketing, more of this sophisticated statistical type of work will soon be available.

Of course, at some point the probability that a customer will respond profitably drops below break-even. At this point, a decision needs to be made as to whether the customer is (1) "dead"/inactive, (2) not worth serving, or (3) just temporarily out of the market. The decision to prune lists is often as crucial as the decision of whom to contact from the list when margins are thin and cost of contact is nontrivial. For low-potential customers, most firms rely on customer-initiated contacts (800 numbers, etc.) and focus company-initiated efforts on high-potential customers. (Note the similarity between this approach and a channel strategy of direct sales to big accounts and the use of distributors for small accounts.)

This discussion has implicitly assumed a single type of solicitation. Obviously, an essentially infinite number can be employed. Hence, in reality the problem is more complex in that different solicitations (formats, specific offerings) need to be tested.

[16]Bruce S. Buchanan and Donald G. Morrison, "Stochastic Modeling of List Falloffs with Implications for Repeat Mailings," *Journal of Direct Marketing* 2 (1988), pp. 7–14.

Moreover, the optimal solicitation may differ by segment or even by individual customer. In essence, this turns the problem of designing customer contact into a market research problem with heavy reliance on sampling and experimental design. Knowing how well most students enjoy that topic and how much space it would take to thoroughly cover it, we leave this to other sources.

Trade Shows

An often overlooked but also often critical channel is trade shows. This multibillion-dollar industry plays a key role in many categories. Boat shows, computer expos, and the like are a constant activity. Trade shows account for 22 percent of business-to-business marketing activities[17] and are important for both channel and final customer contact.

Trade shows provide a way to generate publicity and sales leads as well as actual sales. They also serve as a way to get customer feedback (from a nonrandom sample of potential customers) and competitor information. The negative side of trade shows is that competitors get (early) information about your products as well. Still, for many products, trade shows are make-or-break activities, especially in terms of press coverage. A number of factors influence performance, including preshow promotion booth space, attention-getting techniques, competition, and the number and training of salespeople.[18] Even placement within a show matters; Alcort Sailfish got a major boost when its booth happened to be placed next to the largest boat at the New York Boat Show. Thus, especially for durable goods, a product manager needs to consider when and how to include trade shows in the channel strategy/marketing mix.

Summary

Clearly, a product manager has to determine some approach for getting products and services to customers. As we have noted in this chapter, this task involves first choosing among or selecting a combination of indirect and direct channels. One issue with respect to indirect channels involves selecting which indirect channels to utilize, deciding (jointly with the channels) what is expected of them, and how to compensate them. The other issue regarding indirect channels is to monitor both current volume and profit and trends in volume and profit (see Figure 13–19) and, to the extent possible, control them. Product managers should carefully monitor channels used by competitors lest an important innovation be overlooked. Product managers should also monitor sales through channels not chosen either by them or the competition. So-called gray markets (unauthorized dealers) often account for a large fraction (e.g., 30 percent) of actual sales.

Another major area concerning channel options involves direct solicitation. Besides selecting an approach (in-person sales force, mail, etc.), the product manager

[17]Trade Show Bureau, *Expositions in Today's Marketing Mix* (Denver, 1993).

[18]Srinath Gopalakrishna and Gary L. Lilien, "A Three-Stage Model of Industrial Trade Show Performance," *Marketing Science* 14 (Winter 1995), pp. 22–29.

FIGURE 13–19 Channel Monitoring

		Results			
		Volume		*Profit Contribution*	
Chosen Channels	*Desired Behaviors*	Expected	Actual	Expected	Actual
Agents/reps					
Wholesalers					
Distributors					
Retailers/dealers					

must specify target groups and method of solicitation, as well as the number of solicitations per member of the target group (see Figure 13–20). Of course, expected response rates and profits need to be calculated to check for the reasonableness of the plan and for comparison with actual results. Notice that unlike with advertising and even promotion, it is fairly easy to assess the profit impact of direct solicitation methods such as direct mail. Hence this area lends itself to analytical supervision. It is important to remember that not all customer contacts are equal. Merely finding them is insufficient; they must be satisfied with the interaction. One definition of customer contact is the interaction of communication time (length of contact), the richness of information, and the level of "intimacy"/personal customization,[19] essentially so-called quality time.

An important caveat with respect to direct solicitation has to do with invasion of privacy. Public sentiment in the United States does not universally favor direct solicitation; many view it as unfair and wasteful. Hence caution and good taste are recommended, as is attention to current and future laws governing its use.[20]

At the beginning of this book, we noted a distinction between product-based and market-based organizations. As information about customers becomes available through direct contact (or information sharing with channel members) and computer power and data storage capabilities allow for the capture and essentially instant analysis of the information, a market- (customer-) based organization becomes more desirable. Hence the issue of the value of a customer and the ability to cross-sell other products may outweigh the needs of a particular product. Combined with consumer retailers' focus on category management, the role of the autonomous manager of a narrowly defined brand appropriately decreases. Put differently, an organization structure now tends to include a matrixlike structure in which both brand and market (customer) managers exist, with market managers often the more powerful.

---

[19]Deborah L. Kellogg and Richard B. Chase, "Constructing an Empirically Derived Measure for Customer Contact," *Management Science* 41 (November 1995), pp. 1734–49.

[20]Paul N. Bloom, George R. Milne, and Robert Adler, "Avoiding Misuse of New Information Technologies: Legal and Societal Considerations," *Journal of Marketing* 58 (January 1994), pp. 98–110.

FIGURE 13–20 Direct Marketing Planning

A. Solicitation

	Direct Marketing Plan			**Response**		**Profitability**	
Method	*Target Group*	*Method of Solicitation*	*Number of Contacts*	*Expected*	*Actual*	*Expected*	*Actual*
In-person sales force							
Mail							
Phone							
Computerized							

B. Relationship Maintenance

	Direct Marketing Plan			**Response**		**Profitability**	
Method	*Target Group*	*Method of Solicitation*	*Number of Contacts*	*Expected*	*Actual*	*Expected*	*Actual*
In-person sales force							
Mail							
Phone							
Computerized							

C H A P T E R

14 Managing Service Quality

Overview

As noted in Chapter 1, shortening product life cycles put considerable pressure on product managers to continually innovate. As more competitors enter the marketplace both globally and domestically, products and services are becoming less unique. Thus, product managers continually search for a point of difference to trumpet over a rival's offering as an integral part of the marketing strategy.

Increased competitive pressure has caused product managers to seek new ways to differentiate their products and services. In the 1990s, this source of differentiation is often in the area of customer service. As the CEO of Fanuc Robotics North America has put it, "Everyone has become better at developing products. In robotics, the robot itself has become sort of a commodity. The one place you can differentiate yourself is in the service you provide."[1] As we argue, customer service is one dimension of the product offering that is very difficult to copy because it relies heavily on execution and a strong corporate service ethic, which are often hard to duplicate.

This chapter focuses on the role service quality plays in defining competitive advantage for a product or service. While the vast majority of this book is equally applicable to manufactured products and services, the concept of service quality requires a somewhat different perspective.

For services, service quality is equivalent to product quality and the service *is* the product. This is not a trivial matter for the U.S. economy. As of 1994, services accounted for about 75 percent of gross domestic product and 80 percent of all jobs, and provided a large balance of payment surplus as opposed to the deficit run by the manufacturing sector. Some of the fastest-growing companies in the United States are in the service sector; companies such as ServiceMaster (which fertilizes lawns, kills bugs, and scrubs floors), Waste Management (which may well pick up your garbage),

[1]Ronald Henkoff, "Service Is Everybody's Business," *Fortune,* June 27, 1994, pp. 48–60.

and even traditional manufacturing companies such as IBM and Johnson Controls (a maker of thermostats and energy systems) are experiencing tremendous growth rates in providing services to consumer and industrial markets.

For manufactured products, service quality issues usually surface under the concept of *customer service.* Most often, this is a reactive process in which the service operation kicks in when a customer has a problem getting a piece of software to work, the VCR user's book is unclear (a rather common occurrence), or a building air conditioning system breaks down. However, as the earlier robotics example shows, the way companies react to these situations is an important tool for product differentiation. Customers, whether they are purchasing industrial or consumer products, will tend to return to products when they feel they have been given extraordinary attention. This is true not only in a reactive sense; more and more companies are taking proactive stances when it comes to customer service for manufactured goods by encouraging and rewarding employees who monitor and produce customer satisfaction without first being contacted by customers.

It is interesting how management attention has shifted toward customer service from other "hot" areas. Prior to the development of modern marketing thought and the marketing concept formulated in the late 1950s, competition was (and still is in many product categories) focused on product specifications or features. However, from mid-1960 through the 1970s, the experience curve concept popularized by the Boston Consulting Group focused attention on lowering costs and prices to gain dominant market share in the markets targeted by the product manager. In the 1980s, product quality, as preached by Deming and Jurand and adopted by many Japanese companies, became the buzzword, culminating in the current heated competition for the Malcolm Baldrige National Quality Awards given to both manufacturing and service companies. Although the focus on product specifications and costs has certainly not been eliminated, many companies are turning to service quality and customer service issues as the path to obtaining sustainable competitive advantage.

The automobile brand Lexus highlights the value of a strong commitment to customer service. Lexus consistently scores at or near the top of the J. D. Power surveys of automobile customer satisfaction, even though the cars are not free of defects. An anecdote demonstrates Lexus's commitment to customer service. One California couple had planned a trip to Arizona and intended to drive their new Lexus. Unfortunately, the car had mechanical problems a few weeks prior to the trip. After the car was repaired, it broke down again the day before the trip. The local Lexus dealer flew the couple to Arizona at the company's expense and gave them the free use of a Lexus during their vacation!

What kind of customers did Lexus generate by that approach? Through the use of what is called *service recovery,* the company not only satisfied the customers but probably made them customers for life, with the mechanical problems of their car forgotten. At the cost of two round-trip airfares and a free rental car—under $1,000—the Lexus dealer probably sold several more cars in the future, generating profits that substantially outweighed the cost. This kind of attitude is one reason two-thirds of the people who buy a Lexus have bought one before, the highest repeat purchase rate in the luxury car market.

FIGURE 14–1 The Impact of Customer Retention on Profits

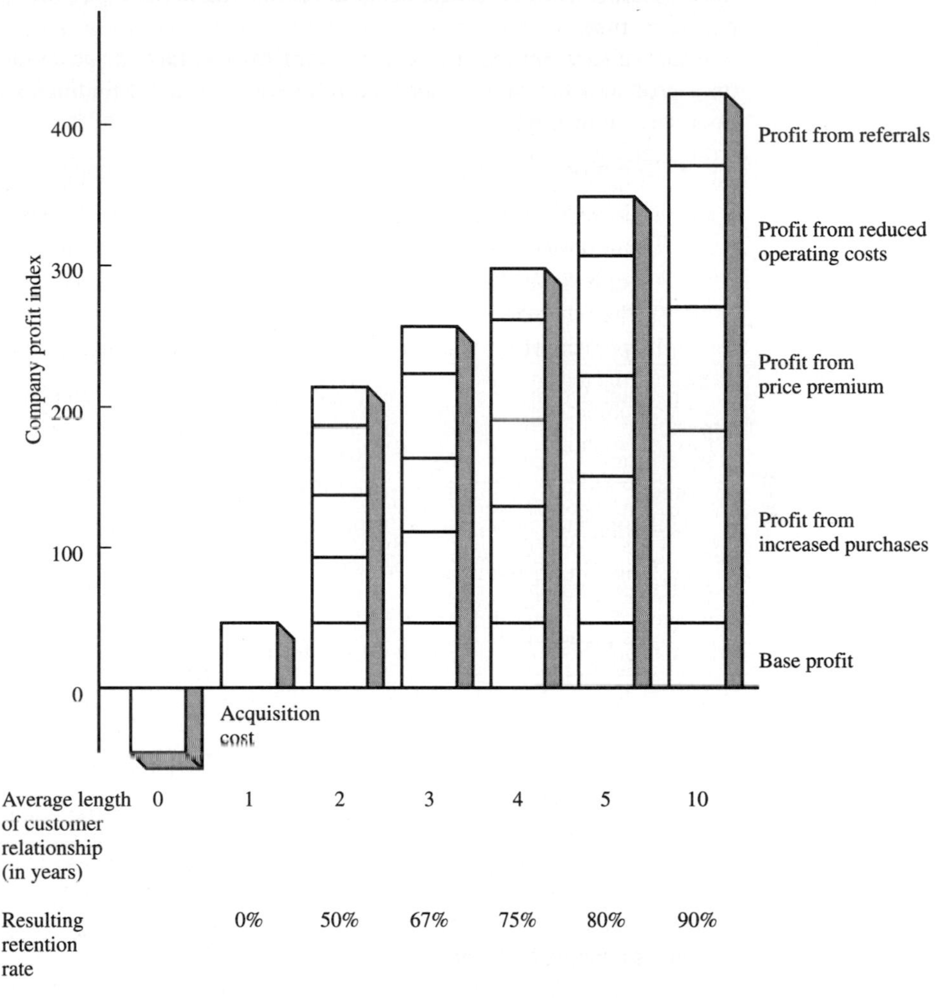

Source: Reprinted by permission of Harvard Business Review, "Zero Defections: Quality Comes to Services," by Frederick F. Reichheld and W. Earl Sasser, Jr., September–October 1990. Copyright © 1990 by the President and Fellows of Harvard College; all rights reserved.

Figure 14–1 shows the value of retaining customers.[2] This figure gives some idea of the amount of profit customer retention programs, such as strong service, can generate. Over time satisfied customers generate profit through increased purchasing,

[2]For further information on this topic, see James L. Heskett, W. Earl Sasser, Jr., and Christopher W. L. Hart, *Service Breakthroughs: Changing the Rules of the Game* (New York: The Free Press, 1990), chap. 3.

less price sensitivity, the lower costs of retention as opposed to new-customer prospecting, and referrals. These numbers, of course, are only broad guidelines, but the main message is clear: Investments in service quality can pay off substantially over a period of time.

Conversely, *not* making such investments can have a substantial negative impact on a product's health. Consider the following anecdotal findings about the results of poor service quality:[3]

- 26 out of 27 customers who have had a bad experience will fail to tell you.
- 91 percent of those who do not complain will not come back.
- The average disgruntled customer tells 9 to 10 other customers (and with today's widespread use of E-mail and mailing lists, it is very easy to tell many others quickly).
- 14 percent of the disgruntled customers tell more than 20 other customers.

In other words, most unhappy customers do not tell you they have had a bad experience with your product or a bad service encounter; they just switch to the competition.[4] (That is, they "exit" rather than "voice.") In addition, unhappy customers are not reluctant to spread the word.

Unhappy customers can be turned around. British Airways found that although 50 percent of customers who chose not to tell the airline about a problem with their experiences switched to other airlines, 87 percent of those with problems who contacted the airline did not defect. The "willing communicators" who volunteered information about a bad service encounter could, in fact, be convinced not to switch, showing the value of encouraging customers to communicate with the company.[5]

Therefore, service quality is an important competitive weapon both in differentiating products and services and in aiding customer retention. However, the concept of service quality needs to be broadly defined. In this chapter, we define service as *all* personal interactions customers have with the product and the company. This broader concept of service is important because ultimately customers determine the meaning of service and act accordingly.

Example: Federal Express

Federal Express is one of the greatest success stories in recent U.S. business history. Founded in 1971, the company grew from revenues of just over $17 million in 1974 to 1995 fiscal year revenues of nearly $10 billion. Many Americans are familiar with the humorous advertising campaign that helped the company grow. However, it is important to realize that Federal Express's outstanding performance is more a result of its

[3]These examples have been collected by the authors over time. The numbers should be taken not literally but more as an indication of the potential disastrous effects of poor service programs.

[4]If you do not believe this, how did you react the last time a waiter at a restaurant asked you how your meal was when you believed the meal and service were mediocre? We bet you said, "Fine."

[5]Charles R. Weiser, "Championing the Customer," *Harvard Business Review,* November–December 1995, pp. 113–16.

commitment to investing in service quality than to having creative advertising. This commitment to its customers culminated in 1990 when Federal Express was the first service company to be awarded the Baldrige award.

Around 1978, the company realized that although it had created the market for overnight delivery by owning its own planes, developing an innovative hub-and-spoke delivery system, and having an excellent record of on-time delivery, the competitive advantage these features provided was not sustainable. Other competitors, such as United Parcel Service (UPS), Emery Air Freight, and the U.S. Postal Service, had either the capabilities or the potential to offer a service with the same products and on-time record (except, perhaps, the U.S. Postal Service).

In addition, except for the airplane operations, all of the company's activities emanated from local stations that handled customer orders, pickup and delivery, sales, and customer service. This resulted in two interrelated problems. First, the rapid growth of the company increased the demands on station personnel beyond their capacity to handle customer inquiries and complaints. Second, these increased demands created service bottlenecks that reduced the efficiency of the operations and threatened product quality.

In 1978, the company decided to attack the problem with the first of a series of significant investments in customer service. First, it developed a computerized central order-taking system, called COSMOS, that became fully operational in early 1980. The COSMOS system was responsible for booking customer sales and tracking customer complaints and left the field stations to do the jobs of picking up and delivering packages and overnight letters, as well as handling sales efforts toward large customers. To send a package, a customer merely had to dial an 800 telephone number. The information from the phone call was then downloaded to the local station that would handle the shipment. Inquiries about the status of shipments were also handled this way. The introduction of COSMOS was soon followed by one of the early applications of bar coding, which allowed customers to find out exactly where their packages were in the system. FedEx again followed up with the installation of 15,000 "Powership" computer terminals at its customers' offices, which allowed customers to track their own shipments as though the goods were moving within the customers' own logistical systems. The most recent innovation is a Windows-based software package, called FedEx Ship, that lets even the smallest customers order pickups, print shipping labels, and track deliveries without using a telephone. Notice this not only makes it easier for the customer but also reduces costs for Federal Express, a so-called "killer application" of information technology. For overseas customers shipping to the United States, FedEx has developed a computerized customs clearing system that alerts U.S. customs officials about incoming international shipments before they arrive.

FedEx's basic product has not changed; the on-time record and the condition of the goods shipped have not markedly improved. However, the "extended" product incorporating the customer service enhancements has improved dramatically. By viewing the expenditures for service as investments rather than expenses for which a measurable return on investment has to be attained quickly, FedEx has been able to maintain its market leadership and generally higher prices. Perhaps even more important, it is difficult for competitors to copy the service enhancements given the magnitude of FedEx's investment and the lead time it has gained. UPS's initial response to a customer tracking system was to provide information via Prodigy, an independent fee-based service, rather than its own system. Thus, FedEx seems to have created a sustainable competitive advantage.

The Service Encounter

Service Quality

How do customers determine whether they have received good service from a supplier? One characteristic of services in general is that due to the intangibility of the "product," perceptions play a heavier role in assessing quality than they do with manufactured products. It is not an exaggeration to say that particularly with services, quality is how the customers perceive it.

Figure 14–2 is one writer's conceptualization of the service quality issue.[6] At the top of the figure, quality is defined in terms of customer perceptions. The final stage of the transaction between the firm and the customer occurs when the customer is assessing the quality of the service encounter, such as purchasing a service or engaging a manufacturer's customer service representative. The right side of the figure describes the customer evaluation process during and after the service contact. The left side depicts the customer's perceptions or forecast of what the service contact will be like. This forecast is often referred to as an *expectation.* Perceived quality of a customer service encounter, therefore, is influenced by a comparison of the expectation or forecast of the quality level to the actual perceived level of quality received.

Expectations are based on a variety of information sources. Clearly, past experience (if any) with the company in a similar situation plays a key role. If a customer called an 800 telephone number to solve a problem with some computer software and had to wait several hours to get through because all the lines were busy, those past experiences will create an expectation for a similar experience in the future. Customer needs also affect expectations; if the software problem is important to the operation of a business, the customer will expect (and hope) to get a quick answer. Other customers affect expectations of quality through the communications of their experiences, also referred to as *word of mouth.* Finally, companies take proactive roles in customer expectation formation through their communications: advertising, promotional material, and the sales force. Advertisements, for example, often tout "24-hour phone service."

The experienced quality (shown on the right side of Figure 14–2) results from an image or a perception formed by the customer after the customer service contact. This perception of the actual quality is based on two components. The first component is the set of features or attributes of the service, labeled "Technical quality: What?" in the figure. In the computer software example, this would be the quality of the advice

[6]See Christian Grönroos, *Service Management and Marketing* (Lexington, Mass.: Lexington Books, 1990).

FIGURE 14–2 A Model of Perceived Quality

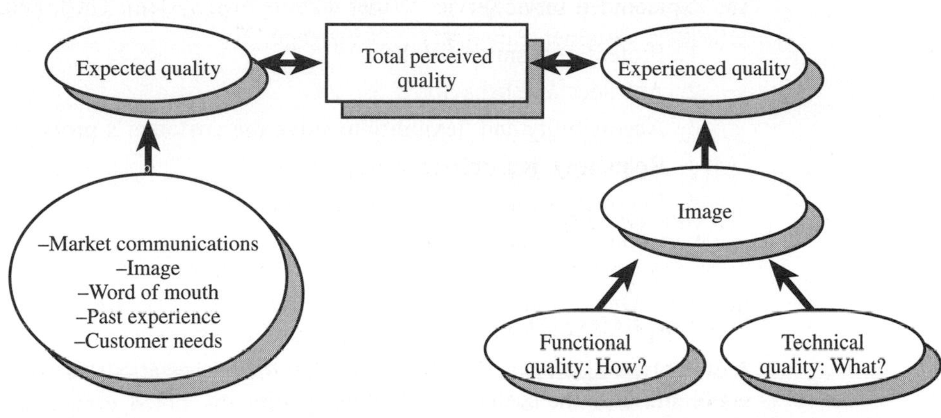

Source: Christian Grönroos, *Service Management and Marketing* (Lexington, Mass.: Lexington Books, 1990), p. 41.

given. This is the narrow view of service quality mentioned earlier in the chapter because it focuses only on the actual features of the encounter. The "Functional quality: How?" component refers to how the service is delivered, that is, the quality of the actual interaction with the company. This could be the friendliness of the telephone service person, how many rings it took before someone answered, and so on. This dimension of service quality is an extended notion that reflects the fact that customers take a broad view of the quality of a service encounter.

Consider a company that has recently purchased a new copier. Two kinds of customer service encounters can occur after the sale. First, the normal kind of service the company would expect is a maintenance call. Such calls may be either routine/scheduled or emergency with emergency calls being negative per se and extremely influential in quality perceptions. The customer forms a perception of the quality of a service call based on the quality of the repair work (technical quality) and the quality of the interaction with the firm, such as how long it took someone to come, whether the person was friendly and well groomed, and so on. To assess quality, the perception also would be matched against the company's expectation based on experience with prior service calls, promises made by the company through salespeople, advertising, and the urgency of the repair.

A second kind of service encounter is seller initiated. This is often called *account management* and entails communicating with the customer even when there is not a repair need or a problem with the service. Evaluating this kind of customer "service" encounter, a proactive move by the seller, would not necessarily involve all the components of Figure 14–2. In this case, technical quality is not really an issue. However, functional quality is critical; in fact, these kinds of ongoing account management activities affect subsequent evaluations of maintenance quality because they have a positive impact on functional quality. In addition, positive expectations of these activities enhance the customer's overall evaluation through the left side of Figure 14–2.

A number of studies have identified the following six factors as being most closely associated with good perceived service quality[7] (the net effect of the expectations and the experienced service):

1. Professionalism and skills.
2. Attitudes and behavior.
3. Accessibility and flexibility to solve the customer's problem.
4. Reliability and trustworthiness.
5. Recovery of negative service encounters.
6. Reputation and credibility.

Gaps in Perceptions of Quality

Inevitably, a discrepancy will arise between the expectations formed about the service encounter and the actual experienced quality. As noted earlier, customers who are upset with poor service tend to talk about it. As also might be expected, they talk more about negative experiences than positive ones.

This asymmetry of the effects of negative and positive discrepancies is theoretically justified by the well-known psychological phenomenon called *loss aversion.*[8] Figure 14–3 shows loss aversion graphically. "Losses" are situations in which the expectations of service quality were higher than the realized quality. "Gains" represent the opposite situation. The curve to the left of the vertical axis demonstrates that losses are more negatively valued than gains are positively valued. In other words, customers react more strongly to unexpectedly poor service than they do to unexpectedly good service.

Negative gaps in perceived service quality (when expectations are higher than delivered quality) can be remedied in two ways. Based on Figure 14–2, the product manager can either lower expectations or raise service quality through improved service features (technical quality) or higher-quality interactions (functional quality). Since expectations are difficult to manage and lowering customer expectations is not usually in the best long-term interest of the product in question, raising service quality is usually chosen. Nevertheless, a good example of managing expectations is how Dell Computer tells a customer that the computer will arrive in five business days when it will actually arrive sooner; sales reps are trained to keep customer expectations low.[9]

However, positive gaps in perceived service quality can also be a problem for a product manager. Consider the retailer Nordstrom, Inc. The folklore about Nordstrom's service ethic is legendary. Since Nordstrom's stores are located mainly on the West Coast, visitors from other parts of the country flock to them when visiting San Francisco, Seattle, and other locations featuring their stores. The strong word-of-mouth effect (the left side of Figure 14–2) creates high expectations. It is possible, however, that on a given visit, Nordstrom could appear to be an average example of a good department store (with a pianist) and the customer could be disappointed. Thus,

---

[7]See Grönroos, *Service Management and Marketing,* p. 47.

[8]See, for example, Daniel Kahneman and Amos Tversky, "Prospect Theory: An Analysis of Decision under Risk," *Econometrica* 47 (1979), pp. 263–91.

[9]Stephanie Losee, "Mr. Cozzette Buys a Computer," *Fortune,* April 18, 1994, p. 113.

FIGURE 14–3 The Concept of Loss Aversion to Service Quality

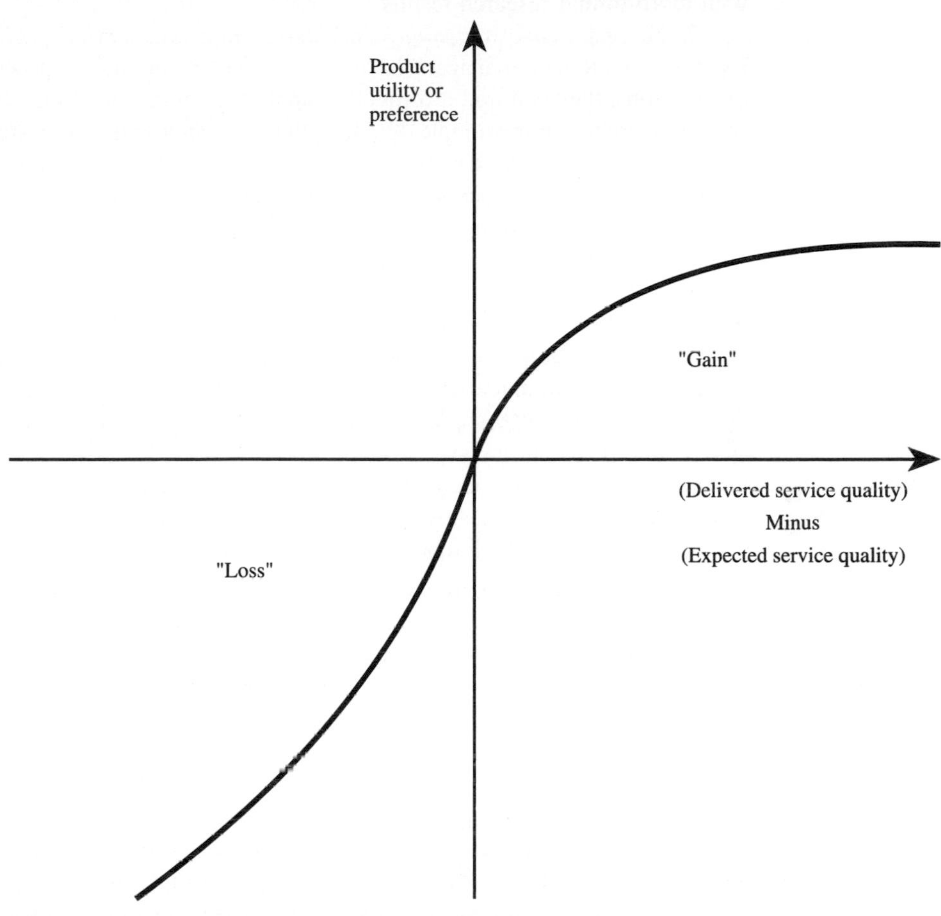

extraordinarily high expectations are doomed to create disappointment. Maintaining quality is especially difficult during periods of rapid expansion, as Nordstrom's has discovered. Restaurants or other products and services that generate strong word of mouth could find themselves in the same situation. Although this is a "problem" that most product managers would love to have, it is still important to understand that customer expectations do drive their ultimate evaluations of quality.

It is possible to categorize the major discrepancies between expectations and realizations into four general types of gaps:[10]

1. *The gap between customers' expectations and management perceptions.* One key problem is that managers often think they know the bases on which customers

[10]Valarie A. Zeithaml, A. Parasuraman, and Leonard L. Berry, *Delivering Quality Service: Balancing Customer Perceptions and Expectations* (New York: The Free Press, 1990).

form expectations but frequently are incorrect. This can often be remedied by conducting focus groups that the product managers attend as well as presenting them with more formal research results.

2. *The gap between management's perceptions and service quality specifications.* Even when product managers have a good understanding of how customers form expectations, they can find it difficult to apply their understanding to the design of the service operation. For example, knowing that computer software customers want quick response to phone calls is not enough; defining what is meant by "acceptable" response time takes discussions with customers and the ability to implement change through employee training programs.

3. *The gap between service quality specifications and service delivery.* Even if the second gap is closed, the objectives will not necessarily be met. That is, simply setting the appropriate response time is still a far cry from actually meeting the targets.

4. *The gap between service delivery and external communications.* As Figure 14–2 shows, communications with customers can have a powerful effect on expectation formation. As noted earlier, some of these are traditional communications such as advertising. Thus, promising 24-hour phone service in advertising can result in a broken promise if implementation is poor. Other kinds of communications can also cause gaps. For example, how many times have you been left waiting at home for a cable TV installer or a plumber who has promised to be there at a certain hour?

In summary, the tasks for the product manager are, first, to understand how important the gap between expected and actual customer service performance is and, second, to realize that this gap can be managed with effective marketing research and implementation.

"Moments of Truth"

The typical service encounter has many points of contact that affect the customer's overall evaluation. However, the points of contact are not all equally important in the customer's mind. Some of these contact points are make-it-or-break-it for the sale or continued relations with the customer. Jan Carlzon, the chairman of SAS, labeled these critical contact points "moments of truth."[11]

One way to understand the locus of these moments of truth is to simulate the customer's interaction with the product or service through a flow diagram. Figure 14–4 shows an example of a flow diagram for a "typical" auto repair shop.[12] The dotted line separates the part of the service that is visible to the customer from the part that is not. The asterisks reflect key service points at which success can be achieved or lost and at which failure most often results. However, *all* points of contact have the potential to create good or bad feelings for the customer. This kind of diagram is very

[11]Jan Carlzon, *Moments of Truth* (Cambridge, Mass.: Ballinger Publishing Company, 1987). Our view of these moments of truth is actually somewhat narrower than Carlzon's, who sees all customer service interactions as being critical.

[12]Ways to create extra customer value and differentiate from competition through, perhaps, creating more boxes in the diagram are discussed later in the chapter.

FIGURE 14–4 A Process-Flow Diagram for the Auto Repair Process

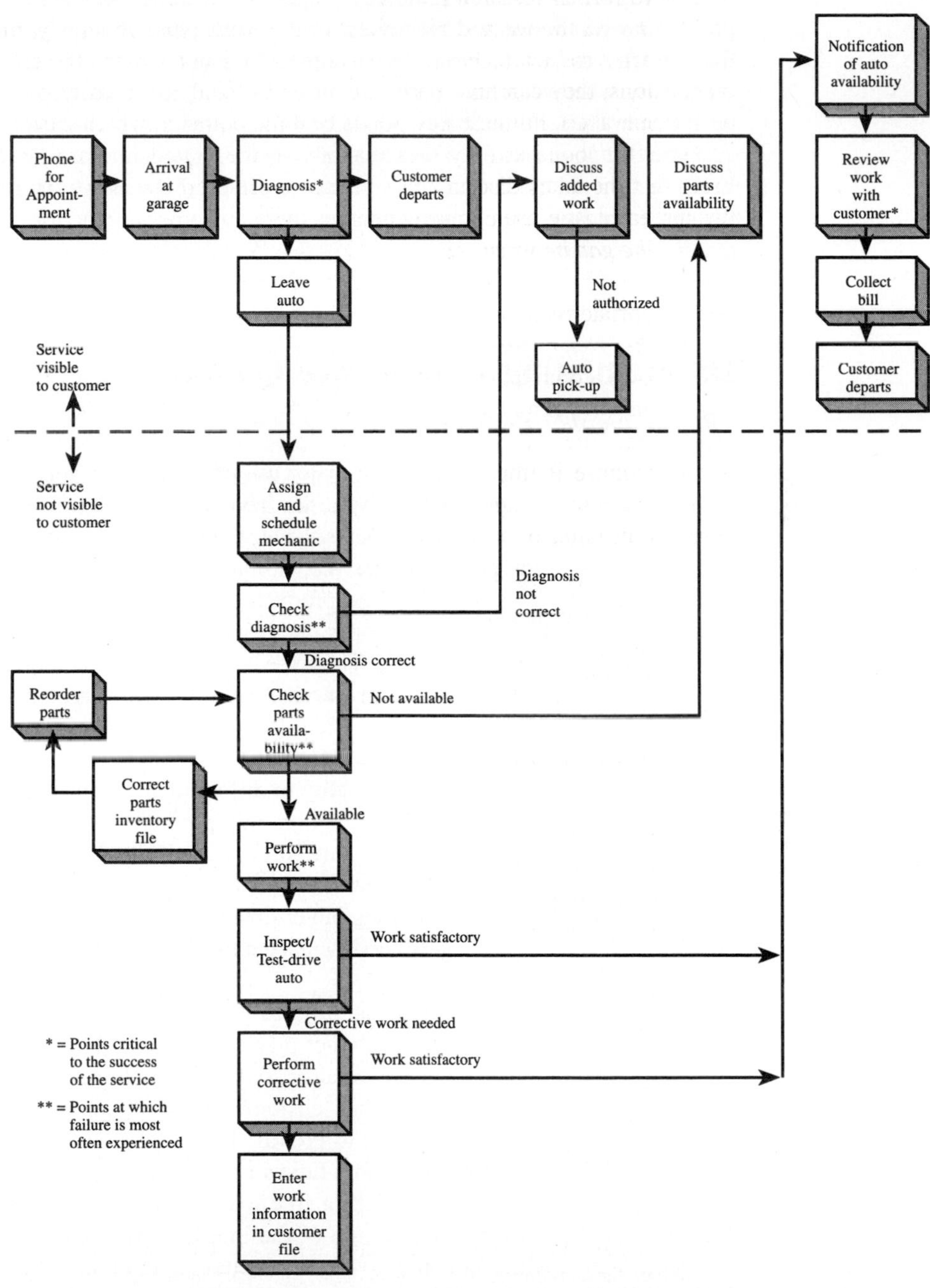

Source: James L. Heskett, W. Earl Sasser, Jr., and Christopher W. L. Hart, *Service Breakthroughs: Changing the Rules of the Game* (New York: The Free Press, 1990), p. 107.

useful because it not only permits identification of the potential trouble spots but also forces the marketing manager to take a customer perspective of the situation.

As Figure 14–4 shows, the key points the customer sees are the diagnosis of the problems with the car and the review of the work plus, obviously, the performance of the car after the work. What the customer does not see are the checks on the initial diagnosis, whether or not parts are in stock, and the quality of the work actually performed. Thus, all these key points become points at which customer loyalty can be sustained or lost, but only the areas above the dotted line are "moments of truth." From the phone call for an appointment to the presentation of the repaired vehicle to the customer, how the company handles these customer interactions affects the service quality evaluation process.

Differentiating with Service Quality

The Augmented Product

As noted earlier in this chapter, one major use of increased levels of customer service is to differentiate the product from the competition. Figure 14–5 portrays this differentiation effort using customer service. Consider the "core" product to be the basic attributes of the product or service, similar to the "technical quality" referred to in Figure 14–2. For a manufactured product, these would be the physical characteristics. For example, for a car, color, weight, gas mileage, and similar characteristics would constitute the core product. The expected product is the core product plus any expectations about the product or service held by the target segment. Thus, the expected car would also feature a certain level of reliability, service from the dealer, prestige obtained from driving it, and so on.

How, then, do we use service quality to differentiate our products? We have noted several times that ultimately all competitors in a product category either offer or have the potential to offer equivalent core products. Thus, it is difficult to achieve differentiation based on product features and attributes. Also, simply meeting expectations is insufficient for maintaining buyer loyalty over an extended period of time. To differentiate, product managers need to reach a third level (shown in Figure 14–5): the *augmented* product.

As an example, we return to the process flow diagram for the automobile service center shown in Figure 14–4. A product manager can use this diagram to check each box for product augmentation potential or look for new boxes to add that go beyond what competitors are offering. In the "customer departs" box at the top of the figure, the normal way is for the customer to provide her or his own transportation or take a shuttle bus to several fixed locations. Lexus and Infiniti dealers (and some others as well) augment the product by offering free loaner cars. In addition, at some Infiniti dealers, even if your car is not the top-of-the-line Q45, the dealer gives you a Q45 to use as the loaner, which not only gives you a better car to drive but also acts as a clever device to induce trading up. Some service centers augment the product by washing customers' cars and filling up the gas tank (new boxes on the "work satisfactory" line). Others send customers reminder notices when their cars should come in for a

Figure 14–5 The Augmented Product

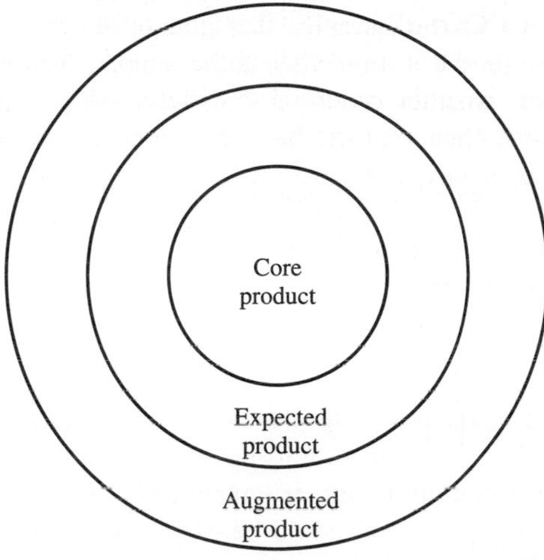

Source: Reprinted by permission of Harvard Business Review. An exhibit from "Marketing Success Through Differentiation—of Anything," by Theodore Levitt, January–February 1980. Copyright © 1980 by the President and Fellows of Harvard College; all rights reserved.

checkup, along with reduced service price coupons (instead of waiting for the customers to phone for an appointment).

A second illustration highlights the extraordinary success of a personal finance computer program called Quicken, marketed by Intuit. Although very successful in its category (as well as the tax preparation category with TurboTax), Intuit is still very small compared to companies such as Microsoft, Corel (WordPerfect), and IBM (Lotus). Intuit has telephone operators who answer technical questions as all other software vendors do. However, its technical support people take extra measures to satisfy customers. If they receive a complicated problem late on a Friday afternoon, the support specialists are likely to work on it over the weekend and call the customer back on Monday.

Put simply, an important job of the product manager is to find ways to augment his or her product. Why are competitors slow to copy some of these features? Why do Lexus and Infiniti offer the services mentioned earlier and U.S. manufacturers do not? Most companies view service as an expense rather than an investment in customer loyalty, because it is difficult to quantify the additional profit generated by investments in customer service but easy to calculate the costs.

Service Guarantees

One way companies augment their products is through service guarantees.[13] Guarantees not only offer the customer some assurance about product quality but also

[13]See Heskett, Sasser, and Hart, *Service Breakthroughs,* chap. 6.

reinforce the brand image at the same time. Some examples are Domino Pizza's promise that you will get your pizza in 30 minutes or you do not have to pay for it (now you receive a reduced-price coupon) and Safeway supermarkets' offer of "Three's a Crowd" service that guarantees the opening of a new checkout counter when any line has more than three people. Although their effectiveness varies, such guarantees have the potential to differentiate a product from competition.

Characteristics of the best service guarantee programs include the following:

1. The guarantee should be unconditional. The customer should not have to be concerned that the company will try to impose a large variety of conditions on the guarantee.

2. The guarantee should address customer needs. In other words, the product manager should know what product characteristics are important to the target segment(s) and focus the guarantee on those. For example, many mail-order personal computer companies offer 30-day, money-back guarantees.

3. The guarantee should have a standard for performance. Whatever its merits, Domino's 30-minute delivery guarantee was clearly stated.

4. The guarantee should be easy to understand and communicate.

5. The guarantee should be meaningful to the customer and the company. If the penalty involves money, for example, the amount should be sufficient that the company will care about how often it is invoked. Fringe Benefits Management, a $9 million company that administers benefits plans, saved a major customer by developing a list of performance standards backed by cash guarantees. For example, if the customer waited more than 40 seconds on hold for a customer service telephone call, Fringe Benefits had to pay a $1,000 penalty, a considerable sum for a company that size.[14]

6. The guarantee should be credible. When the late-night TV ads touting Ginsu knives offer a lifetime guarantee, there is probably some doubt in the minds of potential customers whether the company will be around that long.

Service guarantees are perhaps not appropriate for all kinds of products and services. However, they provide concrete evidence to customers that companies are willing to sacrifice short term profits to cultivate satisfied customers. They can be particularly useful for small companies seeking to differentiate themselves from larger competitors, as in the case of Fringe Benefits Management.

Service Recovery

Obviously the ideal situation is when the product is of such high quality that customers are always delighted. Unfortunately this is almost always prohibitively expensive, if not impossible, to achieve, especially when customer reactions depend on factors beyond the company's control (e.g., their mood). Thus, a critical moment for a product manager occurs when the product or service does not perform up to customer expectations or fails to work properly. How the company reacts to such a situation is crucial for

[14]Michale P. Cronin, "A Guarantee with Teeth," *INC.*, March 1992, p. 93.

maintaining customer relationships. A company can invest in service recovery. For years Microsoft largely serviced its corporate clients using toll-free support lines and partnerships with other service companies. However, Microsoft recently announced plans to set up teams of service employees who will work 24 hours a day to get computers back up and running, visiting corporations in person if necessary.[15]

The problem is, of course, that many times the product manager does not know when expectations are not met, so recovery cannot be implemented. We know that for most products, dissatisfied customers do not tell the company they are unhappy. Thus, a key part of an overall program of service recovery requires being proactive in detecting when customer expectations are not met. Useful devices are follow-up phone calls, exit interviews (e.g., from restaurants), and surveys taken from randomly chosen customers.

A second part of an effective recovery program is an a priori analysis of product failure points. Figure 14–4 indicates where the failure points might be in the automobile servicing illustration (the boxes with double asterisks). This obviously allows the customer service teams to anticipate the kind of recovery with which they are likely to become involved.

Finally, effective service recovery demands significant training and assigning the right people to the job. When service recovery is necessary, customers are typically unhappy because some aspect of the product or service has failed: The package did not arrive, the computer's hard disk has failed, the food is cold, and so on. The people dealing with this situation must be compassionate and good listeners, as well as effective problem solvers.

Turning around a potential disaster can be a tremendous boost to loyalty toward a product or service. For example, an IBM account team was having difficulty overcoming the hostility of a potential major buyer of mainframe processors. Although the potential buyer did own several IBM processors, the company was uninterested in buying any more or in buying peripheral equipment such as tape and disk drives. The account team's basic strategy was to build a new level of confidence from the lower levels of the company's organization that were key influences in the buying decision. Although they were having some success using this approach, one of the breakthrough events that turned the account around was how they handled a failure of one of the installed IBM processors. A large number of IBM personnel worked around the clock to restore the system. Their efforts prompted a laudatory letter from the director of the company's information systems group and went a long way toward improving the relationship. Eventually, the team's efforts resulted in a large order.[16]

Another example witnessed by one of the authors highlights an opportunity lost. Over the last several years, British Airways has been attempting to improve its global image in the area of customer service.[17] On a trip from London to San Francisco, an

---

[15]Don Clark, "Microsoft Beefs Up Customer Services," *The Wall Street Journal,* May 4, 1995, p. B-3.

[16]"International Business Machines (B): Applitronics Account Strategy," Harvard Business School case study 9-581-052.

[17]For a good background on the British Airways efforts, see Steven E. Prokesch, "Competing on Customer Service: An Interview with British Airways' Sir Colin Marshall," *Harvard Business Review,* November–December 1995, pp. 101–12.

unhappy coach passenger complained to a flight attendant that he was only one row from the smoking section and violently disliked inhaling secondary smoke. The customer could have been unobtrusively moved to an unfilled seat in business class (to prevent other coach customers from clamoring for the same benefit), possibly gaining a customer for life at almost zero additional cost (after all, what is the additional cost of the better food and drink?). However, the flight attendant stonewalled the passenger ("I'm sorry, this is your assigned seat"), who undoubtedly switched airlines on his next trip. If one calculates the lifetime value of the customer's potential revenue stream and compares it to the incremental one-time cost, the flight attendant's actions look foolhardy indeed.

Characteristics of a Complete Customer Service Program

A considerable amount of work has focused on customer service. This research has shown that excellent customer service programs have the following elements in common.[18]

1. A marketing strategy.
2. Top management buy-in.
3. The right people.
4. Appropriate product design.
5. An infrastructure to handle customer service.
6. A measurement system.

We explore each of these areas in more depth next.

The Role of Marketing Strategy

As we noted in Chapter 8, it is important that all elements of the marketing mix be consistent with the marketing strategy. Although customer service is not usually formally integrated into the four Ps (price, promotion, product, and place), it is so important that it should be considered a fifth marketing mix element. Which market segments are being targeted and how the product or service is being positioned to those customers dictate how extensive the customer service program should be.

Particularly important, of course, is knowing what features of service are important to the target customers and what their expectations are. If the product is being positioned at the high end—targeted to upscale customers with a high price—their expectations for service will be higher. Therefore, a high-end strategy is usually accompanied by a high level of customer service.

---

[18]See, for example, William H. Davidow and Bro Uttal, *Total Customer Service: The Ultimate Weapon* (New York/Harper & Row, 1989).

However, although we have made a case in this chapter that customer service is becoming more important and can be successfully used as a differentiator, it is not always the case that the strategy and concomitant target customers demand a high service level. In other words, customer expectations are set according to the adage "you get what you pay for." Although they do not offer *poor* service (customers still expect a minimum level of attention), low-priced retailers such as Kmart and Wal-Mart do not offer the level of service Nordstrom does. Nor do customers expect (or even want) such a level of service. Many firms perform self-service; that is they do their own maintenance, or, in the case of Federal Express, place their own orders. Many customers now prefer ATMs to dealing with tellers, and self-service, pay at the pump gasoline purchases. Southwest Airlines charges very low fares and provides low levels of service: no food (unless you consider a bag of peanuts and a soft drink food), no reserved seats, and semiclean planes. However, it is a very successful company because its target customers are price sensitive and have low expectations for the level of service.

Hence it is possible to offer more service than customers are willing to pay for. So at some point using customer service to augment the product may produce a higher price than customer value.

Top Management's Role

Like many other aspects of business, it is difficult to implement any change in an organization or a strategy without the endorsement of top management. A service program needs "top down support," with senior managers demonstrating that they put customer satisfaction at the top of their priority list by maintaining marketing research budgets, by investing in research and development, and generally by taking an investment rather than cost perspective on expenses related to customer retention.

The challenge is to create a service-oriented culture within the company that looks favorably on product managers' efforts to make investments in customer service activities (where appropriate). One characteristic of such a service-oriented organization is the view that customer service is *everyone's* business, not just those individuals in a "customer service" department. Any individual who has contact with customers is, in fact, a customer service representative. It is somewhat ironic that the employees who have the most customer contacts, and therefore more "moments of truth," are often among the lowest paid in the company. These employees include receptionists, repair personnel, cleaning and hotel room maintenance staff, and so on. "Downsizing" (or, as some put it, "rightsizing") has a negative effect on the ability to deliver quality service both by providing fewer personnel to devote to the service and by impacting the attitudes of those who survive the layoffs. One of the great inconsistencies is the tendency of companies to talk about moving from a transaction focus toward long term relationships with customers, while at the same time breaking relationships with employees. If top management is not treating its internal customers well, how does it expect these internal customers to treat end customers well?

Many companies encourage senior managers who have little day-to-day contact with customers to reach out more to them. Motorola, for example, has equipped many of its top managers with pagers and given the numbers to major customers for easier contact. Jan Carlzon of SAS insisted that his top managers rotate through the ticket counters at airports to get a better feel for what is going on there; he often did it himself. At Bergen Brunswig, a distributor of pharmaceuticals, vice presidents must make a minimum of 100 customer sales calls each year to demonstrate top management's commitment to serving customer needs.

Another characteristic of a service-oriented culture is that the company empowers lower-level personnel to handle problems without going through many levels of authority. By cutting the red tape necessary to solve customers' problems, the problems are solved faster and customers' satisfaction levels are higher. In addition, as companies such as American Express have found, by empowering their employees to solve customer problems, the customer service jobs become more interesting and turnover drops.

An example of the importance of top management involvement is General Electric Company's problems with customer service during the mid-1980s.[19] In GE's industrial and power business (turbines, motors, semiconductors, nuclear energy), 40 separate product departments sold through four sales forces. The result was considerable overlap among the customers served by the sales forces and confusion among customers as to who was responsible for solving customer problems. In fact, GE's personnel often transferred responsibility for customer complaints back to the customer rather than looking at the problem from the customer's perspective. GE developed a reputation as a company with which it was difficult to do business.

The top of the GE management organization—Jack Welch (chairman), Leonard Vickers (vice president of corporate marketing), Paul van Orden (executive vice president of consumer marketing), and others—developed an approach to the customer service problem. They grouped the industrial and power products into four major categories: motors, construction equipment, factory automation, and power systems. They appointed customer service managers, veteran GE managers with considerable product experience and interest in solving customer problems, for each of 20 businesses. Then they formed the managers into a customer service task force. Senior GE managers attended the task force meetings and exhorted the task force to effect changes in customer service. By late 1985, improvements were seen in company communications focusing on customer service, surveying customers on quality, training, and information systems to track orders.

Clearly, such a rapid improvement in customer service would not have occurred without the push from top management at GE. However, getting the new philosophy to stick after the initial period of enthusiasm is a difficult task.

Getting the Right People

Naturally no amount of corporate philosophizing or policies will be effective if the implementation is poor. Thus, getting the right people to work on customer service

---

[19]Frank V. Cespedes, "General Electric: Customer Service," Harvard Business School case study 9-588-059, 1988.

issues is critical to a successful effort in this area. We have already discussed the ideas of finding people who are sympathetic and oriented toward problem solving for this kind of work. As some have noted, the new breed of service worker is empathetic, flexible, informed, articulate, inventive, and able to work with minimal levels of supervision. As a result, careful screening of customer service personnel is essential. Further training them in problem solving, not just good telephone manners, is necessary. (Smiling is important but not sufficient.)

A key element in getting the right people *and* getting them to perform well is having an appropriate incentive system. As might be expected, tying employee compensation to customer satisfaction is becoming more common. Marriott Hotels, for example, rewards service groups (e.g., food and beverage) based on maintaining and surpassing quantitative goals based on customer surveys. MCI has instituted a compensation structure for its sales force that is based not only on systems sales but also on satisfaction surveys of customers. To implement these systems, a measurement system must be in place to track levels of customer satisfaction (such systems will be discussed later in this chapter).

The Role of Product Design

In our earlier discussion of Figure 14–4, we noted that it is useful to know the failure points of a system in advance so customer service people can be forewarned about where most of the complaints are likely to occur. Even better, designs should a) try to minimize the need for both routine and emergency service and b) allow for easy service when needed. This can be encouraged by including customer service personnel on new-product design teams. Because of their experiences dealing with customer complaints about earlier generations of the product or service, they can often add useful comments about how to design products to avoid those problems. At the very least, customer service would be forewarned about potential service complaints at a very early stage in the product development process.

Infrastructure

Having the appropriate infrastructure to track customer contacts is also important in designing a customer service system. Some companies design information systems to record all contacts from sales calls to customer inquiries. The tremendous growth in database marketing is due to the rapid advancements in computer technology and the ability to assimilate large amounts of customer data. The purpose of these databases is not just to target customers through direct ("junk") mail and get them to purchase something but also to attempt to develop a relationship with customers that may entail only simple communications. For example, McDonald's attempts to "personalize" its business by getting customers to sign up for children's birthday parties and then sending follow-up birthday cards.

Many firms have established central service centers as a way to a) provide easy access to customers, b) collect data on customers for later use, and c) collect data on problems that enable easy service. USAA is known for its extensive database on customers that allows for both proactive contact (effective solicitations for new products) and effective reactions to questions (by having the customer's entire record available to the personnel who answer incoming calls). Ford has a central system that managed to detect a problem early in one model and allowed it to be fixed before a large-scale recall became necessary. The GE Answer Center deals with 3.1 million calls a year and is the only direct contact the company has with its consumer customers. In addition to the usual problems that account for two-thirds of the calls, 15 percent represent inquiries about products to buy, and hence represent an important marketing opportunity. Having such a service center has become almost a necessity in recent years.

Measurement Systems

To make a customer service system a valuable tool for product managers, some kind of measurement system must be put in place. Measurement enables managers to track levels of customer satisfaction and subsequently reward service personnel based on performance, as well as providing diagnostics for remedial action.

One of the most popular approaches to measuring service quality is the SERVQUAL instrument.[20] The SERVQUAL survey is composed of questions in five categories: tangibles (four questions on dimensions such as appearance of facilities and personnel), reliability (five questions), responsiveness (four questions), assurance (four questions on dimensions such as competence, courtesy, credibility, and security), and empathy (five questions on dimensions such as access or ease of contact, communication, and customer understanding). Each customer surveyed completes one questionnaire measuring expectations of each of the 22 questions and then one for each company or product to measure competitor performance. The SERVQUAL score for a product is the difference between the perception of the dimension and the expectation. A company can then determine its quality of service on each of the five dimensions by taking the average across the questions for that dimension and calculating an overall score. A weighted SERVQUAL score can also be calculated by asking the customer to give importance weights (summing to 1) on each of the five dimensions. Figure 14–6 shows examples of the expectations questions for the four tangible and four reliability questions. Besides using SERVQUAL to calculate service quality perceptions of a product or service, managers can use it to track competition, examine differences among market segments, and track internal service performance.

Some recent work has criticized the SERVQUAL scale. One potential problem is that the expectations questions do not separate what a vendor *should* do from what the vendor *will* do.[21] For example, a customer's expectation of the number of times the phone will ring before it is picked up may differ from how many times the customer thinks it should ring if the company is delivering a good response. Also, the

---

[20]Zeithaml, Parasuraman, and Berry, *Delivering Quality Service,* app. A.

[21]William Boulding, Ajay Kalra, Richard Staelin, and Valarie A. Zeithaml, "A Dynamic Process Model of Service Quality: From Expectations to Behavioral Intentions," *Journal of Marketing Research* 30 (1993), pp. 7–27.

FIGURE 14–6 Example of SERVQUAL Survey

	Strongly Disagree						Strongly Agree
1. Excellent ________ companies will have modern-looking equipment.	1	2	3	4	5	6	7
2. The physical facilities at excellent ________ companies will be visually appealing.	1	2	3	4	5	6	7
3. Employees at excellent ________ companies will be neat appearing.	1	2	3	4	5	6	7
4. Materials associated with the service (such as pamphlets or statements) will be visually appealing in an excellent ________ company.	1	2	3	4	5	6	7
5. When excellent ________ companies promise to do something by a certain time, they will do so.	1	2	3	4	5	6	7
6. When a customer has a problem, excellent ________ companies will show a sincere interest in solving it.	1	2	3	4	5	6	7
7. Excellent ________ companies will perform the service right the first time.	1	2	3	4	5	6	7
8. Excellent ________ companies will provide their services at the time they promise to do so.	1	2	3	4	5	6	7

Source: Reprinted with the permission of The Free Press, a Division of Simon & Schuster, from *Delivering Quality Service: Balancing Customer Perceptions and Expectations* by Valarie A. Zeithamil, A. Parasuraman, and Leonard L. Berry. Copyright © 1990 by The Free Press.

SERVQUAL scale may have to be modified for certain service settings, such as retailing.[22]

Such measurement approaches can even be used by small companies seeking competitive advantage in commodity or highly competitive markets. Granite Rock Company produces concrete, asphalt, sand, and gravel. It has sales of only around $90 million per year, but it is an industry leader in profitability because it charges up to 6 percent higher prices and offers higher-quality service. The company maintains this service quality by regularly monitoring its customers. It not only surveys its customers on their needs but also requests an annual "report card." Granite Rock Company combines the survey data on customer priorities with the report card on its own and competitors' performance levels and produces graphs that are posted on bulletin boards around the company. Thus, measurement is at the heart of its ability to deliver superior customer service.[23]

Of course high scores on satisfaction surveys do not guarantee satisfied customers. For example, in 1990, the General Accounting Office issued a report on a survey of 20 companies that had scored well in the 1988 and 1989 Baldrige competition. One important result was that while responding managers said customer satisfaction levels

[22]James A. Carman, "Consumer Perceptions of Service Quality: An Assessment of the SERVQUAL Dimensions," *Journal of Retailing* 66 (1990), pp. 33–55.

[23]Edward O. Welles, "How're We Doing," *INC.*, May 1991, pp. 80–82.

had increased since then, customer retention remained almost unchanged. Another study reported that in most surveys of customer satisfaction, 85 percent of customers claim to be satisfied but still demonstrate a willingness to switch suppliers.[24]

The Return on Service Quality

We have mentioned several times in this chapter that it is difficult to quantify the return on making investments in customer service and improvements in service quality. In addition, as we just noted, the key result of increased service quality should not be just high scores on satisfaction surveys. What product managers are looking for rather than high satisfaction scores are improvements in actual customer behavior such as increased loyalty. Fortunately, some research attempts to link investments in service to customer retention.[25] The basic concepts of this approach are shown in Figure 14–7.

The key to the approach is to decompose satisfaction levels with an overall process into satisfaction levels with components of those processes. This allows a more targeted approach to investing in service quality as the company will invest in those areas that will deliver the greatest return. This ultimately leads to overall satisfaction and greater customer retention.

For example, Marriott found that customers at full-service Marriotts wanted five things (processes): a great breakfast, fast check-in, fast check-out, clean rooms, and friendly service. It then examined each process to see which subprocess(es) needed the most attention, that is, gave it the greatest leverage to increase satisfaction with the process and ultimately overall satisfaction. With breakfast, the company speeded up service by hiring "runners" who would bring the food to the servers so they would be around when customers wanted them. With check-in, it established a system of allowing customers to get their room keys at the door and preregistering them, bypassing the front desk. For quicker check-out, the bill is slipped under the room doors at 4 AM and the customer just has to sign it. The other two processes were handled by again examining subprocesses.[26]

Internal Marketing

Developing a service culture and a commitment to quality service often involves what is referred to as *internal* marketing.[27] Almost all marketing education is oriented

---

[24]Shelly Reese, "Happiness Isn't Everything," *Marketing Tools,* May 1996, pp. 52–58.

[25]Roland T. Rust, Anthony J. Zahorik, and Timothy L. Keiningham, *Return on Quality: Measuring the Financial Impact of Your Company's Quest for Quality,* (Chicago: Probus Publishing Company, 1994).

[26]Malcolm Fleschner and Gerhard Gschwandtner, "The Marriott Miracle," *Personal Selling Power,* September 1994, pp. 17–26.

[27]See Grönroos, *Service Management and Marketing,* chap. 10.

FIGURE 14–7 **Linking Customer Satisfaction to Retention**

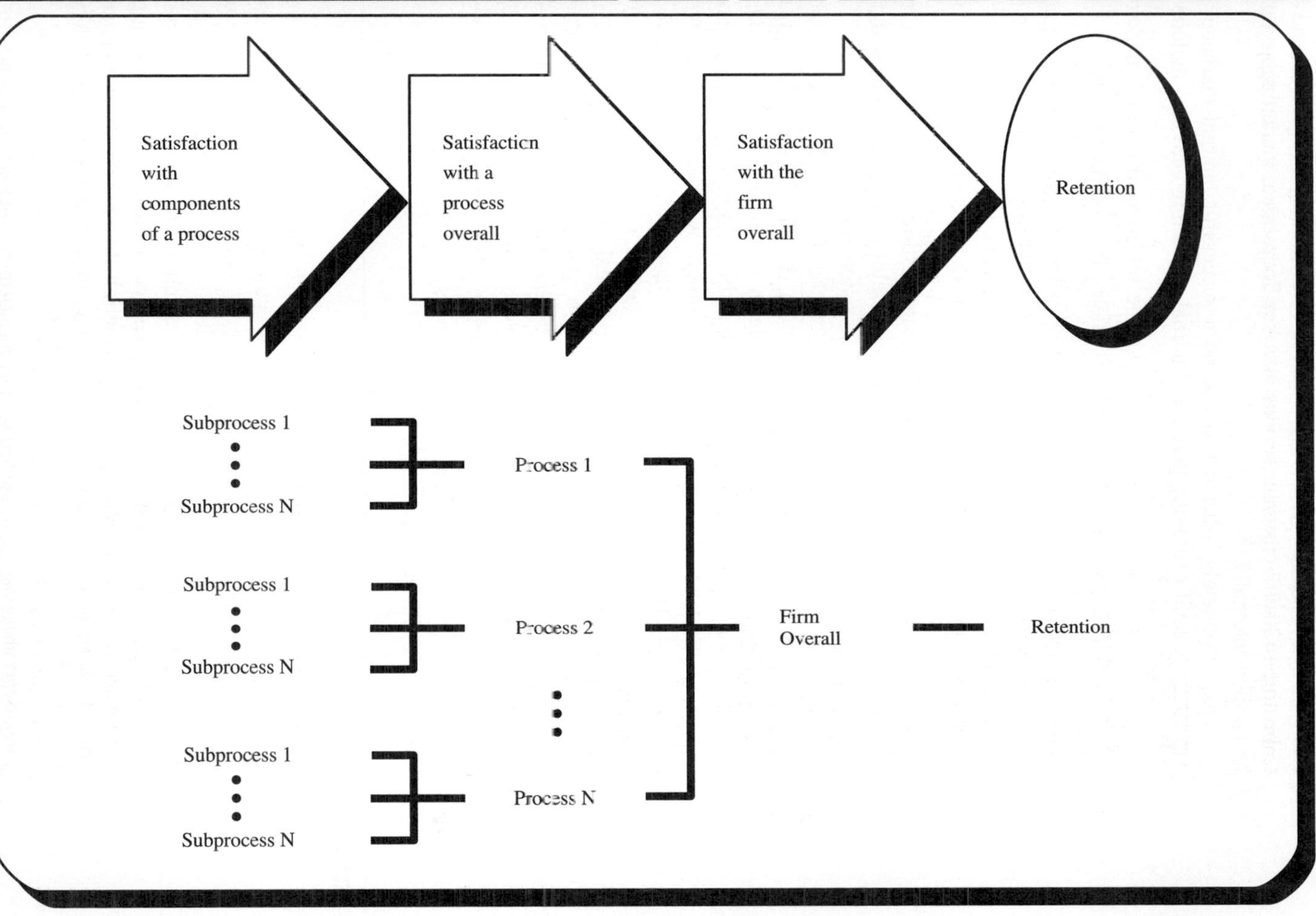

Source: Roland T. Rust, Anthony J. Zahorik, and Timothy L. Keiningham, *Return on Quality: Measuring the Financial Impact of Your Company's Quest for Quality* (Chicago: Probus Publishing Company, 1994).

toward how a product manager should market products and services to external constituents. However, it is clear that to be an effective manager in general, and specifically to be able to "sell" customer service as a key focus area, marketing techniques must be applied internally.[28]

Not surprisingly, what it takes to be a successful internal marketer looks very similar to general marketing practice. Internal marketing activities include

1. Training managers and personnel to be sensitive to internal marketing.
2. Management support and internal interactive communication.
3. Internal mass communication and information support.
4. Support from personnel and human resources.
5. Marketing research.
6. Market segmentation.

The last two points are particularly interesting: They show that the key to successful internal marketing is to treat your colleagues like customers and utilize the same methods for them that you would for customers.

The Federal Express's introduction of the COSMOS system highlights the importance of internal marketing. The system routed all orders through the central telephone facility. However, the salespeople in the local offices who had the job of calling on major clients were concerned that the system would come between them and their customers. Thus, one internal "customer" was the sales force, which had to be convinced that the system could actually make them *more* productive because it could help pinpoint customers who were not buying up to their potential or who were too small to market profitably through personal selling. Another set of internal customers were the financial analysts, who put pressure on the proponents of COSMOS to indicate the level of return on investment. Traditional marketing methods such as brochures and personal selling were used. Thus, one reason the system succeeded is that management recognized early in the process that internal marketing was a key to implementation.

Summary

As noted earlier in this chapter, it looks as though characteristics of a strong customer service program can easily be copied by competitors and therefore cannot contribute to a long-term competitive advantage. However, it should be clear that by examining the characteristics of a strong service effort, it is unlikely they actually can be easily duplicated. For example, it is difficult to emulate the amount of commitment one company's top management has to quality service. Words alone (many companies coin slogans to be used at meetings) do not do the job. In addition, most companies do not invest in sufficient infrastructure to implement a strong service effort. Many do not

[28]Internal marketing can be applied to other management problems, such as how to get the company excited about launching a new product.

believe customer satisfaction can be calibrated, so they do not make the effort to develop a measurement system. In sum, customer service *can* augment the core of an expected product offered in a way that competitors cannot easily copy.

The Marketing Science Institute has sponsored projects in the area of service quality for nearly 15 years. Ten general "lessons" learned about delivering quality service are the following:[29]

1. The lesson of listening to customers.
2. The lesson of reliability.
3. The lesson of basic service: customers expect service companies and customer service operations to do what they are supposed to do.
4. The lesson of service design.
5. The lesson of service recovery.
6. The lesson of surprising customers, that is, exceeding customer expectations.
7. The lesson of fair play: keeping promises, offering honest communications, competent and courteous service.
8. The lesson of teamwork.
9. The lesson of employee research, that is, marketing research on internal customers.
10. The lesson of service leadership, inspired leadership within the organization and service culture.

---

[29]Leonard L. Berry, A. Parasuraman, and Valarie A. Zeithaml, *Ten Lessons for Improving Service Quality,* Report number 93-104, (Cambridge, Mass.: Marketing Science Institute, 1993).

C H A P T E R

15 Financial Analysis for Product Management[1]

Overview

In today's business environment, product managers need to be knowledgeable about the financial dimensions of their jobs as well as the marketing portion. As we noted in Chapter 1, in many companies product managers assume the role of mini-CEOs in that they have complete profit and loss responsibility for their products. In such cases, the product manager must be familiar with *all* aspects of business, including operations management, human resources, and so on. However, besides the analyses marketing managers perform to better understand customers, competitors, and the rest of the external market environment, several other analyses related to the financial aspects of the product's performance are also necessary. As a result, to be part of a firm's overall decision making, product managers must understand the financial implications of their decisions.

Financial decision making is closely related to product strategy. The top part of Figure 8–2 shows that the ultimate objective of product managers is profitability, whether or not the short-term objective in the marketing plan is oriented toward share or profits. The left-hand side of the diagram indicates marketing-oriented activities, such as the decision of whether to seek new segments or to pursue existing customers. However, the right side of the figure indicates activities that are primarily financial, including decisions about cost cutting, improving the sales mix to emphasize products with higher margins, and the like.

Two key kinds of information are important to marketing decision making and strategy development. First, if the product manager is to have profit and loss responsibility or set short- and long-term profit objectives, he or she must have a good understanding of how profits are computed. As any financially oriented manager knows, computing profits is not a straightforward issue. Later in this chapter, we show

[1]This chapter has benefited greatly from discussions with and material obtained from several colleagues, including Rashi Glazer, Noel Capon, and Mac Hulbert.

that there is no such concept as *the* bottom line; in fact, there are at least three ways to calculate the "profitability" of a product. The second kind of information that is critical to a product manager's understanding of financial performance is relevant if there is a product line or many product variants (e.g., different sizes, colors) because it analyzes the performance of different product variants. This is called a *sales* analysis and is also discussed later in this chapter.

The financial analyses described in this chapter can be used in a variety of ways. One way to use either profitability or sales analyses is for planning purposes. As noted in the outline in the appendix to Chapter 2, this prior budgeted or *ex ante* profitability must be reported in a marketing plan. In addition, analysis of the relative sales performances of different product variants can lead to a new marketing strategy or the pruning of a product line.

These analyses can also be used *ex post,* or after the planning period, and at specific intervals within the planning period. Such a use of financial analyses would be for *control* purposes. Obviously, it is important to measure how the company has done or how it is doing, the latter being particularly important for making adjustments during the execution of the plan.

In this chapter, we take a detailed look at several kinds of financial analyses that are very important for product management. Besides the sales and profitability analyses just mentioned above, we describe a strategic approach to control that explicitly links financial to marketing analysis. We also discuss capital budgeting from a marketing perspective.

Sales Analysis

Overview

Consider the advertisement shown in Figure 15–1. Although it undoubtedly overstates the case just a bit, the point made by the graph and the text is clear: In many cases, it is impossible to determine how successful a product or service really is without digging deeper into its sales records. The overall picture can be quite rosy while some real problems can exist in certain channels, regions of the world, sizes, and so on.

This realization leads to the *iceberg principle.*[2] Many of the real problems facing a product manager lie "beneath the water." Like the tip of an iceberg, total sales or profits are the small amount of the mass that is readily visible. However, if the product manager wishes to avoid the fate of many passengers of the *Titanic,* the large amount of mass that is invisible should also be taken into account.

A simple example illustrates the iceberg principle. Suppose the planning horizon coincides with the calendar year and for control purposes, the product manager analyzes her product's sales performance for the first six months, January through June. She finds that sales are $400,000 below objective. Now suppose further that the

[2]The term apparently originated in Richard D. Crisp, *Sales Planning and Control* (New York: McGraw-Hill, 1961).

product is sold in four sizes and, after digging a bit deeper, you find that sales versus objective varies by size:

Size	*Over Objective*	*Under Objective*
1	$ 200,000	
2	160,000	
3	20,000	
4		$780,000
	$ 380,000	$780,000

Thus, the $400,000 figure is a *net* figure that combines $380,000 over objective with $780,000 below objective. Clearly, the problem is severe for size 4.

Taking the analysis one step further by decomposing the sales for size 4 into different geographic regions, produces the following:

Region	*Over Objective*	*Under Objective*
East		$ 1,200,000
Central	$260,000	
South	60,000	
Pacific	100,000	
	$420,000	$ 1,200,000

Again, the problem has now grown into a much bigger one than the initial $400,000 below objective indicated.

Thus, this simple analysis provides two clear benefits. First, the product manager better understands the true magnitude of any problems that exist. Second, potential problem areas are identified. For example, the product manager should focus efforts on size 4 and the East region to attempt to understand why the product is unsuccessful in that size and region and not the others. This evaluation could lead to either eliminating the size, the region, or both or revamping the marketing strategy in those product and geographic segments. However, sales analysis does not explain *why* there are problems; it only pinpoints their location.

The Value of Sales Analysis

In general, sales analysis can be defined as "the gathering, classifying, comparing, and studying of company sales data."[3] Obviously, all firms do the gathering part as a way to measure the performance of their products. However, most companies do not study

[3]See Thomas R. Wotruba, *Sales Management: Planning, Accomplishment, and Evaluation* (New York: Holt, Rinehart & Winston, 1971).

FIGURE 15–1 Why Sales Analyses Are Needed

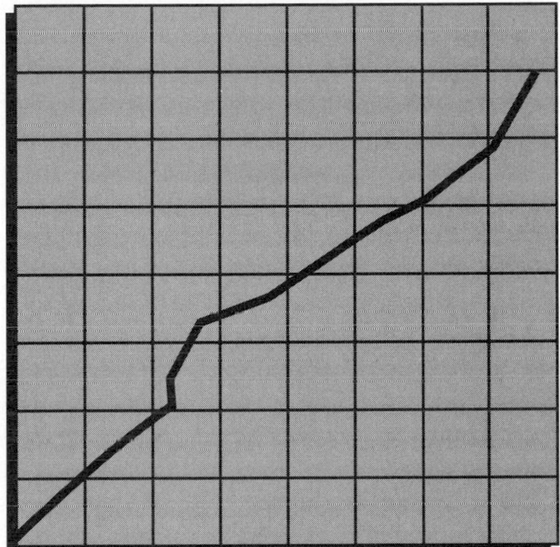

Source: Courtesy of Comshare, Inc.

their sales records systematically. In fact, the advertisement in Figure 15–1 illustrates a common belief that companies fail to analyze their own sales records. As the simple analysis above shows, when compared to some standard of performance (in this case, the stated objective), sales analysis can be a powerful tool in the hands of a product manager.

Figure 15–2 shows the major components of a sales analysis. The four major parts correspond to the following questions.

FIGURE 15–2 Components of Sales Analysis Information

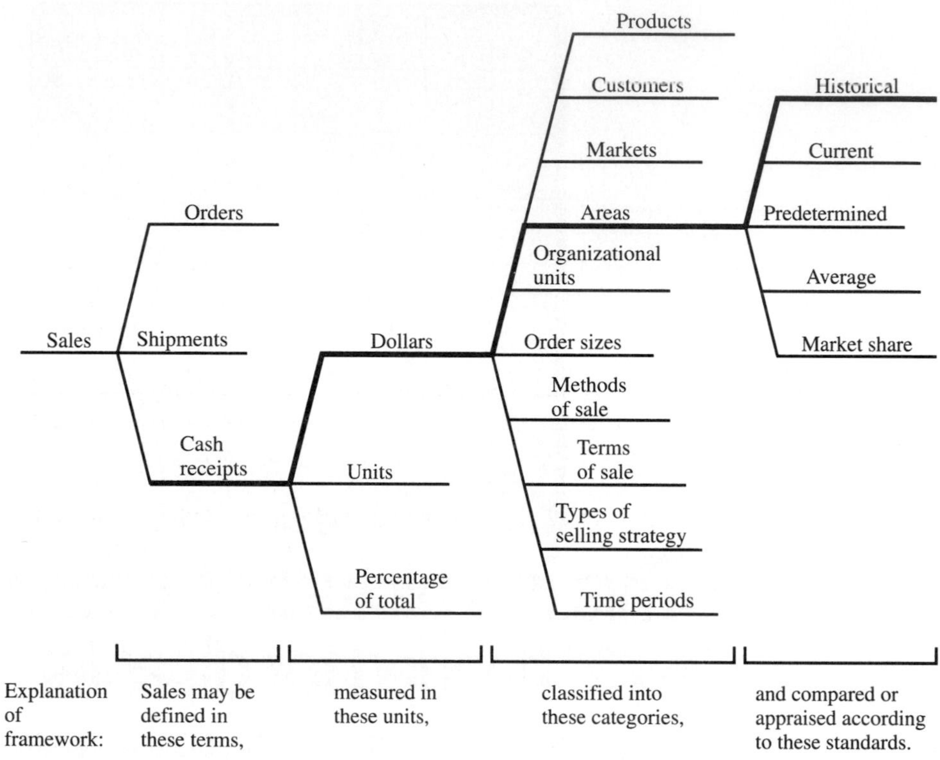

Source: Reprinted from *Sales Management: Text and Cases,* 2nd edition, by Thomas R. Wotruba and Edwin K. Simpson, p. 589, © 1992 by PWS-KENT Publishing Company, by South-Western College Publishing, a division of International Thomson Publishing Inc.

1. How are sales defined? As noted in Figure 15–2, sales can be defined in terms of orders, shipments, or cash receipts. The definition can matter a great deal, particularly for manufactured products. Some companies book sales when the product is shipped, for example, prior to receiving payment for them. Overly zealous managers who are short of sales goals have been known to ship product to themselves to achieve quotas!

2. In what units can sales be analyzed? Sales can be measured in terms of currency, units, or percentage of company sales, among other measures. Currency is useful, particularly when the product can be purchased in a large number of sizes. However, increases in sales in currency terms mask price increases. (Units do not have that problem.) Even when the product is available in different forms (e.g., a cold remedy that is available in both tablet and liquid forms) or sizes, the industry can develop norms of measurement (such as a standard dosage size).

3. In what categories or classifications can the sales data be placed? There are many possibilities here. In the example above, we used geographical area and product

FIGURE 15–3 Sales Analysis Illustration

Size of Order	Number of Orders	Percentage of Total Orders	Sales Value	Percentage of Total Sales	Average Sales Value per Order
Under $10.00	477	17.2	$ 2,599	0.3	$ 5.45
$10–$24.99	462	16.8	8,607	1.0	18.63
$25–$49.99	558	20.3	21,059	2.4	37.74
$50–$99.99	388	14.1	29,798	3.4	76.80
$100–$199.99	151	5.5	23,450	2.7	155.30
$200–$499.99	156	5.7	50,039	5.7	320.76
$500–$1,000.00	209	7.6	163,559	18.7	782.58
Over $1,000.00	352	12.8	576,588	65.8	1,638.03
	2753	100.0	$875,699	100.0	$ 318.09 overall average

Source: Thomas R. Wotruba, *Sales Management: Planning, Accomplishment, and Evaluation* (New York: Holt, Rinehart, & Winston), p. 478.

size. Figure 15–2 shows some other categories. Other common bases of classification are product types, customer types, markets or channels, order sizes, and time periods. Order size is a particularly useful way to break down sales, as shown in Figure 15–3. A situation in which 20 percent of the orders constitute over 80 percent of the sales dollars is not uncommon. In that case, a profitability analysis would show that the small orders not only produce a small percentage of total sales but are also unprofitable to fill.

4. What are the appropriate standards against which the sales can be compared? As Figure 15–2 shows, some of these standards include historical results, current results from another category in the same time period, some predetermined standard such as an objective or quota, averages across the company or some other business unit, and sales relative to market share (such as the share of voice concept discussed in Chapter 11).

Each kind of sales analysis can be denoted by using Figure 15–2 and drawing a line beneath the construct used. As shown, one such analysis could compare historical cash receipts from geographical areas. Naturally, the particular analysis used should be consistent with company recordkeeping, the particular product being analyzed, and the markets in which it is sold.

Roadblocks

If this analysis is so simple yet so valuable, why is it not used more by companies and their product managers? We have identified three reasons.

First, information systems often are not designed with product management in mind. Finance, accounting, manufacturing, operations, and human resource personnel are often key informants about the development of an information system. However, to be useful to a product manager, the system must collect the detailed receipt information and make it available for analysis. If marketing personnel are not queried for their needs when developing the system, the system is not likely to have the characteristics necessary for performing sales analyses.

Second, and related to the first point, financial or accounting personnel have quite different mindsets and perspectives than marketing personnel. Their information needs, training, and background are quite different. The differences can lead to inadequate information and a less than helpful perspective on the value of the information to the company.

Finally, one reason for failing to conduct sales analysis is a lack of internal marketing on the part of product management. As we noted in Chapter 14, a strong internal marketing program is necessary to induce any kind of change within an organization. It is important that marketing personnel be proactive in convincing senior managers who influence information system design that the detailed sales data are important and have value. Otherwise, the different mindsets and backgrounds will continue to dominate the way such systems are designed.

In retailing environments, these kinds of barriers are being broken down with the increasing penetration of optical scanners and point-of-sale (POS) systems. Because each product variant is labeled with a different code, excellent data for sales analyses are being produced for products sold through food, drug, and many discount stores. However, many consumer products and almost all business-to-business products do not benefit from such technology at the present time.

Profitability Analysis

Conventional Product Profit Accounting

A good way to begin this discussion is to use an illustration of an actual financial statement. Figure 15–4 shows an income statement for a hypothetical telecommunications service, referred to as NewCall. The top line indicates that 2 million units of the service were sold during the fiscal year at $5 each for total revenues of $10 million. Subtracted from this revenue figure are expenses related directly to operations such as labor, materials, and certain kinds of operations overhead (utilities, for example). This gives a gross or operating margin of $5.9 million. Finally, all other expenses are subtracted, giving a total profit (loss) of ($100,000).

This approach to computing profits is called a *full-costing approach,* in which all costs associated with a product or service, including corporate overhead, are subtracted from revenues. This is the most popular approach to product profitability accounting. The strength of the full costing approach is that it guarantees that all the costs of the corporation are covered by the products. Another way to say this is that the corporation will be profitable by ensuring that each product is profitable.

However, this approach has some weaknesses that will become apparent as we work through the example. First, given that the product is losing money, is the company better off by dropping NewCall? At first glance, it appears the company

FIGURE 15–4 Typical Income Statement

Product: NewCall Income Statement, December 31, 1996 (000's)		
Revenues (2M units @ $5)		$10,000
Less: Direct labor		2,500
Direct supervision/clerical		500
Social security		255
Materials		5
Operations overhead (plant, etc.)		840
Expenses from operations		4,100
Operating or gross margin		5,900
Less: Advertising	700	
Promotion	200	
Field sales	1,700	
Product management	25	
Marketing management	250	
Product development	150	
Marketing research	175	
Customer service	1,500	
Testing	300	
General and administrative	1,000	
Total expenses		6,000
Operating profit		(100)

would be $100,000 more profitable by eliminating the product. In reality, this turns out not to be the case; the company could actually be worse off.[4] Second, it is difficult to use the full-costing approach to obtain answers to relatively straightforward questions. For example, if revenues increase by 10 percent, what happens to profitability? We develop the ability to address these questions later in the chapter.

Alternative Accounting Systems

We can classify accounting reporting systems into three groups. First, one kind of system is referred to as "financial" or "custodial." Figure 15–4 shows an example of such a system. These systems are good for looking at historical financial results—"how we did." In addition, they are useful for external constituents, such as investors, who may care only about the aggregate or overall financial performance of a company.

Financial reporting systems based on full costing have several problems. First, full-costing methods are inherently unable to link costs, volumes, and profits because different kinds of costs, some of which affect a product's true profitability and some of which do not, are not categorized. The full-cost approach also tends to allocate fixed

[4]This assertion and the later analysis assume there are no opportunity costs of continuing to invest in a product that may generate a lower return on investment than other projects.

costs arbitrarily. For example, a common way to allocate overhead costs such as electricity is by sales volume. Clearly, such costs become difficult to plan because they are almost always variable (as sales volume changes, so do the charges for power). In addition, this approach gives managers a disincentive to raise sales levels because more and more costs are piled on, making the product look less profitable. Finally, these custodial systems fail to draw a distinction between costs that are under the control of the product manager and those that are not. From the product manager's perspective, it is entirely fair to be required to generate more revenues than costs directly attributable to his or her product. However, should a product's profitability, and therefore the manager's evaluation, be a function of how many corporate jets are in the hangar?

A second type of system is performance based. This kind of system is primarily control oriented: It looks at today's performance based on variances from budgets. These variances are useful to pinpoint problems but, like sales analysis, do not provide any answers.

A third kind of system is contribution based. As we show in the next section, its emphasis is on costs the product manager can control, and it makes a clear distinction between fixed and variable costs. Contribution-based systems are for operating managers, and as such they are decision oriented. They permit the manager to look toward the future by being able to generate answers to "what if" kinds of questions.

Our point is not that one system should be used to the exclusion of another but that several kinds of reporting systems are important to provide full information to all levels of management. Corporate jets may be necessary to conduct business, and their costs must be covered by the firm's products. However, should the health of an individual product be damaged by being saddled with a high overhead charge? Another kind of profitability thus indicates how much revenue is generated in excess of costs directly related to marketing an individual product. The more a product manager knows about how profits are calculated, the better equipped she or he is to battle with more senior managers over resource allocation decisions.

Contribution-Oriented Systems

The earlier discussion of Figure 15–4 illustrates one of the "bottom lines" that provides useful information (although with some important limitations) to product managers. A second notion of profitability is called *contribution margin.* Basically, contribution margin is the amount of money left over after variable costs are accounted for that goes toward covering fixed costs. At this point, it is critical to be clear on the different categories of costs.[5]

Figure 15–5 categorizes different kinds of costs that will be useful in our discussion. Variable costs are those that vary directly with total volume of sales or production. Such costs normally include materials (for manufactured products) and

---

[5]Some readers are undoubtedly well versed on the differences among types of costs. However, it is important that we develop a consistent set of definitions for this chapter.

FIGURE 15–5 Cost Classifications

Category	Total Cost	Components	
		Variable	*Fixed*
Operating expenses ($000)			
Direct labor	$ 2,500	2,500	
Direct supervision	500	500	
Social Security	255	255	
Materials	5	5	
Operations overhead	840	200	640
Subtotal:	$ 4,100	3,460	640
Nonoperating expenses ($000)			
Advertising	$ 700		700
Promotion	200		200
Field sales	1,700	200	1,500
Product management	25		25
Marketing management	250		250
Product development	150		150
Marketing research	175		175
Customer service	1,500	240	1,260
Testing	300		300
General and administrative	1,000		1,000
Subtotal:	$ 6,000	$ 440	$5,560
Total	$10,100	3,900	6,200

direct labor (hourly), but they can also include supplies such as packaging. We assume the variable cost per unit remains constant as volume changes.[6]

Fixed costs are more complicated. In general, a cost is fixed if it does not vary in amount with the volume of sales or production. Fixed costs tend to be items such as advertising, customer service, corporate jets, and the like. However, at some level of sales, all costs become variable. That is, rather than being level for any amount of sales, fixed costs often follow a step pattern: They can increase with a large jump in sales but remain level at this new plateau. For example, if the product sells better than expected, additional customer service representatives may have to be hired. Fixed costs can be direct, that is, directly associated with a given product (e.g., advertising), or indirect (e.g., the corporate jet). In addition, programmed fixed costs are highly flexible because they can be increased or decreased at will. Standby fixed costs are difficult to adjust in the short run.

[6]This is not always the case, particularly if the product can exhibit experience curve effects where costs per unit decline with cumulative volume. However, variable costs per unit are usually fixed within a reasonable range of sales or production.

FIGURE 15–6 Classifying Costs: Fixed versus Variable

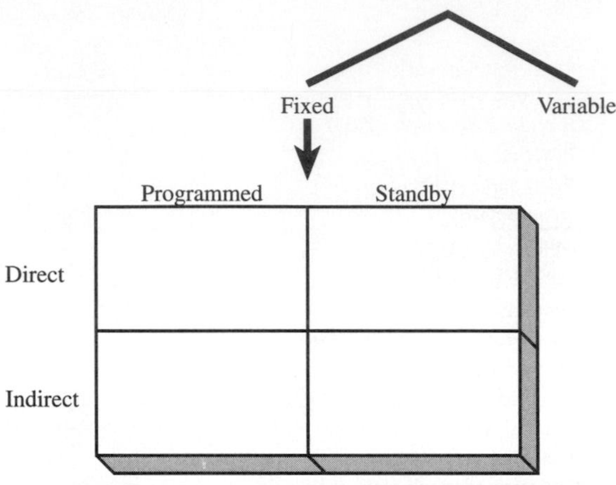

Using these definitions, one can take the numbers in Figure 15–4 and classify them into variable and fixed categories (we will be concerned later with the different categories of fixed costs).[7] Figure 15–6 shows a suggested classification scheme. Examining the operating expenses first (the top part of Figure 15–4), clearly direct labor, social security (a fixed percentage of direct labor), and materials are variable because they depend on sales volume. We assume operations overhead has fixed and variable components. For example, utility bills can vary with production volume and hence may be variable, whereas depreciation of plant and equipment is fixed. Much of the nonoperating expense is fixed except for field sales, which have some commission (fixed percentage of sales) and customer service (on-site service expense is a percentage of the number of units sold).

These newly classified costs can be assembled into a new financial statement, shown in Figure 15–7, called a *contribution margin statement.* The revenues remain the same at $10 million. However, we first subtract the variable costs of $3.9 million, leaving $6.1 million in contribution margin. This is the amount of money left after direct costs of making the product or delivering the service that will go toward covering fixed costs. What is called the contribution or variable margin *rate* is the contribution margin divided by the total sales revenue—in this case, $6.1 million divided by $10 million, or 61 percent. Another way to look at this number is that 61 cents of every dollar of sales goes to covering fixed costs. On a per-unit basis, this translates to $3.05 (61 percent times $5). These will be important numbers in answering some key questions.

Thus, all we have done is reallocate the costs into categories different than those used in the income statement shown in Figure 15–4. Although we have not really

[7]Obviously, the exact classification will vary across individual situations. Figure 15–4 is meant as an illustration only.

FIGURE 15–7 Contribution Margin Statement

Product: NewCall
Income Statement, December 31, 1996
(000's)

Revenues (2M units @ $5)		$10,000
Variable costs		
Direct labor	2,500	
Direct supervision/clerical	500	
Social Security	255	
Sales force commissions	200	
Customer service	240	
Materials	5	
Operations overhead (plant, etc.)	200	
Total variable costs		3,900
Contribution margin (61%)		6,100
Fixed costs		
Operations overhead	640	
Advertising	700	
Promotion	200	
Field sales	1,500	
Product management	25	
Marketing management	250	
Product development	150	
Marketing research	175	
Customer service	1,260	
Testing	300	
General and administrative	1,000	
Total fixed costs		6,200
Operating profit (loss)		(100)

shown yet how this new scheme helps make better decisions, it should already be clear that Figure 15–7 is somewhat easier to interpret. In fact, now we can easily answer the question posed earlier concerning the profit impact of a 10 percent increase in revenues. If revenues increase to $11 million, variable costs also increase by 10 percent to $4.29 million. Since fixed costs remain the same at $6.2 million, the new profit figure would be $510,000, or an increase of $610,000. This would not have been easy to calculate with the statement shown in Figure 15–4.

Using the Contribution Margin Rate

Three basic calculations make use of the contribution margin concept. First, most product managers need to know their *break-even* volume in both units and dollars. This is the amount they need to sell to cover fixed costs. The formulae are:

Break-even in units = Fixed costs/variable margin per unit
Break-even in dollars = Fixed costs/variable margin rate.

The other important concept is the *safety factor,* which is the amount over (or under) the break-even volume currently being sold:

Safety factor = (Current sales volume − Breakeven volume)/Current volume.

Using the information from Figure 15–7, the break-even volume in units is the fixed-cost figure of $6.2 million divided by $3.05 (the contribution margin per unit), or 2,032,787 units. The break-even volume in dollars is $6.2 million divided by 61 percent, or $10,163,934. Clearly, NewCall is operating at below break-even level. As a result, the safety factor is negative: −1.6 percent.

A word of warning about break-even analyses is that they are very short-run oriented because the calculations are based only on one year's results. Even though NewCall is below break-even, it may be a new product and therefore may need more time to establish itself in the marketplace. Overreliance on break-even analyses can result in the company making myopic decisions on products that have considerable promise. However, they are useful benchmarks when used conservatively.

Break-even analysis can also be applied to any incremental change in fixed costs. Suppose the NewCall product manager wishes to hire two additional salespeople at a total cost of $200,000 per year. The sales volume that would have to be generated to cover their salaries (assuming no commission) would be $200,000 divided by .61, or $327,869. Alternatively, if the product manager wishes to spend an additional $100,000 on advertising, $163,934 will have to be generated to break even, assuming no long-term effects of the advertising.

An additional use of the contribution margin information is in profit planning. Suppose the NewCall product manager was given a target of $500,000 profit. The dollar revenues needed would be computed using the following formula:

Target profit break-even = (Target + Fixed costs)/Contribution rate.

Thus, the target profit acts as an additional hurdle to overcome in addition to fixed costs. In dollars, the necessary revenue would be ($500,000 + $6.2 million)/.61, or $10,983,607. In units, the break-even amount would be $6.7 million/$3.05, or 2,196,721 units.

As noted earlier, it is relatively straightforward to calculate the profit impact of increases or decreases in revenues. An increase in revenues of 10 percent increased profits by $610,000. However, the reverse is also true: A decrease in revenues of 10 percent increases the loss by $610,000. It turns out that more fixed cost–intensive businesses suffer when sales drop because there is less revenue to cover the fixed costs. A good example of this problem is the airline industry (and most service businesses in general). The airline industry is characterized by low variable costs (e.g., fuel, food) and extremely high fixed costs (e.g., flight attendants, interest payments on airplanes). This results in price wars for passengers because any empty seats mean lost revenue that can cover fixed costs. Although revenues per passenger drop, the drop can hopefully be offset by greater total revenues per flight. Recessionary periods and products with inherently slow growth rates exacerbate the problem.

In general, products characterized by different variable margin rates have quite different strategic problems. When variable costs are high (contribution margin rates are low), it is important to keep prices high because profit is made on each item sold.

FIGURE 15–8 Break-Even Analysis Table

Percentage Change in Price	Variable Margin Rate (percent)								
	10	*15*	*20*	*25*	*30*	*35*	*40*	*45*	*50*
+25	29	38	45	50	55	58	62	64	66
+20	33	43	50	56	60	64	67	69	72
+15	40	50	53	57	59	70	73	75	77
+10	50	60	67	72	73	78	80	82	83
+5	67	75	80	83	86	88	89	90	91
0	100	100	100	100	100	100	100	100	100
−5	200	150	133	125	123	117	114	113	111
−10		300	200	167	150	140	133	129	125
−15			400	280	200	175	160	150	143
−20				500	300	233	200	180	167
−25					600	350	267	225	200

Divide each table entry by 100. Entries represent the ratio of new unit sales to old unit sales required to break even on a price change for products with various current variable margin rates.

That is, with relatively low fixed costs to cover, profitability is determined by the profit margin on each unit. When fixed costs are high and variable costs are low, sales volume to generate contribution margin to cover the fixed costs becomes critical.

This conclusion is borne out by the figures shown in Figure 15–8. The horizontal dimension is the variable margin rate. Fixed costs increase from left to right. The vertical dimension reflects alternative price changes. The entries in the table are the percentage of new-unit sales to old-unit sales required to break even for a given price change and associated contribution margin rate. Thus, if a product has a 35 percent margin rate and the product manager is thinking of cutting price by 10 percent, sales would have to increase by 40 percent to break even. This occurs because if the price drops, the variable margin rate also drops and less money is left to cover fixed costs. What is alarming is the amount of additional sales needed to break even for even relatively modest price cuts *for any contribution margin rate!* You can see that the airlines benefit to some extent by having contribution margin rates to the right end (or even off) the scale because the higher the margin rate, the less a price cut hurts contribution margin and the lower the incremental volume that has to be generated to break even for any price cut.

Fixed Costs

As we noted earlier, there are different kinds of fixed costs. Programmed direct fixed costs are the kind product managers control and are usually expended for a specific planning period. In other words, they are discretionary. Examples of this kind of costs are advertising, promotion, and the like. Programmed indirect fixed costs are controlled by management but cover several products. Corporate umbrella advertising would fall into this category. Standby direct fixed costs do not change significantly without a major change in operations and are generally not controlled by the product manager in the short run. An example would be costs associated with a production facility that is dedicated to a specific product. Standby indirect fixed costs are typically corporate overhead—the jet, the CEO's salary, and so on. They are not directly related to any specific product, nor are they controlled by the product manager.

The reason for making these distinctions goes back to the notion of profitability and the evaluation of the product manager. For what costs should the manager be responsible? We could argue that the product manager has a primary responsibility to make a profit by generating revenues in excess of variable costs that cover the fixed costs attributable to his or her product—the direct costs, both standby and programmed. In other words, the product manager should be responsible for making a profit based on costs that would exist *only* if the product existed. Any costs that would not disappear if the product were dropped are not the responsibility of the product manager. This is, in fact, a conservative approach because some of the direct standby costs might not disappear at all if the product were dropped. A manufacturing plant, for example, could be adapted for producing another product made by the company.

Figure 15–9 illustrates (based on some assumptions) how these fixed-cost categories can affect the profit picture for a product. The fully allocated cost bottom line is the same, of course (a loss of $100,000), as is the contribution margin bottom line of $6.1 million. However, look at the third "bottom line," that is, the profit picture after subtracting all direct fixed costs. After conservatively subtracting both programmed *and* standby direct fixed costs, NewCall shows a "profit" of $1.835 million! Only after subtracting costs over which the product manager has no control does the product show a loss. We can now answer a question stated earlier in this chapter: In fact, the company would be *worse* off by dropping this money-"losing" product because it is generating $1.835 million that is going toward covering indirect fixed costs.[8] Thus, it is not always clear what profits and losses mean.

In sum, each of the three notions of profit developed in this chapter have pluses and minuses. The full-costing statement (Figure 15–4) is of most interest to top management and external constituents. In addition, ultimately *all* costs of the business must be covered. The contribution margin statement (Figure 15–7) is easy to read and gives a quick idea of how much money is being generated to cover fixed costs. However, it does not make a distinction between indirect and direct fixed costs. Finally, the statement breaking down fixed costs (Figure 15–9) is the most relevant for product management because it clearly states how the product is performing. It also reflects that it is becoming more important to relate product costs to actual activity as opposed to arbitrary allocation methods.[9] However, it is also true that all products sold by a company could be profitable by this measure, but the company would go out of business because the excess funds generated beyond direct costs do not cover indirect costs. To repeat a point we made earlier, product managers must equip themselves with information about the different kinds of profit concepts discussed here to make a better case for an increased share of corporate resources.

---

[8]This assumes that no product substitutes for NewCall in the short run.

[9]See, for example, Robin Cooper and Robert S. Kaplan, "Profit Priorities from Activity-Based Costing," *Harvard Business Review,* May–June 1991, pp. 130–35.

FIGURE 15–9 Income Statement: Direct versus Indirect Fixed Costs

Product: NewCall Income Statement, December 31, 1996		
Revenues (2M units @ $5)		$10,000
Variable costs		
Direct labor	$2,500	
Direct supervision	500	
Social security	255	
Sales force commissions	200	
Customer service	240	
Materials	5	
Operations overhead	200	
Total		3,900
Contribution margin (61%)		6,100
Fixed costs		
Programmed direct:		
Advertising	500	
Promotion	200	
Field sales	1,500	
Product management	25	
Marketing management	200	
Product development	50	
Marketing research	150	
Customer service	400	
Total	3,025	3,075
Standby direct:		
Operations overhead	640	
Testing	300	
General and administrative	300	
Total	1,240	1,835
Programmed indirect:		
Advertising	200	
Marketing management	50	
Product development	100	
Marketing research	25	
Customer service	860	
Standby indirect:		
General and administrative	700	
Total indirect costs	1,935	
Operating profit		(100)

A Strategic Framework for Control

The two financial analyses described thus far can be used both for ex ante budgeting (while the plan is being developed) and for ex post (or after the planning period) control purposes. However, a specific kind of analysis called *variance* analysis is used for control only. In this context, a variance is a discrepancy between a planned figure or objective and the actual outcome. Typically, control in a marketing planning context is limited to some simple variances such as comparing actual advertising expenditures

Figure 15–10 Example of Variance Analysis: Product Alpha

Item	*Planned*	*Actual*	*Variance*
Revenues			
Sales (lbs.)	20,000,000	22,000,000	2,000,000
Price per lb. ($)	0.50	.4773	0.227
Revenues	$10,000,000	$10,500,000	$500,000
Total market (lbs.)	40,000,000	50,000,000	10,000,000
Share of market	50%	44%	(6%)
Costs			
Variable cost per lb. ($)	.30	.30	—
Contribution			
Per lb. ($)	.20	.1773	.0227
Total ($)	4,000,000	3,900,000	(100,000)

Source: James H. Hulbert and Norman E. Toy, "A Strategic Framework for Marketing Control," *Journal of Marketing,* April 1977, p. 13.

to historical averages or market share (using advertising share) or expected versus actual levels of profit or sales. Variance analysis was developed to integrate accounting with concepts from marketing strategy and planning.[10] Like the sales analysis presented earlier, the major benefit of variance analysis is identification of potential problem areas, not diagnosing the causes of the problems.

Figure 15–10 presents possible market results for a hypothetical product, Alpha. As is typical with a variance analysis, the three columns refer to the planned amount, the actual amount, and the difference or variance. The rows describe different quantities of interest. Of particular note are market size and share that link to well-known models of strategic marketing planning, such as the Boston Consulting Group's growth-share matrix.

Figure 15–10 shows an unfavorable contribution variance of $100,000. Assuming the variances are due to marketing-related activities alone, the $100,000 variance could be due to volume variance, that is, selling a different amount than that planned, or a contribution variance. The volume variance is due to variances between planned and actual figures for market size and market share, the two key strategic variables. By decomposing the results in this way, the product manager has a more complete view of where the problems in the product's performance may lie.

Price-Quantity Decomposition

The following terms are used below:

S = Share.
M = Total market size.
Q = Quantity sold in units.
C = Contribution margin per unit.

[10]This section is based on James M. Hulbert and Norman E. Toy, "A Strategic Framework for Marketing Control," *Journal of Marketing,* April 1977, pp. 12–20.

An a subscript denotes actual values, and p denotes planned values. The variance is given by a v subscript.

The price/cost variance is

$$(C_a - C_p) \times Q_a = (.1773 - .20) \times 22{,}000{,}000 = -\$500{,}000.$$

This comes from selling too much at a low margin. In other words, the product is penalized heavily for missing the contribution target. The volume variance is

$$(Q_a - Q_p) \times C_p = (22{,}000{,}000 - 20{,}000{,}000) \times .20 = \$400{,}000.$$

The sum of these variances is the –$100,000 shown in Figure 15–10.

Penetration–Market Size Decomposition

The next stage of the analysis decomposes the volume variance into components due to penetration (market share) and market size. The difference in quantity sold is $Q_a - Q_p$. However, we know that actual quantity is actual share times actual market size, or $Q_a = (M_a \times S_a)$. Likewise, planned quantity $Q_p = (M_p \times S_p)$. Thus, the key to understanding the quantity or volume variance is to understand the variances in share and market size.

The variance in contribution due to market share can be expressed by

$$(S_a - S_p) \times M_a \times C_p,$$

which is

$$(.44 - .50) \times 50{,}000{,}000 \times .2$$
$$= -\$600{,}000.$$

This is offset by the gain from the increased size of the market:

$$(M_a - M_p) \times S_p \times C_p,$$

which is

$$(50{,}000{,}000 - 40{,}000{,}000) \times .5 \times .2$$
$$= \$1{,}000{,}000.$$

Thus, the sum of the two variances, share and market size, nets out to $400,000, which is the quantity variance noted above.

A summary of this analysis is the following:

Planned profit contribution		$4,000,000
Volume variance		
Share variance	($600,000)	
Market size variance	1,000,000	
		400,000
Price/cost variance		(500,000)
Actual profit contribution		$3,900,000

Summary

Who has responsibility for these variances? The market size variance is due to underforecasting the size of the market. In some companies, this is the responsibility of the product manager. However, there are numerous explanations for why the forecast is low. One explanation could be that insufficient exogenous factors such as population growth, government spending, interest rates, and the like were considered. Many times, the forecast is off due to unexpected changes in competitive strategy. In this case, product Alpha's price was lower than planned. The low price can be due to increased price competition, which, if total market demand is price elastic, can cause the market size to increase. This would be difficult to forecast. No matter what the source of the error was, the underforecast resulted in a $1 million favorable variance. However, this is not entirely positive. Market growth greater than expected may have contributed to a set of actions by the product manager that led to loss of competitive position. As the (former) market leader in a fast-growing market, this is a serious loss.

In addition, market share was substantially lower than planned. This also can be due to a large number of factors, but it is usually due less to forecasting errors than to actions by the relevant product managers. In the case of product Alpha, it is possible that the product manager reacted late with a price cut, enabling competitors to gain share. Alternatively, a competitor may have launched a particularly creative advertising campaign. In other words, the market share variance is due more to operational problems than to poor forecasting. This error was particularly damaging, however, costing $600,000 in lost profits.

Clearly, decomposing the $400,000 volume variance into the two components, share and market size, provides more information to the product manager. Like the sales analysis, the $400,000 figure is aggregate and masks substantial underlying numbers. Understanding how market share and size variances contribute to the overall volume variance pinpoints areas for further examination, perhaps organizationally (how do we do our forecasting?) and operationally (how should we react to a competitor's price cut?).

The price/cost variance of –$500,000 is also quite large. However, this variance, although calculated separately, is clearly not independent of the volume variance and its decomposition. The drop in price may well have led to the increased market size. Perhaps the drop in share to 44 percent would have been greater without the lower contribution achieved.

Finally, while the example illustrates the use of this strategic framework for control of a product after the end of the planning period, one major potential application of the approach is for control *during* the execution of the plan. It would clearly be better to understand the variances after 6 months than after 12. Appropriate corrective action can take place and reduce some of the negative variances before the end of the year.

Capital Budgeting

Overview

Product managers often have to weigh alternatives for making incremental changes in a product or for whether or not to introduce a new variant. For example, a workstation product manager may have several options for making product improvements, such as a larger hard disk, a new configuration of the case for a smaller "footprint" on a manager's desk, a better monitor, and so on. These alternative projects have different degrees of potential for expanding sales, market share, or both and thus have different potential financial impact.

The same kind of reasoning can be applied to other kinds of investments made by the product manager. For example, marketing mix expenditures such as advertising, promotion, sales force, and so on can be viewed as projects in the sense that they are investments intended to produce some future cash flow to the firm. Thus, an increase of $1 million in advertising must be weighed against expanding the sales force or even adopting one of the product improvements.

The same mechanism operates at the firm level. Different new-product ideas come from research and development, each with alternative degrees of potential financial success. Like the product manager, senior managers must develop an approach to prioritize investments in new products or major reformulations.

Capital budgeting is an area of finance that deals with this prioritization of projects within a firm.[11] Many readers will already be familiar with the basics of capital budgeting. However, there is rarely any link between what transpires in finance courses and what actually happens in marketing on this topic. For example:

> Marketers and finance people seldom see eye to eye. The marketers say, "This product will open up a whole new market segment." Finance people respond, "It's a bad investment. The IRR (internal rate of return) is only 8%." Why are they so often in opposition?[12]

This section briefly describes the main approaches to rationing resources among a set of risky projects and discusses how marketing issues are heavily related to capital budgeting.

The Basics

Capital budgeting involves five discrete steps:

1. Generating investment proposals.
2. Estimating cash flows for the proposals.
3. Evaluating the cash flows.
4. Selecting projects based on an acceptance criterion.
5. Continually reevaluating the projects after their acceptance.

We focus on the first three steps in this chapter.

Although a detailed discussion is outside the scope of this book, it is clear that marketing management has great influence on alternative investment proposals.[13]

---

[11]All basic finance textbooks deal extensively with capital budgeting. See, for example, James C. Van Horne, *Financial Management and Policy,* 10th ed. (Englewood Cliffs, N.J.: Prentice Hall 1995).

[12]Patrick Barwise, Paul R. Marsh, and Robin Wensley, "Must Finance and Strategy Clash?" *Harvard Business Review,* September–October 1989, pp. 85–90.

[13]See, for example, C. Merle Crawford, *New Products Management,* 4th ed. (Burr Ridge, Ill.: Richard D. Irwin, 1994).

New-product concepts come from contacts with customers such as focus groups, internally from product management, and from a large variety of other sources besides research and development.

Marketing management also generates estimates of cash flows. Product managers or staff personnel develop sales forecasts. They obtain estimates of penetration rates over time from simulated test marketing laboratories, intention-to-buy surveys, and other marketing research sources.

Given that cash flows (after tax) have been estimated, the third step is to evaluate the attractiveness of the different proposals. Again, these could be new products, refinements, or even investments in advertising. The four major methods used to perform this evaluation are

1. Average rate of return.
2. Payback.
3. Internal rate of return.
4. Present value.

Average Rate of Return. This accounting method takes the ratio of the average annual profits after taxes to the average investment in the project. For example, if the average annual profits are $5,000 and the average investment per year in the project is $20,000, the average rate of return is 25 percent. A variant of this method divides the average annual profits by the original investment rather than the average. The return rate can be compared to hurdles used by the firm or other standards. The obvious advantage of this method is that it is simple. However, it ignores the timing of the profits since it values the income from the last year as much as those from the first year.

Payback. This method calculates the number of years it will take to recover the initial investment in the project. It is the ratio of the initial investment over the annual cash flows (not profits as in the average rate of return method). Thus, if the initial investment is $100,000 and the annual cash flow is $20,000, the payback period is five years. If the annual cash flows are not equal, you can still easily calculate the payback period by simply adding the yearly flows up to the point where the initial investment is recovered. The calculated payback period is then compared to a threshold level; if it is less, it is accepted. A major problem with this method is that it ignores cash flows after the payback period. It also does not account for the timing of the cash flows.

Internal Rate of Return (IRR). Most analysts use some kind of discounted cash flow analysis to evaluate projects. The key point is that an equivalent amount of money in the future is not worth as much as it is today. This method and the present value method take account of both the size and the timing of the cash flows returned by a project.

Let r be a rate of interest. Assuming the initial investment in the project occurs at time 0 and n is the last period when cash flows can be expected, the internal rate of return is calculated from the following formula:

$$A_0 = A_1/(1 + r) + A_2/(1 + r)^2 + \cdots + A_n/(1 + r)^n.$$

Therefore, r is the rate that discounts the future cash flows from the project to equal the initial investment (r is the number that equates the right side of the equation with the initial investment, A_0). As with the other methods, r must be compared to an internal hurdle rate or requirement set by management for a project to be accepted. Obviously, this rate should be higher than what is called the "risk-free" rate, the rate the company could get by putting the money in the bank.[14] Unfortunately, in many cases companies probably could do better by doing just that!

Present Value. The net present value of a proposal is

$$NPV = \Sigma A_t/(1 + k)^t,$$

where k is the rate of return the company requires. This is often referred to as the *discount rate* or the firm's *opportunity cost of capital.* Note that when $t = 0$, A is the initial investment and is thus a large negative number. The present value method states that if NPV is greater than 0, the project should be accepted. In other words, you should accept the project if the present value of cash received from it is greater than the present value of cash spent. As might be expected, the internal rate of return and present value methods usually lead to the same decision. However, the NPV method is often favored from a theoretical perspective.

Summary

Clearly, finance and marketing have much to say to each other concerning capital budgeting.[15] Not only are marketing personnel involved with generating projects and projecting cash flow, but the very concept of what makes a good investment is entirely consistent between the two functions. For a new or reformulated product to generate NPV in excess of the investment costs, it must have inherent value to customers and it must satisfy customer needs better than competitive offerings. The capital budgeting process is much more than simply crunching numbers; the sources of the cash flow must be based on the quality of the marketing strategy and the firm's ability to execute the strategy. Unfortunately, it is often difficult to quantify many of the factors that make a new product or other project attractive to marketing management but unattractive to financial executives.

Some ways marketing managers can make project evaluation more responsive to strategic concerns are the following:

1. *Use the right base case.* When normally evaluating a project, the NPV or internal rate of return is compared to some reference point. This is usually an implicit *status quo* option. For example, a new product might cannibalize sales of an existing product. The analysis cannot simply consider the new product as incremental revenue and analyze it that way; it must also consider the lost sales of the old product. This is

[14]Investors usually demand higher rates than the risk-free rate. This depends on industry and market characteristics.

[15]The material in this section is based on Barwise, Marsh, and Wensley, "Must Finance and Strategy Clash?"

particularly important for investments in marketing mix variables, which often have the intent of stifling a competitor's move. For example, sales promotions often cost more money than they generate. A capital budgeting analysis would probably advise not making such expenditures. However, it is possible that without the promotion, market share and profits would have dropped even more. While this is a difficult scenario to quantify, it is quite common.

2. *Select the appropriate time horizon.* In the methods described earlier, the time horizon issue was purposely left vague. Clearly, in attempting to implement all the methods except the payback method, it is necessary to have some estimate of n, the useful life of the project. In many traditional applications of capital budgeting, the project is a piece of capital equipment whose useful life is typically known. Sometimes the time horizon is set arbitrarily. The size of n can affect the NPV or IRR dramatically. For a new product, the stage of the product life cycle would be an important determinant of n. In addition, if a new brand name is being established, the value of the name can linger longer than the exact product or service being launched through extensions and modifications. For a marketing mix variable such as advertising, it is difficult to estimate the useful life of additional expenditure; estimating the carryover effects of advertising has been the topic of much discussion for the past 30 years.[16]

3. *Look at other benefits of the investment.* Often investments create other opportunities. An example mentioned earlier is the creation of a brand name that can be utilized by other products. For example, Arm & Hammer has been successful with its brand of toothpaste. It is possible that the company will eventually design a line of toothbrushes. This spinoff value is difficult to quantify in a conventional capital budgeting process.

4. *Unbundle the costs and benefits.* When Procter & Gamble first introduced disposable diapers, it really made several subinvestments. One major investment was in the marketing of the product because advertising, trade and consumer promotion, packaging, and similar components had to be developed. However, the company also had to develop a proprietary production process to efficiently manufacture the diapers. These are really two separate projects that could have separate NPVs or IRRs.

Thus, it is clear that capital budgeting processes need to include strategic considerations that are relevant to product managers. Performing simple financial analyses does not account for these kinds of considerations, which can significantly alter the way a company allocates resources.

---

[16]In fact, from an accounting perspective, advertising is expensed rather than capitalized because the useful life of $1 of advertising is generally unknown. However, viewing advertising as a possible "project" in a capital budgeting sense still captures the essential trade-offs a product manager has to make among various budgets.

16 Product Management: Back to the Future

Overview

In this book, we have focused on the major job of the product manager: the development of the marketing plan. The plan involves three major components: background analysis, formulation of product strategy, and marketing mix decisions. We considered managing service quality and customer service in Chapter 14, acknowledging the emerging importance of that topic to product management, and suggested that it has become a fifth element of the marketing mix. In addition, we highlighted the importance of financial analysis in the product manager's tool kit. Hence this book presents a set of basic skills and a planning framework that can be used as a template for virtually any product management situation.

However, although there is a set of basic skills with which every product manager should be familiar, the job is evolving due to changes in both the category environment (Chapter 4) and other general business practices. In Chapter 1, we discussed some of the these major changes affecting the product management environment recently:

- New ways to reach customers.
- The data explosion.
- The increased value of brands.
- Shorter product life cycles.
- Increased power of retailers.
- Significant spending on sales promotion versus advertising.
- Pricing and value.
- Increased importance of customer retention programs.
- Increased global competition.

In this final chapter, we briefly review some of the issues likely to have a significant impact on how product managers perform their jobs in the next several years. In particular, we highlight the roles of information technology and the Internet in changing the way marketing and business in general will be conducted through the end of the 1990s.

The Role of Information Technology

In this section, we focus on transaction-based information technology, that is, how information from customer purchases reaches product managers much more quickly today than in the past. Companies spent an estimated $225 billion on information technology hardware in 1995, much of it targeted toward customer-based systems.[1] In the United States, as of 1996, approximately 97 percent of all commodity volume (ACV) moving through grocery stores was being processed by electronic scanners that provide the information to manufacturers and distributors. The number of scanners in discount, drug, and convenience stores is increasing rapidly. By the end of the century, it will be difficult to find a retail outlet that is not equipped with electronic scanners.

For product managers in packaged goods and other categories using distributors or electronic-based delivery (e.g., online banking), this revolution in information based on transactions has and will continue to have profound effects on their jobs. One estimate is that assistant brand managers spend 80 percent of their time working with numbers and data delivered by these kinds of systems. Every day, Bank of America phone representatives field about 100,000 calls from customers who want, among other things, to check a balance or ask about loan rates. The resulting customer information becomes part of a massive database, or data warehouse, that is an important corporate asset for selling additional products and target marketing. Similarly, automated sales force devices such as order entry systems provide detailed and immediately available customer information for business-to-business marketers.

Collecting and disseminating information in businesses has changed dramatically in the last few years.[2] Through improvements in telecommunications and computer technology, more information is being collected at an increasingly rapid pace. This information is usually processed into databases of customer and channel information that is further analyzed for market opportunities. This kind of activity will become increasingly important as Figure 16–1 shows. Marketing, sales, and technology executives believe information on inventory levels, market share, and customer segments will become much more important over the next five years, as will electronic links to customers and sales forces.

As a result of this activity, significant changes have occurred in the amount of information processed, the speed with which the information is transmitted, the way the information is put together or "packaged" for use, and how the information affects organization structures in corporations. These changes affect not only product manager decision making but also the company as a whole and other members of the distribution system, including retailers.

[1]Thomas A. Stewart, "What Information Costs," *Fortune,* July 10, 1995. pp. 119–21.

[2]This section of the chapter is based on Rashi Glazer, "Marketing in Information-Intensive Environments: Strategic Implications of Knowledge as an Asset," *Journal of Marketing* 55 (1991), pp. 1–19.

FIGURE 16–1 Expected Future Importance of Database Technology in Marketing

Marketers wired for tomorrow's technology

Inventory and market share monitoring and databases will lead high-tech marketing, with the highest percentage of executives calling those applications "very important."

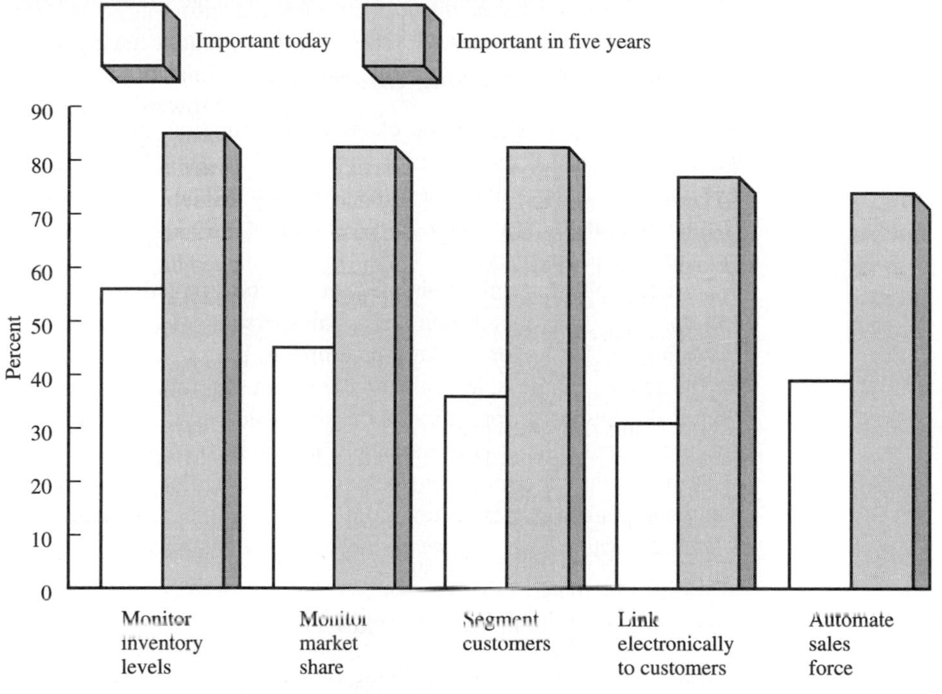

Source: *Advertising Age,* January 25, 1993, p. 30. Reprinted with permission from *Advertising Age,* January 25, 1993.

The Amount of Information Processed

The introduction of POS (point-of-sale) scanners and other technological devices has dramatically increased the quantity of data available for use by the distribution system. POS technology has produced an unprecedented capability to understand customers better, improve inventory control, and affect many other dimensions of business that we will describe in more detail later.

We are only beginning to scratch the surface in using the information being collected; much of the data currently go unanalyzed. Because of the sheer volume of information and the necessity to make decisions quickly in product categories with increased competition, much of the information is being ignored. Current analysis is generally limited to aggregate statistics on sales, market share, and distribution by different kinds of channel members. The rate of information collection has exceeded our abilities to process the information collected and perhaps even goes beyond the need for the information. Thus, in some applications of transaction-based information system (TBIS) technology, a critical bottleneck in the system prevents complete utilization of the data collected.

However, this is changing with the huge investments being made in computing power noted earlier. For example, Burlington Coat Factory Warehouse Corporation, a discount retail clothing chain, has a 1.5 trillion–byte data warehouse assembled from combining daily cash register transactions, factory outputs, inventories, shipments, financial accounting records, and customer data. Burlington uses eight superminicomputers from Seequent Computer Systems to manage the warehouse.[3]

The Speed of Transmitting Information

A second characteristic of the changing information environment is the speed with which managers can receive information. Utilizing satellite-based telecommunications systems, transactions made at retail stores are often instantaneously sent through the channel to manufacturers and, as in the case of Wal-Mart stores (discussed later), often sent directly to suppliers.

Such rapid dissemination of data can be applied in contexts other than POS systems. It is not uncommon for a salesperson, after making a call on a potential customer, to take his or her laptop computer, plug in a telephone cord, fill in a report on the results of the sales call, and transmit the report to the home office where a central database of information about the customer and about competitors' prices and product characteristics is immediately updated. Therefore, rather than waiting weeks or even months for a marketing research firm to collect information from competitors, many companies are now using online databases that are updated after every sales call and made available to anyone in the company.

How Information Is Being "Packaged"

With the large volume of data being produced at such a rapid rate, there is obviously a need to put the data into a form that retailers and other elements of the distribution chain can use. The data therefore have to be collected in a central location and "packaged" (interpreted) in some way to allow decisions to be made based on the information.

Data packages can range from simple forms that show sales and market shares to more sophisticated software programs that make it easy to analyze the data and write reports based on the analyses. The Apollo family of software products marketed by Information Resources, Inc., are examples. These products include Apollo BriefCase, which is based on Microsoft Windows and helps retailers determine how to array brands in a product category on store shelves (called a *planogram*) to maximize profits; that is, it is a category management tool. Figure 16–2 shows a sample screen. Notice that it can show the retailer two kinds of information simultaneously. First, part of the screen reports sales and profits of different brands by UPC (Universal Product

[3]John W. Verity and Russell Mitchell, "A Trillion-Byte Weapon," *Business Week,* July 31, 1995, pp. 80–81.

FIGURE 16–2 Sample Screen from IRI Apollo BriefCase software

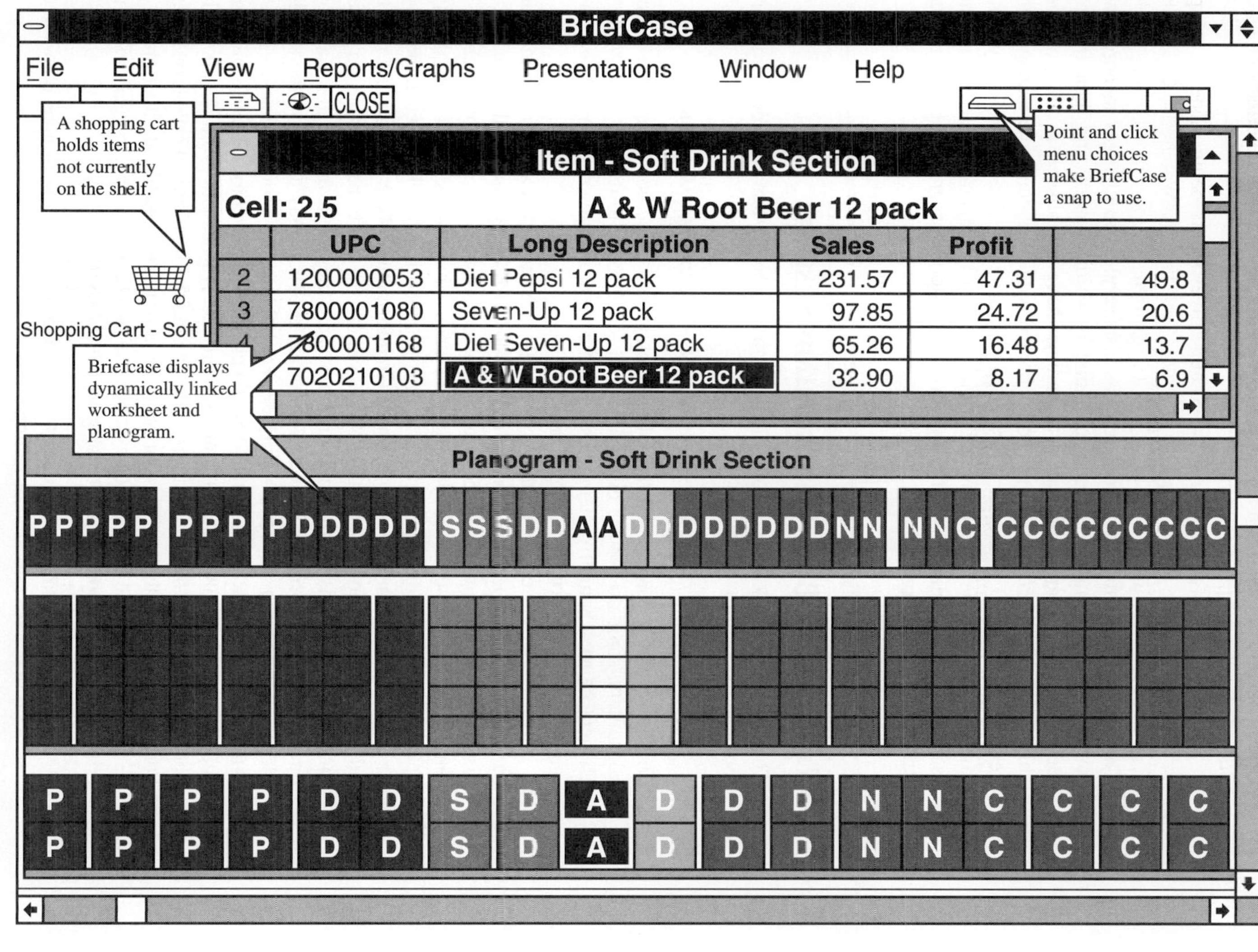
BriefCase
File
Edit
View
Reports/Graphs
Presentations
Window
Help
CLOSE
A shopping cart holds items not currently on the shelf.
Shopping Cart - Soft
Point and click menu choices make BriefCase a snap to use.
Item - Soft Drink Section
Cell: 2,5
A & W Root Beer 12 pack
UPC
Long Description
Sales
Profit
2 1200000053 Diet Pepsi 12 pack 231.57 47.31 49.8
3 7800001080 Seven-Up 12 pack 97.85 24.72 20.6
7800001168 Diet Seven-Up 12 pack 65.26 16.48 13.7
7020210103 A & W Root Beer 12 pack 32.90 8.17 6.9
Briefcase displays dynamically linked worksheet and planogram.
Planogram - Soft Drink Section

Code). Second, the program allows the retailer to see the potential effects on sales and profits of different plans.

Corporate Organizational Structures

The increased amount of information has also resulted in changes in organizational forms in many companies. Companies that view information and their information technology as a major competitive advantage have established a new position, the chief information officer (CIO), who is charged with overseeing the management and development of TBISs and the information they produce. In addition, many organizations have found they can eliminate some layers of management because technology facilitates more rapid flow of information among managers. This has resulted in "flatter" organizational charts.

Transaction-Based Information Systems

The typical textbook diagram of a distribution channel system for a consumer product looks like the following:

Suppliers → Firm → Distributors → Retailers → Consumers.

Of course, not all products follow the same system; some companies sell directly to consumers, some do not use distributors and sell directly to retailers, and so on. Each element of the channel system tries to create loyal customers who will buy a wide range of products from the same firm.

Transaction-based information systems (TBISs) and POS systems are mechanisms used to obtain that loyalty. Assume information is flowing among all elements of the distribution chain and the POS system transmits data from point of purchase at the retailer through the channel system via an electronic network. How does this system help each channel member defend against competition and build customer loyalty? Suppliers to the manufacturer obtain better information about the product mix that is selling and the timing of sales. As a result, they are better able to meet the manufacturers' needs for materials and make sure they are available in the appropriate quantities. Stable trends in the sales of certain products may also give the supplier an incentive to invest in special-purpose equipment for more efficient, lower-cost production. Manufacturers obtain better customer information, know how much to supply distributors and retailers, and get more timely sales and profit data. Distributors obtain similar benefits. In addition, both manufacturers and distributors benefit by building higher switching costs for retailers, a mutually beneficial situation.

In general, these information systems can help the product manager build channel relationships by helping the retailer gain the following:

- Better inventory management through more up-to-the-minute data on which products are and are not selling well.
- Better and more efficient marketing by allowing the retailer to target in-store promotions toward faster-moving brands.
- Greater profits as a result.

Examples of Transaction-Based Information Systems

Wal-Mart. Until he died in 1992, Sam Walton was the richest man in the United States. His Wal-Mart stores sell a wide range of products, from clothes to pharmaceutical and grocery items, and are usually located in rural areas of the country. Wal-Mart became so profitable by being one of the first companies to apply information technology to its distribution system. This distribution system is very simple: The company orders directly from manufacturers, which ship directly to Wal-Mart stores. Wal-Mart designed a satellite-based TBIS that is tied directly both to corporate headquarters in Arkansas and to its merchandise suppliers. Wal-Mart tells manufacturers what to produce and where and when to deliver it. The company requires manufacturers to ship goods already tagged and ready for the selling floor, which eliminates some of the need for warehouse space and processing costs. As a result, Wal-Mart stores need only 10 percent of their total square footage for storage compared to the industry average of 25 percent. When a Wal-Mart store sells a pair of women's size 10 Gitano blue jeans, Gitano replaces them automatically.

Nintendo of America. This video game manufacturer sells its systems through a large number of different kinds of retailers, including toy stores, consumer electronics stores, and variety stores. The company has invested more than $60 million in its Nintendo Inventory Management System (NIMS). Using hand-held computers, Nintendo merchandise representatives collect information at point of sale and transmit the data back to a central warehousing facility in the state of Washington, thus ensuring that each retailer has the appropriate amount of inventory. Not only does the process help the retailer control inventory; it also helps the store plan displays of Nintendo products so it can maximize profits. This investment in stronger retailer relationships has been a major competitive advantage for Nintendo over competitors such as Sega and Sony.[4]

General Electric.[5] GE's traditional method of supplying retailers with large household appliances was to use the industry standard of the "loaded dealer." The theory was that if a manufacturer loaded the dealer with inventory, there would be no room for competitors' products. At the same time, the dealers received the best price from the volume purchase. However, with the rise of the "power" retailers such as Circuit City (see Chapter 13), independent dealers found it too expensive to carry a large stock of any manufacturer's products.

General Electric devised a new system, called Direct Connect, that eliminated the need for retailers to maintain their own inventories of major appliances. Dealers who commit to GE use a computer package that gives them instantaneous access to GE's order-processing system 24 hours a day. This gives them a "virtual" inventory of all the products GE has produced while they carry very little themselves. Dealers get next-day delivery and GE's best price, regardless of order size. In addition, GE gets valuable data on the actual sales of its products. Because of the investment in information technology, GE manufactures in response to consumer demand instead of for inventory.

---

[4]Another good example of this kind of system is the one used by the drug wholesaler McKesson.

[5]This illustration is from Michael Treacy and Fred Wiersema, "Customer Intimacy and Other Value Disciplines," *Harvard Business Review* 93 (January–February 1993), pp. 84–93.

American Greetings. This company is the second largest greeting card manufacturer. American Greetings tested a system to track the sales performance of new cards by adding an extra UPC code keyed to the card's design.[6] This code is then scanned using hand-held computers (like Nintendo) that transmit information directly back to headquarters. Slow-selling designs are quickly replaced, thus helping both the retailer and the company. The sales data thus obtained, as well as consumer demographic data by city blocks, enable American Greetings to tailor its offerings by store. For example, it offers a full gift wrap section in a shop that attracts affluent customers and a smaller section in a store with less well-to-do customers.

Letting Your Customers In

Several writers have noted that a key way for a company to develop long-term customer relations is to let its best customers have access to its databases, that is, create a "dialogue."[7] Some examples are:

- Ingersoll-Rand, a manufacturer of industrial products such as air compressors, extracts data from its systems and makes them available to distributors. For example, any distributor can sit down at a PC or terminal in his or her office and request product pricing, check on inventory availability, place an order, or track the status of an order.
- Rosenbluth International, a travel services company, has a system for its corporate clients that they can check for their travel itineraries and expenses on a daily, weekly, or monthly basis. A new system takes all the available historical travel data for a client to develop specific travel "rules"to follow every time a new travel request is processed.
- Wells Fargo Bank has an interactive service based on its World Wide Web site, where customers can check their account balances, transfer money between accounts, and request information on loans.

New Retail Technology

Some new technology from around the world may soon be widely used in the United States. Examples are:[8]

- *Buying groceries through ATMs.* Italy's Sao Paolo Bank encourages customers to buy groceries and other products through its ATMs, the costs being deducted from their accounts.
- *On-flight ordering.* British Airways has an elaborate system of terminals and computers that allows passengers to order merchandise from their seats. With

---

[6]Judann Pollack, "Role of New Products Puts Scope on SKUs," *Advertising Age,* October 9, 1995, p. 18.

[7]Alice Laplante, "Invitation to Customers: Come into Our Database," *Forbes ASAP,* August 28, 1995, pp. 124–30; Regis McKenna, "Real-Time Marketing," *Harvard Business Review,* July–August, 1995, pp. 87–95.

[8]Allyson L. Stewart-Allen, "Retail Technology Worth Watching," *Marketing News,* January 29, 1996, p. 6.

computer equipment from Olivetti, passengers make selections from catalogs, run their credit cards through a reader, and punch in on a keyboard their addresses or hotels where the goods are to be delivered and on what day. The data are transmitted via satellite.

- *Self-scanning.* SuperTag, a joint venture between South African and U.K. firms, is an electromagnetic tag placed on the side of every product. Shoppers take their purchases to an unmanned check-out desk and place them on a conveyor belt, which passes through an X-ray box that reads the price signals from the tag. Store managers can also wave a "magic" wand that instantly reads the beams of all the tags in the store to take inventory.
- *Talking shelves.* Developed by a Belgian company, a battery-powered computer chip attached to a speaker allows brand managers to promote the brand to customers within a 12-foot range of the shelf. The message is repeated every 30 seconds.

Summary

The information technology revolution in marketing is pervasive. Its pervasiveness is shown in Figure 16–3, which compares information-based marketing to the more traditional approach. As can be seen, all of the major strategic and marketing mix areas, including market segmentation, pricing, advertising, promotion, sales management, channels, new products, and monitoring the progress of marketing plans, have been and will continue to be affected by information technology.

However, as we noted earlier in this chapter, the quantity of information will also increase dramatically. The only way to deal with the information explosion is to use automation to help "package" the information. Certain analyses (e.g., estimating the sensitivity of sales to price) must be automatically produced and made available to managers. However, even if carefully analyzed statistics replace raw information, information overload is still a problem. The eventual solution is some form of artificial intelligence. A small but growing number of researchers are focusing on developing systems that not only analyze data but also provide summary interpretations, often by comparing results to some standard (e.g., statistical significance levels or typical past results) and reporting only exceptional cases.[9]

Another approach is to attempt to discover universal laws, or at least empirical regularities, in the data.[10] For example, as we mentioned earlier, various statistics such as advertising and price elasticities tend to have similar values across a variety of situations.[11] This suggests that meta-analysis, the systematic analysis of general tendencies, will become a more common form of analysis.[12]

---

[9]For an example of such an artificial intelligence system, see John M. McCann, *The Marketing Workbench* (New York: Dow Jones-Irwin, 1996).

[10]See A. S. C. Ehrenberg, *Data Reduction* (London: John Wiley & Sons, 1981), and the special issue of *Marketing Science,* Vol. 13, no. 2, Part 2 of 2, 1995.

[11]Gert Assmus, John U. Farley, and Donald R. Lehmann, "How Advertising Affects Sales: Meta-Analysis of Econometric Results," *Journal of Marketing Research* 21 (February, 1984), pp. 65–74, and Gerard J. Tellis, "The Price Elasticity of Selective Demand: A Meta-Analysis of Econometric Models of Sales," *Journal of Marketing Research* 25 (1988), pp. 331–41.

[12]John U. Farley and Donald R. Lehmann, *Meta-Analysis in Marketing: Generalization of Response Models* (Lexington, MA: Lexington Books, 1986).

FIGURE 16–3 Marketing's Electronic Revolution

	Traditional Marketing	*Information-Driven Marketing*
Segmentation	Uses segments based on demographic and psychographic profiles of current customers or likely converts. Treats individuals with similar profiles as identical.	Uses data about actual behavior to identify customers and prospects and uses statistical models to assess their individual profit potential and value.
Advertising	Communications are designed for the "average" or "typical" member of the target group.	Communications are individualized based on detailed customer information.
Promotion	Promotions are broadcast via FSIs or geographically defined home delivery.	Promotions are tailored based on an individual's past behavior.
Pricing	Price discrimination depends on customer self-selection.	Price discrimination utilizes information about an individual's price sensitivity and is delivered specifically to that individual.
Sales management	Customer data tend to reside with salespeople, who use them to achieve their own goals.	Sales management has access to customer files and can use them to achieve organizational goals.
Distribution channels	Depends on intermediaries or direct selling from sales force.	Direct links to customers. When intermediaries (e.g., retailers) are used, leads and customer relationships are jointly managed.
New products	R&D driven by firm's technology and production system.	New products and services offered on the basis of company affinity with the customer. Serves loyal customer base by selling outsourced products from third parties.
Monitoring	Focus is on tracking market share, sales volume, and profit. Reviews are periodic, usually annual or quarterly.	Greater focus is on customer retention, cost of new customer acquisition, and lifetime value of customer base. Monitoring is generally continuous.

Source: "Bye to 'Assembly Line' Mode of Decisionmaking" B.G. Yovovich *Advertising Age,* October 23, 1995, p. 30. Reprinted with permission.

Product Management and the Internet

Although the Internet, a global network of computers, has been around for many years, it was only in 1995, when the World Wide Web (WWW, or "the Web" for short) was constructed, that marketing applications for the internet became apparent. Prior to 1995, the Internet was used largely by academics for communications purposes or electronically transmitting documents. The WWW is essentially a network of "home pages" where companies, other organizations, and individuals can place information about themselves, communicate with customers, receive communications from customers, and deliver customized messages, products, and services to customers.

Through the use of layers of information called *hypertext,* "hot links" that permit easy flow from one WWW site to another, web search engines or "spiders" that permit a user to search for information by simply typing in a keyword or phrase, and "E-cash," which enables a browser to pay for goods without disclosing credit card information on what may be unsecured communications lines, the WWW became the hottest area of marketing in 1996. Because of the low barriers to entry, the number of commercial home pages now numbers around 50,000 (there are about 200,000 in total) and is growing rapidly as almost every company searches for a web "strategy."

The WWW is not the only source of marketing transactions on the Internet. Internet-based services such as America Online, Prodigy, and CompuServe have been around for the last five years. With a subscription to any of these services, customers can do many of the same things they can do on the web. In addition, the services offer customized programs for subscribers, such as "chat rooms" where teenagers can "talk" online with other teens or with celebrities such as rock stars. A major difference is that access to web sites is free, while one must pay a subscription fee to access the Internet-based services (although all of them also have connections to the WWW).

We focus on two major applications of the Internet and the WWW for product managers: the use of the Internet as a distribution channel and the WWW as an advertising medium. We warn the reader that given the explosive growth in this area, the information presented here will be out of date by the time this book is published. However, no book on marketing, and particularly product management, can omit some discussion of this topic.[13] As we noted in Chapter 1, this is probably the number one trend in product management.

The Internet/WWW as a Distribution Channel

It has been estimated that the market for products being sold using online services should expand from about $900 million in 1995 to over $1.5 billion by 1998, an annual growth rate of about 35 percent.[14] While only 39 percent of U.S. homes have personal computers and fewer have modems, three trends indicate this will change in the near future. First, the prices of personal computers are falling and will continue to fall. In addition, a modem is a basic component of any new system sold today. Second, while current home connections to the Internet are slow, the technology in this area is changing. Some cable TV companies are test marketing cable modems, which provide very-high-speed connections to the Internet. Also, the local telephone companies are beginning (albeit slowly and tentatively) to market ISDN lines to homes and businesses, which also offer higher-speed connections than modems. Third, some companies, such as Oracle, are betting large sums of money on small, Internet-only "computers" that are projected to retail for $500. All these factors will increase the number of people with access to the Internet and obviously increase the potential to sell products.

The Internet offers real advantages to small companies. Since the cost of constructing a web site is reasonably low (although the sky is the limit), a $1 million company can be as accessible to potential customers worldwide as AT&T or Sony.

---

[13]It is also likely that some of the WWW addresses presented in this section and earlier in the book will be obsolete by the time the reader attempts to use them.

[14]Todd Harris, "On-Line and Upward," *FORECAST,* September–October 1995, pp. 22–23.

Small companies that cannot afford the massive databases described earlier in this chapter can communicate with and sell products to their customers and customize these products just as the large companies do. The Internet can "level the playing field" for marketing to potential customers using that channel for purchasing.[15]

Some good examples of how companies are using the Internet and the WWW as a distribution channel are the following:

- Lands' End, the catalog retailer, has a WWW site (http://www.landsend.com) where buyers can visit its Overstocks Store and pick up discounts on overproduced merchandise. In addition, it puts selected products "On the Counter," where prices decrease automatically until they sell out.
- At the Southwest Airlines WWW site (http://iflyswa.com), travelers can make reservations and purchase electronic tickets for travel. Travelers simply arrive at the gate with their reservation numbers and are handed the traditional colored numbered boarding pass.
- As mentioned previously in this book, consumers can buy groceries at home and have them delivered. In Chicago, Boston, and San Francisco, consumers can use Peapod Inc.'s computer software to order groceries from Safeway or Jewel stores. Consumers enjoy real-time savings and weekly specials. They can shop at any hour and sort by attributes such as calories or fat content; the groceries are selected by specially trained Peapod buyers and delivered at a prespecified time for a fee of $6.95 per order plus 5 percent of the grocery total (and a $4.95 per month membership fee). A new WWW-based service, ShoppingLink, is a competitor to Peapod currently in test market.
- One of the most popular WWW sites is c|net (http://www.cnet.com). Through this site, a customer gets access to other WWW sites that sell computer products. The main screen for the "product finder" is shown in Figure 16–4. A user simply clicks on a specific product "button" or enters key words of a product (e.g., "CD-ROM"), and the site immediately links to vendors' WWW sites.
- Even low-tech firms are using the Internet. For example, visitors to the Lukens Steel site (http://steelnet.org/lukens) can send a request for more information, which will be faxed the next morning. SGS Tool Company puts its catalog online (http://sgstool.com) with an automated searching process that allows users to find and order the precise products they need.

Thus, the Internet is becoming the distribution channel of choice for reaching customers who are technically proficient "cyber shoppers." Used in conjunction with other channel options (see Chapter 13), this produces more effective market coverage for product managers at a relatively low cost. It is particularly efficient for reaching customers from all over the world who have as easy access to a WWW site as a customer in the same city.

[15]For some good examples and some potential pitfalls, see Gary McWilliams, "Small Fry Go Online," *Business Week,* November 20, 1995, pp. 158–64.

FIGURE 16–4 Using the WWW as a Distribution Channel: clnet

Click only on a need to know basis

LeadStory.com

c|net product finder

c|net: the computer network

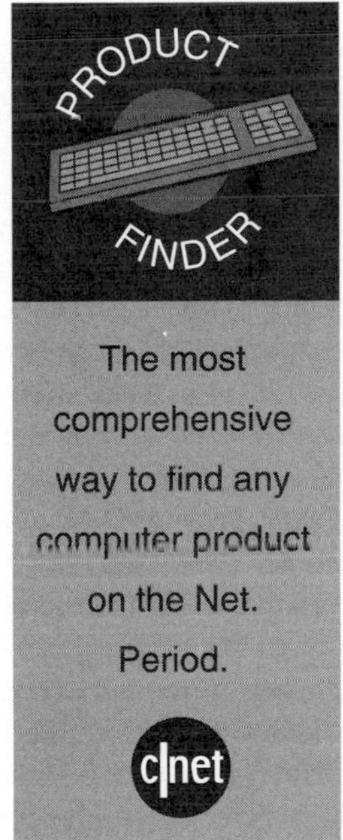

Enter a product or company name: *fast find*

go get it

Or, click on a category: ? what is product finder?

computer systems	peripherals
internet tools	software
gaming	CD-ROMs
networking	online shopping
full alpha list (A-Z)	submit a site

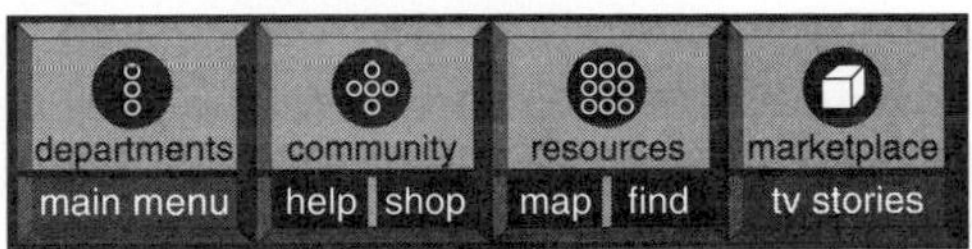

Advertising on the Internet/WWW

As noted in Chapter 11, about $160 billion was spent on advertising in the United States in 1995. Only $12.4 million was spent on advertising over the WWW in the fourth quarter of 1995, a proverbial drop in the bucket.[16] Consistent with the data shown in Figures 11–8 and 11–9, AT&T was the largest spender during this period with a total of $567,000. An example of such an ad by Sprint is shown on the Yahoo! home page in Figure 5–3 (p. 108).

The advantages of advertising on the Internet are obvious. First, you can reach a very targeted audience. Many web sites request descriptive information about the visitor, which not only can be used to define the site's audience but also result in customized ads being shown on the next visit. Many sites are, in fact, a mechanism for delivering an audience rather than selling a product or a service. Second, Internet advertising is very much like direct-response advertising in that customers can link directly to an advertiser's home page and request information, browse a catalog, or buy a product.

Advertising rates on the WWW were initially low, but they are climbing rapidly. Figure 16–5 shows the rates for the most expensive sites in terms of costs per month. Also shown are the estimated number of monthly visitors, the cost per thousand impressions (although it is really only the cost per thousand monthly visitors), and some of the other benefits advertisers receive from the sponsors of the site. As can be seen, a full year of advertising on ESPNet would cost nearly $400,000. While this is cheap compared to national television, a WWW media strategy might include several such sites, thus increasing the costs. Still, large advertisers would probably consider this to be a good investment due to the focused audiences the sites can deliver.

One problem in WWW advertising from a product manager's perspective is audience measurement. The manager would like to measure "eyeballs," that is, how many total exposures an ad receives. However, on a given site visit, customers often go back and forth between hypertext pages rapidly. Measuring the number of times a particular page is on the screen may not be the appropriate measure of exposure, as the screen time may have been very brief. A threshold time amount might be more appropriate before it can count as a "hit." Or the viewer may not scroll all the way down the screen. These issues confront the large number of companies interested in measuring site audiences.[17]

In the end, as with conventional advertising, a product manager, in conjunction with a media specialist, needs to put together a schedule. With so many new pages coming online every week and no centralized source of information about the demographics and buying behavior of the visitors to each site, the task of putting together a WWW advertising schedule is daunting. Naturally, private enterprise is beginning to come to the rescue. A company called Focalink (http://mango.focalink.com) offers a service named MarketMatch that is built from a database of over 450 WWW sites that accept advertising and provides for each site a description of the site, the visitors' psychographic profile, price, a content rating, data on site traffic, and contact information.

---

[16]Debra Aho Williamson, "Web Ad Spending Pegged at $12.4M." *Advertising Age,* December 11, 1995, p 8.

[17]For a good overview of the problems with WWW site measurement and a list of the companies offering measurement services, see Debra Aho Williamson, "Web Searching for a Yardstick," *Advertising Age,* October 9, 1995, pp. 21–24.

FIGURE 16–5 The Web's Most Expensive Sites to Sponsor

Site	Cost per month	Estimated monthly visitors	CPM (impressions)	Comments
1. InfoSeek http://www.infoseek.com	$40,000	3,000,000	$ 13.33	Advertisers receive 3 free keywords. Site offers a variety of packages based on impression levels
2. ESPNet http://espnet.sportszone.com	$33,333	1,600,000	$ 20.83	Cost based on a 3-month sponsorship. Advertiser gets banner on a "franchise" position and a banner rotation through the site
3. Netscape http://www.netscape.com	$30,000	1,000,000	$ 30.00	Cost of the Platinum Program, rotation among the site's highest trafficked pages
4. WebCrawler http://www.webcrawler.com	$22,000	1,000,000	$ 22.00	Rates are for a 4-week period. Approximately 20% of users come from AOL
5. Lycos http://www.lycos.com	$20,000	1,000,000	$ 20.00	Advertisers receive 5 free keywords. Site offers daily banner changes
6. Yahoo http://www.yahoo.com	$20,000	1,000,000	$ 20.00	Rates based on $.02 per page view. Advertiser selects category to sponsor; in most cases, there is only one spot available per category
7. The Dilbert Zone http://www.unitedmedia.com/comics/dilbert	$18,000	1,000,000	$ 18.00	Advertiser receives 1 of 2 banner positions on the home page
8. HotWired http://www.hotwired.com	$15,000	100,000	$150.00	Rates are for a 4-week period. Advertiser's banner is rotated throughout the site
9. Internet Shopping Network http://www.internet.net	$15,000	600,000	$ 25.00	Advertiser's banner appears on home page
10. c/net http://www.cnet.com	$15,000	200,000	$ 75.00	Banner is rotated throughout each page in the site
11. IUMA http://www.iuma.com	$14,000	190,000	$ 73.68	Advertisers share the front page with 3 other sponsors. Also, banners are rotated throughout the site's 4 main sections
12. Pathfinder http://www.pathfinder.com	$10,000	750,000	$ 13.33	
13. Playboy http://www.playboy.com	$10,000	2,000,000	$ 5.00	

Source: *The Traffic Resource (http://www.trafficresource.com). a product of i-traffic, New York.*
Source: Wendy Marx, "Commerce is Slow to Hit the Net," *Advertising Age,* November 20, 1995, p S–6. Reprinted with permission.

Conclusion

Marketing on the Internet/WWW is a brand-new area for product managers. One author offers the following guidelines for marketing "Webonomics":[18]

[18] Evan I. Schwartz, "Advertising Webonomics 101," *Wired,* February 1996, pp. 74–80.

1. Consumers will rarely pay a subscription fee for access to a Web site. People have become used to free information on the WWW.
2. The old models of selling advertising do not apply. As we noted earlier, traditional cost-per-thousand measures (CPM) are not relevant on the WWW.
3. Marketers are on the WWW not for exposure but for results. Even though the technology is wonderful and it is fun to "surf" the web, if companies do not eventually sell more products and services using the web as a channel and a communications medium, it will not be commercially viable; "business" on the web will be reduced to the Winers using it to substitute for holiday greetings cards. (Lehmann still believes in paper.)
4. Customers must be rewarded when they disclose information about themselves. In other words, in exchange for demographic and product use data, customers must get something of value, such as customized information, special deals, and the like. For example, in exchange for information about travel patterns, one of the authors is now on an E-mail list for Cathay Pacific Airlines, where occasionally business-class round-trip seats to Hong Kong are auctioned off at prices beginning at $300. If such special treatments are not forthcoming, customers will no longer give information to site sponsors, the medium will become less attractive to advertisers, and (complementing point 3 above) the other key source of revenue for the web will disappear.

Summary

Undoubtedly other sources of change will pose challenges to product managers in the future. It is very likely that this chapter will be significantly different in the third edition of this book (if we write one), just as it differs from the final chapter in the first edition. As the person serving as the interface between the company and the marketplace, the product manager is particularly vulnerable to any kind of external change in the environment or internal change in the organization.

However, if the product manager sticks to the "basics" of managing existing products as described in this book, any change can be viewed as a potential modification to an existing practice. For example, advertising on the WWW is similar in most respects to advertising decisions in general: There must be an objective, a message strategy, a good fit with the overall communications goals for the product, an evaluation of its effectiveness, and so on. Most important, these changes should be viewed favorably; they often provide an opportunity to achieve differential advantage over competitors, and, from a purely intellectual point of view, they keep the job exciting. If life were simple and the job easy, the pay and opportunities for advancement would be limited. Thus, product managers should be thankful that their task is complex and dynamic.

N A M E I N D E X

SUBJECT INDEX